# AMERICAN

# LITERARY

# CRITICISM

## 1900 - 1950

*by* CHARLES I. GLICKSBERG

 NEW YORK

HENDRICKS HOUSE, INC.

TO

MY MOTHER

# PREFACE

In an anthology of American literary criticism from 1900 to 1950, it is not possible to do more than present the most vital and significant contributions of our time and leave others for only brief, incidental mention. The aim and justification of such a book is primarily to give a cross-section of the critical ideas and methods employed by various eminent and representative critics during the past fifty years. Obviously its chief virtue must be expository and analytical, though there is some attempt at interpretation and evaluation.

Since it would have required a volume of encyclopedic proportions if every twentieth-century writer with some pretensions to critical authority and influence had been included, the editor was compelled to follow some consistent principle of selection. He endeavored to include the work of critics who are representative, significant, and influential. It may be that posterity will pass a different judgment. But no one at present knows what posterity will do, and besides one must accept the limitations, short-sighted as they are, of one's own generation. Sufficient unto our critical day are the evils and errors thereof! All things are relative in a world that is fleeting, subject to the flux of time and the vicissitudes of chance and change. Then, too, objective as one may strive to be, personal preferences will inevitably make themselves felt.

This anthology attempts to exhibit the writings of American critics in some sort of historical perspective. The first half of the twentieth century, when viewed as a whole, does take on clarity of outline and coherence of pattern. Other anthologies have stressed a particular school of thought (Humanism), or a particular method (formalism), or a particular political cause and economic doctrine (Marxism); this collection seeks to present and do justice to all contributions in the field of American literary criticism which have a positive bearing

on the modern critical debate, regardless of their point of view or
political and aesthetic orientation. While individual essays may seem
unrelated to those that come before or after, the selections as a whole
do conform to a consistent, evolving pattern of thought.

The purpose throughout has been to make modern literary trends
understandable through the mediation of the historical approach.
Huneker's impressionism, Spingarn's creative criticism, Van Wyck
Brooks' search for a usable past and his urgent though largely negative analysis of American culture, Mumford's summing up of the
cultural situation in *The Golden Day,* Lewisohn's impassioned plea
for creative freedom, Mencken's flamboyant exploitation of his personality, Woodberry's dignified and eloquent faith in the function of
literature and art, Sherman's steadfast faith in the vitality of the
Puritan heritage, Babbitt's Humanism and More's moral appraisal of
letters, Brownell's insistence on high and exacting critical standards,
Eliot's stress on tradition and classical restraint, Calverton's sociological outlook and the Marxist method Granville Hicks employed
during the thirties, the aesthetic principles and practices used by
such critics as Ransom, Cleanth Brooks, Winters, and Allen Tate,
the rediscovery and reaffirmation of American folk-art and folk-
traditions by Constance Rourke, the concern with psychoanalytic
values and symbols and myths that is characteristic of the work of
Lionel Trilling—all this constitutes a variegated but recognizable
pattern. The pattern takes shape because the work of the critic is
situated within an historical and cultural context. It is expressive of
the dominant forces of its time.

Each selection has been chosen because it was considered intrinsically interesting and significant as an independent unit. But a more
important criterion of selection was its representativeness: to what
degree was it representative of the critic and of the period for which
he spoke? There has been, as a rule, no sacrifice of literary quality
in the search for the representative. The contents should make clear
that while exigencies of space have limited the editor's choice of
material to one essay by a given American critic, no first-rate or
truly significant critic has been omitted.

The arrangement of essays is strictly chronological. Though other
methods of arrangement are surely possible, this method has been
adopted in this case because it promised to yield the best results for

the purpose for which it is intended. Essays have been printed as complete units without excisions and without alterations. The spelling and punctuation of the original text have usually been followed and only obvious printer's errors (and these are relatively few) have been corrected. Even orthographic peculiarities have been preserved. Each selection is preceded by a biographical and critical introduction together with a selective bibliography of the critic's work and of writings about him.

In the preparation of this volume, the editor is principally indebted to Professor Gay Wilson Allen, who initiated the idea for a two-volume anthology of American literary criticism, one covering the nineteenth century and the other the twentieth century. I am deeply grateful to Professor Allen, who will undertake to edit the second volume, for his valuable advice and encouragement in the planning of this anthology, though he is in no way responsible for the selection of the material, the point of view expressed, or the mistakes that may inadvertently have crept in. Dr. Walter Hendricks, the publisher, has been extremely cooperative and genuinely helpful in seeing this book through the press. I owe a great deal more than words can express, to my wife, Dorothy L. Glicksberg, for her unfailing interest in the project, her illuminating suggestions, and her steadfast moral support.

# CONTENTS

# AMERICAN LITERARY CRITICISM
## 1900 - 1950

# INTRODUCTION

## I

AMERICAN literary criticism of the twentieth century seems to reveal no clear-cut line of progression. There is, however, a healthy ferment of change, coupled with a marked trend toward specialization. Criticism, a highly complex art, branches off into a number of different channels, each of which calls for a special kind of training and skill. Criticism, as it develops, becomes historical, textual, semantic, sociological, philosophical, and "scientific," each demanding its own apparatus of scholarship and appropriate technique. Only rarely are these different methods combined in a work which achieves a functional synthesis.

The object of this anthology is not to give a chronologically ordered history of American criticism during the twentieth century but to present material illustrative of some of the major tendencies that were operative in that field during this period of time. It is difficult to discover a single, continuing pattern, a steady flow of what might be called "progress," so that the criticism of 1910, say, would be considered a definite improvement upon the criticism of 1900. That is not the way literary criticism functions. There are currents and counter-currents, action and reaction, eddies and swirls and lengthy detours, but the river, when viewed from a sufficient height, follows a recognizable course. In modern American criticism the main emphases have been psychological, sociological, and aesthetic, though the formal, traditional methods of criticism have never been abandoned.

In presenting the essays included in this volume, there is a distinct advantage in adhering as far as possible to the historical method. It enables us to make some semblance of order out of the seeming confusion and heterogeneity of critical ideas and movements in any period. It discourages the tendency to sum up an age or even a decade by means of some glib generalization or simple formula. Such

3

generalizations, such formulas, are at best only partially true. For each critical trend, especially when it is carried to extremes, generates its own counter-movement. While impressionistic criticism was being enthusiastically practised by H. L. Mencken, there were historical and humanistic critics like Stuart P. Sherman, Irving Babbitt, and Paul Elmer More at work, deploring its exaggerations and exposing its intellectual shortcomings. While the Marxist critics had their day in court during the thirties, the formalist critics like John Crowe Ransom and Allen Tate were insisting on the value of tradition and the importance of making a technically detailed examination of the structural organization and texture of a poem, thus according primacy to the aesthetic rather than the sociological component. All these composite, competing influences, whatever their degree of validity, must be faithfully represented if the picture drawn is to be anywhere near complete.

It is also necessary to trace the evolution of an individual critic in time, from youth to maturity and old age. In each case, especially if the critic possesses a venturesome, questioning mind, will there be found abundant signs of change, if not of growth. Such intellectual development is the resultant of at least two interacting forces: an individual temperament conditioned by its age and environment. The early Van Wyck Brooks, for example, like Oliver Allston, his mature alter ego, is a confirmed idealist, but his attachments later on undergo a conspicuous sea-change. Now, instead of rejecting the culture of his land, he voices an attitude of acceptance, of affirmation, steadfastly treasuring what is most precious and enduring in its heritage, putting at last to good use the usable past which he had formerly set up as a desideratum for the American writer. It is not surprising to find similar symptoms of change in the major American critics. It is not a question of intellectual consistency. The man changes as he grows older and expands his horizon of vision. In addition, social, political, and economic events inevitably leave their impress on his character and mental development. Just as many Socialists abandoned the ideal of internationalism when the First World War broke out, so a number of Marxist critics resigned from the Communist Party or ceased being congenial fellow travelers when the Soviet Union signed the Munich Pact. Furthermore, the minor epidemic of conversion to Communist ideology during the thirties is inconceivable without the impact of the economic depression.

Criticism is thus an act in space-and-time. While the various tendencies not only overlap but conflict (criticism is always a battle over values), the chronological picture, particularly when seen in the sobering perspective of time, is fairly clear-cut. What is more, it is on the whole both reliable and representative. This does not mean that a literary trend is born in one decade, reaches its peak of influence, and then simply declines and gradually disappears from the scene. If it is supported by fruitful, viable ideas, it may persist for some time. It may, for example, continue a tradition inherited from a preceding age. Stuart P. Sherman, in his early work, was deeply influenced by the writing of Matthew Arnold. But the point is that in each period these ideas, whatever their source, will be given a characteristic interpretation. In other words, critical ideas and movements operate within a socio-cultural context. The amount of attention they receive, the influence they wield, the way they are used —all this is determined in large measure by the prevailing climate of opinion. The emergence and feverish development of literary Marxism during the depression-ridden thirties is again a case in point. Another instructive illustration is connected with the hegira of many of the literati to Europe, where they hoped to live the creative life and produce the poems and novels and works of art that a benighted, puritanical, materialistic America prevented them from bringing to birth. Practically all the influential critics of the time joined in these jeremiads against their land. "There are those who can see no good in America, even as there were novelists who could see nothing worthy in the life that they were presenting. They occupy themselves in showing that America started in the gutter and has proceeded to run into the sewer. They call attention loud and long to their belief that the worst of American life is due to her culture, that the best is an accident, and that there is no hope anywhere."[1] Thus the early twenties marked a definite movement of expatriation. And this, too, we can now see, had its historic roots, its economic causes and consequences, as well as its purely aesthetic motivation. The period of self-chosen exile continued until almost the end of the twenties— until the crash of the stock market caused these expatriates to scuttle home.

There is no need to invoke a *Zeitgeist* to account for the rise and fall of critical ideas. In literary criticism, the emergence of an idea or method at any given time, why it is cherished and eagerly adopted, cannot be explained by reference to a hypothetical spirit of the age,[2]

[1] Percy Holmes Boynton, *The Challenge of Modern Criticism* (Chicago, 1931), p. 89.

[2] For a full discussion of this point, see Levin L. Schücking, *The Sociology of Literary Taste* (London, 1944).

but the phenomenon cannot be adequately understood without situating it in the historical process. A critical judgment is an act (an impressionistic utterance, an aesthetic response, an evaluation) committed by some one at some time. What critics think and write cannot be fully understood without reference to what is going on in the nation and the world at large or to what other critics (and writers, too, for that matter) are thinking and writing.

Thus, criticism does not proceed in a vacuum but takes its rise and develops its significant stresses and patterns within a socio-historical matrix; it has a past, but though it is steadied and in part propelled by a vital, ongoing tradition it is also pushed toward the future by unsettling forces of change. Nor does it formulate principles autonomously within its own province; it is closely and inevitably related to the unfolding history of literature wherein it finds its field of operation. What critics feel, think, decree, affirm, and deny, owes much to the body of literature, past and present, which the critic is obliged to consider. The writers put into practice and creatively exemplify what the critic dissects out and analyzes objectively. There is, for example, a close correlation between critical terminology in a particular age and the kind of literary works then in vogue. The process works, of course, both ways. If the writers influence the critics, the latter in turn strongly influence the work of the writer. What the critic tries to do is to interpret in some coherent, systematic fashion the standards of taste that are actually operative, the factors that determine our likes and dislikes.[3]

The historical method of presentation in the field of criticism makes it possible for the reader to trace the genesis, development, and interrelationship of ideas and movements. It also enables him to see, in retrospect, why certain ideas arise at a given time, gather tremendous momentum, and then peter out, while others, however much obscured and out of favor for a time, live on. What is more, it steers clear of the ever-present temptation to treat some movement in isolation, without relating it to what has gone before, even if this movement is only a violent reaction against some dogma of the past. In short, each critical movement must compete against what the past has to offer that is still of some value in the present, just as it must compete against other contenders, newly sprung up, equally determined to dominate the scene. Hence, sometimes, as a strategy

[3] See Austin Warren, "Literary Criticism," in John C. McGalliard, René Wellek, Austin Warren, and Wilbur L. Schramm, *Literary Scholarship* (Chapel Hill, 1941), pp. 133-174.

for survival, a movement may be led to exaggerate its claims unduly, to accentuate the points in which it differs from other critical systems. The historical approach treats critics and their work as part of a complex and continuing tradition. What to a contemporary observer may seem a clotted confusion, a bedlam and babel of strident voices, later takes on definition and clarity of outline and is seen as part of a steady, unbroken movement. Historical insight clarifies and illuminates the critical activity of a period.


## II

The twentieth century in the United States opened with no impressive flourish of critical trumpets. European ideas were infiltrating rapidly and had been doing so, in fact, all through the nineteenth century, but they were at last hearkened to, objectively appraised, and discriminatingly put to use. Modernism was an amalgam of many complex forces and tendencies. It was marked by a lively interest in literatures other than our own. It became involved in the protracted quarrel over realism and naturalism. The literary horizon was definitely broadening. As the tempo of change quickened, there was a widespread, insurgent protest against provincialism in all its forms. A number of writers headed a revolt against hampering conventions and outworn traditions.

Stephen Crane had published his sordid but brilliant naturalistic stories and novels. Frank Norris, turned critic in order to defend his philosophy and practice of fiction, wrote "A Plea for Romantic Fiction," pointing out the salient limitations of realism: its failure to achieve beauty, its preoccupation with minute documented details, its lack of vision. But Romance, by which Norris meant a type of naturalism which departs from the norm and concerns itself with the whole world of passion—the mystery of sex, the depths of evil in the heart of man, all the cruel tragedies of life—exploited unusual incidents, material far removed from the familiar and reassuring aspects of existence, plots spiced with extraordinary adventures and filled with elemental crises. Norris made Zola out to be a writer of Romance. Norris' book, *The Responsibilities of the Novelist* (1903), was eagerly accepted by the young naturalists of the time as a manifesto voicing their aesthetic creed. *McTeague* (1899) vigorously applied the Zolaesque method of naturalism. Interestingly enough, it was Norris who was largely responsible for the acceptance of

Dreiser's first novel, *Sister Carrie* (1900). The two naturalistic novelists joined forces to overcome the massive tradition of genteelism in American letters. Though at the time they were overborne, their followers later fought the battle to a victorious conclusion. The reviewers of *Sister Carrie* were mainly unfavorable in their verdict. Howells, in 1900 still dean of American letters, did not like Dreiser's novel. By that time Howells had given up realism as a lost cause.

William Dean Howells, whose life overlapped that of the twentieth century, lived to see his critical influence repudiated, his work of fiction and his philosophy of realism derided. But as a critic he at least spoke with some degree of authority; he was honest, sincere, penetrating, widely read, and he defended American realism skilfully and consistently, though he did not go far enough in his recommendations as a critic nor in his practice as a novelist to satisfy a later, more rebellious generation.

In 1894 Hamlin Garland had published *Crumbling Idols,* which belongs to the realistic school. Democratic in its faith, strongly influenced by Whitman, it voiced a social as well as individualistic philosophy. Art must serve the common well-being of the race; it must be sociological in orientation and content. Besides upholding truth as part of his creed as a realist, he believed that the purpose of the artist must be to support the cause of justice.

In a cultural sense, the birth of the twentieth century is not coincident with the birth of the year 1900. Though the twentieth century inherited the preceding century's search for a sense of national identity, the creative confidence and courage to establish it was still lacking. It was definitely lacking in the field of literary criticism, where the European and particularly the English influence was still powerful. Critics were on the whole academic and imitative, cautious and conservative, rather than independent and boldly original. Many of the American men of letters found America then wanting in all things of the spirit, in culture, civilization, letters, art, deficient in intellectual vitality, spiritually arrested. Materialism was in the saddle; Mammon ruled the hearts and minds of men. Though Howells stayed in America and staunchly fought for realism, he found himself in the twentieth century in a climate of thought which was utterly uncongenial to his spirit. Though realism had finally come out on top he was not at all consoled, for it was not the kind of realism he cared to sanction. Ironically enough, he was later condemned by the younger critics as an exponent of the genteel tradition, a creative force that had grown tame, respectable, and conservative.[4]

Perhaps it was not until 1914 that the twentieth century first truly dawned in America. Before 1910 there was little criticism of American literature. There was no market for criticism in the magazines. In "Literary Criticism in American Periodicals," originally delivered as a lecture at Yale University in 1914, Bliss Perry underscores what Henry James had noted and lamented in his talk on Balzac, namely, the absence of any informing, constructive criticism.[5] The status of literary criticism had fallen low indeed. There were few intelligent, competent reviews and no genuine criticism. But the critical temper had already made itself felt with the publication of *The Spirit of American Literature,* by John Macy, in 1913, a candid, uncompromising treatment of our life and letters by a critic who rejected the criteria of morality as irrelevant. Literature was no longer to be judged by moral standards. And in 1911 Randolph Bourne had published *Youth and Life,* a collection of challenging essays, intrepid in tone, sounding a call for creative action and leadership on the part of youth. What was needed was a vigorous, fearless criticism. Instead of being recklessly discarded, the old tradition, Bourne held, had to be revaluated, so that what was of enduring worth in it could be assimilated and put to good use. The central issues of American life must be defined and realistically appraised so that American writers might gain not only confidence in their calling but also a helpful sense of direction. If they knew where they were going, and that was the chief task of a healthy criticism to find out, they would have a much better chance of reaching their goal.

Though Hamlin Garland, in *Companions on the Trail* (1931), asserts that American literature is still hopelessly provincial, still in the "hick" stage of culture, the record does not warrant such a pessimistic view of the literary situation. A host of new writers, ignoring Randolph Bourne's warning that a vital, growing literature must have roots in the past, asserted themselves violently—perhaps too violently—by rejecting the past *in toto.* The First World War proved

4 In *Roadside Meetings* (1930), Hamlin Garland records a conversation that he had with Henry James approximately in 1900. Henry James confessed that he had made a mistake in quitting America. If he had to do it over again, he would steep himself thoroughly in America, whereas the mixture of Europe and America had proved disastrous for him, turning him, as a writer and a man, into a hybrid, neither European nor American, alienated, cut off from his own people.
5 Bliss Perry, *The Praise of Folly and Other Papers* (Boston and New York, 1923).

a disruptive but distinctly educative influence. The young men of America, returning from the war in Europe in a disenchanted, embittered, iconoclastic spirit, found much to condemn in the life of their country: its mechanical civilization, its preoccupation with money and material things, its harsh puritanic conservatism. The revolt against the old standards and conventions was on in full force. *Civilization in the United States* (1922), a symposium by thirty Americans, was a militant onslaught, sparing almost no aspect of American civilization from censure: its comstockery, its Philistinism, its hopelessly middle-class mentality. A number of native critics played a leading part in this crusade which angrily repudiated the gods of the American past. In *America's Coming-of-Age* (1915), Van Wyck Brooks called urgently for a usable past, a tradition belonging to this country, which the writer could draw upon in the proud confidence that it would sustain him, but he left no doubt in the reader's mind that the America of his day was crude, unformed, creatively frustrated, and unfulfilled.

These embattled young critics were eagerly listened to; their summons to revolt elicited a vigorous response; social and political conditions at the time lent force and validity to their diagnosis. The defeat of the League of Nations was a disastrous blow to the full-blown democratic idealism with which many young men had entered the war. The post-war years were marked by a tendency to wipe our hands of the unholy mess and allow Europe to stew in its own juice. The period of the twenties was not only cynical but lawless, reckless, irresponsible, neurotic. Though the first quarter of the century was largely imitative and singularly unenterprising, the forces of new life were seething underground, ready to burst forth at the right moment.

Such violent ideological vicissitudes cannot, of course, be accounted for in terms of exact dates. The wave of disillusionment that swept over the land during the aftermath of the First World War led the younger writers to deride and reject the moralistic and philosophic values of what was loosely called Victorianism. These young writers were not only skeptical and irreverent, if not contemptuous, in their attitude toward the venerable figures of the national past, but also bitterly pessimistic. They took pride in the fact that they were dwellers in the waste land. There was no sustaining beauty, no ultimate purpose, no semblance of meaning in life. The deterministic philosophy, as formulated, for example, by Theodore Dreiser, pictured man as a chemism, a tropism, a cog in the gigantic, senselessly

revolving machine of the universe. The naturalistic outlook laid
emphasis on man as part of Nature, not a special creation, not spiritually distinct from and superior to the animals. In this war against
the trammels of the traditional and the theological, even the weapons
of Freudianism were employed with singular effectiveness. The field
of sexual experience, hitherto taboo, was now enthusiastically ex-
plored.

The advance of science worked havoc with the intellectual landscape, upsetting fixed conventions and established beliefs. The
triumph of industrialism and the spread of urbanism introduced
further complexities. The nineteenth-century world with its confidently formulated ethical norms was practically dead. Science gave
man increasing pride in his own powers and assured faith in his individualism, for it vastly extended his control over Nature. Literally
there were no bounds, or so it seemed to him, to his power of mastering his environment by means of the experimental method developed
by science. The country was waking up and making tremendous
progress, now that the frontier was closed and the industrial tempo
stepped up. The swollen tide of immigration added new ethnic elements to the melting pot. The expanding applications of science
helped to loosen the hold religion had on the minds of men. Science
disclosed a new picture of the place man occupied in the universe,
unsupported by divine sanctions, alone but not utterly helpless, depending solely on his own resources. The triumph of industrialism
and technology made it evident that science could not be stopped.

## III

The twentieth century, despite all the shortcomings that we have
listed, witnessed the birth of a critical consciousness unparalleled in
nineteenth-century American literature. Toward the end of the last
century there were, with the possible exception of W. D. Howells and
W. C. Brownell, no native critics capable of producing vital, constructively original criticism, and even Howells, however honest and
forthright in his appraisals, generous in his welcome of newcomers,
was, when judged by modern standards, hardly venturesome. But in
1901, W. C. Brownell in his essay on Matthew Arnold, whose ideas he
warmly espoused, protested against the factitious dualism that had
been set up between critical and creative activity. A passage such as
the following certainly bore witness to the fact that the critical
genius of America was not completely dormant:

What criticism lacks, and what will always be a limitation to its interest and its power, is the element of beauty which it of necessity largely foregoes in its concentration upon truth. It is less potent and less persuasive than poetry, than romance, not because in dealing with literature rather than with life it occupies a lower or less vital field but because its province lies outside the realm of all those puissant aids to cogency and impressiveness that appeal to the sense of beauty and accordingly influence so powerfully not only the intellect but the emotions as well. But of its service to truth there can be no question. Its rôle is not confined to exposition, to interpretation. It is a synthesis of its naturally more or less heterogeneous subject. It is a characterization of art as art is a characterization of nature. And in characterizing, it translates as art itself translates. It is only in criticism that the thought of an era becomes articulate, crystallized, coherently communicated. And real criticism, criticism worthy of its office—criticism such as Arnold's—contributes as well as co-ordinates and exhibits. It is itself literature, because it is itself origination as well as comment, and is the direct expression of ideas rather than an expression of ideas at one remove —either chronicling their effect on the critic after the manner of the impressionists or weighing them according to some detached and objective judicial standard.[6]

That was the conviction, the faith, that native critics stood so sorely in need of: the belief that criticism is itself orgination as well as comment, that it is itself literature. The rebirth of the critical spirit in the United States was caused by a multiplicity of interacting causes. It marked the culmination of the long search for a genuinely national literature, free from colonial leading-strings, no longer abstract or self-consciously aggressive, but concrete and exacting in its demands, satisfied with nothing less than the best, though naturally not by any means agreed as to what constituted the best or how it was to be attained.

It took considerable time before a philosophy of literary history suited to the needs of the nation was developed and put into practice. Howard Mumford Jones, in *The Theory of American Literature* (1948), points out that there should be a constant and fruitful dialectical interplay between literary history and literary criticism, the seminal ideas of one discipline influencing the growth of the other. Genius is situated in a socio-temporal context and owes something to its predecessors and to its contemporaries; but this historical and sociological orientation cannot afford to abandon the task and the responsibility of aesthetic evaluation. Literary history without evalua-

6 W. C. Brownell, *Victorian Prose Masters* (New York, 1928), pp. 168–169.

tive criteria becomes jejune and sterile; literary criticism without historical perspective and insight "grows absolute and inhuman."[7]

The focus of interest in twentieth-century criticism was clearly undergoing a radical shift. Instead of looking forward to a brilliant fulfillment in the future, a renaissance of letters growing out of re-publican institutions, critics like Randolph Bourne and Van Wyck Brooks instituted the quest for a usable past. Challenged was the assumption, commonly taken for granted by many writers and critics in the preceding century, that American literature could not flourish as a separate entity, that it possessed significance and value only in relation to the parent stock of British literature. In the last third of the nineteenth century the demand for creative independence was al-ready making itself felt, especially in the insistent effort to produce the Great American Novel. Difficult questions were being raised and important issues heatedly discussed. To what extent and in what respects was our literature an expression of democratic values? What role could realism play in forging a native, autochthonous literature? Would our literature become regional, even local, instead of seeking to achieve an epic scope and synthesis representative of and embrac-ing the whole nation? What was it specifically that we lacked? Prac-tically all these questions, however couched, voiced a profound dis-satisfaction with things as they were. Finally, literary historians led the long-pending revolt. John Macy's *The Spirit of American Litera-ture* was followed by Parrington's solid contribution, in three vol-umes, *Main Currents in American Thought* (1927–1930), which gave a liberal, Jacksonian interpretation of our literature. Puritan-ism in art and life was at last repudiated, and with it the genteel tradition. As the old literary idols were shattered, neglected figures like Thoreau and Melville were reinstated.

The vigor and fertility of the critical controversies generated dur-ing the first half of the twentieth century afforded striking testimony that American culture was finally coming of age. In demanding that America should not only proclaim but responsibly live up to its lit-erary maturity, putting its full creative potentialities into play, and in calling upon writers to rediscover the native tradition of their land, the critics were actually inspiring numerous writers to greater effort and giving them confidence in their artistic mission in life. In turn, the critics were confirmed in their judgment and immensely

[7] Howard Mumford Jones, *The Theory of American Literature* (Ithaca, 1948), p. 118. See also the chapter on "Literary History," in René Wellek and Austin Warren, *Theory of Literature* (New York, 1949), pp. 263–282.

heartened in their work by the appearance of novelists like Stephen Crane, Theodore Dreiser, Sherwood Anderson, Ernest Hemingway, John Dos Passos, and a host of others. Criticism is obviously most productive and most influential when it is in direct and vital contact with the literature of its time, though criticism in itself constitutes a part of the growing literary movement of a nation.

During the first fifty years American criticism has passed through many metamorphoses; it has been prolific, undeniably alive. Impressionism, humanism, pure aestheticism or "expressionism" modeled on Croce's philosophy of art, creative criticism, liberalism and radicalism and their reflection in *belles lettres* and criticism, the attempt to make literature fundamentally a criticism of life, the steady growth of interest in our native literary tradition, its origins, history, folklore, and development, the reinterpretation of the shaping influence of the frontier, the popular vogue of psychoanalysis and the amazing effect it had on both writers and critics, the sudden emergence of naturalism and a new experimental literature: all these tendencies gave critics a legitimate source of pride, a principle of justification, if one were needed, a cogent reason for continuing the battle with greater energy and conviction. It became more essential than ever before that the critic sharpen his professional tools, put his dictionary of technical terms in order, systematically round out his theory of aesthetics and apply it to the literature of his time and that of the past, to European as well as American letters. As criticism took on a new lease on life, its practitioners, in their search for an efficacious method, necessarily had to dispose of all those ideas and practices (as well as those who advocated them) that stood in the way of the truth as they saw it. The ferment of intellectual activity, the number of articles and books published all dealing with some important aspect of the critical debate, gave proof that a profound resurgence of the critical spirit was under way. There was an enhanced respect for the critical office, not to mention a newly awakened enthusiastic interest in the untapped potentialities of American culture.

Criticism has become of late, and rightly so, a professional concern. Though there are no formal trade-union restrictions, and no monopolistic controls, a writer who wishes to practice the art of criticism must demonstrate his degree of technical competence. Despite the formidable competition he must face, he has an open field. The practical result of his labor, however, must validate his claim to recognition. The field of literary knowledge has grown so complex, so vast, so highly specialized, that one must devote his whole life to it if he expects to succeed. Otherwise he will probably add nothing substantially new or worthwhile to the growing body of critical literature.

The trouble with American criticism at the end of the nineteenth century was that it lacked such trained and devoted practitioners. The established critics were for the most part either genteel amateurs or academic scholars and spokesmen. It is not until the second decade of the present century that we come across a critic, namely, Van Wyck Brooks, who declares that he deliberately chose his calling, that he never desired to be anything else but an American critic.[8] In 1890, there was this void to be filled. There was then not only a surprising lack of faith in the intrinsic merit of American literature but also a singular lack of vital, formative ideas. Since there was no healthy intellectual curiosity, there was little that could be called literary pioneering. Writers looked mainly abroad for leadership, and though they were inclined to be skeptical in temper they had little that was positive to offer.

Here was a splendid opportunity for a new generation of critics. There was a need for new blood, new liberating insights, new causes to espouse. The battle was on for the formulation of sound principles of analysis and methods of appreciation, principles and methods which would be empirically valid, in conformity with the light cast by the intelligence. In short, what was needed was an aesthetic philosophy which would give the writer faith in his calling and at the same time point out to him the incalculably rich but unutilized resources of his own land and people.

To accomplish this, leaders had to spring up who would draft manifestoes, focus ideas, define issues which had to be threshed out, crystallize modes of sensibility, and create definite schools of thought. In addition, faith in the value of the creative life had to be renewed and given public recognition. Otherwise how could a valuable native tradition be inaugurated? How could critics arrive at some common agreement? How could new experimental forms and efforts be encouraged? How could America give birth to an independent and authentically native literature? If American culture was to be brought down to earth and become so firmly rooted in indigenous soil that it could perpetuate itself, it required the services of gifted critical in-

8 Van Wyck Brooks, *The Opinions of Oliver Allston* (New York, 1941), p. 162.

terpreters. But it also required a system of aesthetics, however flexible, born of practice and tested in the fires of discussion, which the critic could apply concretely to a given work of art.

The major problem of American criticism was thus to draw up a comprehensive system of aesthetics that would at the same time do full justice to the structural organization and formal properties of a specific literary work. It could not be taken over bodily from the writings of such nineteenth-century critics as Emerson, Poe, Lowell, and Whitman, illuminating as some of their ideas were. The criticism of the new century had to contend with the emergent future, with forces untried and unprecedented, as well as the traditional. It had, therefore, to be courageous enough to venture on uncharted waters and to rely on its own intuitions and experiences. The counters of nineteenth-century criticism were worn out; the contemporary field of criticism was experimental in temper and outlook. Some critics turned for guidance to Europe, though there was no ground for assuming that such cultural importations would suit our needs. It was clear that the twentieth-century critic would have to forge a method that would rise above the level of judicial academic studies or rank impressionism. Sensibility, however indispensable as an adjunct to the critical act, was not enough.

Fortunately or unfortunately, depending on one's point of view, criticism, like religion, inevitably splits into sects and schisms. Though it may be grouped for purposes of convenience under large categories, such as historical criticism, sociological criticism, there is, even within these categories, no consensus, and no formal agreement as to method. Factional disputes and internal dissension are the rule rather than the exception. Critics are by nature *critical*, especially of each other. John Crowe Ransom, for example, finds much that is wanting or downright wrong in the work of such critics as T. S. Eliot, Yvor Winters, and I. A. Richards, with two of whom he has much in common. Moreover, there is no such thing as a critic who consistently confines himself at all times to one method or point of view. There is bound to be an overlapping of ideologies and principles, an element of change, if not contradiction, in his writing. Temperament invariably plays its part to create differences of emphasis and interpretation. Finally, the critic's moral outlook, his political loyalties, his philosophy of life, and his religion also help to shape his standards and affect his method of evaluation.

Impressionism in criticism, however fallible in some of its extreme applications, is a perennial form of expression. Though interested in the work of art itself, and not in any of its tangential relationships, the impressionist differs from the classicist in repudiating all objective standards of judgment, all aesthetic absolutes and finalities. The source and seat of judgment, if that is what it can be called, resides in the critic himself; he is sole arbiter, and his appreciations and appraisals are conditioned, *mutatis mutandis,* by his temperament, his sensibility, his taste. The impressionist records the adventure of his soul among works of art, his immediate feelings and sensations. Consequently, he is inclined to be subjective, personal, provocative, scattering his ideas and "impressions" broadcast, without regard for the hobgoblin of consistency. There is the contradiction, one among many, that vitiates impressionistic criticism: in one sense it attempts to record with fidelity the effect produced by the work of art under consideration and is therefore, presumably, close to the source of its inspiration; on the other hand, the impressionist defiantly announces that criticism at best cannot escape the personal equation and that his function as critic is fundamentally to be creative, to give vent to his own beliefs and free rein to his own rich personality. As Mencken expressed it in 1919, the critic "makes the work of art live for the spectator; he makes the spectator live for the work of art."[9] It is the tendency on the part of the impressionist to exploit his own personality that often degenerates, as was the case with Huneker and Mencken, into a form of picturesque exhibitionism, the object of which is to display the critic to such advantage that he overshadows the book or author he is examining. That, indeed, in his eyes, constitutes no defect and no handicap at all, since the book under consideration is only a pretext for exhibiting his own idiosyncratic individuality. An equal among equals, he assumes that people will read him not only for what he has to say about a literary production but also and far more for what he has to reveal about himself. But if that is truly his aim, his work seldom outlasts the hour of its publication. As the pendulum of taste swings along its wide arc and new conditions and new modes of sensibility arise, his writing becomes quickly outmoded. He has amused the reader and perhaps quickened his sense of appreciation, but there has been no enlargement of aesthetic insight.

The best example of this tendency to obsolescence on the part of impressionistic criticism is the work of James Gibbons Huneker (1890–1921), a dashing stylist, a bon vivant, a hearty epicure of the arts. Though he was an enthusiastic discoverer of new literary fig-

9 H. L. Mencken, *Prejudices, First Series* (New York, 1919), p. 21.

ures and new movements, especially the experimental writers, artists, and musicians of Europe, his taste was largely undiscriminating in its journalistic exaggerations. At bottom his function was to acquaint the American public with a host of advanced European artists, thinkers, and writers, thus impregnating our culture with new and vital seeds of influence. Unfortunately his utter lack of a critical philosophy, his excessive looseness of judgment, his lack of scrupulously defined and applied standards, together with his strained though picturesque style, have militated against him, and he is today little read or quoted. The curse of the impressionist is that he inaugurates no school and leaves behind him no disciples. As a rule, when the impressionistic critic dies his work dies with him.

Yet American criticism was strongly invigorated by the infusion of Huneker's extraordinary vitality, his inexhaustible gusto. His boundless energy and verve contributed much to neutralize the effete gentility that lay like a blight on the critical writing of the nineties. Long before Mencken appeared on the scene, he engaged in slashing attacks on Philistinism and Puritanism, on morality and propriety as criteria of judgment in the arts. The complete aesthete, the steeplejack of the seven arts, he was ebullient, entertaining, and remarkably productive, even though much of his work was done under the lash of journalistic necessity. Since the time of Poe he was the first American critic who could, through the medium of newspapers and magazines and with the aid of a virile, colorful style, appeal to a wide, literate audience. What made him, despite all his faults, such a desirable influence on the whole was his very eclecticism, his receptivity, his unflagging interest in all movements abroad, though not at home, that betrayed any sign of creative vitality. Should anything unusual be stirring on the continent, whether in music or painting, drama or fiction, philosophy or the dance, he was sure to deliver a vivid report on it. Truly prodigious was his capacity for assimilating and transmitting to his readers the caviar of European letters, art, and thought.

Unfortunately, what he produced was not tough-fibred, responsible criticism based on a sound and consistent point of view supported by a body of genuine if flexible standards, but eclectic impressionism. Over each figure or book or play or musical composition he discharged his luminous rockets of appreciative prose, but without any discernible principle of evaluation. Everything was grist to the critical mill. Everything, so long as it was challengingly new and arresting, was greeted with hosannahs of praise. But what he did—and he was thoroughly honest about his shortcomings—he did superbly well, recording his adventures among continental masterpieces and delivering scintillating eulogies of foreign geniuses. He made the appreciation of arts and letters seem a fascinating game, a unique experience. Conscientiously he carried out his function as importer of the cultural riches of contemporary European thought and art. An ardent impressionist, he at least encouraged a more direct and intimate reading of the text. Though he was widely admired in his time, he brought little to criticism that is destined to endure.

If Huneker possessed superabundant energy and enthusiasm but lacked discrimination and restraint, William Crary Brownell (1851–1928) represented a mediating influence between the solid virtues of Victorianism and the twentieth-century outlook. Though he insisted that there was an organic interconnection between art and life, as an Arnoldian he was drawn more to the gospel of "sweetness and light" than to the naturalistic teachings of men like Darwin, Huxley, and Zola. A seeker after the highest standard of perfection, he found much in American culture that was deplorable. America lacked, Brownell felt, nutritive substance, high seriousness, spiritual density, depth of purpose. If the goal of criticism is to make clear the underlying relationship between literature and life, then the critic is helpless without the support of firmly established standards by which he can judge the quality of literature. That was Brownell's central aim and his distinctive contribution as a critic: he strove to elucidate aesthetic standards derived from the concrete expression of the writer, and his standards in criticism were consistently high and exacting. Judging the corpus of American literature in the light of these standards, he found little that was authentically great.

Brownell at least worked out a fairly coherent critical method. He fixed his attention, not on the technical properties of a work but on those qualities that best characterized a writer, his moral values and spiritual insight, his interpretation of life, as well as his style and principle of construction. He was interested in contemplating, not laws and rules, but such elements as truth, beauty, and goodness. He believed that the critic, after establishing some general conception, must try to give a unified presentation of a physiognomy which constitutes a whole, but without blurring or neglecting the individual features. The whole critical process must be supported by values based on reason, thus eliminating subjective caprice and theoretical preconceptions. American criticism made a huge stride toward maturity with the publication of Brownell's six volumes: *French Traits*

(1889), *French Art* (1892), *Victorian Prose Masters* (1901), *American Prose Masters* (1909), *Criticism* (1914), and *Standards* (1917). Brownell is no impressionist who jumps hastily to conclusions. After conscientiously studying the meaning of a text, he endeavors to evaluate its merit objectively, resisting the pull of temperament and the aberrations of subjectivity. He did not run to extremes; he had the gift for making necessary distinctions. Though by adopting such temperate measures he sacrificed emotional intensity and whole-hearted affirmation, he gained proportionately in balance, in detachment and restraint, in fidelity to the work under consideration, and was thus less liable to go wrong.

If he is fair-minded in praise, he is unsparing when chastisement has to be administered. Those writers who fail to satisfy his standards are roundly taken to task, no matter how exalted their reputation may be in academic or popular esteem. Though he gives Emerson, for example, his due, he also deplores his shortcomings: his limitations of temperament, his deficiencies of sympathy, the lack of organic form and disciplined organization in his work, his want of culture. This is not an isolated instance. It strikes a recurrent motif in his essays on American prose masters. Brownell was convinced that culture can act as a formative as well as disciplining force, checkmating perversities of temperament and providing a sound basis for departures from the established norm. Every art has its conventions which the writer would do well to observe. But life is the substance as well as the subject of literature, and the writer neglects it at his peril. If Brownell categorically rejected the doctrine of art for art's sake, his counsel of decorum, his inveterate demand for the imposition of a severe discipline, unfortunately cabined and confined his sensibility and narrowed his range of sympathy, so that he was prevented from estimating at their true worth the work of the naturalists. Similarly he tended to condemn any form of literary expression that deviated from the ideal he had set up. The result was that he failed to influence the writers whose career he had hoped to guide. Though he is today, like Huneker, virtually unread, he had much to say that was helpful and illuminating.

Until the outbreak of the First World War, however, no notable contributions were made in the field of criticism. The academicians were still in the saddle. George Edward Woodberry, earnest, conscientious, idealistic, was at least aware of the lack of values from which American culture suffered. His books, *America in Literature* (1903), *The Torch* (1905), *The Appreciation of Literature*

(1910), and *Two Phases of Criticism* (1914), reprinted in the *Heart of Man and Other Papers* (1920), were solid and stimulating contributions, written with genuine force of conviction, but he was not, as he himself realized, a herald of the future. *The Sense of Beauty* (1896), by George Santayana, tried to furnish criticism with a psychological base, seeking to arrive at some understanding of how the mind frames aesthetic judgments. Though he used the method of philosophical criticism with polished grace and distinction, his writing left practically no impression on the work of the younger American critics.

Humanism made its appearance in the United States long before it rose to its acme of influence in the late twenties. Paul Elmer More published the first volume of the *Shelburne Essays* in 1904. In 1908, with the publication of *Literature and the American College,* Irving Babbitt fired the opening gun in what was to prove a long and arduous campaign of polemics and preachment. But their vigorous indictment of modern literature and their more positive ideas were overshadowed by the emergence of a school of younger critics determined to break sharply with the traditions of the past, and especially with those of the nineteenth century. They went to great lengths to denounce not only the Victorian worthies but also those who, like Babbitt and More, defended the claims of tradition. Victorianism with its emphasis on decorum became a term of contempt and abuse. The academic taint was to be removed by letting new sources of vital experience flow into literature, by seeking for a new tradition in the heart of America. No restrictive moral compulsives such as the Humanists advocated were to be permitted to hold literature in leash. Brownell's plea for discipline and idealism was laughed out of court, and Huneker, too, eclectic and impulsively eulogistic, fell out of favor. Literature was to root itself in the quickening soil of experience and grow out of perennially fresh and changing reality. The critic, like the writer, was expected to leave his ivory tower and come to grips with American life in all its dynamic complexity, so that a literature realistic in content, truly worthy of the land, could come to birth.

Van Wyck Brooks was the prophetic voice that started the new critical movement. He stressed the cultural shortcomings of America, its sordid materialism, its multiple frustrations, its failure to achieve a principle of organic growth, its unrestrained anarchic individualism in getting and spending, its superficiality and crass vulgarity and competitive mania. If a truly national culture was to be built up, these weaknesses in our collective life would have to be remedied. Instead of being forced to serve acquisitive ends and worshipping the bitch goddess Success, the creative mind must be set free. Ardent spirits among the younger generation immediately responded to the call. *The Seven Arts,* edited by James Oppenheim, Waldo Frank, Van Wyck Brooks, and others, printed essays by Paul Rosenfeld, Theodore Dreiser, and Van Wyck Brooks. In "Life, Art and America," Dreiser thoroughly castigated this country for its hypocritical Puritanism, its fanatical devotion to the art of money-making, its failure to produce artists worthy of the name.[10] Van Wyck Brooks published "The Splinter of Ice," later included in somewhat revised form in *Letters and Leadership* (1918), in which he scored our lack of a tradition, our confirmed opposition to new ideas, our inchoate society, and our native literature, which was anemic because it lacked the sustenance that racial roots can provide. "The history of our literature alone," he then declared, "would be enough to explain our disillusionment, for it chronicles an endless succession of impulses that have spent themselves without being able to grapple, or be grappled by, the soul of the race."[11] Artistically we are still immature. Our national life has been standardized, our human values have surrendered to the drift of circumstance, and our literature is therefore rendered impotent. He was driven to the conclusion that our collective life, on all its levels, was in a state of arrested development. It is because of their subjection to the dominant ideal of material success that our native writers are so badly frustrated; even if they endeavor to combat this ideal, they suffer from damaging repressions. Before a fresh, vital literature can come forth, it must be rooted in the right kind of life. Writers "have to create a fresh respect for experience, a profound sense both in their audience and in themselves of the significance and value of just those things of which literature is the expression."[12] In the same issue, in an article on "Vicarious Fiction," he announced that America needs, above all things, the sense of spiritual adventure, to be absorbed in a vital art. While such counsel was undoubtedly inspiring, it was hardly calculated to suggest any concrete program of action or to make the difficult art of criticism more precise. Essentially Van Wyck Brooks was an idealist sending forth moral appeals for individual and social regeneration.

10 *The Seven Arts,* I (February, 1917), 363–389.
11 *Ibid.,* I (January, 1917), 271.
12 *Ibid.,* p. 280.

A contributing editor to *The Seven Arts*, Randolph Bourne also protested against the domination of our cultural and collective life by the machine. Like Van Wyck Brooks, he had the power of setting other minds on fire as he held up before men the promise of a better life, a liberated and more fruitful culture. An uncompromising critic of American social institutions, interested in philosophy, politics, and education as well as literary criticism, he issued the call for a wider and deeper culture. In the title essay of *History of a Literary Radical* (1920), he describes his transition from a man of letters to an embattled propagandist. He inveighed against our pathetic cultural humility and sense of inferiority. Only through the mediation of art would we finally find fulfillment. "We shall never be able to perpetuate our ideals except in the form of art and literature; the world will never understand our spirit except in terms of art."[13]

Little magazines like *The Dial* and *The Seven Arts* satisfied a genuine need of the time, serving as a kind of testing ground and creative outlet for both writers and critics. They helped, both in England and in America, to inaugurate many a new movement: vorticism, futurism, dada, surrealism, expressionism, philosophical anarchism.[14] In the first issue (December, 1916) of the magazine, *The Soil*, R. J. Coady asserted confidently that American art was not only in the making but that it had already arrived. With this as a preamble he listed what he regarded as noble works of American art: the Panama Canal, the skyscraper, the tug boat, the steamshovel, the steel plants, the docks and aeroplanes, jazz music, Coney Island, the modern dance. Suspicious of abstractions and all absolutes, he insisted that these "arts" are a manifestation of the sensuous and spontaneous life of this land. In his zeal for identifying art with contemporary life in all its exciting diversity, he discovered in auto races, aeroplane stunts, and rodeo shows the same kind of tragic exaltation and instinctual intensity that a Spanish audience feels at a bull fight. Similarly, *The Little Review*, edited by Margaret Anderson, courageously came to the rescue of genius struggling against the incomprehension and even persecution of the compact majority. Margaret Anderson used but one test as the basis for accepting or rejecting manuscripts: art as the expression of personality. Since an artist is an exceptional person, he is bound to have something ex-

[13] Randolph Bourne, *History of a Literary Radical and Other Essays* (New York, 1920), p. 43.
[14] See Frederick J. Hoffman, Charles Allen, and Carolyn F. Ulrich, *The Little Magazine* (Princeton, 1946).

ceptional to say.[15] Though this is a thoroughly vague principle to go by, purely impressionistic, she somehow made it work out successfully. Of the little magazines that specialized in criticism, the most notable during the period between the two wars were *The Dial* (1920–1929), *Hound & Horn* (1927–1934), and *The Symposium* (1930–1933), publishing the work of such critics as T. S. Eliot, John Crowe Ransom, and R. P. Blackmur. *The Dial*, in particular, enlisted the services of a band of critics who were interested in the interrelations of form and concentrated their energy on studying the internal structure of a work. It published the writing of such men as Yvor Winters, Kenneth Burke, and T. S. Eliot.

In the early part of the century the Crocean theory of "expressionism" attracted considerable attention on the part of critics. Like the impressionistic critic, the aesthetic critic is, by theory, primarily concerned with the work of art itself, undistorted by psychological or political preconceptions, removed from its historical context and its milieu. Only when the task of appreciation has been completed, can the work of evaluation begin. Joel E. Spingarn, Croce's disciple, develops many of the ideas that Croce had formulated in his *Aesthetic*. Croce had maintained that the essential aim of criticism is to recover as fully and authentically as possible the experience the author passed through at the time he created his work. By reliving the experience which originally gave rise to the artistic expression, the critic is able to comprehend the inner significance and structure of the art that finally emerged. Hence, though the critic must be historical in his orientation, he revives the past only for the purpose of beholding the work of art as it existed in the moment when the artist produced it. For this task he requires the aid of taste, not a mass of facts; an active imagination, not the accumulated weight of erudition. The creative criticism that Spingarn advocates, rejects all talk of genres and all "scientific" assumptions as to the evolution of literature. The critic must judge each work according to the spirit in which it was written, not according to antecedent rules or standards. Though himself a professor of literature at Columbia University, Spingarn launched a determined attack on academic criticism, with its formal classification of literary productions, its division of works of art into romantic and classical, and its sterile emphasis on the relation of literature to historical origins. Such methods were jejune and spurious, unproductive of genuine critical insight.

15 Margaret Anderson, *My Thirty Years' War* (New York, 1930), p. 134.

The delivery in 1910 of Spingarn's lecture on "The New Criticism," published the following year, precipitated a furious but fruitful controversy, since it forced critics not only to take sides but to define their position. Spingarn did not, however, gain many disciples. In seeking to determine what "standards" to apply in order to measure the degree of achieved excellence, the aesthetic critics were at loggerheads. In his early work, T. S. Eliot was aesthetic in his outlook, judging all literature, past and present, primarily as literature and applying an absolute standard of excellence. But if art is expression, then how differentiate one form of expression from another, and how apply a principle of evaluation? Spingarn's attack on classical rules and on the moral standards of the New Humanists had its constructive aspect, however. It encouraged experimentation and made possible an extended sense of creative freedom. By protesting against the sheer accumulation of facts and challenging the validity of the established faith in historical erudition as an end in itself, it encouraged the critic to fix his attention more closely on the work itself and what it attempted to do, thus paving the way for tendencies in criticism which are still active today.

The "new criticism,"[16] using it in its loose chronological, not Spingarnian sense, was therefore in the nature of a protest against all that was considered conventional, stultifying, and repressive in the social as well as cultural life of America. It was, furthermore, a bold summons to the creative energy of this land, long held in check by materialistic forces, to leap forth and make itself effectively felt. This literary revolt ran the gamut from a fierce denunciation of puritanism and iniquitous capitalism to an impassioned defence of experimentalism in poetry and naturalism in fiction. Though it greatly encouraged writers to have faith in their work and to realize the intrinsic value of the creative life, its contribution to the art of criticism was negative rather than constructive. Norman Foerster describes Randolph Bourne, Van Wyck Brooks, and Lewis Mumford, the leaders of the movement, not as historical critics but as idealistic prophets who judge the present and the past in the light of a bright golden future toward which humanity is moving.[17]

This "new criticism," which began in the second decade and continued in full force during the twenties, had nothing but detestation for all that was conservative and academic, genteel and traditional,

16 The character of "newness" obviously changes constantly in relation to the whirligig of time.
17 Norman Foerster, *Toward Standards*, (New York, 1930), pp. 105–106.

in American life, but it developed no method of analysis. Instead, it stressed the value of experience and recommended faith in America as the basis for an autochthonous literature. Though European cultural importations of a selected kind were made welcome, they were generally used as sticks with which to beat the accursed provincialism that had curbed our growth. There was no incompatibility, however, in encouraging the growth of a truly national literature and in absorbing, insofar as these could prove useful, vital European ideas and influences. Percival Pollard, in *Their Day in Court* (1909), demonstrated that it was possible for a native critic to be keenly appreciative of the work of English and continental writers and still be deeply and discriminatingly interested in the literary contributions of his own countrymen. What these young, iconoclastic critics gave to criticism was an attitude toward life and letters: they were hospitable toward new ideas, realistic in accepting the challenge of new experience, confident that the future belonged to America if once its slumbering and repressed creative forces could be put seriously to work. Though they were diverse in temperament, outlook, and method, that was the one aim they held in common.

H. L. Mencken started a personal campaign against everything in American life that he happened to dislike, from Fundamentalism in the South to the crack-brained speeches made by members of Congress. He had the power of stirring things up. Stridently denunciatory, he fulminated against all that was provincial and puritanic in our national life. Though a matchless satirist and a writer of tremendous verve, he had, like Huneker, whom he admired, no sound principles of criticism to guide him in his work. If he championed writers like Dreiser and Sinclair Lewis at a time when they were still maligned and fighting for recognition, he could with equal conviction acclaim a number of second-rate writers as indubitably great. Toward poetry he was virtually stone-deaf. In short, he was an exuberant impressionist, exhibiting the richness of his soul, and recording brilliantly his reactions to the passing carnival of life and letters in the United States. He held an extremely low opinion of the general run of American critics, men like Stuart P. Sherman, Brownell, Paul Elmer More, William Lyon Phelps, calling them grown-up sophomores, incapable of absorbing new ideas, content to worship at the shrine of the respectable and the traditional.

Mencken's criticism was vigorously expressed but largely negative in spirit and substance. Criticism, he felt, is neither edification nor morality nor science but a creative release, a form of self-expression. There is no final truth to be discovered in aesthetics. It is personality —creative passion and creative force—that makes a work of art or a work of criticism live. "There is, in truth, no such thing as an exact fact in the whole realm of the beautiful."[18] The so-called truths formulated by criticism are relative and shifting. The critic is one who plunges up to his neck in the problems of his time and displays a thoroughgoing aliveness. In brief, he is an artist, not a judge. Despite his pose, Mencken had a considerable gift for appreciation when he genuinely liked an author, and an unparalleled gift for invective when he disapproved of a book or a movement. Unquestionably he succeeded in arousing attention where other critics, sounder in substance and more penetrating in their insight, failed miserably. His essays were alive and widely read, and for a time they imposed their dogmatic taste on both impressionable young writers and on a literate and semi-literate public.

But in his deep-rooted suspicion of theory, in his distrust of the intellect, in his denial that standards of any kind could be brought to bear on the field of criticism, he was part and parcel of the American booboisie that he so mercilessly lampooned. He parted company with them only in his detestation of moral categories as applied to art. Employing a rough and ready touchstone of common sense, he flatly rejected the use of absolutes in the domain of criticism. However, when he abandoned the field of literary criticism and took up the study of the American language, there was no one, really, to take his place. Impressionism, which is not a method but the dramatization of a personality, is essentially inimitable.

Van Wyck Brooks proved a more serious and pervasive influence on the course of literary criticism. What he laid undue stress on was, as we have seen, the theory that our native writers suffered from arrested growth. Theirs was the promise that had never been given the chance to ripen. This doctrine, later retracted or largely modified, was carried to unusual lengths in his books on Henry James and Mark Twain; he even resorted to psychoanalytic techniques to demonstrate how both these writers, aborted in their career as artists, failed to realize the fullness of their genius. Carrying Van Wyck Brooks' thesis and critical method much further, Lewis Mumford, in *The Golden Day* (1926), also discovered a singular warping of the American grain caused by our preoccupation with materialistic pursuits. Like Brooks he saw much in American life that was negative

18 H. L. Mencken, *Prejudices, Fifth Series* (New York, 1926), pp. 202-203.

and depressing: it was crude, raffish, shoddy, vulgar. Inspiring as both these critics were, disseminating fertile ideas in many directions, neither Mumford nor Brooks was particularly helpful in providing criticism with a concrete workable method. Instead they created a tradition of protest and prophecy and the desire for the establishment of an authentic native tradition, a usable past. Both were prophets by temperament, Mumford, as it proved, even more so than Brooks, and though their work played a distinguished part in the evolution of literary criticism in this country it failed to provide the exact discipline that was so badly needed. In a positive sense, their work made writers more sensitively aware of the rich heritage of the past to which they belonged, and the relationship of this past to what American literature could, under ideal conditions, bring forth in the future. Though their prophetic exhortations were not always based strictly on fact—witness the thesis-ridden treatment of the frontier by Mumford and Brooks[19]—they were at their best in encouraging writers to seek out hitherto unexplored or neglected areas of experience; they prepared the soil for naturalism in fiction, they proclaimed their steadfast faith in the potentialities of American genius, they upheld the virtues of vitality and intensity as opposed to the cult of the academic. And their numerous disciples founded "little" magazines to broadcast the new gospel of the creative life. Carried to extremes, this movement degenerated into a pseudo-mystical cult that was attacked for its excesses by both the Agrarians and the Humanists.

While all this was going on, Ezra Pound was waging a literary vendetta of his own. Like Spingarn, he was primarily interested in practicing aesthetic criticism. The concrete experience with a work of art, not a preliminary theory or abstraction, was to form the basis for critical judgment. The aim of criticism was not to draw up a broad system of philosophy but to arrive at a more sensitive and exact appreciation of the work of art. Pound worked out a complex method of his own, based on his enthusiasms and antipathies, and on the works of the past and the present that had influenced him most. As a leader of the experimentalists, he held up the ideal of scrupulous craftsmanship, the need of searching for the exact word. Poetry was to be freed from rhetoric, sentimentality, the abstract, the metaphysical commonplaces of the Victorians. It was the object of the artist to seek out new areas of experience for expression. Par-

[19] See particularly "The Romanticism of the Pioneer," Lewis Mumford, *The Golden Day* (New York, 1926), pp. 47–81.

ticularly he emphasized that the text itself was the locus of value; it must therefore be examined closely and patiently for whatever layers of meaning and overtones of magic it may disclose.

Eccentric, mannered, arbitrary in his judgments, Pound suffered from many of the defects to be found in Huneker's work. An unabashed impressionist, he was convinced that his trained, impeccable taste was a sufficiently valid basis for making critical pronouncements. His personality, however, was so explosively unstable, so contradictory and confused, as to interfere radically with his power of critical judgment. If we read him at all, we read him to catch some of his contagious enthusiasms, especially evident in his "close" studies of writers like Henry James and the French troubadors. The most subjective and dogmatic of critics, he is ill-tempered and even abusive in his literary feuds, in his Bohemian crusade to educate the American public as to the true standards and substance of literature.

While Pound and Spingarn were promulgating their aesthetic ideas, other critics of a liberal frame of mind, opposed to the injustices of the existing social order, were making themselves heard. Hopeful, forward-looking, they envisaged a future which would eradicate the socio-economic evils which prevent man from fulfilling his highest potentialities. Liberalism, an expression of the ingrained moral idealism of the American people, what Stuart P. Sherman would call the genius of America, the saving spirit of Puritanism—liberalism has played a constructive, if intermittent, part in the development of our criticism. With the exception of minor changes in vocabulary there is not much to choose between the "liberalism" of a Stuart P. Sherman after his arrival in New York and that of a Van Wyck Brooks or Ludwig Lewisohn. Critics of this persuasion are as a rule moved to praise highly literature that is in accord with their moral and social beliefs, literature that is experimental, idealistic, and progressive in outlook, not curbed by conventions, growing organically out of life. Like Dreiser and Mencken and Van Wyck Brooks, Ludwig Lewisohn warred against Puritanism and the tendency of our culture to stress narrow moral, parochial, and utilitarian values as opposed to the freedom of the creative life. His views are eloquently presented in *The Creative Life* (1924) and *Expression in America* (1932). Even more pronounced is Parrington's espousal of liberalism in *Main Currents of American Thought*. This was the type of social criticism that Van Wyck Brooks had called for in the hope that it would hasten America's coming-of-age.

The new body of American criticism was intellectually virile, full of fecund ideas, experimental in attitude. In 1926, William A. Drake, editing a volume of American criticism, summed it up by saying: "It is unquestionably more sensitive, more searching, more revealing, more democratic, in an abused word, more *creative*, than it has been at any time in the memory of our generation."[20] Yet he observes the persistence of one signal lack: the lack of a definite aesthetic conception, the result probably, he conjectures, of a long disuse of the reflective faculty. Consequently there are no standards, only a bog of confusion in which each critic exalts his own impressions as the sovereign law.

## IV

At the same time that Mencken and Brooks and Lewisohn and others were attacking Puritanism as the major repressive force in American life, critics were beginning to experiment with the task of applying Freudian theories to the analysis and understanding of literature. In *Freudianism and the Literary Mind*, Frederick J. Hoffman points out that by 1915 psychoanalysis was "fairly well launched in the magazines from which the intellectual of the day drew his information."[21] Many novelists, poets, and critics were deeply interested in psychoanalysis and applied it freely, both to their life and work. Psychoanalysis did more than turn public attention to the fascinating underworld of the unconscious and the complex symbolism of dreams. It encouraged a mania for introspection and self-analysis. People talked loosely but impressively about sublimations and repressions, the Oedipus complex and the inferiority complex. Writers felt that the technique of association revealed in dream analysis could be profitably applied in the field of experimental writing. Some adopted Jung's theory of a collective unconscious. Some critics found that psychoanalysis offered them a new interpretation of human nature, a new source of insight into the dynamics of human behavior. Critics using the Freudian aesthetic contended that poetry resembled the dream in structure, function, and content. Frederick C. Prescott, in *The Poetic Mind* (1922), argued that the dream afforded a revealing clue to the creative imagination. He had published an article on "Poetry and Dreams," in the *Journal of Abnormal Psychology*, reprinted in book form in 1919, which applied

---

20 William A. Drake (ed.), *American Criticism* (New York, 1926), p. vii.
21 Frederick J. Hoffman, *Freudianism and the Literary Mind* (Baton Rouge, 1945), p. 51.

Freudian ideas to poetry on the assumption that poetry is a disguised fulfillment of repressed wishes. The Freudian approach is also used in Conrad Aiken's *Scepticisms: Notes on Contemporary Poetry* (1919). A. A. Brill had translated Freud's *Interpretation of Dreams* into English in 1913.

The Freudian debate was on. Originally Freud had not intended to formulate a psychology of aesthetics, though there were incidental remarks scattered throughout his publications in professional periodicals indicating that his discoveries of "the reasons" for slips of the tongue, neurotic symptoms, and dream formation could also be profitably directed to the analysis of the creative process. Just as the Marxists later seized upon Marx's remarks in his books, his correspondence, and his journalistic articles, to draw up a comprehensive, dogmatic system of aesthetics, so the followers of Freud, taking up the clues the master had thrown out, carried out extensive explorations of the psychoneurotic aspects of literature. While the study of pathological writers—known to be such—may yield some rewarding insights, the analysis of works of art in terms of clinical symptoms is dangerously misleading. Freud's mistake, clearly, was to pigeonhole the artist as a child, and a neurotic child at that. Though Freud modified his theory in various particulars, the fundamental formulation of art as the sublimation of neurotic conflict remained. It was chiefly during the twenties that Freudianism came into its own in this country. Psychoanalysts were kept busy by writers who wished to confess their "sins." In the books of the period, Puritanism and the repressions it inevitably fostered were violently attacked. If these artificial sex repressions could be overcome, then the artist would be free to express himself fully, and thus achieve a measure of creative fulfillment. Converted to psychoanalysis, Floyd Dell, who had himself been psychoanalyzed, hailed Freud as an intellectual discoverer of the same stature as Copernicus, Darwin, and Marx.

The emergence of Freudianism revived the perennial discussion as to the nature of the artist. Was he neurotic or superman? In an article, "The Artist," Alfred Booth Kuttner declared that the artist hovered psychologically between the normal and the neurotic. Following Freud closely he argued that the artist, dissatisfied with life, turns away from reality, and second, that his work is an erotic and egocentric compensation for his myriad frustrations. The artist, in short, represents a stage of fixation which is full of psychic infantilism.[22] These were the ideological excesses to which early disciples of Freud were led. But there was some justification for such intemperate views to be found in the writings of Freud himself. Had Freud not summed up his philosophy of art in an essay published in 1911?

The artist is originally a man who turns from reality because he cannot come to terms with the demand for the renunciation of instinctual satisfaction as it is first made, and who then in phantasy-life allows full play to his erotic and ambitious wishes. But he finds a way of return from this world of phantasy back to reality; with his special gifts he moulds his phantasies into a new kind of reality, and men concede them a justification as valuable reflections of actual life. Thus by a certain path he actually becomes the hero, king, creator, favourite he desires to be, without pursuing the circuitous path of creating real alterations in the outer world. But this he can only attain because other men feel the same dissatisfaction as he with the renunciation demanded by reality, and because this dissatisfaction, resulting from the displacement of the pleasure-principle by the reality-principle, is itself a part of reality.[23]

Psychoanalysis, however, had done aesthetics a serious disservice by emphasizing the pathological aspects of genius. The creative mind was analyzed in the same way as the pathogenic states of paranoia and hysteria. There is nothing wrong in bringing to light the pathological element in literature, when it is manifestly there, but there is no warrant for the assumption that the artist as such is pathological. Even if it is contended that creation is a subtle form of dream life in which conscious and unconscious ingredients are intricately blended or that it is a disguised form of wish-fulfillment, this tells us practically nothing of the gulf which separates the artist from the dreamer. Psychoanalysis is obviously ineffectual in its efforts to account for the formal effects achieved by poetry, for example. The practical contribution psychoanalysis has thus far made to literary criticism is disappointingly small. James Oppenheim, a disciple of Jung, could not see how the unconscious, the product of repressed sexuality, could have been responsible for the birth of *Faust* and *Thus Spake Zarathustra*.[24] Floyd Dell, however, a loyal Freudian, maintained as late as 1930 that repression is as effectual in art as in neuroses. In short, art is interpreted as a

22 *The Seven Arts*, I (February, 1917), 412.
23 Sigmund Freud, *Collected Papers*, tr. by Joan Riviere (London, 1934), IV, 19.
24 James Oppenheim, *American Types* (New York, 1931), pp. 53–54.

symbolic method of leaping across the social barriers erected against incest, the murder of the hated father, narcissism, and homosexuality. "Religion aside, we may say that Art offers us a socially accepted alternative to the neuroses and psychoses which are the socially unacceptable ways of finding relief from lingering infantile anxieties."[25]

During the twenties, writers were attracted to Freudianism because it offered the symbolism of the dream and suggested ways of vitalizing, if not revolutionizing, language. Freudianism helped to sharpen the tool of linguistic communication, revealed its high-powered complexity and dynamic ambiguity, how it can be, and often is, used as a means of evasion or concealment. The poetic metaphor, by being harnessed to the motor of the dream, gained subtlety and psychological depth and richness. Dream language could produce marvelous poetic effects. Hypnagogic images and psychic automatism could become a legitimate, if not always fruitful, mode of literary experimentation. All this intensified the drive to emancipate poetry from the narrow limits of rational discourse. There were heights and depths, motives and paradoxes, ironic subtleties of meaning and obscure needs, which rational speech was incapable of expressing. The unconscious had to be opened up for exploration, repressions had to be overcome, for society straitjacketed and enslaved the organic impulses. The revolution of the word was definitely under way.

The intrusion of Marxist thought further complicated the controversies that raged over Freudian doctrine. Some critics were convinced that Marx and Freud could be reconciled, though in the thirties the general tendency was for Marxists to condemn psychoanalysis as a science because it was conditioned by its middle-class origins and its preoccupation with clinical pathology. The theoretical implications of Freudianism were more fruitful in stimulating numerous writers to experiment with new methods of expression. Some writers, however, preferred Jung's theory of the collective unconscious as well as his exaltation of the creative instinct to Freud's emphasis on the psychopathological aspects of genius and his rigid positivistic outlook. Freudianism, though less dominant than Marxism during the thirties, was subjected to a more thoroughgoing critical scrutiny.

Concretely, Freud's influence led critics to inquire into the nature of poetic genius and the creative process, on the assumption that

[25] Floyd Dell, *Love in the Machine Age* (New York, 1930), p. 384.

the first was essentially neurotic and the second the expression of a wish-fulfillment. Psychoanalytic criticism went even further and found in each literary work a veritable host of clinical symptoms. As Hoffman points out, the critical exploitation of psychoanalysis was often marked by "abuse and misunderstanding. Not only have critics often sinned against good critical sense by forcing the writers of the time into pigeonholes of theory; they have frequently mistreated Freud's original remarks about the psychological nature of the artist."[26]

Edmund Wilson was one of the few critics who utilized psychoanalytic criticism whenever it had anything of substantial value to contribute, but he combined it skilfully with historical criticism. In fact, he was one of those who saw clearly the dangers attendant on a literal application of the Freudian theory of aesthetics. A study of genetic sources may throw a revealing light on the biography and work of a writer, but it is not enough to inspect the personality of an author to ascertain what circumstances shaped it in a given direction. Like Van Wyck Brooks, who had utilized psychoanalytic criteria in his studies of Mark Twain and Henry James, Wilson concluded that Freudianism was too mechanical a science to apply categorically to literature, for it resorts to conjecture when the evidence is slender or non-existent. And Joseph Wood Krutch, in *Experience and Art* (1932), had sensibly declared: "Literature is certainly not a psychological purge any more than it is a sociological treatise. It is not identical with its subject matter and if it teaches anything is never reducible to any terms other than those of literature itself."[27] Bernard DeVoto ridiculed the excesses of psychoanalytic criticism in *Forays and Rebuttals* (1936). In *Minority Report* he punctured its blown-up pretensions with the needle of common sense: "There is an irreducible minimum of speculation in anything that psychoanalysis can say about literature, so long as it cannot study literature in the clinic's dynamic relationship with authors."[28] Neither psychoanalysis nor Marxism, however initially helpful in illuminating the area of literary investigation, can supplant the work the critic must do in order to determine the aesthetic value of literature—a point that Freud himself conceded.

As Kenneth Burke indicated, psychiatric considerations are no

[26] Frederick J. Hoffman, *Freudianism and the Literary Mind* (Baton Rouge, 1945), p. 99.
[27] Joseph Wood Krutch, *Experience and Art* (New York, 1932), p. 12.
[28] Bernard DeVoto, *Minority Report* (Boston, 1940), pp. 177–178.

substitute for aesthetic insight. Sniffing at neurotic symptoms is not the same thing as uncovering and appreciating the intrinsic meaning and function of symbols in a poetic context. But in the first flush of enthusiasm, the abnormal provided the central and controlling perspective, with the result, perhaps natural under the circumstances, that the aesthetic picture was thrown badly out of focus. What psychoanalysis did give a number of critics was a weapon and a vocabulary with which to attack the multiple evils of American civilization: the perverse denial of reality, the flight into dream life, the blighting influence of Puritanism, the sickly evasion of truth. Waldo Frank, for example, harped repeatedly on the repressions from which our native culture suffers. If he found any fault with Freud it was because the latter adhered too strictly to the mechanistic formulation of nineteenth-century science. Edward Dahlberg, a believer in creative criticism, angrily dismissed both psychoanalytic and Marxist criticism:

Away with the scientific, the proletarian and the psychoanalytic fraud in literature,—enough of the maundering truisms on poems and artists, from the Poloniuses upon the Hamlets, from the Jungs, the Otto Ranks, the Plekhanovs, the Trotskys, the Marxists. Enough of, this man is split, that poet is mad, this man is schizoid and that novelist is class-conscious.[29]

Freud's chief contribution to literature was in making clear the irrationality of the modern mind, the power and pervasiveness of unconscious forces at work in our culture.

## V

Two strangely conflicting streams of thought are to be found in the writing of critics concerning the character and destiny of America: one maintains that the future of the world rests in the hands of this country, that it is entrusted with the stupendous task of world leadership. The other attacks the crude, soul-blighting, deadening civilization this wealthy, industrial nation has brought forth and the obsession of the American people with money, materialism, and machinery. Savior and villain, heaven and hell! After the First World War the second attitude predominated: the belief that America is ruled by quantitative, grossly acquisitive standards, and that its people are a race of dollar-worshippers, efficiency-experts, techno-

29 Edward Dahlberg, *Do These Bones Live* (New York, 1941), p. 41.

logical wizards and technologized robots. A number of younger writers, convinced that this was all for the worst in a land of stern Puritanism and sordid materialism, tore up their roots—temporarily, as it proved—and migrated to Europe, particularly to Paris, in a self-sought, self-imposed exile, but not without first making clear the reasons for their disaffection, the cause of their alienation.

Malcolm Cowley's *Exile's Return* (1934) gives us the history of this first period of exile, portraits of the men who took part in it, and what finally drove them home. Historical and economic reasons made them realize finally that there was no avenue of escape, and the religion of art died. The various rationalizations writers had adopted—the escape into art, the escape toward the primitive, the escape by means of expatriation—were no longer effectual. By 1931 writers began the difficult task of readjusting themselves and recasting their values.

When the crash of the stock-market took place in 1929, the literary exiles abroad were shaken out of their isolation. Now that the United States was passing through an unprecedented economic crisis, the writers on the Left Bank were left stranded, without a reason for existence. The period marked the twilight of the Parisian gods. Night fell over the European Parnassus. These politically innocent, untutored exiles suddenly felt the burdens of social responsibility falling upon them. The "lost" generation now discovered that they must find themselves and take their rightful place in the struggle of life. The choice no longer rested in their hands. The depression forced them to scuttle home for safety to the industrial jungle of New York. The story of this period of repatriation and the difficulties it entailed has been told by Samuel Putnam in *Paris Was Our Mistress* (1947). The writer now had to justify his existence in social terms. The proletarian crusade began.

Harold E. Stearns, who had been one of the leaders in this exodus of intellectuals from the shores of America, came home like a prodigal son. After leading the life of a die-hard expatriate in Paris for a number of years, he returned not only converted but enlightened, delighted with America, now pictured as a land of promise and abounding vitality as contrasted with exhausted, decadent Europe, a land of freedom, with a bracing moral climate, with a democracy that is bound to triumph. He found ample confirmation of his new faith in our sexual mores, our business ethics, our science and engineering. How different all this is from the harshly negative appraisal to be found in *Civilization in the United States*, which he had edited in 1922! Thus *America: A Reappraisal* (1937) is an act of atonement and reconciliation.

The expatriate, as R. P. Blackmur points out, was an anti-nationalist in an age of economic nationalism. If much that he did was open to condemnation, he was nonetheless justified in his revolt. "One of the reasons that he went abroad was because of his delusion that the American view that the culture *belonged* abroad and could be *brought from* abroad was right; and another reason was in his corresponding illusion that the symbols of full social unity . . . were actually sustained by an existing and developing tradition."[30] The later expatriates who went abroad after the First World War, until the depression drove them home, afforded convincing testimony that they could find in America no soil where the creative spirit could take root and flourish.

This movement did not take place without arousing considerable protest. Though he encouraged the revolt against American civilization, Mencken, for example, had little sympathy with the Bohemians who fled the air-conditioned nightmare of American life. While others went into voluntary exile, he remained in America,

unshaken and undespairing, a loyal and devoted American, even a chauvinist, obeying all laws that are physiologically obeyable, accepting all the searching duties and responsibilities of citizenship unprotestingly, investing the spare usufructs of my toil in the obligations of the nation, avoiding commerce with men sworn to overthrow the government, contributing my mite toward the glory of the national arts and sciences, enriching and embellishing the native language. . . .[31]

Edgar Lee Masters also protested against this epidemic of expatriation, especially the fallacy on which it was founded, namely, that in the magical atmosphere of Europe the writer could find nourishment and quickening inspiration. The best of our writers, he declared in 1926, stayed at home and discovered their theme and reached creative fulfillment in this land. The handicaps the native environment may impose upon the artist are also the source of his strength and individuality. Like Archibald MacLeish in his poem, "American Letter," he declares: "This country is our fate, and we cannot escape it. For

30 R. P. Blackmur, "The American Literary Expatriate," in David F. Bowers (ed.), *Foreign Influences in American Life* (Princeton, 1944), pp. 134–135.
31 H. L. Mencken, *Prejudices, Third Series* (New York, 1922), p. 59.

myself, I think it probable that America will yet produce one of the
most powerful and distinctive literatures of the world. . . ."[32] He
sees no possibility of a writer ever achieving originality or greatness
by getting away from the roots of his experience. Whatever fruits
exile may produce, they will not be indigenous fruits. To portray
what he knows and what is his own the American writer must stay at
home.

In the twenties, too, an exciting but fortunately short-lived debate
broke out over the relation of the machine to art and civilization.
Lewis Mumford, in *Technics and Civilization* (1934), denounced the
worship of the machine, but *Whither Mankind,* edited by Charles A.
Beard in 1928, protested against this sentimental fear of the machine
and the science and technology on which it was based. Though it had
not yet produced a vigorous, mature art of its own, Beard felt that
it would in time give birth to a functional art. The established attitude, however, especially among the literati, was that the machine
was cruelly destroying our cultural potentialities. In *The Dance of
the Machines* (1929), Edward J. O'Brien personified the machine as
if it were engaged in a diabolical conspiracy to degrade and enslave
mankind. Sherwood Anderson and other writers fell under the same
peculiar obsession. Critics like Waldo Frank labored under the impression that industrialism was somehow fatal to the creative life.
In *Our America* (1919) and *The Re-Discovery of America* (1929),
he betrayed a curious animistic fear of the machine as a generator
of materialism, an anarchic principle, a devouring monster. Louis
Untermeyer, writing on "The Worship of the Machine," declared:
"To regard the machine as destiny is defeatism, which breeds hopelessness, despair, and abdication, and eventually suicide."[33]

But these furious debates on the relation of the machine to the
cultural and creative life of America ceased to be important once
the American economic system broke down in 1929. Gone were the
maudlin complaints about the jungle of the machine, the curse of
Puritanism, the ugliness and sterility of life in this rankly materialistic nation. But before taking up the critical debate that arose during
the depression-ravaged Thirties, it is necessary to discuss the challenge of Humanism.

32 Edgar Lee Masters, "The American Background," in William A. Drake (ed.),
*American Criticism* (New York, 1926), p. 149.
33 Louis Untermeyer, "The Worship of the Machine," *The American Mercury,*
XXII (March, 1931), 256.

## VI

It is inaccurate to speak of Humanism as if it emerged for the first time in the Twenties, for it had never really died. A philosophic evaluation of life, a value-freighted attitude, it represents a more or less permanent expression of the human spirit, manifesting not only a desire for order and restraint but also for some binding ethical discipline. It starts with the fundamental premise that man is not only different from but superior to the animal, and that this superiority consists in his power of controlling his brutish impulses. Like classicism, which it admires, it is opposed to excess, uncurbed enthusiasm, the aberrations of the romantic temperament. The Humanist, believing that man must exercise his god-given will-power, is hostile to the philosophy of deterministic naturalism. What is wrong with naturalism, according to the humanistic doctrine, is that it fails to provide standards. It relies on the contributions of science, without understanding that science is impotent to provide standards of life and of art. Hence the central conflict of this age may well prove to be one between an expanding naturalism and a new humanism.

The very forces that made Humanism seem so attractive for some minds, especially in the academic world, militated against its permanent success. Its gospel of the inner check, its attack on Rousseauistic emotionalism and the cult of the ego and its own, its disparagement of science and its war on the philosophy of determinism, the dualism it set up between man and nature—these tended after a time to repel a postwar generation that had grown accustomed to doubt all things. In *The Critique of Humanism* (1930) and in numerous magazine articles, the dualistic philosophy of Humanism was pulled apart, its fallacies and limitations exposed. However much the opposition might differ on other parts of their program, they were at one in fighting off the attempt to impose moral standards on the integrity of a work of art.

The Humanists, however, were not to be prevented from having their say; their forces were being steadily augmented and they had influential representatives in seats of higher learning throughout the country. In *Humanism and America,* edited by Norman Foerster in 1930, Gorham B. Munson, writing on "Our Critical Spokesmen," hails Babbitt and More as the best living critics of America and regards the years from 1915 to 1930 as in the nature of a tragicomedy. Unselective in his sympathies, Stuart P. Sherman, we are told, lacks the gift of leadership, and the role played by Spingarn, Mencken, and Van Wyck Brooks allegedly illustrates the mediocrity of contemporary American criticism. Though it was opposed to romanticism in all its forms, Humanism did not go far enough to suit T. S. Eliot. It refused to commit itself on the vital matter of supernatural sanctions, setting up the moral and the specifically human as the central norm. Literature was thus to be a medium for exhibiting the measure of self-control the rational imagination could impose on the flux of experience. Here, ready to hand, were the weapons with which to beat down the dangerous heresies of the day: the laxity of impressionism, the mechanistic world-view and interpretation of human nature furnished by naturalism, the "immoral" extravagances and eccentricities of contemporary literature.

In a series of scholarly and impressive works Paul Elmer More gave expression to the basic tenets of the Humanist doctrine, applying to authors of the past and present, chiefly European, the principles of ethical insight and restraint. This preoccupation with the moral element in literature became in time too obsessive; indeed, the chief defect of his writing is that it is too heavily weighted in the direction of philosophy and ethics and too little concerned with the technical requirements of the critical method. In his *Pages from an Oxford Diary* (1937), he complains that it was his misfortune to be too much addicted to literature to be accepted by the philosophers, and too consistently devoted to the method of interpreting art by an ethical criterion to win the approval of literary critics. He was scholarly and high-minded, conscientious, thorough, and eloquent, but his moral prepossessions held his sensibility in check and seriously inhibited his native powers of aesthetic judgment. Before he could accept and approve of a work it had to satisfy his conception of what was ethically right, and if it lacked this saving element, whatever other virtues it might possess, he felt justified in rejecting it. Small wonder that he was opposed to the literature appearing in the Twenties, assailing novelists like Sinclair Lewis, Dreiser, Sherwood Anderson, and John Dos Passos for their naturalistic temper, their contempt for New England Puritanism, their conviction that art has no commerce with morality. In one of his essays, "Modern Currents in American Literature," he describes *Manhattan Transfer* as "an explosion in a cesspool."[34] What American literature needs, he declares, is the "discipline of a classical humanism. . . ."[34a]

---

[34] Paul Elmer More, *The Demon of the Absolute* (Princeton, 1928), p. 63.
[34a] *Ibid.,* p. 76.

Irving Babbitt was the more vigorous personality, a more formidable polemicist. His *bête noir* was Rousseau, the source of all that was emotionally anarchic, irresponsible, and decadent in modern culture. A trenchant stylist, a master of many tongues and literatures, both ancient and modern, he was more interested in combating the influence of pernicious ideas and their embodiment in works of literature than in responding to these works freely and fully and in thus discovering the secret of their creative power. Consistent in his espousal of humanistic principles, he denounced not only Rousseauistic romanticism but also its bastard progeny: humanitarianism, individualism, the shibboleths of freedom, the cult of personality and originality in literature, the perverse emphasis on the experimental, the eccentric, the untraditional. In short, he was a staunch traditionalist, a classicist in his convictions, a die-hard conservative in his tastes. There were sound and tested ideals, he insisted, to which the writer must conform: the ideal of wholeness, of right reason, the ideal of ethical restraint. These were the salutary, disciplining virtues he recommended as a specific remedy against the evils from which modern culture suffered. Impressionism was solipsistic and indefensible; if the critic was to pass judgment with any degree of validity, he must adhere to a norm that does not spring from his capricious personal temperament. Like More, Babbitt arbitrarily condemned modern writers, without elucidating the grounds upon which they are to be excommunicated. The moral criteria of Humanism, when one tries to apply them, prove to be abstract and restrictive, concerned with the ideological content and moral impact of a work rather than with its intrinsic aesthetic qualities. Though it helped to counter some of the excesses of the naturalistic movement, it originated nothing of importance and fell a victim to its own crusading passion and intolerant righteousness.

Humanism achieved nothing in the creative field, its most distinguished contribution being in the domain of criticism. One strongly suspects that the Humanists are interested not so much in literature and art as in the "good life." Babbitt and his followers scold the younger generation of writers severely for their sins and attribute the evils and irresponsibility of contemporary literature to the lamentable influence of Rousseau. Shelley, condemned by Babbitt as the most purely Rousseauistic of the English romantic poets, is dismissed as nothing but an ineffectual dreamer. The most striking limitations of Humanism are revealed in its frontal attack on science, its distrust of empirical experience, its condemnation of the animal instincts and appetites, its wholesale rejection of psychoanalysis. While it argues that the psychological truth of "the higher will" is a mystery that cannot be formulated, it ignores the scientific investigation of the origin and development of morals by such scholars as Malinowski, John Dewey, Westermarck, and Freud. Humanism, denying the reality of the natural order, rejects the concept of the natural man and the idea of the continuity of experience. More, for example, is convinced that the attempt "to represent life as an unmitigated flux . . . means confinement in a mad-house."[35]

The religious character of the Humanist movement appears strongly in the essay on "The Pride of Modernity" (in *Humanism and America*), by G. R. Elliott, who insists that the full spiritual life can be perfected only by the aid of institutional religion. And in *Humanism and Imagination* (1938) he declares that the religious truth is to be found in Christianity and nowhere else. If criticism wishes to see life whole, it must move in the direction of Christianity. Even Paul Elmer More, after seriously weighing the problem, decides that Humanism must be based on religion.

It is not surprising that the most enthusiastic disciples of Humanism were recruited from the academic profession. Stuart P. Sherman, who had while at Harvard fallen under the magnetic spell of his teacher, Irving Babbitt, became for a number of years a devoted follower. So did such critics as Norman Foerster, Harry Hayden Clark, and others. But the Humanist movement was as a whole utterly out of touch with the vital issues confronting the modern mind; it was "reactionary" in outlook, seeking to halt the march of invention and ideas, to impose absolute unity on the flux of experience, to combat the power and limit the validity of science. The radical critics naturally found Humanism to be muddled and ultraconservative. Only here and there are the Humanistic outposts still defended with quiet conviction. The movement has lost whatever commanding position it once held. It is no longer a vital influence in criticism, only an historically outlived memory. Though he does not battle under the standard of Humanism, Yvor Winters certainly has much in common with men like Babbitt and More: there is the same inveterate defence of classical virtues, the same condemnation of eccentric individualism, the same stress on the moral values that literature should exemplify, the same adherence to a system of absolutism.

35 Norman Foerster (ed.), *Humanism and America* (New York, 1930), p. 63.

## VII

Whatever his shortcomings as a literary critic, T. S. Eliot was at least seriously and consistently concerned to formulate a critical method that would be free from the weaknesses to be found in historical, psychological, and sociological interpretations of literature. He is without question the most important and most authoritative critic of our country, if he can be said to belong to us and not to England, far more influential in his writing than either the humanistic or scientific critics. At the outset of his career he could not accept the moralistic bias of the Humanists. As for the impressionists, they were simply unprincipled, wandering at loose ends. The sensibility of a critic must be active, his taste trained, but these must be disciplined by intelligence and controlled by the uses of reason. Before any critical judgment can be passed, the cultivated sensibility must do its work. The way it can best perform its task is by the use of the comparative method. The critic must fix his attention resolutely on the text before him and from that derive his conclusions. Here, Eliot felt, was a check on reckless generalizations and the vagaries of impressionism. The aesthetic preoccupation neutralizes the ethical bias. Moreover, such interest in the inherent qualities of the text, disclosing values immanent in the work of art, rendered superfluous the introduction of biographical details, the intrusion of Marxist ideology or deterministic criteria. Not that the poet was cut off from tradition; the greater the poet the more evident was his indebtedness to a central literary tradition and the discipline it necessarily enforces. In essay after essay, before his conversion to Anglo-Catholicism, T. S. Eliot demonstrated how these tasks should be carried out.

T. S. Eliot's "Tradition and the Individual Talent" is a virtual landmark in modern criticism. Published in 1917, it effectively formulates many of the ideas which were to become the chief stock-in-trade of the new criticism. Impressively defending the role tradition plays in literature, Eliot calls for a reliance on fairly objective standards as opposed to romantic laxness, the flabbiness and inconclusiveness of impressionistic criticism, the cult of genius and uncurbed subjectivity. Rejecting the ethical doctrines of Babbitt, the early Eliot took his stand on such purely literary considerations as structure and style, thus recognizing in poetry a greater degree of complexity than the Humanists, with their formal dualistic principles, could discern. He practiced criticism with grace, urbanity, and distinction, working out a method of analysis that centered on the structure of the poem and how it compared with other poems. Aesthetic criticism had come into its own.

The progress of the artist, Eliot insists, involves a continual extinction of personality. What counts supremely is not the intensity of feeling with which the poet writes but the intensity of his artistic control. Eliot's main thesis, fundamental in his philosophy of aesthetics, is that poetry is essentially an escape from emotions, an escape from the obsessive personality. The great artist forgets himself in his work.

Eliot's transition from purely literary to religious-literary criticism is now pronounced in character. He now holds that though literature as such can be determined only by literary standards, its greatness cannot be measured by such standards. To keep literature and religion in two separate compartments is irrational—and ineffectual. Without the religious synthesis, literature becomes irresponsible and immoral.

The fact that Eliot first published his critical essays in periodicals surely casts no reflection on the quality of the criticism he produces or the value of his books. To regard him, as Stanley Edgar Hyman does in *The Armed Vision,* not as a professional analyst of literature but as a professional poet, is to misrepresent the issue. For Eliot is both poet and critic, and the two functions, far from conflicting, complement each other. Whether or not one agrees with Eliot's critical method and his evaluation of literature, it is impossible not to acknowledge the high seriousness, the profound insight, and the sound scholarship which inform his work, at least before he was led astray by theological absolutes.

A number of critics sprang up, both in England and the United States, who continued this work in aesthetic criticism. Henceforth the text was the point of departure, the focus of primary interest, the basis for aesthetic judgment. In *Axel's Castle* (1931), and in many essays and reviews contributed to periodicals, Edmund Wilson, even though he relied on the historical method, retained a vivid sense of the dynamic qualities of the text before him, its structure as well as meaning. He sketched in the socio-political scene, but only in order to illuminate the poem or novel under consideration.

The one who carried "formal" criticism to its highest point of development was unquestionably Yvor Winters, who insisted on the importance of structural organization and inner coherence, but with this, oddly enough, he coupled a demand for rational discipline and moral values. Alone he fought against the excesses of the experimental modern writers, both "the primitivists" and "the decadents," remorselessly exposing their confusion of thought, their irrationality, their lack of moral insight. In his books and magazine articles, John Crowe Ransom built the foundation for what he calls "the new criticism." Like Allen Tate, he made the analysis of the poetry itself primary; other considerations, social or scientific, political or moral, were secondary. These "new critics" were bent on rediscovering and reaffirming the value of tradition, the value of coherent artistic structure. R. P. Blackmur probably carried this method to its highest degree of perfection, laboring conscientiously over his essays in order to make clear the properties of style and structure in a text, be it poem or novel, and without engaging in the controversies that attracted Ransom and especially Winters. Alert, sensitive, discriminating, imaginatively discerning and subtle in his examination of poetic structure, style, and metaphor, he made of criticism a responsible job of work.

The practitioners of the "new criticism" differ too radically in theory and temperament actually to constitute a school; they represent, rather, a converging stream of tendencies, which rises from a common source of tradition and taste, thought and conviction. Though they possess the fine sensibility and aesthetic responsiveness of the impressionists, they seek to discover value in the work of art itself, and not in extraneous considerations, sociological, positivistic, political, or economic. The literary work is what the writer fashioned, and it is the function of the critic to examine it as closely and sympathetically as he can. Though these formalist critics make use of psychological insights, especially those contributed by Freud, they are not doctrinaire in employing this method. Their concern is fundamentally with developing a sensitive and rewarding critical method. For the most part, however, they are neo-classical in their preferences and opposed, like the Humanists, to many modern influences: scientific monism, the cult of naturalism, economic determinism, romanticism with its vagueness and lack of control, and democratic humanitarianism.

The formalist critics present a fairly good case: criticism, they insist, must sharpen its professional tools, forge a precise nomenclature and method of analysis. Otherwise it is guilty of either specious theorizing or glib impressionism. Formal criticism marks a return to the text, which is used as the field of operation for the interpretation that dialectically emerges. The object of these subtle, painstakingly ingenious interpretations is to reveal the artistry, unconscious as well as deliberate, which went into the making of a poem. Poetry is charged, as I. A. Richards and William Empson had pointed out, with multiple ambiguities and inner tensions, which must be resolved by the aid of critical insight. The language of poetry, according to Cleanth Brooks in *The Well Wrought Urn* (1947), is the language of paradox. The deeper the critic probes, the more rewarding are his findings. For these paradoxes are not the product of ratiocination but the synthesis of emotion and intuition, a kind of surrealist flash and fusion.

There is a definite need for close textual analysis. It is a difficult, challenging, and, when rightly done, highly rewarding discipline. It puts criticism on a responsible basis. The critic can no longer "emote" or reveal the richness of his sensibility. He is tied down by the intention of the poem, the meaning of the lines held in solution, the organic unity of the design. Instead of dealing with generalities, he must analyze the specific properties a poem possesses, its interior structure, its dynamic principle of organization. Consistently applied, this method eliminates biography and sociology and *ad hoc* doctrines as irrelevant. It maintains that the poet meant exactly what he wrote and that the meaning is to be found by a careful study of the poem's imagery, its underlying pattern, rather than by ideological interpretation or impressionistic gush. The only question at issue is how far such a method should be carried. At its worst, this method tends to cut the critic off from life. The poem becomes a complete, autonomous, self-sustaining entity. Any references the poem may have to things outside are taboo. Hence poetry ceases to be an expression or criticism of life and becomes, instead, the vehicle of an experiment in language: it presents conundrums, enigmas, special linguistic and semantic and stylistic problems which it is the province of the critic to explore.

## VIII

Sociological criticism has had many proponents in this country during the past fifty years. It is but a step from contending that literature must serve a moral function to maintaining that it must embody social ideas as well. Hence, if literature is essentially a criticism of life, it should be measured in terms not only of its faithfulness of representation but also of its faithfulness in expressing the social ideal. Literature, therefore, expresses integrated patterns of experience in order, ultimately, to shape and improve the quality of that experience. The adherence to the Puritan tradition, the austere idealism which is native to our literature, was exemplified by Stuart P. Sherman, both in his late and early phase, though more so when he was ponitificating from his academic Zion in the Midwest.

Radical criticism, despite its doctrinaire coating, took its origins from a profound ethical impulse: an impulse expanded and organized so as to include a demand for economic and social reforms of a revolutionary nature, of which literature, all culture in fact, is to be an instrument. Everything is comprehended and accounted for within the framework of dialectical materialism, the philosophical underpinning of Marxism. Here was a doctrine sufficiently comprehensive, militant, and optimistic to appeal to different temperaments among writers, and for different reasons. Capitalism was the master to be destroyed. Whereas politically divergent "liberal" critics such as Ludwig Lewisohn, Van Wyck Brooks, Lewis Mumford, and Waldo Frank had attacked bourgeois civilization, the Marxists based their attack on what they considered to be unimpeachable "scientific" grounds. The shallowness of our native culture, its glorification of individualism, these were the direct expression of a profit-centered capitalist civilization. The Communist critics stressed not the freedom of the individual, not even the so-called freedom of the artist. That was essentially a bourgeois illusion. Rather, the goal was to establish the collective commonwealth, the classless society, in which each would receive according to his needs and give according to his ability. Hence the emphasis on having the writer participate in the labor movement and in the political struggles of his time, championing, of course, the proletarian cause and seeking to produce a proletarian literature that would eventually help to bring about the dictatorship of the proletariat.

Marxist criticism posed a difficult choice between aesthetic and social values. If the economic pressure of capitalist society warped the personality of the artist and adversely conditioned the kind of work he turned out, what then? Marxist criticism, unfortunately, offered no concrete criteria for evaluating a work of art, once its historical genesis and historical relationships in a given period had been determined. For regardless of the economic conditioning to which art in any society is inevitably subjected, its merit and meaning as art still remains to be ascertained.

Upton Sinclair had already called attention, in *Mammonart*

(1925), to the importance of the economic motif in literature. Trotsky's influential book, *Literature and Revolution,* had been published in an English translation in 1924. In 1925 appeared Calverton's *The Newer Spirit,* which employed a form of sociological criticism that treated literature as a reflection of the social and economic conflicts of an age. The socialist *Masses* flourished from 1911 to 1917, under the editorship of Max Eastman and Floyd Dell, as the organ of the literary but still independent left-wing. In *Intellectual Vagabondage* (1926), Floyd Dell traces the rise and fall of different ideas in relation to the economic forces in the environment. At last he came to the conclusion that he must ally himself with the proletariat, the inheritors of the future.

Max Eastman had early espoused the cause of radicalism, and *The Masses* and *The Liberator,* both of which he edited, gave him an outlet for his ideas, but the Stalinist control and coordination of the arts in Russia caused him to change his views. Granville Hicks remained during the Thirties a simon-pure, uncompromising Marxist, who believed that Marxism can be applied not only to all literature but also to all art. Though like Eastman he later left the Communist Party and greatly modified his extremist views, he was, during the period when he helped to edit the *New Masses,* the most influential critic of the left in demanding an economic interpretation of literature according to strict Marxist class-categories. His practice is best illustrated in *The Great Tradition* (1933), which betrays an astonishing neglect of aesthetic values.

Joseph Freeman, a Marxist critic of a pronounced cast, was also active during the Thirties in popularizing Marxist ideas as applied to literature and in formulating the principles which should govern the creation of proletarian literature. In 1935, together with others, he edited *Proletarian Literature in the United States.* At the first American Writers' Congress (1935) he gave a talk on "The Tradition of American Literature," which called on writers to voice their sympathy with the proletarian revolution. A year before that he had declared:

For a long time, Michael Gold and I were the only literary critics in the United States attempting to evaluate art and literature by revolutionary standards. We made many blunders, for we had no real heritage in this field. The *Masses* critics did not, as a rule, accept the Marxist approach to art and literature.[36]

36 Joseph Freeman, "Ivory Towers—White and Red," *New Masses* (September 11, 1934), pp. 21–22.

He does not deny the real backwardness of Marxist criticism in the United States. In his introduction to *Proletarian Literature in the United States*, he emphasizes that the poet expresses a class reality, that all art is class-conditioned. In his autobiography, *An American Testament* (1936), he confesses that the revolutionary movement gave his work and his life meaning, purpose, and vitality.

It soon became evident that this extreme overestimation of the role of social and economic forces in the interpretation of literature would have to be counterbalanced by a more enlightened professional interest in aesthetic problems. The Marxist impulse in American literary criticism was chiefly hortatory and evangelical. Prophetic and propagandistic in tone, it appealed to the conscience of the uprooted intellectuals, especially those who had returned from exile abroad to an America plunged in the trough of an economic depression. Henceforth they resolved to devote themselves to the cause of humanity and enlist as soldiers in the ranks of the proletariat who were fighting the class war. For them it was exhilarating to discover that literature and art were powerful weapons in hastening the advent of the social revolution. At last they had found their true vocation.

Malcolm Cowley illustrates the pilgrimage from Parisian cafés and boulevard brawls to Marxist forums, from a love of Proust and Valéry to a solemn study of Marx and Engels and Lenin, from eccentric aestheticism to the responsibilities of editing *The New Republic*. He developed into a Marxist critic using economic determinants, social perspectives, and class consciousness as his touchstones. There are no universal and timeless human relationships. They change in conformity with broader social changes. A better social philosophy might help writers to produce better plays, poetry, and fiction. The writer cannot cut himself off from society. Yet he balked even then (this was in the mid-Thirties) at the dogmatic application of Marxist principles as a standard of literary values, though he still feels that it is the duty of the writer to engage in the class struggle if he wishes to retain his creative energy and intergrity. But in "Faith and the Future," which appeared in *Whither Revolution?* edited by Irving DeWitt Talmadge in 1941, Cowley shifted his ground and exposed the weaknesses of Communism, just as John Chamberlain, in *The American Stakes* (1940), bidding farewell to his then recent "radical" heresies, announced that he was no longer concerned with what ought to be but with what is, and with what can be salvaged on that basis.

In their revolutionary zeal the Marxists carried their extremism to such lengths that reaction finally set in. The pronounced bias of the movement soon became evident: the tendency to idealize the proletariat and to denounce all opponents as motivated by selfish interests. Even more objectionable was the tendency to apply a mechanical, simplified version of dialectical materialism to all literature and art, without taking the aesthetic component into consideration. Works of literature were systematically tested according to rigid canons of political and ideological orthodoxy. That is what James T. Farrell vigorously protested against in *A Note on Literary Criticism* (1936): namely, the failure of the so-called Marxist critics to take the aesthetic properties of literature into account, thus making literature serve utilitarian and ulterior ends as an arm of propaganda.

With the outbreak of the Second World War, the split in the ranks of the Communist critics and those "fellow-travellers" who practiced Marxist criticism, became even wider. When the report of the third American Writers' Congress, *Fighting Words,* came out, Malcolm Cowley, reviewing it in *The New Republic,* made clear why he, together with a number of other writers, had decided to resign from this organization. He could not accept the explanation of the war which regarded it as a conflict between rival imperialistic powers, just as Granville Hicks could not accept the official "party" interpretation of the treaty of alliance concluded between Soviet Russia and Nazi Germany. That such controversial political issues should engage the attention of literary critics, indicates how far afield criticism had wandered in adopting the philosophy of Marxism.

The critics on the left did not, to be sure, have things their own way. Far from it. They constituted a militantly vociferous, but from the point of view of criticism, professionally inept and hopelessly sectarian minority. Nevertheless, in their messianic righteousness, they raised such an ideological furore that liberal critics were led to make frequent and forceful protests. Henry Hazlitt pointed out that those who dismiss practically all existing culture by invidiously labeling it "bourgeois" are not necessarily Marxists but simply new barbarians, "celebrants of crudity and ignorance."[37] What is even worse, most of the new American "Marxist" critics displayed a deplorable intellectual confusion. Bernard DeVoto, as editor of *The Saturday Review of Literature* from 1936 to 1938, spiritedly com-

37 Henry Hazlitt, "Literature and the 'Class War,'" *The Nation,* CXXXV (October 19, 1932), 362.

batted the excesses of both the Freudian and Marxist critics. Tempered by a profound skepticism, his outlook as a critic was thoroughly eclectic. He had no critical system, he announced, and no intention of formulating one; in fact, that it is logically and psychologically impossible to set up objective standards in criticism. In *The Literary Fallacy* (1944), he maintains that literary critics suffer from inbreeding, a "neurotic" tendency to use literature alone as the measure of cultural value, whereas, to be truly understood, it must be studied and evaluated in relation to its place in the total social, economic, and historical context as one of the vitally significant activities of the human spirit.

There were some critics, however, who never abandoned their faith that the writings of Marx and Engels could provide a *vade mecum* for the literary critic who could apply what they taught boldly and cogently. Bernard Smith, in *Forces in American Criticism* (1939), undertakes the herculean but essentially futile task of interpreting all of American criticism, from the beginning to the present day, in the light of Marxist principles. He states the Marxist thesis briefly as follows:

a work of literature reflects its author's adjustment to society. To determine the character and value of the work we must therefore, among other things, understand and have an opinion about the social forces that produced the ideology it expresses as an attitude toward life. Marxism enables us to understand these forces by explaining the dialectical relationship of a culture to an economy and of that culture to the classes which exist in that economy. At the same time, by revealing the creative role of the proletariat in establishing a communist society, which alone can realize universal peace and well-being, Marxism offers a scale of values.[38]

In *The Armed Vision* (1948), Stanley Edgar Hyman declares that the last possibility of a non-Marxist American criticism disappeared with the death of such men as Randolph Bourne and Vernon Parrington, and that from then on American sociological criticism would have to be Marxist or nothing. Though he differs with the Marxist critics on a number of methodological issues, he seriously proceeds, like them, to examine the writings of Marx in the hope of finding pertinent material on which to base a system of Marxist aesthetics. The quest is in itself indicative of a state of mind which is not uncommon. Whatever Marx may have to say about the decadence of art under capitalism, he is writing tendentiously throughout, and even

[38] Bernard Smith, *Forces in American Criticism* (New York, 1939), pp. 287–288.

at that he is saying nothing that the writers and artists had not discovered themselves. Though Hyman complains of the idiocy of so-
called Marxist criticism, he does so only to clear the way for his own
brand of Marxist criticism, purified and legitimate. It is not Marxist
criticism *per se* that he reprobates but Marxist criticism that fails to
consider aesthetic values. Marxist criticism, he believes, should turn
to the detailed study of literature; it can be used constructively if that
omission is remedied. The assumption throughout is that a valid
Marxist criticism can and will be built on the foundations laid by
Marx, Plekhanov, Lenin, Lunacharsky, and other Soviet aestheticians. Marxism, he declares,

can deal with the social origins and socio-symbolic interrelations of the
work, but it can, in addition, deal with its formal artistic techniques to some
extent in social and historical terms, and in the same terms it can make
rather limited statements of aesthetic value.[39]

Here, then, is an earnest, cautiously qualified, and ingenious attempt
to make the best of two worlds. No reasoned proof, however, is
offered to show why sociological criticism cannot accomplish all that
Marxist criticism is alleged to do, without using its arbitrary class-
categories, its polemical tone, and its revolutionary imperatives.

## IX

In contrast to the messianic Marxists there were skeptical critics
like Carl Van Doren, critics like Henry Seidel Canby who mediated
between extreme points of view, and eclectic critics like Bernard
DeVoto. A vigorous apostle of common sense, a realist in his respect
for facts and what they disclose to the patiently inquiring mind,
DeVoto professes, like Mencken, to eschew all theory, especially
speculations metaphysical, aesthetic, prophetic, and eschatological.
Replying to Edmund Wilson's challenge that he state what principles
support his judgment, he answered cheerfully that he had no such
system and profoundly disbelieved in such systems.[40] This is clearly
an evasion of the issue. The critic cannot forego the attempt nor
shirk the responsibility to coordinate and affirm the ideas which
guide him in the act of judgment and evaluation. Even to repudiate
theory, as DeVoto seems to be doing, is to be guilty of theorizing.

[39] Stanley Edgar Hyman, *The Armed Vision* (New York, 1948), p. 203.
[40] Bernard DeVoto, *Minority Report* (Boston, 1940), p. 164. This article, "Autobiography; or, as Some Call it, Literary Criticism," appeared originally in *The Saturday Review of Literature*, February 13, 1937.

If DeVoto disbelieves in such critical systems it is because he has acquired a deep distrust of absolutes. Positively he describes himself as a pluralist, a relativist, an empiricist, confining himself to the exploration of limited questions, seeking to use methods that can be controlled by facts and the verdict of experience. Experience and common sense: these are what he relies on, and even these are frail reeds to lean on, but at least they are more dependable than the gospel of absolutism, in politics or aesthetics. Since he confines himself to limited objectives, he first seeks to sift out the fact from the theory, the verifiable from that which is visionary. Whereas abstract theory is but a bag of wind, the empirical fact will not let him down.[41] Primarily concerned, in literature, with the individual, he cannot look upon the human tragedy as essentially economic in character; the universal human emotions seem to him more real than the elements of economic conflict. Since he has failed to work out a coherent, all-inclusive system, he is satisfied to move slowly, step by step, trying at all times to be accurate, to document his facts. Thus he prefers to think of himself not as a critic but as a historian or possibly psychiatrist, though he distrusts labels and doubts whether the function of the literary critic can be defined with precision.

In *The Literary Fallacy*, he wars against the whole tribe of American literary critics who are betrayed by theories and preconceptions. Their work is often marked, he charges, by ignorance and folly, *a priori* reasoning, unchecked generalizations. This is how he sums up the nature of "the literary fallacy":

Reduced to general terms, the literary fallacy assumes: that a culture may be understood and judged solely by means of its literature, that literature embodies truly and completely both the values and the contents of a culture, that literature is the measure of life, and finally that life is subordinate to literature.[42]

Here he was reacting strongly against the thesis advanced by such critics as Van Wyck Brooks, Lewis Mumford, Waldo Frank, and others, that America was a desert of crude acquisitiveness and regimented vulgarity, its culture inimical to the flowering of native genius. "Never in any country or any age," he declares hyperbolically, "had writers so misrepresented their culture, never had they

41 Compare this with T. S. Eliot's insistence, as far back as 1923, in "The Function of Criticism," that a critic must have a very highly developed sense of fact. T. S. Eliot, *Selected Essays: 1917–1932* (New York, 1932), 19–22.
42 Bernard DeVoto, *The Literary Fallacy* (Boston, 1944), p. 43.

been so unanimously wrong. Never had writers been so completely separated from the experiences that alone give life and validity to literature."[43]

Almost a decade before this, Gilbert Seldes had presented virtually the same thesis in *Mainland* (1936), denying that literature is the standard by which a nation must be measured. He would provide a heartening corrective to the negative literary approach of critics like Van Wyck Brooks. These men were blind to the rich actuality and achievement of the American past, and they falsified or grossly failed to understand the character of American history or American life. He complains that in the decade of criticism no works appeared to hail the moral grandeur of the pioneer, "the nobility of the businessman, the fine enraptured cultivation of his wife, or even the average decency of the American people."[44] The future, he is convinced, belongs to America.

In our literature and our sports; in popular songs and eccentric religions; in five-and-ten-cent stores and the belt system of producing motorcars; in red barns in New England, silos in Michigan, and bungalows in California; in millions of immigrants and in Browning societies; in Wisconsin and Pittsburgh and Vermont; in Bryan and Henry Ford and John Humphrey Noyes and Emerson, we catch expressions which reveal a character we can call American.[44a]

The relativistic position in criticism was given sober and cogent statement in Frederick A. Pottle's *The Idiom of Poetry* (1942, revised edition issued in 1946). Pottle adopts the mechanistic approach without excluding the psychological one, shifting from one to the other as the context and the occasion demand. He accepts the philosophy of critical relativism: namely, the belief that standards are variable, that judgments are relative to the age in which they are made, that each system is logically consistent within its own framework of assumptions. Hence each critic is right insofar as he applies his standards of judgment consistently; he is wrong if he insists that these judgments are absolute and infallible, true for all time. Tastes change sharply, and there seems to be no reason at all for "concluding that taste grows progressively better, or that the mere passage of time widens literary sympathies and sharpens the critical faculty."[45] Though a critic should proceed to evaluate, and do so

43 *Ibid.*, p. 167.
44 Gilbert Seldes, *Mainland* (New York, 1936), p. 20.
44a *Ibid.*, p. 9.
45 Frederick A. Pottle, *The Idiom of Poetry* (Ithaca, 1946), pp. 28–29.

with all the insight and honest conviction at his disposal, fundamentally all he is evaluating is his own sensibility. The critic cannot get outside of himself, nor can the self of the critic escape the climate of thought of his age, the massive pressure of the sensibility of his time—an idea which Henri Peyre also developed in his study, *Writers and Their Critics* (1944). But the fact that the judgments of the historical critic are necessarily relative does not make them any less valid, so long as he reports the frame of reference within which he operates.

In *New Bearings in Esthetics and Art Criticism* (1943), Bernard C. Heyl points out that it does not matter what judgment the critic passes so long as he furnishes us with the principles, standards, and beliefs that motivate and control his judgments. Relativism is hospitable toward such judgments, since they reveal the temperament of the writer. Given differences of temperament and philosophical preconceptions, differences of opinion are inevitable. People are different, and these differences influence their aesthetic appreciation. Finally, values are relative to time and place. In the preface to *The Private Reader* (1942), Mark Van Doren declares flatly that he has ceased to consider himself a professional critic. The good critic, he feels, knows that his report on whatever reading he had done cannot be complete, that the act of criticism cannot pin down the essence of poetry in definition or analysis. What he particularly deplores is the tendency toward "scientific criticism," the fetish of the "new criticism," with its close scrutiny of texts in the manner of a detective hunting for clues, its search for lurking ambiguities, latent meanings, psychoanalytic symbols, ironic implications. Criticism, he concludes, is too cluttered at present with academic furniture, obsessed with psychology, symbolism, and linguistics.

## X

From this résumé of the chief critical activity in the United States during the past fifty years, certain provisional conclusions emerge. Criticism in America has at last come of age. It is a profession that one can practice with self-respect and a serious sense of responsibility. If there seems to be no reason for believing that literary tastes are improved by the passage of time, there is nonetheless evident a marked increase in the complexity of the critical faculty, a heightened specialization of function. Criticism is no longer pure but mixed with ingredients and insights derived from a bewildering variety of disciplines. The growing feeling that criticism is not only valuable but indispensable could only have arisen as the fruit of extensive practice, the result of varied experimentation and achievement. American criticism has been influential in many fields: in the creation and study of literature, in the art of analysis and interpretation, and in the field of criticism itself, where it has given rise to a methodological art: the criticism of criticism.

The result has been a tremendous enrichment of criticism by its affiliation with and borrowing from the various sciences, but this has also been a source of difficulty and distraction. True enough, criticism has of late been steadily enlarging its content and refining its method by drawing nourishment from such seemingly alien studies as physics, chemistry, anthropology, psychology, mathematics, biology, semantics, sociology, logic, and even politics. The study of such disciplines has vitalized and extended the "science" of criticism. There are critics who announce that they are materialists, naturalists, instrumentalists, pragmatists, relying on the scientific method as the sole reliable guide to the problem of value in both ethics and aesthetics. They have been profoundly influenced by the work of such philosophers as William James, C. S. Pierce, George Herbert Mead, and particularly John Dewey. Nor has this scientific orientation been without gratifying results. Whether we conclude that these results are entirely legitimate, fruitful, and constructive depends, of course, on the aesthetic philosophy we happen to hold. Criticism that is naturalistic, scientifically grounded, takes its stand on the principle of cultural relativity, which relates all forms of knowledge and expression to their causal context. Though behaviorism has attracted few literary critics as disciples, the idea of the Pavlovian conditioned reflex has found its way into criticism and is often used, though without being explicitly acknowledged as such. There are other interesting offshoots of scientific theory and practice.

Unfortunately these amalgamations impose a complex and burdensome responsibility on the critic. It is no longer enough for him to steep himself in the humanities, to master the literary heritage of the past. Now he must wander far afield in search of a method, but the more material he appropriates from the sciences that literary men had formerly despised or ignored the more difficult his task becomes. For he must devise some way of adapting them to his central purpose, he must integrate them with a continuing literary tradition, in order not to become utterly distracted and confused in his aim. After all, as a critic he must devote himself to the specific task of analyzing and evaluating literature. Thus the vast expansion of the universe of knowledge, the steady widening of his intellectual horizons, may prove a handicap as well as a decided benefit. In the attempt to know and assimilate everything that is potentially useful and related to his professional interest (and who can say in advance what study is not germane and helpful?), he may become lost or sidetracked in pursuit of some fascinating but irrelevant goal—irrelevant, that is, to his fundamental job as a critic. He may turn into a scientist or psychologist, moralist, semanticist, propagandist, self-appointed revolutionary, or amateur psychoanalyst.

In addition, his experience with such sciences as psychology, anthropology, sociology, and even biology and physics, has been so recent and so disturbing as to plunge him into confusion. He has not yet succeeded in fully assimilating these new ideas and materials, and consequently he has been guilty at times of indulging in rash generalizations and undiscriminating enthusiasms. The battle that Max Eastman waged so lustily in *The Literary Mind* (1931) still has to be fought out. Some critics, as we have seen, have gone so far as to use the theory of relativity to defend an impressionism that is frankly irresponsible. Even the instrumentalists have defended the relativity of values. How, then, are values determined and validated? By an intuitive choice or by the operation of the scientific method? How are standards to be formed, how are they to be defined, tested, and applied? There the issue is squarely joined. What was eminently useful, however, in thus exploring the value of science for criticism[46] was the realization that the creative faculty is not something uniquely privileged, set apart from the other concerns and interests of men, but that it is, as John Dewey demonstrates in *Art as Experience* (1934), an integral part of all ongoing experience. Profiting greatly from such contacts and cross-fertilization, modern criticism has given birth to new insights, new methods of analysis and interpretation.

Such multiple "distractions" cannot, it seems, be avoided in our time; they are inevitable in an age such as ours when consciousness (and self-consciousness) has been enormously intensified and man is curious not only about the structure of the atom but also the functioning of his own mind. Apparently this is the price that must be paid for the effort to arrive at some new, more inclusive cultural synthesis. Literary criticism during the past fifty years has reflected the major social and ideological conflicts and confusions of the

46 See Herbert J. Muller, *Science and Criticism* (New Haven, 1943).

nation, its struggle to come of age, its strenuous striving to achieve self-realization and cultural independence and identity. It is extremely difficult to discern a definite pattern emerging out of this welter of competing ideas, this battle between the forces of convention and revolt, conservatism and radicalism, individualism and authority, Humanism and naturalism, permanence and change. At first glance all one can make out is a whirlwind of sound and fury, but it does signify something. Every few years a new critical revolution breaks out, but there are also traditional forces at work which act as a stabilizing influence. Each victory is succeeded by a fresh insurgent attack. An experimental movement, a new method, once it succeeds in its initial aims, serves to establish a new technique, a new tradition, a new orthodoxy, which in turn proves after a while cramping and inadequate and must be overthrown or revised.

In the concluding chapter of *The Armed Vision*, Stanley Edgar Hyman attempts to integrate his diverse material and sketch in the outline of what he considers the ideal critic. The assumption he works with is that by including all methods and points of view, one bias will cancel out the other, and thus we can arrive at a balanced, reliable version of the truth. Each critic, under this dispensation, would presumably contribute the best that he has to offer. Thus Edmund Wilson would lend his skill in the art of interpretation and Ezra Pound his concern for poetic and formal values. T. S. Eliot's interest in a central, sustaining tradition would be fused with Parrington's social criticism. The psychoanalytic method as employed by Maud Bodkin, amplified by borrowings from Gestalt, revisionist Freudian, and other psychologies, would be combined with the thoroughgoing Marxist method as practiced by Christopher Caudwell. Nothing, in short, is to be left out except what is not relevant and fruitful.

This ideal integration of all of modern critical method into one super-method could not be on the analogy of stew, with everything thrown at random into the pot, but would have to be on the analogy of construction, with the structure built up, according to an orderly plan on some foundation or around some skeletal framework. What, then, would that foundation, framework, or basis be? The most enthusiastic candidate for the job is Marxism, whose spokesmen have regularly insisted that dialectical materialism is an integrative frame able to encompass and use the newest advances in all fields of knowledge, and in fact must do so to function.[47]

47 Stanley Edgar Hyman, *The Armed Vision* (New York, 1948), p. 397.

The main question, however, is whether Marxism, regardless of its immense accumulations of knowledge from numerous fields, is actually a valid base for constructing a critical synthesis. Does Marxism constitute a comprehensive, reliable foundation for a critical method, when combined with other perspectives and insights? This proposal for a large, all-inclusive framework, even in its ideal state, turns out to be uncritical and eclectic. In criticism as in life the adoption of one choice often necessarily precludes the use of another. If the critic is to psychoanalyze a writer's work, extracting its archetypal symbols and uncovering its underlying pattern of anxiety and oedipal fixation, the psycho-biological orientation immediately stands in the way of applying the Marxist system of interpretation, with its primary interest in the socio-economic roots of art and of human behavior. That is why the critical debate never stops.

Though it is doubtful if in the future criticism will grow by assimilating every field of available knowledge that can be brought to bear on it, the experiment is indeed worth trying, and in any event it is definitely going on. Since this calls for a degree of specialization beyond the capacity of the individual critic, it may be necessary, as Hyman suggests, to experiment with some form of collaboration, or collective criticism. These recurrent conflicts about the aims and methods of literary criticism testify unmistakably to the extraordinary vitality of the critical impulse in American letters. The last word has not been uttered. There is still need for the development of a critical method which will attempt to do full justice to the aesthetic qualities of a literary work. The aesthetic criticism of the future, whatever shape it takes, will not fall victim to the extreme aberrations of psychoanalysis or the militant dogmatism of Marxism. Neither will it be held in check by the fetters of conservatism, whether it call itself Humanism or Neo-Classicism. The work of art will remain the primary datum, to be responded to with freshness and sympathy, but this first-hand response will be strengthened and rounded out by a closer study, and thus culminate finally in a responsible act of critical evaluation.

# JAMES GIBBONS HUNEKER

## (1860–1921)

BORN in Philadelphia on January 31, 1860, Huneker was fortunate in having parents who were sincerely devoted to the arts of music and painting. His early passionate interest in literature precluded the thought of preparing him, as his mother wished, for the priesthood. He studied law for some years at the Law Academy in Philadelphia, but he was not destined for that profession. Unable to shake off his deep passion for the arts, particularly music, he went to Paris, where he studied music at the Sorbonne. There he discovered that he lacked the fundamental talent to become a professional musician. In the meantime, he had developed an appreciation of the beauty and importance of impressionistic art. After returning to the United States, he continued his musical studies and taught the piano for a period of ten years at the National Conservatory in New York City. But it was in journalism that he found his true vocation. From 1891 to 1895 he acted as music and dramatic critic for the *New York Recorder;* from 1895 to 1897 he served as music and dramatic critic on the staff of the *Morning Advertiser.* He worked, too, for such papers as the *New York Sun,* the *New York Times,* and the New York *World.* He ranged far and wide, writing copiously on literary and artistic themes or on any subject that engaged his attention. He traveled frequently to Europe, where he met distinguished personalities in the fields of art and literature and where he gained much of the material that went into the making of his numerous essays and books. His first published book, *Mezzotints in Modern Music,* came out in 1899.

Huneker was constantly under the spur of journalistic necessity, compelled to turn out reams of copy for the printer's devil. Consequently a great deal of his work suffered because it was dashed off hastily, with great vigor but without deep reflection. Another reason for the rapid collapse of his reputation lies in the very qualities that assured him quick recognition during his lifetime: his flamboyant style, his vivid personality, his impressionistic method. A robustious personality, loving life greatly, he is

genuinely responsive to every authentic manifestation of beauty and originality. Though he calls himself a steeplejack of the seven arts, he is neither
an amiable dilettante nor a journalistic amateur. His talents and his exuberant temperament were admirably suited to perform what he considered the prime function of criticism: to stimulate, to awaken in the
reader a desire to return with heightened appreciation and interest to the
original work of art.

His work, however, lacks fundamental insight and unity of design. Its
impressionistic ardors and ecstasies afforded an excellent medium for the
expression of a vital personality. Characteristic of the man is the pride he
takes in his inconoclastic assaults, his explorations and discoveries. Though
his criticism lacked a central, organic principle, it was suffused by a healthy
egotism and a contagious enthusiasm. His critical verdicts are personal
opinions, since they are not based on a philosophical foundation; they are
no more than the record of his tastes, his temperamental preferences and
aesthetic impressions. But he had an enormous hunger for all kinds of experiences, all the varied colors and consummations that life has to offer.
His criticism, free from moral preconceptions, is notable for its catholicity,
its cosmopolitanism, its air of genial and generous tolerance. Therein undoubtedly lies his salient virtue as a critic. A critic, he contends, must be
endowed with the saving quality of humility, so that he will register with
devout fidelity the emotions aroused in him by a masterpiece. Whatever
other gifts the critic may possess, he must be sympathetic and sincere.

Huneker acquired fame by writing with inexhaustible zest about unrecognized or unknown European geniuses, and succeeded in communicating the distinctive quality that characterized their work. Though he
was a splendid purveyor of the best of European culture, his cardinal mistake was that he did not take the work of criticism with sufficient seriousness. Regarding it as preeminently an art, not a science, he had, like
Mencken, a profound contempt for most aesthetic theories. A work was
beautiful and quiveringly alive, one responded to it intuitively, and that
was the ultimate secret and quintessence of criticism.

His impressionistic writing was at least read and made its influence
widely felt. Untrammeled by gentility or tradition, he was caught up by
the creative turmoil and travail of his time. With soaring rhetoric, cascad-
ing wit, and a remarkable capacity for journalistic improvisation, he introduced American readers to a motley band of European artists, musicians, poets, philosophers, and novelists. He penned critical essays on
such figures as Hauptmann, Sudermann, Gorky, Nietzsche, Remy de Gourmont, Strindberg, Shaw, Flaubert, Anatole France, Baudelaire, Villiers de
l'Isle Adam, Ibsen, Stirner, Cézanne, George Sand, Rodin, Wagner, Walt

Whitman, James Joyce, Huysmans, Verlaine, Conrad, Artzibashev, Degas, Matisse, Renoir, Debussy.

What was signally missing in his work was a principle of evaluation which could distinguish between the first- and the second-rate. If a work was imbued with immense vitality, that was all he cared about. Since he never succeeded in working out a rounded body of aesthetic ideas, he had no theory of criticism to guide him. An arch-individualist, he gave us no more than the history of his soul adventuring among masterpieces. Distrusting the abstract categories of philosophy, he did not put much faith in the analyses dictated by pure reason. Concentrated beauty and the diverse intuitive visions of life embodied in art—these were enough for him. Genius was more important than the counters of logic. Though he realized the danger of impressionism when carried to extremes, he did not always avoid it himself. For example, writing on Huysmans, he pens such a vague sentiment as: "He is the virtuoso of the phrase. He is a performer on the single string of self. He knows the sultry harmonics of passion."[1]

But if he failed to formulate a consistent theory of criticism, a fairly consistent aesthetic *attitude* does emerge from his writing. An uncompromising individualist (though he loved in life to rub shoulders with all sorts and conditions of men), he preferred, in the hieratic realm of the arts, the aristocratic genius, the superman. Altruism and humanitarianism were spurious catchwords. He distinguished between true individualism, which is marked by a state of integrity and enlarged, luminous self-consciousness, and the materialistic self-seeking which often mistakenly passes for individualism.

He was opposed to fiction of a doctrinaire stamp, fiction that was too neatly labeled realistic, naturalistic, sociological, or political. Fiction is fundamentally a fine art. The notion of "democratic" art, he declares irritably, is a snare and a curse. There is only good art.[2] The novel with a purpose lacks validity both as a document and as a work of art. Life and literature must be wedded. Fiction must strike deep roots in the soil of experience. In "Cross-Currents in Modern French Literature," he denounces the blight of provincialism in America, its sterile insularity. There is no excuse for provincialism in criticism.

"A critic will never be a catholic critic of his native literature or art if he doesn't know the literatures and arts of other lands, paradoxical as this may sound. We lack aesthetic curiosity. Because of our uncritical parochialism America is comparable to a cemetery of clichés."[3]

---

1 James Gibbons Huneker, *Egoists: A Book of Supermen* (New York, 1910), p. 169.
2 James Gibbons Huneker, *Unicorns* (New York, 1921), p. 92.
  *Ibid.,* pp. 291–292.

Huneker probably drew his own portrait, with mock-seriousness, in "The Critic Who Gossips." It begins, significantly enough, with this confession: "He has a soul like a Persian rug."[4] This gossip-ridden type of critic is fonder of anecdotes than of history. Huneker himself achieved no coherent philosophy of life and with the exception of *Painted Veils* and *Steeplejack,* his autobiography, he produced no single, unified book. In reply to the charge preferred by Percival Pollard that he bowed before the idols of European culture and neglected American culture and art, he asserted that he had gained his living for nearly four decades by writing about the painting, music, literature, and sculpture of his countrymen. Yet the names he is most proud of, the writers with whom he corresponds most frequently, were not Americans but Europeans—English, Celtic, German, French, Scandinavian. All the arts won his hearty allegiance. Because of his rich technical knowledge and capacity for appreciation he could compare not only the literatures of various countries but also the different arts, persevering in his efforts to achieve a synthesis of the seven arts and to interpret one art in terms of another.

His criticism flowed from the richness and vitality of his temperament, but as an impressionist he had no critical ideas of importance to propound and no sound method to formulate. Subjective in his criticism, he denied that criticism was equipped to solve any literary problems. The critic, even at his best, can no more help being prejudiced than he can jump out of his own skin. Beyond setting down the emotions aroused in him by a masterpiece he cannot hope, and should not try, to go. He should concern himself with the technical accomplishment of a work of art, its mastery of form and perfection of style, but even here Huneker did not care to be consistent. Mencken insists that the younger critics owe Huneker a great debt of gratitude for clearing the ground of the rotting lumber of the old criticism.

### BIBLIOGRAPHY

#### TEXT

*Mezzotints in Modern Music.* New York, 1899.
*Melomaniacs.* New York, 1902.
*Overtones: A Book of Temperaments.* New York, 1904.
*Iconoclasts: A Book of Dramatists.* New York, 1905.
*Visionaries.* New York, 1905.
*Egoists: A Book of Supermen.* New York, 1909.
*Promenades of an Impressionist.* New York, 1910.
*Franz Liszt.* New York, 1911.

4 *Ibid.,* pp. 291–292.

*The Pathos of Distance.* New York, 1913.
*Old Fogy: His Musical Opinions and Grotesques.* Philadelphia, 1913.
*Ivory Apes and Peacocks.* New York, 1915.
*New Cosmopolis.* New York, 1915.
*Unicorns.* New York, 1917.
*Bedouins.* New York, 1920.
*Variations.* New York, 1921.
*Steeplejack.* 2 vols. New York, 1920.
*Letters of James Gibbons Huneker,* ed. by Josephine Huneker. New York, 1922.
*Intimate Letters of James Gibbons Huneker,* ed. by Josephine Huneker. New York, 1924.
*Essays by James Gibbons Huneker,* selected with an introduction by H. L. Mencken. New York, 1929.

CRITICISM

DeCasseres, Benjamin, *James Gibbons Huneker.* New York, 1925.
DeMille, George E., *Literary Criticism in America.* New York, 1931, pp. 206–245.
Fay, E. C., "Huneker's Criticism of French Literature," *French Review,* XIV, 130–137 (December, 1940).
Mencken, H. L., *A Book of Prefaces.* New York, 1917, pp. 151–195.
——, *Prejudices, Third Series.* New York, 1922, pp. 65–83.
Smith, Bernard, "Huneker, Man of the Tribe," *Saturday Review of Literature,* X, 49–50 (August 19, 1933).
Smith, Bernard, *Forces in American Criticism.* New York, 1939.

# LITERATURE AND ART*

## I

### CONCERNING CRITICS

THE annual rotation of the earth brings to us at least once during its period the threadbare, thriceworn, stale, flat, and academic discussion of critic and artist. We believe comparisons of creator and critic are unprofitable, being for the most part a confounding of intellectual substances. The painter paints, the composer makes music,

* Reprinted from *Promenades of an Impressionist* by James G. Huneker; copyright 1910 by Charles Scribner's Sons, 1937 by Josephine Huneker; used by permission of the publishers.

the sculptor models, and the poet sings. Like the industrious crow the critic hops after these sowers of beauty, content to peck up in the furrows the chance grains dropped by genius. This, at least, is the popular notion. Balzac, and later Disraeli, asked: "After all, what are the critics? Men who have failed in literature and art." And Mascagni, notwithstanding the laurels he wore after his first success, cried aloud in agony that a critic was *compositore mancato*. These be pleasing quotations for them whose early opus has failed to score. The trouble is that every one is a critic, your gallery-god as well as the most stately practitioner of the art severe. Balzac was an excellent critic when he saluted Stendhal's Chartreuse de Parme as a masterpiece; as was Emerson when he wrote to Walt Whitman. What the mid-century critics of the United States, what Sainte-Beuve, master critic of France, did not see, Balzac and Emerson saw and, better still, spoke out. In his light-hearted fashion Oscar Wilde asserted that the critic was also a creator—apart from his literary worth—and we confess that we know of cases where the critic has created the artist. But that a serious doubt can be entertained as to the relative value of creator and critic is hardly worth denying.

Consider the painters. Time and time again you read or hear the indignant denunciation of some artist whose canvas has been ripped-up in print. If the offender happens to be a man who doesn't paint, then he is called an ignoramus; if he paints or etches, or even sketches in crayon, he is well within the Balzac definition—poor, miserable imbecile, he is only jealous of work that he could never have achieved. As for literary critics, it may be set down once and for all that they are "suspect." They write; ergo, they must be unjust. The dilemma has branching horns. Is there no midway spot, no safety ground for that weary Ishmael the professional critic to escape being gored? Naturally any expression of personal feeling on his part is set down to mental arrogance. He is permitted like the wind to move over the face of the waters, but he must remain unseen. We have always thought that the enthusiastic Dublin man in the theatre gallery was after a critic when he cried aloud at the sight of a toppling companion: "Don't waste him. Kill a fiddler with him!" It seems more in consonance with the Celtic character; besides, the Irish are music-lovers.

If one could draw up the list of critical and creative men in art the scale would not tip evenly. The number of painters who have written of their art is not large, though what they have said is always pregnant. Critics outnumber them—though the battle is really a matter of quality, not quantity. There is Da Vinci. For his complete writings some of us would sacrifice miles of gawky pale and florid mediaeval paintings. What we have of him is wisdom, and like true wisdom is prophetic. Then there is that immortal gossip Vasari, a very biassed critic and not too nice to his contemporaries. He need not indulge in what is called the woad argument; we sha'n't go back to the early Britons for our authorities. Let us come to Sir Joshua Reynolds, whose Discourses are invaluable—and also to be taken well salted; he was encrusted with fine old English prejudices. One of his magnificent sayings and one appreciated by the entire artistic tribe was his ejaculation: "Damn paint!" Raphael Mengs wrote. We wish that Velasquez had. What William Blake said of great artists threw much light on William Blake. Ingres uttered things, principally in a rage, about his contemporaries. Delacroix was a thinker. He literally anticipated Chevreul's discoveries in the law of simultaneous contrasts of colour. Furthermore, he wrote profoundly of his art. He appreciated Chopin before many critics and musicians—which would have been an impossible thing for Ingres, though he played the violin—and he was kind to the younger men.

Need we say that Degas is a great wit, though not a writer; a wit and a critic? Rousseau, the landscapist, made notes, and Corot is often quoted. If Millet had never written another sentence but "There is no isolated truth," he would still have been a critic. Constable with his "A good thing is never done twice"; and Alfred Stevens's definition of art, "Nature seen through the prism of an emotion," forestalled Zola's pompous pronouncement in The Experimental Novel. To jump over the stile to literature, Wordsworth wrote critical prefaces, and Shelley, too; Poe was a critic; and what of Coleridge, who called painting "a middle quality between a thought and a thing—the union of that which is nature with that which is exclusively human"? There are plenty of examples on the side of the angels. Whistler! What a critic, wielding a finely chased rapier! Thomas Couture wrote and discoursed much of his art. Sick man as he was, I heard him talk of art at his country home, Villiers-le-Bel, on the Northern Railway, near Paris. This was in 1878. William M. Hunt's talks on art were fruitful. So are John Lafarge's. The discreet Gigoux of Balzac notoriety has an entertaining book to his credit; while Rodin is often coaxed into utterances about his and other men's work. There are many French, English, and American artists who write and paint with equal facility. In New York, Kenyon

Cox is an instance. But the chiefest among all the painters alive and dead, one who shines and will continue to shine when his canvases are faded—and they are fading—is Eugène Fromentin, whose Maîtres d'autrefois is a classic of criticism. Since his day two critics, who are also painters, have essayed both crafts, George Clausen and D. S. MacColl.

Professor Clausen is a temperate critic, MacColl a brilliant, revolutionary one. The critical temper in either man is not dogmatic. Seurat, the French Neo-Impressionist, has defended his theories; indeed, the number of talented Frenchmen who paint well and write with style as well as substance is amazing. Rossetti would no longer be a rare bird in these days of piping painters, musicians who are poets, and sculptors who are painters. The unfortunate critic occasionally writes a play or an opera (particularly in Paris), but as a rule he is content to echo that old German who desperately exclaimed: "Even if I am nothing else, I am at least a contemporary."

Let us now swing around the obverse side of the medal. A good showing. You may begin with Winckelmann or Goethe—we refer entirely to critics of paint and painters—or run down the line to Diderot, Blanc, Gautier, Baudelaire, Zola, Goncourt, who introduced to Europe Japanese art; Roger Marx, Geoffroy, Huysmans, Camille Mauclair, Charles Morice, and Octave Mirbeau. Zola was not a painter, but he praised Edouard Manet. These are a few names hastily selected. In England, Ruskin too long ruled the critical roost; full of thunder-words like Isaiah, his vaticinations led a generation astray. He was a prophet, not a critic, and he was a victim to his own abhorred "pathetic fallacy." Henley was right in declaring that until R. A. M. Stevenson appeared there was no great art criticism in England or English. The "Velasquez" is a marking stone in critical literature. It is the one big book by a big temperament that may be opposed page by page to Fromentin's critical masterpiece. Shall we further adduce the names of Morelli, Sturge Moore, Roger Fry, Perkins, Cortissoz, Lionel Cust, Colvin, Ricci, Van Dyke, Mather, Berenson, Brownell, and George Moore—who said of Ruskin that his uncritical blindness regarding Whistler will constitute his passport to fame, "the lot of critics is to be remembered by what they have failed to understand." Walter Pater wrote criticism that is beautiful literature. If Ruskin missed Whistler, he is in good company, for Sainte-Beuve, the prince of critics, missed Balzac, Stendhal, Flaubert, and to Victor Hugo was unfair. Yet, consider the Osrics embalmed in the amber of Sainte-Beuve's style. He, like many another critic, was superior to his subject. And that is always fatal to the water-flies.

George III once asked in wonderment how the apples get inside the dumplings. How can a critic criticise a creator? The man who looks on writing things about the man who does things. But he criticises and artists owe him much. Neither in "ink-horn terms" nor in an "upstart Asiatic style" need the critic voice his opinions. He must be an artist in temperament and he must have a *credo*. He need not be a painter to write of painting, for his primary appeal is to the public. He is the middle-man, the interpreter, the vulgariser. The psycho-physiological processes need not concern us. One thing is certain—a man writing in terms of literature about painting, an art in two dimensions, cannot interpret fully the meanings of the canvas, nor can he be sure that his opinion, such as it is, when it reaches the reader, will truthfully express either painter or critic. Such are the limitations of one art when it comes to deal with the ideas or material of another. Criticism is at two removes from its theme. Therefore criticism is a makeshift. Therefore, let critics be modest and allow criticism to become an amiable art.

But where now is the painter critic and the professional critic? "Stands Ulster where it did?" Yes, the written and reported words of artists are precious alike to layman and critic. That they prefer painting to writing is only natural; so would the critic if he had the pictorial gift. However, as art is art and not nature, criticism is criticism and not art. It professes to interpret the artist's work, and at best it mirrors his art mingled with the personal temperament of the critic. At the worst the critic lacks temperament (artistic training is, of course, an understood requisite), and when this is the case, God help the artist! As the greater includes the lesser, the artist should permit the critic to enter, with all due reverence, his sacred domain. Without vanity the one, sympathetic the other. Then the ideal collaboration ensues. Sainte-Beuve says that "criticism by itself can do nothing. The best of it can act only in concert with public feeling . . . we never find more than half the article in print—the other half was written only in the reader's mind." And Professor Walter Raleigh would further limit the "gentle art." "Criticism, after all, is not to legislate, nor to classify, but to raise the dead." The relations between the critic and his public open another vista of the everlasting discussion. Let it be a negligible one now. That painters can get along without professional criticism we know from history, but that they will themselves play the critic is doubtful. And are they any fairer to young talent than official critics? It is an inquiry fraught with significance. Great and small artists have sent forth into the world their pupils. Have they always—as befits honest critics—recognised the pupils of other men, pupils and men both at the opposite pole of their own theories? Recall what Velasquez is reported to have said to Salvator Rosa, according to Boschini and Carl Justi. Salvator had asked the incomparable Spaniard whether he did not think Raphael the best of all the painters he had seen in Italy. Velasquez answered: "Raphael, to be plain with you, for I like to be candid and outspoken, does not please me at all." This purely temperamental judgment does not make of Velasquez either a good or a bad critic. It is interesting as showing us that even a master cannot always render justice to another. Difference engenders hatred, as Stendhal would say.

Can the record of criticism made by plastic artists show a generous Robert Schumann? Schumann discovered many composers from Chopin to Brahms and made their fortunes by his enthusiastic writing about them. In Wagner he met his Waterloo, but every critic has his limitations. There is no Schumann, let the fact be emphasised, among the painter-critics, though quite as much discrimination, ardour of discovery, and acumen may be found among the writings of the men whose names rank high in professional criticism. And this hedge, we humbly submit, is a rather stiff one to vault for the adherents of criticism written by artists only. Nevertheless, every day of his humble career must the critic pen his *apologia pro vita sua*.

## II

### ART IN FICTION

Fiction about art and artists is rare—that is, good fiction, not the stuff ground out daily by the publishing mills for the gallery-gods. It is to France that we must look for the classic novel dealing with painters and their painting, Manette Salomon, by Goncourt. Henry James has written several delightful tales, such as The Liar, The Real Thing, The Tragic Muse, in which artists appear. But it is the particular psychological problem involved rather than theories of art or personalities that steer Mr. James's cunning pen. We all remember the woman who destroyed a portrait of her husband which seemed to reveal his moral secret. John S. Sargent has been credited with being the psychologist of the brush in this story. There is a nice, fresh young fellow in The Tragic Muse, who, weak-spined as he is, prefers at the last his painting to Julia Dallow and a political career. In The Real Thing we recognise one of these unerring strokes that prove James to be the master psychologist among English writers. Any discerning painter realises the value of a model who can take the pose that will give him the pictorial idea, the suggestiveness of the pose, not an attempt at crude naturalism. With this thesis the novelist has built up an amusing, semi-pathetic, and striking fable.

There are painters scattered through English fiction—can we ever forget Thackeray! Ouida has not missed weaving her Tyrian purples into the exalted pattern of her romantic painters. And George Eliot. And Disraeli. And Bernard Shaw—there is a painting creature in Love Among the Artists. George Moore, however, has devoted more of his pages to paint and painters than any other of the latter-day writers. The reason is this: George Moore went to Paris to study art and he drifted into the Julian atelier like any other likely young fellow with hazy notions about art and a well-filled purse. But these early experiences were not lost. They cropped up in many of his stories and studies. He became the critical pioneer of the impressionistic movement and first told London about Manet, Monet, Degas. He even—in an article remarkable for critical acumen—declared that if Jimmy Whistler had been a heavier man, a man of beef, brawn, and beer, like Rubens, he would have been as great a painter as Velasquez. To the weighing scales, fellow-artists! retorted Whistler; yet the bolt did not miss the mark. Whistler's remarks about Mr. Moore, especially after the Eden lawsuit, were, so it is reported, not fit to print.

In Mr. Moore's first volume of the half-forgotten trilogy, Spring Days, we see a young painter who, it may be said, thinks more of petticoats than paint. There is paint talk in Mike Fletcher, Moore's most virile book. In A Modern Lover the hero is an artist who succeeds in the fashionable world by painting pretty, artificial portraits and faded classical allegories, thereby winning the love of women, much wealth, popular applause, and the stamp of official approbation. This Lewis Seymour still lives and paints modish London in rose-colour. Moore's irony would have entered the soul of a hundred "celebrated" artists if they had had any soul to flesh it in. When he wrote this novel, one that shocked Mrs. Grundy, Moore was under the influence of Paris. However, that masterpiece of description and analysis, Mildred Lawson in Celibates—very Balzacian title, by the way—deals with hardly anything else but art. Mildred, who is an English girl without soul, heart, or talent, studies in the Julian atelier and goes to Fontainebleau during the summer. No one, naturally, will ever describe Fontainebleau better than Flaubert, in whose L'Education Sentimentale there are marvellous pictures; also a semi-burlesque painter, Pellerin, who reads all the works on aesthetics before he draws a line, and not forgetting that imperishable portrait of Jacques Arnoux, art dealer. Goncourt, too, has excelled in his impression of the forest and its painters, Millet in particular. Nevertheless, let us say in passing that you cannot find Mildred Lawson in Flaubert or Goncourt; no, not even in Balzac, whose work is the matrix of modern fiction. She is her own perverse, cruel Mooresque self, and she lives in New York as well as London.

In both Daudet and Maupassant—Strong as Death is the latter's contribution to painter-psychology—there are stories clustered about the guild. Daudet has described a Salon on varnishing day with his accustomed facile, febrile skill; you feel that it comes from Goncourt and Zola. It is not within our scope to go back as far as Balzac, whose Frenhofer in The Unknown Masterpiece has been a model for the younger man. Poe, Hawthorne, Wilde, and Robert Louis Stevenson have dealt with the theme pictorial. Zola's The Masterpiece (L'Oeuvre) is one of the better written books of Zola. It was a favourite of his. The much-read and belauded fifth chapter is a faithful transcription of the first Salon of the Rejected Painters (Salon des Refusés) at Paris, 1863. Napoleon III, after pressure had been brought to bear upon him, consented to a special salon within the official Salon, at the Palais de l'Industrie, which would harbour the work of the young lunatics who wished to paint purple turkeys, green water, red grass, and black sunsets. (Lie down, ivory hallucinations, and don't wag your carmilion tail on the chrome-yellow carpet!) It is an enormously clever book, this, deriving in the main as it does from Manette Salomon and Balzac's Frenhofer. The fight for artistic veracity by Claude Lantier is a replica of what occurred in Manet's lifetime. The Breakfast on the Grass, described by Zola, was actually the title and the subject of a Manet picture that scandalised Paris about this epoch. The fantastic idea of a nude female stretched on the grass, while the other figures were clothed and in their right minds, was too much for public and critic, and unquestionably Manet did paint the affair to create notoriety. Like Richard Wagner, he knew the value of advertising.

All the then novel theories of *plein air* impressionism are discussed in the Zola novel, yet the work seems clumsy after Goncourt's Manette Salomon, that breviary for painters which so far back as 1867 anticipated—in print, of course—the discoveries, the experiments, the practice of the naturalistic-impressionistic groups from Courbet to Cézanne, Monet to Maufra, Manet to Paul Gauguin. There are verbal pictures of student life, of salons, of atelier and open air. No such psychologic manual of the painter's art has ever appeared before or since Manette Salomon. It was the Goncourts who introduced Japanese art to European literature—they were friends of the late M. Bing, a pioneer collector in Paris. And they foresaw the future of painting as well as of fiction.

# JOEL ELIAS SPINGARN

## (1875–1939)

BORN in New York City on May 17, 1875, Spingarn graduated from Columbia College at the age of twenty. In 1899, after receiving his Ph. D., he was appointed assistant and tutor in comparative literature at Columbia University. In 1909 he was made full professor. After leaving Columbia University in 1911 he retired to his estate in Amenia. He returned from service in France in the First World War as lieutenant colonel. One of the founders of Harcourt, Brace and Company in 1919, he served as literary editor of that firm until 1932. He was chairman of the National Association for the Advancement of the Colored People from 1913 to 1919. His *History of Literary Criticism in the Renaissance* (1899) was translated into Italian, with an introduction by Benedetto Croce. Spingarn also wrote poetry, delivering the Phi Beta Kappa poem, "The New Hesperides," at Columbia University in 1901.

In the essays first gathered together in 1917 under the title of *Creative Criticism and Other Essays,* Spingarn sounded the tocsin of revolt. Long a student of literary criticism in its historical reaches and editor of a collection of Elizabethan critical essays, he had become a disciple of Croce, whose brilliant expositor and champion he became in the United States. Spingarn's lecture on "The New Criticism" marks a milestone in the history of criticism in the United States. First of all, it inaugurates or reinforces an international movement, the importation of literary and philosophic ideas from abroad, and thus signals the end of provincialism and insularity. Second, it emphasizes not only the autonomy of creative expression but also the autonomy of the critical act. Saved at last from reproach and neglect, criticism is shown to be essentially creative in spirit, a distinction that it shares with the creative activity of the imaginative writer.

By means of the Crocean aesthetic, Spingarn is enabled to divorce criticism from the impressionistic method. Historical criticism, in its search for information about the age and the environment, is guilty of neglecting the work of art. Psychological criticism is rejected on the ground that it

73

concerns itself too much with biographical facts, which are incapable of furnishing a revealing clue to the mystery of the creative imagination. And academic criticism, which follows established rules and precedents, is miles removed from the primary work of art.

Spingarn cuts the Gordian knot of aesthetics by expounding the theory of art as expression. This is not to be mistaken for the sociological theory that literature is an expression of society or the expression of personality. Art is expression and criticism is the study of expression. There is no need for dogmatic pronouncements or traditional canons of judgment. This is the heart of the philosophy of expression as formulated by Croce in *Aesthetic as Science of Expression and General Linguistic,* who reduced criticism to its fundamentals. Once this theory of expression is accepted, the old rules, systems, and doctrines are discarded once and for all. Then, too, the validity of literary genres is exploded. Fundamentally all art is lyrical, all art is expression, regardless of its form or superimposed genre. The Crocean-Spingarn aesthetic eliminates the need for introducing moral judgments on art, for ulterior justification of any kind. To utilize the work of art as a significant social document or as a contribution to morality is to ignore its essential nature and pervert its essential purpose. Creative criticism also dispenses with the belief in literary "evolution," the fallacious theory of "progress" as applied to literature and art. No such standards exist.

Spingarn had a glowing faith in the truth of what he wrote. His essays were unified by a philosophy of aesthetics that was steel-proof against the corrosion of contemporary winds of doctrine. Art, he insisted, is not to be judged by political categories. To confuse poetry with meter and form is even more reprehensible and absurd. What differentiates poetry from prose is imaginative power and nothing else—not meter or rhythm or rhyme. It is not surprising to find him assailing any aesthetic doctrine which fails to recognize the essential "madness" or "inspired state" of the poet. "For the madness of poets," declares Spingarn, heedless of the Freudians, "is nothing more or less than unhampered freedom of self-expression—expression of the real self, and not of mere eccentricity or whim."[1]

In the essay on "The Younger Generation," published in 1922, he stresses the value of youth, youth which incarnates the finest qualities of the creative spirit in its zest for adventure and its bold reconnaissance of the future. This is the spirit which the artist must preserve throughout life if he is not to suffer shipwreck and lapse into impotence. But this is a far cry from the popular fallacy that the most valuable thing to possess is physical

[1] J. E. Spingarn, *Creative Criticism and Other Essays* (New York, 1931), p. 96.

youth. Equally fallacious is the doctrine of ultra-modernity, a disease specially characteristic of our restless age with its emphasis on the cult of youth, a movement which reaches the acme of absurdity in its canonization of the childlike in art. Replying to Mencken's onslaught and defending himself against misrepresentation, Spingarn declares flatly that he is not an advocate of "aestheticism" in any form nor a supporter of "impressionism." But the first stage of the critical process, he maintains, involves the exercise of creative sensibility, an imaginative identification with and assimilation of the work of art. He also inveighs against the notion that poetry can be legitimately classified as "moral" or "immoral." "To say that poetry is moral or immoral is as meaningless as to say that an equilateral triangle is moral and an isosceles triangle immoral."[2] Carrying this even further he declares: "It is not the purpose of poetry to further the cause of democracy, or any other practical 'cause,' any more than it is the purpose of bridge-building to further the cause of Esperanto."[3]

Spingarn's critical writing still makes exciting reading. His essay on "The American Critic," with its outspoken condemnation of all that is shoddy and pedestrian, of scholarship that is archeological rather than alive, still breathes an inspiring spirit of challenge. American criticism is assailed for its want of philosophic insight, its aesthetic insufficiency, its lack of depth and breadth and height of vision. Though he must be free from preconceptions or dogmas of any kind, the critic should possess some general notion of what literature is and attempts to achieve. He has only contempt for those professorial minds that subordinate taste to knowledge, sensibility to factualism. Criticism at its best is sustained not only by a philosophy of aesthetics but also by a philosophy of life, which gives it vital content. The central preoccupation of criticism is with the work of art and not with its background. Though art stems from a personality with its intrinsic moral values, the excellence of art must be judged in and for itself, and not by extrinsic criteria. The first need of American criticism, Spingarn urges, is education in aesthetic thinking. There is, in addition, the need for humane scholarship. Finally, there is great need for training in taste, for a more cultivated sensibility, before a critical judgment can be passed on the imaginative work of the artist. Bernard Smith's summary conclusion that Spingarn's theory "attracted few adherents, founded no school, and is today forgotten,"[4] is only partially true. Spingarn's work is not forgotten, and indirectly his influence still survives.

2 *Ibid.,* p. 217.
3 *Ibid.,* p. 219.
4 Bernard Smith, *Forces in American Criticism* (New York, 1939), p. 284.

BIBLIOGRAPHY

TEXT

*A History of Literary Criticism in the Renaissance.* New York, 1899.
*Critical Essays of the Seventeenth Century,* edited by Joel Elias Spingarn.
    3 vols. Oxford, 1908–09.
*The New Criticism.* New York, 1911.
*A Note on Dramatic Criticism.* Oxford, 1913. (Offprint.)
*Poetry: A Religion.* New York, 1924.
*Creative Criticism and Other Essays.* New York, 1931.
*A Spingarn Enchiridion,* collected by Alain T. Peters. New York, 1929.

CRITICISM

Goldberg, Isaac, "Joel Elias Spingarn," *Stratford Monthly,* I, New Series,
    240–247 (1924).
Mencken, H. L., "Criticism of Criticism of Criticism," *Prejudices, First
    Series.* New York, 1919.
Smith, Bernard, *Forces in American Criticism.* New York, 1939.

## THE NEW CRITICISM*

"WHAT droll creatures these college professors are whenever they talk about art," wrote Flaubert in one of his letters, and voiced the world's opinion of academic criticism. For the world shares the view of the Italian poet that "monks and professors cannot write the lives of poets," and looks only to those rich in literary experience for its opinions on Literature. But the poets themselves have had no special grudge against academic criticism that they have not felt equally for every other kind. For the most part, they have objected to all criticism, since what each mainly seeks in his own case is not criticism, but uncritical praise. "Kill the dog, he is a reviewer," cried the young Goethe; and in our own age William Morris expressed his contempt for those who earn a livelihood by writing their opinions of the works of others. Fortunately for criticism, it does not live by the grace of poets, to whom it can be of small service at its best, but by the grace of others who have neither the poet's genius nor the critic's insight. I hope to persuade you this evening

* Reprinted from J. E. Spingarn, *The New Criticism.* Copyright 1911 by Columbia University Press.

that the poets have been mistaken in their very conception of the critic's craft, which lives by a power that poets and critics share together. The secret of this power has come to men slowly, and the knowledge they have gained by it has transformed their idea of Criticism. What this secret is, and into what new paths Criticism is being led by it, is the subject of my lecture to-night.

At the end of the last century, France once more occupied the centre of that stage whose auditors are the inheritors of European civilization. Once more all the world listened while she talked and played, and some of the most brilliant of her talk was now on the question of the authority of Criticism. It is not my purpose to tell you (what you know already) with what sober and vigorous learning the official critics of the *Revue des deux Mondes* espoused the cause of old gods with the new weapons of science, and with what charm and tact, with what grace and suppleness of thought, Jules Lemaître and Anatole France, to mention no others, defended the free play of the appreciative mind. Some of the sparks that were beaten out on the anvil of controversy have become fixed stars, the classical utterances of Criticism, as when Anatole France described the critic not as a judge imposing sentence, but as a sensitive soul detailing his "adventures among masterpieces."

To have sensations in the presence of a work of art and to express them, that is the function of Criticism for the impressionistic critic. His attitude he would express somewhat in this fashion: "Here is a beautiful poem, let us say 'Prometheus Unbound.' To read it is for me to experience a thrill of pleasure. My delight in it is itself a judgment, and what better judgment is it possible for me to give? All that I can do is to tell how it affects me, what sensations it gives me. Other men will derive other sensations from it, and express them differently; they too have the same right as I. Each of us, if we are sensitive to impressions and express ourselves well, will produce a new work of art to replace the work which gave us our sensations. That is the art of criticism, and beyond that criticism cannot go." We shall not begrudge this exquisite soul the pleasure of his sensations or his cult of them, nor would he be disconcerted if we were to point out that the interest has been shifted from the work of art to his own impressions. Let us suppose that you say to him: "We are not interested in you, but in 'Prometheus Unbound.' To describe the state of your health is not to help us to understand or to enjoy the poem. Your criticism constantly tends to get away from the work of art, and to centre attention on yourself and your feelings." But his answer would not be difficult to find: "What you say is true enough. My criticism tends to get farther and farther from the work of art and to cast a light upon myself; but all criticism tends to get away from the work of art and to substitute something in its place. The impressionist substitutes himself, but what other form of criticism gets closer to 'Prometheus Unbound'? Historical criticism takes us away from it in a search of the environment, the age, the race, the poetic school of the artist; it tells us to read the history of the French Revolution, Godwin's 'Political Justice,' the 'Prometheus Bound' of Aeschylus, and Calderon's 'Magico Prodigioso.' Psychological criticism takes me away from the poem, and sets me to work on the biography of the poet; I wish to enjoy 'Prometheus Unbound,' and instead I am asked to become acquainted with Shelley the man. Dogmatic criticism does not get any closer to the work of art by testing it according to rules and standards; it sends me to the Greek dramatists, to Shakspere, to Aristotle's 'Poetics,' possibly to Darwin's 'Origin of Species,' in order that I may see how far Shelley has failed to give dramatic reality to his poem, or has failed to observe the rules of his *genre;* but that means the study of other works, and not of 'Prometheus Unbound.' Aesthetics takes me still farther afield into speculations on art and beauty. And so it is with every form of criticism. Do not deceive yourself. All criticism tends to shift the interest from the work of art to something else. The other critics give us history, politics, biography, erudition, metaphysics. As for me, I re-dream the poet's dream, and if I seem to write lightly, it is because I have awakened, and smile to think I have mistaken a dream for reality. I at least strive to replace one work of art by another, and art can only find its *alter ego* in art."

It would be idle to detail the arguments with which the advocates of the opposing forms of Criticism answered these questionings. Literary erudition and evolutionary science were the chief weapons used to fight this modern heresy, but the one is an unwieldy and the other a useless weapon in the field of aesthetic thought. On some sides, at least, the position of the impressionists was impregnable; but two points of attack were open to their opponents. They could combat the notion that taste is a substitute for learning, or learning a substitute for taste, since both are vital for Criticism; and they could maintain that the relativity of taste does not in any sense affect its authority. But these arguments are not my present concern; what I wish to point out is that the objective and dogmatic forms of Criticism were fighting no new battle against impressionistic Criti-

cism in that decade of controversy. It was a battle as old as the
earliest reflection on the subject of poetry, if not as old as the sensitiveness of poets. Modern literature begins with the same doubts,
with the same quarrel. In the sixteenth century the Italians were
formulating that classical code which imposed itself on Europe for
two centuries, and which, even in our generation, Brunetière has
merely disguised under the trappings of natural science. They
evolved the dramatic unities, and all those rules which the poet
Pope imagined to be "Nature still but Nature methodized." But at
the very moment when their spokesman Scaliger was saying that
"Aristotle is our emperor, the perpetual dictator of all the fine arts,"
another Italian, Pietro Aretino, was insisting that there is no rule
except the whim of genius and no standard of judgment beyond
individual taste.

The Italians passed on the torch to the French of the seventeenth
century, and from that day to this the struggle between the two
schools has never ceased to agitate the progress of Criticism in
France. Boileau against Saint-Évremond, Classicists against Romanticists, dogmatists against impressionists,—the antinomy is deep
in the French nature, indeed in the nature of Criticism itself. Listen
to this: "It is not for the purpose of deciding on the merit of this
noble poet [Virgil], nor of harming his reputation, that I have
spoken so freely concerning him. The world will continue to think
what it does of his beautiful verses; and as for me, I judge nothing,
I only say what I think, and what effect each of these things produces on my heart and mind." Surely these words are from the lips
of Lemaître himself! "I judge nothing: I only say what I feel." But
no, these are the utterances of the Chevalier de Méré, a wit of the
age of Louis XIV, and he is writing to the secretary of that strong-
hold of authority, the French Academy. For some men, even in the
age of Boileau, criticism was nothing but an "adventure among
masterpieces."

No, it is no new battle; it is the perpetual conflict of Criticism. In
every age impressionism (or enjoyment) and dogmatism (or judgment) have grappled with one another. They are the two sexes of
Criticism; and to say that they flourish in every age is to say that
every age has its masculine as well as its feminine criticism,—the
masculine criticism that may or may not force its own standards on
Literature, but that never at all events is dominated by the object
of its studies; and the feminine criticism that responds to the lure
of art with a kind of passive ecstasy. In the age of Boileau it was the

masculine type which gave the tone to Criticism; in our own, outside of the universities, it has certainly been the feminine. But they continue to exist side by side, ever falling short of their highest powers, unless mystically mated,—judgment erecting its edicts into arbitrary standards and conventions, enjoyment lost in the mazes of its sensuous indecision.

Yet if we examine these opposing forms of Criticism in our own age, we shall find, I think, that they are not wholly without a common ground to meet on; that, in fact, they are united in at least one prepossession which they do not share with the varying forms of Criticism in any of the earlier periods of its history. The Greeks conceived of Literature, not as an inevitable expression of creative power, but as a reasoned "imitation" or re-shaping of the materials of life; for Aristotle, poetry is the result of man's imitative instinct, and differs from history and science in that it deals with the probable or possible rather than with the real. The Romans conceived of Literature as a noble art, intended (though under the guise of pleasure) to inspire men with high ideals of life. The classicists of the sixteenth and seventeenth centuries accepted this view in the main; for them, Literature was a kind of exercise,—a craft acquired by study of the classics, and guided in the interpretation of nature by the traditions of Greek and Roman art. For these men Literature was as much a product of reason as science or history. The eighteenth century complicated the course of Criticism by the introduction of vague and novel criteria, such as "imagination," "sentiment," and "taste." But with the Romantic Movement there developed the new idea which coördinates all Criticism in the nineteenth century. Very early in the century, Mme. de Staël and others formulated the idea that Literature is an "expression of society." Victor Cousin founded the school of art for art's sake, enunciating "the fundamental rule, that expression is the supreme law of art." Later, Sainte-Beuve developed and illustrated his theory that Literature is an expression of personality. Still later, under the influence of natural science, Taine took a hint from Hegel and elaborated the idea that Literature is an expression of race, age, and environment. The extreme impressionists prefer to think of art as the exquisite expression of delicate and fluctuating sensations or impressions of life. But for all these critics and theorists, Literature is an expression of something, of experience or emotion, of the external or internal, of the man himself or something outside the man; yet it is always conceived of as an art of expression. The objective, the dogmatic, the impressionistic critics of our day may set for themselves very different tasks, but the idea of expression is implicit in all they write. They have, as it were, this bond of blood: they are not merely man and woman, but brother and sister; and their father, or grandfather, was Sainte-Beuve. The bitter but acute analysis of his talent which Nietzsche has given us in the "Twilight of the Idols" brings out very clearly this dual side of his seminal power, the feminine sensitiveness and the masculine detachment. For Nietzsche, he is "nothing of a man; he wanders about, delicate, curious, tired, pumping people, a female after all, with a woman's revengefulness and a woman's sensuousness, a critic without a standard, without firmness, and without backbone." Here it is the impressionist in Sainte-Beuve that arouses the German's wrath. But in the same breath we find Nietzsche blaming him for "holding up objectivity as a mask"; and it is on this objective side that Sainte-Beuve becomes the source of all those historical and psychological forms of critical study which have influenced the academic thought of our day, leading insensibly, but inevitably, from empirical investigation to empirical law. The pedigree of the two schools thereafter is not difficult to trace: on the one side, from Sainte-Beuve through *l'art pour l'art* to impressionism, and on the other, from Sainte-Beuve through Taine to Brunetière and his egregious kin.

French criticism has been leaning heavily on the idea of expression for a century or more, but no attempt has been made in France to understand its aesthetic content, except for a few vague echoes of German thought. For the first to give philosophic precision to the theory of expression, and to found a method of Criticism based upon it, were the Germans of the age that stretches from Herder to Hegel. All the forces of philosophical thought were focused on this central concept, while the critics enriched themselves from out this golden store. I suppose you all remember the famous passage in which Carlyle describes the achievement of German criticism in that age. "Criticism," says Carlyle, "has assumed a new form in Germany. It proceeds on other principles and proposes to itself a higher aim. The main question is not now a question concerning the qualities of diction, the coherence of metaphors, the fitness of sentiments, the general logical truth in a work of art, as it was some half century ago among most critics; neither is it a question mainly of a psychological sort to be answered by discovering and delineating the peculiar nature of the poet from his poetry, as is usual with the best of our own critics at present: but it is, not indeed exclusively, but inclusively of its two other questions, properly and ultimately a question of the essence and peculiar life of the poetry itself. . . . The problem is not now to determine by what mechanism Addison composed sentences and struck out similitudes, but by what far finer and more mysterious mechanism Shakspere organized his dramas and gave life and individuality to his Ariel and his Hamlet. Wherein lies that life; how have they attained that shape and individuality? Whence comes that empyrean fire which irradiates their whole being and appears at least in starry gleams? Are these dramas of his not veri-similar only, but true; nay, truer than reality itself, since the essence of unmixed reality is bodied forth in them under more expressive similes? What is this unity of pleasures; and can our deeper inspection discern it to be indivisible and existing by necessity because each work springs as it were from the general elements of thought and grows up therefrom into form and expansion by its own growth? Not only who was the poet and how did he compose; but what and how was the poem, and why was it a poem and not rhymed eloquence, creation and not figured passion? These are the questions for the critic. Criticism stands like an interpreter between the inspired and the uninspired; between the prophet and those who hear the melody of his words and catch some glimpse of their material meaning but understand not their deeper import."

I am afraid that no German critic wholly realized this ideal; but it was at least the achievement of the Germans that they enunciated the doctrine, even if they did not always adequately illustrate it in practice. It was they who first realized that art has performed its function when it has expressed itself; it was they who first conceived of Criticism as the study of expression. "There is a destructive and a creative or constructive criticism," said Goethe; the first measures and tests Literature according to mechanical standards, the second answers the fundamental questions: "What has the writer proposed to himself to do? and how far has he succeeded in carrying out his own plan?" Carlyle, in his essay on Goethe, almost uses Goethe's own words, when he says that the critic's first and foremost duty is to make plain to himself "what the poet's aim really and truly was, how the task he had to do stood before his eye, and how far, with such materials as were afforded him, he has fulfilled it." This has been the central problem, the guiding star, of all modern criticism. From Coleridge to Pater, from Sainte-Beuve to Lemaître, this is what critics have been striving for, even when they have not succeeded; yes, even when they have been deceiving themselves into thinking that they were striving for something else. This was not the ideal of Aristotle when he tells us that the critic may censure a work of art as "irrational, impossible, morally hurtful, self-contradictory, or contrary to technical correctness." This was not Boileau's standard when he blamed Tasso for the introduction of Christian rather than pagan mythology into epic poetry; nor Addison's, when he tested "Paradise Lost" according to the rules of Le Bossu; nor Dr. Johnson's, when he laments the absence of poetic justice in "King Lear," or pronounces dogmatically that the poet should not "number the streaks of the tulip." What has the poet tried to do, and how has he fulfilled his intention? What is he striving to express and how has he expressed it? What impression does his work make on me, and how can I best express this impression? These are the questions that nineteenth-century critics have been taught to ask when face to face with the work of a poet.

The theory of expression, the concept of Literature as an art of expression, is the common ground on which critics have met for a century or more. Yet how many absurdities, how many complicated systems, how many confusions, have been superimposed on this fundamental idea; and how slowly has its full significance become the possession of critics! To accept the naked principle is to play havoc with these confusions and complications; and no one has seen this more clearly, or driven home its inevitable consequences with more intelligence and vigor, than an Italian thinker and critic of our own day, Benedetto Croce, who has received of late a kind of official introduction to the English-speaking world in the striking compliment paid to him by Mr. Balfour in a recent Romanes Lecture. But I for one needed no introduction to his work; under his banner I enrolled myself long ago, and here re-enroll myself in what I now say. He has led aesthetic thought inevitably from the concept that art is expression to the conclusion that all expression is art. Time does not permit, nor reason ask, that we should follow this argument through all its *pros* and *cons*. If this theory of expression be once and for all accepted, as indeed it has been partly though confusedly accepted by all modern critics, the ground of Criticism is cleared of its dead lumber and its weeds. I propose now merely to point out this dead lumber and these weeds. In other words, we shall see to what conclusions the critical thought and practice of a century have been inevitably converging, and what elements of the old Criticism and the old literary history are disappearing from the new.

In the first place, we have done with all the old Rules. The very conception of "rules" harks back to an age of magic, and reminds the modern of those mysterious words which the heroes of the fairy-tales are without reason forbidden to utter; the rules are a survival of the savage *taboo*. We find few arbitrary rules in Aristotle, who limited himself to empirical inductions from the experience of Litera-ture; but they appear in the later Greek rhetoricians; and in the Romans empirical induction has been hardened into dogma. Horace lays down the law to the prospective playwright in this manner: "You must never have more than three actors on the stage at any one time; you must never let your drama exceed five acts." It is unneces-sary to trace the history of these rules, or to indicate how they in-creased in number, how they were arranged into a system by the classicists of the sixteenth and seventeenth centuries, and how they burdened the creative art of that period. They were never without their enemies. We have seen how Aretino was pitted against Scaliger, Saint-Évremond against Boileau; and in every age the poets have astounded the critics by transgressing rules without the sacrifice of beauty. But it was not until the end of the eighteenth century that the Romanticists banished them from the province of Criticism. The pedantry of our own day has borrowed "conventions" from history and "technique" from science as substitutes for the outworn formulae of the past; but these are merely new names for the old mechanical rules; and they too will go, when criticism clearly recog-nizes in every work of art an organism governed by its own law.

We have done with the *genres,* or literary kinds. Their history is inseparably bound up with that of the classical rules. Certain works of literature have a general resemblance and are loosely classed to-gether (for the sake of convenience) as lyric, comedy, tragedy, epic, pastoral, and the like; the classicists made of each of these divisions a fixed norm governed by inviolable laws. The separation of the *genres* was a consequence of this law of classicism: comedy should not be mingled with tragedy, nor epic with lyric. But no sooner was the law enunciated than it was broken by an artist impatient or ignorant of its restraints, and the critics have been obliged to explain away these violations of their laws, or gradually to change the laws themselves. But if art is organic expression, and every work of art is to be interrogated with the question, "What has it expressed, and how completely?" there is no place for the question whether it has conformed to some convenient classification of critics or to some law derived from this classification. The lyric, the pastoral, the epic, are abstractions without concrete reality in the world of art. Poets do not write epics, pastorals, lyrics; they express themselves, and this expression is their only form. There are not, therefore, only three, or ten, or a hundred literary kinds; there are as many kinds as there are individual poets. But it is in the field of literary history that this error is most obvious. Shakspere wrote "King Lear," "Venus and Adonis," and a sequence of sonnets. What becomes of Shakspere, the creative artist, when these three works are separated from one another by the historian of poetry; when they lose their connection with his single creative soul, and are classified with other works with which they have only a loose and vague relation? To slice up the history of English Literature into compartments marked comedy, tragedy, lyric, and the like, is to be guilty of a complete misunderstanding of the meaning of Criticism; and literary history becomes a logical absurdity when its data are not organically related but cut up into sections, and placed in such compartments as these.

We have done with the comic, the tragic, the sublime, and an army of vague abstractions of their kind. These have grown out of the generalizations of the Alexandrian critics, acquiring a new lease of life in the eighteenth century. Gray and his friend West corresponded with each other on the subject of the sublime; later, Schiller distinguished between the naïf and the sentimental. Jean Paul was one of many who defined humor, and Hegel among those who defined the tragic. If these terms represent the content of art, they may be relegated to the same category as joy, hate, sorrow, enthusiasm; and we should speak of the comic in the same general way in which we might speak of the expression of joy in a poem. If, on the other hand, these terms represent abstract classifications of poetry, their use in criticism sins against the very nature of art. Every poet re-expresses the universe in his own way, and every poem is a new and independent expression. The tragic does not exist for Criticism, but only Aeschylus, Shakspere, Racine. There is no objection to the use of the word tragic as a convenient label for somewhat similar poems, but to find laws for the tragic and to test creative artists by such laws as these is simply to give a more abstract form to the outworn classical conception of dramatic rules.

We have done with the theory of style, with metaphor, simile, and all the paraphernalia of Graeco-Roman rhetoric. These owe their existence to the assumption that style is separated from expression, that it is something which may be added or subtracted at will from the work of art. But we know that art *is* expression, that it is complete in itself, that to alter it is to create another expression and therefore to create another work of art. If the poet, for example, says of springtime that " 'Tis now the blood runs gold," he has not employed a substitute for something else, such as "the blood tingles in our veins"; he has expressed his thought in its completeness, and there is no equivalent for his expression except itself.

> "Each perfect in its place; and each content
> With that perfection which its being meant."

Such expressions are still called metaphors in the text-books; but metaphor, simile, and all the old terms of classical rhetoric are signs of the zodiac, magical incantations, astrological formulae, interesting only to antiquarian curiosity. To Montaigne they suggested "the prattle of chambermaids"; to me they suggest rather the drone and singsong of many school-mistresses. We still hear talk of the "grand style," and essays on style continue to be written, like the old "arts of poetry" of two centuries ago; but the theory of styles has no longer a real place in modern thought; we have learned that it is no less impossible to study style as separate from the work of art than to study the comic as separate from the work of the comic artist.

We have done with all moral judgment of Literature. Horace said that pleasure and profit are the end of art, and for many centuries the critics quarreled over the terms "pleasure" and "profit." Some said that poetry was meant to instruct; some, merely to please; some, to do both. Romantic criticism first enunciated the principle that art has no aim except expression; that its aim is complete when expression is complete; that "beauty is its own excuse for being." If the achievement of the poet be to express any material he may select, and to express it with a completeness that we recognize as perfection, obviously morals can play no part in the judgment which criticism may form of his work. No critic of authority now tests literature by the standards of ethics.

We have done with "dramatic" criticism. The theory that the drama is not a creative art, but a by-product of the physical exigencies of the theatre, is as old as the sixteenth century. An Italian scholar of that age was the first to maintain that plays are intended to be acted on a stage, under certain restricted physical conditions, and before a large and heterogeneous crowd; dramatic performance has developed out of these conditions, and the test of its excellence is the pleasure it gives to the mixed audience that supports it. This idea was taken hold of by some of the German romanticists, for the purpose of justifying the Shaksperean drama in its apparent diver-

gence from the classical "rules." Shakspere cannot be judged by the
rules of the Greek theatre (so ran their argument), for the drama is
an inevitable product of theatrical conditions; these conditions in
Elizabethan England were not the same as those of Periclean Athens;
and it is therefore absurd to judge Shakspere's practice by that of
Sophocles. Here at least the idea helped to bring Shakspere home to
many new hearts by ridding the age of mistaken prejudices, and
served a useful purpose, as a specious argument may persuade men
to contribute to a noble work, or a mad fanatic may rid the world of
a tyrant. But with this achievement its usefulness but not its life was
ended. It has been developed into a system, and become a dogma of
dramatic critics; it is our contemporary equivalent for the "rules"
of seventeenth-century pedantry. As a matter of fact, the dramatic
artist is to be judged by no other standard than that applied to any
other creative artist: what has he tried to express, and how has he
expressed it? It is true that the theatre is not only an art but a business, and the so-called "success" of a play is of vital interest to the
theatre in so far as it is a commercial undertaking. The test of
"success" is an economic test, and concerns not art or the criticism of
art, but political economy. Valuable contributions to economic and
social history have been made by students who have investigated
the changing conditions of the theatre and the vicissitudes of taste
on the part of theatrical audiences; but these have the same relation
to criticism, and to the drama as an art, that a history of the publisher's trade and its influence on the personal fortunes of poets
would bear to the history of poetry.

We have done with technique as separate from art. It has been
pointed out that style cannot be disassociated from art; and the false
air of science which the term "technique" seems to possess should
not blind us to the fact that it too involves the same error. "Technique is really personality; that is the reason why the artist cannot
teach it, why the pupil cannot learn it, and why the aesthetic critic
can understand it," says Oscar Wilde, in a dialogue on "The Critic
as Artist," which, amid much perversity and paradox, is illumined
by many flashes of strange insight. The technique of poetry cannot
be separated from its inner nature. Versification cannot be studied
by itself, except loosely and for convenience; it remains always an
inherent quality of the single poem. Milton's line:—

"These my sky-robes spun out of Iris' woof"

is called an iambic pentameter; but it is not true that artistically it has something in common with every other line possessing the same succession of syllables and accents; in this sense it is not an iambic pentameter; it is only one thing; it is the line:—

"These my sky-robes spun out of Iris' woof"

We have done with the history and criticism of poetic themes. It is possible to speak loosely of the handling of such a theme as Prometheus by Aeschylus and by Shelley, of the story of Francesca da Rimini by Dante, Stephen Phillips, and D'Annunzio; but strictly speaking, they are not employing the same theme at all. Each artist is expressing a certain material and labeling it with an historic name. For Shelley Prometheus is only a label; he is expressing his artistic conception of life, not the history of a Greek Titan; it is the vital flame he has breathed into his work that makes it what it is, and with this vital fiame (and not with labels) the critic should concern himself in the works of poets.

We have done with the race, the time, the environment of a poet's work as an element in criticism. To study these phases of a work of art is to treat it as an historic or social document, and the result is a contribution to the history of culture or civilization, without primary interest for the history of art. "Granted the times, the environment, the race, the passions of the poet, what has he done with his materials, how has he converted poetry out of reality?" To answer this question of the Italian De Sanctis as it refers to each single work of art is to perform what is truly the critic's vital function; this is to interpret "expression" in its rightful sense, and to liberate aesthetic Criticism from the vassalage to *Kulturgeschichte* imposed on it by the school of Taine.

We have done with the "evolution" of Literature. The concept of progress was first applied to Literature in the seventeenth century, but at the very outset Pascal pointed out that a distinction must here be made between science and art; that science advances by accumulation of knowledge, while the changes of art cannot be reduced to any theory of progress. As a matter of fact, the theory involves the ranking of poets according to some arbitrary conception of their value; and the ranking of writers in order of merit has become obsolete, except in the "hundred best books" of the last decade and the "five-foot shelves" of to-day. The later nineteenth century gave a new air of verisimilitude to this old theory by borrowing the term "evolution" from science; but this too involves a fundamental misconception of the free and original movement of art. A similar misconception is involved in the study of the "origins" of art; for art has no origin separate from man's life.

> "In climes beyond the solar road,
>   Where shaggy forms o'er ice-built mountains roam,
>   The Muse has broke the twilight-gloom";

but though she wore savage raiment, she was no less the Muse. Art is simple at times, complex at others, but it is always art. The simple art of early times may be studied with profit; but the researches of anthropology have no vital significance for criticism, unless the anthropologist studies the simplest forms of art in the same spirit as the highest; that is, unless the anthropologist is an aesthetic critic.

Finally, we have done with the old rupture between genius and taste. When Criticism first propounded as its real concern the oft-repeated question: "What has the poet tried to express and how has he expressed it?" Criticism prescribed for itself the only possible method. How can the critic answer this question without becoming (if only for a moment of supreme power) at one with the creator? That is to say, taste must reproduce the work of art within itself in order to understand and judge it; and at that moment aesthetic judgment becomes nothing more nor less than creative art itself. The identity of genius and taste is the final achievement of modern thought on the subject of art, and it means that fundamentally the creative and the critical instincts are one and the same. From Goethe to Carlyle, from Carlyle to Arnold, from Arnold to Symons, there has been much talk of the "creative function" of Criticism. For each of these men the phrase held a different content; for Arnold it meant merely that criticism creates the intellectual atmosphere of the age,—a social function of high importance, perhaps, yet wholly independent of aesthetic significance. But the ultimate truth toward which these men were tending was more radical than that, and plays havoc with all the old platitudes about the sterility of taste. Criticism at last can free itself of its age-long self-contempt, now that it may realize that aesthetic judgment and artistic creation are instinct with the same vital life. Without this identity, Criticism would really be impossible. "Genius is to aesthetics what the ego is to philosophy, the only supreme and absolute reality," said Schelling; and without subduing the mind to this transcendental system, it remains true that what must always be inexplicable to mere reflection is just what gives power to poetry; that intellectual curiosity may amuse itself by asking its little questions of the silent sons of light, but they vouchsafe no answer to art's pale shadow, thought; the gods are kind if they give up their secret in another work of art, the art of Criticism, that serves as some sort of mirror to the art of Literature, only because in their flashes of insight taste and genius are one.

# GEORGE EDWARD WOODBERRY
## (1855–1930)


BORN at Beverly, Massachusetts, on May 12, 1855, Woodberry was educated at Phillips Exeter and then attended Harvard University. After graduating from Harvard, he taught at the University of Nebraska and served for a short period on the staff of *The Nation*. From 1882 to 1891 he settled down to literary work, contributing material to the *Atlantic Monthly* and acting as literary editor of the *Boston Post*. His distinguished life-work began in 1891 when he was appointed professor of English at Columbia University. Upon his retirement from his teaching duties in 1904 he devoted his time to writing and lecturing.

His was a long and fruitful writing career. His first book, *A History of Wood Engraving* (1883), was followed by his biographies of Poe (1885, revised in 1919), Hawthorne (1902), and Emerson (1907). These books gained him a substantial reputation as a scholar and critic. His critical and literary essays breathe a deep and genuine love of literature. Though his work is at present largely neglected, he was an inspiring teacher and highly stimulating critic. His interests covered a wide and varied field. Taking all of Western culture as his demesne, he treated foreign as well as native writers, the past as well as the present, with sympathetic understanding.

The breadth and range of Woodberry's love of literature in all its varied forms is vividly evidenced in *The Appreciation of Literature* (1907), as well as in such volumes as *Studies in Life and Letters* (1890), *The Torch* (1905), *Great Writers* (1907), and *The Inspiration of Poetry* (1910). He approached literature not as so much dead matter to be dissected into its component parts, classified, and studied in relation to the milieu, the moment, and the race, but as a vital expression of life. Scholarly without ever becoming pedantic, he never sacrificed the spirit for the letter. Consistently he develops the theme that literature is the foremost of the humanities, one of the most efficacious means of making man more completely human. The appreciation of literature does not depend upon following a set of rules or a body of critical principles but in being responsive to impressions, in being

91

fully alive, open to all the rich suggestions that emanate from a work of art. For the universality of a literary work is an ever-widening circle that begins with the writer's own life and reaches out to include all of humanity. It does more than communicate experience; it communicates experience clarified and ordered. All three approaches to literature—the aesthetic, the historical, and the psychological—are useful, indeed indispensable, if the essential significance of a work is to be brought forth. The characteristic value of a literary work, however, is to be found in its being a work of literature. The aim and end of literature is not instruction but insight into the mysteries of life and fate. To know the truth of life in all its infinite variety —that is the goal in view.

Woodberry rejects the Crocean-Spingarn conception of creative criticism, primarily for the reason that it eliminates both judgment and interpretation and becomes a kind of irresponsible private appreciation enacted in the consciousness of the critic. Adhering to a more traditional conception of criticism, he argues that the world of art possesses an absolute value which it transmits to its works. Once they are born and given to the world, works of art become public possessions, subject to the vicissitudes of time; since they are part of the world of culture, they enter inevitably into relations with other monuments of culture. By thus taking their place in the continuum of time and tradition, they give rise to a history of art, becoming an integral part of a temporal order. When considered from the point of view of their development in time, they fall within the scope of historical criticism.

Woodberry had little sympathy for what passed itself off as scientific criticism: theories which emphasize the objective factors in the genesis and growth of art. These exhaustive labors of analysis and documentation are beside the point, for they tend to get further and further away from the work of art itself, substituting facts and theories for first-hand insight and aesthetic appreciation. If we are to re-create the work of art as it existed in the mind of the artist, we must make sure that our reconstruction is true to the mind and vision of the artist, and for that the historical method is imperative. Though art is universal in its appeal, it manifests itself in diverse ways. The spirit of the past must therefore be reproduced as faithfully as possible. That is the only way to re-create the work of art as it originally came to life in the mind of the artist. Here Woodberry approaches the philosophy of relativism, though without being aware of its modern implications. Other races, other civilizations, create works of art that are to us not only unfamiliar but enigmatic, sometimes bafflingly unintelligible. Art cannot be forced within a logical framework of abstract categories; it can be known only in the concrete. That is why Woodberry clings to historical criticism as the only way of preparing himself for the task of aesthetic criticism.

The function of judgment, however, must also be exercised. It is a mistake on the part of the Crocean to limit the critic too narrowly to the aesthetic field, arbitrarily preventing him from inquiring into the state of the artist's mind or to judge the value of his completed work. Once a work is produced it is a source of intellectual and moral values which may be harmful or beneficial in their effect. Even if the genius behind the work is supremely original, breaking new ground, discovering new forms and devising new methods of expression, the artist does not depart entirely from the uses of the past. Techniques may be legitimately analyzed in the light of tradition. Works of art, part of a long-continuing tradition and long-developed craft, incorporate communal interests and enduring moral values. Criticism must follow the guide of reason in passing judgment on the intellectual and moral values implicit in a work of art. For art cannot be divorced from the life of reason. The mind shapes the material of art as it shapes the material of life, with this difference, that in the former there is the triumph of creatively imposed order and achieved unity.

Historical criticism is but one phase of the critical process. There is the objective expression, the work of art, as perceived by our senses and charged with the artist's personality, his symbols, his vital meanings. If in criticism there is a diversity of interpretation, that is inevitable, since we stamp the artist's image with our own personality, creating it anew each time. Art is thus never fully apprehended; inexhaustible in its power of suggestions, it is never finished, ever growing richer in significance. Then, too, rooted temperamental differences produce differences in appreciation. Each one has his own aesthetic preferences and antipathies, so that we cannot ever re-create the work of art exactly as it existed in the artist's mind at the time he produced it.

If that is a serious handicap, there is ample compensation in the knowledge that with each age the work of art takes on new and fresh accretions of meaning as we strive to master its mystery and assimilate its substance. Art progressively emancipates itself from the mind of its original begetter and enters upon a life of its own, and its immortality lies precisely in this continual renewal in the minds of those who respond to it. Liberal in temper, Woodberry believed in the quality of the universal. Civilization grows by absorbing all that is rich and vital in alien cultures and civilizations. He deplores race prejudice and contempt for the foreigner in American life. His profound love for literature at its best, literature as an inspiring and spiritualizing force, is effectively communicated in his critical work. His "A New Defense of Poetry" which was first printed in *Heart of Man* in 1899, is still worth reading.

BIBLIOGRAPHY

TEXT

*Edgar Allen Poe*. New York, 1885; 1909.
*Heart of Man*. New York, 1899.
*Makers of Literature*. New York, 1901.
*Nathaniel Hawthorne*. Boston, 1902.
*The Torch*. New York, 1903.
*America in Literature*. New York, 1903.
*Swinburne*. New York, 1905.
*Great Writers*. New York, 1907.
*Ralph Waldo Emerson*. New York, 1907.
*The Appreciation of Literature*. New York, 1909.
*The Inspiration of Poetry*. New York, 1911.
*Wendell Phillips*. Boston, 1912.
*Two Phases of Criticism*. Boston, 1914. (Privately printed.)
*Collected Works*. 6 vols. New York, 1920.
*Literary Memoirs of the Nineteenth Century*. New York, 1921.
*A Scholar's Testament;* two letters from George Edward Woodberry to J. E. Spingarn. Amenia, 1931. (Privately printed.)
*Selected Letters*, with an introduction by Walter de la Mare. Boston and New York, 1933.

CRITICISM

Calverton, V. F., *The Newer Spirit*. New York, 1925, pp. 153–155.
Erskine, John, "George Edward Woodberry," *Bulletin of the New York Public Library*, XXXIV, 275–279 (May, 1930).
Hawkins, R. R., "A List of Writings by and about George Edward Woodberry," *Bulletin of the New York Public Library*, XXXIV, 279–296 (May, 1930).
Hovey, R. B., "George Edward Woodberry: Genteel Exile," *New England Quarterly*, XXIII, 504–526 (December, 1950).
Ledoux, L. V., *The Poetry of George Edward Woodberry*. New York, 1917.
——, "George Edward Woodberry," *Saturday Review of Literature*, VI, 638 (January 11, 1930).
Rosenberg, J. N. and Benét, W. R., "George Edward Woodberry: Two Estimates," *New York Herald-Tribune Books*, IX, 1–2 (July 9, 1933).
Thwing, C. F., "George Edward Woodberry," *Harvard Graduate Magazine*, XXXVIII, 433–443 (June, 1930).

## ESTHETIC CRITICISM*

Is it an error to relegate art to the dead past and translate it into history? Works of art are not like political events and persons; they do not pass at once away. The Hermes of Praxiteles is still with us. Is it really the same Hermes that it was when it was made? Is its personal identity a fixed state, or does its personality, like our own, change in the passage of time? May it not be the nature of art to cast off what is mortal, and emancipate itself from the mind of its creator? Is it truly immortal, still alive, or only a stone image forever the same—a petrifaction, as it were, of the artist's soul at a certain moment? or is it possible, on the other hand, that such a life really abides in art as to make what is immortal in the work greatly exceed that mortal and temporary part which historical criticism preserves? Let us ignore the historical element, and consider what is left in the critical act, still conceived as a re-creation of the image, but the re-creation of the image before us apart from any attempt to realize what was in the artist's mind, or with only a passing reference to that.

Expression is the nucleus of the artist's power. What is expression? It is the process of externalizing what was in the artist's mind, in some object of sense which shall convey it to others. The material used may be actual form and color, as in painting and sculpture; or imaginary objects and actions through the medium of language, as in literature; or pure sound, as in music; always there is some material which is perceived by the senses and intelligible only through their mediation. Slight, indeed, would be the artist's power and inept his skill, if he should not so frame the lineaments of his work as to stamp on the senses of all comers the same intelligible image, and give for the bodily eye what the bodily eye can see in picture, statue or story. The work of art, however, is not merely the material object, but that object charged with the personality of the artist. It is in his power to make that charge effective that his true faculty of expression lies. The material object—form, color, action, sound— is enveloped in his feeling; the words he uses are loaded with his meanings and tones. His personality is immaterial, and cannot be bodied forth; hence, the most essential and significant part of what

* Reprinted from *Heart of Man and Other Papers* by George Edward Woodberry, copyright, 1920, by Harcourt Brace and Company, Inc. Delivered first as a lecture at Kenyon College in 1913. Privately printed in 1914 together with the other lecture on "Historical Criticism."

he expresses, that which clothes the material object with its spirituality, is dependent in a supreme degree on suggestion, on what can be only incompletely set forth, on half-lights and intimations, and the thousand subtleties which lie on the borderland of the inexpressible.

In so far as a work of art is a thing of nature, it can be expressed materially with the more adequacy; in so far as it is a thing of the spirit, of personality, it is less subject to complete and certain expression; and in all art there are these two elements. In that process of re-creating the image which we are now examining the mind's fortune with these two elements is unequal; so far as the material part is concerned, normal eyes will see the same thing, normal intelligence will grasp the same thing, in figure, action and event; but when it is a question of realizing the spirit, differences begin to emerge and multiply. Rifts of temperament and varieties of experience between artist and spectator make chasms of misunderstanding and misappreciation. How diverse are the representations in the mind finally, as revealed in our tastes and judgments! The same image, mirrored in individuals, becomes radically different in opposed minds, and each is apt to believe that his own is the true and only one. It is commonplace that every reader thinks that he is Hamlet. What a number of Hamlets that makes! It is a commonplace also that this ease of identification with a character is a test of genius in a writer and ranks him in power and significance. Those who create so are called the universal writers. Whence arises this paradox, so common in art, of infinite diversity in identity? It comes from the fact that, so far from realizing the image as it was in the artist's mind and receiving it charged with his personality merely, it is we ourselves who create the image by charging it with our own personality. In this creation we do not simply repeat in ourselves his state of mind and become as it were ghosts of him who is dead; but we originate something new, living and our own. There is no other way for us to appropriate his work, to interpret it and understand it. The fact is that a work of art, being once created and expressed, externalized, is gone from the artist's mind and returns to the world of nature; it becomes a part of our external world, and we treat it precisely as we treat the rest of that world, as mere material for our own artist-life which goes on in our own minds and souls in the exercise of our own powers in their limitations. Our appropriation of art is as strictly held within these bounds as is our grasp upon the material world.

It is one of the charms of art that it is not to be completely under-

stood. In an age in which so high a value is put upon facts, information, positive knowledge, it is a relief to have still reserved to us a
place apart where it is not necessary to know all. The truth of science
is stated in a formula of mathematics, a law of physics, a generalization of one or another kind; it is clear, and it is all contained there;
in each specific case there is nothing more to be known. The truth of
art is of a different sort; it does not seem to be all known, finished
and finally stated, but on the contrary to be ever growing, more rich
in significance, more profound in substance, disclosing heaven over
heaven and depth under depth. The greatest books share our lives,
and grow old with us; we read them over and over, and at each
decade it is a new book that we find there, so much has it gained in
meaning from experience of life, from ripening judgment, from the
change of seasons in the soul. The poetry of Wordsworth is a typical
instance of such a book. It is the same with the artists, with sculptors and musicians. Art of all sorts has this lifelong increment of
value, and whoever has experienced this easily realizes to what a
degree and how constantly the reader's intelligence, cultivation and
experience are controlling and limiting factors in his power to appropriate what is before him. In art he appropriates only a part of
what the work contains. It is thus that the great artists, Shakespeare,
Dante, Virgil, are lifelong studies.

A second but powerful limitation lies in those differences of temperament, just referred to, which have an arbitrary potency in appreciation. The practical man is, as a rule, really self-excluded from
the field of art; but, inside the field, the stoic will not make much of
Byron nor the cynic of Shelley. In certain arts, such as the many
kinds of prints, a special training of the eye and some technical
knowledge of processes must be acquired before one really sees what
the eye itself must discover in the engraving in order to apprehend
its subtle qualities. The way, however, is most commonly blocked by
certain inhibitions which are so lodged in the mind by education and
opinion that they effectively paralyze any effort at re-creation. I remember once, years ago, when I was myself a student, meeting on a
western train out of Buffalo a clergyman who kindly engaged me in
conversation; and I, being a boy, repaid his interest by flooding him
with my enthusiasms for George Eliot and Scott, who happened to
be then my ascendant stars. I recall well his final reply: "Young
man," he said, "I never read anything that isn't true." What an
inhibition that was, in his literary and artistic career! I have since
wondered if he found much to read. Ideal truth, as you perceive, had

never dawned upon his mind—and that is the finer and happier part of truth. The prejudice of the early New England church against the theater is a curious instance of an inhibition that rendered nugatory a great historic branch of art, the drama; and it is the more singular, viewed as a religious phenomenon, because of the great place the drama held in religion itself in Catholic countries and especially in medieval times. What Puritan could read the sacred drama of Spain with any understanding? I have friends who object to war as a theme of verse, and the praise of wine by the poets is anathema in many quarters. These are all examples of moral inhibitions bred in the community and operating against great divisions of literature. What a sword of destruction that would be which would strike Mars and Bacchus from the world's poetry! The American inhibition, however, which best illustrates what I have in mind, is that which rejects the nude in sculpture and painting, not only forfeiting thereby the supreme of Greek genius and sanity, but to the prejudice, also, of human dignity, as it seems to me. Such inhibitions in one way and another exist in communities and individuals; the appreciation of literature, and of art in general, is subject to them; and I cite these examples to bring out clearly how true it is that, almost involuntarily and unconsciously, in re-creating the work of art we remake it in ourselves and not in its own world, and the meaning we charge it with is our own personality and not that of its original creator. If I look with shamed eyes at Hermes, Narcissus and Venus, the shame is mine, and not the sculptor's; if I cannot read the old verses on Agincourt with sympathy and delight in their heroic breath, the poverty of soul is mine, not Drayton's. In every way, the responsibility for what we make of art, in re-creating it, springs from what we are.

It is plain that, in consequence of our various limitations in faculty, knowledge, experience, temperament and working always with some subjection to communal ideas and tastes, we must suffer many losses of what the work of art originally contained and fall short of realizing it as it was in the artist's mind. On the other hand there is some compensation in the fact that the work itself may take on new meanings that the artist did not dream of; for, in returning to the external world and becoming a part of our real environment, the work of art has resumed that plastic quality which belongs to the world of nature and makes it material for us to mold our own souls in. The essence of the work, its living power for us, is not what the artist put in it, but what we draw from it; its world-value is not what it was to the artist, but what it is to the world. It is common enough for the reader to find meanings in a book that the writer did not consciously put there; there is much in personality that the artist himself is not aware of, and also there may be much in the work which he does not attend to, and hence there is excess of significance in both ways; and moreover, the reader may respond to the work with greater sensitiveness than belonged to the creator and in new ways. Thus arises the paradox which I often maintain, that it is not the poet, but the reader, who writes the poem.

This is more plainly seen when literature is looked at under the changing lights of time. New ages appropriate the works of the past by accomplishing a partial transformation in them, and unless art is capable of such a remaking, it cannot last; it becomes merely archaic, historic, dead—a thing for the scholar's museum. Homer has delighted ages, but it is through his capacity to live again in the battle-loving and travel-loving hearts of men; it is not because later generations have read the "Iliad" and the "Odyssey" as the Greeks read or heard them. Each age reads something into the text, as we say, and this "reading-in" is incessant in the history of art. It is well illustrated in the criticism of Pater, so frequently called creative criticism, and especially in his "Marius, the Epicurean,"—a marvelous blend of the modern spirit with ancient material—but such "reading-in" is his most brilliant achievement in all his essays, whether they treat of Greek gods, like Dionysus, or French gallants, or Roman gentlemen; all his figures are developed in the dark chamber of his own singularly sensitive and refined artistic temperament. The same phenomenon occurs as characteristically, though in so contrasted a way, in the Puritan rehabilitation of the Old Testament at the time of the Civil War, when Agag and Naboth and their lives served as the eternal pattern of the ideal for the Roundheads; and at the present day one often hears in orthodox churches a discourse which, so far as its figures and colors are concerned, always reminds me of antique tapestry and seems to belong to some Oriental art of expression rather than to our own tongue, manners and ideas. Literature, and indeed all art, has this magic to change the meaning without altering the signs. It was thus that the picturesque and mythologic side of Paganism, the poetic part, was taken up, absorbed and reëmbodied in the Catholicism of southern Europe, and lives to this day, little changed in outward seeming, by the old Mediterranean shores. Indeed, in much modern poetry I often find the necessity of translating the old signs into fresh meanings in order to keep the language alive to me. Poetic imagery is none too abundant, take it all together; we cannot afford to sacrifice much of it. Instead of abolishing battle and the wine-cup, the gods and the heroes, the Old Testament, and what not, it will be far wiser to use them in the service of our new ideals. Art, taken either as a language or in its individual works, has not one meaning, but many. This is a part of the poet's subtle mystery that he declares he knows not what.

If you have followed these remarks with any sympathy and I have conveyed to you my belief that each of us has the artist-soul, continually engaged in its own creations, you will readily comprehend that works of art are not to me historical monuments valuable for the information they give of the past, nor even artistic entities to be known apart from ourselves and as they were in the artist's mind; but rather such works are only raw material, or at least new material, for us to make our own statues and pictures and poems out of; or, in a word, to create the forms of our own souls out of; for the soul must be given forms in order to be aware of its being, to know itself, truly to be. The soul moves toward self-expression in many ways, but in finding forms for itself the soul discovers its most plastic material in the world of art. It is in forms of ideality that the soul hastens to clothe itself; and while it is possible for us to elaborate such forms from the crude mass of nature, as the first artists did, yet later generations are the more fortunate in that they possess in art and literature a vast treasure of ideality already elaborated and present. Works of art thus constitute a select material wherein the artist-soul that is in each of us can work, not only with our own native force of penetration and aspiration, but, as it were, with higher aid—the aid of genius, the aid of the select souls of the race. It is true that the re-creation of old art which we accomplish is our own personal act, and cannot be otherwise; but the way is made easier for us, doors are opened, directions are indicated, light is shed on forward and unknown paths, sympathy, guidance and courage are given to us by companionship with the works of those, our forerunners, who have lived long in the soul's own world and left their testimony for us so far as we have skill to read in their text and understand in their spirit. This is the true service of art—of the poets, painters, musicians—to prepare the material of the soul's life so that those who are less fortunately endowed and more humble may more readily put on the spiritual garment that all must wear if they are to be souls, indeed, and live above the bodily sphere. There are other ways than art, it is true, by which the soul comes into its own; but in the way of art it is by re-creating in ourselves the past forms of the spirit, vitally appropriating them and charging them with our own life, that we win most directly and happily to true self-knowledge of the wonderful creature that man is.

It has become plain, I trust, in what sense it is indeed true that it is the nature of art to cast off what is mortal and emancipate itself from the mind of its creator, and thus to enter upon a life of its own, continually renewed in the minds of those who appropriate it. This is its real immortality—not the fact that it lasts through time, but that it lives in the souls of mankind. I am fond of biography, and few are the pleasures of the literary life that are more pure and precious than the quiet and unknown companionship which biography may establish between ourselves and those whose works have endeared to us their persons and interested us in their human fortunes as if they were friends; but I am always glad when time has destroyed all merely mortal record of them, and there remains only their work—only the "souls of poets dead and gone." It is only when fame shrinks to that narrow limit of the book or the deed, that it rises to its height. The Greek Anthology is a book of pure immortality because it has brought down with it so little of the alloy of temporal personality; and that clarity of fame, which seems almost a peculiarity of classical literature and antique art, gathering all its luster often into one lonely name, is due, perhaps, most to this freedom from human detail. The poet, the sculptor, has come to live only in his work, where the immortal part of him found expression and lodgment while he was yet alive; all else was dust, and is in the tomb which is appointed for mortal things. It is better so, when the poet's memory itself becomes ideal, and the imagination paints its Dante and carves its Shelley after the image of the pure soul they left on earth when they departed hence. Even that soul, that personality which they incarnated in their art, suffers changes and refinement. Only that element abides which can enter continuously and permanently into the souls of men, according to their several grades of being—only that which can live in humanity; the rest fades away with time. And then this miracle arises that into the soul of Virgil, for example, enters a Christian soul, new-born, and deepening its pathos; and not Virgil only, but many others, are, as it were, adopted into the race itself and become the ever growing children of the human spirit, ideals and fathers of ideals through ages. That is earthly immortality—the survival and increment of the spirit through time. Thus arises another paradox, that as art begins by being charged with personality, it ends by becoming impersonal, solving the apparent contradiction in the soul universal, the common soul of mankind. Each of us creates art in his own image—it seems an infinite variable; and yet it is the variable of something identical in all—the soul. I often think that in the artistic life, and its wonderful spiritual interchange through the re-creation in each of the ideals of all, there is realized something analogous to the religious conception of the communion of saints, especially when one considers the impersonality of art in its climax of world-fame; for the communion of saints is not a communion of individual with individual, but of each one with all. It is thus in the artistic life that one shares in the soul universal, the common soul of mankind, which yet is manifest only in individuals and their concrete works. Art like life has its own material being in the concrete, but the spiritual being of both is in the universal.

We have come then, in our examination of criticism, or, in other words, of the act of appreciation, to the point I indicated earlier upon opening the subject, where criticism appears to be a private affair, a deeply personal act, such that every one of us must be his own artist. Each of us has the artist-soul, and if we enter truly into the world of art, it is not merely as spectators, but as participants, as ourselves the artists. It is on this activity of the soul in its artist-life that the whole subject concentrates its interest. I reminded you that from time to time in history our ancestors encountered successively alien literatures, and as each was in turn appropriated, a Renaissance resulted. It is thus that civilization has grown in body and quality, ever enriching itself by what it absorbs from this and that particular race and age. Nothing can exceed in folly the policy and temper that would isolate nations and races one from another; it is from the intermingling of all, with their various gifts and labors, that the greatest good finally comes; and no sign of the times is so disturbing to me as the present reactionary tendency in America apparent in the growth of race-prejudice and a jealous contempt of the foreigner. In this respect the life of the individual is like that of nations. If he grows, it is often by a Renaissance attending the introduction of something novel into his life. You are all familar with the splendid burst of the human spirit which attended the re-discovery of the ancient classic world in Italy, and you will recall how at a later time the re-discovery of the Middle Ages occasioned a similar flowering of art in the Gothic Renaissance, so variously fruitful in its turn in the last century. The parallel is easily found in individual life; such a profound and developing experience was the Italian journey for Goethe, the study of Plato and the Greek dramatists for Shelley, mythology for Keats—and everywhere in literary biography one finds illustrations.

The most arresting trait of the artist-life, as one begins to lead it, is that it is a life of discovery. It is not truth that is discovered, but faculty; what results is not an acquisition of knowledge, but an exercise of inward power. The most wonderful thing in the soul is the extraordinary latency of power in it; and it is in the artist-life, in the world of art, that this latent power is most variously and brilliantly released. What happens to you when you begin to see, really to see, pictures, for example? It is not that a new object has come within the range of your vision; but that a new power of seeing has arisen in your eyes, and through this power a new world has opened before you—a world of such marvels of space, color and beauty, luminosity, shadow and line, atmosphere and disposition, that you begin to live in it as a child begins to learn to live in the natural world. It is not the old world seen piece-meal; it is a new world on another level of being than natural existence. So, when you begin to take in a poem, it is not a mere fanciful arrangement of idea and event added to your ordinary memory of things; new powers of feeling have opened in your heart that constitute a fresh passion of life there, and as you feel it with lyric and drama, a significance, a mystery, a light enter into the universe as you know it, with transforming and exalting power. To the lover of pictures the visible world has become something other than it was—even nature herself flowers with Corots and Manets, coruscates with Turners and Claudes, darkens with Rembrandts; to the lover of poetry also the visible world has suffered change and lies in the light of Wordsworth or of Shelley, but much more the invisible world of inward life is transformed into visions of human fate in Aeschylus and Shakespeare, into throbs of passion in Dante and Petarch, into cries of esctasy and pain in how many generations of the poets worldwide. It is not that you have acquired knowledge; you have acquired heart. To lead the artist-life is not to look at pictures and read books; it is to discover the faculties of the soul, that slept unknown and unused, and to apply them in realizing the depth and tenderness, the eloquence, the hope and joy, of the life that is within. It is by this that the life of art differs from the life of science: its end is not to know, but to be. The revolt against the historical treatment of art arises from feeling that in such treatment art loses its own nature, and that what is truly life, and has its only value as life, is degraded into what is merely knowledge. I appreciate the worth and function of knowledge, and join with Tennyson in recognition of her rightful realm, but add with him—

> "Let her know her place;
> She is the second, not the first."

The first place is held by life. It is against the substitution of knowledge for life in scholarship, especially in the literary and artistic fields, that the protest is made.

A second main trait of the artist-life of the soul, for which I am, as it were, pleading, is that it is a life of growth by an inward secret and mysterious process. There is nothing mechanical in it; it is vital. It was this aspect of the soul's life which Wordsworth brought so prominently forward, and made elemental in his verse, advocating a "wise passiveness" in the conduct of the mind:

> "Think you, 'mid all this mighty sum
> Of things forever speaking,
> That nothing of itself will come,
> But we must still be seeking?"

"Consider the lilies, how they grow: they toil not, neither do they spin." That is the type of the artist-soul; in the artist-life there is neither toiling nor spinning. In an economical civilization like ours, leisure is apt to be confounded with indolence, and it is hard to see how the poet watching

> "the sun illume
> The yellow bees in the ivy bloom,"

is not an idler in the land. Especially is it hard to see how things will come without planning. In our own day planning has become an all-engrossing occupation. A belief in organization has spread through the country, and is applied in all quarters of life, as if success were always a matter of machinery, and preferably of legislative machinery. Even in the churches, which have been the home of spiritual force, organization plays an ever increasing part, as if failure in driving-force could be made up for by appliances in the machine; to a certain extent this is possible, but the driving force is not the machine. The practical reason so occupies all the field of our life that the result is to belittle and destroy whatever has not its ground of being in the useful. Art, by its own nature, excludes the useful.

Art, in its creative process, discards the instrumentality of means to an end, in the sense of planning and intention; its process is inspirational, as we say—a secret and mysterious growth. The artist, in generating his work—the poem, statue, picture—does not plan it; it comes to him. And when we, in our turn, look at what he has figured, or read what he has expressed, we do not plan what the result—the re-creation—will be in us; one of the most precious qualities of art is the divine surprise that attends its reception and realization in ourselves. There is a part of life where planning, the adjustment of means to an end, organization, and all that belongs in the practical sphere, has its place; but the growth of the soul proceeds on other principles and in another realm. This is Eucken's text. Our bodies and our mortal interests are subject to the world of use; but our spirituality, our immortal part, is above use. The artist-life of the soul—and the soul's life is characteristically artistic —lies in the self-revelation of its own nature, and this is a growth which takes place in a world of beauty, passion, adoration—in a word, of ideality, where what Wordsworth calls "our meddling intellect," the practical reason, has small part.

I well know how opposed this doctrine is to the ruling spirit of our time, which shrinks our lives to the limits of an economical and mechanical sphere, to use Eucken's phrases, and accustoms us to the dominance of their precepts and methods. Art with difficulty finds room among us. It is not by accident that our most literary temperament, Henry James, and our two great artists, Whistler and Sargent, have had their homes abroad, and that from the beginning the literature and art of America have often had their true locality on a foreign soil. Yet, whatever may be the seeming, it is always true that the soul grows, it is not made; and the world of art is chiefly precious to us because it is a place for the soul's growth.

A third main trait of the world of art is that it is a place of freedom. I have already alluded to this briefly. It is not merely that the soul is there freed from the manacles of utility and has escaped from the great burden of success in life; that is only the negative side. It has also, on the positive side, entered into a realm of new power, the exercise of which is its highest function. The soul transcends nature, and reconstitutes the world in the image of its own finer vision and deeper wisdom, realizing ideality in its own consciousness and conveying at least the shadow of its dream to mankind. It transcends nature in creating form. The Hermes of Praxiteles, whether or not one knows it is Hermes and discerns in it the godlike nature, gives to all ages a figure such as nature never shaped. The soul, also, in its artist-life, transcends nature in idea; each of us, in reading the play, may believe he is Hamlet, but each is well aware that he is identifying himself with a more perfect type of himself, such as is known only to the mind's eye. And, similarly, the soul transcends nature in the field of the relations of things; it builds up an Arcadia, an earthly Paradise, an ideal state, a forest of Arden, an island-kingdom of Prospero, a Round Table, a School of Athens, a Last Judgment, a legend of the Venusberg—what not?—so vast and various is the imaginary world wherein the soul from the beginning has bodied forth that inner vision and wisdom in which it finds its true self-consciousness. So great is its freedom there that, as is often said, it transcends also the moral world, and so far as morals belong in the sphere of mere utility and social arrangement, this must be granted; but the subject is too large and complicated to be entered upon here. I allude to it only to emphasize and bring out fully the doctrine that the soul exercises in its artist-life an unchartered freedom; for it is not concerned there with practical results of any kind, but only with the discovery of its nature, both active and passive. The fruit of this large freedom is the ideal world, in which each realizes his dream of the best. It is here that experiments are made, that revolutions sometimes begin; for the ideal, as I have said, once expressed, passes back into the ordinary world, and there it may be made a pattern, a thing to be actualized, and it falls under the dominance of the practical reason and has this or that fortune according to the wisdom or folly of mankind at the time. The ideal world is very mutable in different ages and races; and history is full of its débris. It is not an everlasting city set in the heavens that shall some time descend upon the earth in a millennium; it is a dream, the dream of the soul in its creative response to the world about it. Yet there is nothing insubstantial about the dream; however unrealized in the external world of fact, it is spiritually real, for it is lived in the soul—it is the conscious life of the soul. There are times, however, when the ideal world does enter into the actual world, and partly permeate it, if it does not wholly master it. The classic, the chivalric, the Christian world attest the fact, broadly; and in individual life how must we ourselves bear witness to the mingling in ourselves of the poets' blood—which is the blood of the world. In the intimacy of this communion is our best of life, and it is accomplished solely by the re-creation in us, in our minds and hearts, our hopes, admirations and loves, of what was first in the artists of every sort, according to our capacity to receive and reëmbody in our own spiritual substance their finer, wiser, deeper power. Their capacity to enter thus into the life of humanity is the measure of their genius, and our capacity to receive the gift is the measure of our souls.

Such in its main lines is the artist-life of the soul, a life of discovery, of growth, of freedom; but what is most precious in it, and most characterizes it, is a prophetic quality that abides in its experiences. The poets are often spoken of as prophets, and in history the greatest are those most lonely peaks that seem to have taken the light of an unrisen dawn, like Virgil, whose humanity in the "Aeneid" shines with a foregleam of the Christian temperament, or like Plato, whose philosophy in many a passage was a morning star that went before the greater light of Christian faith in the divine. But it is not such poets and such prophecy that I have in mind. I mean that in our own experiences in this artist-life with the poets, sculptors and musicians there abides the feeling that we shall have, as Tennyson says, "the wages of going on"—there is our clearest intimation of immortality. Wordsworth found such intimations in fragments of his boyhood and youth. I find them rather in fragments of manhood and maturer life. Life impresses me less as a birth initially out of the divine into mortal being than as birth into the divine at each step of the onward way. I am always fearful that in such statements, and in such a discourse as this has been, I may seem to be speaking of exceptional things, of life that is only for the select and methods that are practicable only for the few and for men especially endowed with rare temperaments. Nothing could be further from my own belief. The artist-life of the soul is common to all, as soon as the soul begins to be and breathe, for it is in the world of art that the soul lives. The child with his picture-book and the dying Laureate reading the Shakespearian "Dirge" in the moonlight lead the same life and follow the same method. The boy with Homer, the sage with Plato—it is all one: each is finding his soul, and living in it. The herb of grace grows everywhere. I have never such firm conviction of the divine meaning that abides in our life as when I notice how the soul puts forth its flower in the humblest lives and in the most neglected places, what deeds of the spirit are simply done by the poor and almost as if they did not know it. It is true that human life is an animal existence, and the sphere of the useful is primary in it; the necessity for earning one's food, building one's lodging, caring for one's offspring, governs our days and years; but if I am in favor of social betterment and a more just economic order in the state to

lessen the burden of common life and free it from an animal enslave-
ment, it is not that I am thinking so much of what is called the welfare of the masses, in the sense of comfort. It is because I desire for
them the leisure which would leave their souls room to grow. I
should be sorry to see material comfort, which is an animal good,
become the ideal of the state, as now seems the tendency. We are all
proud of America, and look on our farms and workshops, the
abundance of work, the harvest of universal gain dispersed through
multitudes reclaimed from centuries of poverty—we see and proclaim the greatness of the good; but I am ill-content with the spiritual
harvest, with the absence of that which has been the glory of great
nations in art and letters, with the indifference to that principle of
human brotherhood in devotion to which our fathers found greatness and which is most luminous in art and letters; our enormous
success in the economical and mechanical sphere leaves me unreconciled to our failure to enter the artistic sphere as a nation.

There is always, however, as you know, "a remnant." It is true
that the conditions of our time almost enforce upon our citizens,
especially as they grow old and become absorbed in the work of the
world, so abundant and compelling here—it is true that these conditions almost enforce a narrowly practical life. But there is one
period of life when this pressure is less felt, and when nature herself
seems to open the gateways for this artist-life that I have been speaking of: it is youth. I hope some random sentence, perhaps, may have
made it easier for some one of you who are young, to believe in that
world, to follow its beckoning lights and to lead its life.

# WILLIAM CRARY BROWNELL
## (1851–1928)

THOUGH stemming from New England stock, William Cary Brownell
was born in New York City and brought up in Buffalo. After graduating
from Amherst in 1871, he entered the field of journalism, working first as
a reporter and then as city editor on the *New York World*. He then joined
the staff of *The Nation*, edited by E. L. Godkin. A decisive turn in his
fortunes took place when he departed with his wife for a period of study
abroad, chiefly in France. As a result of these experiences he composed his
two books, *French Traits* (1889) and *French Art* (1892). In January,
1888, he became editor and adviser to Charles Scribner's Sons, a position
which he held to the time of his death.

*French Traits, An Essay in Comparative Criticism* seeks to discover the
qualities peculiar to French culture and to determine how far they can be
profitably transplanted to American soil. *French Art* further exemplifies
his developing critical method, its judicious balance and discriminating insight, its capacity for viewing a problem in the round, without impassioned
partisanship or shrill polemics. Though Brownell began his career with a
study of French culture and art, he had a genuinely interested eye cocked
all the time on the American scene. His critical writings usher in the
twentieth century. In some respects he was out of touch and certainly out
of sympathy with the developments of the new age, its philosophy of
change, its naturalistic temper, its industrialism and technology. By taste
and temperamental inclination he belonged with the Victorians, whom he
so greatly admired. *Victorian Prose Masters* (1901) and *American Prose
Masters* (1909) are the two books in which he applies his critical principles
to the works of the age in which he had been brought up. It is not surprising
that he finds many points of kinship with a figure like Matthew Arnold,
whom he strongly resembles in aim and outlook. Like Arnold he did not
confine himself to the aesthetics of literature but endeavored to formulate
the conditions essential to the good life. From Arnold, too, he derived his
high estimate of the function of intelligence in the critical process.

In *Criticism* (1914) and *Standards* (1917), he works out his critical philosophy and lays the basis for the practice of his "art." Brownell knew very well what he was about; he was concrete, suggestive, thoroughly informed, acute, and illuminating. With patient tact and unfailing sympathy he tried to discover and appraise in every work of art its quickening element of personality. The critic, according to Brownell, should know thoroughly not only his own literature but also the literatures of Europe, ancient and modern, the majestic sweep of history, the fine arts, the contributions of philosophy, but all these should be unified by a personal, coherent philosophy of life. For it is this philosophy which will lend unity and individuality, character and consistency to his judgments. Even in *Victorian Prose Masters* he had pointed out that though the sole artistic standard is fitness, the adaptation of means to end, the formal qualities of beauty "depend upon the artist's personality and are inseparable from it."[1] It is the critic's job to examine the degree to which the artist has succeeded in expressing the fullness of his vision in concrete, aesthetically effective terms. Restricted in scope is that type of criticism which limits itself to a consideration of the technical aspects of literature. The writer should not expect from the critic technical aid which belongs properly to the classroom. In short, Brownell maintains that criticism is a special province of literature, with a technique of its own. Since every literary work expresses a personality, what the critic must concern himself with is not so much the material expression as the mind behind it; not the technical properties of the writing but the moral values that emerge from it.

The way to achieve unity in criticism is to develop some general conception, steadily adhered to and elaborated, the details supplementing and supporting the general conception. Criticism must achieve a synthesis if it is to have the organic qualities to be found in the work of Matthew Arnold. But this general conception must not be carried to excess, for then it degenerates into special pleading or barren formulas and becomes excessively theoretical, and such theoretic criticism is fatally untrustworthy. The theory must grow out of and derive its authority from examples of permanent value; the critic must strive to solve the mystery of the human personality as embodied in literature. That is the crown and consummation of critical effort.

*Standards* underscores a number of salient deficiencies in American culture: its crudity, its craving for sensations, its emphasis on undisciplined individualism. *The Genius of Style* (1924) stresses further the need for discipline as a counterbalance to the anarchic forces in American culture. In this volume Brownell makes abundantly clear his love of the classic

---

[1] W. C. Brownell, *Victorian Prose Masters* (New York, 1928), p. 6.

characteristics of order and restraint, style being defined as that integral factor in a work of art which preserves in every part some sense of the form of the whole. Like Matthew Arnold he exalts nobility of expression, high disinterestedness, forgetfulness of self, devotion to the ideal. If the writer is to pursue the ideal of perfection, he must transmute instinct and impulse into character and control. Life is the inescapable material of art, but art must order and control the experiences of life which it seeks to utilize.

Though Brownell had much in common with Humanists like More and Babbitt, he was regarded by the faithful as being doctrinally "impure." The Humanists appreciated his insistence on high standards in literature, but they felt that he was never a Humanist in the strict sense of the term, because he responded too much to the humanitarian optimism characteristic of America. Harry Modean Clark maintains that it is an error to classify Brownell as a Humanist, since he was at variance with the Humanists in most of the critical standards he upheld.[2]

Though Brownell lacked intensity, the capacity for passionate, large-souled utterance and rousing affirmations, this lack was compensated by a scrupulous regard for intelligence undistorted by easy emotionalism. In his search for standards he trusted the head rather than the heart, feeling that values must be intellectually justified before they can be accepted and applied. The influence his work exerted was on the whole both salutary and liberating. Whatever revisions we may wish to introduce in his work, his emphasis on standards as a corrective for temperamental impressionism was all to the good. Unlike Bernard Smith who speaks disparagingly of Brownell, Stuart P. Sherman is generous yet discriminating in his estimate of Brownell's value as a critic. He doubts whether any other critic

"is more abundantly supplied with those general ideas in which the permanent value of critical writing largely resides: and I am not acquainted with any other who has quite so pertinently, intelligently, and intelligibly applied his general ideas to the real cultural problems of our time—I mean the definition of culture's own standards, the creation of a cultural ideal, the description of culture's business in a modern democracy."[3]

Effectively using the theories and literary influences active in Europe, Brownell carried on the tradition of humane letters where Arnold left off.

Even if we disagree with some of Brownell's critical judgments, we cannot help being impressed by his method of carefully analyzing a work in

[2] Harry Modean Campbell, "Was W. C. Brownell a New Humanist?," in *Studies in English*. Department of English, the University of Texas, 1945–1946. The University of Texas Press, Austin, 1946, pp. 172–176.

[3] Introduction to W. C. Brownell, *American Prose Masters* (New York, 1923), p. xix.

order to determine its strength and weakness, his habit of documenting each evaluation by copious references to the text under consideration. He eschews generalizations or theories that are not supported by relevant and illuminating details. Each judgment is based on reflection as well as painstaking analysis. The organic unity of structure that he demanded of literature he seeks to impose on his criticism, which is an art in its own right. An urbane critic, Brownell is bent on keeping the balance even, on judging a writer's work as a whole. If he is generous and fair-minded, he is never sentimentally indulgent, refusing to allow kindness or patriotic motives to influence his judgment. He will not compromise his high standards. He takes no pleasure in reprobation; it is simply a necessary, if unenviable, part of the critical function.

The critical temperament is reflective by nature. "Criticism is not the product of reading, but of thought. To produce vital and useful criticism, it is necessary to think, think, and think, and then, when tired of thinking, to think more."[4] Brownell's prime distinction as a critic is that he labored earnestly to erect a set of standards that would be free of the taint of impressionism and the futile pedantry of academic criticism. The only standard, as he saw it, that could maintain itself in a complex age and world such as ours is the standard founded on reason. Unfortunately the predominance of intelligence in his criticism constitutes a source of weakness as well as strength, for it inhibited his emotional response to art. He could not let himself go. Yet his positive virtues are indisputable: his discriminating sense of values, his disciplined insight, his intelligent analysis of works of art. He prepared his critical essays with the same concentrated intensity that the artist lavishes on his work, except that he relied on rational reflection before revealing his own feelings.

BIBLIOGRAPHY

TEXT

*French Traits*. New York, 1889.
*French Art*. New York, 1892.
*Victorian Prose Masters*. New York, 1901.
*American Prose Masters*. New York, 1909.
*Criticism*. New York, 1914.
*Standards*. New York, 1917.
*The Genius of Style*. New York, 1924.
*Democratic Distinctions in America*. New York, 1927.
*The Spirit of Society*. New York, 1927.

4 W. C. Brownell, *American Prose Masters* (New York, 1923), p. 255.

*William Crary Brownell: An Anthology of His Writings.* Edited by Gertrude Hall Brownell. New York and London, 1933.

CRITICISM

Bandler, Bernard, II, "The Humanism of W. C. Brownell," *Hound & Horn,* II, 205–222 (1929).
*W. C. Brownell: Tributes and Appreciations.* New York, 1929. (Privately printed.)
Ch'ên, Mei-chên (Chiang), *William Crary Brownell.* Philadelphia, 1946. (Bibliography, pp. 90–93.)
Foerster, Norman (ed.), *Humanism and America.* New York, 1930.
Harper, George McLean, *John Morley and Other Essays.* Princeton, 1920.
Mercier, Louis J. A., *Le mouvement humaniste aux États-Unis.* Paris, 1928.
——, "W. C. Brownell and Our Neo-Barbarians," *Forum,* LXXXI, 376–381 (June, 1929).
Sherman, Stuart P., *Points of View.* New York, 1924.
——, *Critical Woodcuts.* New York and London, 1926.
Sturgis, R. "William Crary Brownell as Critic on Fine Art," *International Monthly,* V, 448–467 (April, 1902).
Wharton, Edith, "William C. Brownell," *Scribner's,* LXXXIV, 596–602 (November, 1926).
——, *A Backward Glance.* New York and London, 1934.

## III

## CRITERION*

Its equipment established, criticism calls for a criterion. Sainte-Beuve says somewhere that our liking anything is not enough, that it is necessary to know further whether we are right in liking it— one of his many utterances that show how thoroughly and in what classic spirit he later rationalized his early romanticism.

The remark judges in advance the current critical impressionism. It involves more than the implication of Mr. Vedder's well-known retort to the time-honored philistine boast, 'I know nothing of art, but I know what I like': 'So do the beasts of the field.' Critical impressionism, intelligent and scholarly, such as that illustrated and advocated by M. Jules Lemaître and M. Anatole France, for ex-

* Reprinted from *Criticism* by W. C. Brownell; copyright 1914 by Charles Scribner's Sons, 1942 by Gertrude Hall Brownell; used by permission of the publishers.

ample, though it may, I think, be strictly defined as appetite, has certainly nothing gross about it, but, contrariwise, everything that is refined. Its position is, in fact, that soundness of criticism varies directly with the fastidiousness of the critic, and that consequently this fastidiousness cannot be too highly cultivated, since it is the court of final jurisdiction. It is, however, a court that resembles rather a star chamber in having the peculiarity of giving no reasons for its decisions. It has, therefore, at the outset an obvious disadvantage in the impossibility of validating its decisions for the acceptance of others. So far as this acceptance is concerned, it can only say, 'If you are as well endowed with taste, native and acquired, as I am, the chances are that you will feel in the same way.'

But it is of the tolerant essence of impressionism to acknowledge that there is no certainty about the matter. And, in truth, the material to be judged is too multifarious for the criterion of taste. Matthew Arnold's measure of a successful translation: that is, the degree in which it produces the same effect as the original to a sense competent to appreciate the original, is an instance of a sensible appeal to taste: first, because the question is comparatively simple; and secondly, because in the circumstances there can be no other arbiter. But such instances are rare, and the very fact that so much matter for criticism still remains matter of controversy proves the proverb that tastes differ and the corollary that there is no use in disputing about them. It is quite probable that M. France would find M. Lemaître's plays and stories insipid, and quite certain that M. Lemaître would shrink from the strain of salacity in M. France's romance. High differentiation and the acme of aristocratic fastidiousness, which both of these critics illustrate, manifestly do not serve to unify their taste. There *is* no universal taste. And criticism to be convincing must appeal to some accepted standard. And the aim of criticism is conviction. Otherwise actuated it must be pursued on the art-for-art theory, which, in its case at least, would involve a loss of identity. Recording the adventures of one's soul among masterpieces, which is M. France's variant of Eugène Véron's definition of landscape,— the first formal appearance of the idea, I think,—'painting one's emotions in the presence of nature,' must be a purely self-regardant exercise unless the reader has an answering soul and can himself authenticate the masterpieces.

Feeling the unsatisfactoriness of the impressionist's irresponsibility, the late Ferdinand Brunetière undertook a campaign in opposition to it. He began it, if I remember aright, in his lectures in

this country nearly twenty years ago. These lectures, however, and
the course of polemic which followed them excelled particularly, I
think, in attack. They contained some very effective destructive
criticism of mere personal preference, no matter whose, as a final
critical criterion. Constructively, on the other hand, Brunetière was
less conclusive. In a positive way he had nothing to offer but a defense of academic standards. He harked back to the classic canon—
that canon in accordance with which were produced those works
designed, as Stendhal says, 'to give the utmost possible pleasure to
our great-grandfathers.'

The case might perhaps have been better stated. Brunetière was
devoted to the noble French literature of the seventeenth century.
The august had no doubt a special attraction for the self-made
scholar. Out of reach the aristocratic always looks its best—the less
attainable the more admirable. But though he became a distinguished
scholar, Brunetière retained the temperament of the schoolmaster,
which was either native to him or the result of belated acquaintance,
however thorough, with what French impatience calls the *déja-vu*.
It was because he had so explicitly learned that he wished always to
teach.

Now there is nothing strictly to teach save the consecrated and
the canonical, whereas criticism is a live art, and contemporaneous-
ness is of its essence. Once codified, it releases the genuine critic to
conceive new combinations,—the 'new duties' taught by 'new occasions,'—and becomes itself either elementary or obsolete. It is
important to know which, of course, as Wordsworth's failure successfully to recast the catalogue of the poetic *genres,* noted by
Arnold, piquantly attests. Moreover in his devotion to the seventeenth, Brunetière was blind to the eighteenth century,—as well
as, by the way, heedless of Voltaire's warning that the only bad style
is the *style ennuyeux;* his style alone devitalized his polemic in favor
of prescription. Finally, instead of winning adherents for him, this
ardent advocacy of authority took despotic possession of his entire
mind and gathered him to the bosom of religious and political reaction.

Whatever our view of criticism, it is impossible at the present day
to conceive it as formula, and the rigidity of rules of taste is less
acceptable than the license permitted under the reign of taste un-
regulated, however irregular, individual, and irresponsible. In spite
of the logical weakness of the impressionist theory, it is to be observed that a high level of taste, uniform enough to constitute a very

serviceable arbiter, at least in circumstances at all elementary, is practically attainable; and as a matter of fact is, in France at least, often attained. For in criticism as elsewhere it is true that we rest finally upon instinct, and faith underlies reason. The impressionist may properly remind us that all proof, even Euclidian, proceeds upon postulates.

The postulates of criticism, however, are apt unsatisfactorily to differ from those of mathematics in being propositions taken for granted rather than self-evident. The distinction is radical. It is not the fact that everybody is agreed about them that gives axioms their validity, but their self-evidence. Postulates that depend on the sanction of universal agreement, on the other hand, are conventions. Universal agreement may be brought about in a dozen ways. It may be imposed by authority, as in the case of classic criticism, or it may develop insensibly, illogically, and indefensibly; it may derive, not from truth but from tradition, or it may certainly be the result of general reaction, and promptly crystallize with a rigidity equivalent to that from which it is just emancipated. Examples would be superfluous. The conventions of romanticism, realism, impressionism, symbolism, or what-not, are no more intrinsically valid than those underlying the criticism of academic prescription, as is attested by this variability of the universal agreement which is their sanction.

The true postulates of criticism have hardly varied since Aristotle's day, and impressionism itself, in imagining its own an advance upon them, would be in peril of fatuity. Yet even sound intuitions, fundamental as they may be, do not take us very far. Pascal, who though one of the greatest of reasoners is always girding at reason, was obliged to admit that it does the overwhelming bulk of the work. 'Would to God,' he exclaims, 'that we had never any need of it, and knew everything by instinct and sentiment! But nature has refused us this blessing; she has, on the contrary, given us but very little knowledge of this kind, and all other knowledge can only be acquired by reasoning.' But even if intuitions had all the importance claimed for them, it would still be true that *conventions* are extremely likely to be disintegrated by the mere lapse of time into what every one sees to have been really inductions from practice become temporarily and more or less fortuitously general, and not genuine intuitive postulates at all. Still clearer is the conventionality of the systems erected upon them, beneath which as a matter of fact they customarily lie buried. All sorts of eccentricity are incident to elaboration, of course, whether its basis be sound or unsound.

So that, in brief, when the impressionist alleges that a correct judgment of a work of literature or art depends ultimately upon feeling, we are quite justified in requiring him to tell us *why* he feels as he does about it. It is not enough for him to say that he is a person of particularly sensitive and sound organization, and that his feeling, therefore, has a corresponding finality. In the first place, as I have said, it is impossible to find in the judgments derived from pure taste anything like the uniformity to be found in the equipment as regards taste of the judges themselves. But for all their fastidiousness these judges are as amenable as grosser spirits to the test of reason. And it is only rational that the first question asked of them when they appeal to the arbitrament of feeling should be: Is your feeling the result of direct intuitive perception, or of unconscious subscription to convention? Your true distinction from the beasts of the field surely should lie, not so much in your superior organization resulting in superior taste, as in freedom from the conventional, to which even in their appetites the beasts of the field, often extremely fastidious in this respect, are nevertheless notoriously enslaved. In a word, even if impressionism be philosophically sound in the impeachment of reason unsupported by intuitive taste, it cannot dethrone reason as an arbiter in favor of the taste that is not intuitive but conventional. The true criterion of criticism therefore is only to be found in the rationalizing of taste.

This position once reached, it is clear that the only way in which the impressionist, however cultivated, can be at all sure of the validity of the *feeling* on which he bases his judgment is by the exercise of his reasoning faculty. Only in this way can he hope to determine whether his 'impression' originates in a genuine personal perception of the relations of the object producing it to some self-evident principle of truth or beauty, or proceeds from habit, from suggestion, from the insensible pressure of current, which is even more potent than classic, convention. Absolutely certain of achieving this result, the critic can hardly expect to be. Nothing is more insidious than the conventional. Civilized life is continually paying it tribute in innumerable ways. Culture itself, so far as it is uncritical, is perhaps peculiarly susceptible to it. But the critic can discharge his critical duty only by approximating this certainty as nearly as possible, by processes of scrutiny, comparison, and reflection, and in general that arduous but necessary and not unrewarding exercise of the mind involved in the checking of sensation by thought.

There is nothing truistic at the present time in celebrating the thinking power, counselling its cultivation and advocating its application—at least within the confines of criticism where the sensorium has decidedly supplanted it in consideration. Nor, on the other hand, is there anything recondite in so doing. It is as plain as it used to be remembered that it is in 'reason' that a man is 'noble,' in 'faculty' that he is 'infinite,' in 'apprehension' that he is 'like a god.' The importance of his exquisite sensitiveness to impressions is a *post*-Shakespearean discovery. I certainly do not mean to belittle the value of this sensitiveness, in suggesting for criticism the advantages of its control by the thinking power, and in noting the practical disappearance of the latter from the catalogue of contemporary prescription. If my topic were not criticism, but performance in the field of American imaginative activity, to belittle taste would at the present time be unpardonable. The need of it is too apparent. The lack of it often cheapens our frequent expertness, ruptures the relation between truth and beauty, and is responsible for a monotonous miscellaneity that is relieved less often than we could wish by works of enduring interest.

It cannot, however, be maintained that the standard of pure taste is a wholly adequate corrective for this condition even in the field of performance. At least it has been tried, and the results have not been completely satisfactory. We have in literature more taste than we had in days when, perhaps, we had more talent. (I exclude the domain of scholarship and its dependencies, in which we have made, I should suppose, a notable advance.) But the very presence of taste has demonstrated its insufficiency. In general literature, indeed, if its presence has been marked, its effect is not very traceable, because it has been mainly exhibited in technic. It can't be said, I think, to have greatly affected the substance of our literary production. In two of the arts, however, taste has long had full swing with us—the arts, I mean, of architecture and sculpture; and the appreciation it has met with in these is, though general, not rarely of the kind that confuses the merits of the decorative with those of the monumental, and the virtues of adaptation with those of design. A rational instead of a purely susceptible spirit, dictating constructive rather than merely appreciative and assimilative activity, might have been more richly rewarded in these fields—might even have resulted in superior taste.

In the restricted field of criticism, at all events, the irresponsibility of pure temperament seems currently so popular as to imply a general belief that reasoning in criticism died with Macaulay and is as defunct as Johnson, having given place to a personal disposition which perhaps discounts its prejudices but certainly caresses its predilections as warrant of 'insight' and 'sympathy.' Yet our few star examples in current criticism are eminently critics who give reasons for the hope that is in them; and certainly American literature has one critic who so definitely illustrated the value of the thinking power in criticism that he may be said almost to personify the principle of critical ratiocination. I mean Poe. Poe's perversities, his cavilling temper, his unscrupulousness in praise if not in blame, his personal irresponsibility, invalidate a great deal of his criticism, to say nothing of its dogmatic and mechanical character. But at its best it is the expression of his altogether exceptional reasoning faculty. His reasons were not the result of reflection, and his ideas were often the crotchets Stedman called them; but he was eminently prolific in both, and his handling of them was expertness itself. His ratiocination here has the artistic interest it had in those of his tales that are based on it, and that are imaginative as mathematics is imaginative. And his dogmas were no more conventions than his conclusions were impressions. His criticism was equally removed from the canonical and the latitudinarian. If he stated a proposition he essayed to demonstrate it, and if he expressed a preference he told *why* he had it.

Poe's practice is, indeed, rather baldly ratiocinative than simply rational, and its felicity in his case does not, it is true, disguise its somewhat stark, exclusive, and exaggerated effect. I do not cite M. Dupin as an example of the perfect critic. There is something debased—not to put too fine a point upon it—in the detective method wherever used. It is not merely subtle, but serpentine—too tortuous and too terrene for the ampler upper air of examination, analysis, and constructive comment. Reason is justified of her children, not of her caricaturists. But if the answer to the question Why? which I have noted as her essential monopoly (since prescription precludes and impressionism scouts the inquiry), be challenged as an advantage to criticism, I think its value can be demonstrated in some detail.

The epicurean test of the impressionist, let me repeat, is of course not a standard, since what gives pleasure to some gives none to others. And some standard is a necessary postulate, not only of all criticism, but of all discussion or even discourse. Without one, art must indeed be 'received in silence,' as recommended by the persistently communicative Whistler. In literature and art there are, it is true, no longer any statutes, but the common law of principles is as applicable as ever, and it behooves criticism to interpret the cases that come before it in the light of these. Its function is judicial, and its business to weigh and reason rather than merely to testify and record. And if it belongs in the field of reason rather than in that of emotion, it must consider less the pleasure that a work of art produces than the worth of the work itself. This is a commonplace in ethics, where conduct is not approved by its happy result but by its spiritual worthiness. And if art and literature were felt to be as important as ethics, the same distinction would doubtless have become as universal in literary and art criticism. Which is of course only another way of stating Sainte-Beuve's contention that we need to know whether we are right or not when we are pleased. And the only guide to that knowledge—beyond the culture which, however immensely it may aid us, does not automatically produce conformity or secure conviction—is the criterion of reason applied to the work of ascertaining value apart from mere attractiveness. The attractiveness takes care of itself, as happiness does when we have done our duty.

At all events, aside from its superior philosophic satisfactoriness, thus indicated, a rational—rather than either an academic and authoritative or an impressionist and individual—criticism is especially useful, I think, at the present time, in two important particulars. It is, in the first place, especially fitted to deal with the current phase of art and letters. Of this phase, I take it, freedom and eclecticism are the main traits. Even followers of tradition exercise the freest of choices, tradition itself having become too multifarious to be followed *en bloc*. On the other hand, those who flout tradition and pursue the experimental, illustrate naturally still greater diversity. Both must ultimately appeal to the criterion of reason, for neither can otherwise justify its practice and pretensions. Prescription is a practical ideal if it is coherent; it loses its constituting sanction the moment it offers a choice. And experiment attains success only when through proof it reaches demonstration. In either case a criterion is ultimately addressed which is untrammeled by precedent and unmoved by change; which is strict without rigidity, and seeks the law of any performance within and not outside it; which demands no correspondence to any other concrete, but only to the appropriate abstract; which, in fact, substitutes for a concrete ideal a purely abstract one of intrinsic applicability to the matter in hand.

It exacts titles, but they may be couched in any form, or expressed in any tongue but that of irrationality. No more the slave of schools than the sponsor of whim, it does not legislate, but judges performance, in its twofold aspect of conception and execution, in accordance with principles universally uncontested.

In the next place, no other criterion is competent to deal critically with the great question of our day in art and letters alike, namely, the relation of reality to the ideal. No other, I think, can hope to preserve disentangled the skein of polemic and fanaticism in which this question tends constantly to wind itself up into apparently inextricable confusion. Taste, surely, cannot. Taste, quite comprehensibly, I think, breathes a sigh of weariness whenever the subject of 'realism' is mentioned. Nevertheless, 'realism' is established, entrenched, and I should say impregnable to the assaults of its more radical and numerous foes, more particularly those of the art-for-art's-sake army. It is too fundamentally consonant with the current phase of the Time-Spirit to be in any present danger. But it is only reason that can reconcile its claims with those of its censors by showing wherein, and to what extent, 'realism' is really a catholic treatment of reality, and not a protestant and polemic gospel of the literal.

Reality has become recognized as the one vital element of significant art, and it seems unlikely that the unreal will ever regain the empire it once possessed. Its loss, at all events, is not ours, since it leaves us the universe. But it is obvious that 'realism' is often in practice, and not infrequently in conception, a very imperfect treatment of reality, which indeed not rarely receives more sympathetic attention in the romantic or even the classic household. Balzac is a realist, and at times the most artificial of great romancers. George Sand is a romanticist, and a very deep and fundamental reality not rarely underlies her superficial extravagances. Fundamentally, truth —which is certainly none other than reality—was her inspiration, as, fundamentally, it certainly was not always Balzac's. 'Realism' has made reality our touchstone. But it is not a talisman acting automatically if misapplied. To mistake the badge for the credentials of a doctrine is so frequent an error because it is irrational, and close-thinking, being difficult, is exceptional. Exponents of 'realism,' such as that most admirable of artists, Maupassant, are extraordinarily apt in practice to restrict the field of reality till the false proportion results in a quintessentially unreal effect. Every detail is real, but the implication of the whole is fantastic. Why? Because the ideal is excluded. The antithesis of reality is not the ideal, but the fantastic.

This is, I think, the most important distinction to bear in mind in considering the current realistic practice in all the arts. I refer of course to what we characterize as the ideal in general—not to the particular ideal whose interpenetration with the object constitutes the object a work of art and measures it as such. But for that matter the ideal in general may be conceived as having a similar relation to reality. Since it is a part of the order of the universe,—of reality, that is to say,—it is obviously not antithetic to it. On the other hand, the fantastic is essentially chaotic by definition though often speciously, attractively, and at times poetically garbed in the raiment of order—the poetry of Coleridge or the compositions of Blake, for example. The defect of this kind of art *is* its lack of reality, and its consequent comparative insignificance. But it is no more ideal for that reason than *Lear* or the Venus of Melos. This is still more apparent in the less artistic example of Hawthorne's tales, where in general the fantasticality consists in the garb rather than the idea, and where accordingly we can more readily perceive the unreality and consequent insignificance, the incongruous being more obvious in the material than in the moral field. But it is the special business of criticism at the present time of 'realistic' tyranny to avoid confusing the ideal with the fantastic, to avoid disparagement of it as opposed to reality, and to disengage it from elements that obscure without invalidating it.

*Ivanhoe,* for example, is fantastic history, but the character of the Templar is a splendid instance of the ideal inspiring, informing, intensifying, incontestable reality. In *Le Père Goriot,* on the other hand, in which the environment and atmosphere are realistic to the last degree, the protagonist is the mere personification of a passion. These are, no doubt, subtleties. But they are not verbal subtleties. They are inseparable from the business of criticism. And they impose on it the criterion of reason rather than that of feeling, which cannot be a standard, or that of precedent and prescription, which is outworn.

Finally,—and if I have hitherto elaborated to excess, here I need not elaborate at all,—no other than a rational criterion so well serves criticism in the most important of all its functions, that of establishing and determining the relation of art and letters to the life that is their substance and their subject as well.

## METHOD

AND a rational criterion implies a constructive method. In itself
analysis reaches no conclusion, which is the end and aim of reason.
Invaluable as is its service in detail, some rational ideal must under-
lie its processes, and if these are to be fruitful they must determine
the relations of the matter in hand to this ideal, and even in dissection contribute to the synthesis that constitutes the essence of
every work of any individuality. The weak joint in Sainte-Beuve's
armor is his occasional tendency to rest in his analysis. It is the finer
art to suggest the conclusion rather than to draw it, no doubt, but
one should at least do that; and I think Sainte-Beuve, in spite of
his search for the *faculté maîtresse* and his anticipation of the race,
the *milieu,* and the moment theory so hard worked by Taine, occasionally fails to justify his analysis in this way; so that his result
is both artistically and philosophically inconclusive. Now and then
he pays in this way for his aversion to pedantry and system, and the
excessive disinterestedness of his curiosity.

It would certainly be pedantry to insist on truly constructive
criticism in every *causerie du lundi* in which a great critic may quite
pardonably vary his more important work with the play for which
he has a *penchant.* But on the other hand truly constructive criticism
does not of necessity involve rigidity. It implies not a system, but
a method—to employ the distinction with which Taine defended his
procedure, but which assuredly he more or less conspicuously failed
to observe. It prescribes, in every work of criticism, a certain independence of its subject, and imposes on it the same constructive
obligations that it in turn requires of its theme. A work of criticism
is in fact as much a thesis as its theme, and the same thematic treatment is to be exacted of it. And considered in this way as a thesis, its
unity is to be secured only by the development in detail of some
central conception preliminarily established and constantly referred
to, however arrived at, whether by intuition or analysis. The detail
thus treated becomes truly contributive and constructive in a way
open to no other method. We may say indeed that all criticism of
moment, even impressionist criticism, has this synthetic aspect at
least, as otherwise it must lack even the appearance of that organic
quality necessary to effectiveness. And when we read some very

interesting and distinguished criticism—such as the agglutinate and amorphous essays of Lowell, for example—and compare it with concentric and constructive work,—such as *par excellence* that of Arnold,—we can readily see that its failure in force is one of method as well as of faculty.

On the other hand, the constructive method is peculiarly liable to excess. If the central conception it is concerned with is followed out in detail without the checks and rectifications of analysis—the great verifying process—we have the partisanship of Carlyle, the inelasticity of Taine, the prescriptive formulary of Brunetière. The spirit of system stifles freedom of perception and distorts detail. Criticism becomes theoretic. And though theoretic criticism may be, and in fact is not unlikely to be, artistically effective, it is fatally untrustworthy, because it is bent on illustrating its theory in its analysis, instead of merely verifying such features of its central conception as analysis will confirm. Against such intuitive extravagance as Carlyle's the advantages of remarkable insight may fairly be set off. The academic prescriptions of Brunetière, too, have a distinct educational value—the results of a high-class literary scholiast are always technically instructive, however lacking they may be in the freedom and impressionability sanctioned by a criterion less rigid for being purely rational, and committed to no body of doctrine, traditional or other.

It is, however, the historical method of criticism that chiefly illustrates constructive excess. This method has at present probably the centre of the stage; and though there is in France a distinct reaction from the supremacy of Taine and in favor of Sainte-Beuve's sinuous plasticity, the method itself maintains its authority. Taine was an historian and a philosopher rather than a critic, and his criticism is accordingly not so much criticism illuminated by history and philosophy as philosophic history. The data of literature and art under his hand become the 'documents' of history, of which in a scientific age we hear so much. His thesis once established, however, as historical rather than literary or aesthetic, too much I think can hardly be said for his treatment. Classification has the advantage of clearing up confusion, and the value of a work like the *History of English Literature* appears when one recognizes its paramount merit as resident in the larger scope and general view of history in which of necessity purely individual traits are to some extent blurred if not distorted. These indeed may very well be left to pure criticism whose precise business they are. But the historic method in pure criticism is held quite independently of Taine's authority. Scherer, for example, arguing against 'personal sensations' in criticism, maintains that from the study of a writer's character and of his period the right understanding of his work issues spontaneously. This is excellent prescription for the impressionist, although Scherer doubtless means by 'personal sensations,' personal *judgment* also, and thus minimizes or indeed obliterates perhaps the most essential element of all in criticism, the critic's own personality. Scherer's practice, precisely owing to his personality, far excelled his theory, as to which Arnold reminded him of Macaulay, who certainly knew his writers and their period, but in whose mind a right understanding of their works occasionally failed spontaneously to issue.

In fine, the historic method, great as have been its services to criticism and truly constructive as it is, has two erroneous tendencies. It tends generally to impose its historical theory on the literary and aesthetic facts, to discern their historical rather than their essential character; and, as inelastically applied, at all events, it tends specifically to accept its 'documents' as final rather than as the very *subjects* of its concern. Taine furnishes a striking instance of the latter practice. I have never myself been able to agree with those of his opponents, who, like Brunetière, rested in the comfortable assurance that his whole theory was overthrown by the fact that the ordinary Venetian gondolier of the period was the product of the influences that also produced Tintoretto. One might as well hold that immunity in some cases is not the result of the vaccine that fails to take in others; the causes of such differences in either physiology or history being perhaps, so far as they are not obvious, too obscure for profitable discussion compared with the causes of resemblances. But from the critical point of view it *is* a legitimate objection to his rigorous application of his method that he is led by it to consider so disproportionately *causes*, which are the proper subject of history, rather than *characteristics*, which are the true subject of criticism; to deem the business finished, so to say, when it is explained, and, comparatively speaking, to eschew its estimation.

As to the other tendency, that of imposing historical theory on critical data, it is a commonplace that history itself, which has been luminously called philosophy teaching by examples, sometimes suffers from the submergence of its examples by its philosophy. In criticism the result is more serious because, viewed in the same light, its 'examples' have a far more salient importance. They are themselves differentiated philosophically in a high degree, and it is correspondingly difficult successfully to treat them merely as pieces of some vaster mosaic. On large lines and in an elementary way, this may of course be usefully done, but the work belongs in general I think rather to the class-room than to the forum of criticism. In the latter place their traits call for a treatment at once more individually searching and more conformed to an abstract, ideal, independent, and rational standard—for the application to the data they furnish of the *ideas* they suggest, not the theory they fit.

Now, in the true critical field of independent judgment, however enlightened by culture and fortified by philosophic training, we know very well that theory means preconception. And, carried into any detail of prescription, preconception is as a matter of fact constantly being confuted by performance. Divorced from the ideas proper to each performance, reposing on a formula derived in its turn from previous performance become accepted and consecrate, it is continually disconcerted. New schools with new formulae arise as if by some inherent law, precisely at the apogee of old ones. And preconception, based as it perforce is upon some former crystallization of the diverse and undulating elements of artistic expression, is logically inapplicable at any given time—*except* as it draws its authority from examples of permanent value and enduring appeal, in which case no one would think of calling it preconception at all. It may be said, to be sure, that philosophically this view, in excluding theory, degrades criticism to an altogether ancillary station— the business of merely furnishing data for an historical synthesis. But I am disinclined to accept this implication until the possibility of an historical synthesis at all comparable in exactness with the critical determination of the data for it is realized or shown to be realizable. The monument that Sainte-Beuve's critical essays constitute is, in spite of their disproportionate analysis, far otherwise considerable than the fascinating historical and evolutionary framework within which Taine's brilliant synthesis so hypnotizes our critical faculty.

In general effect, moreover, Sainte-Beuve's work is itself markedly synthetic. What a complete picture it presents, at the same time continually illustrating the truth that the wiser business of criticism is to occupy itself with examples and the ideas they evoke, not with theories and the systems they threaten! For with examples we have the essential elements of unity 'given'; it is actual, not problematical. And—impersonal theses of course aside—in criticism of the larger kind as distinct from mere reviewing or expert commentary, by examples we mean, practically, personalities. That is to say, not *Manfred,* but Byron, not the Choral Symphony, but Beethoven. I mean, naturally, so far as personality is expressed in work, and do not suggest invasion of the field of biography except to tact commensurable with that which so notably served Sainte-Beuve. There is here ample scope for the freest exercise of the synthetic method. For personality is the most concrete and consistent entity imaginable, mysteriously unifying the most varied and complicated attributes. The solution of this mystery is the end of critical research. To state it is the crown of critical achievement. The critic may well disembarrass himself of theoretical apparatus, augment and mobilize his stock of ideas, sharpen his faculties of penetration, and set in order all his constructive capacity, before attacking such a complex as any personality, worthy of attention at all, presents at the very outset. If he takes to pieces and puts together again the elements of its composition, and in the process or in the result conveys a correct judgment as well as portrait of the original thus interpreted, he has accomplished the essentially critical part of a task demanding the exercise of all his powers.

And I think he will achieve the most useful result in following the line I have endeavored to trace in the work of the true masters of this branch of literature, the born critics whose practice shows it to be a distinctive branch of literature, having a function, an equipment, a criterion, and a method of its own. This practice involves, let me recapitulate, the initial establishment of some central conception of the subject, gained from specific study illuminated by a general culture, followed by an analysis of detail confirming or modifying this, and concluding with a synthetic presentation of a physiognomy whose features are as distinct as the whole they compose—the whole process interpenetrated by an estimate of value based on the standard of reason, judging the subject freely after the laws of the latter's own projection, and not by its responsiveness to either individual whim or formulated prescription. This, at all events, is the ideal illustrated, with more or less closeness, by not only such critics as Sainte-Beuve, Scherer, and Arnold, but such straightforward apostles of pure good sense as Sarcey and Émile Faguet.

*How* the critic conducts his criticism will of course depend upon his own personality, and the ranks of criticism contain perhaps as great a variety of types and individuals as is to be found in any other field of artistic expression. For, beyond denial, criticism is itself an art; and, as many of its most successful products have been entitled 'portraits,' sustains a closer analogy at its best with plastic portraiture than with such pursuits as history and philosophy, which seek system through science. One of Sainte-Beuve's studies is as definitely a portrait as one of Holbein's; and on the other hand a portrait by Sargent, for example, is only more obviously and not more really, a critical product than are the famous 'portraits' that have interpreted to us the generations of the great. More exclusively imaginative art the critic must, it is true, forego. He would wisely, as I have contended, confine himself to portraiture and eschew the panorama. In essaying a 'School of Athens' he is apt, rather, to produce a 'Victory of Constantine.' His direct aim is truth even in dealing with beauty, forgetting which his criticism is menaced with transmutation into the kind of poetry that one 'drops into' rather than attains.

I have dwelt on the aesthetic as well as the literary field in the province of criticism, and insisted on the aesthetic element as well as the historic in the culture that criticism calls for, because in a very true and fundamental sense art and letters are one. They are so at all events in so far as the function of criticism is concerned, and dictate to this the same practice. Current philosophy may find a pragmatic sanction for a pluralistic universe, but in the criticism of art, whether plastic or literary, we are all 'monists.' The end of our effort is a true estimate of the data encountered in the search for that beauty which from Plato to Keats has been virtually identified with truth, and the highest service of criticism is to secure that the true and the beautiful, and not the ugly and the false, may in wider and wider circles of appreciation be esteemed to be the good.

# THOMAS STEARNS ELIOT

## (1888–1965)

Born in St. Louis in 1888, Eliot attended Harvard University where he heard such men as Santayana and Babbitt lecture. After graduating from Harvard and receiving two degrees, the A.B. and the A.M., he went to Oxford and the Sorbonne for further study. From 1914 up to the present time he has been living in England. His *Poems* came out in 1920, and *The Waste Land* (published in 1922) won *The Dial* award as the most worthy contribution to American literature for that year. In 1927 he became a British subject.

As a critic he sought to establish standards not touched by Victorianism or the Romantic movement. The seventeenth-century poets and writers had something substantial and permanently valuable to offer the moderns, and with their example before him he endeavored to reconstruct the critical taste of his period. The "Metaphysical" school of poets were reinstated in favor as models of excellence, elegance, and compressed ironic wit. As a result of Eliot's labors, modern criticism took a new turn, becoming structural in its analysis, concerned with aesthetic criteria in general and with the close examination and explication of the text in particular.

As a literary critic, Eliot in his early work allows no extra-literary preoccupations to distract his mind and distort his judgment. His reviews, which are really carefully prepared critiques, never pass beyond the work itself, which remains the focal point of interest. His studies of the Elizabethan dramatists, for example, are judiciously done, stimulatingly written, arousing in the reader a desire to renew his acquaintance with these writers. His critical observations gleam with multiple implications and light up far stretches of territory. In an essay on John Ford, he will suddenly declare that Shakespeare cannot be judged adequately by one or two plays, not even by his best and mature work. All of Shakespeare must be known before any single part can be known.[1]

T. S. Eliot's philosophy of criticism is admirably summed up in "Tradi-

[1] T. S. Eliot, *Selected Essays: 1917–1932* (New York, 1932), p. 179.

tion and the Individual Talent." Eliot does not believe in the autotelic function of criticism. Whatever may be true of art, criticism "must always profess an end in view, which, roughly speaking, appears to be the elucidation of art and the correction of taste."[2] Just as the writing of poetry involves a continual extinction of personality, so criticism should not indulge in a display of egotism on the part of its practitioners. The critic should rely not on personal but communal authority, the stay of tradition. Not that criticism does not play an important part in creative work. The creative mind is during the period of composition critically alert and active. In fact, the greater the writer the more acute and discriminating is his critical faculty. Hence Eliot has no use for the psychoanalytic aesthetic that would reduce the artist to a registering machine of the unconscious.

If the critic is not to go astray, he must develop a sustaining sense of fact. By doing so he is saved from the pitfall of impressionism, from subjectivity and what is loosely called "appreciation." Many "interpretations" of works of art have no foundation, since there is no way of confirming them objectively, of determining how much is valid and how much has been gratuitously dragged in. Interpretation can best be relied upon when it is not interpretation at all "but merely putting the reader in possession of facts which he would otherwise have missed."[3] Eliot is certain of one thing: namely, that facts cannot corrupt taste.

What Eliot enjoys doing, and what indeed he does best, is textual criticism, comparative criticism. He loves to compare lines of verse, to trace the evolution of prosody, to judge comparative degrees of merit. Few things, he declares, are more important to a nation than the invention of a new form of verse, for by it the language is enriched and the sensibility transformed. Rejecting Lamb's distinction between drama and literature, he argues that there is no truth in the assumption that poetry and drama are two distinct things. In protest against the tendency to treat Shakespeare as primarily a philosopher, Eliot dénies that the poet is concerned with the communication of thoughts; the poet who "thinks" is expressing but the emotional equivalent of thought, and that requires intense intellectual effort. Shakespeare did not project a coherent, affirmative philosophy of life, since he was not expressing philosophical views; he was occupied with the more difficult task of transforming human actions into the stuff of poetry. Poetry is no substitute for philosophy or religion.

Eliot tries to dispose of the vexed problem of belief in poetry by doubting whether belief proper enters into the activity of a great poet.

2 "The Function of Criticism," *Ibid.*, p. 13.
3 *Ibid.*, p. 20.

"That is, Dante, qua poet, did not believe or disbelieve the Thomistic cosmology or theory of the soul; he merely made use of it, or a fusion took place between his initial emotional impulse and a theory, for the purpose of making poetry. The poet makes poetry, the metaphysician makes metaphysics, the bee makes honey, the spider secretes a filament; you can hardly say that any of these agents believes: he merely does."[4]

As for the problem of expressing emotion in the form of art, the artist must find what Eliot calls an "objective correlative": the group of objects or events which have the power of evoking a particular emotion.[5]

Eliot's conversion to Anglo-Catholicism was marked by a slow but radical modification of his whole theory and practice of literary criticism. From then on he was no longer concerned to keep morality and theology out of poetry, provided that they were the right kind of morality and theology. Once Eliot became converted to Anglo-Catholicism, he could no more keep his religious beliefs out of his criticism than he could keep them out of his poetry. Christianity, he argues against Matthew Arnold and Irving Babbitt, cannot be preserved without its central belief in the supernatural. The religious emphasis comes out strongly in his attck on the limitations of Humanism as expounded by Irving Babbitt and Norman Foerster. The Humanist, by suppressing the divine, is left with a human element which may quickly degenerate to the animal level. Humanism, to be efficacious and maximally useful, should rely on the religious view. In "Second Thoughts About Humanism," Eliot compactly sums up his position:

"There is no avoiding that dilemma: you must be either a naturalist or a supernaturalist. If you remove from the word "human" all that the belief in the supernatural has given to man, you can view him finally as no more than an extremely clever, adaptable, and mischievous little animal."[6]

By this time we are almost completely removed from the realm of literary criticism, as Eliot practised it with distinction in the past. Though he possesses an exceptionally trained sensibility, wide erudition, and a power of concise, epigrammatic statement, he has grown increasingly conservative and conformist not only in politics and religion but also in literature. In *The Use of Poetry and the Use of Criticism* (1933), Eliot holds that criticism, far from being a symptom of decadence or impotence, is an organic part of the literary life of a people. At this time he still perceives the danger that lurks in any attempt to relate poetry very closely to a religious or social or political system of values. Poetry should not be defined in terms of something else.

[4] T. S. Eliot, *Selected Essays: 1917–1932* (New York, 1932), p. 118.
[5] *Ibid.*, pp. 124–125.
[6] *Ibid.*, p. 397.

Despite these cautions, Eliot in "Religion and Literature" frankly declares that literature and religion should not be separated. The ethical and religious ideal should complete the act of literary criticism. Paradoxically enough, he asserts that it is literature read for pleasure, rather than literature read for moral edification, which has the most profound effect upon us. Catholic thought, Eliot is nevertheless convinced, can save us from the extreme of humanitarianism, whereas no system of social or political reform can possibly help us.

Religion can vitalize and fructify literature. Without morals that grow out of tradition and orthodoxy, the accent on personality becomes alarmingly great, and this stress on the eccentric and the singular gives rise to the self-defeating cult of "self-expression." To counteract this heresy, the reality and pervasiveness of Evil must be reaffirmed. In *After Strange Gods* (1934), Eliot concludes that in an unsettled age such as ours tradition must be corrected and strengthened by the restraint of Christian orthodoxy. This is carried even further in *The Idea of a Christian Society* (1940), which contains little that has any bearing on the problems of literary criticism. The religious orientation, the Anglo-Catholic emphasis, obtrudes persistently and disturbingly into his literary criticism—witness his latest opus, *Notes Towards the Definition of Culture* (1949)—to a point where it ceases to be criticism and becomes dogmatic theology.[7]

[7] For a fairly extensive bibliography of books, reviews, and articles dealing with T. S. Eliot, consult *T. S. Eliot: A Selected Critique,* edited by Leonard Unger, New York, 1948.

### BIBLIOGRAPHY

#### TEXT

*Ezra Pound: His Metric and Poetry*. New York, 1917.
*The Sacred Wood*. New York, 1921.
*Homage to John Dryden*. London, 1924.
*For Lancelot Andrewes*. London, 1928.
*Dante*. London, 1929. (Poets on Poets, No. 2.)
*Selected Essays: 1917–1932*. New York, 1932.
*John Dryden: The Poet, The Dramatist, The Critic*. New York, 1932.
*The Use of Poetry and the Use of Criticism*. London, 1933.
*After Strange Gods*. New York, 1934.
*Essays Ancient and Modern*. New York, 1936.
*The Idea of a Christian Society*. New York, 1940.
*The Classics and the Man of Letters*. London, 1942.
*The Music of Poetry*. Glasgow, 1942.
*Notes Towards the Definition of Culture*. New York, 1949.
"From Poe to Valéry," *The Hudson Review*, II, 327–342 (Autumn, 1949).
*Poetry and Drama*. Cambridge (Mass.), 1951.

CRITICISM

Brombert, Victor H., *The Criticism of T. S. Eliot*. New Haven, 1949.
Costello, Mary Cleophas, *Between Fixity and Flux*. Washington. D. C., 1947.
Daniells, J. H., "T. S. Eliot and His Relations to T. E. Hulme," *The University of Toronto Quarterly*, II, 380–396 (1933).
Gallup, Donald, *A Bibliographical Check-list of the Writings of T. S. Eliot*. New Haven, 1947.
Glicksberg, Charles I., "T. S. Eliot as Critic," *Arizona Quarterly*, IV, 225–236 (Autumn, 1948).
Hyman, Stanley Edgar, "T. S. Eliot and Tradition in Criticism," in *The Armed Vision*. New York, 1948, pp. 73–105.
Matthiessen, F. O., *The Achievement of T. S. Eliot*. New York, 1947.
McGreevy, Thomas, *Thomas Stearns Eliot*. London, 1931.
Nicholl, A., "Eliot and the Revival of Classicism," *English Journal*, XXIII, 269–278 (1934).
Rajan, B. (ed.), *T. S. Eliot: A Study of His Writings by Several Hands*. London, 1947.
Ransom, John Crowe, *The New Criticism*. Norfolk, 1941.
Savage, D. S., *The Personal Principle*. London, 1944.
Schwartz, Delmore, "T. S. Eliot as International Hero," *Partisan Review*, XII, 199–206 (Summer, 1945).
Stephenson, E. M., *T. S. Eliot and the Lay Reader*. London, 1944.
Taupin, Rene, "The Classicism of T. S. Eliot," *Symposium*, II, 64–82 (January, 1932).
Vivas, Eliseo, "The Objective Correlative of T. S. Eliot," *American Bookman*, I, 7–18 (Winter, 1944).
Tindall, William Y., "The Recantation of T. S. Eliot," *American Scholar*, XVI, 431–437 (1947).
Unger, Leonard (ed.), *T. S. Eliot: A Selected Critique*. New York, 1948.
Weiss, Ted, "Eliot and the Courtyard Revolution," *Sewanee Review*, LIV, 289–307 (Spring, 1946).
Winters, Yvor, "T. S. Eliot," in *The Anatomy of Nonsense*. Norfolk, 1943, pp. 120–167.

TRADITION AND THE INDIVIDUAL TALENT*

In English writing we seldom speak of tradition, though we occasionally apply its name in deploring its absence. We cannot refer

* Reprinted from *Selected Essays: 1917–1932* by T. S. Eliot, copyright, 1932, by Harcourt, Brace and Company, Inc.

to "the tradition" or to "a tradition"; at most, we employ the adjective in saying that the poetry of So-and-so is "traditional" or even "too traditional." Seldom, perhaps, does the word appear except in a phrase of censure. If otherwise, it is vaguely approbative, with the implication, as to the work approved, of some pleasing archaeological reconstruction. You can hardly make the word agreeable to English ears without this comfortable reference to the reassuring science of archaeology.

Certainly the word is not likely to appear in our appreciations of living or dead writers. Every nation, every race, has not only its own creative, but its own critical turn of mind; and is even more oblivious of the shortcomings and limitations of its critical habits than of those of its creative genius. We know, or think we know, from the enormous mass of critical writing that has appeared in the French language the critical method or habit of the French; we only conclude (we are such unconscious people) that the French are "more critical" than we, and sometimes even plume ourselves a little with the fact, as if the French were the less spontaneous. Perhaps they are; but we might remind ourselves that criticism is as inevitable as breathing, and that we should be none the worse for articulating what passes in our minds when we read a book and feel an emotion about it, for criticizing our own minds in their work of criticism. One of the facts that might come to light in this process is our tendency to insist, when we praise a poet, upon those aspects of his work in which he least resembles any one else. In these aspects or parts of his work we pretend to find what is individual, what is the peculiar essence of the man. We dwell with satisfaction upon the poet's difference from his predecessors, especially his immediate predecessors; we endeavour to find something that can be isolated in order to be enjoyed. Whereas if we approach a poet without this prejudice we shall often find that not only the best, but the most individual parts of his work may be those in which the dead poets, his ancestors, assert their immortality most vigorously. And I do not mean the impressionable period of adolescence, but the period of full maturity.

Yet if the only form of tradition, of handing down, consisted in following the ways of the immediate generation before us in a blind or timid adherence to its successes, "tradition" should positively be discouraged. We have seen many such simple currents soon lost in the sand; and novelty is better than repetition. Tradition is a matter of much wider significance. It cannot be inherited, and if you want it you must obtain it by great labour. It involves, in the first place, the historical sense, which we may call nearly indispensable to any one who would continue to be a poet beyond his twenty-fifth year; and the historical sense involves a perception, not only of the past-ness of the past, but of its presence; the historical sense compels a man to write not merely with his own generation in his bones, but with a feeling that the whole of the literature of Europe from Homer and within it the whole of the literature of his own country has a simultaneous existence and composes a simultaneous order. This historical sense, which is a sense of the timeless as well as of the temporal and of the timeless and of the temporal together, is what makes a writer traditional. And it is at the same time what makes a writer most acutely conscious of his place in time, of his own con-temporaneity.

No poet, no artist of any art, has his complete meaning alone. His significance, his appreciation is the appreciation of his relation to the dead poets and artists. You cannot value him alone; you must set him, for contrast and comparison, among the dead. I mean this as a principle of aesthetic, not merely historical, criticism. The necessity that he shall conform, that he shall cohere, is not onesided; what happens when a new work of art is created is something that happens simultaneously to all the works of art which preceded it. The existing monuments form an ideal order among themselves, which is modified by the introduction of the new (the really new) work of art among them. The existing order is complete before the new work arrives; for order to persist after the supervention of novelty, the *whole* existing order must be, if ever so slightly, altered; and so the relations, proportions, values of each work of art toward the whole are readjusted; and this is conformity between the old and the new. Whoever has approved this idea of order, of the form of European, of English literature will not find it preposterous that the past should be altered by the present as much as the present is directed by the past. And the poet who is aware of this will be aware of great difficulties and responsibilities.

In a peculiar sense he will be aware also that he must inevitably be judged by the standards of the past. I say judged, not amputated, by them; not judged to be as good as, or worse or better than, the dead; and certainly not judged by the canons of dead critics. It is a judgment, a comparison, in which two things are measured by each other. To conform merely would be for the new work not really to conform at all; it would not be new and would therefore not be a work of art. And we do not quite say that the new is more valuable because it fits in; but its fitting in is a test of its value—a test, it is true, which can only be slowly and cautiously applied, for we are none of us infallible judges of conformity. We say: it appears to conform, and is perhaps individual, or it appears individual, and many conform; but we are hardly likely to find that it is one and not the other.

To proceed to a more intelligible exposition of the relation of the poet to the past: he can neither take the past as a lump, an indiscriminate bolus, nor can he form himself wholly on one or two private admirations, nor can he form himself wholly upon one preferred period. The first course is inadmissible, the second is an important experience of youth, and the third is a pleasant and highly desirable supplement. The poet must be very conscious of the main current, which does not at all flow invariably through the most distinguished reputations. He must be quite aware of the obvious fact that art never improves, but that the material of art is never quite the same. He must be aware that the mind of Europe—the mind of his own country—a mind which he learns in time to be much more important than his own private mind—is a mind which changes, and that this change is a development which abandons nothing *en route*, which does not superannuate either Shakespeare, or Homer, or the rock drawing of the Magdalenian draughtsmen. That this development, refinement perhaps, complication certainly, is not, from the point of view of the artist, any improvement. Perhaps not even an improvement from the point of view of the psychologist or not to the extent which we imagine; perhaps only in the end based upon a complication in economics and machinery. But the difference between the present and the past is that the conscious present is an awareness of the past in a way and to an extent which the past's awareness of itself cannot show.

Some one said: "The dead writers are remote from us because we *know* so much more than they did." Precisely, and they are that which we know.

I am alive to a usual objection to what is clearly part of my programme for the *métier* of poetry. The objection is that the doctrine requires a ridiculous amount of erudition (pedantry), a claim which can be rejected by appeal to the lives of poets in any pantheon. It will even be affirmed that much learning deadens or perverts poetic sensibility. While, however, we persist in believing that a poet ought to know as much as will not encroach upon his necessary receptivity and necessary laziness, it is not desirable to confine knowledge to whatever can be put into a useful shape for examinations, drawing-rooms, or the still more pretentious modes of publicity. Some can absorb knowledge, the more tardy must sweat for it. Shakespeare acquired more essential history from Plutarch than most men could from the whole British Museum. What is to be insisted upon is that the poet must develop or procure the consciousness of the past and that he should continue to develop this consciousness throughout his career.

What happens is a continual surrender of himself as he is at the moment to something which is more valuable. The progress of an artist is a continual self-sacrifice, a continual extinction of personality.

There remains to define this process of depersonalization and its relation to the sense of tradition. It is in this depersonalization that art may be said to approach the condition of science. I, therefore, invite you to consider, as a suggestive analogy, the action which takes place when a bit of finely filiated platinum is introduced into a chamber containing oxygen and sulphur dioxide.

## II

Honest criticism and sensitive appreciation are directed not upon the poet but upon the poetry. If we attend to the confused cries of the newspaper critics and the *susurrus* of popular repetition that follows, we shall hear the names of poets in great numbers; if we seek not Blue-book knowledge but the enjoyment of poetry, and ask for a poem, we shall seldom find it. I have tried to point out the importance of the relation of the poem to other poems by other authors, and suggested the conception of poetry as a living whole of all the poetry that has ever been written. The other aspect of this Impersonal theory of poetry is the relation of the poem to its author. And I hinted, by an analogy, that the mind of the mature poet differs from that of the immature one not precisely in any valuation of "personality," not being necessarily more interesting, or having "more to say," but rather by being a more finely perfected medium in which special, or very varied, feelings are at liberty to enter into new combinations.

The analogy was that of the catalyst. When the two gases previously mentioned are mixed in the presence of a filament of platinum, they form sulphurous acid. This combination takes place only if the platinum is present; nevertheless the newly formed acid contains no trace of platinum, and the platinum itself is apparently unaffected; has remained inert, neutral, and unchanged. The mind of the poet is the shred of platinum. It may partly or exclusively operate upon the experience of the man himself; but, the more perfect the artist, the more completely separate in him will be the man who suffers and the mind which creates; the more perfectly will the mind digest and transmute the passions which are its material.

The experience, you will notice, the elements which enter the presence of the transforming catalyst, are of two kinds: emotions and feelings. The effect of a work of art upon the person who enjoys it is an experience different in kind from any experience not of art. It may be formed out of one emotion, or may be a combination of several; and various feelings, inhering for the writer in particular words or phrases or images, may be added to compose the final result. Or great poetry may be made without the direct use of any emotion whatever: composed out of feelings solely. Canto XV of the *Inferno* (Brunetto Latini) is a working up of the emotion evident in the situation; but the effect, though single as that of any work of art, is obtained by considerable complexity of detail. The last quatrain gives an image, a feeling attaching to an image, which "came," which did not develop simply out of what precedes, but which was probably in suspension in the poet's mind until the proper combination arrived for it to add itself to. The poet's mind is in fact a receptacle for seizing and storing up numberless feelings, phrases, images, which remain there until all the particles which can unite to form a new compound are present together.

If you compare several representative passages of the greatest poetry you see how great is the variety of types of combination, and also how completely any semi-ethical criterion of "sublimity" misses the mark. For it is not the "greatness," the intensity, of the emotions, the components, but the intensity of the artistic process, the pressure, so to speak, under which the fusion takes place, that counts. The episode of Paolo and Francesca employs a definite emotion, but the intensity of the poetry is something quite different from whatever intensity in the supposed experience it may give the impression of. It is no more intense, furthermore, than Canto XXVI, the voyage of Ulysses, which has not the direct dependence upon an emotion. Great variety is possible in the process of transmutation of emotion: the murder of Agamemnon, or the agony of Othello, gives an artistic effect apparently closer to a possible original than the scenes from Dante. In the *Agamemnon,* the artistic emotion approximates to the emotion of an actual spectator; in *Othello* to the emotion of the protagonist himself. But the difference between art and the event is always absolute; the combination which is the murder of Agamemnon is probably as complex as that which is the voyage of Ulysses. In either case there has been a fusion of elements. The ode of Keats contains a number of feelings which have nothing particular to do with the nightingale, but which the nightingale, partly, perhaps, because of its attractive name, and partly because of its reputation, served to bring together.

The point of view which I am struggling to attack is perhaps related to the metaphysical theory of the substantial unity of the soul: for my meaning is, that the poet has, not a "personality" to express, but a particular medium, which is only a medium and not a personality, in which impressions and experiences combine in peculiar and unexpected ways. Impressions and experiences which are important for the man may take no place in the poetry, and those which become important in the poetry may play quite a negligible part in the man, the personality.

I will quote a passage which is unfamiliar enough to be regarded with fresh attention in the light—or darkness—of these observations:

> And now methinks I could e'en chide myself
> For doating on her beauty, though her death
> Shall be revenged after no common action.
> Does the silkworm expend her yellow labours
> For thee? For thee does she undo herself?
> Are lordships sold to maintain ladyships
> For the poor benefit of a bewildering minute?
> Why does yon fellow falsify highways,
> And put his life between the judge's lips,
> To refine such a thing—keeps horse and men
> To beat their valours for her? . . .

In this passage (as is evident if it is taken in its context) there is a combination of positive and negative emotions: an intensely strong attraction toward beauty and an equally intense fascination by the ugliness which is contrasted with it and which destroys it. This balance of contrasted emotion is in the dramatic situation to which the speech is pertinent, but that situation alone is inadequate to it. This is, so to speak, the structural emotion, provided by the drama. But the whole effect, the dominant tone, is due to the fact that a number of floating feelings, having an affinity to this emotion by no means superficially evident, have combined with it to give us a new art emotion.

It is not in his personal emotions, the emotions provoked by particular events in his life, that the poet is in any way remarkable or interesting. His particular emotions may be simple, or crude, or flat. The emotion in his poetry will be a very complex thing, but not with the complexity of the emotions of people who have very complex or unusual emotions in life. One error, in fact, of eccentricity in poetry is to seek for new human emotions to express; and in this search for novelty in the wrong place it discovers the perverse. The business of the poet is not to find new emotions, but to use the ordinary ones and, in working them up into poetry, to express feelings which are not in actual emotions at all. And emotions which he has never experienced will serve his turn as well as those familiar to him. Consequently, we must believe that "emotion recollected in tranquillity" is an inexact formula. For it is neither emotion, nor recollection, nor, without distortion of meaning, tranquillity. It is a concentration, and a new thing resulting from the concentration, of a very great number of experiences which to the practical and active person would not seem to be experiences at all; it is a concentration which does not happen consciously or of deliberation. These experiences are not "recollected," and they finally unite in an atmosphere which is "tranquil" only in that it is a passive attending upon the event. Of course this is not quite the whole story. There is a great deal, in the writing of poetry, which must be conscious and deliberate. In fact, the bad poet is usually unconscious where he ought to be conscious, and conscious where he ought to be unconscious. Both errors tend to make him "personal." Poetry is not a turning loose of emotion, but an escape from emotion; it is not the expression of personality, but an escape from personality. But, of course, only those who have personality and emotions know what it means to want to escape from these things.

### III

ὁ δὲ νοῦς ἴσως Θειότερόν τι καὶ ἀπαθές ἐστιν.

This essay proposes to halt at the frontier of metaphysics or mysticism, and confine itself to such practical conclusions as can be applied by the responsible person interested in poetry. To divert interest from the poet to the poetry is a laudable aim: for it would conduce to a juster estimation of actual poetry, good and bad. There are many people who appreciate the expression of sincere emotion in verse, and there is a smaller number of people who can appreciate technical excellence. But very few know when there is an expression of *significant* emotion, emotion which has its life in the poem and not in the history of the poet. The emotion of art is impersonal. And the poet cannot reach this impersonality without surrendering himself wholly to the work to be done. And he is not likely to know what is to be done unless he lives in what is not merely the present, but the present moment of the past, unless he is conscious, not of what is dead, but of what is already living.

# VAN WYCK BROOKS
## (1886–1963)

BORN in Plainfield, New Jersey, on February 16, 1886, Van Wyck Brooks was educated at Harvard University, from which he graduated in 1917. He taught for a period of two years at Leland Stanford University, did some editorial work for the *Standard Dictionary, World's Work,* and Doubleday, Page and Company, and then settled down to his life's work as a critic. His first book, *The Wine of the Puritans,* came out in 1908, followed by *The Malady of the Ideal* in 1913. In 1917 and 1918 he was associate editor of *The Seven Arts Magazine.* From 1920 to 1924 he was connected with *The Freeman.* In 1927, in collaboration with Paul Rosenfeld, Alfred Kreymborg, and Lewis Mumford, he edited the first issue of *American Caravan. The Dial* in 1923 awarded him the prize of two thousand dollars for distinguished service to literature. Though he has devoted himself chiefly to the study of the literature of his own country, he possesses a cosmopolitan range of interests and a wide but discriminating literary background.

The views expressed in *America's Coming-of-Age* (1915) and *Letters and Leadership* (1918) had much to do with the awakening of literary activity in America. They preached a new note of courage and confidence in the creative life at a time when native energies were misdirected toward materialistic exploitation and financial buccaneering. Brooks called for the conservation and free expression of our finest spiritual resources, urgently demanding that our native genius be given the opportunity to make its distinctive contribution to world culture. That is the categorical imperative sounded in his early work: our writers must strive to live creatively and to live completely, and do so in the name of some great corporate ideal. That is the faith, that is the vision, we require, and to discover that faith, to formulate that vision at its best, is the special task of American criticism.

Few American writers have taken up the art of criticism with more single-minded devotion. What is more to the point, he has been, from the start, singularly content to be an *American* critic, American in fibre, American in outlook, American in tradition. It is altogether fitting that in his autumnal years he should seek to keep this native tradition alive. That was the fundamental motive which drove him to undertake historical writing, namely, the hope that in this way he would stiffen the moral backbone of American writers, promote their maturity, and give them secure possession of a usable past, a sense of their group history, a common heritage, the knowledge that they were part of a rich and responsible tradition. A number of writers were inspired by his method and his message.

"Much of Randolph Bourne's ironic rejection of the pragmatists, many of the apocalyptical plunges of *Our America,* much of the appreciation of American art done by other critics, are movements made through the open door opened by Brooks when he organized for American literature the ancient and honorable manner of criticism popularly associated with the name of Taine. . . ."[1]

All this helps to explain why Brooks' later writing is more affirmative and hopeful in tone, so unlike in its attitude of acceptance to the predominantly negative temper reflected in *America's Coming-of-Age* and *Letters and Leadership.* But these books endeavored to fill a definite need at the time: the lack of a searching and responsible literary criticism. American literature if it is to come of age must resolutely face those forces in the national life which keep it submerged and provincial—its materialism, its acquisitive spirit, its unregenerate individualism.

Van Wyck Brooks' change of heart is evident as early as 1934. In his preface to *Three Essays on America* (1934), he deplores his former bearding of the native prophets, his tendency to reject the New England poets of the nineteenth century and to discover only arrested growth and sterility in the life and literature of his land. *Opinions of Oliver Allston* (1941) reveals Brooks in a subdued, mellow mood. He now finds much in America to praise and admire. He no longer believes in the value of the psychoanalytic method as applied to the writing of biography, thus rendering dubious the validity of his books on Henry James and Mark Twain. Though he has not abandoned his socialist ideals, his sympathies are ethical and humanitarian rather than narrowly economic and doctrinaire. As an idealist he cannot accept the strict determinism that lies at the base of dialectical materialism. His most striking traits as a critic are his goodness, his kindliness, his tolerance, his disinclnation to debunk and denounce and find fault. In an age of frantic money-making and meretricious

[1] Paul Rosenfeld, *Port of New York* (New York, 1924), pp. 46–47,

cults of all kinds, he has never compromised his integrity. James T. Farrell may attack him as one of "the league of frightened Philistines," but whatever weaknesses he may possess he cannot be accused of joining forces with the Philistines.

To appreciate the nature and extent of the change that has come over Brooks, all one has to do is to turn to *The Opinions of Oliver Allston* and compare its judgments and evaluations, item by item, with those he voiced in 1915 and 1918. Gone is the condemnation of the evil of Puritanism. In addition, he has made his peace with his native land, and in book after book, exploring the golden age of American letters, he seeks to establish the tradition of which he had written so persuasively in his younger years. But the personality that shines through his maturer work, while less challenging and prophetic, is the same sensitive, conscientious, integrated personality that he revealed in his early work. There is the same earnest groping for truth, the same love of the best that has been thought and said, the same habit of interlarding his prose with felicitous quotations from his extensive reading. As for the charge that his transcendental idealism prevents him from coming to grips with his subject or that he has deserted the arena of contemporary criticism to become the historian of a romantically idealized past, he does not deny that he is an idealist or that he has turned of late to historical subjects. He simply insists that all this is the result of the evolution of his mind, and therefore inescapable. His scholarship and historical writing provide him with heavier ammunition for the battle he is still waging.

Brooks believes in the autonomy of literature as opposed to the views held by the materialistic determinists. Idealism, he contends, is the dominant tendency in all literature, particularly so in American literature. Certain elements in man are constant, and it is this constancy which can furnish the base for standards in criticism. If these standards exist, then the objectivity of literary truth stands vindicated. Convinced of the central importance of tradition, he now finds fault with the writers of his time because they are so nihilistic in outlook. Their view of the nature of man is not one that he can accept. What he finds objectionable in writers like Faulkner and Dos Passos is their conviction that life is inescapably ugly and sordid and vile. Whatever good they did by calling attention to present evils was more than neutralized by their bleak, uncompromising pessimism. Van Wyck Brooks refuses to look upon life as contemptible, without nobility of purpose, without a future. Therefore he turns for solace and strength to writers who are positive and soul-sustaining, men who have faith in the freedom of the human will and in the destiny of mankind. If literature is to live, this is the germ of faith that it must contain, and this was the germ present in all truly great literature. An internationalist, Brooks maintains that the international spirit, the international mind, can best be achieved by sinking one's roots into his native soil. That is why, in *The Flowering of New England* (1936), *New England: Indian Summer* (1940), and *The Times of Melville and Whitman* (1948), he is devoting himself to the task of exploring and revaluating the heritage of his country, its usable past. That is the affirmation he wishes to make as a way of counterbalancing the negativism of his age.

### BIBLIOGRAPHY

#### TEXT

*Wine of the Puritans*. London, 1908.
*The Malady of the Ideal*. New York, 1913.
*John Addington Symonds*. New York, 1914.
*The World of H. G. Wells*. New York, 1915.
*America's Coming-of-Age*. New York, 1915.
*Letters and Leadership*. New York, 1918.
*The Ordeal of Mark Twain*. New York, 1920.
*The Pilgrimage of Henry James*. New York, 1925.
*Emerson and Others*. New York, 1927.
*The Life of Emerson*. New York, 1932.
*Sketches in Criticism*. New York, 1932.
*Three Essays on America*. New York, 1934.
*The Flowering of New England*. New York, 1936.
*New England: Indian Summer*. New York, 1940.
*On Literature Today*. New York, 1941.
*The Opinions of Oliver Allston*. New York, 1941.
*The World of Washington Irving*. New York, 1944.
*The Times of Melville and Whitman*. New York, 1947.
*A Chilmark Miscellany*. New York, 1948.

#### CRITICISM

De Voto, Bernard, *The Literary Fallacy*. Boston, 1944.
Dupee, F. W., "The Americanism of Van Wyck Brooks," *Partisan Reader*. New York, 1946, pp. 363–377.
Farrell, James T., *The League of Frightened Philistines*. New York, 1945.
Foerster, Norman, *Towards Standards*. New York, 1930.
Glicksberg, Charles I., "Van Wyck Brooks," *Sewanee Review*, XLIII, 175–186 (April–June, 1935).
Hyman, Stanley Edgar, "Van Wyck Brooks and Biographical Criticism," *The Armed Vision*. New York, 1948, pp. 106–126.
Kenton, Edna, "Henry James and Van Wyck Brooks," *Bookman*, LXII, 152–157 (October, 1925).

Kohler, Dayton, "Van Wyck Brooks," *College English*, II, 629–639 (April, 1941).
Maynard, Theodore, "Van Wyck Brooks," *Catholic World*, CXL, 412–421 (January, 1935).
Rosenfeld, Paul, *Port of New York*, New York, 1924.
Smith, Bernard, *Forces in American Criticism*. New York, 1939.
Van Doren, Carl, *The Roving Critic*. New York, 1923.
Wellek, René, "Van Wyck Brooks and a National Literature," *American Prefaces*, VII, 292–306 (Summer, 1942).

## THE LITERARY LIFE IN AMERICA*

AMONG all the figures which, in Mrs. Wharton's "The Age of Innocence," make up the pallid little social foreground, the still more pallid middle distance, of the New York of forty years ago, there is none more pallid than the figure of Ned Winsett, the "man of letters untimely born in a world that had no need of letters." Winsett, we are told, "had published one volume of brief and exquisite literary appreciations," of which one hundred and twenty copies had been sold, and had then abandoned his calling and taken an obscure post on a women's weekly. "On the subject of *Hearthfires* (as the paper was called) he was inexhaustibly entertaining," says Mrs. Wharton; "but beneath his fun lurked the sterile bitterness of the still young man who has tried and given up." Sterile bitterness, a bright futility, a beginning without a future: that is the story of Ned Winsett.

One feels, as one turns Mrs. Wharton's pages, how symbolic this is of the literary life in America. I shall say nothing of the other arts, though the vital conditions of all the arts have surely much in common; I shall say nothing of America before the Civil War, for the America that New England dominated was a different nation from ours. But what immediately strikes one, as one surveys the history of our literature during the last half century, is the singular impotence of its creative spirit. That we have and have always had an abundance of talent is, I think, no less evident: what I mean is that so little of this talent succeeds in effectuating itself. Of how many of our modern writers can it be said that their work reveals a con-

* Taken from *Emerson and Others* by Van Wyck Brooks, published and copyright 1927 by E. P. Dutton & Co., Inc., New York.

tinuous growth, or indeed any growth, that they hold their ground tenaciously and preserve their sap from one decade to another? Where, to speak relatively, the characteristic evolution of the European writer is one of an ever-increasing differentiation, a progress towards the creation, the possession of a world absolutely his own (the world of Shaw, the world of Hardy, the world of Hamsun, of Gorky, of Anatole France), the American writer, having struck out with his new note, becomes—how often!—progressively less and less himself. The blighted career, the arrested career, the diverted career are, with us, the rule. The chronic state of our literature is that of a youthful promise which is never redeemed.

The great writer, the *grand écrivain,* has at the best of times appeared but once or twice in America: that is another matter. I am speaking, as I say, of the last half century, and I am speaking of the rank and file. There are those who will deny this characterization of our literature, pointing to what they consider the robust and wholesome corpus of our "normal" fiction. But this fiction, in its way, corroborates my point. What is the quality of the spirit behind it? How much does it contain of that creative element the character of which consists in dominating life instead of being dominated by it? Have these novelists of ours any world of their own as distinguished from the world they observe and reflect, the world they share with their neighbors? Is it a personal vision that informs them, or a mob-vision? The Danish writer, Johannes V. Jensen, has described their work as "journalism under exceptionally fortunate conditions." Journalism, on the whole, it assuredly is, and the chief of these fortunate conditions (fortunate for journalism!) has been the general failure of the writers in question to establish and develop themselves as individuals: as they have rendered unto Caesar what was intended for God, is it any wonder that Caesar has waxed so fat? "The unfortunate thing," writes Mr. Montrose J. Moses, "is that the American drama"—but the observation is equally true of this fiction of ours—"has had many brilliant promises which have finally thinned out and never materialized." And again: "The American dramatist has always taken his logic second-hand; he has always allowed his theatrical sense to be a slave to managerial circumstance." The two statements are complementary, and they apply, as I say, to the whole of this "normal" literature. Managerial circumstance? Let us call it local patriotism, the spirit of the times, the hunger of the public for this, that or the other: to some one of these demands, these promptings from without, the "normal" American writer always allows himself to become a slave. It is the fact, indeed, of his being a slave to some demand from without that makes him "normal"—and something else than an artist.

The flourishing exterior of the main body of our contemporary literature, in short, represents anything but the integrity of an inner well-being. But even aside from this, one can count on one's two hands the American writers who are able to carry on the development and unfolding of their individualities, year in, year out, as every competent man of affairs carries on his business. What fate overtakes the rest? Shall I begin to run over some of those names, familiar to us all, names that have signified so much promise and are lost in what Gautier calls "the limbo where moan (in the company of babes) still-born vocations, abortive attempts, larvae of ideas that have won neither wings nor shapes"? Shall I mention the writers —but they are countless!—who have lapsed into silence or involved themselves in barren eccentricities, or who have been turned into machines? The poets who, at the outset of their careers, find themselves extinguished like so many candles? The novelists who have been unable to grow up, and remain withered boys of seventeen? The critics who find themselves overtaken in mid-career by a hardening of the spiritual arteries? Our writers all but universally lack the power of growth, the endurance that enables one to continue to produce personal work after the freshness of youth has gone.

Such is the aspect of our contemporary literature; beside that of almost any European country, it is indeed one long list of spiritual casualties. For it is not that the talent is wanting, but that somehow this talent fails to fulfill itself.

This being so, how much one would like to assume, with certain of our critics, that the American writer is a sort of Samson bound with the brass fetters of the Philistines and requiring only to have those fetters cast off in order to be able to conquer the world! That, as I understand it, is the position of Mr. Dreiser, who recently remarked of certain of our novelists: "They succeeded in writing but one book before the iron hand of convention took hold of them." There is this to be said for the argument, that if the American writer as a type shows less resistance than the European writer it is plainly because he has been insufficiently equipped, stimulated, nourished by the society into which he has been born. In this sense the American environment is answerable for the literature it has produced. But what is significant is that the American writer *does* show less resistance; and as literature is nothing but the expression of power, of the creative will, of "free will," in short, is it not more accurate to say, not that the "iron hand of convention" takes hold of our writers, but that our writers yield to the "iron hand of convention"? Samson had lost his virility before the Philistines bound him; it was because he had lost his virility that the Philistines were able to bind him. The American writer who "goes wrong" is in a similar case. "I have read," says Mr. Dreiser, of Jack London, "several short stories which proved what he could do. But he did not feel that he cared for want and public indifference. Hence his many excellent romances." *He did not feel that he cared for want and public indifference.* Even Mr. Dreiser, as we observe, determinist that he is, admits a margin of free will, for he represents Jack London as having made a choice. What concerns us now, however, is not a theoretical but a practical question, the fact, namely, that the American writer as a rule is actuated not by faith but by fear, that he cannot meet the obstacles of "want and public indifference" as the European writer meets them, that he is, indeed, and as if by nature, a journeyman and a hireling.

As we see, then, the creative will in this country is a weak and sickly plant. Of the innumerable talents that are always emerging about us there are few that come to any sort of fruition. The rest wither early; they are transformed into those neuroses that flourish on our soil as orchids flourish in the green jungle. The sense of this failure is written all over our literature. Do we not know what depths of disappointment underlay the cynicism of Mark Twain and Henry Adams and Ambrose Bierce? Have we failed to recognize, in the surly contempt with which the author of "The Story of a Country Town" habitually speaks of writers and writing, the unconscious cry of sour grapes of a man whose creative life was arrested in youth? Are we unaware of the bitterness with which, in certain letters of his later years, Jack London regretted the miscarriage of his gift? There is no denying that for half a century the American writer as a type has gone down to defeat.

Now why is this so? Why does the American writer, relatively speaking, show less resistance than the European writer? Plainly, as I have just said, because he has been insufficiently equipped, stimulated, nourished by the society into which he has been born. If our creative spirits are unable to grow and mature, it is a sign that there is something wanting in the soil from which they spring and the conditions that surround them. Is it not, for that matter, a sign of some more general failure in our life?

"At the present moment," wrote Mr. Chesterton in one of his early essays ("The Fallacy of the Young Nation"), struck by the strange anaemia of so many American artists, "at the present moment the matter which America has very seriously to consider is not how near it is to its birth and beginning, but how near it may be to its end. . . . The English colonies have produced no great artists, and that fact may prove that they are still full of silent possibilities and reserve force. But America has produced great artists and that fact most certainly means that she is full of a fine futility and the end of all things. Whatever the American men of genius are, they are not young gods making a young world. Is the art of Whistler a brave, barbaric art, happy and headlong? Does Mr. Henry James infect us with the spirit of a school-boy? No, the colonies have not spoken, and they are safe. Their silence may be the silence of the unborn. But out of America has come a sweet and startling cry, as unmistakable as the cry of a dying man." That there is some truth behind this, that the soil of our society is arid and impoverished, is indicated by the testimony of our own poets. One has only to consider what George Cabot Lodge wrote in 1904 in one of his letters: "We are a dying race, as every race must be of which the men are, as men and not accumulators, third-rate"; one has only to consider the writings of Messrs. Frost, Robinson, and Masters, in whose presentation of our life, in the West as well as in the East, the individual as a spiritual unit invariably suffers defeat. Fifty years ago, J. A. Froude, on a visit to this country, wrote to one of his friends: "From what I see of the Eastern states I do not anticipate any very great things as likely to come out of the Americans. . . . They are generous with their money, they have tenderness and quiet good humor; but the Anglo-Saxon power is running to seed and I don't think will revive." When we consider the colorlessness and insipidity of our latter-day life (faithfully reflected in the novels of Howells and his successors), the absence from it of profound passions and intense convictions, of any representative individuals who can be compared in spiritual force with Emerson, Thoreau and so many of their contemporaries, its uniformity and its uniform tepidity, then the familiar saying, "Our age has been an age of management, not of ideas or of men," assumes indeed a very sinister import. I go back to the poet Lodge's letters. "Was there ever," he writes, "such an anomaly as the American man? In practical affairs his cynicism, energy and capacity are simply stupefying, and in every other respect he is a sentimental idiot possessing neither the interest, the capacity nor the desire for even the most elementary processes of independent thought. . . . His wife finds him so sexually inapt that she refuses to bear him children and so drivelling in every way except as a money-getter that she compels him to expend his energies solely in that direction while she leads a discontented, sterile, stunted life. . . ." Is this to be denied? And does it not in part explain that lovelessness of the American scene which has bred the note of a universal resentment in so much of our contemporary fiction? As well expect figs from thistles as men from such a soil who are robust enough to prefer spiritual to material victories and who are capable of achieving them.

It is unnecessary to go back to Taine in order to realize that here we have a matrix as unpropitious as possible for literature and art. If our writers wither early, if they are too generally pliant, passive, acquiescent, anaemic, how much is this not due to the heritage of pioneering, with its burden of isolation, nervous strain, excessive work and all the racial habits that these have engendered?

Certainly, for example, if there is anything that counts in the formation of the creative spirit it is that long infancy to which John Fiske, rightly or wrongly, attributed the emergence of man from the lower species. In the childhood of almost every great writer one finds this protracted incubation, this slow stretch of years in which the unresisting organism opens itself to the influences of life. It was so with Hawthorne, it was so with Whitman in the pastoral America of a century ago: they were able to mature, these brooding spirits, because they had given themselves for so long to life before they began to react upon it. That is the old-world childhood still, in a measure; how different it is from the modern American childhood may be seen if one compares, for example, the first book ("Boyhood") of "Pelle the Conqueror" with any of those innumerable tales in which our novelists show us that in order to succeed in life one cannot be up and doing too soon. The whole temper of our society, if one is to judge from these documents, is to hustle the American out of his childhood, teaching him at no age at all how to repel life and get the best of it and build up the defences behind which he is going to fight for his place in the sun. Who can deny that this racial habit succeeds in its unconscious aim—to produce sharp-witted men of business? But could anything be deadlier to the poet, the artist, the writer?

Everything in such an environment, it goes without saying, tends to repress the creative and to stimulate the competitive impulses. A certain Irish poet has observed that all he ever learned of poetry he got from talking with peasants along the road. Whitman might have said almost as much even of New York, the New York of seventy years ago. But what nourishment do they offer receptive spirits to-day, the harassed, inhibited mob of our fellow-countrymen, eaten up with the "itch of ill-advised activity"—what encouragement to become anything but automata like themselves? And what direction, in such a society, does the instinct of emulation receive, that power-ful instinct of adolescence? A certain visitor of Whitman's has described him as living in a house "as cheerless as an ash-barrel," a house indeed "like that in which a very destitute mechanic" might have lived. Is it not symbolic, that picture, of the esteem in which our democracy holds the poet? If today the man of many dollars is no longer the hero of the editorial page and the baccalaureate ad-dress, still, or rather more than ever, it is the "aggressive" type that overshadows every corner of our civilization; the intellectual man who has gone his own way was never less the hero. Many, in short, are the elements in our society that contribute to form a selection constantly working against the survival of the creative type.

It is certainly true that none of these unfavorable conditions could have had such a baleful effect upon our literature if there had been others to counteract them. An aristocratic tradition, if we had ever had it, would have kept open among us the right of way of the free individual, would have preserved the claims of mere living. "It is curious to observe," writes Nietzsche in one of his letters, "how anyone who soon leaves the traditional highway in order to travel on his own proper path always has more or less the sense of being an exile, a condemned criminal, a fugitive from mankind." If that is true in the old world, where society is so much more complex and offers the individual so much more latitude, how few could ever have had the strength in a society like ours, which has always placed such a premium on conformity, to become and remain themselves? Is it fanciful indeed to see in the famous "remorse" of Poe the traces left by this dereliction of the tribal law on the unconscious mind of an artist of unique force and courage? Similarly, a tradition of volun-tary poverty would have provided us with an escape from the im-portunities of bourgeois custom. But aside from the fact that even so simple a principle as this depends largely for its life on precedent (Whitman and the painter Ryder are almost alone among latter-day

Americans in having discovered it for themselves), aside from the fact that to secede from the bourgeois system is, in America, to subject oneself to quite peculiar penalties (did it ever occur to Mark Twain that he *could* be honorably poor?)—aside from all this, poverty in the new world is not the same thing as poverty in the old: one has only to think of Charles Lamb and all the riches that London freely gave him, all the public resources he had at his disposal, to appreciate the difference. With us poverty means in the end an almost inevitable intellectual starvation. Consider such a plaint as Sidney Lanier's: "I could never describe to you" (he writes to Bayard Taylor) "what a mere drought and famine my life has been, as regards that multitude of matters which I fancy one absorbs when one is in an atmosphere of art, or when one is in conversational relationship with men of letters, with travellers, with persons who have either seen, or written, or done large things. Perhaps you know that, with us of the younger generation in the South since the war, pretty much the whole of life has been merely not dying." That is what poverty means in America, poverty and isolation, for Lanier, whose talent, as we can see today, was hopelessly crippled by it, was mistaken if he supposed that there was anything peculiar to the South in that plight of his: it has been the plight of the sensitive man everywhere in America and at all times. Add to poverty the want of a society devoted to intellectual things and we have such a fate as Herman Melville's in New York. "What he lacked," says Mr. Frank Jewett Mather, "was possibly only health and nerve, but perhaps, even more, companionship of a friendly, critical, understanding sort. In London, where he must have been hounded out of his corner, I can imagine Melville carrying the reflective vein to literary completion." Samuel Butler was not entirely mistaken when he jotted down the following observation in his notebook: "America will have her geniuses, as every other country has, in fact she has already had one in Walt Whitman, but I do not think America is a good place in which to be a genius. A genius can never expect to have a good time anywhere, if he is a genuine article, but America is about the last place in which life will be endurable at all for an inspired writer of any kind."

To such circumstances as these, I say, the weakness of our literary life is due. But the lack of great leaders, of a strong and self-respecting literary guild (the one results from the other)—is not this our chief misfortune? In the best of circumstances, and considering all the devils that beset the creative spirit, a strong impulse is scarcely enough to carry the writer through: he must feel not only that he is doing what he wishes to do but that what he is doing *matters*. If dozens of American writers have fallen by the wayside because they have met with insuperable obstacles, dozens of others have fallen, with all their gifts, because they have lost interest in their work, because they have ceased to "see the necessity" of it. This is just the point where the presence of a leader, of a local tradition, a school, a guild, makes all the difference. "With the masters I converse," writes Gauguin in his journal. "Their example fortifies me. When I am tempted to falter I blush before them." If that could have been true of Gauguin, the "Wolf," who walked by himself as few have walked, what shall we say of other men whose artistic integrity, whose faith in themselves, is exposed every day to the corroding influences of a mechanized civilization? It would be all very well if literature were merely a mode of "having a good time": I am speaking of those, the real artists, who, with Nietzsche, make a distinction (illusory perhaps) between "happiness" and "work," and I say that these men have always fed on the thought of greatness and on the propinquity of greatness. It was not for nothing that Turgenev bore in his memory, as a talisman, the image of Pushkin; that Gorky, having seen Tolstoy once, sitting among the boulders on the seashore, felt everything in him blending in one happy thought, "I am not an orphan on the earth, so long as this man lives on it." The presence of such men immeasurably raises the morale of the literary life: that is what Chekov meant when he said, "I am afraid of Tolstoy's death," and is it not true that the whole contemporary literature of England has drawn virtue from Thomas Hardy? The sense that one is *working in a great line:* this, more than anything else perhaps, renews one's confidence in the "quaint mania of passing one's life wearing oneself out over words," as Flaubert called it, in the still greater folly of pursuing one's ego when everything in life combines to punish one for doing so. The successful pursuit of the ego is what makes literature; this requires not only a certain inner intensity but also a certain courage, and it is doubtful whether, in any nation, any considerable number of men can summon up that courage and maintain it unless they have *seen the thing done.* The very notion that such a life is either possible or desirable, the notion that such a life exists even, can hardly occur to the rank and file: some individual has to start the ball rolling, some individual of extraordinary force and audacity, and where is that individual to be found in our modern American literature? Whitman is the unique instance, for Henry

James was an exile; and Whitman was not only essentially of an earlier generation, he was an invalid who folded his hands in mid-career.

Of those others what can we say, those others whose gifts have fitted them to be our leaders? Howells once observed of the American drama that "mainly it has been gay as our prevalent mood is, mainly it has been honest, as our habit is, in cases where we believe we can afford it." In this gently ironical pleasantry one seems to discern the spirit of the literature of the age preceding ours. But it was Howells himself who, in order to arrive at the doctrine that "the more smiling aspects of life are the more American," deliberately, as he has told us, and professed realist that he was, averted his eyes from the darker side of life. And Mark Twain suppressed his real beliefs about man and the universe. And Henry Adams refused to sponsor in public the novels that revealed what he considered to be the truth about American society. At its very headwaters, as we see, this modern literature of ours has failed to flow clear: the creative impulse in these men, richly endowed as they were, was checked and compromised by too many other impulses, social and commercial. If one is to blame anything for this, it is the immense insecurity of our life, which is due to its chaotic nature; for one is not entitled to expect greatness even of those who have the greatest gifts, and of these men Adams was alone secure; of Howells and Mark Twain, frontiersmen as they were, it may be said that they were obliged to compromise, consciously or unconsciously, to gain a foothold in the one corner of the country where men were able to exist as writers at all. But if these men were unable to establish their independence (and one has only to recall the notorious Gorky dinner in order to perceive the ignominy of their position), what can one expect of the rank and file? Great men form a sort of wind-shield behind which the rest of their profession are able to build up their own defences; they establish a right of way for the others; they command a respect for their profession, they arouse in the public a concern for it, an interest in it, from which the others benefit. As things are, the literary guild in America is not greatly respected, nor does it too greatly respect itself. In "My Literary Passions," Howells, after saying that his early reading gave him no standing among other boys, observes: "I have since found that literature gives one no more certain station in the world of men's activities, either idle or useful. We literary folk try to believe that it does, but that is all nonsense. At every period of life among boys or men we are accepted when they are at leisure and want to be amused, and at best we are tolerated rather than accepted." That is ironical too, but a little pathetic as well. Imagine Gorky or Hamsun or Bernard Shaw "trying to believe" that literature gives him a certain station in the world of men's activities! Howells, conscientious craftsman that he was, instinctively shared, in regard to the significance of his vocation, the feeling of our pragmatic philosophers, who justify the intellectual life by showing how useful it is—not to mention Mr. R. W. Chambers, who has remarked that writers "are not held in excessive esteem by really busy people, the general idea being—which is usually true—that literature is a godsend to those unfitted for real work." After this one can easily understand why it is that our novelists take such pains to be mistaken for business men.

So much for the conditions, or at least a few of them, that have prevented our literature from getting its head above water. If America is littered with extinct talents, the halt, the maimed and the blind, it is for reasons with which we are all too familiar; and those to whom the creative life is the principle of human movement look on this wreckage of everything that is most precious to society and ask themselves what our fathers meant when they extolled the progress of our civilization. But let us look facts in the face. Mr. Sinclair Lewis says that we are in the midst of a revival and that we are too humble in supposing that our contemporary literature is inferior to that of England. That we are in the midst of a revival no one doubts, but it is the sustained career that makes a literature; without the evidence of this we can hope much but we can affirm nothing. And what we can see is that, with all its hope, the morale of the literary profession in this country is just what its antecedents have made it. I am reminded of the observation of a friend who has reason to know, that the Catholic Church in America, great as it is in numbers and organization, still depends on the old world for its models, its taskmasters and its inspiration; for the American priest, as a rule, does not feel the vocation as the European feels it. I am reminded of the American labor movement which, prosperous as it is in comparison with the labor movements of Europe, is unparalleled for the feebleness of its representatives. I am reminded of certain brief experiences in the American university world which have led me to believe that the professors who radiate a genuine light and warmth are far more likely to be Russians, Germans, Englishmen, Dutchmen, and Swedes than the children of '76. The hostility of the pioneers to the special career still operates to prevent in the American mind the powerful, concentrated pursuit of any non-utilitarian way of life. Considered with reference to its higher manifestations, life itself has been thus far, in modern America, a failure. Of this the failure of our literature is merely emblematic.

Mr. Mencken, who shares this belief, urges that the only hope of a change for the better lies in the development of a native aristocracy that will stand between the writer and the public, supporting him, appreciating him, forming as it were a *cordon sanitaire* between the individual and the mob. That no change can come without the development of an aristocracy of some sort, some nucleus of the more gifted, energetic and determined, one can hardly doubt. But how can one expect the emergence of an aristocracy outside the creative class, and devoted to its welfare, unless and until the creative class itself reveals the sort of will that attracts its ministrations? "The notion that a people can run itself and its affairs anonymously is now well known to be the silliest of absurdities." Thus William James, in defence of the aristocratic principle; and what he says is as applicable to literature as to every other department of social life. But he continues: "Mankind does nothing save through initiatives on the part of inventors, great and small, and imitation by the rest of us—these are the sole factors alive in human progress. Individuals of genius show the way, and set the pattern, which common people then adopt and follow." In other words, so far as literature is concerned, the burden of proof lies on the writer himself—which brings one back to a truism: it is not for the public or any aristocratic minority within the public to understand the writer, it is for the writer to create the taste by which he is understood. Is it not by this indeed (in a measure, at least) that we recognize the creator?

Certainly if our contemporary literature is not respected, if it has not been able to rally to its support the sensitive public that already exists in this country, it is partly because this literature has not respected itself. That there has been every reason for this makes no difference; that it has begun to respect itself again makes no difference either, for when a people has lost confidence in its literature, and has had grounds for losing confidence, one cannot be surprised if it insists a little cynically upon being "shown." The public supported Mark Twain and Howells and the men of their generation, it admired them for what was admirable in them, but it was aware, if only unconsciously, that there was a difference between them and the men of the generation before them; and in consequence of this the whole stock of American literature fell. But those who insist in our day that America prefers European writers to its own because America is still a colony of Europe cannot ignore the significant fact that at a time when America was still more truly colonial American writers had all the prestige in this country that European writers have at present; and it is not entirely because at that time the country was more homogeneous. Poe and Thoreau found little support in the generation I speak of, as Whitman found little support in the generation that followed it. On the other hand, there were no European writers (and it was an age of great writers in Europe) who were held in higher esteem in this country than Hawthorne, Emerson, Motley and one or two others almost equally distinguished, as well from a European as from an American point of view; there were few, if any, European writers, in fact, who were esteemed in this country as highly as they. How can one explain it? How can one explain why, at a time when America, in every other department of life, was more distinctly colonial than it is now, American literature commanded the full respect of Americans, while today, when the colonial tradition is vanishing all about us, it so little commands their respect that they go after any strange god from England? The problem is far from simple, but among its many explanations one can hardly deny that there were in that period a number of writers of unusual power, who made the most of their power and followed their artistic conscience and who by this fact built up a public confidence in themselves and the literature they represented. Does it matter at all whether we today enjoy these writers or not? They were men of spiritual force, three or four of them: that is the important point. If the emerging writers of our epoch find themselves handicapped by the scepticism of the public, they have only to remember that they are themselves for the most part in the formative stage and that they have to live down the recent past of their profession.

Meanwhile, what constitutes a literature is the spiritual force of the individuals who compose it. If our literature is to grow it can only be through the development of a sense of "free will" on the part of our writers themselves. To be, to feel oneself, a "victim" is in itself not to be an artist, for it is the nature of the artist to live, not in the world of which he is an effect, but in the world of which he is the cause, the world of his own creation. For this reason, the pessimistic determinism of the present age is, from the point of view of literature, of a piece with the optimistic determinism of the age that is passing. What this pessimistic determinism reveals, however, is a *consciousness of the situation:* to that extent it represents a gain, and one may even say that to be conscious of the situation is half the battle. If we owed nothing else to Mr. Dreiser, we should owe him enough for the tragic sense of the waste of American life which his books communicate. It remains true that if we resent this life it is only a sign of our weakness, of the harm we have permitted this civilization to do us, of our imperfectly realized freedom; for to the creative spirit in its free state the external world is merely an impersonal point of departure. Thus it is certain that as long as the American writer shares what James Bryce called the "mass fatalism" of the American people, our literature will remain the sterile, inferior phenomenon which, on the whole, it is.

"What we want," wrote Henry Adams in 1862 to his brother Charles, "is a *school.* We want a national set of young men like ourselves or better, to start new influences not only in politics, but in literature, in law, in society, and throughout the whole social organism of the country—a national school of our own generation. And that is what America has no power to create. . . . It's all random, insulated work, for special and temporary and personal purposes. And we have no means, power or hope of combined action for any unselfish end." *That is what America has no power to create.* But can it be said that any nation has ever created a school? Here we have the perfect illustration of that mass fatalism of which I have spoken, and Henry Adams himself, in his passivity, is the type of it. Secure as he was, uniquely secure, why did he refuse to accept the responsibility of those novels in which he expressed the contempt of a powerful and cultivated mind for the meanness of the guiding element in American society? In the darkest and most chaotic hours of our spiritual history the individual has possessed a measure of free will only to renounce it: if Henry Adams had merely signed his work he might by that very fact have become the founder of the school that he desired. But it is true that in that generation the impulses of youth were, with extraordinary unanimity, focussed upon a single end, the exploitation of the continent; the material opportunities that American life offered were too great and too all-engrossing, and it is unlikely that any considerable minority could have been rallied for any non-utilitarian cause. Sixty years later this school remains the one thing necessary: the reforestation of our spiritual territory depends upon it. And in more than one sense the times are favorable. The closing of the frontier seems to promise for this country an intenser life than it has known before; a large element of the younger generation, estranged from the present order, exists in a state of ferment that renders it highly susceptible to new ideas; the country swarms with half-artists who have ceased to conform to the law of the tribe but have not accepted the discipline of their own individual spirits. "What I chiefly desire for you," wrote Ibsen to Brandes at the outset of his career, "is a genuine, full-blooded egoism, which shall force you for a time to regard what concerns you yourself as the only thing of any consequence, and everything else as non-existent. . . . There is no way in which you can benefit society more than by coining the metal you have in yourself." The second half of this rather blunt counsel of perfection is implied in the first, and it connotes a world of things merely to name which would be to throw into relief the infantility of the American writer as a type. By what prodigies of alert self-adaptation, of discriminating self-scrutiny, of conscious effort, does the creative will come into its own! As for ourselves, weak as too many of us are, ignorant, isolated, all too easily satisfied, and scarcely as yet immune from the solicitations of the mob, we still have this advantage, that an age of reaction is an age that stirs the few into a consciousness of themselves.

# STUART P. SHERMAN

## (1881–1926)

Born in Anita, Iowa, on October 1, 1881, Stuart P. Sherman spent his boyhood in California and New England. He attended Williams College, where he won a place on the staff of the *Williams Literary Monthly*, becoming its editor in his senior year. After graduating from Williams in 1903, he went on a three-year fellowship to Harvard, where he came under the influence of the redoubtable Irving Babbitt. In 1904 he received the degree of A.M. and in 1906 his doctorate, at Harvard. In 1906 he was appointed to an instructorship in English at Northwestern University, but soon transferred his services to the University of Illinois, serving there as associate professor of English from 1909 to 1911, and as a full professor from 1911 to 1924. His wide-ranging scholarship, his pronounced gift as a lecturer, his various critical essays and books, soon gained him considerable recognition. During the First World War he staunchly supported the cause of the Allies, writing a pamphlet on *American and Allied Ideals*. In April, 1924, he received a call to become literary editor of the *New York Herald Tribune*, a position of commanding importance in which he was able to exercise substantial influence as a critic. His distinguished career was cut short when he drowned on August 21, 1926.

He played his part in the battle of critical ideas in the first quarter of the twentieth century. His first volume, *Matthew Arnold: How to Know Him* (1917) not only won him his spurs as a scholar but also set him on his way as a critic following the Arnoldian tradition. His next venture, *On Contemporary Literature* (1917), was the record of his humanistic crusade against naturalism, which he equated with animalism. Significantly enough, this volume is dedicated to Paul Elmer More. In examining writers like Dreiser and Wells, Sherman seeks to determine the philosophy that underlies their work as well as the craftsmanship that shaped it. In his representation of life, the novelist or poet also expresses a criticism of life. No writer can pretend that he is above the battle, unprejudiced and uncommitted. Some point of view he must inevitably espouse if he is to write at

161

all. Sherman is heartened by the signs of a reaction against naturalism, led by such men as Brownell, Babbitt, and More. The inner check is the force which opposes the push of instincts, the pressure of the biological impulses.

The mental and spiritual revolution wrought by the First World War turned Sherman into a militant nationalist, a devout patriot. In *Americans* (1922), he selects ten figures as embodying the central and enduring American tradition: the tradition of Puritanism. This book attempts to work within and rightly appraise the national tradition, and particularly to judge and evaluate contemporary letters in the light of the past. The spirit of America assures him that love of his country, her history and her culture, her traditions, is not in opposition to the ideal of fraternal humanity. Fulminating against H. L. Mencken and Ludwig Lewisohn, he speaks disparagingly of "the militant hostility of alien-minded critics towards what they conceive to be the dominant traits of the national character."[1] Mary M. Colum points out that Sherman suffered from two prejudices throughout his life as a critic: "a prejudice against the alien-minded and a prejudice in favor of the Puritan, and with a firm conviction that these two sorts of people were peculiar to America."[2]

*The Genius of America* (1923) represents an heroic effort to apply moral standards to literature. Sherman strenuously defends the Puritan against all detraction, portraying Puritanism as a vital creative impulse, a profound spirit of protest, in American life. He writes with passionate, even prophetic conviction, exalting the continuous power of the national life as it is exemplified in its great men, the bearers and transmitters of our source of spiritual and creative energy. In the title essay, "The Genius of America," he not only defends the inextinguishable spirit of Puritanism but also attacks the aesthetic theories of Spingarn, especially the latter's contention that beauty has nothing to do with morals or democracy. As a critic Sherman is convinced that the artist, since he lives in society, is burdened with a great moral responsibility.

In *Points of View* (1924) there are symptoms of a growing change in his intellectual outlook. He has begun to discover some saving virtues in contemporary writers he had formerly castigated. In *Critical Woodcuts* (1926), we find striking evidence of the change that came over him after he had assumed editorship of the book-review section of the *New York Herald Tribune*. His removal to New York liberalized his point of view

---

[1] Stuart P. Sherman, *Americans* (New York, 1922), p. 25.

[2] In her essay, "Stuart Sherman," printed in the *Saturday Review of Literature*, June 26, 1926, and reprinted in William A. Drake (ed.), *American Criticism* (New York, 1926), pp. 38–39.

and led him gradually to break away from the Humanism he had formerly embraced.

Though some of the books and authors Sherman treats of in *The Main Stream* (1927) are already "dated," his essays and reviews still hold our interest by virtue of their gusto, their vivid style, and their penetrating insight. *The Emotional Discovery of America and Other Essays* (1932), a posthumous collection of miscellaneous essays, exhibits Sherman's catholic range of interests, his vibrant aesthetic sensibility, his rich capacity for experience, and his ability to grow and develop. He writes with lively zest, combining earnestness of vision with eloquence of style. "The Emotional Discovery of America," which was delivered as an address before the American Academy of Arts and Letters, furnishes a statement of his credo as a critic, and particularly of his attitude toward America. In *Toward Standards*, Norman Foerster assails Stuart P. Sherman as being a practitioner of historical criticism and a journalist reviewing the fluctuating fashions in taste, rather than a critic in the humanistic sense.[3]

On the whole, Sherman, as an apostle of American culture and the Puritan tradition, was opposed to the iconoclastic spirit of the moderns. Temperamentally he was drawn to the conservative element in life and the traditional forces in literature. According to him, the greatest heroes of civilization, our most influential and profound spiritual leaders, were Puritans at heart, men who insisted upon discipline as a means of achieving a better life. It is hard to say what kind of critic Sherman would have developed into had death not cut his life short, but it is clearly evident that he would have been far more sympathetic toward the moderns, continuing to discover virtues where formerly he had detected not only faults but flagrant vices. As literary editor of the *New York Herald Tribune*, he had come to appreciate the character of the common man and welcome the experimental quality of modern fiction, even that produced by the naturalists.

## BIBLIOGRAPHY

### TEXT

*Matthew Arnold.* Indianapolis, 1917.
*On Contemporary Literature.* New York, 1917.
*Americans.* New York, 1922.
*The Genius of America.* New York and London, 1923.
*My Dear Cornelia.* Boston, 1924.
*Points of View.* New York and London, 1924.

[3] Norman Foerster, *Toward Standards* (New York, 1930), p. 90.

*Critical Woodcuts.* New York and London, 1926.
*The Main Stream.* New York and London, 1927.
*Shaping Men and Women.* Edited by Jacob Zeitlin. Garden City, 1928.
*The Emotional Discovery of America and Other Essays.* New York, 1932.
*The Life and Letters of Stuart P. Sherman,* ed. by Jacob Zeitlin and Homer
 Woodbridge. 2 vols. New York, 1929.

CRITICISM

Burgum, Edwin Berry, "Stuart P. Sherman." *English Journal,* XIX, 137–
 150 (February, 1930).
Calverton, V. F., *The Newer Spirit.* New York, 1925.
De Mille, George E., *Literary Criticism in America.* New York, 1931.
Elliott, G. R., "Stuart Sherman and the War Age," *Bookman,* LXXI,
 173–181 (April–May, 1930).
——, *Humanism and Imagination.* Chapel Hill, 1938.
Munson, Gorham B., *The Dilemma of the Liberated.* New York, 1930.
Warren, Austin, "Humanist into Journalist," *Sewanee Review,* XXXVIII,
 357–365 (July–September, 1930).

# VIII

## THE POINT OF VIEW IN AMERICAN CRITICISM*

Delivered as a lecture on the William Vaughn Moody foundation at the University of Chicago, May 10, 1922.

Were you looking to be held together by lawyers?
Or by arguments on paper? or by arms?
Nay, nor the world, nor any living thing, will so cohere.

WHITMAN

The teacher of the coming age must occupy himself in the study and
explanation of the moral constitution of man more than in the elucidation
of difficult texts.

EMERSON

There is that in me—I do not know what it is—but I know it is in me.
Wrench'd and sweaty—calm and cool then my body becomes;
I sleep—I sleep long.

* Reprinted from *The Genius of America* by Stuart P. Sherman; copyright 1923 by
Charles Scribner's Sons, 1951 by Ruth Sherman; used by permission of the publishers.

I do not know it—it is without a name—it is a word unusual;
It is not in any dictionary, utterance, symbol.
Something it swings on more than the earth I swing on;
To it the creation is the friend whose embracing awakes me.
Perhaps I might tell more. Outlines! I plead for my brothers and sisters.
Do you see, O my brothers and sisters?
It is not chaos or death—it is form, union, plan—it is eternal life—it is
    Happiness.

WHITMAN

ACCORDING to all the critics, domestic and foreign, who have prophesied against America during the last hundred years, the great and ever-present danger of a democratic society lies in its tendency to destroy high standards of excellence and to accept the average man as a satisfactory measure of all things. Instead of saying, like Antigone in the drama of Sophocles, 'I know I please the souls I ought to please,' democracy, we are told, is prone to dismiss the question whether she has any high religious obligation, and to murmur complacently, 'I know I please the souls of average men.' I propose to examine a little the origins of this belief, and then to inquire whether it is justified by the present condition of our civilization, as reflected in our current literature. In the course of the inquiry I shall at least raise the question whether the average man is as easy to please as he is ordinarily supposed to be.

At the very foundation of the Republic, the menace of the average man was felt by a distinguished group of our own superior men, including Washington, John Adams, Hamilton, and many other able and prosperous country gentlemen. To them the voice of the people was not the voice of God, but the clamor of a hydra-headed monster, requiring to be checked and bridled. Thus, at the outset of our civilization, they established a point of view and they instituted a criticism, which were unfriendly to the average man and his aspirations and to all his misguided friends. They possessed, for example, certain standards of character and manners, which they applied with some austerity to what they regarded as the vulgar Jacobinism of Thomas Paine, to the disintegrating demagoguery of Jefferson, to the cosmopolitan laxity of Franklin, and to all the tendencies of French radicalism towards leveling by law the inequalities created by law and by nature.

Edmund Burke explained England's relative immunity to the equalitarian speculations of the French by this fact: 'We continue,' he said, 'as in the last two ages, to read more generally, than, I believe, is now done on the Continent, the authors of sound antiquity. These occupy our minds. They give us another taste and turn, and will not suffer us to be more than transiently amused with paradoxical morality.' Now, it is insufficiently recognized that, in the third quarter of the eighteenth century, America, like England, was at the height of her classical period—I mean the period when statesmen, poets, and painters most deliberately and successfully imitated the example of the ancients. The public characters of Washington and his friends, like those of Burke and his friends, were in the grand style, were in a style more or less consciously moulded upon that of the great republicans of England, Rome, and Athens. From Cromwell and Milton, and, above all, from the heroes of Plutarch, the friends of Washington inherited the ardor and the elevation of their public spirit, and, at the same time, their lofty disdain for the vulgar herd and a conviction that the salvation of the people depended upon the perpetuation of their own superiorities.

At its best, near the source, and on its positive side, there is something very august and inspiring in the utterances of this old Roman or aristocratic republicanism. It is not far from its best in the letters of Abigail Adams.

Glory, my son [she writes to John Quincy Adams], in a country which has given birth to characters, both in the civil and military departments, which may vie with the wisdom and valor of antiquity. As an immediate descendant of one of these characters, may you be led to an imitation of that disinterested patriotism and that noble love of country, which will teach you to despise wealth, titles, pomp, and equipage, as mere external advantages, which cannot add to the excellence of your mind, or compensate for the want of integrity or virtue.

It is not difficult to despise 'wealth, pomp, and equipage,' when one is adequately supplied with them; John Quincy Adams, accordingly, found his occasion for pride in the excellence of his mind and in his integrity and virtue. And, true to his breeding, he maintained, like Coriolanus, a kind of passionate and scornful opposition to the vulgar mob. In 1795, he writes to his mother that France will remain without the means to form a Constitution till she has exploded the doctrine of submission to and veneration for public opinion. A little later, he admits to his father that 'the struggle against a popular clamor is not without its charms in my mind.'

There he sounds the rallying cry of our great conservative tradition. I shall not ask here whether the creative ardor of the aristocratic spirit which we observed in the mother is not already beginning to be transformed in the son to a certain ardor of repression. Nor am I concerned here to trace the evolution of this Roman-American pride from its pure high source, down through the ages, till it re-appears in aristocratic republicans of our own times, who still find a charm in opposing the popular clamor. I am thinking of the railway magnate, author of the celebrated phrase, 'The public be damned'; and I am thinking of our most aggressive literary critic, a professed Federalist, who remarked the other day in language savoring a bit, perhaps, of the Roman decadence: 'I don't care a damn what happens to the Republic after I am dead.'

We must pause here, however, long enough to recall that the classical models of society, which the more conservative of our fore-fathers kept in their minds' eye, rested upon a slave population, and that the government which they actually set up countenanced, in opposition to the plebeian taste of Paine and the demagoguery of Jefferson, a slave population. It is a question of more than academic interest to-day, whether or not the government which they set up necessarily implies the continued existence of an illiterate peasantry.

Those who believe that the salvation of the people depends upon the perpetuation of their own superiorities are likely, in the long run, to make the end subservient to the means, to grow rather careless about the salvation of the people and rather over-careful about the preservation of their own superiorities. They incline, also, to a be-lief that these superiorities can best be perpetuated through their own offspring—a belief which, so far as I can learn, is inadequately supported by statistics. On this assumption, however, they endeavor to make a kind of closed corporation of their own class, and seek to monopolize for it the administration of government, the possession of property, the enjoyment of higher education and culture, and the literary production of the country.

These tendencies, as we know, appeared very early in the history of the Republic. John Adams nearly ruined himself in 1787 by his frank declaration that wealth and birth should be qualifications for the Senate. Hamilton, at the same time, put forth his proposals for restraining the vulgar herd by perpetuating wealth and the leader-ship of established families in the nearest possible American imita-tion of the British monarchical and aristocratic system.

The irrepressible conflict provoked by such attempts to check the rich fecundity and the unpredictable powers of our colonial 'populace' is ordinarily presented to us as a contention over political principles. In its most comprehensive aspect, it may profitably be regarded as rather a conflict of religions. The short interval between the adoption of the Constitution and the end of the eighteenth century is the period of antique Republicanism triumphant, dominated by the religion of the superior man. In 1800, this religion received a blow in the election of Jefferson, the St. Paul of the religion of the populace, who preached faith, hope, and charity for the masses. In 1828, the religion of the superior man received a still more ominous blow, when the fiery, pistoling rough-rider from Tennessee, Andrew Jackson, defeated John Quincy Adams. At this reverse to the sons of light, John Quincy Adams lost his faith in God, the God of superior men.

We have recently had, from the fourth eminent generation of the Adams family, Brooks, Charles Francis, and Henry, a voluminous commentary upon the effort of 'the heirs of Washington' to stand against the popular clamor and uphold their great tradition. On the whole, if we may trust their testimony, it has been a tragically unavailing effort. In Boston and Cambridge and in a few tributary villages in old New York and Washington, on a few great plantations of Virginia and the Carolinas, the civilization which the superior men contemplated obtained a struggling foothold before the Civil War. And this civilization achieved some literary expression in the classical oratory of Webster, in the fine old English gentility of Irving's prose, and in the pale provincial flowering of our New England poetry. Sanguine observers saw in this literary renascence promise that the intrenched intelligence and culture of the settled, civilized East was to take and hold the mastery in the national life.

But for Henry Adams, at least, that hope ended with his return from England in 1868. He discovered, when he went to Washington to offer his services in carrying on the great tradition—he discovered that the great tradition was broken. There had taken place, not merely a Civil War, but a far more fundamental revolution. He and his kind, bred on the classics, and versed in law and European diplomacy, were anachronisms, survivors out of the classical eighteenth century, belated revelers in the Capitol. A multitude of unknown or ignored forces had developed in his absence, and had combined to antiquate him, to extrude him from the current of national life, and to incapacitate him for a place in the public councils. This singular new nation was no respecter of grandfathers. It took its superior men wherever it found them. It picked its chief statesman out of a log cabin in Illinois, its chief military hero out of an Ohio tannery, its most eminent poet from a carpenter's shop, and its leading man of letters from a pilot-house on the Mississippi. Such standards! Henry spent a life-time elaborating his grand principle of the degradation of energy, to explain to himself why the three grandsons of two presidents of the United States all ended miserably: one as President of the Kansas City Stock Yards; one as a member of the Massachusetts Bar; while one had sunk to the level of a Professor of History at Harvard.

From the point of view of these antique republicans, the period from the Civil War to the end of the nineteenth century proves the truth of all the prophesies against the average man. This is the period of triumphant democracy—meaning, of course, the triumph, not of the political party, but of the religious principle. In this epoch, the gates of opportunity open as never before to the populace, to the new men. What are the results? Throughout the period, the steadily waning influence of Eastern intelligence and culture in the national life, steadily increasing immigration from the peasant stocks of Europe, expansion of the population into new western territory, prosperity of industrial pioneers, rise of the railway magnate, the iron-master, the organizer of large-scale production of material commodities—immense rewards and glory for supplying the average man what the average man, at that particular moment, wanted and had to have.

Midway in this epoch, one of its heroes, Andrew Carnegie, wrote a book which he called *Triumphant Democracy*—a work which exults and rejoices in the goodness and greatness of American life. It was an industrial captain's reply to the foreign critics who had flitted across the country year after year, like ravens, boding disaster. It was a reply from the point of view of a Scotch radical, a self-made man, who could compare the poor little Scotch town of Dunfermline, where the revolution in machinery had ruined his father, to the booming city of Pittsburgh, Pennsylvania, where the same revolution had made him one of the masters of his generation.

Carnegie's point of view was inadequate. He offered no effective answer to the savage criticism which Dickens had made of our civilization forty years earlier, when he pictured the democracy as brutal, boisterous, boastful, ignorant, and hypocritical. He made no effective reply to Carlyle, who had cried twenty-two years later than Dickens, 'My friend, brag not yet of our American cousins! Their quantity of cotton, dollars, industry and resources, I believe to be almost unspeakable; but I can by no means worship the like of these.'

Matthew Arnold, a critical friend of ours, far more friendly to our political institutions and to our social organization than Carlyle, dropped in upon us at about the time that Carnegie published his book. 'The trouble with Carnegie and his friends,' said Arnold, 'is that they have no conception of the chief defect of American life; namely, that it is so dreadfully uninteresting.' This dullness, he explained, was due to the average man's quite inadequate conception of the good life, which did not go beyond being diligent in business and serving the Lord—making money and observing a narrow code of morality.

The particularly hopeless aspect of our case, Arnold thought, was that we, as a people, seemed quite unconscious of our deficiencies on the human side of our civilization. We displayed a self-satisfaction which is 'vulgarizing and retarding.' Nationally we were boasters, or, as we say nowadays, 'boosters.' 'The worst of it is,' he continues, 'that this tall talk and self-glorification meets with hardly any rebuke from sane criticism over there.' He cites some examples; and then he adds that, 'the new West promises to beat in the game of brag even the stout champions I have been quoting.'

Now, no Englishman will ever fathom the mystery of Uncle Sam's boasting. No outsider can ever know, as we all know, how often, out of the depths of self-distrust and self-contempt and cutting self-criticism, he has whistled to keep his courage up in the dark, and has smiled reassuringly while his heart was breaking. Still, if you look into the literature of the period, you find that there is much warrant for Arnold's strictures, though not always precisely where he found it. The little boasts of men like Lowell and Thomas Wentworth Higginson and Brander Matthews are only Yankee whistling, the turning of the trodden worm, a decent pride in the presence of 'a certain condescension in foreigners.' Lowell knew a man, he says, who thought Cambridge the best spot on the habitable globe. 'Doubtless God could have made a better, but doubtless He never did.' I myself am fond of declaring that the campus of the University of Illinois is finer than the meadows of Christ Church College, Oxford. But no one in America thinks anything a whit the finer for what an academic person has said in its favor. Nor, on the other hand, does anyone, outside academic circles, think anything in America a whit the worse for what a foreign critic has said against it. The Chicago

journalists, for example, with true Jacksonian hilarity, ridiculed
Arnold and, after his departure, stigmatized him as a 'cur.'

The only criticism which ever, as we say, 'gets across' to the
Jacksonian democracy is that which comes from one of their own
number. The really significant aspects of our self-complacency in
Carnegie's time were reflected in the popular literature of the period
by writers sprung from the new democracy, self-made authors, who
flattered the average man into satisfaction with his present state and
his average achievement. I am thinking of Western writers, like
Joaquin Miller and Riley and Carleton and Bret Harte and Mark
Twain. I am thinking of the romantic glamour which these men
contrived to spread over the hard rough life and the rougher characters of the middle-borderers, the Argonauts, and the Forty-Niners.

You recall the method. First, they admit certain facts—for picturesque effect. For example, these settlers of the Golden West, they
say, included a few decent men, but they were in great part the riffraff
of the world—foreign adventurers, offscourings of Eastern cities,
uncouth, red-shirted illiterates from the Middle States, lawless, dirty,
tobacco-spitting, blaspheming, drunken, horse-thieves, murderers,
and gamblers. And then, with noble poetic vision, they cry: 'But
what delicacy of sentiment beneath those shaggy bosoms! What
generosity and chivalry under those old red shirts! Horse-thieves,
yet nature's noblemen! Gamblers and drunkards, yet kings of men!'
'I say to you,' chants 'the poet of the Sierras,' 'that there is nothing
in the pages of history so glorious, so entirely grand, as the lives of
these noble Spartan fathers and mothers of Americans, who begot
and brought forth and bred the splendid giants of the generation
that is now fast following the setting sun of their unselfish and all
immortal lives.'

Here is the point of view of the Jacksonian democracy in its romantic mood. This, in general, was the point of view of Mark Twain,
the most original force in American letters and, on the whole, the
most broadly representative American writer between the close of
the Civil War and the end of the century. Most of us have enough
pioneer blood in our veins, or in our imaginative sympathies, to love
Mark Twain nowadays. But academic people, they tell us,—and
they tell us truly,—had little to do with establishing his earlier
reputation. He neither flattered them nor pleased them. He pleased
and flattered and liberated the emotions of that vast mass of the
population which had been suppressed and inarticulate. He was the
greatest booster for the average man that the country ever produced.

Confident in the political and mechanical and natural superiorities conferred upon every son of these States by his mere birth under the American flag, Mark Twain laughed at the morality of France, the language of Germany, the old masters of Italy, the caste system of India, the imperialism of England, the romances of Scott, the penal laws of the sixteenth century, and at the chivalry of the court of King Arthur—he laughed at all the non-American world, from the point of view of the average American, stopping only from time to time to pat his countrymen on the back and to cry, like Jack Horner, 'What a brave boy am I!' To make a climax to the bold irreverence of this Jacksonian laughter, he laughed at New England and at all her starchy immortals.

In the *Connecticut Yankee at King Arthur's Court,* published in 1889, we hear the last full-hearted laughter of triumphant democracy. Twain himself became sombre in his later years; he became cynical, and touched with misanthropy. I cannot go here, in any detail, into the causes for the darkening of his outlook. The most interesting of these causes, perhaps, was that Mark Twain had one foot over the threshold of a new age, our present era, which I shall call the era of critical and pessimistic democracy. He had begun to emerge, as I think we are all now beginning to emerge, from the great romantic illusion about the average man, namely, that liberty or equality or any kind of political recognition or literary exploitation, or even economic independence, can make him a happy or a glorious being.

Poets and novelists, since the French Revolution, have fostered this romantic illusion in a laudable but misdirected effort to bestow dignity upon the humblest units of humanity. They liberated the emotion for a religion of democracy. They did little to give to that emotion intelligent direction.

You will recall Wordsworth's poem called 'Resolution and Independence.' The poet, wandering on the moor in richly gloomy thought, comes upon a poor old man, bent, broken, leaning over a pool, gathering leeches for his livelihood. The poet questions him how it goes with him. The old man replies, quietly enough, that it goes pretty hard, that it is going rather worse; but that he still perseveres and manages to get on, in one way or another. Whereupon Wordsworth falls into a kind of visionary trance. The old peasant looms for him to a gigantic stature. He becomes the heroic 'man with the hoe'; a shadowy shape against the sky; man in the abstract, clothed in all the moral splendor of the poet's own imagination.

This same trick of the fancy Hardy plays with his famous dairy-maid, Tess of the D'Urbervilles. She is but an ignorant, instinctive, erring piece of Eve's flesh. Yet, says Hardy, drawing upon the riches of his own poetic associations, 'The impressionable peasant leads a larger, fuller, more dramatic life than the pachydermatous king.' Thereupon he proceeds to invest the dairy-maid with the tragic emotions and import of a heroine of Thebes or Pelops' line. He infers, by a poetic fallacy, that she is as interesting and as significant to herself as she is to him.

I will take one other case, the hero of a recently translated novel, Knut Hamsun's *Growth of the Soil*. Here we have an illiterate peasant of Norway, going into the public land almost empty-handed; gradually acquiring a pig, a cow, a woman, a horse, building a turf-shelter, a cowshed, a cabin, a mill—and so, little by little, toiling like an ox, becoming a prosperous farmer, owner of rich lands and plentiful flocks and herds. It is, in a sense, a very cheerful book, a sort of new *Robinson Crusoe*. Its moral appears to be that, so long as men stick to the soil and preserve their ignorance and their natural gusto, they may be happy. It is a glorification of the beaver, the building animal. It is an idealization of the peasant at the instinctive level.

The trick of the literary imagination in all these cases is essentially the same as that which Bret Harte played with his Argonauts, and Miller and Riley with their Indiana pioneers, and Mark Twain with his Connecticut Yankee. We are changing all that.

I chanced the other day upon an impressive new American novel, strikingly parallel in some respects to Hamsun's *Growth of the Soil*, but utterly different from it in the mood and the point of view. I refer to the story of Kansas life, called *Dust*, by Mr. and Mrs. Haldeman-Julius. Here again we have the hardy pioneer, rough, dirty, and capable, entering on the new land, with next to nothing but his expectations; acquiring a pig, a hut, cattle, and a wife; and gradually 'growing up with the country' into a prosperous western farmer, with stock in the bank, and a Cadillac, and electric lights in the cow-barns, and kerosene lamps in the house. Our human beaver in America, toiling with the same ox-like fortitude as Isak in Norway, achieves the same material success. But—and this is the difference —the story is one of unrelieved gloom ending in bitter tragedy. Why this sustained note of gloom? Why has our Kansas tale none of the happy gusto of Hamsun's *Growth of the Soil?* Because the Kansas farmer is not content with the life of a peasant. Because our Kansas authors refuse to glorify man on the instinctive level, or to disguise the essential poverty and squalor of his personal life with a poetic fallacy. The book is written from a point of view at which it is apparent that our civilization has failed to solve the human problem.

Since the time of *The Connecticut Yankee* and Carnegie's *Triumphant Democracy,* our literary interpreters have been gradually shifting their ground. They are giving us now a criticism of life from a position at which it is possible to see through the poetic illusion about the average man. Making an effort now to·see him as he really is, our authors are reporting that he is not satisfied with his achievements, he is not happy, he is very miserable. The most hopeful aspect of American literature to-day is its widespread pessimism. I call this symptom hopeful, because it is most fully exhibited by precisely that part of the country, and by those elements of the population, which were thought forty years ago to be most addicted to boasting and most deeply infected with the vulgarizing and retarding self-complacency of the Philistine, the red-shirted Jacksonian from Missouri. This pessimism comes out of Wisconsin, Minnesota, Illinois, Indiana, Missouri, Kansas, and California; from the sons and daughters of pioneer farmers, country doctors, small-town lawyers, and country editors; from the second generation of immigrant stock, German, Swedish, Scotch, Irish; from the hungry, nomadic semi-civilization of the West.

I call this Western pessimism auspicious, because it is so sharply critical, and because the criticism is directed, not so much against the political and economic framework of society as against the kind of personalities which this society produces, and against the quantity and quality of the human satisfactions which these personalities have at their disposal. It is directed against that defect in our civilization which Arnold pointed out; it is so lacking in elevation and beauty; it is so humdrum, so dreadfully uninteresting; it fails to appease the vague yet already acutely painful hunger of the average man for a good life. 'Beguile us no longer,' cry the new voices; 'beguile us no longer with heroic legends and romantic idyls. The life which you celebrate is not beautiful, not healthy, not satisfying. It is ugly, obscene, devastating. It is driving us mad. And we are going to revolt from it.'

The manifestation of this spirit which, at the present moment, is attracting most attention is what Mr. Van Doren, in his interesting book on *Contemporary American Novelists,* has called 'the revolt from the village.' I need only remind you of that long series of narratives, beginning in the early eighties with E. W. Howe's *Story of a*

*Country Town,* and followed by Hamlin Garland's *Main Travelled
Roads,* Mr. Masters's *Spoon River Anthology,* Sherwood Anderson's
*Winesburg, Ohio,* Sinclair Lewis's *Main Street,* Zona Gale's *Miss
Lulu Bett,* and the novel of which I have already spoken, *Dust,* by
Mr. and Mrs. Haldeman-Julius.

But the interesting pessimistic and critical note in our current
literature is by no means confined to representations of country life
and the small town. Take Mrs. Wharton's pictures of metropolitan
society, from *The House of Mirth* to *The Age of Innocence,* remembering only that Mrs. Wharton cannot be classed as a Jacksonian;
then consider the dreary wide wilderness of Mr. Dreiser's picture of
big business; Ben Hecht's story of a city-editor in *Erik Dorn;* Mr.
Cabell's *Cream of the Jest;* Mr. Norris's broad picture of the California scene in *Brass;* Mr. Fitzgerald's account of the younger
generation in *The Beautiful and Damned;* Mr. Hergesheimer's admirable new novel, *Cytherea;* and, finally, Mr. Lewis's *Babbitt.*

Here we are invited to consider a class of which the discontent
cannot be explained by their struggle with the churlishness of the
soil and the rigor and tragic whimsicality of the elements. Most of
the characters, indeed, have reached a level at which even the economic struggle is as much a pastime as a necessity. They are business
men and their womenkind, with a sprinkling of professional men,
people who, as we say, know 'how to live,' people who live expen-
sively, purchasing with free hand whatever gratifications are available for the senses. Nevertheless, if we may trust their interpreters,
these people, too, are dreadfully uninteresting to one another, alternating between a whipped-up excitement and a stifled yawn. Their
entire stratum of society is permeated by a terrible ennui. Jaded with
business and card-parties, Mr. Hergesheimer's persons, for example,
can conceive no relief from the boredom of the week but to meet at
one another's houses at the week-ends and, in a state of half-maudlin
tipsiness, kiss one another's wives on the stairs. Even when the
average man is sheltered on all sides, weariness, as Pascal says,
springs from the depths of his own heart and fills the soul with its
poison. Our 'bourgeoisie,' no less than our 'peasantry,' are on the
verge of a cultural revolt; they are quarreling with the quality of
their civilization.

Now, at the time when a man quarrels with his wife, either one of
two interesting things may happen. He may elope with his neighbor's
wife for Cuba, fancying for the moment that she is the incarnation
of all his unsatisfied desires, the divine Cytherea. Or this man and

his old wife may turn over a new leaf and put their relations on a more satisfactory basis. Which course will be followed depends on the power of self-criticism which the interested persons possess.

This is a parable, with wide possibilities of social application. Our average man, in town and country, is quarreling with his wife, that is to say, with our average American civilization. If he listens to certain counselors who appeal to certain of his instincts and to his romantic imagination, his household, the material civilization which he has slowly built up out of the dust by faithfully working on certain traditional principles—this household will be in danger of disruption. If, on the other hand, his discontent with himself and his human conditions is adequately diagnosed, and if an adequate remedy is accepted, then he will look back upon this period of pessimism as preliminary to the redintegration of the national spirit and its expression in literature. Which course will be followed depends in no small measure upon our power of criticism, which, in its turn, depends upon an adequate point of view.

The elder critics in the academic tradition have in general not dealt sympathetically, or even curiously, with the phenomena. Fixed in an inveterate fidelity to the point of view established by the early classical Americans, they look with a mingling of disdain and abhorrence upon our impious younger world, as upon

> a darkling plain
> Where ignorant armies clash by night.

The critics, on the other hand, who are endeavoring to deal sympathetically and curiously with the phenomena, are utterly unorganized; are either without standards of judgment, or in a wild state of confusion with regard to their standards. They are making efforts to get together; but they have no principle of integration. I have not time to do more than mention some of their incongruous points of view.

A man whose hearty geniality touches the affections of us all, Mr. William Allen White, proposed the other day, as an integrating principle, the entire abandonment of all standards and a general adoption of the policy of live and let live. His theory of universal sympathy, which he miscalls 'the democratic theory in criticism,' would, if applied, destroy both criticism and democracy.

Our journalistic critics in general, conscious of the incompatibility between their private beliefs and the political and economic interests which they serve, tend at the present time, I should say, to adopt the point of view of universal cynicism.

In order precisely to escape from the troublesome clashes of political, social, and moral judgment, in order to escape, in other words, from the real problem of critical redintegration, another group has adopted the aesthetic point of view, and has made a feeble effort to revive in America, with the aid of the Crocean philosophy, the doctrine of art for art's sake.

I will mention, finally, one other point of view, to which an increasing company of the younger writers are repairing, which we may call for convenience the Freudian point of view. The champions of this point of view attempt a penetrating diagnosis of all the maladies of American civilization, with the assistance of the new psychology. To sum up their findings briefly, they hold that the trouble with American life is, at the root, due to age-long and cankering inhibitions, attributable to our traditional Puritanism. The remedy is a drop to the instinctive level; the opening of the gates to impulse; a free and spontaneous doing as one pleases in all directions.

Popular Freudianism is, perhaps, the most pestilential of all the prevailing winds of doctrine. Yet its champions have penetrated, I believe, nearer to the heart of our difficulty, they are nearer to an adequate point of view and an integrating principle, than any of the other seekers. They at least recognize that the kingdom of disorganization is within the individual breast. The fact that they approach so near to the true destination, and yet fall short of it, renders their counsels peculiarly seductive and peculiarly perilous.

They are right when they attribute the central malady of our civilization to suppressed desires. They are tragically wrong if they believe that this malady is due to the suppression by religion of any specific isolable physical instinct. They are tragically wrong if they think that this malady can be cured by the destruction of religious restraint and the release of any specific isolable physical instinct. When they prescribe, as many of them do with as much daring as they can muster, giving a new and large licence, for example, to the sexual impulses; when they prescribe, as if with the countenance of fresh scientific discoveries, the restoration of the grand old liberative force of alcohol; when they flatter any of the more or less disciplined instincts of our animal nature with the promise of happiness in emancipation, they are offering us intoxicants, anodynes, opiates, every one of which has been proved, by the experience of innumerable generations, hopeless even to accomplish any permanent alleviation of the malady which they profess to cure. And when they attack the essential religious principle of Puritanism,—its deep human passion for perfection,—they are seeking to destroy the one principle which can possibly result in the integration of the national life.

Now, as I talk with the members of the beautiful younger generation which comes through my class-room year after year, I find that the Freudians are profoundly mistaken in their analysis of human nature. The deepest craving of these average young men and women is not to be unbound, and released, and to be given a license for a free and spontaneous doing as they please in all directions. They recognize that nature and environment and lax educational discipline have made them beings of sufficiently uncoördinated desires and scattering activities.

What they deeply crave is a binding generalization of philosophy, or religion, or morals, which will give direction and purpose, which will give channel and speed, to the languid diffusive drift of their lives. The suppressed desire which causes their unhappiness is a suppressed desire for a good life, for the perfection of their human possibilities. The average unreflective man does not always know that this is, in fact, his malady. And in the blind hunger and thirst of his unenlightened nature, he reaches out eagerly for opiates and anodynes, which leave him unsatisfied. But what the innermost law of his being demands, what his human nature craves, is something good and great that he can do with his heart and mind and body. He craves the active peace of surrender and devotion to something greater than himself. Surrender to anything less means the degradation and humiliation of his spirit.

This is the tragedy involved in any surrender to subordinate passions or instincts. I think that our current pessimistic literature indicates that our average man is discovering this fact about his own nature, and that, therefore, like the sinner made conscious of guilt, he is ripe for regeneration; he is ready for the reception of a higher culture than he has yet enjoyed.

Democratic civilization suffereth long, because it is always waiting for the hindmost to catch up with the middle. It is always reluctant to consign the hindmost to the devil. But, in the long run, I do not believe that the history of our civilization is going to verify the apprehensions entertained by our old Roman-Americans regarding the average man. To one whose measure of national accomplishment is not the rich flowering of a small aristocratic class, but the salvation of the people, the choices of the average man in the past do not conclusively prove the danger of giving him what he wants. In his first period, he wanted a stable government; and he got it, and wholeheartedly glorified the political and military heroes who gave it to him. In his second period, he wanted a rapid and wide diffusion of the material instruments of civilized life; he got them, and wholeheartedly glorified the industrial heroes who provided them. In his third period, the average man is growing almost as scornful of 'wealth and pomp and equipage,' as John Quincy Adams. The captains of industry are no longer his heroes; they have communicated to him what they had of virtue for their hour. What the average man now wants is the large-scale production and the wide diffusion of science, art, music, literature, health, recreation, manners, human intercourse, happiness—the best to be had; and he is going to get them and to glorify wholeheartedly the heroes of culture who provide them for him.

The great civilizations of the world hitherto have been integrated in their religion. By religion I mean that which, in the depths of his heart, a man really believes desirable and praiseworthy. A great civilization begins to form when men reach an agreement as to what is desirable and praiseworthy. The leading Athenians, in their best period, reached such an agreement; and that is why, whether you meditate on their art, their poetry, or their philosophy, whether you gaze at the frieze of the Parthenon, or read a drama of Sophocles, or the prayer of Socrates, you feel yourself in the presence of one and the same formative spirit—one superb stream of energy, superbly controlled by a religious belief that moral and physical symmetry are the most desirable and praiseworthy things in the outer and the inner man.

The prospects for our American civilization depend at present upon our capacity for a similar religious integration. Our present task is, primarily, to become clear in our minds as to what is our own formative spirit. The remedy for our present discontents is indicated by the character of the malady. The remedy is, first, to help the average man to an understanding of his own nature, so that he may recognize more fully what part the things of the mind and the imagination may play in the satisfaction of his suppressed desires. It is to help him to recognize that even an intellectual and imaginative life will yield him little content unless it is organized around some central principle and animating purpose. It is to give the average man what the literature of our pessimistic democracy has at last proved that he wants, namely, an object to which he can joyfully surrender the full strength of his soul and body.

But this is not the whole of the remedy. It is necessary, at the same time, to persuade the superior men that the gods of the old Roman-American aristocrats have forsaken them, and that the time has come when even they may safely accept the purified religion of democracy. To oppose it now is to oppose the formative spirit of our national life and to doom one's self to sterility. The remedy is, in short, to effect a redintegration of the national will on the basis of a genuinely democratic humanism, recognizing as its central principle the duty of bringing the whole body of the people to the fullest and fairest human life of which they are capable.

The point of view which I advocate is not, as it has been called, moralistic. It is essentially religious. And the religion of an intelligent man is not a principle of repression, any more than it is a principle of release. Religion binds us to old morals and customs so long as they help us towards the attainment of our object; but it releases from old morals and customs as soon as they impede our progress towards that object. The object gives the standard. Confronted with heirlooms or with innovations, one's first question is, does this, or does it not, tend to assist the entire body of the people toward the best human life of which they are capable? Advance to this point of view, and you leave behind you universal sympathy, universal cynicism, universal æstheticism, and the black bats of the Freudian cave. You grasp again a power of choice which enables you to accept or reject, with something of that lost serenity which Socrates displayed when he rejected escape from prison and accepted the hemlock. You recover something of that high elation which Emerson displayed when he said: 'I am primarily engaged to myself to be a public servant of all the gods, to demonstrate to all men that there is intelligence and good-will at the heart of things, and ever higher and higher leadings.'

# H. L. MENCKEN
## (1880–1956)

A SLASHING critic of his generation, H. L. Mencken plunged joyously into practically every controversy that agitated the country from 1919 to 1930, never giving quarter, speaking his mind freely. He was actively engaged not only in the practice of literary criticism but also in social, political, and economic debates. Now that his energies are chiefly occupied in carrying on his philological work, it is possible to view him dispassionately and objectively from a perspective of time that does not distort the value of his contribution. Conservative in matters political and economic, he was contemptuous of all that was stuffy and repressive in the Victorian tradition, its taste, its morality, its artistic conventions. The rigorous testing of everything, literary or otherwise, by the acids of skepticism and the touchstone of common sense—that was the critical method (if he can be said to have a method at all) he used with considerable skill and daring. Keen, self-confident, truculent, dogmatic in his pronouncements, yet fundamentally irreverent in attitude, he challenged established values, using his formidable powers of invective to demolish all that ran counter to his conception of truth and intrinsic excellence.

A versatile and indefatigable journalist all his life, Mencken wrote with amazing ease and power. He was born in Baltimore, on September 12, 1880, of parents who had emigrated from Germany. From the start, Mencken manifested an interest in literary pursuits, composing verses at an early age and even trying his hand at the composition of music. This interest in music has persisted. After a brief period of schooling, he took up journalism with tremendous gusto. He began his journalistic career as a reporter on the *Baltimore Morning Herald* in 1899, and he has continued writing for newspapers, on and off, ever since. In 1908 he served as literary critic of *The Smart Set,* and in 1914 became co-editor with George Jean Nathan of that magazine, which passed out of existence in 1923. It was not until the founding of *The American Mercury* in 1924 that Mencken gained national prominence. From 1924 until 1933 the magazine not only pre-

181

sented his point of view but attacked every section of the United States, and every person in it, that gave any evidence of narrowness or stupidity. Mencken's strength lay chiefly in the art of "debunking." He derived intense delight from deflating the Elmer Gantrys and Babbitts of America, the political windbags in the halls of Congress, the blindness and timidity of the professorial mind, and especially the doctrines of the New Humanists.

He was outspoken, aggressive, prolific, full of provocative ideas. In addition to his frequent contributions to the newspapers, he continued to publish books regularly. He brought forth a book of poetry and two plays, he edited the work of Henrik Ibsen and Eugene Brieux, but his first significant work of criticism was *George Bernard Shaw, His Plays* (1905). In 1908 he published *The Philosophy of Friedrich Nietzsche,* another writer from whom he derived many of his leading ideas.

As a full-fledged critic, his most important contributions consisted of stimulating and challenging essays which treat of a multitudinous variety of subjects, anything that happened to engross his attention: literature, music, politics, personalities. His best known and most influential work as a critic is to be found in his six volumes of *Prejudices,* which reveal him at his best and worst: opinionated, irate, invigorating, forceful. He voiced his political, ethical, and religious views in *Notes on Democracy* (1926), *Making a President* (1922), *A Treatise on the Gods* (1930), and *A Treatise on Right and Wrong* (1934). He is a rare combination of political conservative, eminently satisfied with the *status quo,* and unregenerate skeptic questioning all sanctities and certitudes, but his judgments in literary criticism, as in politics, are by no means impeccable.

The essays from the sophisticated *Smart Set* and *The American Mercury,* which Mencken reprinted in his *Prejudices,* set the tone of his acceptances and rejections. He despised not only the academic but also the utopian mind as exemplfied in the work of H. G. Wells, Henry George, and Thorstein Veblen. Yet say what one will in dispraise of Mencken, he has at least been fairly consistent in his *attitude.* The Samuel Johnson of twentieth-century criticism in America, he applied the standard of common sense with extraordinary effectiveness. Pungent, inconoclastic, possessed of a trenchant style, he was the most bellicose exponent of impressionism the country had ever beheld. Like Huneker, he had no critical ideas to offer except his own vital and often violent reactions to books and personalities, but these reactions were presented with so much saliency and picturesque forcefulness as to make exciting, if not always illuminating, reading.

Despite his lack of a critical method, he championed many good causes. He denounced Puritanism and the aridity of the cultural life of this land. An intransigent individualist he vehemently asserted the need for full freedom in the arts, condemning any attempt to censor the new naturalistic literature that was springing up. As editor of *The American Mercury*, he virtually dictated the tone and temper of letters during the stormy twenties, giving writers an outlet for their work and imbuing them with faith in their creative mission. With all his limitations, he was a vitalizing force. The cutting edge of his style, his power of caricature and devastating satire, his love of startling paradoxes, were in evidence early in life, while he was still in his twenties. The later Mencken is implicit in the book he wrote on Nietzsche. From Nietzsche he derived his conception of the aristocracy, his contempt for the mob, his conception of absolute individualism, his hatred of the sham of democracy. His statement regarding Nietzsche applies equally well to himself:

"He believed that it was only by constant skepticism, criticism and opposition that progress could be made, and that the greatest of all dangers was inanition. . . . Such was his mission, as he conceived it: to attack error wherever he saw it and to proclaim truth wherever he found it."[1]

During his most productive years, Mencken's chief contribution to literary criticism was that he made literature come to life, infusing his own exuberant vitality into the critical act and infecting the reader with his own enthusiasms and prejudices. Indeed, he regards this as one of the prime functions of the critic. Holding such views, Mencken was bound to have little use for the theories and categories drawn up by critics, what he satirically referred to as "the criticism of criticism of criticism." Art as morality, art as psychology, art as play, art as a vicarious form of immortality, art as philosophy, history, politics, sociology, science, or pure pedantry—as a thoroughgoing impressionist he had nothing but contempt for the various aesthetic systems that reigned in the marketplace of criticism. The critic must purge himself of his moral and political dogmas —Mencken does not, of course, follow his own prescription—and learn to enter with sympathy and insight into the mind that fathered the work, thus recapturing some of the creative passion that once moved the artist. There is a creative force at work in criticism as in other forms of art. Another criterion of excellence in criticism is the power of the critic to let himself go, and Mencken certainly suffered from no serious inhibitions. What he liked he liked heartily and what he disliked he damned in no uncertain terms. Mencken thus communicates a lusty, picturesque personality delighting in its "prejudices," its non-conformity, its negations, its sturdy common sense.

The really competent critic must be an empiricist, and facts disprove the

---

[1] H. L. Mencken, *The Philosophy of Friedrich Nietzsche* (Boston, 1908), p. 201.

reality of the iridescent dreams conjured up by American critics of a glorious future for American culture. The literature of our time, like the literature of our past, is colorless, shallow, emasculated, hopelessly imitative and mediocre, incapable of giving birth to original ideas. The cause of this unfortunate development lies in our political beliefs, our morals, and our religion; in our lack of a civilized aristocracy that would be skeptical in temper, giving the writer intelligent criticism and enlightened appreciation.

Mencken's prejudices are part and parcel of his "consistency." He can argue that there is no such thing as inspiration, the free flow of ideas in writing being simply a function of the digestive tract, a blood-conditioned, physiological process. The critic, Mencken is convinced, is either a middle-man, a sober retailer of the ideas of other men, or else he is a creative artist in his own right, impelled by an inner necessity to understand life and to express himself. This faith in the autotelic function of criticism is reinforced by a remarkable gusto. What Mencken looks for and values in literature is the element of vitality. Unfortunately this search for vitality in contemporary letters led him to neglect or grossly underestimate the major figures of our national past. Though he performed a salutary service in his time, he is not a profound or original critic.

The chief weakness of Mencken as a critic is that he measures every-thing by personal standards. If he happens to dislike poetry, then he dismisses it as no more than a reassuring fiction set to music, "chiefly produced and esteemed by peoples that have not yet come to maturity."[2] Mencken's admirers hail him as a creative critic who communicates a vital sense of life and who reaches to the roots of a work of art. Isaac Goldberg considers Mencken essentially an aesthetic critic, "and what is more, an aesthetic critic in an almost Crocean sense."[3] A more recent critic, how-ever, speaks of Mencken as liquidating "the American past when he initi-ated the American future. There were some other curious elements in his thinking: a rather slippery logic, a sacrifice of sobriety to the appeal of bravado, for he never hesitates to affirm violently what he had just as violently denied."[4] Mencken wrote at such high voltage that logical con-sistency was of necessity sacrificed to brilliance of effect. Despite all his splenetic railing at American civilization for its countless faults and follies, Mencken has devoted his later years to a work of "expiation." He has undertaken a monumental investigation of the American language. *The American Language,* including *"Supplement One"* and *"Supplement Two,"* may very well constitute his most lasting bid for fame. In this work

2 H. L. Mencken, *Prejudices, Third Series* (New York, 1922), p. 162.
3 Isaac Goldberg, *The Man Mencken* (New York, 1925), p. 248.
4 Maxwell Geismar, *The Last of the Provincials* (Boston, 1947), pp. 12–13.

Mencken, like Van Wyck Brooks in composing the literary history of his people, is supplying the basis for a viable American tradition.

### BIBLIOGRAPHY

#### TEXT

*George Bernard Shaw*. Boston and London. 1905.
*The Philosophy of Friedrich Nietzsche*. Boston, 1908.
*A Little Book in C Major*. New York, 1916.
*A Book of Prefaces*. New York, 1917.
*Prejudices, First Series*. New York, 1919.
*Prejudices, Second Series*. New York, 1920.
*Prejudices, Third Series*. New York, 1922.
*Prejudices, Fourth Series*. New York, 1924.
*Prejudices, Fifth Series*. New York, 1926.
*Notes on Democracy*. New York, 1926.
*Prejudices, Sixth Series*. New York, 1927.
*James Branch Cabell*. New York, 1927.
*Treatise on the Gods*. New York, 1930.
*Selected Prejudices*. New York, 1927.
*The American Language*. New York, 1936.
*Happy Days*. New York, 1940.
*Newspaper Days*. New York, 1941.
*Heathen Days*. New York, 1943.
*The American Language. Supplement I*. New York, 1945.
*The American Language. Supplement II*. New York, 1947.
*The Days of H. L. Mencken*. New York, 1948.
*A Mencken Chrestomathy*. New York, 1949.

#### CRITICISM

Angoff, Charles, "Mencken Twilight," *North American Review*, CCXLVI, 216–232 (Winter, 1938–39).
Babbitt, Irving, *On Being Creative and Other Essays*. Boston and New York, 1932.
Boyd, Ernest A., *H. L. Mencken*. New York, 1925.
Brooks, Van Wyck, *Sketches in Criticism*. New York, 1932.
Cabell, James Branch, *Some of Us*. New York, 1930.
Calverton, V. F., "H. L. Mencken: A Devaluation," *Modern Monthly*, X, 7–11 (December, 1936).
Canby, H. S., *American Estimates*. New York, 1930.
DeCasseres, Benjamin, *Mencken and Shaw*. New York, 1930.
Frey, Carroll, *A Bibliography of the Writings of H. L. Mencken*. Philadelphia, 1924.
Geismar, Maxwell, *The Last of the Provincials*. Boston, 1947.

Harrold, C. F., "Two Critics of Democracy," *South Atlantic Quarterly,*
    XXVII, 130–141 (April, 1928).
Harris, Frank, *Contemporary Portraits* (4th series). New York, 1923.
Harrison, J. B. *A Short View of Menckenism in Menckenese.* Seattle, 1927.
Kemler, Edgar, *The Irreverent Mr. Mencken.* Boston, 1950.
Manchester, William, *Disturber of the Peace.* New York, 1951.
*Menckenia.* New York, 1928.
Nathan, George Jean, *The Intimate Notebooks of George Jean Nathan.*
    New York, 1932.
Rascoe, Burton, et al., *H. L. Mencken.* New York, 1920.
Sherman, Stuart P., *Americans.* New York, 1922.
——, *Critical Woodcuts,* New York, 1926.

## FOOTNOTE ON CRITICISM*

NEARLY all the discussions of criticism that I am acquainted with start off with a false assumption, to wit, that the primary motive of the critic, the impulse which makes a critic of him instead of, say, a politician, or a stockbroker, is pedagogical—that he writes because he is possessed by a passion to advance the enlightenment, to put down error and wrong, to disseminate some specific doctrine: psychological, epistemological, historical, or æsthetic. This is true, it seems to me, only of bad critics, and its degree of truth increases in direct ratio to their badness. The motive of the critic who is really worth reading—the only critic of whom, indeed, it may be said truthfully that it is at all possible to read him, save as an act of mental discipline—is something quite different. That motive is not the motive of the pedagogue, but the motive of the artist. It is no more and no less than the simple desire to function freely and beautifully, to give outward and objective form to ideas that bubble inwardly and have a fascinating lure in them, to get rid of them dramatically and make an articulate noise in the world. It was for this reason that Plato wrote the "Republic," and for this reason that Beethoven wrote the Ninth Symphony, and it is for this reason, to drop a million miles, that I am writing the present essay. Every-

* Reprinted from *Prejudices, Third Series,* by H. L. Mencken, by permission of Alfred A. Knopf, Inc. Copyright 1922 by Alfred A. Knopf, Inc.

thing else is after-thought, mock-modesty, messianic delusion—in brief, affectation and folly. Is the contrary conception of criticism widely cherished? Is it almost universally held that the thing is a brother to jurisprudence, advertising, laparotomy, chautauqua lecturing and the art of the schoolmarm? Then certainly the fact that it is so held should be sufficient to set up an overwhelming probability of its lack of truth and sense. If I speak with some heat, it is as one who has suffered. When, years ago, I devoted myself diligently to critical pieces upon the writings of Theodore Dreiser, I found that practically every one who took any notice of my proceedings at all fell into either one or two assumptions about my underlying purpose: (*a*) that I had a fanatical devotion for Mr. Dreiser's ideas and desired to propagate them, or (*b*) that I was an ardent patriot, and yearned to lift up American literature. Both assumptions were false. I had then, and I have now, very little interest in many of Mr. Dreiser's main ideas; when we meet, in fact, we usually quarrel about them. And I am wholly devoid of public spirit, and haven't the least lust to improve American literature; if it ever came to what I regard as perfection my job would be gone. What, then, was my motive in writing about Mr. Dreiser so copiously? My motive, well known to Mr. Dreiser himself and to every one else who knew me as intimately as he did, was simply and solely to sort out and give coherence to the ideas of Mr. Mencken, and to put them into suave and ingratiating terms, and to discharge them with a flourish, and maybe with a phrase of pretty song, into the dense fog that blanketed the Republic.

The critic's choice of criticism rather than of what is called creative writing is chiefly a matter of temperament—perhaps, more accurately of hormones—with accidents of education and environment to help. The feelings that happen to be dominant in him at the moment the scribbling frenzy seizes him are feelings inspired, not directly by life itself, but by books, pictures, music, sculpture, architecture, religion, philosophy—in brief, by some other man's feelings about life. They are thus, in a sense, secondhand, and it is no wonder that creative artists so easily fall into the theory that they are also second-rate. Perhaps they usually are. If, indeed, the critic continues on this plane—if he lacks the intellectual agility and enterprise needed to make the leap from the work of art to the vast and mysterious complex of phenomena behind it—then they *always* are, and he remains no more than a fugelman or policeman to his betters. But if a genuine artist is concealed within him—if his feelings are in any sense profound and original, and his capacity for self-expression is above the average of educated men—then he moves inevitably from the work of art to life itself, and begins to take on a dignity that he formerly lacked. It is impossible to think of a man of any actual force and originality, universally recognized as having those qualities, who spent his whole life appraising and describing the work of other men. Did Goethe, or Carlyle, or Matthew Arnold, or Sainte-Beuve, or Macaulay, or even, to come down a few pegs, Lewes, or Lowell, or Hazlitt? Certainly not. The thing that becomes most obvious about the writings of all such men, once they are examined carefully, is that the critic is always being swallowed up by the creative artist—that what starts out as the review of a book, or a play, or other work of art, usually develops very quickly into an independent essay upon the theme of that work of art, or upon some theme that it suggests—in a word, that it becomes a fresh work of art, and only indirectly related to the one that suggested it. This fact, indeed, is so plain that it scarcely needs statement. What the pedagogues always object to in, for example, the *Quarterly* reviewers is that they forgot the books they were supposed to review, and wrote long papers—often, in fact, small books—expounding ideas suggested (or not suggested) by the books under review. Every critic who is worth reading falls inevitably into the same habit. He cannot stick to his task: what is before him is always infinitely less interesting to him than what is within him. If he is genuinely first-rate—if what is within him stands the test of type, and wins an audience, and produces the reactions that every artist craves—then he usually ends by abandoning the criticism of specific works of art altogether, and setting up shop as a general merchant in general ideas, *i. e.*, as an artist working in the materials of life itself.

Mere reviewing, however conscientiously and competently it is done, is plainly a much inferior business. Like writing poetry, it is chiefly a function of intellectual immaturity. The young literatus just out of the university, having as yet no capacity for grappling with the fundamental mysteries of existence, is put into writing reviews of books, or plays, or music, or painting. Very often he does it extremely well; it is, in fact, not hard to do well, for even decayed pedagogues often do it, as such graves of the intellect as the New York *Times* bear witness. But if he continues to do it, whether well or ill, it is a sign to all the world that his growth ceased when they made him *Artium Baccalaureus*. Gradually he becomes, whether in or out of the academic grove, a professor, which is to say, a man devoted to diluting and retailing the ideas of his superiors—not an artist, not even a bad artist, but almost the antithesis of an artist. He is learned, he is sober, he is painstaking and accurate—but he is as hollow as a jug. Nothing is in him save the ghostly echoes of other men's thoughts and feelings. If he were a genuine artist he would have thoughts and feelings of his own, and the impulse to give them objective form would be irresistible. An artist can no more withstand that impulse than a politician can withstand the temptations of a job. There are no mute, inglorious Miltons, save in the hallucinations of poets. The one sound test of a Milton is that he functions as a Milton. His difference from other men lies precisely in the superior vigor of his impulse to self-expression, not in the superior beauty and loftiness of his ideas. Other men, in point of fact, often have the same ideas, or perhaps even loftier ones, but they are able to suppress them, usually on grounds of decorum, and so they escape being artists, and are respected by right-thinking persons, and die with money in the bank, and are forgotten in two weeks.

Obviously, the critic whose performance we are commonly called upon to investigate is a man standing somewhere along the path leading from the beginning that I have described to the goal. He has got beyond being a mere cataloguer and valuer of other men's ideas, but he has not yet become an autonomous artist—he is not yet ready to challenge attention with his own ideas alone. But it is plain that his motion, in so far as he is moving at all, must be in the direction of that autonomy—that is, unless one imagines him sliding backward into senile infantilism: a spectacle not unknown to literary pathology, but too pathetic to be discussed here. Bear this motion in mind, and the true nature of his aims and purposes becomes clear; more, the incurable falsity of the aims and purposes usually credited to him becomes equally clear. He is not actually trying to perform an impossible act of arctic justice upon the artist whose work gives him a text. He is not trying with mathematical passion to find out exactly what was in that artist's mind at the moment of creation, and to display it precisely and in an ecstasy of appreciation. He is not trying to bring the work discussed into accord with some transient theory of æsthetics, or ethics, or truth, or to determine its degree of departure from that theory. He is not trying to lift up the fine arts, or to defend democracy against sense, or to promote happiness at the domestic hearth, or to convert sophomores into right-thinkers, or to serve God. He is not trying to fit a group of novel phenomena into the orderly process of history. He is not even trying to discharge the catalytic office that I myself, in a romantic moment, once sought to force upon him. He is, first and last, simply trying to express himself. He is trying to arrest and challenge a sufficient body of readers, to make them pay attention to him, to impress them with the charm and novelty of his ideas, to provoke them into an agreeable (or shocked) awareness of him, and he is trying to achieve thereby for his own inner ego the grateful feeling of a function performed, a tension relieved, a *katharsis* attained which Wagner achieved when he wrote "Die Walküre," and a hen achieves every time she lays an egg.

Joseph Conrad is moved by that necessity to write romances; Bach was moved to write music; poets are moved to write poetry; critics are moved to write criticism. The form is nothing; the only important thing is the motive power, and it is the same in all cases. It is the pressing yearning of every man who has ideas in him to empty them upon the world, to hammer them into plausible and ingratiating shapes, to compel the attention and respect of his equals, to lord it over his inferiors. So seen, the critic becomes a far more transparent and agreeable fellow than ever he was in the discourses of the psychologists who sought to make him a mere appraiser in an intellectual customs house, a gauger in a distillery of the spirit, a just and infallible judge upon the cosmic bench. Such offices, in point of fact, never fit him. He always bulges over their confines. So labelled and estimated, it inevitably turns out that the specific critic under examination is a very bad one, or no critic at all. But when he is thought of, not as pedagogue, but as artist, then he begins to take on reality, and, what is more, dignity. Carlyle was surely no just and infallible judge; on the contrary, he was full of prejudices, biles, naïvetés, humors. Yet he is read, consulted, attended to. Macaulay was unfair, inaccurate, fanciful, lyrical—yet his essays live. Arnold had his faults too, and so did Sainte-Beuve, and so did Goethe, and so did many another of that line—and yet they are remembered to-day, and all the learned and conscientious critics of their time, laboriously concerned with the precise intent of the artists under review, and passionately determined to set it forth with god-like care and to relate it exactly to this or that great stream of ideas—all these pedants are forgotten. What saved Carlyle, Macaulay and company is as plain as day. They were first-rate artists. They could make the thing charming, and that is always a million times more important than making it true.

Truth, indeed, is something that is believed in completely only by persons who have never tried personally to pursue it to its fastnesses and grab it by the tail. It is the adoration of second-rate men —men who always receive it at second-hand. Pedagogues believe in immutable truths and spend their lives trying to determine them and propagate them; the intellectual progress of man consists largely of a concerted effort to block and destroy their enterprise. Nine times out of ten, in the arts as in life, there is actually no truth to be discovered; there is only error to be exposed. In whole departments of human inquiry it seems to me quite unlikely that the truth ever *will* be discovered. Nevertheless, the rubber-stamp thinking of the world always makes the assumption that the exposure of an error is identical with the discovery of the truth— that error and truth are simple opposites. They are nothing of the sort. What the world turns to, when it has been cured of one error, is usually simply another error, and maybe one worse than the first one. This is the whole history of the intellect in brief. The average man of to-day does not believe in precisely the same imbecilities that the Greek of the fourth century before Christ believed in, but the things that he *does* believe in are often quite as idiotic. Perhaps this statement is a bit too sweeping. There is, year by year, a gradual accumulation of what may be called, provisionally, truths—there is a slow accretion of ideas that somehow manage to meet all practicable human tests, and so surive. But even so, it is risky to call them absolute truths. All that one may safely say of them is that no one, as yet, has demonstrated that they are errors. Soon or late, if experience teaches us anything, they are likely to succumb too. The profoundest truths of the Middle Ages are now laughed at by schoolboys. The profoundest truths of democracy will be laughed at, a few centuries hence, even by school-teachers.

In the department of æsthetics, wherein critics mainly disport themselves, it is almost impossible to think of a so-called truth that shows any sign of being permanently true. The most profound of principles begins to fade and quiver almost as soon as it is stated. But the work of art, as opposed to the theory behind it, has a longer life, particularly if that theory be obscure and questionable, and so cannot be determined accurately. "Hamlet," the Mona Lisa, "Faust," "Dixie," "Parsifal," "Mother Goose," "Annabel Lee," "Huckleberry Finn"—these things, so baffling to pedagogy, so contumacious to the categories, so mysterious in purpose and utility— these things live. And why? Because there is in them the flavor of salient, novel and attractive personality, because the quality that shines from them is not that of correct demeanor but that of creative passion, because they pulse and breathe and speak, because they are genuine works of art. So with criticism. Let us forget all the heavy effort to make a science of it; it is a fine art, or nothing. If the critic, retiring to his cell to concoct his treatise upon a book or play or what-not, produces a piece of writing that shows sound structure, and brilliant color, and the flash of new and persuasive ideas, and civilized manners, and the charm of an uncommon personality in free function, then he has given something to the world that is worth having, and sufficiently justified his existence. Is Carlyle's "Frederick" true? Who cares? As well ask if the Parthenon is true, or the C Minor Symphony, or "Wiener Blut." Let the critic who is an artist leave such necropsies to professors of æsthetics, who can no more determine the truth than he can, and will infallibly make it unpleasant and a bore.

It is, of course, not easy to practice this abstention. Two forces, one within and one without, tend to bring even a Hazlitt or a Huneker under the campus pump. One is the almost universal human susceptibility to messianic delusions—the irresistible tendency of practically every man, once he finds a crowd in front of him, to strut and roll his eyes. The other is the public demand, born of such long familiarity with pedagogical criticism that no other kind is readily conceivable, that the critic teach something as well as say something—in the popular phrase, that he be constructive. Both operate powerfully against his free functioning, and especially the former. He finds it hard to resist the flattery of his customers, however little he may actually esteem it. If he knows anything at all, he knows that his following, like that of every other artist in ideas, is chiefly made up of the congenitally subaltern type of man and woman—natural converts, lodge joiners, me-toos, stragglers after circus parades. It is precious seldom that he ever gets a positive idea out of them; what he usually gets is mere unintelligent ratification. But this troop, despite its obvious failings, corrupts him in various ways. For one thing, it enormously reënforces his belief in his own ideas, and so tends to make him stiff and dogmatic—in brief, precisely everything that he ought not to be. And for another thing, it tends to make him (by a curious contradiction) a bit pliant and politic: he begins to estimate new ideas, not in proportion as they are amusing or beautiful, but in proportion as they are likely to please. So beset, front and rear, he sometimes sinks supinely to

the level of a professor, and his subsequent proceedings are interesting no more. The true aim of a critic is certainly not to make
converts. He must know that very few of the persons who are susceptible to conversion are worth converting. Their minds are intrinsically flabby and parasitical, and it is certainly not sound
sport to agitate minds of that sort. Moreover, the critic must always harbor a grave doubt about most of the ideas that they lap
up so greedily—it must occur to him not infrequently, in the silent
watches of the night, that much that he writes is sheer buncombe.
As I have said, I can't imagine any idea—that is, in the domain of
æsthetics—that is palpably and incontrovertibly sound. All that I
am familiar with, and in particular all that I announce most vo-
ciferously, seem to me to contain a core of quite obvious nonsense.
I thus try to avoid cherishing them too lovingly, and it always
gives me a shiver to see any one else gobble them at one gulp.
Criticism, at bottom, is indistinguishable from skepticism. Both
launch themselves, the one by æsthetic presentations and the other
by logical presentations, at the common human tendency to accept
whatever is approved, to take in ideas ready-made, to be responsive
to mere rhetoric and gesticulation. A critic who believes in anything absolutely is bound to that something quite as helplessly as
a Christian is bound to the Freudian garbage in the Book of Revelation. To that extent, at all events, he is unfree and unintelligent,
and hence a bad critic.

The demand for "constructive" criticism is based upon the same
false assumption that immutable truths exist in the arts, and that
the artist will be improved by being made aware of them. This
notion, whatever the form it takes, is always absurd—as much so,
indeed, as its brother delusion that the critic, to be competent, must
be a practitioner of the specific art he ventures to deal with, *i. e.*,
that a doctor, to cure a belly-ache, must have a belly-ache. As
practically encountered, it is disingenuous as well as absurd, for
it comes chiefly from bad artists who tire of serving as performing
monkeys, and crave the greater ease and safety of sophomores in
class. They demand to be taught in order to avoid being knocked
about. In their demand is the theory that instruction, if they could
get it, would profit them—that they are capable of doing better
work than they do. As a practical matter, I doubt that this is ever
true. Bad poets never actually grow any better; they invariably
grow worse and worse. In all history there has never been, to my
knowledge, a single practitioner of any art who, as a result of "con-

structive" criticism, improved his work. The curse of all the arts, indeed, is the fact that they are constantly invaded by persons who are not artists at all—persons whose yearning to express their ideas and feelings is unaccompanied by the slightest capacity for charming expression—in brief, persons with absolutely nothing to say. This is particularly true of the art of letters, which interposes very few technical obstacles to the vanity and garrulity of such invaders. Any effort to teach them to write better is an effort wasted, as every editor discovers for himself; they are as incapable of it as they are of jumping over the moon. The only sort of criticism that can deal with them to any profit is the sort that employs them frankly as laboratory animals. It cannot cure them, but it can at least make an amusing and perhaps edifying show of them. It is idle to argue that the good in them is thus destroyed with the bad. The simple answer is that there *is* no good in them. Suppose Poe had wasted his time trying to dredge good work out of Rufus Dawes, author of "Geraldine." He would have failed miserably—and spoiled a capital essay, still diverting after three-quarters of a century. Suppose Beethoven, dealing with Gottfried Weber, had tried laboriously to make an intelligent music critic of him. How much more apt, useful and durable the simple note: "Arch-ass! Double-barrelled ass!" Here was absolutely sound criticism. Here was a judgment wholly beyond challenge. Moreover, here was a small but perfect work of art.

Upon the low practical value of so-called constructive criticism I can offer testimony out of my own experience. My books are commonly reviewed at great length, and many critics devote themselves to pointing out what they conceive to be my errors, both of fact and of taste. Well, I cannot recall a case in which any suggestion offered by a constructive critic has helped me in the slightest, or even actively interested me. Every such wet-nurse of letters has sought fatuously to make me write in a way differing from that in which the Lord God Almighty, in His infinite wisdom, impels me to write —that is, to make me write stuff which, coming from me, would be as false as an appearance of decency in a Congressman. All the benefits I have ever got from the critics of my work have come from the destructive variety. A hearty slating always does me good, particularly if it be well written. It begins by enlisting my professional respect; it ends by making me examine my ideas coldly in the privacy of my chamber. Not, of course, that I usually revise them, but I at least examine them. If I decide to hold fast to them, they are

all the dearer to me thereafter, and I expound them with a new
passion and plausibility. If, on the contrary, I discern holes in them,
I shelve them in a *pianissimo* manner, and set about hatching new
ones to take their place. But constructive criticism irritates me. I
do not object to being denounced, but I can't abide being school-
mastered, especially by men I regard as imbeciles.

I find, as a practicing critic, that very few men who write books
are even as tolerant as I am—that most of them, soon or late, show
signs of extreme discomfort under criticism, however polite its terms.
Perhaps this is why enduring friendships between authors and critics
are so rare. All artists, of course, dislike one another more or less,
but that dislike seldom rises to implacable enmity, save between
opera singer and opera singer, and creative author and critic. Even
when the latter two keep up an outward show of good-will, there is
always bitter antagonism under the surface. Part of it, I daresay,
arises out of the impossible demands of the critic, particularly if he
be tinged with the constructive madness. Having favored an author
with his good opinion, he expects the poor fellow to live up to that
good opinion without the slightest compromise or faltering, and this
is commonly beyond human power. He feels that any let-down com-
promises *him*—that his hero is stabbing him in the back, and making
him ridiculous—and this feeling rasps his vanity. The most bitter of
all literary quarrels are those between critics and creative artists, and
most of them arise in just this way. As for the creative artist, he on
his part naturally resents the critic's air of pedagogical superiority
and he resents it especially when he has an uneasy feeling that he
has fallen short of his best work, and that the discontent of the
critic is thus justified. Injustice is relatively easy to bear; what
stings is justice. Under it all, of course, lurks the fact that I began
with: the fact that the critic is himself an artist, and that his creative
impulse, soon or late, is bound to make him neglect the punctilio.
When he sits down to compose his criticism, his artist ceases to be a
friend, and becomes mere raw material for his work of art. It is
my experience that artists invariably resent this cavalier use of
them. They are pleased so long as the critic confines himself to the
modest business of interpreting them—preferably in terms of their
own estimate of themselves—but the moment he proceeds to adorn
their theme with variations of his own, the moment he brings new
ideas to the enterprise and begins contrasting them with their ideas,
that moment they grow restive. It is precisely at this point, of course,
that criticism becomes genuine criticism; before that it was mere

reviewing. When a critic passes it he loses his friends. By becoming an artist, he becomes the foe of all other artists.

But the transformation, I believe, has good effects upon him: it makes him a better critic. Too much *Gemütlichkeit* is as fatal to criticism as it would be to surgery or politics. When it rages unimpeded it leads inevitably either to a dull professorial sticking on of meaningless labels or to log-rolling, and often it leads to both. One of the most hopeful symptoms of the new *Aufklärung* in the Republic is the revival of acrimony in criticism—the renaissance of the doctrine that aesthetic matters are important, and that it is worth the while of a healthy male to take them seriously, as he takes business, sport and amour. In the days when American literature was showing its first vigorous growth, the native criticism was extraordinarily violent and even vicious; in the days when American literature swooned upon the tomb of the Puritan *Kultur* it became flaccid and childish. The typical critic of the first era was Poe, as the typical critic of the second was Howells. Poe carried on his critical jehads with such ferocity that he often got into law-suits, and sometimes ran no little risk of having his head cracked. He regarded literary questions as exigent and momentous. The lofty aloofness of the don was simply not in him. When he encountered a book that seemed to him to be bad, he attacked it almost as sharply as a Chamber of Commerce would attack a fanatic preaching free speech, or the corporation of Trinity Church would attack Christ. His opponents replied in the same Berserker manner. Much of Poe's surviving ill-fame, as a drunkard and dead-beat, is due to their inordinate denunciations of him. They were not content to refute him; they constantly tried to dispose of him altogether. The very ferocity of that ancient row shows that the native literature, in those days, was in a healthy state. Books of genuine value were produced. Literature always thrives best, in fact, in an atmosphere of hearty strife. Poe, surrounded by admiring professors, never challenged, never aroused to the emotions of revolt, would probably have written poetry indistinguishable from the hollow stuff of, say, Prof. Dr. George E. Woodberry. It took the persistent (and often grossly unfair and dishonorable) opposition of Griswold *et al* to stimulate him to his highest endeavors. He needed friends, true enough, but he also needed enemies.

To-day, for the first time in years, there is strife in American criticism, and the Paul Elmer Mores and Hamilton Wright Mabies are no longer able to purr in peace. The instant they fall into stiff professorial attitudes they are challenged, and often with anything but urbanity. The *ex cathedra* manner thus passes out, and free discussion comes in. Heretics lay on boldly, and the professors are forced to make some defense. Often, going further, they attempt counter-attacks. Ears are bitten off. Noses are bloodied. There are wallops both above and below the belt. I am, I need not say, no believer in any magical merit in debate, no matter how free it may be. It certainly does not necessarily establish the truth; both sides, in fact, may be wrong, and they often are. But it at least accomplishes two important effects. On the one hand, it exposes all the cruder fallacies to hostile examination, and so disposes of many of them. And on the other hand, it melodramatizes the business of the critic, and so convinces thousands of bystanders, otherwise quite inert, that criticism is an amusing and instructive art, and that the problems it deals with are important. What men will fight for seems to be worth looking into.

# LUDWIG LEWISOHN
## (1883–1955)


BORN in Berlin, on May 30, 1883, Ludwig Lewisohn came to the United States in 1890. His parents settled in South Carolina. After graduating from the College of Charleston in 1901, he attended Columbia University, which awarded him a master's degree in 1903. He left Columbia without revising his dissertation for the doctorate, and entered upon editorial work and free-lance writing. In 1910 he secured a position teaching German at the University of Wisconsin. From 1911 to 1919 he was a member of the German Department at Ohio State University. After coming to New York he took up editorial work on the staff of *The Nation* in 1919, becoming for a time its dramatic critic. He lived abroad for a period of ten years. Of late he has been actively identified with the Zionist movement.

Lewisohn is a scholar, a creative critic, a scrupulous craftsman whose work is informed with high seriousness and moral passion. His books, he maintains, are not the expression of purely literary opinions but personal confessions rendered in more or less objective terms, weapons used in the unending struggle of life. The function of the critic, like that of the poet, is to save mankind. In his criticism as in his novels, Lewisohn has been consistently autobiographical. This is an intrinsic and inescapable part of his method. The truths he has discovered in his own mind he seeks to pass on to mankind. In 1915 appeared his first book, *The Modern Drama, An Essay in Interpretation,* an attempt to evaluate the dramatic contributions of France, Germany, and England during the last three decades. Then Lewisohn was commissioned to edit the plays of Gerhart Hauptmann, translating sixteen of the twenty-eight in the collection. *The Spirit of Modern German Literature* (1916), which consists of lectures delivered at the University of Wisconsin, helped to advance his reputation as a scholar and critic. Judicial canons, he feels, need no longer be employed in the serious appraisal of books. For art is born of an impassioned experience of life, and what the critic needs is, not historical erudition or fixed rules but a deep feeling for the inherent quality of life, a sensitive and exact perception of beauty.

In 1919 Lewisohn edited *A Modern Book of Criticism,* which gave him an opportunity to drive home, both by precept and example, the critical ideas and ideals in which he believed. Criticism was no genteel, elegant diversion but a preoccupation with those profound and eternal forces which control the life of man. Denying the truth of the Humanist position, he declares ringingly:

"For I love beauty in all its forms and find life tragic and worthy of my sympathy in every manifestation. I need no hierarchical moral world for my dwelling-place, because I desire neither to judge nor to condemn. Fixed standards are useless to him whose central passion is to have men free."[1]

In *Up Stream* (1922) Lewisohn wrote the history of his struggle to gain academic and literary recognition. *The Drama and the Stage* (1922) is an example of Lewisohn's prose at its best. For him the theatre, like poetry, like all literature, has the primary liberating function of serving and saving mankind. This is the method of all art, realistic or romantic. Just as the dramatist communicates his vision of life, so the dramatic critic in discussing plays uncovers the drama of his own mind. *The Creative Life* (1924), a collection of essays from the files of *The Nation,* rises above the level of the journalistic by virtue of its direct communication of passion and faith. Lewisohn's glorification of the creative life, in its necessary revolt against materialism and the deadening influence of an industrial environment, the opposition he sets up between the artist as seeker and the complacent bourgeois ensconced in his office, the contrast drawn between the ideal of personal freedom and the calloused morality of the business world—these still strike home, but they are now history, not prophecy.

Lewisohn's development as a critic was fundamentally changed by his conversion to Judaism. Slowly it dawned upon him that only by spiritual solidarity with his people could he work out his personal salvation. *Mid-Channel* (1929) records the various stages of his spiritual wayfaring and how he came at last to the conviction that the Jews must not renounce their racial heritage but become the spokesmen of their folk. A book of essays containing literary criticism, impressions of travel, and personal reminiscences, *Cities and Men* (1927) again stresses the need for leading the creative life. He announces that he is a romanticist in his insistence on speaking out freely, but a classicist in his recognition of the need for re-

---

[1] Ludwig Lewisohn (ed.), *A Modern Book of Criticism* (New York, 1919), p. iii.

interpreting the funded experience of the past. *Expression in America* (1932) is Lewisohn's magnum opus. In it he not only formulates his critical principles but applies them boldly, sometimes dogmatically, to the body of American literature. He relies not only on the aesthetic canons of vitality and creative force but also on the psychological criteria borrowed from the writings of Sigmund Freud.

Literature, Lewisohn declares, is expression. The writer, if his work is to endure, must body forth a world that is complete and convincing, beautiful and true. Since art is the expression of the totality of the writer's being in its relation to humanity and the cosmos, the ultimate result of that expression must necessarily be moral. Art is thus fundamentally a criticism of life. And criticism is far more than a report on the contents of a book or a formal yardstick for measuring its literary merit. It reaches to the heart of life and thought; it involves the whole man.

When in the thirties the center of interest shifted from the life creative to the life political and economic, Lewisohn did not ignore the challenge. In *The Permanent Horizon* (1934), his moral sublimity makes itself felt not only in his earnestness and emphasis of tone but also in his tendency to anathemize all those who do not subscribe to his views. As a disciple of Freud, and for other reasons as well, Lewisohn cannot accept the economic interpretation of life and literature advanced by the Marxists. If our civilization is riddled with ugly evils, they can be eliminated by rational means, without resort to fratricidal conflict. For society is not an economically determined mechanism. Man is himself a determining factor.

Lewisohn endeavors to communicate what he considers unimpeachable and eternal truths; his mission, he feels, is to redeem and preserve those immemorial virtues of freedom and justice which constitute the good life. It is easy to deride this Faustian mission, but it is silly and decidedly unfair to label him a reactionary. Like Krutch and Mumford, he is a sincere and gifted liberal who will not surrender his faith in those saving principles —freedom of thought and conscience and expression, the integrity of the individual soul, the need for intelligent thinking and the practice of social justice—which he has inherited from the great liberal thinkers of the past. He calls for the emergence of a neo-idealistic literature, attacking materialism, economic determinism, mechanism, and causality.

BIBLIOGRAPHY

TEXT

*German Style.* New York, 1910.
*The Modern Drama.* New York, 1915.

*The Spirit of Modern German Literature*. New York, 1916.
*The Poets of Modern France*. New York, 1918.
(ed.), *A Modern Book of Criticism*. New York, 1919.
*The Drama and the Stage*. New York, 1922.
*Up Stream*. New York, 1922.
*The Creative Life*. New York, 1924.
*Cities and Men*. New York, 1927.
*Mid-Channel*. New York, 1929.
*Expression in America*. New York, 1932.
*The Permanent Horizon*. New York, 1934.
*The Magic Word*. New York, 1950.

### CRITICISM

Brande, Dorothea, "Mr. Lewisohn Interprets America," *American Review*, II, 189–198 (December, 1933).
Cestre, Charles, "Une grande histoire philosophique de la littérature américaine," *Revue Anglo-Américaine*, XII, 302–317 (1935).
Gillis, Adolph, *Ludwig Lewisohn*. New York, 1933.
Goldberg, Isaac, "Ludwig Backstream Lewisohn," *American Spectator*, II, 13–14 (October, 1936).
Mersand, Joseph, *Traditions in American Literature*. New York, 1939.
Sherman, Stuart P., *Americans*. New York, 1922.
Wise, James Waterman, *Jews Are Like That*. New York, 1928.

## CREATIVE CRITICISM*

WE are witnessing a new battle of the books. Well-armed champions take the field; armor gleams in the sunlight; now and then speeds a poisoned dart. To the natural man, who lives by his passions rather than by his reason, there is something agreeable even in this bloodless fray. The traditionalist who is busy rationalizing his emotional life is hopelessly engaged in it. The liberal, on the contrary, who is sworn to the service of reason, must recall with Bacon that "where there is so much controversy, there is many times little inquiry," and address himself steadily to the latter task.

The first object of such inquiry must be the character of the traditionalist himself. He is one in whom a set of æsthetic perceptions has become interwoven with ancestral pieties. Thus his opinions

* From *The Creative Life* by Ludwig Lewisohn, published by Liveright, copyright 1924, Boni and Liveright, Inc.

are, as Johnson put it, "so complicated with his natural affections
that they cannot easily be disentangled from the heart." He loves the
ivied wall, the studious cloister, the cadence of great verses heard
in youth. His heart is tenacious and betrays him into believing only
the familiar to be beautiful and only the customary to be true. He
can sustain the harmony of his inner life only by vast exclusions. As
the world grows more turbulent and surges nearer to his quiet
threshold, he begins to fear for his inner security and becomes
petulant and bitter. He is convinced that he stands for noble things.
And subjectively he is quite right. Only, in the world of reality the
noble traditions which he loves and guards have gone down to ir-
revocable defeat. Thus as a humanist he loves his country. "Dulce
et decorum est pro patria mori." By means of a poetic tradition he
excludes from his consciousness the sordidness and tyranny of the
state. At crucial historic moments he, like the great leaders of his
caste, Gilbert Murray and Wilamowitz-Möllendorf, thinks not of
economic facts but of Latin verses and Greek examples and suc-
cumbs to the shame of hatred and intolerance. He does not see that
the restraints and conformities he councils by the light of his tradition are inextricable from the false idealisms of war and slavery
amid which they arose, and that the variety and unbridled multi-
formity he holds to be barbarous have some small chance, at least,
of giving mankind both liberty and peace. He fixes his vision upon
a beautiful campus or a stately ceremonial and will not yield to the
aching consciousness of slum and trench. He lives in an ideal realm
of images and values where the disastrous cries of the world cannot
reach him, and the speech of those who seek a contact with the wild
totality of things sounds harsh and strident to his ear.

In every country he is, of course, an impassioned though decorous
nationalist, eager to preserve the traditions that have shaped his
people's spiritual life. In America he is hard put to it. The great
voices in our brief national past are few and they do not speak on
his side. Emerson understood his emotional basis and disposed of
it in one sharp sentence: "Once you saw phœnixes; they are gone;
the world is not therefore disenchanted." "The philosophy we want,"
Emerson continued, "is one of fluxions and mobility." Accordingly
he declared that "the quality of the imagination is to flow and not
to freeze," and that, above all, "the value of genius to us is in the
veracity of its report." Nor did he spare our traditionalist in the
sacred citadel of the personal life. "In this great society wide lying
around us, a critical analysis would find very few spontaneous ac-

tions. It is almost all custom and gross sense." Is it not precisely this custom and gross sense that our contemporary traditionalist defends in the name of phœnixes that are gone? It is, assuredly, the spontaneous and liberating action that he dreads. Whitman, "sworn poet of every dauntless rebel the world over," will give him even smaller comfort. "He going with me leaves peace and routine behind him." Whitman's request was the quest of naked reality "even in defeat, misconception, and imprisonment—for they too are great." At last the traditionalist turns to Mark Twain to meet an even ruder repudiation: "I think a man's first duty is to his honor. Not to his country and not to his party." And yet more cruelly: "Each person in the human race is honest in one of several ways, but no member of it is honest in all the ways required by—by what? By his own standard. Outside of that, as I look at it, there is no obligation upon him." Mark Twain, it is clear, had pierced the fallacy of selective sympathies, of living by exclusions, and had solved the problem of toleration by understanding that the truth of human action is found within the soul. It is the holding of moral absolutes, he declared, and their imposition on others that is the cause of every injustice and cruelty in the world. "Truth is good manners; manners are a fiction."

Our American traditionalist, as a matter of fact, though he is perfectly sincere, uses the names of Emerson and Whitman and Mark Twain in a slightly decorative fashion. His heart is elsewhere. It is with the Puritan tradition against which each of the three rebelled. It is with ancestral, not with insurgent voices. It is on the side of a spiritual frugality that has ended in meagerness, and of a moral code that has drained and enfeebled life. For it is not, one fears, of the heroic moment of Puritanism that he thinks, of the moment in history when Puritanism, too, was a force of liberation and revolt. That moment is embodied in the author of the "Areopagitica" and him our traditionalist in reality belittles and betrays. He appeals to the Pilgrim Fathers. And it is true that they came to find liberty for themselves. But the liberty they sought was indeed a selective ideal and included the liberty to burn witches and scourge Quakers. Bradford's name is an ominous one to which to appeal in the modern world. There were those, we are told in "New England's Memorial," who "pretended a great zeal for liberty of conscience, but endeavored to introduce such a liberty of will as would have proved prejudicial, if not destructive, to civil and church societies." And to these were added "many of that pernicious sect called Quakers, whose opinions are a composition of many errors." That has a curiously contemporary sound and flavor. It might have been written into the resolutions of defense committees or the promulgations of censors. Yet in his innermost mind our traditionalist clings to that spirit. He defends it and identifies it with the spirit of our national life. And, in a sense, it has unhappily become so. We live by Bradford rather than by Emerson and sedulously cultivate a civilization which Matthew Arnold called "the very lowest form of intelligential life which one can imagine as saving." It is our Puritan cities and countrysides that might well have wrung from him the cry: "Can any life be imagined more dismal, more hideous, more unenviable?" It is Arnold's perception that liberal American criticism shares; it is his task that we seek here to accomplish. The world has changed; the philosophical background of our effort is not quite his. But our aim is his own, the aim "of making human life, hampered by a past it has outgrown, natural and rational."

To accomplish this aim the American spirit must be liberated for a new contact with reality. The anterior assumptions of the Puritan tradition must be broken down. The light of a free criticism must be turned on values that no longer work. The creative spirit in literature and life arises invariably from an immediate relation to the undistorted nature of things. No traditionalist has ever founded a tradition, though he may, like Dante, sum one up. The home of human civilization is not in any given set of forms but in the mind itself. It is the undue hardening of particular forms that threatens recurrently to destroy it. "We want a ship in these billows we inhabit!" Emerson exclaims. "An angular, dogmatic house would be rent to chips and splinters." The house has been rent. Our conservative critics huddle in its damp chambers trying to mend the roof. They have, as always in such periods, the support of the official forces of society. Yet that very fact should give the nobler of them pause. When have the forces of the world ever befriended the forces of the spirit? Meanwhile the liberal critic pursues his task. Like the modern poet he seeks, as Arnold said of Goethe, "to interpret human life afresh and to supply a new spiritual basis for it." It is not an easy task in a slothful and intolerant world; it is hard that spirits caught in a web of their own emotions should join powers with whom they have in reality nothing in common, and cast the first stone.

Those whom their friends at times and their enemies more frequently call "the younger intellectuals" have not always armored themselves either wisely or sufficiently against inevitable jibes and darts. Protesting against the painful tightness of an over-regimented

society, they have been accused of wanting to run amuck; repudiating dead tradition, they have had flung at them the supposedly
withering words of promiscuity and license. In these final retorts
there lurks a fallacy which a schoolboy ought to be able to discover.
But most of us are mere nominalists; ugly words seem to fill us with
awe; they seem suddenly to rise before us like walls we cannot scale.
Thus kindly and by no means stupid people have been permitted to
suppose that certain blameless literary gentlemen in our midst wreck
homes before breakfast and use no beverage but gin.

The popular fallacy which the younger intellectuals have not
guarded against is that it is possible to act without choice simply
because you are tired of one particular and monotonous choice. What
the Elder Critics have, in effect, said to them is strictly analogous to
this: "What, you will not eat the wholesome and manly porridge of
our ancestors? No doubt you feed on babies' bones." And the readers
of the conservative press echo: "They feed on babies' bones." The
younger intellectuals have airily forgotten to answer: "But, dear
people, there is cream of wheat and wheatena and hominy and corn-
flakes and puffed rice and new things yet uninvented. It is you who
are coarse; it is you who exercise no choice and are therefore promis-
cuous; it is we who are fastidious and selective and delicate and
conscientious and austere. You speak of us as undisciplined. You do
not know what discipline is. To narrow the possible choices of life
is to eliminate discipline more and more. Your true conservatives are
the animals whose habits know no change in a thousand generations.
They practice no discipline, for they need none."

The familiar line from Wordsworth's "Ode to Duty" will make
the point quite clear. "Me," wrote the poet with that inversion which
now seems quainter to us than it should, "me this uncharter'd freedom tires." Now a wholly unchartered freedom is, of course, not
possible to a man who is neither drunk nor mad. All sane human
action is motivated and into its motivation enter not only desire but
moral and aesthetic preferences, economic urges and repressions,
social loves and fears. The sum of such motives is the charter of a
given action. What the Elder Critics, without quite daring to say it,
have meant is that there is but one charter for civilized action. Experience contradicts this flatly, and what the younger intellectuals
have tried to do is to seek within experience new, more liberal, more
gracious charters according to which men may live. Far from repudiating self-discipline they have insisted upon the necessity of its
exercise. What they have disliked is herd-discipline masquerading as

self-discipline and the mechanical adherence to charters that do not arise from the needs of the soul.

For the sources of our charters of action, for the shaping of beautiful motives, they have gone to a rational culture. For it is the precise virtue of culture that it makes for high and fastidious choice in both art and life and yet gives free play to personality and prevents the individual from lapsing into the herd unit. Thus they have, as their accusers have never tired of saying, talked a great deal about the self. They have not meant an undisciplined self; they have meant a self that draws the powers of its discipline from within, that chooses its duties, creates its charter, and thus can never lose that moral harmony and freshness of impulse without which the fairest-seeming actions have no true virtue at their core. Even as artists who survey the same scenes and actions will weave them into utterly different yet equally beautiful works, so, upon this view, the same material will be shaped into many kinds of life—all beautiful, all moral, all disciplined, each exercising its freedom according to a charter which itself has found.

The critic's character, like the poet's, has undergone many transformations in the course of time. During long ages the didactic notion of the critic prevailed, and learned and self-satisfied men cling to it still. According to this notion, which commends itself easily to superficial thinking, the critic is an expert in fixed rules by which art is to be judged. He handles standards, both moral and aesthetic, very much as a draper does his yardstick. No subtlety of learning or refinement of reasoning changes the character of the didactic critic to whose gigantic futility the history of his craft bears eloquent witness. His anterior assumptions always invalidated his judgments, and his divine yardstick turned out to be the weapon of his angry prejudices. The scientific critic, a type that flourished mightily but briefly, is both more amiable and less pretentious. But he is the victim of an analogy of deadly falseness. You can classify phenomena that are identical—moons, beetles, rocks. You cannot classify phenomena that are unique. There is no "évolution des genres" because, closely looked upon, there are no "genres." There are only individuals expressing their personal sense of life in art; and there are the imitators of these individuals who do not count.

The impressionists were fully aware of the sterility of both the didactic and the scientific methods. They sought to disengage the peculiar aroma of books and pictures and, being frankly subjective, produced many pages of beautiful creative literature. But they restricted themselves a little narrowly to æsthetic considerations and, conscious always of their reaction against the older schools, hesitated to assume the critical functions which they had seen so absurdly exercised. A gentle pessimism haunts all their books, and the elegiac sense of the passing of a world from which their own souls were not yet wholly estranged. If Sainte-Beuve wrote "the natural history of minds," the impressionists clung timidly to the history of their own minds. They paid homage to the dead rules of criticism by not daring to proceed without them beyond the autumnal gardens of their own souls.

It is at this point that the modern critic parts company with the masters whom he has loved and from whom he has learned so much. His is a hardier and a cooler nature. Skepticism does not wound his heart and the perception of change leaves him quite untroubled. He has shifted his whole point of vision and has no inner or outer need of any comfortable absolutes. For he sees art as an integral part of the life-process, as the life-process itself growing articulate through chosen personalities. That it should do so at all, that life should speak in terms of beauty—this is to him the central and sufficient fact which satisfies the "idealistic" cravings of his mind. Beauty exists—there is his heartening and transcendent truth. In beauty he admits differences of method, of growth, and degrees of intensity; he admits no moralistic qualifications of better or worse, higher or lower, through the choice of one sort of subject matter rather than another or one technique of expression rather than another. Veracity of substance and intensity of expression are his sole tests. He may privately entertain the opinion that certain kinds of subjects and certain technical methods have actually made for veracity and intensity more often than others. But he is eager to have that opinion refuted and the realm of beauty thus enlarged. He knows nothing of a beauty that is wrong or immoral. He knows, negatively, only the false or the feeble expression that misses its own inherent aim through disloyalty to experience or through failure in articulateness. Wherever deep experience attains intense expression, there is art.

This critic, like the poet, is born and can hardly be made. The reading of many books will help him little unless he has the sense of life, unless its throb comes to him even through alien speech and remote forms. No partisanship must curb his humanity, no prejudice blunt the sensitiveness of his spirit. He must be himself a seeker after beauty, after the expression that makes life luminous and rich; he must be able to identify his own self with men and things. And he must be sensitive to the general drift of the many lives that make the world, and neither expect romantic expansiveness in small and rigid societies nor the severities of classical synthesis in an age of democratic revolution. He must share imaginatively the life of other periods and very practically that of his own. The passions of its freest minds must be his also, though at the core he may always keep a touch of coolness to save his inner processes from hardening even in the best of causes. His highest aim will always be to keep his perception of the relation of literature to life firm and unclouded, lest in the ardor of his personal seeking he fall into the old error of condemning passions he does not share or opinions to which he is hostile. All life must be his province. If it is, he cannot go far wrong in his dealings with art. If he has been, directly or vicariously, a part of all human experience, the expression of no form of it can startle or befog his mind.

His function in modern society is a grave and arduous one. He must constantly reinterpret the past for the uses of the present, in order that it may contribute to the creation of that cultural atmosphere which is his final practical aim. Thus he will illustrate the continuity and oneness of art as the expression of life, and thus establish at once the validity and use of the art of his own contemporaries. This art he will be careful to interpret in relation to the vital forces from which it springs, in order that by its reaction on its audience it may serve to establish the cultural environment within which the experience of individuals can be most free and rich. None will be more acutely aware of this interaction between art and life than himself, or do more to clarify it and make it effectual. The expression of life in art reacts on life. Poets create new moods in love for their hearers; dramatists have altered the structure of society. It will be the critic's task to heighten and increase this enrichment and liberation of life. He will seek to make art, which expresses life, re-enter life through the sharpened senses of all capable of receiving its impressions.

The virtue of this program of the modern critic is that it translates the severest spiritual efforts into direct social action, and yet leaves him serene and detached. To free souls through the ministry of art, to create an atmosphere in which that freedom may be exercised and art itself may thrive—these are the ends for which he will unceasingly labor. The purely æsthetic has not lost its magic or its glow for him. But it needs no nursing. It will appear whenever the source of art, which is experience, is kept untrammeled, strong, and full.

The notion of a necessary connection between the critical and the creative functions has rarely been entertained in America. Our older critics and historians of literature made it a vigorous custom to mention none but the dead and gave their struggling contemporaries the barren consolation that posterity would be just. This custom was wholly derived from England. In France and Germany the danger has often been the contrary one and critical theory has, during many periods, shot beyond creative practice. Today the makers of a vigorous young literature among us turn to criticism a not unhopeful if not wholly trusting eye. They are often touchingly humble. Their very crudities and imperfections constitute a silent question. What answer do they receive?

From the group of critics which, by a strange irony, is the self-appointed guardian of the national shrine, they meet with irritated repudiation. They should not be what they are. The frank absurdity of such an attempt to stop the cosmic processes with a monkey-wrench renders it negligible. But other and wiser and more liberal voices do not often present to the poet, the novelist, the playwright, a more fruitful message. They are sympathetic, they are benignant. Their councils, however, can be summed up in the Horatian maxim to turn over the great Greek exemplars by night and by day. And they are impelled toward a certain insistence on this point because one or two of the very liberal critics to whom our younger men of letters actually turn, do not, in fact, make enough of the classics and seem themselves often at the mercy of tempestuous prejudices and perverse moods. Thus one, with all the resources of his energetic mind and athletic style, announced but the other day that poetry must always be puerile because it is neither as intellectual as prose nor as abstractly emotional as music.

The advice to turn to the classics is, clearly, healthier and more saving than that. But it must not be given in the spirit of the rhetorician; it must not regard the classics as norms of practice but as examples of the creative spirit in action. There is the critic who is learned in the Homeric controversy and in the versification of Shakespeare as an historical test. It is not he who can make the classics seem either friendly or useful. But there is another critic who knows how, on a certain night at Tibur, the Falernian stung the palate of Horace and his friend Thaliarchus, who has shared the pang of Dante's heart when the vision of the living Beatrice Portinari had so shattered the poet that his friends feared for his life, who has caroused with the young Shakespeare and Falstaff and their friends at some gabled tavern, who has been with Goethe at Sesenheim and in Venice and has dreamed with Shelley of the liberation of mankind and worshiped Emilia Viviani at her convent gate. This critic understands how such experiences grew into the works of art that express and commemorate them. He has lived with the classics and looked into his own heart and has mastered the character of the creative process itself. It is by virtue of this knowledge that he can guide others in the transmutation of life into art, in both the freedom and the self-discipline that are involved, in the realization of their personalities through an expression that shall have a timeless accent, in the embodiment of their unique and necessary aims.

The artist, then, should be taught to live with the classics. But he should live with them in order, if possible, to become a classic in his turn. And often he can live with them best by imitating their example but neglecting their works. "Nous voulons la beauté nouvelle!" exclaims a remarkable young French poet. In order to be like the classics he repudiates them. To him as to them the world is new and beautiful and tragic and inexpressibly his own. This day and its experiences are his; this morning is the beginning of the world.

> Et si je danse sur les tombes
> C'est pour que la beauté du monde
> Soit neuve en moi tous les matins!

It is this living spirit of the freedom of all great and original literature that our critic will seek to communicate to his contemporaries. His understanding of it will also guide him in his opinions of work accomplished. Amid the heavy standardization of thought and taste and ethical reaction that often weighs so heavily on our national life, he will guard and direct every precious flicker of personality and never tire of driving home the force of Goethe's maxim:

> Ursprünglich eignen Sinn
> Lass dir nicht rauben!
> Woran die Menge glaubt
> Ist leicht zu glauben!

But he will never lose sight of that creative process by which alone such originality of vision can become art. There must be, not this or that form, but form; not this or that technique, but organization. For raw experience is meaningless save to him who has felt it. Art is communication. Its symbols must be both concrete and universal. It speaks for one, but its voice must reach mankind.

"If, then," the professor said, stroking his beard unquietly, "if, then, you allow no standards or certain tests by which the worth of a piece of literature can be established, how are we either to learn or to teach? What are we to study and what are we to transmit as of assured fruitfulness and value?"

"You are, if I may say so," the critic answered thoughtfully, "too proud and too humble at once. You are too proud because you are afraid to spend your time on anything except the perfect and the permanent; you are too humble because you will not let yourself realize that by the exercise of the thought and sensibilities of just such men as you the perfect and permanent is established, is, I had almost said, created."

The professor shook his head. "You go fast. Take up your two points separately. Life is short and feverish. It is not pride that forbids us spending our time on anything but the best."

"The best," the critic repeated slowly. "You work with such hard concepts. There are, I think, several kinds of best. There is, of the one kind, the Pharmaceutria of Vergil. The hexameters are beautiful and liquid beyond description. But as you hear their music you are also a little flattered and sustained in your favorite moods by knowing that it has sounded across so many centuries. You recall, too, that Macaulay thought a certain passage in the poem the loveliest and most loving in Latin poetry. And it is, indeed, charming in itself. But some of its charm is also in the very antiquity of that little lad who sighed for his sweetheart in the orchard. And is not mere antiquity in itself, quite like novelty in itself, an adventitious source of interest though, I should grant you at once, by far the nobler?"

The professor smiled. "Your psychology is sound even if it is a little like prying. But I am curious to hear about your other kind of best."

"Let us suppose," the critic said, "that a novel appears with a style and form of but mediocre quality and also, so far as we can see, with little chance of being remembered for many years to come. But let us suppose, further—for it happens every year—that this novel renders and thus clarifies some vital and widespread experience of the men and women who live today so accurately and so closely that life itself is a little changed and its difficulty a little mitigated—would you not recognize there, too, a value of the best kind?"

"But what has it to do with art?" the professor asked.

"Nothing, if you limit art to a few simple gestures permanently molded. But the majority of men are not connoisseurs of such beauty. Life is, as you said, short and feverish. They do not want to die before they have learned to live."

"Are the classics barren in that respect?"

"No, but insufficient. 'Non omnia possumus omnes.' How true but how cold and general. Also, it is didactic—a maxim pronounced from without. We need experience more than maxims."

The professor shook his head. "It seems to me that we began by talking about one thing and are now talking about another. I am acquainted with the modern doctrine of art as expression. I understand it though it means little to me. On the basis of it I am not unwilling to grant you an excellence in literature made up of such elements as you have described. I still desire to know how, without norms or standards, we are to recognize among the works of this or any age those that will be permanent because their beauty will be, like the beauty of the Pharmaceutria, permanently persuasive to the souls of men."

"You want," the critic said, choosing his words carefully, "a recognition before the fact which cannot come because it is not born until after the fact. The friends of Vergil by believing in the permanence of his poem began to create it. Their equals in sensitiveness and insight approved that judgment in generation after generation. Separately these judgments were subjective and independent of external norms in every instance. Collectively, however, the agreement of so many identical subjective reactions over so long a period of time came to constitute the only kind of objectivity we know at all. I said you were too humble and I meant that you will not take toward some contemporary work the attitude that Vergil's friends took and so begin the creation of that permanence in beauty which you crave."

"But suppose I have not their good fortune and my subjective decision is reversed?"

The critic smiled. "The extremes of humility and pride are one," he said. "You are too humble to judge because you are too proud to take the chance of having judged wrongly. You want the safeguard of standards in order to avoid the risks of human fate."

"I do not admit your picture of human fate," the professor cried, "as excluding the recognizably transcendent and eternal! Where are we to rest in this mad flux?"

"We are in it," the critic said sadly. "No shore is visible. I refuse to suppose a shore because I am weary at moments. Life and art create their values from within. Here or nowhere is eternity."

The professor arose. "I refuse to live in such a world!"

The critic smiled again. "That is an old and frequent cry. Your classics have not taught you their great lesson of resignation. But that cry grants my case. I, at least, have a chance of being more useful than you who ask for a moon you do not even see."

"It is better to ask for a moon that does not exist than to consent to a moonless world."

"Ah, you idealists," the critic said, "you offer a fine and heroic spectacle for us in our leisure hours. But we who are meek do the work that needs to be done upon the earth and perhaps we shall, as it was foretold of us, inherit it after all."

The Very Young Critic was vexed. "With all possible respect," he said, "I don't see that all your talk about Plato and the consensus of mankind and the great moral tradition gets you anywhere. You wouldn't be reading Plato himself if he hadn't been such a charming writer. And in his most charming thing 'The Banquet' there are both incidents and doctrines that, well—they don't exactly fit into your scheme."

The Graybeard smiled. "I was aware that you had probably read nothing of Plato except 'The Banquet' and that probably again in the version and interpretation of Shelley. The fact remains that man is distinguished from the brutes by having built up a spiritual universe of values and traditions and ideals within this sensible world. That is the City of God in which Sophocles and Plato, Dante and Shakespeare are the rulers. There is beauty enough in that city. But that beauty is the expression of the highest aspirations of the race. To be disloyal to those aspirations is to tear down the walls of the city which noble spirits in many centuries have built against the winds of paganism and license and degradation and despair."

The Very Young Critic who limped a little when he walked had a rather flippant expression. "I notice that your walls didn't keep out the war. That was some example of degradation and despair!"

"To those who didn't grasp its purpose and meaning!" The Graybeard grew a little red in the face. "Of course, if I'm talking to a pacifist or a pro-German . . ."

"Not at all," said the Very Young Critic, "though I confess your City seemed a little queer with Goethe out of it. I'm fed up on both the war and its consequences. The whole thing seems pretty rotten. And one can't help noticing that the moral old gentlemen got us into the great mess and can't get us out. That's one big reason why I repudiate, so far as art goes, the expression of moral values. Such expression is futile. Beauty is the absolute good, a beauty that is, so far as possible, remote from the muddle of practical things. It's their concern with that muddle which ruined Shaw and Wells. An exquisite, abstract pattern is the same yesterday, today, and forever."

The Graybeard could contain himself no longer. "Young man," he said, "that's twaddle. We heard that twaddle in the nineties. Where are those twaddlers now? How did Oscar Wilde end?"

The Critic of Forty had been listening patiently. "I don't like to see you two quarreling," he said at last, "because there's no fundamental difference between you."

"Oh, isn't there though!" the Very Young Critic chirped. The Graybeard smiled his disdain.

"Why, no," said the Critic of Forty. "You're like two people in a ship. The ship is on the rocks; her bottom's fouled; her sails are rags and her masts in splinters. Most of the passengers are dead, the rest and the crew are rotten with scurvy. You two happened to be in the first cabin and happened to have private supplies. So you talk. One of you," he turned to the Graybeard, "says: 'This is the noble ship on which my fathers sailed. Their charts are as near an approach to absolute truth as man can reach. Let no one rock the boat. So long as we stick to this ship and these charts we are, at least, upholding the dignity that befits man, the traditions of our race and nation, and defeating the savagery of human nature.' And you," he grinned in the direction of the Very Young Critic, "reply: 'Well, things look bad but no doubt you're right. Let's fiddle a tune!'"

The Graybeard looked severe. "Parables and analogies are notoriously misleading. A skipper's charts may not be absolutely accurate. He'll do no better by throwing them overboard."

"It's not a question," the Critic of Forty said, "of tolerably inaccurate charts, but of such as are necessarily and demonstrably misleading. But I shall drop my analogy. To talk about a beautiful abstract pattern except in the arts of decoration is meaningless. Literature, at all events, since it deals with the actions and passions of men, must express both the values which men hold and live by and the author's attitude to those values which is, in turn, the necessary expression of his own. Hence literature can no more avoid moral and philosophical and even political and economic issues than a man can jump out of his skin."

The Graybeard looked benign. "Precisely," he said.

The Critic of Forty smiled. "Ah, but you're forgetting how I started. I agree with you that literature is practical and moral and I do not agree with our young friend, who doesn't really agree with himself, that it can be abstracted from morals and practice. But you mean one set of morals and one kind of practice. You are thinking of a set of morals long formulated and a kind of practice long agreed upon. And you want literature to illustrate these. You want, if you'll forgive my returning to my feeble illustration, to keep on poring over the old charts while the ship goes utterly to pieces and the rest of the passengers and the crew die in agony. That's not what I want. I want literature within its own field to coöperate with both the critical and creative movement by which the human intelligence must reconstruct the moral and practical basis of life, if life is to persist at all. We have followed the old charts. We have built up institutions and enacted codes and compelled obedience. And we are on the rocks. Two-thirds of mankind is sick in body. *All* of mankind is sick in soul. And one of you says: 'Let us go on precisely as before. At least we shall be moral and dignified.' And the other says: 'Let us have an agreeable time.' As though that were to be had for the wanting. Literature must go upon a voyage of discovery. It must immerse itself in a study of human nature as human nature really is; it must be uninhibited by such catch-words as 'license,' 'savagery,' 'dignity'; it must co-operate with the reason in discovering what is fit and beautiful for such a being as man in such a world as the present. That effort, unhampered by myth and superstition and the cold touch of the dead who knew less than we, has never been attempted. It is being made today. It is being made everywhere. But the new fiction in England and, especially in America, is our best example. These writers are intensely preoccupied with morality—"

The Graybeard snorted and arose. "With immorality you mean, sir! You talk like a Bolshevik!"

The Very Young Critic smiled sunnily. "No, only like a professor."

The Critic of Forty quoted something about "pectora cæca." His older friend reflected that a gentleman's education was often wasted; his younger coolly whistled.

It must have been some schoolman, in either the mediæval or the modern sense, or else an angry philologist, who first established the dichotomy—critical, creative. The man, whoever he was, did a great deal of harm and wasted the time of unborn generations. He fixed in the mind of the public the notion that the critic is, in the words of Dr. Johnson, a barren rascal, a man who has failed at art and so takes to the business of belaboring his betters. Hence it is but natural that from time to time, up to this very moment, the critics arise and protest that they are artists in their own right, that their function is a creative one, that neither Zoilus nor Gifford is their necessary prototype.

They invent fine and sound theories to prove their point. They declare that, as poets create men, so they create poets, that they establish cosmogonies, project visions, release passions. They are wroth and plaintive by turns. In their irritation they pour out their scorn over philologists and commentators and professors. They seem never to realize that their heat is superfluous, that the simplest appeal to the history of literature, to the history of criticism proves their point.

Perhaps they have been kept from making this appeal by what looks like a bad beginning. No one ever accused the father of criticism of verse or creative rapture. But Aristotle, we are to remember, was, like Hegel or Spencer, an encyclopedic philosopher who included a theory of the arts in his system. He was not, in the deeper and narrower sense, a critic. With him must be classed all the pure æstheticians who are dedicated to a philosophical discipline and not to literature at all.

So soon as we reach the critics proper all doubt disappears. We meet Horace whose "Epistola ad Pisones" had so long and finally so unhappy an influence; we meet Dante with his great treatise on the speech of the folk; we meet the first very great, fully equipped critic of the modern world in the person of John Dryden. In the eighteenth century our proofs multiply. Boileau was an eminent poet according to the standards of his period; so was Johnson; Lessing was dramatist, epigrammatist—in the sense of the ancients—and a creator of prose; Goethe was—Goethe. In the romantic and post-romantic periods the critics are all artist natures, all "diverse and undulating," all intense and visionary. We need but think of Cole-

ridge, Lamb, Hazlitt. The latter, the greatest of them, poured all his
creative ardor into critical form and established, more than anyone
else, the artistic independence of that form. Sainte Beuve was a true
poet even though the "Causeries" have overshadowed the "Poèsies
de Joseph Delorme," Lemaître a dramatist and writer of *contes*,
Gourmont a "maker" in every field. If we must omit Brunetière,
more scholastic philosopher than critic anyway, we are rewarded
by the names of Matthew Arnold, who will some day, perhaps, seem
the most lasting of the Victorian poets, of Walter Pater, that arduous
artist in prose who wrote the "Imaginary Portraits" and "Marius
the Epicurean," of quite minor contemporaries, such as Edmund
Gosse, whose verse is as felicitous as their critical prose. If we
desired merely to multiply names, there are Lowell and Poe, Andrew
Lang and Austin Dobson; there is an overshadowing one that we
have reserved for the last—the name of Anatole France.

It is evident, then, that criticism, like the lyric, the play, the
novel, is one of the various forms through which the creative temper
communicates its sense "of man, of nature, and of human life." Its
mood is often more cerebral than the moods of the other forms. But
even that is often more apparent than real, and there as passages in
Hazlitt and Heine, Pater and Lemaître that are as impassioned as a
lyric and as stirring as a drama, without ever abandoning the true
movement and method of critical form. We suspect, indeed, that
the cry, criticism is not creation, has come in the past and comes in
the present chiefly from critics who are not critics at all, from an-
notators of textbooks, academic *feuilletonistes* in newspapers and
popular magazines, from all those who, in the rude Carlylean phrase,
have no "fire in their belly," and are anxious to make that lack a
note of excellence in themselves and a mark of the craft to which
they pretend.

All our best writers jeer at the academicians. The pedagogue and
scholar—alas that the two are nearly always convertible terms—
must by this time be inured to contumely. Perhaps he bears it with
a grin; perhaps he bears it with indignation. It is certain that he has,
so far, not spoken very articulately in his own defense. At meetings
of scholars the matter is either not discussed, or else the scholars
seek escape by trying to evade their own characteristic function and
calling, and merge into the universally respected realms of the
practical and the efficient.

One must not be severe on them. The proper defense of learning is a difficult one in America today. Even before the war the holders of notable professorships, especially in the humanities, in history, literature, and philosophy, gained an unfortunate distinction. They defended the obviously outworn, celebrated the shoddy, closed their minds to the living humanities that were being reborn in the world about them. During the war there was here, as elsewhere, scarcely one saving voice among their ranks. Professors of German repudiated Goethe; professors of philosophy suddenly discovered that Kant was a vicious fellow; philologists were almost tempted to rename Grimm's law on the principle which, for some years, turned sauerkraut into Liberty Cabbage.

Today, then, the scholar has no friend. The liberal literati jeer, the really progressive students snicker, the public rests more firmly in its old, inane contempt. It is time for a protest, however gentle, to be raised; it is time for a reconsideration of the matter. Permanent and precious values are at stake. They, like all others, have been contaminated by the world, by ugly passions, by loud prejudices and sordid ambitions. They remain in their essential nature uninvalidated. Merely to sneer at pedagogues and dryasdusts is dangerous; it is dangerous to youth; it is in the last analysis dangerous to those living representatives of the humanities who have done it most.

Not all professors are hundred-percenters, not all professors are academic overlords. There are the academic helots—helots against their will and vision, helots through the weaknesses bred of their very strength. In every seat of learning there are those who love learning, who do pass their lives of poverty and renunciation of the world in study and reflection, who are in truth what they are meant to be, the memory of the race. Where are their fruits? it will be asked. These men are not often highly articulate; their products, "pickled away," in the words of a university wit, in the technical journals, do not make very alluring reading. Between "Babbitt" and the last book of Lytton Strachey it is not easy to become absorbed in a laboriously written article on the Old English Riddles, or variants on the last mystery transcribed in Paris, or an investigation of the relation of the pseudo-Vergilian poems to the style and temper of the poet's authentic works.

It is not easy. But if you closely consider these ill-written and perhaps dull pages, there arises the vision of lives that are austere and not ignoble, that the world has always needed and will always need, lives that are profitable to the salvation of us all. The scholar's study is shabby; his books are many, but there is no pomp of binding or of first editions; his table is in disorder; his papers are stained by the ashes of his pipe; there is a rag rug on the floor and the poor man has to sneak out now and then to "tend" the furnace so that his wife and children do not take cold. And yet, unless his salary is quite too pitifully small, he is usually a very cheerful mortal. Business does not allure him, nor common pleasures. He does not lust after power; he is neither epicure nor æsthete; the glories of this world seem little and remote to him. He loves truth so far as his vision can grasp it; he loves the ripe and permanent things in literature and thought; he seeks to add, however humbly, to the history and understanding of them. Yes, he tends to grow narrow, to love the "Æneid" less and his contribution to Vergilian exegesis more. Well, he is human. He doesn't hustle or boost; he is against the forces of bigness and jazz, against the temptation of mere actuality, immediacy, speed, and glitter. By all means let us scorn as loudly as we please the presidents and deans and glossy masters of the academic mart, and laugh out of countenance, if we can, the fashionable professors who praise seventh-rate uplift literature in the popular magazines. But let us not forget the shabby fellow with grizzled hair and slightly stooping shoulders, and slightly reeking pipe who spends his life with things beautiful and worthy of the mind of man, who, even while he is chatting with you, is seeing Chaucer on a summer's day or has just discovered precisely why, one rainy day at Tibur, Horace broke off in the middle of a verse, or is aglow with a new explanation—suggested, by Heaven, in neither Smelfungus nor Oberwellinghausen—of a strangely obscure passage toward the end of "Beowulf."

The learned who insist on being severely judicious even in their sprightly moods assure us that a reviewer of books can never be a critic. The reason they give us is not new. It is an academic commonplace; it has been promulgated as an axiom in a hundred classrooms and seminars. The reviewer, we are assured, cannot be a critic because the subject of his comment is the immediate and contemporary. Once more we are regaled with the quotation that the criticism of our contemporaries is only conversation and instructed that the entire history of the critic's craft bears out the argument to the utter rout of the reviewer.

But does it? Or are we facing a slightly petrified tradition? There are, at least, examples to give us pause. The judgment of contemporaries has not always been absurd nor has the perspective of time always saved mighty critics from terrible blunders. Take Ben Jonson on Shakespeare. Combine the two aspects of his judgment, the "would he had blotted a thousand" with "he was not of an age but for all time." Is that not sovereign and final—far more so than either the "inspired barbarian" theory of the Age of Reason or the undiscriminating idolatry of the Romantics? No one has bettered Goethe's estimate of Schiller; Johnson was far sounder on Pope than on Milton; Matthew Arnold was magnificent on Wordsworth whom he had known in the flesh and inconceivably mistaken on Shelley who died in the year of his birth. Jules Lemaître's "Les Contemporains" and Remy de Gourmont's "Livres des Masques" have all the marks of authentic criticism and permanent literature; even the severe and academic Brunetière wrote, not ineffectually or foolishly, on the novelists of his day.

But is there not, the academicians will ask—in the departments of English they will be thinking of Cowley, the stock or classical example—is there not an inevitable tendency to overestimate contemporary work? The answer will depend on the precise meaning of the word overestimate. We are undoubtedly tempted to mistake immediate values for eternal ones and the virtues of actuality for those of permanence. But these immediate and actual values and virtues are intensely real ones, a truth which the academic critic will not grasp. It is, for instance, highly questionable whether the writings of, let us say, Mr. Sherwood Anderson have the rich universality of appeal and the permanent preciousness of speech that must characterize the humblest classic. What is not questionable is that he expresses—expresses at times by his very dumbness—a mood, attitude, yearning, that are of the highest actuality and importance to this moment in the spiritual history of America. He may not speak to the twenty-first century; he speaks to and for last year and this and the next. He speaks for a certain civilization in certain moods as, to compare smaller things to greater, Tennyson spoke for certain years and moods in the religious history of the English people. Those moods are gone. The stature of the poet assumes truer proportions. But those years and moods were. We must understand them to understand what followed.

There is no reason why the intelligent reviewer of the latest books may not be a critic in the finest sense by keeping the distinction between temporary and permanent values in his consciousness. Literature is more than a game, and the academic diversion of arranging dead writers in correct hierarchies of rank is the most negligible department of criticism. The reviewer who, because he has experienced it deeply, can show his readers persuasively and eloquently how a given contemporary work expresses, interprets, clarifies that life which we are all trying to live and make more rational and beautiful, is exercising a more fruitful critical function than the learned academician who balances weightily the claims of Milton, Wordsworth, Shelley to the second place in the roll of British poets. If our reviewer of a contemporary work thinks that, in addition to its immediate and vital appeal and significance, it has the qualities of permanence too, he is, at worst, making a mistake that time is sure to right. At best he may be another Ben Jonson saying the final words early instead of late.

A distinguished critic has justly and acutely analyzed the attitudes toward life that form the background of much recent literature. He sums these up very tellingly and declares that the world which these authors see is "chaotic, incoherent, meaningless," a scene of "moral confusion." To mere hopelessness of there being any intelligible world, to mere jumble and a sort of brazen pride in it, he ascribes the welter of concrete fact that is poured forth, the uncritical and almost unselective heaping of detail upon detail, the shamelessness which characterizes James Joyce's "Ulysses" and sundry related works. He admits, of course, that if the world seems merely chaos to an artist it is his right and his business to communicate the sense of chaos through his works; for himself he clings—here we are quite at one with him—to the eternal value of "self-control" (this term we should want rather rigidly defined), "clear thinking," and the eager search for "delight and beauty."

We have here a rough description of two attitudes: that of the more or less expressionistic artist; and that of the humanist critic who deplores the present state of literature, but will not permit himself to be illiberal toward it, who is a good deal of a Pyrrhonist himself but longs a little for the fleshpots of certitude and order.

There is, we think, a third attitude, more fruitful, more hopeful than either of these. This attitude is still to be found behind many of those works of the day, in several languages, which have not gone to the paralyzing extremes of expressionistic technique. This third attitude is an old and very simple one. It is one of neither affirmation nor negation; it is one of inquiry. It is allied to the attitude of the scientist who marshals his great array of facts, of data, neither to show that they have no meaning, nor, if he is a true scientist, to prove that they have some particular meaning which gives him an emotional "kick," but to find out precisely what their meaning is.

It requires but the briefest reflection to show that the "moral confusion" of our world is largely due to a failure to apply that attitude of inquiry. Question any contemporary on a difficult and intricate matter of human conduct, and he will either give you a meaningless answer, i.e., he will fling at you a moral fiction which he believes no more than you, but which saves him the trouble of being either thoughtful or just, or else he will throw up his hands in utter helplessness, in utter refusal to rush in where the fools trample with their iron heels.

Now it seems that the virtue of the literature which, though the name has become discredited, is still naturalistic in temper and method, is that it did and does approach the moral world in a spirit of free inquiry, that it neither pretends to know the road to salvation and order nor to deny the existence of one, but is very earnestly in quest of it. Such a work as Theodore Dreiser's "The 'Genius,' " for instance, despite the desperate banality and meanness of a hundred passages, does, through its massive, faithful, broodingly absorbed, agonizedly seen record of certain central and moving facts concerning human life, widen the boundaries of true experience, deepen the perception of familar things, approach the disorganized world of conduct in a way of wondering hope and serious questioning. The naturalist, in brief, asks: What shall we do to be saved in such a world as this? In such a world as this, be it observed, man being what he is. And the first step is, obviously, to show us what the world is actually like, and what forms human conduct, conditioned in the essential nature of man, does actually take. In some such manner the heaping up of detail, the huge pouring forth of the concrete in recent literature, is to be both explained and justified. We have not yet reached the stage of interpretation; we cannot yet build up an intelligible world. We shall not reach that stage for years, perhaps not for generations. Salvation is far off. But again the analogy of the sciences should help us. In regard to morals we are still in what might be called the alchemistic and astrological age. We are still in the grip of fiction and superstition. We must have patience and bear with the artists who give us facts and confessions, in order that some day the age of chemistry and astronomy may dawn upon that world of conduct and spiritual values which is the supreme concern of us all.

# V. F. CALVERTON
## (1900–1940)

BORN in 1900, V. F. Calverton (George Goetz) came of age intellectually when war broke out in Europe. He attended Johns Hopkins University. In 1923 he founded and edited *The Modern Quarterly,* later converted into *The Modern Monthly.* Although he was sympathetic with Communism, he never joined the Communist Party. His visit to Soviet Russia in 1927 served to disillusion him and he became an independent radical. The *New Masses* "honored" his defection from the ranks of the ideologically orthodox by devoting an entire issue to a violent attack on him, accusing him of plagiarism and other "sins." He was literary editor for the Book League of America and for a time editor for the Macaulay Company. He gave many lectures throughout the land, as well as in Canada and Europe. He was opposed to America's participation in the Second World War. He died in 1940 while at work upon his autobiography, *Between Two Wars.*

V. F. Calverton played a prominent part in the development of Marxist criticism in this country. The aesthetic theories implicit in any body of literature, Calverton argues in *The Newer Spirit* (1925), are an expression of the society in which they emerge. The social system itself is but the product of the material conditions of the time. Class concepts shape and determine the aesthetic consciousness. Every revolution in ideas is a consequence of a revolution in the social structure. These are abstract formulas that obviously furnish no concrete criteria of aesthetic evaluation. It is not surprising that Calverton later abandoned this mechanical system of aesthetics.

In *Sex Expression in Literature,* Calverton develops the thesis that the literary manifestations of the sexual impulse are determined by economic forces. Sex attitudes are socially conditioned. In *The Bankruptcy of Marriage,* he analyzes the history and present status of sexual morality, emphasizing how values change from age to age in conformity with changes in the economic structure of society. Calverton edited two symposia in collaboration with Samuel Schmalhausen, *Sex in Civilization* and *The New Generation.*

223

From the point of view of literary criticism, Calverton's most substantial book is *The Liberation of American Literature* (1932), an attempt to interpret American literature in terms of a Marxian analysis of class ideologies.

"His book is concerned not so much with literary history or criticism as with the structure and development of social forces in America. Aesthetic evaluation is subordinated to Marxist analyses of the particular ideology underlying an author's work. Books are but the crystallization of a class view. . . . Before a valid critical method can be formulated, the class basis of American literature must be examined and appraised."[1]

Calverton devotes himself only to those aspects of our richly varied literary history which support his case.

In *The Making of Man,* which Calverton edited, he formulates a theory which purports to show that class factors determine the formation of cultural compulsives, and that class interests are the decisive element in the evolution of these compulsives in history. The theory of cultural compulsives is further amplified in *The Passing of the Gods.* In *The Awakening of America,* Calverton clearly indicates that he regards an exclusive preoccupation with economic forces in analyzing the causative process in history, as inadequate and misleading. His last work, completed just before his death, is *Where Angels Dared to Tread.*

Calverton forcefully refuted what he called the pollyannistic fallacy, namely, that proletarian literature must be optimistic in content. Virtually on the same level was the vulgar belief that tragedy expressed the psychology of a decadent bourgeois class. "Tragedy still remains," he declared, "under proletarian auspices or any other, the most inspiring form of art. After all, even under the most auspicious proletarian regime tragedy will continue, however changed it may become in its manifestations. As sensitive human beings, we can never, under any regime, escape the tragic sense of life."[2]

Written in 1937, this testifies to a sensitive awareness of the fact that the categories of art are more inclusive than those of politics. It is not possible, Calverton held, to construct a sound critical method out of the scattered remarks on literature to be found in the writings of Marx and Engels. Marxism is an historical method, not an aesthetic tool. "All Marxism can do," declares Calverton, "is to enlighten critics as to the nature of historical processes, but it cannot help critics a whit in the matter of deciding whether

[1] Charles I. Glicksberg, "V. F. Calverton: Marxism without Dogma," *Sewanee Review,* XLVI (July–September, 1938), 342.
[2] Charles I. Glicksberg, "Calverton and Marxist Literary Criticism," *The Modern Quarterly,* XI (Fall, 1940), 58.

Eschylus was a greater artist than Sophocles, or whether Thomas Mann is a greater novelist than Sigrid Undset."[3]

The Marxist method, it is clear, cannot prove of much help in the task of critical evaluation.

Calverton adopted this position not because he was abjuring established Marxist principles but because he found them totally inadequate to explain the facts which constitute the early history of America. He possessed an amazingly fertile mind. In a period of fifteen years he turned out books and articles with a prodigal hand: books dealing with Negro culture, anthropology, American literature, religion, sociology, American history. It was his very versatility which in part militated against his achieving a solid reputation as an "authority" in one field. Apparently he had no ambitions in that direction. He sowed his seed and then passed on to fields and pastures new.

His evolution as a critic betrayed a pattern of consistency, but the consistency was dynamic rather than static. He drew a distinction between Marxian criticism, which involved an analysis of a specific work in terms of its structure and design, and the Marxian interpretation of literature, which is concerned with social meaning and purpose, with ideological content and determinate ends. In short, it was not enough to condemn a writer's work as bourgeois or decadent; the critic must analyze this work in terms of its literary qualities and attempt to determine how these qualities are related to and spring out of the social context. The internal dynamics of art, the problem of craftsmanship and literary excellence, must not be neglected in an obsessive concern with abstract ideologies. The critic must therefore be sensitive, discriminating, gifted with intuition, the power of solving aesthetic problems. No one was better aware of the flagrant shortcomings of what in America passed itself off as Marxist criticism than Calverton. In any estimate of American literary criticism during the twenties and thirties, Calverton's contribution will have to be recognized as a seminal force.

## BIBLIOGRAPHY

### TEXT

*The Newer Spirit.* New York, 1925.
*Sex Expression in Literature.* New York, 1926.
*The Bankruptcy of Marriage.* New York, 1928.
*For Revolution.* New York, 1932.
*The Liberation of American Literature.* New York, 1932.

[3] *Ibid.,* p. 59.

*The New Ground of Criticism.* Seattle. 1930.
*The Passing of the Gods.* New York, 1934.
*The Awakening of America.* New York, 1939.
*Where Angels Dared to Tread.* New York, 1941.

CRITICISM

V. F. Calverton Memorial Issue. *The Modern Quarterly,* XI, 7–60 (Fall, 1940).
Glicksberg, Charles I., "V. F. Calverton," *Sewanee Review,* XLVI, 338–351 (July–September, 1938).
Ramsey, David and Calmer, Alan, "The Marxism of V. F. Calverton," *New Masses,* VIII, 9–17 (January, 1933).
Stork, A., "Mr. Calverton and His Friends," *International Literature,* No. 3, 97–124 (July, 1934).

# SOCIOLOGICAL CRITICISM OF LITERATURE*

THE time when literature was considered the product of a supernatural afflatus or peculiar impartation of spirit or impulse has disappeared. The passing of this notion has been a very simple and perceptible phenomenon. Explanations and descriptions of it have been legion. The advance of science with its revelations of both sidereal and terrestrial activity, and the consequent decline of otherworldly conceptions, the change from the deductive to the inductive method, created a different attitude toward man and his achievements. The change and progress in thought and science have been an inevitable reflection of the steady transforming material conditions of present and past centuries. Creative and critical composition, if we must make that division for the moment, have altered both in style and substance with each of the vicissitudes of social evolution. The criteria of excellence have varied with each advancing epoch. Literature of the "impossible" and "improbable" cast, which fascinated one age, suffices but to dull and stupefy another; pictures of court and chivalry, the gilded pageantry of palace and field, the sunny romance of knight and lady, which captivated the imagination of artists and critics of olden centuries, no longer allure. The demand for the inevitable and the real becomes as vital a part

* Reprinted from *The Newer Spirit. A Sociological Criticism of Literature,* by V. F. Calverton, published by Liveright, copyright 1925, Boni and Liveright, Inc.

of the literary creed as the scientific. The tendencies of art, religion, and science are but the interwoven threads of the social texture.

Theories of scientific criticism urged by Hennequin and J. M. Robertson[1] are no more than the necessary extension of sociological development into the critical realm. The idea of Mr. Mencken that the excellency of an author's writing may depend upon nothing more exalted than the activity of his pylorus, and Mr. W. Huntington Wright's, that literary creation is merely a form of physico-chemical reaction, are likewise similar manifestations of the sociological trend. The application of the biographical method to criticism is but part of this same phase. Taine's progress in the examination of literature as the product of telluric and social environment is no more singular, although more happily significant. All are common, and in no way surprising, expressions of our modern age of industrial and scientific growth. They could be characteristic of no other age.

As we continue to cautiously and minutely study the literature of any race or period, then, we eventually discover that all of the theories and concepts, the dicta and shibboleths, of creative and critical effort are but the outgrowths of the social system in which they have their being, and which in turn is the product of the material conditions of the time. This point we shall illustrate at considerable length. Under feudalism, for instance, we shall show that the literary conceptions which prevailed were in consonance with the social structure and did not change until the latter began to alter. In similar manner we shall picture the changes in social environment that brought with them the different literary concepts and tactics of the eighteenth and nineteenth centuries. And finally we shall consider the complex expansion of science and industry during the latter part of the nineteenth and beginning of the twentieth centuries, and its effects upon the form and substance of contemporary literature.

Social classes develop within one another. There is no fixed line of demarcation to determine the precise moment of their birth and extinction. Caused by newly arising conditions, they spring into existence slowly or swiftly according to the nature of the exigency, and for a considerable period are quite overlapping entities. The bourgeois class, for example, was a gradual growth in the very heart of feudal society. Developing primarily as a result of the industrial changes circling about the Renaissance: the inventions of gun-

[1] See Robertson's *New Essays Toward a Critical Method.*

powder,[2] printing with movable type, the compass, the manufacture of paper on a large scale, and the extension of commerce with the Orient, it did not become permanently dominant until the disappearance of feudalism, or cause any enduring changes in literature until the beginning of the eighteenth century. That does not mean, as some might suppose, that previous to the eighteenth century, literature was entirely unaffected by its rise, but that the effects were too scattered and incoherent to create a distinct and lasting change of literary trend. In the seventeenth century, for instance, the bourgeois class in England rose in successful rebellion against the nobility, and for eleven years established a government of their own, which was characterized by all the extensions and restrictions of the puritanic bourgeois conceptions of the period. The progress of theatrics was temporarily interrupted, and the mundane in literature was supplanted by the religious. The romantic poetry of the Elizabethans was succeeded by the somber metaphysical lyrics of Daniel, Breton, Donne and Herbert. The change, however, though sharp, was ephemeral. The Restoration brought with it a swift return to the older conceptions and manners. The recoil, for a time, was virulent and excessive. This bourgeois incursion then, as we shall see, wrought no fundamental and permanent change in esthetic theory or practice. Nevertheless, coming as a consequence of economic difficulties forced upon them by the tyrannic taxation of the king, it furnishes incontestable proof of the rising potency of the bourgeois class at the time. It was not to be until some decades later, however, that its class concepts were to become a steadily ruling element in the social and esthetic consciousness.

The attitude toward tragedy that prevailed throughout the feudal period and continued to persist over much of Europe until the bourgeois revolution of 1789, is interesting and conclusive illustration of this division of class-psychology caused by the existing types of social structure. Since the time of Aristotle, and certainly many years before, though we have no written records to certify it, tragedy has been considered the loftiest form of literary art, and to its construction have been devoted the highest artistic energies of man. The psychological reasons, reduced to their material motives, why tragedy has been conceived in such exalted fashion—which would carry us into the problems of "catharsis," the nature of physiological

2 This, of course, was originally invented by the Chinese, but was first applied to warfare by the Occidentals, who used it in this capacity as early as the battle of Crecy in 1346.

reaction, universal pessimism, the intellectual ennui of civilization—
need not be discussed in this treatise. The presence of the conception
is what we are immediately concerned with, and its process of change
is what we must subject to analysis.

Feudal society, dependent upon agricultural production, was the
necessary outgrowth of the various systems of slavery that preceded
it. Its apex, the nobility, was the class that determined and fostered
the leading conceptions of the age; the manners of court, the practice of chivalry, the system of judicature, the pursuance of the arts,
the metaphysics of the period—all were products of the peculiar
agrarian system of production and distribution that then existed.
The religious class, in possession of extensive and fertile lands,
came in conflict with the nobility only when the latter threatened
usurpation of such territory, and in general worked for the perpetuation of the feudal regime. The burghers of the town, as we
mentioned earlier in our discussion, became influential only as feudalism started to decline.[3] And these esthetic and ethical concepts
which prevailed, and that were but the patent reflections of the
character of the reigning class, were defended with sincere and unremitting zeal and justified as "absolute."

There is perhaps no clearer evidence of precisely how the ideas
of a community, those of its artists and critics, statesmen and metaphysicians, are determined by the nature of material conditions,
from which arise the structure of society, than that afforded by the
esthetic concept of tragedy. Until the eighteenth century, when the
bourgeois class had acquired sufficient power to exert a permanent
influence upon social conceptions, the attitude towards tragedy was
uniformly feudal and aristocratic. The distinction between higher
and lower drama, tragedy and comedy, throughout the Middle Ages
and extending to the decline and decrease of feudalism, was considered by critics as being fundamentally a distinction of social
status. Tragedy could be concerned only with noble characters—
the illustrious—and to conceive it as being written about a bourgeois protagonist would have been literary sacrilege. If, for a moment, we consider the writings of that French classicist, Abbe
d'Aubignac (1604-76), we shall discover an explicit statement of
this attitude. Tragedy, says d'Aubignac, "inheres not in the nature
of the catastrophe but in the rank of persons." The other French

3 The rise of these burghers, in fact, was one of the main causes of the decline of
the feudal system, although it in turn was the result of still more underlying material causes.

classicists were equally firm in their position. Pellitier, Ronsard, de Laudun, Vauquelin de la Fresnay, Pelet de la Mesnardière, each supported the aristocratic theory of tragedy, and wrote as if a deviation from it were an impossibility. Voltaire, a radical in so many things, and whose death occurred only eleven years before the bourgeois revolution in France, was certain that tragedy required characters elevated above the common level. Even Joubert, in the memorable *Encyclopedie*, declared that tragedy is "the imitation of the lives and speech of heroes, subject by their elevation to passions and catastrophes as well as to the manifestations of virtues, of the most illustrious kind." It must not be forgotten that at the time the *Encyclopedie*, under the organization of Diderot, made pretensions to advance to modernism, unrivaled by any other literary or scientific production. The Italian humanists in no case dissented from the aristocratic theory of tragedy. The German pseudo-classicists, Opitz and Gottsched, the directors of literary taste in Germany during a century and a half, the former during the most of the seventeenth and the latter during the first half of the eighteenth, were in avowed agreement with the classicist attitude. In his *Buch von der Deutschen Poeterey* (1624), Opitz gave the aristocratic interpretation to poetry, and later in *Versuch einer Critische Dichtkunst vor die Deutschen* in 1730, Gottsched continued the same criticism. The following quotation from Opitz, for instance, clearly represents the attitude of these German classicists toward tragedy:

"Tragedy . . . seldom permits the introduction of people of humble or common deeds, because it deals only with royal decrees, murders, despairs, slaughters of fathers and children, fires, incests, wars and rebellions, lamentations, outcries, sighs, and the like. Comedy has to do with ordinary matters and persons; it speaks of weddings, banquets, games, tricks and knaveries of serving men, bragging foot-soldiers, love affairs, frivolity of youth, avarice of old age, match-making, and such things which daily occur among the common people."

Gottsched, in his *Critische Dichtkunst*, expresses in terms no less unequivocal the same sentiment:

"If you wish to make a comedy of your subject, the persons must be citizens; for heroes and princes belong in a tragedy. Tragedy is distinguished from comedy only in this, that, instead of laughter, it tries to arouse wonder, terror and pity; therefore it usually concerns itself with men of birth only, who are conspicuous by their rank, name, and appearance. In an epic, which is the masterpiece of all poetry, the persons must be the most impressive in the world, kings, heroes, and great statesmen, and everything in it must sound majestic, strange and wonderful."

The very titles of certain of the romances and tragedies of the period are an interesting and significant index to its social trend: Bucholz's *Pleasant Romance of the Christian Royal Princes Herculiscus and Herculadisla and their Princely Company* (1659); Ziegler's *The Asiatic Banise, or Bloody but Courageous Pegu, Based on Historic Truth but Covered with the Veil of a Pleasing Story of Heroic Love-Adventure* (1688); and Lohenstein's *The Magnanimous General Arminius, with his Illustrous Thusnelda, Held up to the German Nobility as an Honourable Example and for Praiseworthy Emulation* (1689).

But do we discover dissenting voices in England at the time?— England to which so many panegyrics of liberty have been dedicated. The attitude of their artists and critics is clear and inflexible. For tragedy only the great can be characters; the "dignity of persons," to employ the phrase of Ben Jonson used in this reference, is a necessity if tragedy is to possess elements of the sublime. Such was the avowed attitude of Stubbes, Puttenham, Gosson, Webbe, and Harrington, the eminent critics in the era of the romantic drama, and no deviation from it is to be noted in the writings of Ben Jonson, whom we quoted above, or any of the Restorationists. Rymer contended that tragedy "required not only what is natural, but what is great (noble) in nature." Both Congreve and Dryden declared in favor of the aristocratic conception of tragedy; in Dryden's words, "tragedy, as we know, is wont to image to us the minds and fortunes of noble persons," and in those of Congreve, tragedy "distinguishes itself from vulgar poetry by the dignity of its characters." Even Oliver Goldsmith, the son of a poor curate, a pale struggling genius acquainted with all of the pain and torture of deprivation, maintained that "the distresses of the mean (the middle and poorer classes) by no means affect us so strongly as the calamities of the great." There is no question, therefore, that the aristocratic conception of tragedy was not an isolated, sporadic phenomenon, but a widespread, generally accepted theory.[4]

[4] For certain data presented in this essay credit must be acknowledged to Kuno Francke's *History of German Literature,* and to some of the literary research of William H. Hudson and Ernest Crosby, each of which authors caught hints of the effects of material conditions but in no fundamental sense attempted to coördinate the facts assembled. The coördination is what is significant.

The dramas of Shakespeare can be taken as fitting example of application of the feudal concept. There have been many, aside from Tolstoi and Shaw, who have attacked Shakespeare for what they call his narrowness of vision, his bigoted reverence for the aristocracy and blatant contempt for the rabble. We might as well attack Plato for considering soldiers an important class in the state, a class to be studied and promoted, and fighting an art to be developed and practiced—or Aristotle for not condemning slavery, the institution that made it possible for Greece at the time to progress and flourish. These strictures, of course, remain, the environment that produced them notwithstanding. It is the environment, however, that makes them explicable—and inevitable. Shakespeare did nothing more than represent the esthetic conceptions of his period. In weaving every tragedy about the struggles of the noble and the illustrious, he violated no concept of his age. Both the commoner and the bourgeois were subjects of humor and satire, the means of affording comedy to the situation and relaxing tenseness in the drama. The humbler classes, as they were called, appear often under titles themselves ludicrous enough to indicate the nature of their treatment: Quince, the Carpenter; Snug, the Joiner; Starveling, the Tailor; Smooth, the Silkman; Bottom, the Weaver; and Flute, the Bellows-maker. In *A Midsummer Night's Dream,* for instance, most of the trades are ridiculed. In all of Shakespeare's works with but a few exceptions, one in *Richard II,* where we find a loyal servant, another in *Cymbeline,* still another in *King Lear,* several in *Timon of Athens,* one in *A Winter's Tale,* two in *Anthony and Cleopatra*—all servants, shepherds or soldiers, who are pictured as faithful and honest—we find unflattering pictures of both proletarian and tradesman. Of the lower class as a whole, the dramatist is even more satirical. In one place characterized as "hempen-homespuns," another as "the barren sort," in still another as "mechanic slaves, with greasy aprons, rules and hammers"; he goes still further in *Coriolanus* to speak of the "stinking breath of the commoner" and decrying them as "the mutable, rank-scented many," "garlic eaters," "multiplying spawn," "worthless peasants," "rude unpolished hinds," all phrases consistent with the aristocratic attitude of the time. In *Hamlet,* Shakespeare laments the seeming rise of the lower strata and declares that "the age has grown so picked, that the toe of the peasant comes so near the heel of the courtier, he galls his kibe." Then in *Henry IV* he sneers at the famous rebellion of Wat Tyler, the "damned commotion," which he describes as coming "in base and abject routs, led on by bloody youth, guarded with rags, and countenanced by beggary." In *Pericles* the dramatist proclaims that "princes are a model, which heaven makes like to itself," and in *Henry VI* he has the Duke of York denounce the "mean-born man," and in *Henry VI* Joan of Arc is made to speak of her "contemptible estate." This material instead of being viewed as disturbing and disappointing should rather be considered as satisfying and convincing to the scientific critic, who studies literature as the product of the material conditions that created the society and all of the appurtenances which were necessary to its literary expression. This reference to Shakespeare was made only because his works so excellently illustrate how the esthetic and ethical ideas of the feudal period were expressed in literature, and stand out in such sharp and striking contrast to the changing conceptions of later centuries.

And from whence could such a conception arise? The Hegelian idealist with his thesis of the absolute might attempt to explain it as the logical development of the absolute idea. But, to us, this appears ridiculously illogical. Besides, the coördinates of absolutist logic are as maddeningly elusive as the motions of a will-o'-the-wisp. On the other hand, we can readily perceive how such a conception, of necessity, must have arisen from the material conditions that had created the feudal regime. As long as the nobility remained the ruling class, the administering and not the administered, it would be a sociological solecism to expect ideas to be other than reflections of the aristocratic, courtly attitude. In no instance in history do we discover such a solecism. The aristocratic conception of tragedy, therefore, continued as long as feudalism existed, and when the system of feudalism could no longer function—the declining nobility steadily becoming more and more dependent upon the rising bourgeois—and had to recede in favor of another system of more adequate and satisfactory dimensions, the concept faded into a myth. That this process of the decline and disappearance of the aristocratic concept was purely a matter of change of social environment, which at basis was due to the failure of feudalism to adapt itself to the demands of its growing communities, was unquestionably proven by the sequence of "bourgeois" tragedy, concomitant with the ascent of the bourgeois class.

In England feudalism experienced a more rapid retrogression than in any other European country. Due to its peninsular location, which afforded a sense of security and protection, a merchant class was an early historical necessity, and in correspondence with the growth of towns and commerce this class became augmented. In France, for example, where the land was part of the continent, without peninsular advantages or handicaps, the bourgeois class did not revolt until over one hundred and forty years after the bloody revolution of the bourgeois in England. As a consequence, we find bourgeois concepts, political and esthetic, developing in England long before. France, and Voltaire's letters, therefore, appear in no way singular. The political and judicial liberty for which England, in every history, has been so conspicuously noted, then, was ultimately the result of this geographic factor.

In England, it follows, if our logic be correct, we should locate the first deviations from the aristocratic conception. And so we do. The play that is commonly referred to as marking the origin of *tragedie bourgeoise* in England is Lillo's *The London Merchant* which was staged by Theophilus Cibber in 1731. The tragedy of this play is concerned with the moral decay and execution of a merchant's apprentice, George Barnwell, whose end was so dismal because he failed to live a life of sincerity and rectitude. In brief, the play is an encomium of bourgeois virtues made emphatic by frequent moral lessons and sharp condemnation of all wayward traits. This play received more comment and laudation than perhaps any other play of the century. It was acted before crowded audiences, night after night in the heat of midsummer, and drew the patronage and praise of poet and critic. Within a few years five authorized editions of it were printed. Pope, amid the clamor of court and forum, gave the tragedy his commendation. Later the play won the attention and admiration of Rousseau, Marmontel, Prévost, Lessing, Goethe, Schiller, and the extravagant eulogy of Diderot. In 1796 its theme was worked into a novel by Thomas Skinner Surr, and afterwards memoirs of George Barnwell and a life history were written. It was acted by a number of famous actors and actresses, among whom were Charles Kemble, Mrs. Siddons, and Sir Henry Irving. Considered by our present dramatic standards, *The London Merchant* is a fifth-rate production. Its homilies are ludicrous, its characters, including the merchant Thorowgood, stilted and unnatural, and its points of dramatic intensity almost laughably unconvincing. From a historical standpoint, however, as we have noted, the tragedy is significant.

It is necessary to admit, of course, that *The London Merchant* was not the first tragedy in English which was constructed about bourgeois characters. No social movement can be said to have expressed itself in any single moment or episode; the expression is usually gradual and hints at its coming long before its arrival. In Heywood's *A Woman Killed with Kindness* we have an early suggestion of the rising trend and in Otway's *The Orphan,* Southern's *Fatal Marriage,* and Rowe's *The Fair Penitent* we meet with even more marked evidence of the Domestic Tragedy. Yet none of these tragedies possess the thoroughly bourgeois character of *The London Merchant,* or, for that matter, of the two famous plays that followed Lillo's tragedy: *The Gamester* and *The Mysterious Husband,* and cannot be considered as anything more than mild and minor predecessors.

As the bourgeois class, with the steady decline of feudalism, continued to rise in other countries, the aristocratic conception waned. In Germany, for instance, we find Lessing acting the part of the revolutionist. His play *Miss Sarah Simpson,* which appeared in 1755, was the first German tragedy of bourgeois life. His achievement in this drama was very similar to that of George Lillo in *The London Merchant* and Edward Moore in *The Gamester.* This, of course, was a complete departure from the theories of Opitz and Gottsched, and later was explained and justified by Lessing in his critical writings. It is important to observe here that with all his radical notions as to dramatic theme and technique, and even his attack upon Frederick, he still clung to a kind of nationalist sentiment[5] that the internationalist of the twentieth century would ridicule. Had industry developed, science grown, commerce expanded, cities enlarged, and intercourse taken on the world-wide aspect of late decades, Lessing, with his other radical characteristics, in turn would have forsaken the tiniest vestige of nationalism. In *Minna von Barnhelm* he devoted himself to a description of "a people beginning to feel itself again as a whole, and to be again conscious of national responsibilities." It would be illogical, from a sociological viewpoint, to expect Lessing to have been otherwise. In *Emilia Galloti* (1772) he fought against the oppression of the bourgeois by the aristocracy; from the play, according to Francke, can be traced the beginnings of the battles carried on by the *Sturm und Drang* movement. In France, Nivelle de la Chaussée and Diderot were the innovators of the *tragedie bourgeoise,* and later Saurin, the author of *Beverly,* an adaption of Moore's *Gamester,* in the century following, extended the *tragedie bourgeoise* to include a wider scope.

So long as the supremacy of the bourgeois remained unquestioned,

5 St. 101, Works 7, 474.

which was certainly the case until the appearance of the modern utopians,[6] Pierre le Roux, Fourier and Saint Simon, there could be but two kinds of ethical and esthetic conceptions, one dominant, the bourgeois, the other recessive or vestigial, the aristocratic. If we take America during the period immediately following the Revolutionary War, we shall discover a fruitful illustration of the effects of bourgeois ascendency. One would scarcely expect, nor does he find, in a country that has just experienced a triumph of its bourgeois,[7] a literature devoted to the praise either of its aristocracy or its proletariat. In a nation where Madison and Pinckney disagreed as to the three classes for which the Constitution should provide, Madison being in favor of the landed, the commercial, and the manufacturing, and Pinckney in favor of the professional, the landed, and the commercial, neither believing the proletariat worthy of consideration, it would be contrary to social evolution to find literary themes revolving about the tragic struggles and tribulations of the proletarian characters. In no work of the period do we see the proletarian accepted as fit character for tragedy, or his adversity pictured in bold but sympathetic line and color. Irving used him as a source of sport and satire, Cooper as a frontiersman to combat his fantastic, rainbow-plumed Indians, and Franklin as suitable object for bourgeois sermons on thrift and wisdom. Neither can the verse of Freneau, Barlow, Hopkinson and Drake, nor the prose of Jefferson, Washington or Brockden Brown be said to have treated him in gentler fashion. In England, as we have described, the proletarian now served as material for wit and comedy. In France and Germany, where de la Chaussée and Lessing had emancipated the stage from the aristocratic conception, the proletarian had to be likewise, by esthetic necessity, subservient to the bourgeois, the ascending class.

In the first stages of capitalism the distinction between the bourgeois and the proletarian is not as wide and definite and not so difficult to bridge as in its later stages, when, through the increase and concentration of its mass, it steadily dispossesses and enlarges its

6 Unless we wish to begin with Godwin's *Political Justice* (1793) which, in one sense, can be used as a starting point for the modern utopians.

7 For information as to the American Revolution's representing a clear victory for the merchant class, the bourgeois, the reader may refer to A. M. Symons' *Social Forces in American History,* or to more orthodox historians and their work, such as Farrand's *Development of the U.S.,* Schlesinger's *Colonial Revolution,* or McMaster's *History of the People of the United States.* Beard, likewise, can be used in this reference, or James Oneal.

lower element and fortifies and narrows its upper. As this dispossession process continues, unless there be some disturbing and deceptive factor, such as the free-land policy, which we found in America during the nineteenth century, the class-consciousness of the dispossessed class grows in ratio with the degree of dispossession. Until this process has developed and intensified there is no significant class-organization, and without organization a class cannot impress itself upon the activity of a society, or function as a determinant of its basic conceptions. During this period, the incipiency of capitalism, for instance, the bourgeois exercised supreme and unquestioned authority; the first labor unions did not organize in America until about 1805 or 1810, over forty-five years after the beginning of the Industrial Revolution, and their organization approximated nothing extensive or involved until the 60's or 70's. The Haymarket episode, of course, weakened the purpose and temporarily wrecked much of this later complexity of organization. These labor organizations, distinct products of class-consciousness,[8] came as the inevitable result of the increasing concentration of capital. With this steady rise of the proletarian, his organization into a definite class with definite class-interests, and with the acquisition of certain educational privileges necessary to his expression, society was driven into acknowledgment of the reality and importance of his existence, and as a consequence he became a force in the molding of social conceptions. James Russell Lowell, despite his miserably inferior *Vision of Sir Launfal* and a number of his classic prejudices, was one of the voices of this trend. In his Birmingham address in 1884, just two years before the Haymarket riot, he revealed how very profoundly the rise of the proletariat had affected his ideas and changed his attitude:

"What is really ominous of danger to the existing order of things is not democracy (which, properly understood, is a conservative force), but the Socialism which may find a fulcrum in it. If we cannot equalize conditions and fortunes any more than we can equalize the brains of men—and a very sagacious person has said that 'where two men ride of a horse, one must ride behind'—we can yet, perhaps, do something to correct these methods and influences that lead to enormous inequalities, and to prevent their growing more enormous. . . . Communism means barbarism, but Socialism means, or wishes to mean, coöperation and community of in-

[8] The swift spread of this class-consciousness was due in good part to the fact that the free-lands in the West had been largely consumed.

238 AMERICAN LITERARY CRITICISM

terests, sympathy, the giving to the hands not so large a share as to the brains, but a larger share than hitherto in the wealth they must combine to produce—means, in short, the practical application of Christianity to life, and has in it the secret of an orderly and benign reconstruction."

Although this is what we should classify as sentimental or utopian socialism, it nevertheless is an interesting reflection of the movement of thought caused by the change in material conditions which brought the proletariat into economical and political significance.

Walt Whitman was a finer product of this trend. Into more genuinely poetic, although more mystical, phraseology did he put its aspirations and dreams. With Whitman we find the proletarian no longer the inferior, the source of sport and travesty, but a being infused with the same elements of power and excellence as the heroic general or statesman, a being capable of the deepest thoughts and feelings, and of the profoundest struggle and tragedy. A little over a century earlier, Whitman—but he would not have been the Walt Whitman we know because he would have been made by different conditions—would have sung of other heroes and embodied in his poetic philosophy nothing of the spirit of the proletarian. Instead of a hymn to *A Common Prostitute* he would have bemoaned the fateful end of a princess, or perhaps the daughter of a Thorowgood, and instead of crying that "no one thing in the universe is inferior to another thing," that "behind each mask was a kindred soul," he would have crooned the songs of a priest or composed madrigals to stupid, courtly dames or romantic and prurient maidens.

It is important at this point to note likewise the indisseverable connection between the nature of literary technique and the stage of development of society. Hitherto we have shown how the social conceptions that prevail determine the substance of literature, but not how the form, the technique, the very manner in which the composition is constructed, is determined also by the same material conditions that created the social conceptions. We shall draw only one parallel, which will prove sufficient evidence to establish the premise. This time, to introduce variety, we shall take the novel for our illustration. The first novels, if we exclude such ollapodrida as Petronius' *Satyricon,* Cervantes' *Don Quixote,*[9] Sidney's *Arcadia,* Mrs. Manley's *The Power of Love, in Seven Novels* (1720), appeared in England during the heyday of bourgeois supremacy.

[9] Macaulay called *Don Quixote,* which it should be remembered appeared quite a number of years before *Pamela,* "certainly the best novel in the world beyond all comparison."

Exactly nine years after the staging of *The London Merchant*, Richardson's *Pamela* was printed.[10] Although *Pamela* was parodied by Fielding in *Joseph Andrews*, and the general spirit of the Richardson novels for a time was satirized also by Smollett and Sterne, it was succeeded by *David Simple* and Goldsmith's *Vicar of Wakefield*, both novels dedicated to a similar exaltation of bourgeois virtues. But we are not concerned here with an analysis of the substance of the novel, as we are in the case of the drama, but with its form, which renders further dissection of content at this point entirely superfluous.

The more carefully we notice the history of fiction, and the novel need only serve as one instance, we are immediately impressed by the evolution from the impossible to the improbable, thence to the probable and finally to the inevitable. To many, even to the American critic, we dare say, who first recorded this feature, this evolution seems a quite unaccountable affair. That the mythical, legendary romances of Arthur and the Round Table should have prevailed in the four or five centuries following the Norman Conquest, and finally been crystallized into the memorable *Morte d'Arthur* in 1485, all "impossible" in content, is nothing strange nor unexpected to the scientific critic. The fierce encounters of knights, with the perilous enemies of the forest, giants, dragons, mystical swords that could be drawn only with an enchanting sign or whisper, charms evoked by the wicked sorcery of medieval magicians, made up the category of fascinating "impossibilities." *The Castle of Otranto*, *The Champion of Virtue*, Matthew Lewis' *The Monk*, the weird stories of Mrs. Radcliffe, even Godwin's *St. Leon*, can be classified also in the "impossible" group. The romance of castle and field, which was carried on in the tragedies of the Elizabethans and all of the seventeenth and early eighteenth century dramatists, under more realistic and convincing guise, marked the advance to the improbable and probable stage. The nineteenth century, for instance, was the century for the "probable" in fiction, although the grotesque tales of Poe and Hoffman are clear evidence of the survival of the improbable and even a phase of the impossible trend. Romantic fiction is all a vestige of these older trends, each produced by different stages of social structure. That certain of these trends should persist after the social environment that caused them has declined and disappeared does not mean that a surprising or confusing element has been intro-

---

10 It is curious to note also that in France Marivaux's novel *Marianne*, based upon similar plot and purpose, was published several years earlier than *Pamela*.

duced into the historical process. It would be surprising and confusing if such remnants of the old ideology did not from time to time spring into print. By our very knowledge of the law of cause and effect we can easily see that the advance of a new social system though it achieved a change in the dominant esthetic and ethical ideas cannot hope to annihilate at once, or in a generation or two, all of the remains of those conceptions that have been forced to recede into the background. There are still royalists in France, although political democracy has been almost a universally accepted theory in the countries of the civilized world.

It was not until science advanced into its later stages, when the reactions of the mind and body as well as those of matter came to be recognized as following the same inescapable law of cause and effect, that the idea of the inevitable could assume scientific form. Prediction, the aim of science, now became possible in mental as well as physical things, and the causal law attained the extensions necessary to undermine beliefs in chance and the fortuitous. Without the rise of science, which was part of the development of the capitalist system, the idea of the inevitable would never have emerged from its religious raiment, and esthetic conceptions would have been but scantily affected by its existence. At the time that prose and poetic fiction possessed the impossible and improbable cast, the human mind, ignorant of natural law and scientific generalization, demanded nothing more of its literary substance; when knowledge advanced, however, and reality began to be sifted from myth, the literary form became modified in accordance with the nature of the advance. In pace with the progress of science, therefore, did metamorphosis in literary practice result. At the present time, the twentieth century, and also during the latter part of the nineteenth, particularly after the appearance of *The History of Civilization in England, The Origin of Species* and *Das Kapital*, realism of the inevitable character developed. The realism of Sterne, Smollett, and even Fielding, was not the realism that the nineteenth and twentieth centuries require; the former was more plastic, yielding, without the quality of the inevitable, the undeviating necessity, such as we find exemplified in the novels of Hardy and Conrad. The inflexible criterion of modern realism is "inevitability." Situations must flow inevitably from each other; characters must perform only those actions which, in the nature of their being, it was impossible for them not to perform. There must be no appeal to mere possibility or probability if the fiction is to convince. Although the large category of so-called popular magazines of the amorous, snappy and adventurous variety, with which every civilized country is flooded, and the Wrightian and Corellian novels, still cling to the improbable and probable types— hence their success as investments, but failures as literature—there is not a single significant literary periodical or author that would dare publish material of such character. This evolution in structure, then, has been but a reflection of the rise of the scientific attitude, itself a product of the capitalist system, which brought with it a fuller understanding of the essence and inevitability of human reaction.

We see, then, that in literature, besides its content, the choice and arrangement of incident, the description and analysis of character, are likewise determined by environment. Now let us turn to the literature that followed Whitman, the literature of the late 90's and the twentieth century. The rise of labor organizations, a necessity for the expression of proletarian class-consciousness which was described on a previous page, was and is a constant factor in driving proletarian conceptions to the foreground. Without this rise and the impression of the proletarian upon society, novels and dramas with proletarian protagonists, treated in the serious and searching manner befitting a tragic study, would never have attained expression. This point cannot be emphasized too strongly for those idealist critics who are so prone to view the changes in literary tendencies as developments of the absolute idea or more whimsical alterations of interest and motive.

A glance at the literature of any country in which the proletariat has become a force in the social organization will reveal how very marked the literature has become by its rise. The literary artist in these lands comes to recognize that there is a soul in the common man, that the proletarian is not without his tragic affections and aspirations. And the study of these affections and aspirations becomes the subject for tragedies as elevated and sublime as those of *Œdipus* and *Athalie*. Dramas like *The Weavers, Strife,* and *Beyond the Horizon,* built about the sufferings of those of the proletariat, become masterpieces of dramatic art, and novels like *Tess of the d'Urbervilles, Frau Sorge,* and *Sons and Lovers,* stories concerned with the misery and anguish of the dispossessed class, are accepted as tragedies of genuine and vital character. It should not be thought that proletarian tragedy, if such we must call it in contradistinction to the aristocratic and bourgeois, began in any particular year or with any special book, but rather that it sprang up gradually as the proletariat became more and more a class demanding social consideration. As early as 1864 in the Naturalist novel, *Germinie Lacerteux*, the Goncourts dealt with the tragic life of a servant girl,[11] and de Maupassant, although many of his stories are concerned solely with the bourgeois, gave tragic significance to the fate of Maitre Hauchecorne, the poor Norman in *A Piece of String*. These characters were treated in a different manner than was Richardson's seamstress, the difference being the consequence of the different ages in which the works appeared. Hugo, of course, in many instances gave sympathetic though romantic description to the proletarian, the description, nevertheless, usually interlarded with appeals to bourgeois virtues and sentimentality. And Zola, with all of his brutality, did not fail to see and depict the strength as well as the ofttimes deep-rooted viciousness of proletarian character. All of these men, it should be noted, wrote after the revolution of 1848.

It is not until contemporary times, however, that we begin to see a steady and opulent literature growing up about the proletarian. Pierre Hamp, in France, for example, in that one collection of his stories entitled *People*, has seen great and insprinig tragedy in the life of *The Sweet Smeller* and *The Potato Sisters*. Joyce in more than one place in *Dubliners*, particularly in *The Little Cloud*, realizes the tragedy of the drab—and what is so drab as the life of a proletarian? And if we turn to American literature we meet with a very striking picture of the new concept—shall we call it the proletarian concept? Certainly it would be neither rash nor hasty criticism to say that among the most important pieces of fiction that have appeared in America during the last two decades, three works stand out very distinctly: *Ethan Frome*, by Edith Wharton; *Winesburg, Ohio*, by Sherwood Anderson, and *Sister Carrie*, by Theodore Dreiser. The protagonists in these books are proletarians and without exception

[11] In the preface we find an interesting and illuminating statement of the Goncourts' position: "Living in the nineteenth century, at a time of universal suffrage, and democracy, and liberalism, we asked ourselves whether what are called the 'lower orders' had no claim upon the Novel; whether the people—this world beneath a world—were to remain under the literary ban and disdain of authors who have hitherto maintained silence regarding any soul and heart that they might possess. We asked ourselves whether, in these days of equality, there were still for writer and reader unworthy classes, misfortunes that were too low, dramas too foul-mouthed, catastrophes too base in their terror. We became curious to know whether Tragedy, that conventional form of a forgotten literature and a vanished society, was finally dead; whether, in a country devoid of caste and legal aristocracy, the miseries of the lowly and the poor would speak to interest, to motion, to piety, as loudly as the miseries of the great and rich; whether, in a word, the tears that are wept below could provoke weeping like those that are wept above."

the histories of their lives are woven into the texture of strange and telling tragedy. To many this fact, if it has been recognized, has not seemed to deserve notice. Yet it is of utmost significance. It mirrors the advance of the proletariat. It is additional proof that literature is the product of sociology, and can only be satisfactorily approached, studied and criticized by the sociological method.

It is because most of us today believe that the life-experience of the proletarian offers as purifying material for tragedy as that of the bourgeois or aristocrat, that we fail to realize how very brief, in historical duration, has been the existence of this attitude. The mere existence of an idea or conception too often gives the delusion of permanence.[12] What must be realized is the social process that has brought about the conditions necessary for the creation of this conception. In understanding this process, however, we do not mean to conclude that all these artists who, in their work, embody this conception are aware of the sociological factors that have made it a part of the civilization. In the greater number of instances, on the contrary, the attitude prevails, in spite of ignorance of its cause. The attitude becomes a kind of social-reflex.

As scientific critics we cannot expect any form of society to be finally permanent, and if, as Polybius predicted, which is scarcely possible, the rise of the proletariat should be followed by an era of confusion and change, and result in the restoration of monarchy and a new system of slavery, we should discover different ethical and esthetic concepts arising to replace the proletarian. The point that must be stressed, nevertheless, is that any such change, reversion to monarchy or despotism,[13] can flow only from necessary alterations in material conditions.

Although revolutions in esthetics are due to revolutions in ideas, every revolution in ideas is a consequence of a revolution in the social structure that the prevailing material conditions have produced.

---

12 See *An Economic Approach to the Yellow Problem* by the author, which appeared in April 12th issue of *The New Leader*.

13 These terms are used in the manner that they were applied by Montesquieu.

# LEWIS MUMFORD
## (1895–      )


BORN of middle-class parents in Flushing, Long Island, on October 19, 1895, Lewis Mumford was educated in the New York schools. He attended the College of the City of New York, where he pursued such studies as politics, philosophy, and English, later shifting to the study of sociology and architecture. During the First World War he served as a radio operator in the American navy. In 1919, after contributing reviews to *The Dial,* he became an associate editor of that magazine. He published many articles in various liberal, literary, and architectural periodicals. In addition, he delivered lectures on various subjects, especially literature and architecture, at various institutions.

Far-ranging in his interests, Lewis Mumford does not confine himself to literature, which is but one of his many-sided pursuits. His vision of humanity and the good life conditions his critical doctrine, but unlike the literary critics whose interests are purely aesthetic he has tried, at every stage of his development, to acquire accurate, thorough, first-hand knowledge—and that often of a specialized character—before venturing to diagnose the complex condition of Western culture. For Mumford the great crime of modern civilization is the progressive mechanization of life, which has degraded man instead of contributing to his intellectual emancipation, his leisure, his means of enjoyment. The machine, instead of being used to satisfy human desires, became an object of idolatrous worship, with the standards of mechanical efficiency and worldly success set up as the ultimate ideal. The contemplative arts, the arts that fulfill the needs of the inner world, must be cherished on their own account. In his essay, "The Arts," which appeared in *Whither Mankind,* Mumford declares:

"To deny that the machine can produce art is a fallacy; to believe that everything the machine produces is excellent art is also a romantic fallacy. To curb the machine and limit art to handicraft is a denial of opportunity. To extend the machine into provinces where it has no function is likewise a denial of opportunity."[1]

[1] Charles A. Beard (ed.), *Whither Mankind* (New York, 1928), p. 303.

Mumford's first book, *Story of Utopias* (1922) was followed by *Sticks and Stones* (1924), an attempt to evaluate architecture in terms of civilization. The future of American civilization, he believes, depends on the ability of the people not only to utilize wisely their heritage from the past but also to change their present attitudes and to project fresh forms into which their creative energies may flow. In *The Golden Day* Mumford, after exposing the tragic weakness of the life led by the pioneers, discusses the rich contributions made by the writers of the Golden Age. Emerson was the morning star, Thoreau the dawn, and Whitman the high noon of the movement. According to Mumford, the mission of creative thought

"is to gather into it all the living sources of its day, all that is vital in the practical life, all that is intelligible in science, all that is relevant in the social heritage and recasting these things into new forms and symbols, to react upon the blind drift of convention and habit and routine. Life flourishes only in this alternating rhythm of dream and deed: when one appears without the other, we can look forward to a shrinkage, a lapse, a devitalization. . . . What is valid in idealism is the belief in this process of re-molding, re-forming, re-creating, and so humanizing the rough chaos of existence."[2]

Mumford, however, gives a distorted picture of the frontier because he fails to view it in its proper historical perspective.

*The Brown Decades* (1931), subtitled "A Study of the Arts in America, 1865–1895," explores the achievements of that period, especially as exemplified in the arts—architecture, engineering, landscape designing, and painting. He feels it is time to stop bewailing the shortcomings and vices of American culture. Because of their exclusive interest in literature, critics have overlooked the creative vitality of the Brown Decades. What was vital in the art and life of that period did not perish with the coming of an aggressive imperialism.

Originally intending to compose a study of the machine, the city, religion, society, and the human personality, Lewis Mumford found that the materials on technics were so abundant that he had to abandon the plan, and incorporate in later works his analysis of the relation of the machine to architecture and other phases of civilization. *Technics and Civilization* (1934) makes a sober, documented investigation of the cultural preparations of the machine age, its origins and evolution, its present-day development and the outlook for the future. Mumford criticizes severely the foundations on which the natural sciences rest, their assumption that the measured, time-sequence picture of the universe is a true one,

2 Lewis Mumford, *The Golden Day* (New York, 1926), p. 166.

whereas in reality it does not include the total report of common human experience, reflecting only those aspects which can be observed and measured. Science flourished and accomplished much because it extruded all considerations of art and poetry and life that did not fall within its narrow compass. Man is a free agent, creating the conditions under which he lives, and not the passive slave of circumstances. If he can control the forces of Nature, why not those of the machine? While *Technics and Civilization* does not deal directly with the problems peculiar to literature or literary criticism, it is one of the most important books of our time, for in it Mumford attempts to clarify and crystallize those humane values which are fundamental to Western civilization. We must build up, he declares, "more organic centers of faith and action in the arts and in society and in the discipline of personality."[3] In the conception of this work he was deeply influenced by Sir Patrick Geddes and by vital thinkers like Victor Branford and Thorstein Veblen.

Mumford has carried the same central theme forward even more convincingly in *The Culture of Cities* (1938) and in *The Condition of Man* (1944). In the latter book he argues that man needs much more than economic security; he needs the cultivation of his personality, the stimulation of art, a vital interest in living, participation in the great society, creative release. The human personality must in the future become the touchstone of value. To *The Critique of Humanism* (1930) he contributed the essay, "Toward an Organic Humanism," in which he not only reveals the limitations of both the New Humanists and the New Mechanists but also states his philosophy of life. Personality is the crown and consummation of social achievement.[4]

Mumford has also written *Faith for Living* (1940) and *Men Must Act* (1939), the former book voicing his fears concerning our sick and possibly dying civilization and proposing some drastic remedies. It is an impassioned call to the democracies to wake up from their pragmatic slumber before it is too late. In a slashing polemic, "The Faith of Lewis Mumford," James T. Farrell calls attention to Mumford's ideological contradictions and confusion, his abandonment of science and reason, and his cultivation of a form of moral mysticism.

"He is one of the outstanding spokesmen among the war intellectuals. To those of us who have said that this war will not solve the major problems of our society and that it is a war for empire and world domination, the war

3 Lewis Mumford, *Technics and Civilization* (New York, 1934), p. 373.
4 C. H. Grattan (ed.), *The Critique of Humanism* (New York, 1930), p. 357.

intellectuals replied that the Second World War was not a continuation of its predecessor, on a new stage, but totally different in character."[5]

*Values for Survival* (1946), dedicated to his son Geddes, who died in the Second World War, is a collection of articles which elaborate a single theme that has increasingly dominated the mind of Mumford: What shall modern man do to be saved? One chapter, "Program for Survival," is in effect a continuation of the final chapter of *The Condition of Man.*

## BIBLIOGRAPHY

### TEXT

*The Story of Utopias.* New York, 1922.
*Sticks and Stones.* New York, 1924.
*Aesthetics.* Amenia, New York, 1925. (Pamphlet.)
*The Golden Day.* New York, 1926.
*American Taste.* New York, 1929.
*Herman Melville.* New York, 1929.
*The Brown Decades.* New York, 1931.
*Technics and Civilization.* New York, 1934.
*The Culture of Cities.* New York, 1938.
*Men Must Act.* New York, 1939.
*Faith for Living.* New York, 1940.
*The South in Architecture.* New York, 1941.
*The Condition of Man.* New York, 1944.
*Values for Survival.* New York, 1946.

### CRITICISM

Farrell, James T., *The League of Frightened Philistines.* New York, 1945.
Foerster, Norman, *Towards Standards.* New York, 1930.
Frank, Waldo, *In the American Jungle.* New York, 1937.
Glicksberg, Charles I., "Lewis Mumford and the Organic Synthesis," *Sewanee Review,* XLV, 55–77 (January–March, 1937).

## *ENVOI**

ENTERING our own day, one finds the relations of culture and experience a little difficult to trace out. With the forces that have

---

5 James T. Farrell, *The League of Frightened Philistines* (New York, 1945), p. 129.

* Reprinted from *The Golden Day* by Lewis Mumford, published by Boni and Liveright, copyright 1926, Boni and Liveright, Inc., used by permission of the author.

come over from the past, it is fairly easy to reckon: but how these are being modified or supplanted by new efforts of experience and new stores of culture one cannot with any assurance tell. Is Robert Frost the evening star of New England, or the first streak of a new dawn? Will the Dewey who is struggling to step outside his old preoccupations influence the coming generation, or will the more passive and utilitarian thinker continue to dominate? Will our daily activities center more completely in metropolises, for which the rest of the country serves merely as raw material, or will the politics and economics which produce this state give place to programs of regional development? What is the meaning of Lindsay and Sandburg and Mrs. Mary Austin? What is the promise of regional universities like Nebraska and North Carolina and New Mexico? May we look forward to a steady process of re-settlement; or will the habits of nomadry, expansion, and standardization prevail?

The notion that the forces that are now dominant will inevitably continue and grow stronger will not stand a close examination. Those who take refuge in this comfortable view are merely accepting facts as hopes when they think this would be desirable, or hopes as facts, when they profess that it is unavoidable. The effort of an age may not lead to its prolongation: it may serve to sharpen its antithesis and prepare the way for its own demise. So the stiffening of the old Renaissance motifs in the Eighteenth Century did not lead to their persistence: they formed the thorny nest in which Romanticism was hatched. It was in the decade of Watt's steam engine that Percy's *Reliques* were published; it was in the decade of the steamboat that Scott published his Waverley novels. Romanticism, for all its superficialities, gave men the liberty to breathe again; out of the clever imitations of Chatterton grew Wordsworth, and out of the meretricious Gothic of Walpole, Hugo and Viollet-le-Duc took possession anew of Notre Dame. I do not say that the Romantic poets changed the course of industrialism; but they altered the mood in which industrialism was received and quickened the recognition of its potentialities for evil, which a blind and complacent utilitarianism might have ignored for generations.

We have seen American culture as formed largely by two events: the breakdown of the medieval synthesis, in the centuries that preceded America's settlement and by the transferal to the new soil of an abstract and fragmentary culture, given definitive form by the Protestants of the Sixteenth Century, by the philosophers and scientists of the Seventeenth Century. Faced with the experience of the

American wilderness, we sought, in the capacity of pioneers, to find a new basis for culture in the primitive ways of forest and field, in the occupations of hunter, woodman, miner and pastoral nomad: but these occupations, practiced by people who were as much influenced by the idola of utilitarianism as by the deeper effort of the Romantic Movement, did not lead towards a durable culture: the pioneer environment became favorable to an even bleaker preoccupation with the abstractions of matter, money, and political rights. In this situation, the notion of a complete society, carrying on a complete and symmetrical life, tended to disappear from the minds of every one except the disciples of Fourier; with the result that business, technology, and science not merely occupied their legitimate place but took to themselves all that had hitherto belonged to art, religion, and poetry. Positive knowledge and practical action, which are indispensable elements in every culture, became the only living sources of our own; and as the Nineteenth Century wore on, we moved within an ever narrower circle of experience, living mean and illiberal lives.

The moving out of Europe was not merely due to the lure of free land and a multitude of succulent foods: it pointed to cultural vacancy. For three centuries the best minds in Europe had either been trying to get nourishment from the leftovers of classic culture or the Middle Ages, or they had been trying to reach some older source of experience, in order to supplement their bare spiritual fare. Science built up a new conception of the universe, and it endowed its disciples with the power to understand—and frequently to control—external events; but it achieved these results by treating men's central interests and desires as negligible, ignoring the fact that science itself was but a mode of man's activity as a living creature, and that its effort to cancel out the human element was only a very ingenious human expedient. In America, it was easy for an Emerson or a Whitman to see the importance of welding together the interests which science represented, and those which, through the accidents of its historic development, science denied. Turning from a limited European past to a wider heritage, guiding themselves by all the reports of their own day, these poets continued the old voyages of exploration on the plane of the mind, and, seeking passage to India, found themselves coasting along strange shores. None of the fine minds of the Golden Day was afraid to welcome the new forces that were at large in the world. Need I recall that Whitman wrote an apostrophe to the locomotive, that Emerson said a steamship sailing promptly between America and Europe might be as beautiful as a star, and that Thoreau, who loved to hear the wind in the pine needles, listened with equal pleasure to the music of the telegraph wires?

That practical instrumentalities were to be worshiped, never occurred to these writers; but that they added a new and significant element to our culture, which the poet was ready to absorb and include in his report upon the universe, was profoundly true. It is this awareness of new sources of experience that distinguishes the American writers of the Golden Day from their contemporaries in Europe. That the past was merely provisional, and that the future might be formed afresh were two patent generalizations which they drew directly from their environment. These perceptions called, of course, for great works of the imagination; for in proportion as intelligence was dealing more effectually with the instrumentalities of life, it became more necessary for the imagination to project more complete and satisfying ends. The attempt to prefigure in the imagination a culture which should grow out of and refine the experiences the transplanted European encountered on the new soil, mingling the social heritage of the past with the experience of the present, was the great activity of the Golden Day: the essays of Emerson, the poems of Whitman, the solitary musings of Melville all clustered around this central need. None of these men was caught by the dominant abstractions: each saw life whole, and sought a whole life.

We cannot return to the America of the Golden Day, nor keep it fixed in the postures it once naturally assumed; and we should be far from the spirit of Emerson or Whitman if we attempted to do this. But the principal writers of that time are essential links between our own lives and that earlier, that basic, America. In their work, we can see in pristine state the essential characteristics that still lie under the surface: and from their example, we can more readily find our own foundations, and make our own particular point of departure. In their imaginations, a new world began to form out of the distracting chaos: wealth was in its place, and science was in its place, and the deeper life of man began again to emerge, no longer stunted or frustrated by the instrumentalities it had conceived and set to work. For us who share their vision, a revival of the moribund, or a relapse into the pragmatic acquiescence is equally impossible; and we begin again to dream Thoreau's dream—of what it means to live a whole human life.

A complete culture leads to the nurture of the good life; it permits the fullest use, or sublimation, of man's natural functions and activities. Confronted by the raw materials of existence, a culture works them over into new patterns, in which the woof of reality is crossed by the warp of desire. Love is the type of desire in all its modes; and in the recent emergence of a handful of artists who by the force of their inner life have seen the inessential and makeshift character of a large part of the daily routine, there is perhaps the prophecy of a new stream of tendency in American life.

Henry Adams, in his *Education,* observed that the American artist, in distinction to all the great writers of classic times, seemed scarcely conscious of the power of sex; he was aware of neither a Virgin nor a Venus. In the works of Sherwood Anderson, Edna Millay, Eugene O'Neill, and Waldo Frank this aversion has disappeared: human passion comes back to the scene with almost volcanic exuberance, drawing all the habits and conventionalties and prudences in its wake. It is through brooding over their sexual experience that Mr. Anderson's characters begin to perceive the weaknesses, the limitations, the sordidness of the life about them: they awaken with the eagerness of a new adolescence to discover, like the father in *Many Marriages,* that what seemed to them "real life," the externalisms, the business arrangements, the neat routine of office and factory, was in fact an unrelated figment, something which drew upon a boyish self that made sandpiles, whittled sticks, or played soldier and wanted to be captain. Whereas the deep and disruptive force that rouses them, and makes beauty credible and desire realizable, is not, as the Gradgrinds would have it, a dream at all, but the prelude to every enduring reality.

Desire is real! Sherwood Anderson's people come to this, as to a final revelation. But if sexual desire, why not every human desire? In full lust of life man is not merely a poor creature, wryly adjusting himself to external circumstances: he is also a creator, an artist, making circumstances conform to the aims and necessities he himself freely imposes. "Sooner murder an infant in its cradle," wrote William Blake, "than nurse unacted desires;" and in the deep sense of Blake's application, this covers every aspect of life, since a failure of desire, imagination, and vision tends to spread over into every activity. Practical intelligence and a prudent adjustment to externalities are useful only in a secondary position: they are but props to straighten the plant when it begins to grow: at the bottom of it all must be a soil and a seed, an inner burgeoning, an eagerness of life. Art in its many forms is a union of imaginative desire, desire sublimated and socialized, with actuality: without this union, desires become idiotic, and actualities perhaps even a little more so. It is not that our instrumental activities are mean: far from it: but that life is mean when it is entirely absorbed in instrumental activities. Beneath the organized vivacity of our American communities, who is not aware of a blankness, a sterility, a boredom, a despair? Their activity, their very lust, is the galvanic response to an external stimulus, given by an organism that is dead.

The power to escape from this sinister world can come only by the double process of encountering more complete modes of life, and of reformulating a more vital tissue of ideas and symbols to supplant those which have led us into the stereotyped interests and actions which we endeavor in vain to identify with a full human existence. We must rectify the abstract framework of ideas which we have used, in lieu of a full culture, these last few centuries. In part, we shall achieve this by a criticism of the past, which will bring into the foreground those things that have been left out of the current scheme of life and thought. Mr. A. N. Whitehead's *Science and the Modern World,* and Mr. Victor Branford's *Science and Sanctity* are landmarks towards this new exploration; for they both suggest the groundwork of a philosophy which shall be oriented as completely towards Life as the dominant thought since Descartes has been directed towards the Machine. To take advantage of our experience and our social heritage and to help in creating this new idolum is not the smallest adventure our generation may know. It is more imaginative than the dreams of the transcendentalist, more practical than the work of the pragmatists, more drastic than the criticisms of the old social revolutionists, and more deeply cultural than all our early attempts to possess the simulacra of culture. It is nothing less than the effort to conceive a new world.

*Allons! the road is before us!*

# PAUL ELMER MORE

## (1864–1937)

PAUL ELMER MORE, born in St. Louis on December 12, 1864, graduated from Washington University with an A.B. After receiving his Master of Arts degree in 1892, he was impelled to take up the study of Sanskrit and Pali and comparative religion. During his stay at Harvard University he formed a lifelong friendship with Irving Babbitt. More was on the faculty at Harvard and Bryn Mawr, but teaching he decided was not his life work. The religious problem troubled him acutely. Like Milton at Horton, he retired in 1897 to Shelburne, New Hampshire, living there as a virtual hermit, but with the intention not merely of devoting himself intensively to a studious life but also of achieving some lasting, unifying faith. He read widely and deeply, composing the essays that later went into the *Shelburne Essays*. After this period of voluntary retirement, he became literary editor of the *Independent*. From 1903 to 1909 he served as literary editor of the New York *Evening Post*. From 1909 to 1914 he held the influential position of editor-in-chief of *The Nation,* giving the magazine a distinctly literary tone. Then he settled down at Princeton. Scholar, critic, and Humanist, More turned at last devoutly to the Christian tradition for salvation.

The *Shelburne Essays,* most of which were produced from 1901 to 1914, mark an important contribution to American criticism, though one cannot accord them the greatness ascribed to them by More's enthusiastic biographer, Robert Shafer.[1] Most of the essays illuminate some phase of literary criticism, and are impressive for their solidity of substance, their able presentation of a point of view not given sufficient attention in modern letters.

More is a critic who from the start of his career spent his energies in seeking for a body of universal standards, the unifying principle that would give meaning and direction to his life. The best statement of his

[1] Robert Shafer, *Paul Elmer More and American Criticism* (New Haven, 1935), p. 112. He goes so far as to place More's work above that of Matthew Arnold.

253

critical method is to be found in "The Demon of the Absolute." Adamant in his hostility to the philosophy of naturalism that dominated modern literature, More consistently sought to apply ethical criteria to the examination and evaluation of letters; he had no interest in formulating a method by means of which the critic, undistracted by ethical standards, could decide why one work was superior or inferior to another. As a Humanist More posited a dualism between the animal and the human, the lower and the higher self. The individual is left helpless unless he learns to control his animal impulses and conforms to the disciplined restraint exercised by the inner check. Unlike Babbitt, however, More drew closer and closer to the religious synthesis, finally embracing Anglo-Catholicism.

Few critics can compare with More in depth, range of scholarship, close knowledge and appreciation of literature, ancient and modern, and above all, in distinction of style. His richly stored mind can bring its resources to bear on whatever subject is under discussion. Though he is both penetrating and illuminating, he makes some startling mistakes in literary judgment. His deep-seated bias against humanitarianism makes itself felt in his essay on "The Religious Ground of Humanitarianism." For him there is this eternal truth to which the mass of men are strangely blind: namely, that the things of this world pass away; the personal self with all its ephemeral desires is a peculiarly stubborn illusion that must be transcended. Whatever progress humanity has made is due to the activity of its great men working within the framework of competition, and it is only just that they should receive their proper material reward. This note of ingrained conservatism runs strongly through More's later writings. No amount of sentimental yearning will alter the laws of society, which are fixed.[2]

Like Babbitt, More contends that the intellectual life of our time has its source in Rousseau more than in any other man, and he holds Rousseau chiefly responsible for our moral laxity, our sentimental humanitarianism, our illusions of liberty and progress, natural religion and innate goodness. All these theories were fallacious because they did not take account of the cleft in man's nature, the dualism that is rooted in the omnipresent sense of evil. Even in literature does this dualism manifest itself, underlying the passages of poetry that move us most deeply. "It may even be used— though with extreme caution—as a test to discriminate the higher from the lower realm of artistic intuition."[3] In the preface to *The Drift of*

[2] Paul Elmer More. *Shelburne Essays*. First Series. (Boston and New York, 1904), p. 250.
[3] Paul Elmer More, *Shelburne Essays*. Sixth Series. (New York and London, 1909), p. 22.

*Romanticism* (1913), More replies to those who took him to task for forcing writers whose work was instinct with beauty into a Procrustean ethical framework instead of responding aesthetically to this beauty. More declares that he does not practice the kind of criticism "that limits itself to looking at the thing in itself, or the parts of a thing as they successively strike the mind."[4] The critic who beholds the larger relations, the central drift and ultimate consequences of a dominant movement, is to be forgiven if he dwells on these rather than the particular aesthetic qualities of a book or author. If this movement constitutes a grave danger to society, then there is no justification for ignoring it. Like Goethe, More identifies classicism with health and romanticism with disease.

It is not surprising to find More taking issue with the man of science, directing his heaviest fire at Huxley, the champion of Darwinism and scientific thought. Science is unacceptable to More on the ground that it presents us with a closed mechanical system, determined in all its parts; it therefore disposes of spontaneity, the free action of the will, and the fascinating, complex world of the inner life. Like Babbitt, he sums up his opposition by arguing that science and romanticism, though they seem at odds, have much in common. Naturalism is undesirable because it denies the authority of religion and the truth of supernatural intuition. Formally art can rise to a high standard of excellence only if the imagination of the artist is disciplined by the inner check.

More's literary criticism cannot be adequately understood without reference to his lifelong quest for religious unification. *Pages from an Oxford Diary* (1937) indicates that More possessed a more complex, emotionally richer personality than his writings on literature alone would lead us to suspect. He found peace of mind by becoming a conscious Platonist, coupling his Platonism with faith in Christianity. More finally came to believe in the existence of a personal supernatural agent at work, finding the evidence for theism everywhere present on the face of the earth.

Robert Shafer defends More against the attacks of other critics, particularly against the charge that he paid little attention to his contemporaries. The index to *Shelburne Essays* indicates the wide range of More's interests as a critic, but of the 117 essays only twenty-three are devoted to American literature. He has dealt with such writers as Henry Adams, T. B. Aldrich, Emerson, Jonathan Edwards, Benjamin Franklin, Freneau, Hawthorne, Lafcadio Hearn, William James, Longfellow, Poe, Thoreau, Walt Whitman, but it is difficult to recall a single one of these essays which voices unqualified appreciation or hearty acceptance. Certainly he

4 Paul Elmer More, *The Drift of Romanticism. Shelburne Essays*. Eighth Series. (Boston and New York, 1913), p. vii.

is much more at home in the spacious field of English literature; the traditional, time-honored names of the Anglo-Saxon literary heritage far outweigh in number the writers of his own time and land.

For range of subject matter, depth of insight, sound and far-reaching erudition and stylistic excellence, it is difficult to come across an American critic in the early part of the twentieth century who rivals him. His critical work has suffered, however, precisely because he adhered so inflexibly to moral standards in the evaluation of literature. The Humanism he advocated was conservative, exclusive, often intolerant. Such moralistic inflexibility blinded him to the virtues of Proust and the originality of Joyce. As a Humanist, More was convinced that beauty cannot be cut off from meaning and value. Though literature is measured by the working of the imagination, great literature must combine imaginative richness with nobility of content.[5]

## BIBLIOGRAPHY

### TEXT

*A Century of Indian Epigrams.* Boston, 1898.
*Benjamin Franklin.* Boston, 1900.
*Shelburne Essays.* First Series. New York and London, 1904.
*Shelburne Essays.* Second Series. New York and London, 1905.
*Shelburne Essays.* Third Series. New York and London, 1905.
*Shelburne Essays.* Fourth Series. New York and London, 1906.
*Shelburne Essays.* Fifth Series. New York and London, 1906.
*Shelburne Essays. Studies of Religious Dualism.* Sixth Series. New York and London, 1909.
*Shelburne Essays.* Seventh Series. New York and London, 1910.
*Nietzsche.* Boston and New York, 1912.
*The Drift of Romanticism. Shelburne Essays.* Eighth Series. Boston, 1913.
*Aristocracy and Justice. Shelburne Essays.* Ninth Series. Boston, 1915.
*Platonism.* Princeton, 1917.
*With the Wits. Shelburne Essays.* Tenth Series. Boston and New York, 1919.
*A New England Group and Others. Shelburne Essays.* Eleventh Series Boston and New York, 1921.
*The Religion of Plato.* Princeton, 1921.
*Hellenistic Philosophies.* Princeton, 1923.
*The Christ of the New Testament.* Princeton, 1924.
*Christ the Word.* Princeton, 1927.
*The Demon of the Absolute.* Princeton, 1928.

[5] See "How to Read Lycidas," Paul Elmer More, *On Being Human* (Princeton and London, 1936).

*The Catholic Faith.* Princeton, 1931.
*The Sceptical Approach to Religion.* Princeton, 1934.
*Selected Shelburne Essays.* New York, 1935.
*On Being Human.* Princeton, 1936.
*Pages from an Oxford Diary.* Princeton, 1937.

## CRITICISM

Bandler, B., "Paul Elmer More," in C. H. Grattan (ed.), *A Critique of Humanism.* New York, 1930, pp. 281–297.

Brett, George S., "Paul Elmer More: A Study," *University of Toronto Quarterly,* IV, 279–295 (April, 1935).

Brown, S. G., "Paul Elmer More as Critic," *Sewanee Review,* XLVII, 476–497 (October, 1939).

Elliott, G. R., "The Religious Dissension of Babbitt and More," *American Review,* IX, 252–265 (Summer, 1937).

Foerster, Norman (ed.), *Humanism and America.* New York, 1930.

Gregory, Horace, "On Paul Elmer More and His Shelburne Essays," *Accent,* IV, 140–149 (Spring, 1944).

Leander, Folke, *Humanism and Naturalism.* Göteborg, Sweden, 1937.

——, "More—'Puritan á Rebours,'" *American Scholar,* VII, 438–457 (Autumn, 1938).

Lewisohn, Ludwig, *Expression in America.* New York, 1932.

More, L. P., "Shelburne Revisited." *Sewanee Review,* XLVIII, 457–460 (October, 1940).

Morrow, Felix, "The Serpent's Enemy." *Symposium,* I, 168–193 (April, 1930).

Munson, G. B., *Destinations.* New York, 1928.

Mercier, Louis J. A., *The Challenge of Humanism.* New York, 1933.

Peck, Harvey W., "Some Aspects of the Criticism of Paul Elmer More," *Sewanee Review,* XXVI, 63–84 (January, 1918).

Parkes, H. B., "Paul Elmer More: Manichean," *Hound & Horn,* V, 477–483 (April-June, 1932).

Peters, Alain T. (ed.), *A Spingarn Enchiridion.* New York, 1929.

Ransom, John Crowe, *God Without Thunder.* New York, 1930.

Richards, P. S., "The Religious Philosophy of Paul Elmer More," *Criterion,* XVI, 205–219 (January, 1937).

Shafer, Robert, *Paul Elmer More and American Criticism.* New Haven, 1935.

Sherman, Stuart P., *Americans.* New York, 1922.

——, *The Emotional Discovery of America.* New York, 1932.

Smith, Bernard, *Forces in American Criticism.* New York, 1939.

Stamm, Rudolf, "Paul Elmer Mores Suche nach einer lebendigen Tradition," *Englische Studien,* LXXII, 58–72 (October, 1937).

Wilson, Edmund, *The Triple Thinkers.* New York, 1938.

Young, M. O., *A Bibliography of Paul Elmer More*. Princeton, 1941.
Zabel, M. D., "An American Critic," *Poetry*, L, 330–336 (September, 1937).
Zeitlin, Jacob (ed.), "Stuart P. Sherman and Paul Elmer More: Correspondence," *Bookman*, LXX, 43–53 (September, 1929).

## THE DEMON OF THE ABSOLUTE*

HOWEVER it may have been a couple of decades ago, there are few men today bold enough, or blind enough, to deny the presence of certain demons in human society,—the Moloc of violence, the Beelzebub of treachery, the Belial of lying flatteries, the Mammon of gold, the Mephistopheles of scepticism, and others of the Stygian Council escaped through the open gates of hell. And I suppose that not many educated men today, looking back upon history, will doubt that these disturbers of the peace have always been stalking over the world, plying their trade of malice, though the worst of them, the hobgoblin of fear, may have been unchained only since the War. But there is one demon who retains so much of celestial glamour, who so wears the robe of authority, that he still moves about unnoticed or passes for an angel of light. And the mischief of his art is that the finer minds are often those most subject to his wiles. I mean the Demon of the Absolute.

This Demon of the Absolute is nothing else but rationalism, what Francis Bacon called the *intellectus sibi permissus,* or, if you wish it in plainer English, reason run amuck. Now reason, so long as it is content to accept the actual data of experience, is manifestly one of our diviner faculties; at every step in life it is our guide and friend, and without it we can do nothing wisely or prosperously. And that is why it becomes so dangerous when, disregarding "matters of fact, those unconcerning things," it sets up its own absolutes as the truth and asks us to act thereupon. For there are no absolutes in nature; they are phantoms created by reason itself in its own likeness, delusions which, when once evoked, usurp the field of reality and bring endless confusion in their train. Their close is chaos, in which Anarchy rules supreme. You can trace their disastrous effects in philosophy ever since Parmenides and Heraclitus in ancient days

* Reprinted from *The Demon of the Absolute* by Paul Elmer More, copyright, 1928, Princeton University Press; used by permission of the publishers.

started the pretty wrangle, still going on, between the metaphysicians who conceive the ultimate reality of things as immutable unity and those who reduce the universe to pure flux and multiplicity. You can see the Demon at work in politics whenever men begin to contend for some final unchecked authority in the State, whether it be lodged in a monarch or in all the people. It has wrought havoc in religion by presenting to faith the alternative between an absolute omnipotent God or no God at all, and between an infallible Church or undisciplined individualism. But nowhere has it produced more stupid contrariety than among the critics of art and literature.

## I. STANDARDS

If you doubt the malignity of the Demon in the field of criticism open one of Mr. H. L. Mencken's popular volumes of *Prejudices*. You will find his pages scintillating hell-fire in the manner of the damnatory clauses in the Athanasian Creed. You will learn that "Brownell argues eloquently for standards that would bind an imaginative author as tightly as a Sunday-school superintendent is bound by the Ten Commandments and the Mann Act. Sherman [this was before that genial writer had listened to the lure of Broadway] tries to save Shakespeare for the right-thinking by proving that he was an Iowa Methodist—a member of the local Chamber of Commerce, a contemner of Reds, an advocate of democracy and the League of Nations, a patriotic dollar-a-year-man during the American scare. . . . And Babbitt, to make an end, gives over his days and nights to deploring Rousseau's anarchistic abrogation of 'the veto power' over the imagination, leading to such 'wrongness' in both art and life that it threatens 'to wreck civilization.' "

If I have omitted my own name from this elegant diatribe, it is not because I was too obscure to escape the attention of Mr. Mencken and his ilk. Alas, no; *et tacitum vivit sub pectore vulnus*. Perhaps, in fact, the simplest and most direct way to deal with the matter will be to give a little of my sad experience in those days, now beginning to be remote, when I was an editor and frequent writer of essays. I used to solace myself then with the boast that I was at once the least read and most hated author in existence. Other writers I admitted might be more hated, and I hoped that a few were less read; but the combination I claimed for myself as a unique distinction.

The watchword among the wolves was given by a Brooklyn newspaper in the statement that a certain book of mine was "pathetic

when it was not disgusting." There was a finality about that which I
could not but admire. Sometimes the attack was more picturesque.
I remember, for instance, coming into the Century Club one morning
for breakfast and being greeted on the steps by Professor Dunning,
that rare gentleman now gone to his rest, with the quizzical remark,
"And so you were one of those who gave the hemlock to Socrates!"
followed, when I expressed my surprise, by the query, "Haven't you
seen the last issue of the *New Republic?*" Well, I picked up the
magazine, and discovered that to its reviewer a recent book of mine
on Platonism proved me to be such a one as would have joined the
murderers of Socrates had I been living at the time. And not content
with this the writer, grasping at the most awful insult in his vocabulary, declared that I had the temper of a banker and resembled the
late J. P. Morgan. Imagine it; imagine the exasperation of a reviewer
brought to such straits of fatuity!

A good deal of this splutter of indignation might be attributed to
the naïve cause avowed by a lady in the *North American Review:*
"I do not like you, Dr. Fell; The reason why I cannot tell." And to
such a mood I would bow in silence. Who would undertake to defend his own amiability? But other critics had a very definite reason
for their animosity, a reason which might have lifted the debate out
of the petty range of personalities, though to my sorrow it did not.
For example, one of my excited adversaries took the occasion of a
couple of books by John Cowper Powys to make comparisons that,
to speak mildly, were not meant to be agreeable. "Mr. Powys," he
observed, "is what is currently termed a subjective critic. Only, perhaps, in America are there people left who object to that sort of
criticism and seek for some cosmic footrule with which to measure
works of art." In contrast with the true subjective critic I was then
named as a specimen of the "arid" sort who think they have a cosmic
footrule in their pocket. Another gentleman, in "A Note on Criticism" contributed to a New York review, was, if possible, even more
explicit. It is the hidebound critic, he averred, who ought to be reminded of the true meaning of culture, and not "the avid child who
can digest green apples where later he won't be able to stand the
delicate monstrosities of Katherine Fullerton Gerould." And then
the reviewer added, like Jove scattering his bolts upon the just and
the unjust, " 'Wholesome' boys are spanked every day for reading
detective stories which delight"—strange fellowship in joy—Elihu
Root and Charles E. Hughes and myself. Whether Mr. Root and
Mr. Hughes indulge in the secret vice of reading detective stories I

do not know; it is awful to contemplate such depravity. As for my poor self, I might have suspected that, by coupling my name so unexpectedly with two distinguished statesmen, the reviewer intended a compliment, had he not held me up elsewhere in the article as a deplorable case of the madness that comes from rejecting "the irresponsibility of temperament" and searching for "a true criterion of criticism."

There you have it. The cat is out of the bag, that Demon of the Absolute who has played such pranks with philosophy and politics and religion, and is now let loose in the pleasant garden of letters. On one side is set up a monster of pedantry and over against him is ranged the genius who champions a complete irresponsibility of temperament.

To all which I would say that this denunciation of standards by souls enamoured of æsthetic adventure is very pretty if taken as rhetoric, but has no connexion with facts. Has there ever been a sane critic who thought he had a cosmic footrule in his pocket, or believed he could measure the value of a work of art by some infallible standard? Sane critic, I say, for I do remember an article by an eminent psychologist which undertook to create an absolute scale for measuring the merits of style. With the audacity of an experimenter used to laboratory methods he gave a series of quotation, ranging from college exercises up to acknowledged masterpieces, and marked them by percentages, as if he had been correcting a paper in mathematics. He then proceeded to show how, with these specimens as a testing scale, any one could take a paragraph of English and rate it as so many per cent good or bad, without fear of contradiction. The results were excruciatingly funny; but the fellow, as I said, was a laboratory psychologist, and a psychologist of that school has been described as a student who investigates the mind, having first acknowledged that he has no mind to investigate. And I remember another scholar, not a psychologist but a professor of English in a large university, who promulgated a somewhat similar scheme for establishing literary values of a more complicated sort. He had discovered that the effect of a piece of literature depended on its possession of ten qualities—such as pathos, humour, sublimity, and the like. To each of these qualities he allowed ten points or less, so that a perfect piece of writing, having all the qualities in the highest degree, by a simple process of addition would be graded one hundred per cent, and so on down the scale. The scheme possessed the ease and infallibility of a problem in arithmetic; it was a veritable cosmic footrule, and the perplexities of the critic were forever ended. The only difficulty was in the application of the rule. As I recollect the measurements actually made by the learned inventor, in a long list of tested books *Beside the Bonnie Briar Bush* stood at the top as the greatest work of literature ever produced, while *Hamlet* was far down towards the bottom. And so of the students of this distinguished pedagogue I fear it might be said:

> The hungry sheep look up, and are not fed,
> But swoln with wind and the rank mist they draw,
> Rot inwardly, and foul contagion spread;
> Besides what the grim wolf—

this academic wolf being no other than those so-called utilitarian pursuits that ever stand ready to draw off the ill-fed students of the humanities.

If the foes of standards have in mind such freaks of criticism as these, let us bid them Godspeed. No sane critic believes that questions of taste can be settled by an absolute rule like problems in arithmetic. But is there any more sanity in setting up an absolute law of irresponsibility?

Luther once likened our human nature to a drunkard on horseback: prop him up on one side, and over he topples on the other. The simile is apt, and applies to taste as well as to morals. As soon as we are convinced that no absolute standard exists, forthwith we flop to the other extreme and swear that there are absolutely no standards at all; so hard is it to keep the middle path of common sense. And so behind the light-armed skirmishers of the press whom, to say the truth, no one takes very seriously, we have scholars like Mr. Spingarn, who, with the inverted sort of pedantry common today, teach a ready public that art is only expression and criticism only impression, and that no one need bother to hunt for standards of taste, which are not and never were. And worse than that, we have sober philosophers like Lord Balfour, arguing for pure relativity of taste on metaphysical grounds:

> That is for every man most lovable which he most dearly loves. That is for every man most beautiful which he most deeply admires. Nor is this merely a reiteration of the old adage that there is no disputing about tastes. It goes far deeper; for it implies that, in the most important cases of all, a dispute about either love or beauty would not merely be useless: it would be wholly unmeaning.

These men, I assert, and not the champions of reasonable standards of taste, are the veritable addicts of the Absolute and slaves of
the Demon. They theorize very persuasively, but have their conclusions any relation to fact? Is it true that admiration so varies with
time and place, and from individual to individual, that no common
sense of beauty is discoverable which can be used as a basis of conversation and to which appeal can be made in argument? If my theme
were the plastic arts, it would be sufficient to adduce the indisputable
truth that the forms and pictures prized as lovely by the Orient do
sooner or later obtain due recognition in the West, and *vice versa*.
However it be with minor eccentricities, the supremely beautiful
things in Greece and Italy and India and China are beautiful for
all the world. But for our convenience we may look rather to the
extraordinary absence of local and temporal barriers in lyrical
poetry. When Simonides composed his epitaph for the Spartans who
fell at Thermopylæ:

O passer by, tell the Lacedæmonians that we lie here obeying their
orders—

he used words that would carry the same poetic thrill to all men of
all lands. Perhaps you will say that the emotion expressed by
Simonides is so simple, the language so devoid of ornament or metaphor or fancy, that the couplet is scarcely to be reckoned as poetry.
I think no one acquainted with the Greek would raise such an objection; but let it pass. Let us take one of the epigrams of the Anthology,
written by a poet of no particular reputation and replete with the
imagery of pagan superstition:

Do thou, who rowest the boat of the dead in the water of this reedy lake,
for Hades, stretch out thy hand, dark Charon, to the son of Cinyras, as he
mounts the ladder by the gangway, and receive him. For his sandals will
cause the lad to slip, and he fears to set his feet naked on the sand of the
shore.

That is one of the trifles of art, yet its pathetic beauty could touch
the heart of an American, Lafcadio Hearn, who had made his home
in the far Orient, and who set by its side for comparison a *tanka* (a
lyric confined to thirty-one syllables) of a Japanese governor on the
death of his son:

As he is so young, he cannot know the way. . . . To the messenger of the
Underworld I will give a bribe, and entreat him, saying: "Do thou kindly
take the little one upon thy back along the road."

Surely there is a common ground of feeling and taste even in these minor things, something that overleaps all estrangement of land and race and age. So, to come nearer home, Ben Jonson, "Saint Ben," as Herrick called him, Briton to the core of him, could cull a few phrases scattered through the very prosaic letters of Philostratus, and weave them into a song which, given the knowledge of the English tongue, will find an echo in the heart of any lover of beauty the world over:

> Drink to me only with thine eyes,
>     And I will pledge with mine;
> Or leave a kiss but in the cup,
>     And I'll not look for wine.
> The thirst that from the soul doth rise,
>     Doth ask a drink divine:
> But might I of Jove's nectar sup,
>     I would not change for thine.

And Goethe, alone amidst the trees and the mountains, in the wide silence of a summer night, once wrote in German what a Chinese, centuries ago and far away by the shores of the Yangtse River, might have expressed in his own metrical form:

> *Ueber allen Gipfeln*
> *Ist Rub.*

But we have no need to multiply examples. It is a simple fact, not a theory, that in the matter of taste there is still that which is not confined by the boundaries of space or nullified by the process of time, and which makes the whole world kin. This is not to say that we can lay down any absolute law of agreement; but it does mean, emphatically, that certain standards of taste exist which approximate, more or less, to universality. It is a direct challenge to the veracity of those who would stop our mouths with the dictum that a debate about either love or beauty is not merely useless, but wholly unmeaning.

If only the henchmen of the press, who have been seduced by the prophets of the flux, would act consistently on the principle that there is no disputing about tastes! But this is the curious fact: just so surely as you meet with one of these relativistic critics, you will find him pretty soon uttering the most savage and exemplary judgements against those who disagree with him. This Mr. Powys, for instance, who is regarded as a model of adventurous and irrespon-

sible sympathy, can slash about when he pleases with a cutting assurance which hints at a bowie-knife in his pocket, however he may
eschew cosmic footrules. But the really test case is the great Anatole
France, the flowing philosopher *par excellence,* from whom so many
of our late-emancipated youth have borrowed their literary creed, to
the effect that criticism is a continual adventure of the soul, a kind
of freebooting romance for the curious and enlightened. Well, one
day, in the course of his *Vie Littéraire,* Anatole France felt obliged
to write about a certain novel, *La Terre,* which no amount of adventurous sympathy could make him like, which, in fact, he heartily
disliked; and this is how he sums up his condemnation of the author:
"He [M. Zola] has no taste, and I have come to believe that the
want of taste is that mysterious sin spoken of by the Scripture, the
greatest of sins, which alone will never be pardoned."

In other words, when Anatole France laid aside theory and spoke
his real mind, he could judge as incisively as M. Brunetière or any
other avowed doctrinaire; and admittedly he judges from a central
principle of his nature, which he calls taste. How, indeed, could it be
otherwise? Every man likes certain things and dislikes certain other
things; more than that, every man likes a certain class of things and
dislikes a certain other class of things, and praises or dispraises by
a standard, whether he names it taste or refuses to acknowledge that
it has a name.

## II. Tradition

The simple truth is that every man, unless he be a dumb idiot,
has a standard, more or less consciously chosen, by which he judges,
and when the "irresponsibles" exhibit such fury at the sound of the
word, they are merely throwing dust in our eyes to confuse the issue.
The real question is not whether there are standards, but whether
they shall be based on tradition or shall be struck out brand new by
each successive generation or by each individual critic. And first of
all is there in fact any discoverable tradition of taste, or do we deceive ourselves in imagining its existence?

The relativists, like Lord Balfour, point to the mistakes of criticism in the past, and particularly to its failure to recognize great
works of original genius on their first appearance. They take a
ghoulish glee in quoting the sentences of Jeffrey and Gifford and
the other anti-romanticists of the early nineteenth century. And
what, they ask, shall we expect of "official" criticism which says that

*The Excursion* will never do, tells a certain young surgeon's apprentice named Keats to go back to his gallipots, and has no better description of Shelley's poems than "convulsive caperings of Pegasus labouring under colic pains"? Well, those much-maligned maligners are like the devil in one respect at least: they are not so black as they are painted. There were fools among them, no doubt; and our own feeble-minded are not all in asylums. But if those who take most delight in decrying Jeffrey, for instance, would condescend to read what they abuse, they would find that his taste was generally good, and that most, not all, of the things he condemned were worthy of condemnation. They might learn, too, that the despised Gifford's chief work, in *The Baviad* and *The Mæviad,* was to bring contempt upon the "namby-pamby madrigals" and "splay-foot doggrel," the "motley fustian, neither verse nor prose," of a horde of much-lauded poets now well forgotten. As Scott said, he "squabashed the Della Cruscans at one blow." I suspect that one of the things we most need in our own day is just a *Baviad* to pillory some of the lawless men who are trampling down the wild thyme of Parnassus.

I am far from saying that Gifford and his tribe were always judicious or generous. I do say, however, that where they failed it was precisely because they were not in the tradition, but pronounced sentence from the narrow and ephemeral point of view of the pseudo-classic, not the classic, school. Those who scold these errant critics as an illustration of the complete relativity of taste, forget that they do so by virtue of the validity of a larger tradition. It is with tradition as it is with standards: because tradition is not absolute and infallible, men are prone to cry out that there is no tradition. That is a habit deep-rooted in human nature, hard to eradicate. No intelligent man supposes that tradition is a scale fixed once and forever in all its *nuances* of valuation; but it is a simple matter of history, nevertheless, that a long tradition of taste does exist, wavering and obscure on its outskirts, growing steadier and more immutable as we approach its center. Let us take a poet who stands in this central tradition and follow his fortunes, briefly by necessity, in general estimation. We shall see, I think, that the law of taste is the least changeable fact of human nature, less changeable than religious creeds, far less changeable than scientific theories. The advent of Christianity has left it untouched, and the waning of faith does not trouble it. The hypotheses of science—elemental spirits, and phlogiston, corpuscular and undulatory explanations of light, atoms and ions and the continuum, catastrophism and natural selection—come and pass and come again, while the central tradition of taste is still the same. Wars and revolutions alter everything, but not this. It is like the sea:

> Man marks the earth with ruin, his control
> Stops with the shore.

If anything in history seems to be settled it is the position of Homer among the Greeks. To him they turned for the source of literature, the mirror of conduct, the fountain-head of all right thinking and all right speaking. He was the guide of the young, the philosopher of the middle-aged, the friend of the old. Not that his acceptance was absolute. Plato, though he could write of Homer in terms of adoration, also censured him harshly for his familiar treatment of the gods; and there was a crabbed grammarian named Zoilus, who won the epithet *Homeromastix,* scourge of Homer, for his systematic abuse of the poet. But these exceptions only prove that a solid fact need not be an absolute fact. And what Homer was to the Greeks, he continued to be to the Romans until the old civilization passed away.

With the coming of the Dark Ages—significant name—there is a change. The Greek language was almost forgotten in the West, and as a consequence the *Iliad* and *Odyssey* were little read. Nevertheless, the tradition was not lost, nor even totally eclipsed, and with the revival of learning it emerges once more, never again, let us hope, to be darkened. There were, however, several curious and, in part, contradictory currents in Renaissance criticism which for a while prevented the complete acknowledgment of Homer's literary supremacy. For one thing, owing to the language of the *Æneid* and to the ease with which Christian ideas could be read into various passages, Virgil had supplanted Homer through the Middle Ages as the master poet; and the scholars of the Renaissance, despite their pose of general rebellion, were too deeply involved in the spirit of the immediate past to escape its æsthetical restrictions without a long struggle. And the theory of the new criticism, with its insistence on the authority of reason and on the authority of age, tended to uphold the superiority of the Latin epic. These two principles of authority were clearly and definitively formulated by Scaliger in his *Poetice,* published in 1561, and were applied to the tradition of taste with childlike confidence. "Homer's genius," he says (*Poetice,* v, 2), "was the  greatest; his art was of such a character that he seems rather to have happened on it than to have cultivated it. Wherefore there is no reason for surprise if I find in him a certain Idea of nature, but not art. . . . Then Virgil, having received art from Homer in this rude state, raised it by his selective study of nature and his judgement to the highest point of perfection. . . . As in the very circle of our life there are many things, yet few give pleasure, and still fewer raise admiration; so many things would insinuate themselves into the breast of the poet, but not all are to be admitted. He who follows the example of Virgil prefers therefore to exclude an occasional good thing which might give pleasure, rather than admit anything which can offer even the suspicion of offence."

Here you will see how Scaliger applies to Homer and Virgil the false notion of reason as a faculty superior to, and in a sense hostile to, the creative imagination—the notion underlying pseudo-classic art and pseudo-classic criticism, which, strange as it may sound, is still confused with the true classic by some of our belated scholars. It is easy to understand how such a theory worked against the full and frank recognition of Homer as an artist.

The other principle formulated by Scaliger was oddly inconsistent in its operation. Like the Renaissance scholars in general he was imbued with respect for authority as a power synonymous with age. Now, in accordance with this law the *Iliad* as the older poem ought to be the better, and this undoubtedly would have been Scaliger's avowed opinion were it not that he stood committed to the greater regularity and art of Virgil. Instead, therefore, of comparing Homer with Virgil on the basis of authority by virtue of age, he switches aside and makes his comparison between the *Iliad* and the *Hero and Leander* of Musæus, really a late production of the sixth century after Christ, but by a confusion of its author with the mythical Musæus held to be a work of the remote pre-Homeric age. Scaliger was too sound a critic at heart not to see that the actual matter of the *Hero and Leander* was relatively slight and insignificant; but he had his hypothesis ready, like a true philologian. He imagined that this poem was a mere *parergon* of the mighty bard of antiquity and that the serious works of Musæus and Orpheus and their coevals had been lost. "If Musæus," he says, "had written those things which Homer wrote, we may suppose that he would have written them far better." And as it is, "the style," if not the substance, "of Musæus is far more polished and elegant than Homer's."

Now this triple judgement of Scaliger on Homer and Virgil and Musæus bears closely on the true nature of tradition. It shows, I think, that in his heart of hearts Scaliger was quite awake to the

surpassing genius and art of Homer, but was seduced by current
theories to express opinions not entirely in accord with his actual
taste as determined by the criterion of pleasure. And one can follow
this deflexion of expressed opinion right through the reign of pseudo-
classicism. Let me illustrate what I mean by two familiar examples
taken from English literature. One cannot read Pope's *Preface to
the Iliad* without feeling his preference of the poet he was translating; yet so deeply ingrained in his mind was the Renaissance notion
of the opposition between reason and inventive genius that he could
not omit a formal comparison of the two ancient epics on the basis
of this contrast. "No author or man," he says, "ever excelled all the
world in more than one faculty; and as Homer has done this in
invention, Virgil has in judgement. Not that we think that Homer
wanted judgement, because Virgil had it in a more eminent degree;
or that Virgil wanted invention, because Homer possessed a larger
share of it; each of these authors had more of both than perhaps any
man besides, and are only said to have less in comparison with one
another. Homer was the greater genius, Virgil the better artist. In
one we most admire the man, in the other the work." And so on. For
our other illustration we may take the absurd wrangle that was the
occasion of Swift's *Battle of the Books*. Does any one suppose that
Sir William Temple and Boyle or any other champion of the *Epistles
of Phalaris* got more satisfaction out of reading those frigid exercises in rhetoric than from the genuine masterpieces of Greek prose?
Certainly they did not; yet because they believed these *Epistles*
to be from the hand of the Sicilian tyrant and so endowed with the
authority of primitive age, they did not hesitate to cross swords for
them with the terrible Bentley himself. At least one of the false
theories of pseudo-classicism, the sheer authority of age, was so
damaged in that battle that it has had little force since then to de-
flect the straight line of tradition.

Homer was to come to his own with the revival of Romanticism,
though here again the mischievous inheritance of the Renaissance
can be seen at work. The romanticists were, and are, quite as convinced as any pseudo-classicist of the inherent hostility between
reason and imagination, between judgement and genius; only they
take the opposite side and bestow all their praises on imagination, as
they understand it, and genius. Hence you will find a succession of
scholars in the nineteenth century, particularly in Germany, who
made much of the spontaneity and naïveté of the *Iliad*, likening it
to the untutored ballads of the people, and comparing it in this

respect favourably with the *Æneid,* which they were wont to belittle as a product of reflective judgement and conscious art. On the whole I am inclined to believe that the justice of tradition has come nearer to suffering a real perversion from these romantic sentimentalists than from the rationalists of the pseudo-classical school.

But withal the tradition still abides, and promises to abide. There are, of course, men today, like our late professional endower of libraries, who affect to look down on the *Iliad* as the work of a barbarous age. But if you investigate their opinion, you will find that it is warped by some extraneous theory, such as a crude pacifism which thinks it uncivic to enjoy a tale of fighting, or an equally crude evolutionism which measures excellence unflinchingly by the criterion of newness. And you will commonly find, moreover, that these faddists have not read the poem in the original, that is, properly speaking, have not read it at all, and so ought to be put out of court. The verdict of those who have a right to judge is almost without exception that in Homer we have the nearest approach to pure poetry, and that everything since is in a way derivative and secondary.

At any rate, I do not see how one can study the history of taste honestly without acknowledging this fact of the enduring permanence of the Homeric tradition. His place, you will observe, has not been absolutely fixed; it has deflected a little to this side and to that in accordance with the changing theories of criticism, but it has always moved close to a central point—like the North Star, which moves about at a slight distance from the axis of the sky. As we depart further and further from this core of tradition, our literary judgements become less certain and the probability of variation grows greater; but the central truth is not affected. Those who deny the validity of tradition are like watchers of the heavens who should set their eyes on the wandering planets of the ecliptic and from these alone should infer that there was no possibility of a Polar Star.

### III. The Criterion

At this point a wary antagonist might break in with a seasonable objection. All this, he will say, is very well, but it scarcely touches the real issue. I will grant that standards do exist, in the sense that for all men certain works of art possess qualities which they instinctively or consciously use as a criterion of taste. I will even grant the existence in the past of those traditional standards on which you lay so much stress. But what is it to me though a hundred generations of mankind have united in acclaiming the merits of this or that poem; is that any reason why I should admire the same thing? The truth is that our relativists, who dwell with such satisfaction on the errors of authoritative criticism, are not so much concerned with disproving the existence of traditional standards as they are with establishing their own right to independence of taste.

Well, tradition does not *create* standards; to suppose that it did would be to fall into the pseudo-classical error of regarding age as a criterion of excellence. But tradition may be evidence that certain works of art embody qualities which it is very much our concern to appreciate, and which we have every reason to use as a criterion. To understand why this is so we must look a little into the nature of these criteria on which standards are formed. And here, luckily, we have the help of one who, as the first of romantic critics in English, ought to possess, and does possess, high credit among the relativists of today. "As it was my constant reply," Coleridge says in his *Biographia Literaria,* "to authorities brought against me from later poets of great name, that no authority could avail in opposition to TRUTH, NATURE, LOGIC, and the LAWS OF UNIVERSAL GRAMMAR; actuated too by my former passion for metaphysical investigations; I laboured at a solid foundation, on which permanently to ground my opinions, in the component faculties of the human mind itself, and their comparative dignity and importance. According to the faculty or source, from which the pleasure given by any poem or passage was derived, I estimated the merit of such poem or passage. As the result of all my reading and meditation, I abstracted two critical aphorisms; . . . first, that not the poem which we have *read,* but that to which we *return,* with the greatest pleasure, possesses the genuine power, and claims the name of *essential poetry.* . . . Be it however observed, that I excluded from the list of worthy feelings, the pleasure derived from mere novelty in the reader, and the desire of exciting wonderment at his powers in the author."

Coleridge is verbose and wanders as usual, but his "solid foundation" resolves itself clearly enough into these four rules:

First: That the value of a work of art is not determined primarily by authority, but is a question of truth and nature.

Secondly: That our sense of truth and nature in a work of art is the pleasure we derive from it. To this notion, that the aim of art is to give pleasure, Coleridge returns frequently in the course of his rambling treatise,

Thirdly: Coleridge asserts that pleasures vary in value and importance by a criterion of permanence. For instance, other things being equal, we place a higher value on a poem which continues to interest us on a second or third perusal than on one which interested us a first time, but bores us a second time.

Fourthly: He asserts that pleasures vary also in value and importance by a criterion of quality, that is, in accordance with the faculty of the mind which is concerned.

Now to the first and second of these principles I do not see how the most truculent individualist can object; taken alone they might even appear to support the position for which he is contending. And the same thing, I suppose, might be said of the third and fourth principles, were it not for certain inferences which too patently can be drawn from them. In these inferences lies the very crux of the question at issue.

To take the third proposition: if it be true that pleasure is a criterion of value in a work of art, and if one element of comparison between two pleasures be their relative degree of permanence, if, that is to say, other things being equal, we instinctively prefer the pleasure that endures the longer, then is there not, on the face of it, a strong probability that the book which has been read with interest by a hundred generations of men, while other books have been read and forgotten, is the one which will maintain its interest for the individual reader, if he will give it a fair chance? At least the burden of proof rests upon those who would deny such an analogy.

Let me ask for indulgence if I speak from my personal experience. It was my custom for a number of years, while I enjoyed the schoolman's privilege of leisurely vacations, to pass my summers on the coast of Maine, and there each season, within sight and sound of Homer's eternal sea, to read through the *Iliad* and *Odyssey* alternatively, not indeed shedding tears like the captive of Calypso, who

>Day after day, from beach and rocky caves,
>Looked out upon the waste of untamed waves—

but filled with "the sober certainty of waking bliss," such as no other reading has ever afforded me. I do not give this experience as in any way peculiar to myself. On the contrary, Homer has kept his place in tradition just because he has offered this uncloying pleasure to all who are prepared to take it. Possibly some book written today might have the same power, but, considering the actual destinies of literature past and present, the chances are a million to one against it—*habent sua fata libelli.*

Tradition, it is well to repeat, is not in itself a quality of excellence, but merely evidence of such qualities; and the question is still to be answered, why these poets—Homer and Virgil and Dante and Shakespeare and Milton and the other genuine classics—have attained their preeminence, and why they are able to afford us a permanence of delight such as we cannot get from ephemeral productions.

First of all they have this power, I think, because they appeal to what is universal in human nature, rather than to what is temporary and accidental. But this quality of universality needs to be defined, since it is of a double source, and in one of its aspects is the aim of a sort of art which can be called anything but classical. Men lose their differences and show the common ground of humanity when they rise to the height of their being and when they sink to its lowest substratum. There is a striking passage at the opening of the ninth book of the *Republic* in which Plato tells of the lawless desires that lurk in the breast of every man, even the most virtuous, silent by day when the man's will is awake, but sometimes in his sleep going forth to accomplish their filthy ends.[1] Yes, the beast is in all of us, and it is possible to attain a kind of universality by rousing it, and feeding it with suggestions, until it dominates the soul. This is the truth that the naturalists have learned. There is in fact a whole school of writers in Russia and Austria and Germany and Scandinavia who are trading on it systematically; and recently the same theory of art has begun to hold up its head in England and America. We have among us a growing number of pithecoid creatures, who know enough of art to understand that its appeal should be to the universal in human nature, but are not sufficiently educated to perceive that the true universal of art is of quite another order than the bestial. These naturalists forget that permanence of pleasure is a prime requisite of good art, or, remembering it, are blind to the fact that the pleasure derived from the inverted order of universality is of all kinds the quickest to cloy. This is not a matter of theory but of experience. Take Zola's *La Terre,* or any other of his novels in which the principle of naturalism was first worked out systematically, is it possible to imagine any normal man returning to such a book year after year, with ever-heightened enjoyment? Naturalism

[1] Pretty much all the truth of Freudianism can be found in the Platonic and Stoic theory of dreams.

may conceivably fascinate by the shock of surprise, or may conceivably interest for a while by the intensity of the emotions it excites, but surprise and intensity are the least stable factors of pleasure, and, if they appeal to the animal within us, they pass quickly to satiety and from satiety to disgust. As Shakespeare's Friar Laurence said, in words that might be applied to naturalism long before Anatole France reviewed *La Terre*, it is but "the unreasonable fury of a beast":

> These violent delights have violent ends,
> And in their triumph die.

The universality of true art is of quite another order than this, and leads to the fourth of our criteria. It will be remembered that Coleridge, besides grading pleasures by the standard of permanence, distinguished them "according to the faculty or source" from which they were derived. Man, he would say, is not simple in his being, but dual; there is in all men the lurking beast, but there is also in all men a faculty of control whether you call this higher element reason or the divine or the supernatural. The error of the naturalist is to regard men as simple, or as natural in the sense of having no other nature than animal instincts. He seeks the universal there where, according to his imperfect psychology, it can alone be found, and the puppet world of his vision is like Cassio's: "I have lost the immortal part of myself, and what remains is bestial." The true artist, on the contrary, is aware indeed of the bestial in man, but sees also something else, and in that something else looks for the meaning of life.

I do not say that the artist, by this law of our double being, is restricted in his representation of nature to what is pure and innocent; very far from that. Homer and Shakespeare and Turgeniev, all the poets and dramatists and novelists in the great tradition, have not blenched before a world shaken, as the world we know is shaken, by passionate ambition and furious desire. Nor is the true artist one who takes upon himself the office of preacher, to rail unseasonably against the shortcomings and vices of the life he is portraying; very far from that. Rather he is one who, by the subtle, insinuating power of the imagination, by just appreciation of the higher emotions as well as the lower, by the revelation of a sad sincerity, shall I call it, in his own soul, gives us always to feel that the true universal in human nature, the faculty by which man resembles man as a being different from the beast, is that part of him that is "noble in reason," the master and not the slave of passion. True art is thus humanistic rather than naturalistic; and its gift of high and permanent pleasure is the response of our own breast to the artist's delicately revealed sense of that divine control, moving like the spirit of God upon the face of the waters.

So far I seem to see my way clear. If you should ask me by what rhetorical devices or by what instrument of representation one poem or one work of art appeals more successfully than another to the higher faculty within us, how, for instance, Milton's *Paradise Lost* accomplishes this end better than Blackmore's *King Arthur,* though both poems were written with equally good intentions, I would reply frankly that the solution of this problem of the imagination may be beyond my powers of critical analysis. And, fortunately, I am not here concerned with artistic means but with artistic results. I could at least say to the questioner, with a good deal of assurance, that, if he would read honestly both *Paradise Lost* and *King Arthur,* however he might feel towards Milton's epic he would find his pleasure in Blackmore's epic less in kind and quality. No power on earth, not even the desire to rout an adversary, could make him read Blackmore a second time.

But there is still a difficulty. Why, if these criteria are inherent in human nature, are not they themselves universally acknowledged? Whence the obvious fact that the tradition of taste is so widely rejected today by those who make a boast of modernism? "I know," we can hear one of these gentlemen say, "that past generations of men pretended to find their fullest artistic satisfaction in Homer and Shakespeare and Milton and others of the illustrious dead; but I do not. I won't say much about Homer, since he is Greek to me; but Bernard Shaw gets more pleasure from his own plays than from Sophocles and Shakespeare and Racine rolled together, and so do I. And as for your Milton, I have heard college professors declare that no one now reads *Paradise Lost* except under compulsion, and I know that I and my friends are vastly more entertained by the meandering prose of Mr. Joyce's *Ulysses* than by all the formal epics ever composed. The past was in leading-strings, but we have suddenly grown alive and, I may add, honest."

Well, our sceptical friend is certainly honest, and he seems to be pretty wide awake; but is he educated? Now education embraces many things: it does not despise the most humble and utilitarian pursuits; it is largely occupied with the bare acquisition of knowledge; it aims to strengthen the muscles of the body and to tighten the fibres of the brain; but, above all, it is, or should be, a discipline of the soul in the appreciation of pleasure and pain. Do not suppose that such a discipline is a light or unimportant matter. If you will read the ninth book of Plato's *Republic* and the introductory books of the *Laws,* you will see how, to the eye of that keenly observant philosopher, the whole of human conduct, whether for good or for evil, is dependent on the right appreciation of pleasure and pain, and how deeply the welfare of the State is concerned with the education of youth in just this field. Teach a boy to take pleasure in things that are fine and pure and strong and of good repute, and you have prepared him for a life wholesome and happy in itself and useful to the community.

Certainly, at least, the standards of taste are involved in this discipline. That faculty of the soul which responds to the higher and more permanent pleasures of art is, no doubt, present in all men, and is thus potentially universal; but it may be, and commonly is, dormant until awakened by external stimulus. For the reason that its activity means a steady choice among our natural inclinations and impulses, demanding self-control and, in a way, self-abnegation, it comes to full fruition only by exercise that at first may be painful and repellent to the natural man. By nature men are prone to grasp at the nearest and easiest pleasure, and to shirk the labour necessary for the higher and more permanent pleasure. They are even inclined to question the reality of the higher and more permanent pleasure, until it has been forced upon their recognition by the experience of others. And just here is the function of tradition. The very essence of education is not to confirm the young mind in its natural temperament, in its tendency to pursue the present and easier pleasure, but to set before it the stirring example of those who have found their joy and consolation in the higher things, forcing it by a tender compulsion, painful perhaps at the moment, but leading gradually to the liberty of endless delight, to taste of these things for itself and to acquire the right to judge of them whether they be indeed full of pleasantness for the awakened soul. Education is the ability to judge. The educated man is he who has the right to pronounce on the standards of taste, because he has had experience of both the higher and the lower pleasures. I am not upholding any priggish or superhuman ideal. The educated man will not have lost his appreciation of the commoner things at their time and in their degree. He will enjoy the wholesome books that are of the moment and make no pretension to permanence or elevation; you will remember that our relativistic friends have even charged Mr. Root and Mr. Hughes, whether for honour or for dishonour, with finding a secret satisfaction in detective stories and penny-dreadfuls. But the educated man is one who has also been trained to know that highest and most enduring pleasure which is derived from the few great books selected and approved by the verdict of tradition. And in that power of enjoyment he will feel himself set free from his own petty limitations, and made a humble companion of those who share the heritage of time.

I suspect that these sticklers for the liberty of taste against the judgements of mankind are in the main simply uneducated; being untrained to feel the higher and more permanent pleasures of art, they grasp at any ephemeral work that offers an easy flattery of the lower elements of their nature, and swear there is nothing else. It may sound a bit paradoxical to reduce the rebellion against standards to so simple a matter as imperfect education, and, indeed, that phrase does not tell the whole story. The merely uneducated man is likely to be indifferent to standards rather than actively hostile, or he may be a modest fellow who knows what he has missed, and would never think of raising his ignorance into a "cosmic footrule." There is a cause, a trait of character, behind the belligerence of ignorance. The belligerents themselves call it "irresponsibility of temperament" or the "spirit of romantic adventure," or may dignify it as a "philosophy of relativism"; but it has another name, which I hesitate to mention. In fact, I should not have courage to pronounce the invidious phrase at all, had it not been spoken long ago by those whose insight into human nature gave them the right to speak. Even Matthew Arnold, when he came to explain the common hostility to academic standards, thought it safer to take refuge behind a venerated authority, and quoted Spinoza's maxim that "the two great bans of humanity are self-conceit and the laziness coming from self-conceit"; and he might have appealed to a more ancient philosopher than Spinoza—to none other than Buddha, who also traced the origin of all evil, ethical and æsthetic, to this source. That, then, the spirit of indolence and conceit, is the animating cause behind the bitterness of those who proclaim against standards. It is the indolence, moral in some, intellectual in others, that revolts from such discipline as would enable a man to judge between the higher and the lower pleasure; it is the conceit that makes him cling tenaciously to his naked temperament as a better guide than the voice of tradition.[2] Standards there are, and all men judge by them; but there is a vast difference between the standards of education and those of a self-satisfied ignorance. Unfortunately, there is a theory abroad today, formulated and preached by a preposterous body of pedagogues, which professes to have found in this indolence and conceit the corner-stone of education.

That is the new thing, so far as there is anything new, in the world today; not indolence and conceit, which are as ancient as humanity, but the philosophy which justifies them under the title of absolute relativism. That is the present disguise of the Demon as he stalks abroad, instilling his venom into the innocent critics of the press.

## IV. THE FETISH OF PURE ART

It is a nice question to ask whether belief in the absolute irresponsibility of the artistic temperament has engendered the modern ideal of absolute art, or the contrary. Which is first, the complacency of conceit or of theory? For myself I am willing to leave the solution of such a problem to the Demon himself, who alone knoweth his own mind; but from the *Æsthetic*[3] of Signor Croce, the most epoptic hierophant of the demonic mysteries in these days, I can see how nearly the two absolutes are related, and can get some glimpse of the procedure of the metaphysical mind at its highest point of activity.

Now Signor Croce, though really himself a child of Hegel, makes good sport of the theoretical æstheticians in the train of Kant and Hegel who define art as pure hedonism, or pure moralism, or pure conceptualism; and so far he does well. You might suppose he was taking the ordinary and sensible point of view, viz., that art must of course give pleasure, and must be psychologically moral (not pedantically so), and must contain ideas, but that it is a false sort of simplification to define art itself therefore *as* pleasure, or *as* morals, or *as* ideas. If such were the motive behind Croce's antipathy to the Teutonic æsthetics of the last century, he would seem, as I say, to be pleading for the liberty of common sense against the absolutism of the Demon; but he too quickly dispels any such illusion. "Art," he

2 Anatole France, for example, was highly educated intellectually, and as a matter of fact his critical judgements are generally sound and in conformity with the great tradition. But his philosophy of life was tainted with moral indolence, which betrays itself in his literary productions and to some extent in his critical standards.

3 *Nuovi Saggi di Estetica,* 1920.

declares, "which *depends* on morals or pleasure or philosophy *is* morals or pleasure or philosophy, and not art at all." Now what kind of logic is this that argues: Because art is not pure pleasure, therefore pure art is absolved from the need of giving pleasure; because art is not pure morals, therefore pure art is absolved from any concern with morals? One might as well say, *e.g.*, that cookery which is relished for the pleasure it gives *is* pleasure, and not cookery at all; therefore cookery has nothing to do with pleasure. It is the old story of Luther's drunken man on horseback: prop him up on one side and over he flops on the other. Because one absolute is not true, therefore the contrary absolute must be true; because art which gives pleasure is not definable simply as pleasure, therefore art is a hieratic abstraction entirely independent of pleasure.

But if such a theory of art would seem to be buzzing in a metaphysical vacuum, it is not without its very practical aspect, whether as cause or effect. "The artist," says Signor Croce, coming down abruptly to earth, "is always above blame morally and above censure philosophically." There you have it, the claim to irresponsibility, so dear to our militant gentlemen of the press, vested in the authority of an awesome name. I do not suppose many of our emancipated writers are deeply versed in the thin dialectic of æsthetics, but they understand pretty well what is meant when they are told that in their work as creative artists they need not concern themselves with the ethical laws supposed to govern life or with the dull maxims of truth.

It may be a question, as I have said, whether the great Neapolitan has risen from the popular lust of irresponsibility to his theory of independent art or has condescended to the lower level from the heights of abstract reasoning. In either case the next step, from a definition by negation to a definition by affirmation, carries him into an altitude beyond the reach of any earthly telescope. Art, he has shown, is absolutely not pleasure or morals or philosophy; it just absolutely *is*—but is what? In the answer to this question I seem to hear no human voice but the very diction of the Demon. Otherwise I cannot understand whence the avowed foe of Kantian and Hegelian abstractions has derived his positive definition of art, which of all abstractions is the most abstract and of all absolutes the most absolute. "Art is intuition," he says, that and nothing else; not the vision of something, mind you, but pure vision. Or, if you desire more words in your definition, you may have it thus: "An aspiration inclosed in the circle of a representation, that is art; and in it the aspiration exists solely by the representation, and the representation solely by the aspiration." Which words, if they mean anything, signify, I suppose, that art is of the spirit of pure creativeness, a reaching out towards a goal which is non-existent until visualised by the very act of reaching out. Such a definition may engage the attention of metaphysicians; in my common-place mind, frankly, it draws blank. I do not comprehend what is meant by aspiring towards that which is non-existent until we visualise it by aspiring.

Croce is the pope of the new school, and as such ought to be immune from the questioning of the lay intelligence. For a more accessible exposition of the ideas stirring the young modernists I turn to the distinguished critic and philosopher of Spain, José Ortega y Gasset, and in particular to his essay published under the significant title of *The Dehumanization of Art*.[4] Unless I mistake his language, Señor Ortega finds little satisfaction æsthetically in the extreme products of the movement he describes. But he believes that it is not the function of a critic to value works of art in accordance with his own taste or distaste. And especially today, when more than ever before it is a characteristic of art to divide mankind sharply into those who comprehend and those who do not, the business of criticism should be to enter into the intention of the artist, and not to judge his work from some alien point of view, least of all to condemn. Well, Señor Ortega in a sense comprehends; he states the various theories adopted by the *jóvenes* to justify their adventurous ways with admirable perspicuity and precision—and with that final confusion at the back of his mind which enables him to speak as one who belongs intellectually to the movement, however practically his taste may lag a little behind its utmost advance.

The central thesis of Señor Ortega's book, which at once justifies his title and summarizes the most advanced attitude towards art, is exactly this: "To rejoice or suffer with the human lot which a work of art may incidentally suggest or present to us, is a very different thing from the true artistic pleasure. More than that: this occupation with the human element of the work is essentially incompatible with pure æsthetic fruition."[5]

That clearly is the voice of the Demon once more, appealing to the same lust for an irresponsible absolute as inspires the Crocean

4 *La Deshumanización del Arte*, Madrid, 1925.

5 *Alegrarse o sufrir con los destinos humanos que, tal vez, la obra de arte nos refiere o presenta, es cosa muy diferente del verdadero goce artístico. Más aún: esa ocupación con lo humano de la obra es, en principio, incompatible con la estricta fruición estética.*

æsthetics. And now art is to be not only independent of morals but in its essence divided altogether from human nature; and if it still aims to please, its pleasure is of a kind peculiar to itself and unrelated to the coarse fodder of life. Suppose, to take the illustration given by Señor Ortega, a notable man is lying at the point of death. His wife will be standing by his bed, a physician will be counting his pulse, while elsewhere in the house a reporter awaits the news and a painter is engaged to depict the scene. All four persons—wife, physician, reporter, painter—are intent upon the same fact, but with varying degrees of intimacy and with different kinds of interest. To the wife the event is an occasion of grief and anxiety; she is, as it were, a part of it; whereas to the artist, at the other extreme, the situation is entirely divested of human sympathy or sentiment: "his mind is set solely on the exterior, on certain lights and shadows, certain chromatic values." And so it happens that if the natural emotions felt on such an occasion by the wife, the physician, and even to a lesser degree by the news-reporter, are what the ordinary man (the "philistine" or "bourgeois" of the older romantic jargon) regards as the real stuff of life, then art to the ordinary man is removed to a sphere of incomprehensible unreality. "An artistic object," says Señor Ortega, "is artistic only in the measure in which it ceases to be real." Hence, in the scene just described, the actual death-bed and the artist's picture of it are two things "absolutely different (*completamente distintos*)." We may interest ourselves in one or the other; in one case we live with, or in, the event, in the other case we "contemplate" an object of art as such, with æsthetic pleasure perhaps, but with no human emotions. Just in so far as the picture shows any feeling for, or awakens in ˙the beholder any response to, the significance of death, it falls below the high function of art. The tragedy of loss, the frustration of ambition, the humility of surrender, the consolations of hope, the victory of love, the sanctities of religion,—any shadow of these resting upon the canvas will detract from the purity of æsthetic pleasure. The artist and the connoisseur in the presence of death find only an occasion for certain lines and colours. And further, as our power of contemplation becomes more refined, we cease to discern (or, if we are artists, to paint) even the unreal representation of a real event; a picture will cease to depend on, or suggest, any subject whatsoever. For art is like a window through which we look out upon a garden. The ordinary man sees only the flowers and leaves beyond, and is so absorbed in these as to be quite unaware of the pane of glass, the more so as the glass is purer and clearer. But with effort we can make ourselves conscious of the medium through which we are looking; and as our vision is thus concentrated on the glass, the garden fades into a confused blotch of colours or even passes out of conscious perception altogether.

That is Señor Ortega's vivid metaphor for the Crocean theory of art as pure intuition—which he professes to reach, however, by no theorizing of his own but from study of the actual practice of certain of the *jóvenes*. For those who believe in the divine mission of art the elevation of society might seem to lie in obeying the command of Mr. Skionar in Peacock's *Crotchet Castle:* "Build *sacella* for transcendental oracles to teach the world how to see through a glass darkly." It all sounds rather funny to me. But I hope I am not laughing at an unfair caricature. What else in fact is the meaning of those sapient critics, who might join me in repudiating the language of metaphysics, yet insist that in judging a picture we shall pay no heed to the subject represented but consider it as pure representation, or who say that the value of a work of art depends not at all on the character of the human experience put into it but only on the sincerity of self-expression?—as if there were some mystical virtue in self-expression even when the self has no experience worthy to be expressed. It is, in fact, pedantic talk of this sort in the mouths of respected critics that indicates how far the depredations of the Demon have extended into the realm of common sense.

As for the creators, so called, there may be a young votary of art here and there who is trying honestly to put these abstractions into practice; and for him, I should suppose, the goal of dehumanization and derealization will have been attained when his pictures are simplified to a cunning design of line and colour with no suggestion of a definite subject, or still further to a spread of pure colour with no design at all; his music to a pure tone without melody or even variation; his poems to a succession of beautiful words unsullied by sense. That would seem to be the nearest practical equivalent to seeing a pure pane of glass. One wonders why the pilgrim of vacuity should be so slow and hesitant in his progress towards so easy a mark. Perhaps he foresees that absolute art, so reached, will cease to be art at all. Perhaps he has a foreboding that the prize if obtained would not be very valuable. It is hard to imagine the pleasure or profit to be derived from concentrating one's attention upon a pane of transparent glass until one sees nothing through it; most of us would prefer to retain our impure perception of the flowers in

the garden beyond. Despite the majestic logic of youth we persist in
thinking that such a picture as Leonardo da Vinci's *Last Supper* is
a truer work of art than the deftest whirl of colours ever painted;
that the *Æneid* is richer in poetical joy than *Kubla Khan* (not to
mention the latest lyric from the American colony in Paris); that
Bach's *Mass in B Minor* is still a miracle and a rapture of sound.
Yet all these—the painting and the epic and the mass—are brim-
ming with human emotion and with a brooding sense of the eternal
values of life. They are great for various reasons, no doubt; but
certainly among those reasons is the fact that they are not art at all
as the modernists would have us believe.

The simple truth is that the effort to create pure art is nothing
more than idolatry to a fetish of abstract reason—unless you prefer
to ticket it as empty conceit—and could never engage the practical
interest of any but a few witless cranks. There is a profound confusion in Señor Ortega's interpretation of what is happening among
the mass of the younger artists, as indeed there is often in their own
statement of what they are endeavouring to do. They may be seeking an absolute, but it is not an absolute of purity in any sense of the
word.

Now I grant at once that there is a difference between art and
life, that the attitude of the painter, to return to the old illustration,
is not identical with that of the wife in the house of mourning. There
is in art a change, a transmutation, a something taken away and a
something added. "Art," said Goethe, "is art only because it is not
nature." And Aristotle, perhaps, had the same truth in mind in his
famous theory of the purgation of the human passions. In that
sense we can accept a maxim that comes from Japan: "Art lies in
the shadowy frontiers between reality and unreality."[6] The point I
would make is the falseness and futility of the logical deduction that
art can therefore dispense with the stuff of humanity or nature, or
can weigh anchor and sail off into a shoreless sea of unreality. What
has actually happened is this. Always the great creators have taken
the substance of life, and, not by denying it or áttempting to evade
its laws, but by looking more intently below its surface, have found
meanings and values that transmute it into something at once the
same and different. The passions that distract the individual man
with the despair of isolated impotence they have invested with a
universal significance fraught with the destinies of humanity; the

[6] *Masterpieces of Chikamatsu, the Japanese Shakespeare,* translated by Asataro
Miyamori, p. 48.

scenery of the material world they have infused with suggestions of an indwelling otherworld. And so by a species of symbolism, or whatever you choose to call it, they have lifted mortal life and its theatre to a higher reality which only to the contented or dust-choked dwellers in things as they are may appear as unreal. That, for instance, is precisely what Perugino has achieved in his picture of a death-scene entitled the Mystic Crucifixion, where pain and grief and the fear that clutches the individual heart in its hand of ice have been transmuted into a drama of divine redemption through suffering, while the tender burgeoning of spring thrown up against the far-off juncture of earth and sky gives hints of a mode of exist-ence in joyous and infinite freedom. Even the lesser creators, those who in innocence of spirit have undertaken merely to reproduce what they see, may have done so with a clarity and largeness of vision capable of working a magic alchemy of which they themselves per-haps never dreamed.

That was the tradition of agelong practice; it is what we mean, or ought to mean, by classical. And then, after the devastating material-ism of late eighteenth-century philosophy there came a change of ideals. The veritable feeling for the otherworld and for spiritual values was lost, while at the same time the new school, stirred with vague aspirations, was not satisfied with a simple and, in its way, wholesome naturalism. Above all these prophets of the romantic movement, as we designate it, revolted from the restrictive rules of an art which was neither classical nor innocently naturalistic, but pseudo-classical, and which had developed from one side of the Renaissance. They too perceived that no great art was possible with-out escape from the levelling tyranny of natural law, and, being unable to transcend nature, seeing indeed no higher reality into which nature could be raised, they sought freedom by sinking be-low nature. In painting, as Mr. Mather has shown with fullness of knowledge and admirable acumen, this process of escape meant "a successive elimination of academic authority, imagination, memory, fidelity to nature, and nature itself. It would seem as if the last sacrifice had been made; but no. In all these rejections and in the most grotesque experiments the painter had retained his seriousness and self-respect. This too went by the board in a brief moment after the War, when the Dadaists bade the artist create in a mood of joyous bluff, meanwhile mocking himself and his world. The oft-repeated demonstration is complete once more—the latter end of expansive Romantic individualism is Romantic disillusionment and

Romantic irony."[7] And the same history might be given of modern
music and literature, though in the case of the latter the disinvolu-
tion, by reason of the medium employed, is more complicated. For
instance the liberation of art from the moral obligations of life, so
vaunted by Mr. Cabell and others of the left wing in America as a
new achievement, is really contemporaneous with the romantic movement. At least as far back as 1837 we find George Sand declaring that
by almost universal consent the arts have become accomplices in
this strange tendency towards "amoralism." Now conscientious
theorists may hold that amoralism is a step in the direction of freedom; in practice it became commonly a mere euphemism for immorality, not to say vulgar indecency. The climax of the movement in that direction was reached in the realism of Zola and others
who, quite frankly and systematically and "scientifically," made
human nature coterminous with the bestial in man. Art may have
been emancipated from one set of bonds, but it was wrapt and en-
folded and constricted in a bondage tenfold straiter. It may have
been dehumanized in the sense that it had repudiated the government of reason which to the older humanists was the distinguishing
trait of man as man; it certainly was not purged of its attempt to
evoke passions which on a lower plane are *menschlich allzu menschlich.*

As a matter of fact the radical writers of today who are accomplishing anything of magnitude are still predominantly of that
school of realism. But a few restless souls, those in particular whom
Señor Ortega has in mind, driven on by the despotic Demon of the
Absolute, have not been content to abide in this halfway house. They
see clearly enough that art has not been purified by such realism,
but mixed and muddied by deliberate opposition to the ethical interpretation of life; they will detach art from even that poor remnant
of deliberation which made a selection among the elements of composite human nature with a certain regard, though an inverted
regard, for moral values. They hold deliberation to be the foe of
liberation. Hence the later theory, exemplified in English by James
Joyce, that art shall not reproduce a picture of life as the humanist
sees it, or even from the inverted point of view of the realist, but for
its subject matter shall descend to what they call the pure "stream of
consciousness." The hero of fiction shall have no will, no purpose, no
inhibition, no power of choice whether for good or evil, but shall be
merely a medium through which passes an endless, unchecked,

7 *Modern Painting,* by Frank Jewett Mather, Jr., p. 375.

meaningless flux of sensations and memories and emotions and impulses.

And so the limit of elimination has been reached—at least the practical limit, since below the stream of consciousness there would seem to remain nothing to represent save bottomless inanity. But this fact is to be noted: though the process of evolution may seem to have been carried on in the name of absolute art, the actual goal attained is an absolute of quite another order; there has been no true liberation, but a progressive descent in slavery. As, successively, one after another of the higher elements of our composite nature has been suppressed, a lower instinct has taken its place. The submergence of the humanistic conception of man as a responsible creature of free will has been accompanied by an emergence of the romantic glorification of uncontrollable temperament; this has been supplanted by a realistic theory of subjection to the bestial passions, and this, at the last, by an attempt to represent life as an unmitigated flux, which in practice, however it be in literature, means confinement in a mad-house. The practitioners of the newest art call themselves *surréalistes,* super-realists; they flatter themselves, they are sub-realists. Art may be dehumanized, but only in the sense that, having passed beyond the representation of men as undifferentiated from animals, it undertakes to portray them as complete imbeciles. To speak of the works produced by the boastful modern school as pure art is, from any point of view, mere bluff. By their fruits you shall know them. Turn the pages of the little magazine published in Paris under the title of *Transition,* wherein Mr. Joyce and a group of denationalized Americans and Americanized Frenchmen collaborate to their own mutual satisfaction: you will there find what the Simon-pure article is in theory and practice. For instance a certain M. Louis Aragon,—described by his admiring introducer as "an intellectual on a lifelong holiday, a twentieth century pilgrim with a pack of words on his back," etc.,—expounds the theory thus:

Reason, reason, o abstract day-phantom, I have already driven you from my dreams. And now I am at the point where they are ready to blend with the realities of appearance. There is no longer room only for me. In vain reason denounces the dictatorship of sensuality. In vain it puts me on guard against error. Error is here the queen. Come in, Madame, this is my body, this is your throne. I pat my delirium as I would a beautiful horse. . . . Nothing can assure me of reality. Nothing, neither the exactness of logic nor the strength of a sensation, can assure me that I do not base it on the delirium of interpretation.

And so M. Aragon, concluding "that only the syllables of reality are artistically usable," exemplifies the new style:

> *Ité ité la réa*
> *Ité ité la réalité*
> *La réa la réa*
> *Té té La réa*
> *Li*
> *Té La réalité*
> *Il y avait une fois LA RÉALITÉ.*

Such is the manifesto of Super-realism, "the Freudian period," as the addicts of the stream of consciousness call it, "to the realistic misconception." Their title, I have said, is a pretty mistake for sub-realism; but they are not mistaken in their claim to have reached a kind of absolute. At least I cannot imagine what lower level of imbecility may still be honoured with the name of art.

(If any votary of "pure art" chances to read this essay, he will say: So Keats and Milton were treated by critics of their age.)

# IRVING BABBITT

## (1865–1933)

Born in Akron, Ohio, Irving Babbitt graduated from Harvard, after which he went to the Sorbonne for two years of study. After holding an instructorship in Romance languages at Williams College, he was appointed to a position as instructor in French at Harvard, becoming a full professor in 1912. In addition to his voluminous writing, he lectured widely. In 1930 he was elected to the American Academy of Arts and Letters.

As a critic he sought to analyze the deplorable breakdown of the Humanist tradition and to discover the reasons why, since the time of Bacon and Rousseau, Classicism and Christianity were overthrown. The Humanism he envisaged rested upon immediate intuition and the collective wisdom of the past. Tirelessly Babbitt and his disciples preached the need for spiritual discipline, for exercising the vital inner check. An acknowledged leader of the group that had gathered about him, Babbitt wrote with authority and tremendous power of conviction. A formidable dialectician and propagandist, a profound scholar, he used his learning, imbued as it was with moral passion and insight, to excellent effect, attacking the enemy—"the modernists"—with implacable militancy. What the New Humanists fought for so earnestly had much to do with the nature of literature and the function of criticism. Central to their faith was the principle of dualism: the conflict between the two opposed forces in the soul of man, the natural and the human, the animal and the divine.

In his first book, *Literature and the American College* (1908), Babbitt voiced the credo of the New Humanists. In this volume are shadowed forth many of the themes Babbitt would elaborate at much greater length and with a vast wealth of erudition in his later books: the salvationary discipline of the classics, the dangerous subjectivity and pathological introversion of modern literature, with its indulgence in reveries, unconscious fantasies, and unbridled sentimentality. In *The New Laokoön* (1910), Babbitt deplores the rampant confusion in the arts caused by the romantic movement. This is an even more concentrated assault on romanticism and

288

its bastard child, naturalism. Naturalism, Babbitt insists, grows naturally
and inevitably out of the romantic temper and outlook.

Whatever Babbitt writes is stamped with his individuality of style,
character, and conviction. From the start he had a message to preach and
he never wavered in carrying out his self-imposed mission, that of redeeming our culture from barbarism and decadence. If his dogmatism is the
measure of his limitations, it is also the source of his enduring strength.
His anti-naturalistic animus led him to fulminate against romanticism and
to assail Rousseauism as chiefly responsible for the degeneration of modern
literature. Unlike Sainte-Beuve, Babbitt is primarily interested not in
personality but in writers as representatives of ideas. The true critic, he
feels,

"has to have a knowledge and sympathy broad enough to compass all the
modes of literary expression, and then—an even more difficult task—he
must bring this knowledge and sympathy under the control of the strictest
judgment. Only in this way can we hope to render a verdict that will
finally be ratified by the good sense of the world."[1]

This implies that the critic must possess a definite and central point of
view. This in turn means that he must not surrender to the influence of
romantic sympathy, for then all that we get is impressionistic appreciation.

*The Masters of Modern French Criticism* (1914) presents the leading
ideas of the French critics of the nineteenth century and endeavors to
analyze the fundamental causes of the anti-intellectualism dominant in
the twentieth century. With the triumph of the principle of relativity in
science and literature, and the abandonment of outer standards, criticism
obviously ran the danger of growing anarchic, at the mercy of every eccentric and undisciplined sensibility. Standards must be inwardly apprehended, taste must be subordinated to the higher claims of our nature.
*Rousseau and Romanticism* (1919) is a spirited, all-out attack on romanticism in its different forms. In reality it is a manifesto directed against the
naturalistic philosophy of life. As a corrective for the philosophy of relativity and change promulgated by men like Bergson, Croce, and Dewey,
Babbitt would substitute a oneness that is always changing. To contemplate the infinite variety of things is to cultivate the romantic attitude; to
perceive the unity underlying manifoldness is to adopt the classical attitude. There is a distinct connection between the scientific spirit and the
spirit of romance. The romantic critic conceives of genius as something
purely temperamental, when actually the critic should test each work of
art "by some standard set above both his own temperament and that of

1 Irving Babbitt, *Spanish Character and Other Essays*. Edited by Frederick Manchester, Rachel Giese, and William F. Giese. (Boston and New York, 1940), p. 32.

the creator."[2] In opposition to the free expression of expansive desires, the Humanist would start with what he considers a fact of immediate experience—the presence in the individual of a vital check. "After all to be a good humanist is merely to be moderate and sensible and decent:"[3]

Babbitt's conception of literature and life is fundamentally ethical and Aristotelian. Like the author of *The Poetics*, he believes that art deals not with the isolated or exceptional, but with that which is probable or necessary. An ethical basis is needed. Babbitt is essentially making a plea for discipline and conformity. His whole system of ethics is based on a dualism between temperamental excess and wise self-control. Babbitt draws up a list of those writers who are romanticists, and therefore beyond the pale, and those writers who follow the human law. Dante, Aristotle, and St. Augustine are mentioned with approval, but Shelley and Blake, Rousseau, Hugo, Baudelaire, and Swinburne are harshly condemned. Babbitt brands the psychology fathered by Freud as a view of life that applies to the degenerate but not to the normal man.

All his life Babbitt was engaged in formulating those standards which would be most fruitful and effective in preparing the way for the best development of literature. He called upon the critic to draw up a philosophy of life which both writers and critics could accept. Humanistic standards, he urged, would safeguard us against the irresponsibility and impressionism, the naturalism and anarchy rampant in our day. Rejecting the scientific conception of man as a biological creature, Babbitt set up the ideal of man as master over himself, free to choose his destiny, and capable of choosing wisely, if he follows the guidance of the past and imposes self-control by applying the mandate of the ethical will. A critic of the first order, Babbitt engaged in the struggle, practically a crusade, to establish exact and viable standards according to the ideal of Humanism.

### BIBLIOGRAPHY

#### TEXT

*Literature and the American College.* Boston and New York, 1908.
*The New Laokoön.* Boston, 1910.
*The Masters of Modern French Criticism.* Boston, 1912.
*Rousseau and Romanticism.* Boston, 1919.
*Democracy and Leadership.* Boston and New York, 1924.
*On Being Creative.* Boston and New York, 1932.
*Spanish Character,* ed. by Frederick Manchester, Rachel Giese, and William F. Giese. Boston and New York, 1940. (Contains bibliography.)

[2] Irving Babbit, *Rousseau and Romanticism* (New York and Boston, 1919), p. 65.
[3] *Ibid.,* p. xxi.

CRITICISM

Blackmur, R. P. "Humanism and the Symbolic Imagination," *Southern Review*, VII, 309–325 (Autumn, 1941).

Eliot, T. S., *For Lancelot Andrewes*. London, 1928.

——, "The Humanism of Irving Babbitt," *Forum*, LXXX, 37–44 (July, 1928).

Elliott, G. R., "T. S. Eliot and Irving Babbitt," *American Review*, VII, 442–454 (September, 1936).

——, *Humanism and Imagination*. Chapel Hill, 1938.

Fausset, Hugh, *The Proving of Psyche*. London, 1929.

Foerster, Norman (ed.), *Humanism and America*. New York, 1930.

Leander, Folke, *Humanism and Naturalism*. Göteborg (Sweden), 1937.

MacCampbell, Donald, "Irving Babbitt," *Sewanee Review*, XLIII, 164–174 (April, 1935).

Manchester, F. and Shepard, O., *Irving Babbitt*. New York, 1941.

Mather, F. J., "Irving Babbitt," *Harvard Graduate Magazine*, CLXVI, 65–84 (December, 1933).

Mercier, Louis J. A., *The Challenge of Humanism*. New York, 1933.

——, "The Legacy of Irving Babbitt," *Harvard Graduate Magazine*, XLII, 327–347 (June, 1934).

More, Paul Elmer, "Irving Babbitt," *The University of Toronto Quarterly*, III, 129–145 (January, 1934).

Morell, Ray, "Wordsworth and Professor Babbitt," *Scrutiny*, I, 375–383 (March, 1933).

Munson, Gorham B., *Destinations*. New York, 1928.

——, *The Dilemma of the Liberated*. New York, 1930.

Richard, Christian, *Le mouvement humaniste en Amérique*. Paris, 1934.

Russell, F. T., "The Romanticism of Irving Babbitt," *South Atlantic Quarterly*, XXXII, 399–411 (October, 1933).

Shafer, Robert, "The Definition of Humanism," *Hound & Horn*, III, 533–557 (July, 1930).

Sypher, Wylie, "Irving Babbitt: A Reappraisal," *New England Quarterly*, XIV, 64–76 (May, 1941).

Wilson, Edmund, "Notes on Babbitt and More," *New Republic*, LXIV, 115–120 (March 19, 1930).

# THE CRITIC AND AMERICAN LIFE*

A FREQUENT remark of the French about Americans is: 'They're children'; which, interpreted, means that from the French point of

* The selections from *On Being Creative and Other Essays*, by Irving Babbitt, are reprinted by permission of and arrangement with Houghton Mifflin Company, the authorized publishers. Copyright 1932 by Irving Babbitt.

view Americans are childishly uncritical. The remark is relevant only in so far as it refers to general critical intelligence. In dealing with the special problems of a commercial and industrial society, Americans have shown that they can be abundantly critical. Certain Americans, for example, have developed a critical keenness in estimating the value of stocks and bonds that is nothing short of uncanny.[1] The very persons, however, who are thus keen in some particular field are, when confronted with questions that call for general critical intelligence, often puerile. Yet in an age like the present, which is being subjected to a constant stream of propaganda in everything from the choice of its religion to its cigarettes, general critical intelligence would seem desirable.

As a matter of fact, most persons nowadays aspire to be not critical but creative. We have not merely creative poets and novelists, but creative readers and listeners and dancers. Lately a form of creativeness has appeared that may in time swallow up all the others—creative salesmanship. The critic himself has caught the contagion and also aspires to be creative. He is supposed to become so when he receives from the creation of another, conceived as pure temperamental overflow, so vivid an impression that, when passed through his temperament, it issues forth as a fresh creation. What is eliminated in both critic and creator is any standard that is set above temperament and that therefore might interfere with their eagerness to get themselves expressed

This notion of criticism as self-expression is important for our present subject, for it has been adopted by the writer who is, according to the *Encyclopaedia Britannica*,[2] 'the greatest critical force in America'—Mr. H. L. Mencken. Creative self-expression, as practiced by himself and others, has, according to Mr. Mencken, led to a salutary stirring up of the stagnant pool of American letters: 'Today for the first time in years there is strife in American criticism. . . . Heretics lay on boldly and the professors are forced to

1 This was written before the collapse of the great common stock bubble in the autumn of 1929. It then became evident that what the financial leaders of the 'boom' period lacked was not so much expertness in their own field as general critical intelligence—especially some working knowledge of the ways of Nemesis. There were of course honorable exceptions. The late Paul M. Warburg showed that he was one of them when he remarked, apropos of the so-called business cycle, that 'it is a subject for psychologists rather than for economists.' [What is involved] 'is the answer to the question: How long—in industry, commerce and finance—does the memory of painful experiences prevent human greed and conceit from regaining control, etc.'

2 Thirteenth edition. In the fourteenth edition we are informed that Mr. Mencken is a satirist rather than a critic.

make some defence. Often going further they attempt counter-attacks. Ears are bitten off, noses are bloodied. There are wallops both above and below the belt.'

But it may be that criticism is something more than Mr. Mencken would have us believe, more in short than a squabble between Bohemians, each eager to capture the attention of the public for his brand of self-expression. To reduce criticism indeed to the satisfaction of a temperamental urge, to the uttering of one's gustos and disgustos (in Mr. Mencken's case chiefly the latter) is to run counter to the very etymology of the word which implies discrimination and judgment. The best one would anticipate from a writer like Mr. Mencken, possessing an unusual verbal virtuosity and at the same time temperamentally irresponsible, is superior intellectual vaudeville. One must grant him, however, certain genuine critical virtues —for example, a power of shrewd observation within rather narrow limits. Yet the total effect of his writing is nearer to intellectual vaudeville than to serious criticism.

The serious critic is more concerned with achieving a correct scale of values and so seeing things proportionately than with self-expression. His essential virtue is poise. The specific benefit he confers is to act as a moderating influence on the opposite insanities between which mankind in the lump is constantly tending to oscillate—oscillations that Luther compares to the reelings of a drunken peasant on horseback. The critic's survey of any particular situation may very well seem satirical. The complaint that Mr. Mencken is too uniformly disgruntled in his survey of the American situation rather misses the point. Behind the pleas for more constructiveness it is usually easy to detect the voice of the booster. A critic who did not get beyond a correct diagnosis of existing evils might be very helpful. If Mr. Mencken has fallen short of being such a diagnostician, the failure is due not to his excess of severity but to his lack of discrimination.

The standards with reference to which men have discriminated in the past have been largely traditional. The outstanding fact of the present period, on the other hand, has been the weakening of traditional standards. An emergency has arisen not unlike that with which Socrates sought to cope in ancient Athens. Anyone who is untraditional and seeks at the same time to be discriminating must almost necessarily own Socrates as his master. As is well known, Socrates sought above all to be discriminating in his use of general terms. Before allowing one's imagination and finally one's conduct to be controlled by a general term, it would seem wise to submit it to a Socratic scrutiny.

It is, therefore, unfortunate that at a time like the present, which plainly calls for a Socrates, we should instead have got a Mencken. One may take as an example of Mr. Mencken's failure to discriminate adequately, his attitude towards the term that for several generations past has been governing the imagination of multitudes —democracy. His view of democracy is simply that of Rousseau turned upside down, and nothing, as has been remarked, resembles a hollow so much as a swelling. A distinction of which he has failed to recognize the importance is that between a direct or unlimited and a constitutional democracy. In the latter we probably have the best thing in the world. The former, on the other hand, as all thinkers of any penetration from Plato and Aristotle down have perceived, leads to the loss of liberty and finally to the rise of some form of despotism. The two conceptions of democracy involve not merely incompatible views of government but ultimately of human nature. The desire of the constitutional democrat for institutions that act as checks on the immediate will of the people implies a similar dualism in the individual—a higher self that acts restrictively on his ordinary and impulsive self. The partisan of unlimited democracy on the other hand is an idealist in the sense the term assumed in connection with the so-called romantic movement. His faith in the people is closely related to the doctrine of natural goodness proclaimed by the sentimentalists of the eighteenth century and itself marking an extreme recoil from the dogma of total depravity. The doctrine of natural goodness favors the free temperamental expansion that I have already noticed in speaking of the creative critic.

It is of the utmost importance, however, if one is to understand Mr. Mencken, to discriminate between two types of temperamentalist —the soft and sentimental type, who cherishes various 'ideals,' and the hard, or Nietzschean type, who piques himself on being realistic. As a matter of fact, if one sees in the escape from traditional controls merely an opportunity to live temperamentally, it would seem advantageous to pass promptly from the idealistic to the Nietzschean phase, sparing oneself as many as possible of the intermediary disillusions. It is at all events undeniable that the rise of Menckenism has been marked by a certain collapse of romantic idealism in the political field and elsewhere. The numerous disillusions that have supervened upon the War have provided a favoring atmosphere.

The symptoms of Menckenism are familiar: a certain hardness and smartness and disposition to rail at everything that, rightly or wrongly, is established and respected; a tendency to identify the real with what Mr. Mencken terms 'the cold and clammy facts' and to assume that the only alternative to facing these facts is to fade away into sheer romantic unreality. These and similar traits are becoming so widely diffused that, whatever one's opinion of Mr. Mencken as a writer and thinker, one must grant him representativeness. He is a chief prophet at present of those who deem themselves emancipated but who are, according to Mr. Brownell, merely unbuttoned.

The crucial point in any case is one's attitude towards the principle of control. Those who stand for this principle in any form or degree are dismissed by the emancipated as reactionaries or, still graver reproach, as Puritans. Mr. Mencken would have us believe that the historical Puritan was not even sincere in his moral rigorism, but was given to 'lamentable transactions with loose women and fiery jugs.' This may serve as a sample of the assertions, picturesquely indiscriminate, by which a writer wins immediate notoriety at the expense of his permanent reputation. The facts about the Puritan happen to be complex and need to be dealt with very Socratically. It has been affirmed that the point of view of the Puritan was stoical rather than truly Christian, and the affirmation is not wholly false. The present discussion of the relationship between Puritanism and the rise of capitalism with its glorification of the acquisitive life also has its justification. It is likewise a fact that the Puritan was from the outset unduly concerned with reforming others as well as himself, and this trait relates him to the humanitarian meddler or 'wowser' of the present day, who is Mr. Mencken's pet aversion.

Yet it remains true that awe and reverence and humility are Christian virtues and that there was some survival of these virtues in the Puritan. For a representative Puritan like Jonathan Edwards they were inseparable from the illumination of grace, from what he terms 'a divine and supernatural light.' In the passage from the love and fear of God of an Edwards to the love and service of man professed by the humanitarian, something has plainly dropped out, something that is very near the center. What has tended to disappear is the inner life with the special type of control it imposes. With the decline of this inner control there has been an increasing resort to outer control. Instead of the genuine Puritan we then have the humanitarian legalist who passes innumerable laws for the control of people who refuse to control themselves. The activity of our uplifters is scarcely suggestive of any 'divine and supernatural light.' Here is a discrimination of the first importance that has been obscured by the muddy thinking of our half-baked intelligentsia. One is thus kept from perceiving the real problem, which is to retain the inner life, even though one refuse to accept the theological nightmare with which the Puritan associated it. More is involved in the failure to solve this problem than the Puritan tradition. It is the failure of our contemporary life in general. Yet, unless some solution is reached by a full and free exercise of the critical spirit, one remains a mere modernist and not a thoroughgoing and complete modern; for the modern spirit and the critical spirit are in their essence one.

What happens, when one sets out to deal with questions of this order without sufficient depth of reflection and critical maturity, may be seen in Mr. Sinclair Lewis's *Elmer Gantry*. He has been lured from art into the writing of a wild diatribe which, considered even as such, is largely beside the mark. If the Protestant Church is at present threatened with bankruptcy, it is not because it has produced an occasional Elmer Gantry. The true reproach it has incurred is that, in its drift toward modernism, it has lost its grip not merely on certain dogmas but, simultaneously, on the facts of human nature. It has failed above all to carry over in some modern and critical form the truth of a dogma that unfortunately receives much support from these facts—the dogma of original sin. At first sight Mr. Mencken would appear to have a conviction of evil—when, for example, he reduces democracy in its essential aspect to a 'combat between jackals and jackasses'—that establishes at least one bond between him and the austere Christian.

The appearance, however, is deceptive. The Christian is conscious above all of the 'old Adam' in himself: hence his humility. The effect of Mr. Mencken's writing, on the other hand, is to produce pride rather than humility, a pride ultimately based on flattery. The reader, especially the young and callow reader, identifies himself imaginatively with Mr. Mencken and conceives of himself as a sort of morose and sardonic divinity surveying from some superior altitude an immeasurable expanse of 'boobs.' This attitude will not seem especially novel to anyone who has traced the modern movement. One is reminded in particular of Flaubert, who showed a diligence in collecting bourgeois imbecilities comparable to that

displayed by Mr. Mencken in his *Americana*. Flaubert's discovery
that one does not add to one's happiness in this way would no doubt
be dismissed by Mr. Mencken as irrelevant, for he has told us that
he does not believe in happiness. Another discovery of Flaubert's
may seem to him more worthy of consideration. 'By dint of railing
at idiots,' Flaubert reports, 'one runs the risk of becoming idiotic oneself.'

It may be that the only way to escape from the unduly complacent
cynicism of Mr. Mencken and his school is to reaffirm once more
the truths of the inner life. In that case it would seem desirable to
disengage, so far as possible, the principle of control on which the
inner life finally depends from mere creeds and traditions and assert
it as a psychological fact; a fact, moreover, that is neither 'cold'
nor 'clammy.' The coldness and clamminess of much so called
realism arises from its failure to give this fact due recognition. A
chief task, indeed, of the Socratic critic would be to rescue the
noble term 'realist' from its present degradation. A view of reality
that overlooks the element in man that moves in an opposite direction from mere temperament, the specifically human factor in short,
may prove to be singularly one-sided. Is the Puritan, John Milton,
when he declares that 'he who reigns within himself and rules passions, desires, and fears is more than a king,' less real than Mr.
Theodore Dreiser when he discourses in his peculiar dialect of 'those
rearranging chemisms upon which all the morality or immorality of
the world is based?'

As a matter of fact, according to the degree and nature of the
exercise of the principle of control, one may distinguish two main
types of realism which may be denominated respectively religious
and humanistic: as the principle of control falls into abeyance, a
third type tends to emerge, which may be termed naturalistic realism.
That the decline of the traditional controls has been followed by a
lapse to the naturalistic level is indubitable. The characteristic evils
of the present age arise from unrestraint and violation of the law of
measure and not, as our modernists would háve us believe, from
the tyranny of taboos and traditional inhibitions. The facts cry to
heaven. The delicate adjustment that is required between the craving for emancipation and the need of control has been pointed out
once and for all by Goethe, speaking not as a Puritan but as a clear-
eyed man of the world. Everything, he says, that liberates the spirit
without a corresponding growth in self-mastery is pernicious. This

one sentence would seem to cover the case of our 'flaming youth' rather completely.

The movement in the midst of which we are still living was from its inception unsound in its dealing with the principle of control. It is vain to expect from the dregs of this movement what its 'first sprightly running failed to give.' Mr. Carl Sandburg speaks of the 'marvelous rebellion of man at all signs reading "Keep off." ' An objection to this purely insurrectional attitude is that, as a result of its endless iteration during the past century and more, it has come to savor too strongly of what has been called 'the humdrum of revolt.' A more serious objection to the attitude is that it encourages an unrestricted and merely temperamental liberty which, paradoxically enough at first sight, affords the modern man no avenue of escape from the web that is being woven about him by the scientific determinist.

Realists of the current type are in point of fact intimately allied with the psychologists—glandular, behavioristic, and psycho-analytical—who, whatever their divergences among themselves, unite in their deterministic trend and therefore clash fundamentally with both religious and humanistic realists. The proper method of procedure in defending the freedom of the will would seem to be to insist upon it as a fact of experience, a fact so primary that the position of the determinist involves an evasion of one of the immediate data of consciousness in favor of a metaphysical dream. What is genuinely experimental in naturalistic psychology should of course be received with respect; but the facts of which it takes account in its experiments are unimportant compared with the facts it either neglects or denies. Practically it is running into grotesque extremes of pseudo-science that make of it a shining mark for the Socratic critic.

Here at all events is the issue on which all other issues finally hinge; for until the question of moral freedom—the question whether man is a responsible agent or only the plaything of his impulses and impressions—is decided, nothing is decided; and to decide the question under existing circumstances calls for the keenest critical discrimination. Creation that is not sufficiently supported by such discrimination is likely to prove premature.

One may illustrate from Mr. Dreiser's *American Tragedy,* hailed in certain quarters as the 'Mount Everest' of recent fiction. He has succeeded in producing in this work something genuinely harrowing; but one is harrowed to no purpose. One has in more than full measure the tragic qualm but without the final relief and enlargement of spirit that true tragedy succeeds somehow in giving, and that without resort to explicit moralizing. It is hardly worth while to struggle through eight hundred and more very pedestrian pages to be left at the end with a feeling of sheer oppression. The explanation of this oppression is that Mr. Dreiser does not rise sufficiently above the level of 'rearranging chemisms,' in other words, of animal behavior. Tragedy may admit fate—Greek tragedy admits it—but not of the naturalistic variety. Confusion on this point may compromise in the long run the reputation of writers more eminent than Mr. Dreiser—for example, of Thomas Hardy. Fatalism of the naturalistic type is responsible in large measure for the atmosphere of futility and frustration that hangs heavily over so much contemporary writing. One finally comes to feel with a recent poet that 'dust' is the common source from which

> stream
> The cricket's cry and Dante's dream.

Anyone who admits reality only in what derives from the dust, whether in a cricket or a Dante, must, from the point of view of the religious or the humanistic realist, be prepared to make substantial sacrifices. In the first place, he must sacrifice the depth and subtlety that arise from the recognition in some form of the duality of man's nature. For the interest that may arise from the portrayal of the conflict between a law of the spirit and a law of the members, the inordinate interest in sex for its own sake promoted by most of the so-called realists is a rather shabby substitute. A merely naturalistic realism also involves the sacrifice of beauty in almost any sense of that elusive term. Closely related to this sacrifice is the sacrifice of delicacy, elevation, and distinction. The very word realism has come to connote the opposite of these qualities. When we learn, for example, that someone has written a realistic study of a great man, we are sure in advance that he has devoted his main effort to proving that 'Plutarch lied.' The more the great man is reduced to the level of commonplace or worse, the more we feel he has been 'humanized.'

Mr. Sherwood Anderson has argued ingeniously that, inasmuch as we ourselves are crude, our literature, if it is not to be unreal and factitious, should be crude likewise. But the writer who hopes to achieve work of importance cannot afford to be too deeply immersed in the atmosphere of the special place and passing moment. Still less can he afford to make us feel, as writers like Mr. Anderson and Mr. Dreiser and Mr. Sinclair Lewis do, that, if there were any lack of vulgarity in what they are depicting, they would be capable of supplying the defect from their own abundance. More is involved here than mere loss of distinction. We have come, indeed, to the supreme sacrifice that every writer must make who does not transcend a naturalistic realism. He must forego the hope of the enduring appeal—the hope that every writer worthy of his salt cherishes in some degree. In the absence of humanistic or religious standards, he is prone to confound the real with the welter of the actual, and so to miss the 'grandeur of generality.'

Certain books in the current mode are so taken up with the evanescent surfaces of life that they will survive, if at all, not as literature but as sociological documents. The very language in which they are written will, in a generation or two, require a glossary. So far from imposing an orderly pattern on the raw material of experience, they rather emphasize the lack of pattern. The resulting effect, to borrow a phrase from the late Stephen Crane, who has had a marked influence on the recent movement, is that of a 'cluttered incoherency.' As an extreme example of the tendency one may cite *Manhattan Transfer* by John Dos Passos. In the name of reality, Mr. Dos Passos has perpetrated a literary nightmare. Such a work would seem to have slight value even as a sociological document; unless, indeed, one is prepared to admit that contemporary Manhattan is inhabited chiefly by epileptic Bohemians.

'It is as much a trade,' says La Bruyère, 'to make a book as it is to make a clock'; in short, literature is largely a matter of technique. The technique of *Manhattan Transfer* is as dubious as its underlying philosophy. Neither can be justified save on the assumption that the aim of art is to exaggerate the clutter and incoherency of the mundane spectacle instead of eliciting its deeper meaning. Technique counts for even more in poetry than in prose. It would be possible to base on technical grounds alone a valid protest against the present preposterous overestimate of Walt Whitman. Fundamental questions need, in these very untraditional days, to be critically elucidated with a view to right definition if the poet is not to lack technique or still worse, if he is not, like certain recent practitioners of free verse, to be hagridden by a false technique. It evidently concerns both the form and substance of poetry, whether one define it with Aristotle as the portrayal of representative human action, or whether one define it with Mr. Carl Sandburg as a 'mystic, sensuous mathematics of fire, smokestacks, waffles, pansies, people, and purple sunsets.'

There is no doubt much in the America of today that suggests a jazzy impressionism. Still our naturalistic delinquence has probably not gone so far as one might infer from poetry like that of Mr. Sandburg or fiction like that of Mr. Dos Passos. The public response to some of the realistic novels has been considerable: allowance must be made however for the *succès de scandale,* also for the skill attained by the modern publisher in the art of merchandizing. The reputation of certain books one might mention may be regarded as a triumph of 'creative' advertising. What has been created is a mirage of masterpieces where no masterpieces are. It is well also to remember in regard to some of the works that have been most discussed that, so far from being an authentic reflection of the American scene, they are rather a belated echo of certain European movements. For it is as certain that in our literary and artistic modes we follow Europe—usually at an interval of from five to forty years—as it is that we lead Europe in our bathtubs and sanitary plumbing. Anyone who resided in Paris in the nineties and later in America, will, as I can testify from personal experience, have the sense of having lived through the same literary fads twice. Mr. Dreiser reminds one of Zola and his school. The technique of Mr. Dos Passos recalls that of the Goncourts. Our experimenters in free verse have followed in the wake not merely of Walt Whitman but of the French symbolists, and so on.

We shall presently begin to hear of certain new developments in French literature and critical thought that point, though indecisively as yet, to a radical departure from what has been the main current since the eighteenth century and in some respects since the Renaissance. It is well that we should become familiar with the writers who reveal in different ways this latest trend—notably with Maritain, Maurras, Lasserre, Seillière, and Benda; for they give evidence of a quality of cerebration that is rare in our own literati. At the same time we should not adopt with our usual docility the total outlook of any of these writers: for no one of them has worked out a point of view exactly adapted to our requirements. In general, it is not fitting that a great nation at the very height of its power should go on indefinitely trailing after Europe. It is time for us to initiate something of our own. This does not mean that we should proceed forthwith to inbreed our own 'originality.' It means almost the exact opposite. The most original thing one could do nowadays would be to question the whole theory of originality as mere temperamental overflow and self-expression that has prevailed from the 'geniuses' of the eighteenth century down to one of our youthful and very minor bards who aspires to 'spill his bright illimitable soul.'

A genuinely critical survey would make manifest that the unsatisfactoriness of our creative effort is due to a lack of the standards that culture alone can supply. Our cultural crudity and insignificance can be traced in turn to the inadequacy of our education, especially our higher education. Mr. Mencken's attack on the 'professors' is therefore largely justified; for if the professors were performing their function properly Mr. Mencken himself would not be possible. One must add in common justice that the professors themselves, or at least some of them, are becoming aware that all is not well with existing conditions. One could not ask anything more perspicacious than the following paragraph from a recent report of Committee G to the American Association of University Professors:

American education has suffered from the domination, conscious or unconscious, direct or indirect, of political and sentimental, as well as educational, theories that are demonstrably false. If the views of some men are to prevail the intellectual life of the country is doomed; everybody except the sheer idiot is to go to college and pursue chiefly sociology, nature study, child study, and community service—and we shall have a society unique only in its mediocrity, ignorance and vulgarity. It will not do to dismiss lightly even so extreme a view as this; it is too indicative. Such influences are very strong, their pressure is constant; and if education has largely failed in America it has been due primarily to them.

In short, as a result of the encroachments of an equalitarian democracy, the standards of our higher education have suffered in two distinct particulars: first, as regards the quality of students; second, as regards the quality of the studies these students pursue. The first of these evils is generally recognized. There is even some prospect of remedial measures. Certain institutions, Harvard, for example, without being as yet severely selective, are becoming more critical of the incompetent student. On the other hand, there seems to be less hope than ever of any righting of the second and more serious evil—the failure to distinguish qualitatively between studies. The main drift is still towards what one may term the blanket degree. (Dartmouth, for example, has just merged its bachelor of arts and bachelor of science.) Yet rather than blur certain distinctions it would have been better, one might suppose, to use up all the letters of the alphabet devising new degrees to meet the real or supposed educational needs of the modern man. To bestow the A.B. degree indiscriminately on a student for whom education has meant primarily a specialization in chemistry and on one for whom it has meant primarily an assimilation of the masterpieces of Greek literature is to empty it of any effective meaning. At the present rate, indeed, the time may come when the A.B. will not throw much more light on the cultural quality of its recipient than it would, if, as has been suggested, it were bestowed on every American child at birth.

It goes without saying that those who have been lowering and confusing educational standards have been profuse in their professions of 'service.' A critical examination, not merely of American education but of American life at the present time will almost necessarily hinge on this term. The attitude of the Socratic critic towards it is not to be confounded with that of Mr. Mencken and the 'hard-boiled' contingent. 'When a gang of real estate agents,' says Mr. Mencken, 'bond salesmen, and automobile dealers get together to sob for Service, it takes no Freudian to surmise that someone is about to be swindled.' But if one entertain doubts about this current American gospel, why waste one's ammunition on any such small fry? Other and more exalted personages than the members of the Rotary Club at Zenith have, in Mr. Sinclair Lewis's elegant phrase, been 'yipping for Service.' If one is to deal with this idea of service Socratically, one needs to consider it in its relation to the two figures who have rightly been taken to be the most representative in our cultural background—Benjamin Franklin and Jonathan Edwards. Franklin's idea of service is already humanitarian. Edwards' idea is still traditionally Christian—service not of man but of God. What Franklin stood for is flourishing prodigiously at the present moment, so much so that he may perhaps be defined in his chief line of influence as the great superrotarian. What Edwards stood for is, on the other hand, largely obsolete or survives only in the form of habits, which, lacking doctrinal support, are steadily declining along with the whole Puritan culture.

Intermediary types are possible. One may in one's character reflect the Puritan background and at the same time in one's idea of service derive rather from Franklin. Precisely that combination is found in the most influential of our recent educational leaders—the late President Eliot. A legitimate admiration for his personal qualities should not interfere with the keenest critical scrutiny of his views about education, for the two things stand in no necessary connection. Practically this means to scrutinize the humanitarian idealism that he probably did more than any other man of his generation to promote. In this respect most of the heads of our institutions of learning have been and still are understudies of President Eliot.

In an address on the occasion of his ninetieth birthday President Eliot warned his hearers against introspection, lest it divert them from a wholehearted devotion to service. Between this attitude and a religious or humanistic attitude there is a clash of first principles. Both humanism and religion require introspection as a prerequisite of the inner life and its appropriate activity. With the disappearance of this activity what is left is the outer activity of the utilitarian, and this leads straight to the one-sided cult of material efficiency and finally to the standardization that is, according to nearly all foreign critics and many of our own, a chief American danger. We cannot return to the introspection of the Puritan. We shudder at the theology an Edwards would impose as the condition of his 'divine and supernatural light.' Yet it does not follow, as I have already suggested, that we should reject the inner life itself along with this theology. One may recognize innumerable incidental advantages in the gospel of service and yet harbor an uneasy suspicion withal that in the passage from the older religion to the modern humanitarian dispensation something vital has disappeared, something for which neither the outer working of the utilitarian nor again the expansive sympathy of the sentimentalist can offer an equivalent.

The problem of the inner life is very much bound up with two other problems that are now pressing for solution in our higher education and have as yet found none: the problem of the specialist and the problem of leisure. The man of leisure is engaged in an inner and specifically human form of activity, a form that is, according to Aristotle, needful if he is to compass the end of ends— his own happiness. The question is whether one should consent like the specialist to forego this activity and to live partially and as a mere instrument for the attainment of some outer end—even though this end be the progress of humanity. We are beginning to hear a great deal nowadays about the 'menace' of leisure. It has been estimated that with the perfecting of mechanical devices the man of the future will be able to satisfy his material wants by working not more than four hours a day. It is vain to anticipate that the rank and file will use this release from outer activity intelligently unless the leaders, notably those in high academic station, show the way. The notion of true leisure is the ultimate source of the standards of any education that deserves to be called liberal. When even a few of our college and university presidents show that they are thinking to some purpose on the nature of leisure it will be time enough to talk of 'America's coming of age.'

As it is, our institutions of learning seem to be becoming more and more hotbeds of 'idealism.' Their failure, on the whole, to achieve standards as something quite distinct from ideals, on the one hand, and standardization, on the other, may prove a fact of sinister import for the future of American civilization. The warfare that is being waged at the present time by Mr. Sinclair Lewis and others against a standardized Philistinism continues in the main the protest that has been made for several generations past by the temperamentalists, hard or soft, against the mechanizing of life by the utilitarian. This protest has been, and is likely to continue to be, ineffectual. The fruitful opposite of the standardized Philistine is not the Bohemian, nor again the hard temperamentalist or superman, as Mr. Mencken conceives him, but the man of leisure. Leisure involves an inner effort with reference to standards that is opposed to the sheer expansion of temperament, as it is to every other form of sheer expansion.

Perhaps a reason why the standards of the humanist are less popular in this country than the ideals of the humanitarian is that these standards set bounds to the acquisitive life; whereas it seems possible to combine a perfect idealism with an orgy of unrestricted commercialism. It is well for us to try to realize how we appear to others in this matter. Our growing unpopularity abroad is due no doubt in part to envy of our material success, but it also arises from the proneness of the rest of the world to judge us, not by the way we feel about ourselves, but by our actual performance. If we are in our own eyes a nation of idealists, we are, according to a recent French critic, M. André Siegfried,[3] a 'nation of Pharisees.' The European, M. Siegfried would have us believe, still has a concern for the higher values of civilization, whereas the American is prepared to sacrifice these values ruthlessly to mass production and material efficiency.

It is easy to detect under this assumption the latest form of a 'certain condescension in foreigners.' The breakdown of cultural standards is European as well as American. It is not clear that M. Siegfried himself has an adequate notion of the form of effort that

---

[3] See his volume *Les États-Unis d'aujourd'hui* (1927), translated under the title *America Comes of Age.*

can alone serve as a counterpoise to the one-sided activity of the utilitarian. At the same time his anatomy of our favorite ideal of service is not without interest. This ideal opposes no effective barrier to our expansiveness. An unchecked expansiveness on the national scale is always imperialistic. Among the ingredients of a possible American imperialism M. Siegfried enumerates the American's 'great self-satisfaction, his rather brutal sense of his own interests, and *the consciousness, still more dangerous, of his "duties" towards humanity.'* M. Siegfried admits however that our imperialism is likely to be of a new and subtle essence, not concerned primarily with territorial aggrandizement.

A proper discussion of Mr. Siegfried's position as well as of other issues I have been raising would transcend the limits of an essay. My end has been accomplished if I have justified in some measure the statement with which I started as to the importance of cultivating a general critical intelligence. James Russell Lowell's dictum that before having an American literature we must have an American criticism was never truer than it is today. The obvious reply to those who call for more creation and less criticism is that one needs to be critical above all in examining what now passes for creation. A scrutiny of this kind would, I have tried to show, extend beyond the bounds of literature to various aspects of our national life and would converge finally on our higher education.

We cannot afford to accept as a substitute for this true criticism the self-expression of Mr. Mencken and his school, unless indeed we are to merit the comment that is, I am told, made on us by South Americans: 'They are not a very serious people!' To be sure, the reader may reflect that I am myself a critic, or would-be critic. I can only express the hope that, in my magnifying of the critical function, I do not offer too close a parallel to the dancing-master in Molière who averred, it will be remembered, that 'all the mistakes of men, the fatal reverses that fill the world's annals, the shortcomings of statesmen, and the blunders of great captains arise from not knowing how to dance.'

# KENNETH BURKE

## (1897–    )

BORN in Pittsburgh on May 5, 1897, Burke was educated at Ohio State University and at Columbia. After some editorial work for the Bureau of Social Hygiene in New York City, he became in 1927 music critic for *The Dial*. A brilliant and prolific writer, he has produced literary criticism, book reviews, stories, translations, and fiction, much of which was contributed to such periodicals as *The Nation* (he was its music critic from 1933 to 1935), *The New Republic, The Southern Review,* the *Bookman, Broom,* the *Symposium, Vanity Fair, The Little Review, Hound & Horn,* and a number of others. In 1928 he won *The Dial* award of two thousand dollars for distinguished service to American letters. In 1935 he was granted a Guggenheim Fellowship.

As a critic Burke enlisted from the start in the ranks of the "opposition." In *Counter-Statement* (1931), Burke advanced the principle of polarity or the achievement of perspective through incongruity, which plays such an important part in his literary criticism. Primarily interested in tracing the working out of symbolic action in literature, he applies his critical theory to such writers as Thomas Mann, Gide, Pater, and Flaubert. The section called "Lexicon Rhetoricae" is highly suggestive, a kind of judgment-machine designed to clarify critical issues and to make the nature of controversy more definite.

For his method of analysis, Burke is largely indebted to the work of such men as I. A. Richards and C. K. Ogden in *The Meaning of Meaning.* In *Permanence and Change* (1935), his primary object is to achieve terminological exactitude by reducing meanings, which are essentially social in origin and purpose, to their component elements. Terms are defined, placed in novel juxtaposition with related terms, viewed from opposed angles of vision, till they lose their conventional connotations. The "reasons" and motivations of one group of thinkers prove to be the "rationalization" of another school of thought. Dewey's concept of occupational psychosis enables Burke to examine in a new light the factor

307

of interest in many problems arising in sociology and criticism. Burke's method, consistently carried out, is to turn established linguistic and conceptual categories upside down and inside out. Indeed, he urges "that planned incongruity should be deliberately cultivated for the purpose of experimentally wrenching apart all those molecular combinations of adjective and noun, substantive and verb, which still remain with us."[1] Influenced by the Marxian outlook as well as by Dewey's instrumentalism, Burke seeks to formulate an occupational morality.

In *Attitudes Toward History* (1937) Burke examines and tests on a number of writers the dual frames of acceptance and rejection, on the ground that concepts embody attitudes. We are for or against people and also for and against the ideas or functions these people represent. Burke's treatment of the poetic categories—the epic, the satire, the elegy, burlesque, the grotesque, the didactic—and his study of the symbolic structures they contain, yield novel results. His primary purpose is simply to indicate that however free aesthetic enterprise may be, it is necessarily held down by historical forces: "the poetic forms are symbolic structures designed to equip us for confronting given historical or personal situations."[2] What he has attempted to do is twofold: to invent a dictionary of critical terms, definitions that will supply a more flexible and relativistic language to fit the complexities of modern life, and second, to split apart words that are bound to one category and transfer them to another mode of association. This process he calls "casuistic stretching," a process inherent in the structure of language, for each concept contains its opposite in solution. Burke's method owes a great deal to the work of such men as I. A. Richards, C. K. Ogden, Bentham, Marx, Freud, and Dewey.

In *The Philosophy of Literary Form* (1941), Burke has undertaken the difficult and ambitious task of re-examining and reappraising the fundamental principles and practices of literary criticism, interpreting literature in terms of situations and strategies. As in his other work, he is primarily interested in the nature of symbolic action, particularly as it is embodied in literature, and how to recognize and interpret these various modes of symbolic action. Though he does write on "Motives and Motifs in the Poetry of Marianne Moore" and "Symbolic Action in a Poem by Keats," the specific criticism of books is relegated to a subordinate role. He is interested in disclosing the underlying pattern of motivation which is to be found in poetic situations, believing that he can work out an objective psychology of aesthetics by means of such analyses. His suggested procedure for analyzing the symbolic act in a work of art is to search for

1 Kenneth Burke, *Permanence and Change* (New York, 1935), p. 157.
2 Kenneth Burke, *Attitudes Toward History* (New York, 1937), I, 42.

significant "leads," for dramatic alignments, for a cluster of telltale imagery, hoping in this way to discover what the poem is doing for the poet and thus gain insight into the fundamentals of structural relations. Though he grants the assumption that the focus of critical analysis must be brought to bear upon the structure of the work itself, he feels that his proposed method can be applied to events within and outside the locus of the poem.

*A Grammar of Motives* (1945) takes up the motivational aspects of literature and relates them to what is involved in human behavior. The basic categories of thought are exemplified in this universal tendency to attribute motives to human actions. He arranges his drama into five parts: Act, Scene, Agent, Agency, Purpose, though aware all the time that they are highly complex and that they constantly overlap. His method he calls "dramatism," in that it treats thought and language behavioristically as modes of action. In this study Burke departs from literary criticism and enters the labyrinthine caves of metaphysical speculation. Just as Sir Thomas Browne dearly loved a mystery, so Kenneth Burke is overfond of ambiguities which he can clear up dialectically, strongly reminding one of William Empson in this respect.

Though Burke tries hard to bring these abstractions down to earth and apply them to social processes as well as literary works, his concern with literature is incidental rather than primary. The writer, the poem, the novel, the play, is but an illustration of a tendency, a semantic strategy for encompassing a situation. Psychology, Marxism, Freudianism, semantics, metaphysics, anthropology, linguistics, symbolic logic, instrumentalism, sociology, all these are brought to bear on the study of literature, with the not unexpected result that the literary work often gets lost or obscured in the process.

## BIBLIOGRAPHY

### TEXT

*Counter-Statement*. New York, 1931.
*Permanence and Change*. New York, 1935.
*Attitudes Toward History*. 2 vols. New York, 1937.
*The Philosophy of Literary Form*. Baton Rouge. 1941.
*A Grammar of Motives*. New York, 1945.
"Kinds of Criticism," *Poetry*, LXVIII, 272–282 (August, 1946).
*A Rhetoric of Motives*, New York, 1950.

### CRITICISM

Duffey, Bernard, "Reality as Language," *Western Review*, XII, 132–145 (Spring, 1948).

Glicksberg, Charles I., "Kenneth Burke," *South Atlantic Quarterly*, XXXVI, 74–84 (January, 1937).

Hyman, Stanley Edgar, "Kenneth Burke and the Criticism of Symbolic Action," *The Armed Vision*. New York, 1948, pp. 347–394.

Munson, Gorham B., "In and about the Workshop of Kenneth Burke," *Calendar*, III, 129–141 (July, 1926).

——, *Destinations*. New York, 1928.

Parkes, Henry B., *The Pragmatic Test*. San Francisco, 1941.

Nemerov, Howard, "A Note on the Terms of Kenneth Burke," *Furioso*, II, 29–42 (Spring, 1947).

Warren, Austin, "Kenneth Burke," *Sewanee Review*, XLI, 225–236, 344–363 (April-June, 1933; July-September, 1933).

## APPLICATIONS OF THE TERMINOLOGY*

HIERARCHY. Many aspects of a writer's merit, being wholly outside him, change independently of him (as is particularly the case with the changes in ideology and in the predominant aspects of a social situation). Every poem is, in a sense, an "occasional" poem —and it is somewhat a matter of accident whether the occasion for which the poem was written continues frequently to recur. (Or, for that matter, the situation for which a work is written may become more widespread at a later date than at the time of its production— in which case the work may seem to a later age more apropos than it did to its own. This eventuality likewise may be more to a writer's good fortune than to his credit.) In asking that literature produce one sort of effect rather than another, we should be asking that literature fit one sort of situation rather than another.[1]

There are two general bases of critical exhortation. (1) We may have a concept of an ideal situation, and insist that literature be written in accordance with this ideal situation; or (2) We may have a concept of a contemporary situation, and insist that literature be written in accordance with this contemporary situation. The first method is absolutist: it seeks to determine once and for all what kind of literature is categorically superior to what other kinds of

* From *Counter-Statement*, copyright, 1931, by Kenneth Burke. Reprinted by permission of Harcourt, Brace and Company, Inc.

[1] A work may be said to "fit" a situation in two ways. It may fit as a corrective to the situation—or it may be said to "fit" simply because the situation enables it to be well received. The two ways are not necessarily opposed, but are often opposed.

literature. The second method is relativistic, or historical: it holds
that if literature is to be written for an ideal situation at a time
when the actual situation is far from ideal, writers must sacrifice the
appositeness of art in the interests of a purely academic concept of
"perfection." The first method would decide *in absoluto* whether
literature should provide bread or cake; the second method would
have to say "sometimes bread—sometimes cake, according to the
'needs' at the particular moment." The second method may seem, on
the face of it, more readily defensible—but it has difficulties of its
own, and though all the absolutists were silenced, there would still
be endless bickerings among the relativists, since a given situation
can be interpreted in many ways, and thus may be shown to have
diametrically opposite "needs." In one respect, however, the advocates of the second method now have the advantage: the advocates
of the first method, while holding to the categorical superiority of
some literature (as the Neo-Humanists), have yielded much to the
ways of historical or relativistic thinking, and have sought to defend
their brands of art, not solely in accordance with a concept of perfection, but also as being apposite to the contemporary scene. Yet a
particular brand of art cannot be at once categorically superior and
best fitted for all situations in history, since the situations in history
change so greatly that, by being better fitted to deal with one, a
brand of art would necessarily be worse fitted for dealing with others.

Thus, some absolutist critics, having hit upon a distinction between "yea-saying" and "nay-saying," ask that literature be not a
protest, but an affirmation. But who says "yea" badly has nay-said
—and one is almost certain to say "yea" badly if he and his contemporaries are living in a pig-sty. Insofar as we may look upon
literature as an incipient form of action (in the pitting of some assumptions against others, the poet leaves us with an implied code
of conduct), we might reasonably expect literature to say "yea" or
"nay" purely in accordance with the kind of action demanded by
the times. We do not categorically praise one remedy above another
unless both are intended to cure the same illness in the same type
of patient. And insofar as life is a solving of problems, to praise
categorically a certain kind of solution (a certain brand of art) is to
praise a method regardless of the problem (which would be like
advocating the use of nothing but quadratic equations, though the
problem to be solved had no concern with quadratic equations—
nor is the analogy so far-fetched, as there are certain kinds of honest
outcry to which the tests of "affirmation" are totally irrelevant).

The last decade has counted many attacks upon Rousseau. Rousseau's principles, according to his modern opponents, have led to vast absurdities. Let us, to simplify the issue, grant their contentions, though there are many who would attribute our difficulties to too little Rousseau rather than to too much. But even if we granted the contentions of his opponents, we should not overlook the fact that any principles can lead to vast absurdities, if only because principles persist and grow in popularity long after they have gained the end for which they were formulated. And in outlasting their original beneficent function, they take on a maleficent function, for instead of running counter to the situation which they were designed to correct, they may now be carrying to excess the situation which they served to bring about. Indeed, we might almost say that the predominance of a principle is *per se* evidence that this principle has outlived its usefulness; for by the time it has penetrated from the busy centers of thought to the sluggish periphery of mankind, the situation for which it was designed has certainly altered.

As for the "class-romantic" dichotomy, and the many feuds arising from the attempt first to define the distinctions between them and then to extol one at the expense of the other, we might attempt a distinction of our own, based upon a slightly different definition of dualistic and monistic thinking. The classicists have, in general, praised dualistic thought, conceiving of the individual as the balancing of opposite principles, and they have accused the romantic of being monistic, or one-sided. They have pointed out that a monistic principle contains no basis of correction—that its "logical conclusion" is not distinguishable from its "reduction to absurdity." The romantic, however, can likewise lay claim to a dualistic system, having for opposites the principle which he stands for and the principle represented by the society against which he revolts. His "individualism" never for a moment permits him to forget the "enemy" —and indeed, to be effective, he must have a great understanding of the "enemy," must to an extent encompass the "enemy."

It seems that, at a time when many people are living dissatisfactorily, the romantic dualism (of "oneself against society") will be the more useful mode of correction (as one "establishes his equilibrium by leaning"). Classicism, however, would seem particularly useful at precisely that time when a monistic principle has come to have considerable weight against the "opposition" and is threatening to become the predominant influence in turn. At this point classicism might serve to hold the two principles in fusion, to prevent as long as possible either from gaining upon the other. Classicism might thus be called the flowering of a romantic excess. The nature of its insight is determined by the romantic emphases out of which it arises. When the battle has been fought, it can attempt to prolong the amenities of peace.

So much for the two under ideal conditions. Each can be misused. We can have classicists, extolling affirmation and poise, when a small class happens to be enjoying a privileged way of life out of which much order and charm can be extracted by the fortunate. We can have romantics, calling for rebellion, simply because their morbid vanity has been injured. The weaknesses of each position have been soundly attacked by the members of the other camp. But as for the entire picture of the two types (classic "repose" and romantic "disturbance") we must realize that either represents a selection from the normal experiences of a day, which have both their classic and romantic aspects. "Poise" and "decorum" are as much an arbitrary simplification as "rebellion," and it is only by denying some aspects of our day that we could categorically rule out one type in favour of the other.

ART AND "LIFE." The exhortation that the artist "deal with life" is confusing, particularly as it is hard to understand how he could deal with anything else. When applied to novels, the slogan seems to mean that the artist should give us characters which seem "life-like," should show them doing things which seem "natural," and should tell his tale in a simple, running style which is unobtrusive and permits the reader to follow it unawares. Yes, however strongly critics insist that these be the traits of the novel, they are not the traits of lyric poetry, and thus are not always essential to the process of "dealing with life." The fact is that much of the world's greatest literature lacks the "life-like" characters and the "natural" actions and the "conversational" manner which one can find, or thinks he can find, in even inferior fictions of the nineteenth century. To this extent, therefore, we may seem justified in interpreting the exhortation to "deal with life" as an exhortation to preserve certain conventions of nineteenth-century prose fiction.

Other critics mean by the phrase "deal with life" that the artist should deal with specific "problems" of the day. Thus, we have the proletarian critic, who asks that the writer never close his eyes to labour disputes, slum conditions, political outrages, etc. "Dealing with life," by this system, usually contains all the requirements listed above, plus an attack upon the "evasiveness" of a writer who devotes himself, say, to historical idylls depicting the life of the cultured rich on Greek islands of antiquity. The proletarian critic will call such an idyll bourgeois literature of "escape." He will say that it is welcomed by bourgeois readers because its phantasy enables them to forget the harsh realities underlying their prosperity. Incidentally, in pursuing such a line of attack he overlooks entirely the effect which a "Utopian" literature may have in sharpening a reader's dissatisfaction with the contemporary scene. For the very book that may serve a reader as an "evasion" while he is reading it, may make reality seem all the more unappealing when he is not reading (psychoanalysis having led us to forget how, but a few years ago, the "escape" literature of love romances was condemned by educators, not because it enabled the readers to "accept" the world as it was, but because by contrast it made the facts of everyday life very unacceptable).

Underlying the proletarian attitude is the assumption that literature must be "useful," that it must serve to eradicate certain forms of social injustice, and that it can eradicate these forms of injustice only by dealing with them specifically. It overlooks entirely the fact that there is the pamphlet, the political tract, the soap-box oration, to deal with the specific issues of the day, whereas the literature of the imagination may prepare the minds in a more general fashion. That is, a great work, dealing with some hypothetical event remote in history and "immediacy," may leave us with a desire for justice —and the political speaker may profit by this equipment when he shows his hearers that some particular situation in his particular precinct is unjust. There must be a literature which upholds such an equipment in the abstract, if the social reformer is to find something in us to which he can appeal when advocating reforms in the particular. It is fortunate for the proletarian reformer that so much of art is written in defiance of his injunctions.[2]

Again, by the exhortation that literature "deal with life," we often mean that literature should be popular. For it is obvious that if a

[2] In one respect, however, art may serve his purposes very well. If a political doctrine which he advocates is repugnant to most people, the artist may "naturalize" it by depicting very humane types of people who hold to this doctrine (thus pitting the reader's assumptions as to "likable people" against his assumptions as to the degradation of the doctrine). Such a procedure militates against a naïve but basic tendency on the part of mankind to associate an abhorrent doctrine with one specific kind of abhorrent person (an association which probably explains why nearly every heretic sect was generously credited with "unnatural practices," as are the victims of morphine today).

book engrosses one reader, it has "dealt with life" so far as he is concerned, though all the rest of mankind find it trivial and unconvincing. Accordingly if, knowing that a book has in the present or past engrossed a few readers, we insist that it does not deal with life, we must mean that it should engross more readers.

To consider the entire issue from the standpoint of the Lexicon:

A writer is engaged in the producing of effects upon his readers. He may seek to produce such effects as appeal to a large audience, or to a small audience, or to a particular kind of audience (as an audience of workingmen, or an audience of scholars). Thus he will aim to produce the sort of effects which certain people (presumably more or less like himself) will find appealing. He will manipulate their ideology, he will exploit his and their own patterns of experience, he will symbolize by one set of modes or another (he may prey upon their sense of injustice, for instance, by depicting the maltreatment of a slave on a Greek island of antiquity, or by an account of child labour conditions in the cotton mills—and whether he use the "antique" modes or the "modern," he is dealing with life if he awakens in his readers such rage against injustice as he intended to awaken).

A work deals with life for a great many people when it symbolizes such patterns of experience as characterize a great many people and ramifies the Symbol by such modes of experience as appeal to a great many people. It may, in so doing, prove its unfitness to deal with life for others, who require other kinds of Symbolization and who happen—whether through their way of living or through the conventions of their art—to demand that the Symbols be ramified in other modes of experience. A fiction designed for an audience of workingmen, for instance, may give such pictures of life among the wealthy as could never be said by the wealthy to deal with life. But these pictures, however inaccurate, "deal with life" so long as they serve as Symbols for arousing in the workingmen such emotions as the artist wished to arouse. One must realize that many works of the past which now seem "hollow" are hollow because they were so well adapted to "dealing with life" under their particular set of conditions (they were "occasional poems" for occasions so specific that the occasions are not likely to recur). We may further recall our account of the vaudeville actor's witticism in Spain (Lexicon: Topic 26, "The Symbolically and formally 'charged' "). Transferred to America at present, the witticism would be completely "hollow." But the day may come when we too have been "waiting for seven years." The witticism will then "deal with life." We must realize, on this point, that when to "deal with life" means to exploit "burning issues" (as the popular magazines often attempt to do) the author is choosing the readiest means of producing his effects, the means which happen to be most effective at the moment (as would a playwright "exposing" vice conditions at a time when the public was much exercised over a crusade against vice rings).

In conclusion: The most "unreal" book in the world can properly be said to "deal with life" if it can engross a reader (that is, if it is an "occasional poem" written for the particular sort of occasion which happens to characterize the reader's own life or stage of life). Some ages will prefer (as in the time of Lyly) such persiflage and gallantry as never was. But we must not overlook the fact that, however "artificial" such a style may be, the feeling behind it, the love of ceremony which it symbolizes, is as "natural" and "spontaneous" as any other emotion. For many people the emphases of today may be such that this love of ceremony seems trifling and malapropos; for them, not only the exaggerated *désinvolture* of a Lyly, but even the fluent badinage of Restoration Comedy, will seem not to "deal with life." And the author who would get general credit for "dealing with life" must give more attention to other emphases, other forms of the conventional and unreal which happen at the moment to be deemed more "natural."

OBJECTIVE-SUBJECTIVE. In the "great ages," when drama flourishes, art is "objective." That is, the artist gets his effects primarily by the exploitation of the current ideology. In the society of the times there are many implicit judgments, a general agreement as to what is heroic, what cowardly, what irreligious, what boorish, what clever, etc.,—the playwright thus being able to affect his audience by endowing his characters with these various traits. The advantages of such a method are obvious. The artist may easily obtain the maximum of "impersonality." If he is at peace with the world, he may manipulate those aspects of the current ideology which make for comedy; if he is gloomy, he may exploit the implicit judgments of the day to produce tragedy; but beyond this, his personal bias need not intrude at all.

Racine's prefaces to his plays illustrate to perfection the "objective" method of composition. They disclose how, using the contemporary ideology of vice and virtue, of nobility and disgrace, he would put a character together almost like mixing the ingredients in a cooking recipe, balancing vices and virtues, sympathetic and anti-pathetic traits, purely from the standpoint of the attitude which he intended to arouse in his audience. Thus: "In Euripides and Seneca, Hippolyte is accused of actually violating his mother-in-law: *vim corpus tulit.* But here he is accused of only having entertained the thought. I wanted to spare Thésée a confusion which would have made him less appealing to the audience." Or again: "As for the character of Hippolyte, I noticed that ancient writers blamed Euripi-des for having depicted him as a philosopher so free of all imperfec-tions that the death of this young prince aroused much more indig-nation than pity. I thought that I should give him some weakness which would make him somewhat guilty towards his father, though without taking from him any of that magnanimity with which he protects the honour of Phèdre and accepts suffering rather than ac-cuse her. I consider as weakness the passion which he felt in spite of himself for Aricie, who is the daughter and the sister of his father's mortal enemies." Or of Phèdre: "I am not surprised that this charac-ter had so happy a success in the days of Euripides, and that it has still succeeded so well in our era, since it has all the qualities which Aristotle requires of the tragic hero, and which are adapted to the arousing of pity and terror." And of the play *Iphigénie:* "Thus the outcome of the play is drawn from its very foundations; and one has but to see it acted to realize what pleasure I have provided for the audience, both by saving at the end a virtuous princess in whom the audience has come to take such an interest during the course of the tragedy, and in saving her by some other means than by a miracle [i.e., the *deus ex machina*] which the audience could not have ac-cepted because they could not have believed in it."[3]

This dramatic or objective method (of composing one's symbols from the standpoint of the effect desired) is weakened in proportion as the ideology which the dramatist relies upon is weakened. And in time an ideology must weaken, either through processes of exhaus-tion, or through the encroachment of new material which the ideology cannot encompass. As this weakening progresses, the artist will necessarily become less "objective." On finding the ideology im-paired, he will look for some other kind of certainty to take the place of it. He will, in art, search for something which is equivalent to Descartes' *"cogito, ergo sum"* in metaphysics: he will, that is,

---

[3] Perhaps we should mention, as a particular instance of Racine's manipulation of the ideology current in his times, his great reliance upon the concepts of honour which distinguished the "aesthetic" of the court.

tend to found his art upon an irreducible minimum of belief. This irreducible minimum is, obviously, his personal range of experiences, his own exaltations and depressions, his specific kinds of triumph and difficulty. Wherefore, he will tend to symbolize his particular "pattern of experience"—his art will become "subjective." Some critics will decry this development as a kind of self-indulgence on the part of the artist: but they might with equal justice salute the accuracy of the artist in making the change. In any event, the most vigorous and enterprising artists will be found to be the ones who have manifested this "subjective" tendency most thoroughly, while the hackmen, the Broadway playwrights and the writers of purely commercial fiction, will be found to rely greatly upon the remaining vestiges of the ideology (often they use aspects of the ideology which, though brought into confusion by new matter, still flourish in "backwoods of the mind" not yet affected by the force of the new matter; and just as often they exploit certainties of the moment, as a financial panic, or a wave of patriotism in war times—among this group being also those objective writers who have, in recent years, been working the vein of "youthful sophistication").

In summary: the objective writer attempts to make effective Symbols; the subjective writer attempts to make Symbols effective (that is, constructs a Symbol as the replica of his own pattern of experience, and having constructed it, schemes to find ways of making it effective).

The distinction might throw some light upon the "enigma of Hamlet." Shakespeare, as dramatist at a time when an ideology was flourishing (consider, for instance, what advantages the author of *Othello* had over a modern playwright who, under the disturbances of recent psychological tenets, would attempt a tragedy of jealousy built upon a concept of chastity) was adept at the composition of effective Symbols. His plays were constructed from the standpoint of the effect to be produced; and with the exception of Hamlet, when a character in Shakespeare becomes "enigmatic," or unusually complex, we can account for the phenomenon by discovering that Shakespeare has stretched the mould of the character slightly in order to gain some momentary theatrical effect. That is, he seems to feel that the theatrical effect will be startling enough and engrossing enough in itself to make the audience overlook the fact that the consistency of the character is somewhat violated (a trick which would probably have remained undisclosed had not so many patient scholars taken to studying the characters as characters, and gone to painful lengths in trying to explain away inconsistencies which can readily be explained from the standpoint of dramatic expediency). In the case of Hamlet, however, the matter is different. There are diffuse and confusing aspects of Hamlet which cannot be explained from the standpoint of a desired effect, for the effect itself is muddled. Was Hamlet constructed in the "subjective," "non-dramatic" manner? Does he symbolize a specific pattern of experience? Did Shakespeare, for one reason or another, renounce the dramatist's method? Mr. Eliot has noted the similarity between this play and the sonnets. Could we not carry the similarity to the point of noting the non-dramatic element in both, the predominant characteristic shared by both as Symbols of a pattern—with the one notable difference that Hamlet is a product of the author's maturity? If the Symbol of Hamlet was developed, not from the standpoint of effectiveness, but as the reduplication of a pattern, we should have some explanation for the hypertrophied "character-depiction" of, let us say, Act II, Scene II, with its obvious complaining and settling of "personal scores" outside the limits of fiction.

It is, of course, no new thing to "explain" Hamlet as Shakespeare. Our distinction might simply make more precise the nature of Hamlet's "failure." Some private difficulties, we may suppose, became so intense that, despite the flourishing of the ideology, Shakespeare for once could not content himself with merely arousing tragic feelings— he had to symbolize the pattern of his own particular tragedy. Mr. Eliot has suggested that Shakespeare may, at this time, have read Montaigne—a very acute suggestion, since it may be true in essence whether or not it is true in actuality. For in this play Shakespeare shows a tendency towards the least dramatic of all ways of thinking, the "essayistic." The essayist, in contrast with the dramatist, can dispense with a maximum of certainty in ideology. If a code is crumbling he can, with all the convenience in the world, say so. Whereas the dramatist exploits beliefs, the essayist can devote himself precisely to the questioning of beliefs. And it is at least an interesting accident that in this play, where the playwright displays something very close to bafflement, his protagonist states with resignation: "Why, then, 'tis none to you; for there is nothing either good or bad, but thinking makes it so," a thought which undermines the very foundations of a dramatist, since it suggests that he is getting his effects out of an almost gratuitous or arbitrary ideology, and that subsequent impairments of the ideology—which are totally beyond his management—may imperil the vigour of his results.

There is evidence that in this, the most "subjective" of Shakespeare's plays, the playwright's confusions were both practical and aesthetic, that the bleakness of his outlook arose from a concomitant questioning of both his life and his artistic methods. Such a double difficulty would be sufficient to overwhelm any man, and force him into "personal complaint," the symbolizing of his experiential pattern.

At a later date, however, when the ideology of our culture was threatening to disintegrate under the effect of many new influences brought to bear upon it, a writer would not require such great personal stress to embrace the literature of "confession," the subjective. We may suppose that a skilled dramatist, writing at a time when an ideology was intact, could be induced only under pressure of great anguish to symbolize a specific pattern of experience—whereas this readjustment could be accepted by artists of a later age with almost no discomfiture whatever, since they had never found the ideology powerful enough for them to build a method upon its full utilization.[4]

4 This is not offered as an alternative explanation to Mr. Eliot's. As a matter of fact, I believe that it is little more than Mr. Eliot's explanation rephrased. As stated in *The Sacred Wood* the argument runs: "The only way of expressing emotion in the form of art is by finding an 'objective correlative'; in other words, a set of objects, a situation, a chain of events which shall be the formula of that *particular* emotion; such that when the external facts, which must terminate in sensory experience, are given, the emotion is immediately evoked. If you examine any of Shakespeare's more successful tragedies, you will find this exact equivalence; you will find that the state of mind of Lady Macbeth walking in her sleep has been communicated to you by a skilful accumulation of imagined sensory impressions; the words of Macbeth on hearing of his wife's death strike us as if, given the sequence of events, these words were automatically released by the last event in the series. The artistic 'inevitability' lies in this complete adequacy of the external to the emotion; and this is precisely what is deficient in *Hamlet*. Hamlet (the man) is dominated by an emotion which is inexpressible, because it is in *excess* of the facts as they appear. And the supposed identity of Hamlet with his author is genuine to this point: that Hamlet's bafflement at the absence of objective equivalent to his feelings is a prolongation of the bafflement of his creator in the face of his artistic problem. Hamlet is up against the difficulty that his disgust is occasioned by his mother, but that his mother is not an adequate equivalent for it; his disgust envelops and exceeds her. It is thus a feeling which he cannot understand; he cannot objectify it, and it therefore remains to poison life and obstruct action. . . . To have heightened the criminality of Gertrude would have been to provide the formula for a totally different emotion in Hamlet; it is just *because* her character is so negative and insignificant that she arouses in Hamlet the feeling which she is incapable of representing." Thus, Mr. Eliot concludes: "We must simply admit that here Shakespeare tackled a problem which proved too much for him. Why he attempted it at all is an insoluble puzzle; under compulsion of what experience he attempted to express the inexpressibly horrible, we cannot ever know. . . ." Agreed: that we probably "cannot ever know." We may, however, insist that the trend of subjective writing since Shakespeare's time would give us greater authority for identifying Hamlet as Shakespeare than Mr. Eliot here seems to acknowledge. For it is precisely when a Symbol is created as a parallel to life rather than as a recipe for obtaining certain effects, that such "Hamletic" confusions generally arise.

POETRY AND ILLUSION. Since certain things were believed, and poets used these beliefs to produce poetic effects, the beliefs became "poetic." But in the course of time contrary things came to be believed, with the consequence that the earlier beliefs were now called "illusions." And noting that so much of the world's poetry had been built upon what were now called illusions, the critics argued in a circle: The illusions, they said, were poetic, and in the loss of the illusions through science we face the death of poetry through science. The difficulty lay in the assumption that illusions were inherently "poetic"—whereas they had been made "poetic" by the fact that poets had constructed poetry upon them.[5]

Ambitious writers have selected the "death of tragedy" as an instance of science's destructive effect upon the highest poetry. Tragedy, they have observed, was developed out of a sense of theological or metaphysical stability; man was dignified; he had some direct or personal relationship with the forces of the cosmos; his problems were of vast importance in the universal scheme. But the "illusions" of tragedy are slain by the scientific point of view, which leaves us too humiliated for the noble, godlike posturings of tragedy, wherein man shares the "mystic participation" which M. Lévy-Bruhl attributes to the savage: that sense of the universe as being personally with him or against him. Tragedy is ruined, they say, when the "illusion" of man's personal connection with superhuman processes is lost, when he is looked upon as a mere species of animal that happens to inhabit a planet for a certain number of years between its birth and its extinction. This "death of tragedy" (and thus, the death of the very essence of poetry) is manifested already as an inability to write great tragedies—and in time it will even be manifested as an inability to appreciate the great tragedies already written. Such is, in essence, the position of those who hold to a fundamental opposition between poetry and science—and it has been stated with much fervour and fluency by Mr. Krutch in his volume *The Modern Temper*.

Mr. Krutch combines under his concept of tragedy both the tragic drama and the tragic spirit. Once a distinction is made between them, however, the issue may look less discouraging. The death of the tragic drama we should attribute to the crumbling of an ideology,

5 It is not necessary to assume that there is anything inherently dignified about the earth's being the centre of the universe. But poets must erect a structure of human dignity upon something, and if the earth happens to be thought the centre of the universe, they may find this a convenient belief upon which the structure of human dignity can be erected. Whereupon, in questioning the belief, science may seem to question human dignity itself.

as previously explained. The highly fluctuant nature of our thinking at the present time makes more naturally for the essayistic than the dramatic—and the death of tragedy is a natural corollary of this general situation. The question of "poetic illusions" need not enter.

In the matter of the tragic spirit, however, there seems to be no essential abatement at all. For if tragedy is a sense of man's intimate participation in processes beyond himself, we find that science has replaced the older metaphysical structure with an historical structure which gives the individual man ample grounds to feel such participation. What science has taken from us as a personal relationship to the will of Providence, it has re-given as a personal relationship to the slow, unwieldy movements of human society. It is to the greatest credit of Nietzsche that he made this readjustment so thoroughly, turning from the "tragic dignity" of theology to the "tragic dignity" of history, and showing that if there was something "poetic" in the sense of a stable metaphysical structure personally concerned with the fate of man, there can be something equally "poetic" constructed out of the "illusion" or belief now current, the sense of the individual's place in an historical process. In another way the same readjustment was made by Pater in his *Marius the Epicurean,* where the "tragic fallacy" arises from our sense of Marius's close personal relationship to deep alterations in the mentality of peoples. Mr. Krutch himself, had he admitted a distinction between the tragic drama and the tragic spirit, would not have become involved as he does in the task of disproving his own thesis at the close of his book. For having said that tragedy is dead, and that it is dead because the new scientific "truths" have destroyed the tragic "illusions," he ends: "Some small part of the tragic fallacy may be said indeed to be still valid for us, for if we cannot feel ourselves as great as Shakespeare did, if we no longer believe in either our infinite capacities or our importance in the universe, we know at least that we have discovered the trick which has been played upon us and that whatever else we may be we are no longer dupes." He will accept the full responsibilities of this "truth," though the "truth" deprive him of something so edifying, so necessary to the most wholesome human expansiveness, as tragedy: "If death for us and our kind is the inevitable result of our stubbornness, then we can only say, 'So be it.' Ours is a lost cause and there is no place for us in the natural universe, but we are not, for all that, sorry to be human. We should rather die as men than live as animals." He pictures those of his kind watching simpler men who, through having gone less far in their thinking, enjoy certain vital advantages (high among which is "tragic importance"). But though recognizing the advantages that lie with the simple, those of his kind will follow their thoughts even to disaster. Such are Mr. Krutch's obdurate conclusions.

Now, tragedy as a mechanism is based upon a calamitous persistence in one's ways. It is "nobler" when the persistence is due to a moral stability on the part of the hero than when it is due to a mere misunderstanding. What, then, if not the formula for tragedy is this position of Mr. Krutch? He will take a personal stand in relation to a *historic* process (the historic process being in this instance the loss of certain magical or theological or metaphysical "illusions" based upon "non-scientific" systems of causality)—and in this stand he will persist at all hazards. It is good to have a writer display so well the basic machinery for a modern tragedy in a book heralding the death of all tragedy.

Wordsworth, in his preface to the *Lyrical Ballads,* has stated the opposite position quite succinctly. If science, he says, "should ever create any material revolution, either direct or indirect, in our condition, and in the impressions which we habitually receive," the poet will carry "sensation into the midst of the objects of the science itself. The remotest discoveries of the Chemist, the Botanist, or Mineralogist, will be as proper objects of the Poet's art as any upon which it can be employed, *if the time should ever come* [our italics] *when these things shall be familiar to us, and the relations under which they are contemplated by the followers of these respective sciences shall be manifestly and palpably material to us as enjoying and suffering beings.*" Which is to say, by our present terms, that if an ideology of science obtains general credence, the poet will poetize it by using it for the production of emotional ("human," "poetic") effects. It is not surprising that this statement should have been made by one whose poetry is a simplification, a utilization of "what is left," rather than an attempt to incorporate much new material. For this simplification itself indicated an appreciation of the fact that an ideology was in a state of remaking—it showed a determination to use only so much of the "certain" as remained fairly intact (which was, for him, sensation, or nature, and the sentiment arising from the exaltation of natural processes).

The primary objection to science so far has been the instability of its beliefs, though this does not apply to the general principles of scientific method (the acceptance of scepticism as a major principle of guidance)—and some few doctrines do seem on the road towards "canonization." High among them will probably be the concept of time as a "fourth dimension" (Mr. J. H. Woodger, in his *Biological Principles*, has shown that this concept can serve far beyond the sphere of mathematics). Psychology has perhaps added the word "compensation" as a permanent warning in our terminology of human conduct, and the various aspects of "transference" will probably continue to be stressed. Into the great wilderness of argument and prognostication by statistics we are doubtless permanently launched. A tendency to think in terms of processes will most likely supplant the tendency to think in terms of entities, whereupon "good" and "evil," with all their present concealed shades in our ratings of a "man of character," may be supplanted by such concepts as "adjustment" and "maladjustment." Above all else, the qualities that go with "heroism" will be altered—and not vacillation, but assurance, may be looked upon as the first signs of mental decay. Possibly the Einstein cosmogony will be "naturalized"—whereupon we could have the foundations for a new Dante or Lucretius. And as for dignity, whatever kind of dignity survives will not be based upon a theory of cosmic favouritism, but upon a scheme of human potentialities, a conception of what man "could be" (such a turn from metaphysical to psychological foundations as we have saluted in Nietzsche).

Already there are many new elements to be "poetized." But insofar as the poet "looks before and after," or "binds together by passion and knowledge the vast empire of human society," he cannot at this time be concerned with the new alone. He will, if he is sensitive to the entire situation, retreat slowly (or advance slowly, as one prefers), relinquishing only what must be relinquished, retaining the vocabulary of past beauty so long as he can bring himself to feel its validity, yet never closing his eyes in the interests of comfort and respite, but continually testing the valves and wheels of his poetic mechanism, and not for a moment attempting to conceal from himself the fact that some part or other is outworn. It is quite likely that for each belief science takes from us, some other belief will be placed in its stead. That a new belief seems more "difficult" or less "poetic" need trouble us little, for the difficulty is not inherent, but arises from the fact that we must alter old methods—and if an old belief existed long enough for genial poets to make it poetic, a new and contrary belief must necessarily seem unpoetic until it in turn has been exploited by a poet.

CONVENTIONAL FORM ("categorical expectation"). The matter of conventional form has brought out the extremes of aesthetic acuity and aesthetic bluntness. The rise of conventions may be due to exceptional imaginativeness and accuracy; their preservation may be due to the most inaccurate and unimaginative kinds of pedantry. A reader may, for instance, have come to expect a certain formal contrivance regardless of the effect which this contrivance is best able to produce—and his expectancy may be so imperious that he will condemn the slighting of this form even in an author who is aiming at different effects. Yet in violating a convention, an author is undeniably violating a major tenet of form. For he is disappointing the expectations of his audience; and form, by our definition, resides in the fulfilment of an audience's expectations. The only justification which an author may have for thus breaking faith with his audience is the fact that categorical expectations are very unstable and that the artist can, if his use of the repetitive and progressive principles is authoritative enough, succeed in bringing his audience to a sufficient acceptance of his methods. And as the history of art fully testifies, if the changes in conventional form are introduced to obtain a new stressing, to produce a kind of effect which the violated convention was not well able to produce, but which happens to be more apropos to the contemporary scene, the changes may very rapidly become "canonized" in popular acceptance and the earlier convention may seem the violator of categorical expectancy. All of which may be, in our terminology, the equivalent for Wordsworth's statement that the poet creates the taste by which he is judged.

The issue is further complicated by the fact that resistance to a change in convention may be due to a sensitive appreciation of the convention, to a thorough training in it and familiarity with it. A sonnet in four-foot metre would not scandalize the average salesman. Haydn greatly resented Beethoven's liberties with the sonata-form; yet a modern audience, in finding them acceptable, does not show greater musicianship. The modern audience may simply be insensitive to the issue as Haydn's thorough training enabled him to feel it. For such reasons an innovator may find a more enthusiastic reception among those whose training is defective, particularly if he is aiming at effects which are more apropos to their experiences.

As a handy illustration of the best and weakest aspects of conventional form, we may take the history of the chorus as developed in Greek tragedy. During the incunabula of tragedy, when a tragedy was still the "goat-song," there was not as yet an appreciable element of drama in this predominantly religious festival. The ceremony was wholly choric: there were no individual actors, though the leader of the chorus sometimes contributed antiphonally to the songs. Gradually this antiphonal aspect of the leader was stressed until he split from the chorus entirely, becoming a more or less independent "actor," while a new choric leader took over his former function. Greek tragedy broke clear of these origins and manifested purposes distinct from them when Aeschylus, adding a second actor, subordinated the chorus to the dialogue of the two. The result was the tragedy as codified by Aristotle.

The process continued, Sophocles adding a third character to the *dramatis personae*. In both Aeschylus and Sophocles the chorus was integral to the effects desired. They produced the sort of drama for which the convention was best fitted. The ethic meditations of the chorus, the air of solemn comment and understanding they frequently impart to the action, the gravity of their criticism and prophesyings —all such contribute to the impression of sublimity and determination characteristic of the tragedies at their best. Subsequently, however, the purposiveness of the chorus diminished. Euripides began to seek effects which the chorus was not best qualified to produce (effects distinctive of a more "intimate" or realistic drama). At the same time, his art was a "reversion." He sought to reaffirm some qualities which were more characteristic of the "goat-song." As is often the case with the godless, he took a keen interest in the primitive forms of religion—and thus, at the very time when he was aiming at effects to which the chorus was not wholly adapted, he restored to the chorus much of the importance which it had possessed before Aeschylus. He stressed the chorus as a *convention*, "formalizing" it and divorcing it from the action of the play. But if Euripides stressed the conventionality of this convention, in other writers the purely conventional aspects of its appeal are present without such methodological stressing. At certain periods in their plays, the audience could expect a choric punctuation of moral maxims, much as the steps in the plot of a Chinese drama are marked by the striking of gongs. The conventional form was now so slightly associated with the purposes of drama that, as Aristotle complains, the choric numbers were hardly more than incidental music: playwrights worked up a store of choric numbers which they released at fitting intervals, the themes being as well suited to one place in the play as another, or to one play as another.

When the continuity of the tragedy was restored in England, the chorus was at first preserved (due, it is said, to the maintaining of this convention in the plays of Seneca, who was the model for English playwrights). In time the chorus was dropped entirely: the Elizabethan playwrights were nearer to the effects of Euripides than of Aeschylus—and with the tragedy now so far from its origins, and with an audience which had no training in the ways of classic tragedy, the chorus lacked any authority for inclusion on the grounds of conventional form. As Elizabethan tragedies were not written to be sung through masks, so they were not written in a vein in which the unreality of a chorus's moralizings could have been anything but an obstacle. (Perhaps Wagner's "music-drama" is, in this one respect, closer to the aesthetic of the Greek tragedy.)

Elizabethan tragedy did, however, seek ceremonious effects which were akin to those of the chorus. The proscenium speech was not merely "tolerated": it was requisite to such effects. Diction, in all the distinctly tragic scenes, was cast in a mould to suggest the grandiose, the heightened. Tragedy was no longer sung—but it was ranted. Hence appropriate conventions were developed—the set speech, or monologue, being one of them. There is good cause to believe that the monologue was enjoyed exactly as an aria in Italian opera. Subsequently, as tragedy developed towards the "realistic," becoming the tragedy not of exceptional people but of "you and me," the appeal of the frankly recitative monologue diminished. After being *enjoyed* as conventional form, it was next *tolerated* as conventional form, and finally developed into a mere convenience for slovenly playwrights, a kind of "aside" for imparting necessary information to the audience, whereas the new effects required the complete elimination of such a device. It clung, however, until the time of Ibsen—and fittingly, was not dismissed here until Ibsen turned from verse to prose.

Yet as evidence that the conventional forms, at the heyday of their usage, serve a very accurate purpose, we have Andreyev's restoration of the chorus's function in *The Life of Man*. In this play Andreyev sought, though imperfectly, to regain the effects of Aeschylean and Sophoclean tragedy—the sense of fatalistic guidance which each of these playwrights utilized so well to make the audience feel that not the author, but the nature of things, was moving the story. Thus, Andreyev invented the character of Someone in Gray Called He, who stood about the edges of the play, aloof from its action, prophesying, moralistically commenting upon the allegorical destiny of these humble characters, and in all important respects except the matter of eloquence rediscovering the purpose of the Greek chorus as an instrument in procuring one kind of dramatic effect. And similarly, we might make clearer the functional value of the monologue in Shakespeare by pointing out that his tragic effects approach those of Greek tragedy insofar as a character's meditations upon his own fate can substitute for the part of the detached chorus in Aeschylus and Sophocles (though witches, ghosts, and portents are also greatly relied upon to make the audience feel more the hand of the cosmos than that of the playwright).

In summary we may note the dual aspect of conventional form: It thrives when the audience expects it and also requires the kind of effects which it is best able to produce; but it becomes an obstacle if it remains as categorical expectancy at a time when different effects are aimed at. But we should note two further aspects of the subject:

First: the absence of marked conventional contrivances often leads to a kind of "one-time" convention which is liked purely as an innovation. Thus, we may see one play constructed as an "aria da capo," another borrowing quick change of scene from the motion picture, another built upon the convention that people speak out their innermost thoughts (restoration of the aside); or for a season we restore the old "thriller" of the eighties; or a great musician will adopt some historical manner for fifteen minutes—and in all such cases we enjoy the convention purely because of its transiency. If another man repeated the performance, we should thunder against him as eagerly as we applauded the first. Yet a convention is most fruitful, obviously, when it is stable enough for many men to converge upon the exploitation of it.[6] (It is for this reason that the stock characters of Broadway drama are to be taken seriously; for how can they, by the sheer laws of probability, be used so often without something good eventually coming of them?)

Our second consideration is: Categorical expectancy does not only make for inclusions; it also makes for exclusions. In expecting how things *will be,* we expect by implication how they *will not be.* Much of the difficulty with imaginative prose today lies in the fact that our categorical expectations require a manner poorly adapted to the

---

[6] The matter of the Greek chorus may give us some insight as to the nature of "invention" in art. The Greek chorus was not "invented" by Aeschylus; it was adapted to a new purpose. In all probability, had the whole idea of the chorus been an innovation, he could not have succeeded in making his use of the chorus generally acceptable. Similarly, in adding a second actor, he did not innovate, but simply carried a process one step further. An artist probably works nearest to impunity if his innovations are adaptations of this sort.

fuller potentialities of prose. We are at the end of a "conversational" trend in prose, a trend which has proved its high value in purely informative writing, but acts as an impoverishment when the informative is not primarily aimed at. Nothing more clearly displays the occasional tyranny and arbitrariness of conventional form than this contemporary insistence upon a "narrative" style of prose. If a prose-writer departs from it, he is called artificial, though not one of his sentences has the obvious artificiality of verse (this verse, meanwhile, being deemed "natural"). The reader of modern prose is ever on guard against "rhetoric," yet the word, by lexicographer's definition, refers but to "the use of language in such a way as to produce a desired impression upon the hearer or reader."

Rhetoric. As a final instance of the hazards of convention, we might with profit examine the history of this word's decay. In accordance with the definition we have cited, effective literature could be nothing else but rhetoric: thus the resistance to rhetoric *qua* rhetoric must be due to a faulty diagnosis. To an extent, this resistance is a revolt against an over-emphasizing of the traditionally ceremonious (since inferior "rhetoricians," in their attempt to be "eloquent," confined themselves to such material as had been made "eloquent" by earlier and more talented artists). As such the resistance is wholesome and commendable enough. But much of the resistance is also due to a mistake in critical nomenclature. As artists no longer wished to produce the kinds of effect which the devices of the rhetoricians were designed to produce, they overshot the mark —and to turn against a specific method of specific rhetoricians, they persuaded themselves that they were turning against rhetoric *in toto*. Thus, since the rhetorical procedure had become identified as the art of appeal, the artist who chose to appeal in other ways felt that he had given up any attempt to appeal at all. This led, above all, to a denigration of form (formal devices being a major portion of the rhetorician's lore); and the one factor in keeping such denigration of form from doing great damage was the artist's tendency to preserve many more aspects of form than he was aware of. Once again the issue was improperly diagnosed—and in revolting against certain kinds of form, the artist persuaded himself that he was revolting against form in general.

Now, slogans are always bungling. They must somewhat overstate their case to get what they are after. And the overstatement of the case against "rhetoric" undeniably served a salutary end. But it has left us with too wide a distrust, and a tendency to discountenance the use of pronounced formal contrivances even in a writer who might use them to produce such effects as they were designed to produce. If the respect clung too long, the distrust now threatens equally to outlast its usefulness. In particular this distrust militates against the retention or rediscovery of old values which cannot be permanently eliminated without considerable impoverishment of art. Their temporary elimination was wholesome, since it made other emphases possible, enabling us to develop an "imperceptible" variety of prose which flowers in the information-giving of the best journalism and narratives. But in this matter the zest of discovery has long since abated; the billions of "conversational" words turned out yearly by our country's presses cannot, as sentences, delight us further. The major tenet of eloquence (maximum of formal and Symbolic "charge") must be reaffirmed if prose *qua* prose is to be enjoyed. Yet such a reaffirmation must overcome the resistance of "categorical expectancy," must temporarily at least violate the principles of conventional form, must risk seeming "unnatural" until the present decrees as to the "natural" are undone.

The reversal is not unthinkable. Already an objection to the barrenness of much modern prose is arising in many quarters. And though a critic recently asked himself "by what confusion the contemporaries of Mozart were led to praise as 'natural' musical compositions as elaborately formal as his," it almost seems that in the few months since this sentence was written, Mozart's musical compositions have again become "natural."

So, to capitulate: One aims at effects; whatever effects he desires, he can in all humility be assured that they are "natural," since his desire could not possibly be anything other than natural; and if he finds the present categorical expectancies obstructive to his purposes, he may be justified in violating these expectancies and in allowing his procedures to be viewed as an oddity, as peripheral, on the chance that other men may eventually join him and by their convergence make such procedures the "norm."

# JOSEPH WOOD KRUTCH
## (1893–      )

BORN on November 25, 1893, in Knoxville, Tennessee, Joseph Wood Krutch attended the University of Tennessee, from which he graduated in 1915. Though early interested in science, he shifted to the study of literature, taking his graduate work in the English Department at Columbia University, from which he received his Master of Arts degree in 1916 and his doctorate in 1923. Though he has taught English at Vassar and at Columbia (he is now a professor of English at Columbia University), he is primarily a writer rather than a teacher. In 1924 he was appointed dramatic critic and associate editor of *The Nation,* becoming one of its editors in 1932. In 1930 he was awarded a Guggenheim Fellowship, using the leisure thus granted him to work on *Experience and Art* (1932), a book on the aesthetics of literature.

After the publication of *Comedy and Conscience after the Restoration* (1924) and his study of Poe in 1926, he attracted considerable attention when *The Modern Temper* appeared in 1929, a work which effectively analyzes the philosophic dilemma of the disillusioned post-war generation. His object is to diagnose a state of mind and to show that Nature is indifferent to the human values which men cherish. Science, by shattering the old anthropomorphic universe, has intensified man's sense of alienation. Science has destroyed man's most fundamental myth, his need for some stable moral order, some established standards of conduct. A choice, Krutch feels, must be made between an existence essentially animal in character and one which aspires to purely human values.

In the chapter, "The Tragic Fallacy," he undertakes to demonstrate why we no longer have the capacity to write tragedies. Modern man has lost the power of imposing a unified, metaphysically satisfying meaning upon life, and tragedy presupposes faith in the importance of man and of his life upon earth. This conception of tragedy has been attacked by Mark Harris in *The Case for Tragedy* (1932). Krutch, in brief, is hostile to mechanical

331

progress and the scientific outlook because they have tended to rob man of the feeling that he plays a central role in the drama of life.

Joseph Wood Krutch is not the type of critic who founds schools, launches movements, vigorously combats heresies, and arouses wild enthusiasm or antipathy. His is not the truculent iconoclasm of a Mencken, the impassioned idealism of a Ludwig Lewisohn, the mystical prophetic fervor of a Waldo Frank, the religious orthodoxy of a T. S. Eliot, the controversial ardor and dogmatism of an Irving Babbitt; he is poles removed from the messianic zeal of the Marxist critics; yet he has probably been far more influential than his analytical, impersonal prose would lead one to suspect. If he has presented no comprehensive and rounded system of aesthetic values, it is because he does not believe that such a unification is possible at present in the realm of criticism. Incurably skeptical, he distrusts all codified systems, all dogmatic affirmations, all authoritarian solutions, whether masquerading in the guise of religion or philosophy, science or aesthetics. The critic cannot hope to escape the conditioning of his temperament, the limitations inherent in his mass of apperceptions. This does not mean that he must surrender to a random and irresponsible impressionism. If he wishes to escape these pitfalls, he must strive, as far as possible, to objectify his subjective impressions, to discriminate, to get as close as he can to the text he is considering, yet he cannot entirely overcome the bias of his temperament and his past history. Hence differences in judgment are inevitable, and there is no reason for deploring such an outcome.

In *Experience and Art,* Krutch goes to great pains to set forth the conditions that beset the act of critical analysis and appraisal, the dangers and difficulties that confront the most conscientious critic, and the reason why a "science of criticism" is an ideal impossible of attainment. The psychological explanation of literature is fallible because it is so narrow in its scope of application, limiting itself to those works which take their origin in pathological states and are therefore calculated to confirm its initial thesis. Krutch explicitly denies the truth of the conclusion "that all works of literature are to be accounted for and dismissed as the day-dreams of a child or the relatively harmless delusions of border-line cases."[1]

Though as a skeptic Krutch has pointed out that no system can ever satisfy all the needs of the human spirit, he has at least attempted to formulate his leading ideas in the field of criticism. Even relativism has its internal coherence and consistency if it is defended with any degree of logic, and Krutch's appeal is to the legitimacy of reason even when he

1 Joseph Wood Krutch, *Experience and Art* (New York, 1932), p. 32.

reveals its inadequacies. Criticism is an art rather than a science. What one group of critics affirms another categorically rejects. If critics differ among themselves that is inevitable, for what they deal with is not the empirically given but that which the imagination creates. It does not matter what ideological variations abound so long as man is free to choose one and support it with ardent conviction. There are all sorts of lives, and all sorts of aesthetic systems, religions, philosophies, and arts.

There are no absolutes in the field of criticism, just as there are none that can be logically demonstrated in sociology or morality or politics. The attempt to assign an absolute value to art cannot be successful, even if we postulate as our norm a mature person trained sufficiently in literature to be competent to make the necessary discriminations and pass reliable judgment. No "normal" critic actually exists, whose judgment may be identified with the work itself. No man is completely representative. The relativity of values in art is inescapable. Our tastes change, our old enthusiasms are discarded. And who shall say at what age the aesthetic judgment is closest to the truth? There are no eternally fixed hierarchies of value, no standards by which we can assign measures of excellence. Nevertheless, Krutch maintains that literary criticism still has a considerable field in which it may disport itself without dogmatism. In dealing with particular works it may be discriminatingly analytical and proceed to judge with relative detachment what he calls their functional effectiveness.

Even such methods are only relatively impersonal. No matter what the type of criticism employed, it inevitably involves the personality of the critic. Impressionism cannot be avoided, it can only be safeguarded against. One may yield to the influence of the purely personal elements or struggle against it; the first gives rise to impressionism, the other to so-called "objective criticism."

"We can ask only that the critic shall be aware of the personal nature of his reactions as well as of the arbitrary character of his standards, and that, just in proportion as he fails to maintain an absolute detachment, he will cultivate that underlying skepticism which softens the dogmatism from which we cannot escape so long as we undertake to say anything at all."[2]

As an intellectual he is inclined to support capitalism because he is interested in preserving the priceless qualities of reason and detachment, tolerance and understanding, which the social revolution threatens to overthrow.

2 Joseph Wood Krutch, *Experience and Art* (New York, 1932), p. 189.

BIBLIOGRAPHY

TEXT

*Comedy and Conscience after the Restoration.* New York, 1924.
*Edgar Allan Poe.* New York, 1926.
*The Modern Temper.* New York, 1929.
*Five Masters.* New York, 1930.
*Experience and Art.* New York, 1932.
*Was Europe a Success?* New York, 1934.
*The American Drama since 1918.* New York, 1939.
*Samuel Johnson.* New York, 1944.
*Henry David Thoreau.* New York, 1948.
*The Twelve Seasons.* New York, 1949.

CRITICISM

Beach, J. W., "Mr. Krutch and Ideal Values in Literature," *International Journal of Ethics*, XLVIII, 487–497 (July, 1938).
Glicksberg, Charles I., "Joseph Wood Krutch," *Sewanee Review*, XLVI, 77–93 (January-March, 1936).
Harris, Mark, *The Case for Tragedy.* New York, 1932.
Hoffman, Ross J. S., "Mr. Krutch and Europe," *American Review*, IV, 56–66 (November, 1934).
Larrabee, A., "Prufrock and Joseph Wood Krutch," *Accent*, III, 115–121 (Winter, 1943).

## THE FUNCTION OF CRITICISM*

FULLY developed schools of art usually inspire systems of esthetics which accompany and defend them. Sometimes the artists themselves, aware that they have departed from tradition, sketch out a theory intended to justify their novel processes. Sometimes, on the contrary, it is the first admirers of the new methods who assume the duty of demonstrating that these methods correspond either to the discovery or the rediscovery of the true nature and purpose of art. And yet, inevitable as this process is, it is notoriously true that really first-class work usually long outlives the theory which was supposed to justify it, and the taste, however variable it may be, is generally more stable than those rationalizations of it which constitute criticism.

Nothing could, in this connection, be more instructive than to compare a certain passage in Vasari with a certain better-known paragraph in Pater. Both of these commentators felt a very particular admiration for the Mona Lisa of Da Vinci, and yet it would be impossible to guess from their two descriptions of its qualities that the same picture was in question. Pater is concerned with certain spiritual qualities which he believes it to have been the painter's purpose to suggest. Vasari is concerned almost exclusively with the accuracy with which the realistic details of a face have been reproduced and, in fact, bases no inconsiderable part of his appreciation upon such things as the rendering of the bloom of the cheek and the imitation of each separate eyelash.

Nor is it to be supposed that we have here to do with nothing except a personal idiosyncrasy, for in general the men of the Renaissance attributed a very great importance to that accuracy of imitation which most modern painters so utterly abominate, and we need look at no more than the writings of the past hundred years to realize that theories of literature have been at least as discordant as theories of painting.

In the first place, the whole conception of the function of criticism was twice inverted during the course of the century. When it began, the critic was firmly seated in the judge's chair, and was generally expected to pronounce an author guilty or innocent in accordance with the laws of the republic of letters. Then romanticism unseated him, and fifty years after the heyday of the autocrats the critic himself was proclaiming the purely personal character of his opinions and boasting of the fact that he merely subjected himself to the influence of his author in order to discover what that author was about. The "judgment" had given way to the "impression," and "myself in connection with Shakespeare" was the accepted formula. But though that attitude is still common enough, it is no longer undisputed. In the minds of many estheticians it is "impersonality" rather than "sensitivity" which is the mark of really valuable criticism, and the more advanced of the intellectualist critics have once more seated themselves upon the judge's chair. Nor has change been any less obvious in the accepted criteria for the evaluation of individual works of art.

Indeed, rival systems have contradicted one another so flatly that it might almost seem as though new groups of critics had set up shop by the simple process of inverting the cardinal doctrine of their competitors, and as though ingenuity had been exhibited chiefly in the discovery of new sets of opposing aims or qualities which could be championed. Thus the Tolstoyan contention that the only valid test of literary value is moral usefulness is met by the esthete's proclamation that morality has nothing whatsoever to do with the matter, and by his determination to demonstrate the fact by selecting the most morally repulsive materials as well as the most morally perverse conclusions. Thus also a Bernard Shaw, speaking for the creators of a whole school of drama and fiction, declares that "happiness and beauty are by-products"—by-products of, that is to say, that earnest social conviction and earnest social purpose which another school is ready to denounce as not only wholly foreign to the purpose of art but utterly destructive of even any capacity for a genuine esthetic experience. And if these examples will serve as illustrations of the violence of disagreement which has existed between confidently asserted opinions concerning the relationship of literature to morals and sociology, even briefer allusions to other such contradictory contentions must suffice.

Flaubert convinces his admirers that the *sine qua non* of literature is style, and that style is characterized by its continual employment of the one precise and accurate word which perfectly defines the idea or the thing; but Verlaine, in a scarcely less well-known and scarcely less influential passage, banishes from literature whatever *is* precise, and calls for the nebulous, the vague, and the ambiguously evocative. Another whole school professes to have discovered the secret of art in its expressiveness. It assumes that a work is valuable in so far as it reveals or expresses the man behind it, but the critics who form this school appear wholly oblivious of the fact that another and a newer school finds the *absence* of any obvious personality in a piece of literature one of the signs of its authentically literary character, and exalts above everything else an objective detachment, especially in poetry. Even this is not all, for just as psychology seems just about to define the nature of that relationship (long assumed to exist) between the poet and the dreamer, Paul Valéry announces with Orphic finality that "whoever says poetry says the very opposite of dream."

Nor—it must be remembered—were any of these mutually destructive contentions lightly advanced or lightly held. Not only was each the product of a passionate conviction, but each was illustrated by works of very considerable merit, which seemed to owe their excellence to the fact that they embodied a recognition of the principle in question. Each was, moreover, the occasion of a very considerable body of interesting critical writing, and gave currency to the names of certain critics, each of whom was, for a time at least, the center of a genuine cult, whose members not only spread the doctrine of their master, but very often adopted toward the uninitiated that attitude of condescension which is the true mark of the disciple.

It is, for example, not long since the expressionistic theories of Croce (known in America chiefly through Spingarn's *Creative Criticism*) were on the tip of every knowing commentator's tongue, but new leaders—T. S. Eliot, for example—are now in fashion, and these same commentators now assume toward those tainted with a taste for the "expressive" the same pitying contempt formerly reserved for those who did *not* realize that only "expression" really counted. Sometimes one wonders, indeed, whether or not the more condescending reviewers fully realize how wholly incompatible are the doctrines of the leaders who replaced one another in such rapid succession. Anatole France's Pyrrhonic skepticism—the limitless relativism of his critical principles—had hardly been understood until some, at least, began to babble of "standards"; Remy de Gourmont's rationalistic, materialistic, and analytic approach was still known chiefly to the illuminati when it began to be bruited about that the really advanced in literary matters were now interested chiefly in metaphysics, mathematics, and a "synthesis," or that they had, at the very least, thrown away their copy of *La Disassociation des Idées* in order to thumb the pages of Valéry's *Soirée avec M. Teste* and Eliot's *The Sacred Wood*.

There was even, for a time, a not wholly understandable doubt concerning the side of the fence upon which some of the leading creative writers were to be sought. Thus some naïve persons supposed that Joyce and Eliot represented only the most advanced stage of "decadence," that theirs was merely a cynicism, a skepticism, and a general "je m'en f—tism" which had only carried them farther upon the road previously taken by their less extravagant predecessors. But it was, of course, soon discovered that Joyce and Eliot were, on the contrary, austere classicists following in the footsteps of Homer and of Dante, and that one of them at least was headed irresistibly toward the church. This discovery, moreover (and purely incidentally), corresponded roughly in time with the discovery that the physical sciences, instead of being, as it had commonly been supposed, materialistic and atheistic, were on the contrary mystical and pious.

Perhaps the criticism of literature should be a science, and perhaps science should be what it pretends that it is—positive knowledge of external phenomena arrived at by processes of experiment and of induction wholly uninfluenced by prejudice or desire. But it is evident enough that, at least in their more usual manifestations, neither is either. The conclusions of science are, on the contrary, commonly neither positive nor wholly uninfluenced by the temperamental prejudices of scientists; and criticism, which so frequently and so radically changes the premises which determine its aims, methods, and standards, does not achieve either an exactitude or a detachment equal even to those of science. But if criticism is not a science, then it must—if we accept the conventional dichotomy—be an art, and it is indeed, just because of its artistic character that its premises are subject to such frequent variation. For art, it must be remembered, owes its charm to the fact that it is so freely plastic.

Man is surrounded by stubborn facts, even when he does not recognize some of them as such. The universe in which he lives is a universe given to him, and there is little that he can alter as radically or as frequently as he would like. But art is a realm of human freedom; it is perpetually being remolded in accordance with human desires, some of which are no more than temporary and wayward fancies; and the world of imagination is delightful exactly because it is so much less stubborn that the world of fact. Human society could not endure if the human nature of one epoch were actually as different from the human nature of the next as artists commonly represent it to be—if, for example, the men of the twentieth century were actually as different from the men of the nineteenth as the characters of D. H. Lawrence are different from the characters of Thackeray. Neither would literature be the continuous thing which it is if its whole character varied as rapidly and as radically as changing critical attitudes would seem to call desirable. But just as human society gains a kind of stability from the very physiological and instinctive bases of human behavior, so the continuity of literature is maintained by aims and methods and functions which remain the same despite certain variations and despite the emphasis upon these variations which critical theories provoke.

Nor is it this plasticity alone which suggests that criticism is an art, for the actual function which it performs is the function of all art, since it rationalizes and gives temporary form to our experiences with literature just as literature rationalizes and gives temporary form to our experiences with Nature. What we ask of a novel, for example, is an arrangement of the facts we know in accordance with an intellectual and emotional scheme acceptable to our minds. We expect it to read some sort of order into the bewildering complexity of phenomena, to show how a sequence of events may be interpreted in a way which justifies our attitude toward life, and to find a place for those standards and judgments and preferences which we cherish. But criticism does for the world of art what art does for the world of phenomena. It sets up those same imaginary boundaries and establishes those same quasi-absolutes which literature finds itself obliged to create when it undertakes the task of providing us with a thinkable and feelable schematization of the material with which it deals. Nor is this all, for just as literature serves to suggest and direct experiments in living, so too criticism serves to suggest and direct experiments in writing. Like literature again, it helps to formulate those creeds which may be changed to-morrow but which, by the very fact that they are believed, give courage and strength and determination to the man who is writing a book as well as to the man who is molding a life.

Life and literature may flow on, and neither may be what it seems, but the phenomena of both can be understood only when art has translated them into logical terms. The critic—usually, at least—is only endeavoring to make Art—which is to say, a logical whole—out of the separate phenomena of literature, just as the novelist or the poet is endeavoring to make Art out of the separate phenomena of nature. Critics, like poets, differ among themselves because critics, like poets, are dealing with a realm which is not given to man but created by him—with a realm in which, and for this very reason, values are not so much discovered as brought into being by a fiat of the imagination.

## II

A familiarity with the history of human opinion and its variability does not, however, produce skepticism—except in the minds of those who are already temperamentally inclined toward it. Hence, it is hardly to be expected that critics should cease to advance general opinions concerning the nature and function of art merely because they know how widely such opinions have differed from one another in the past, and it is, perhaps, not at all desirable that they should do so. Convictions of some sort are necessary for effective writing, either creative or critical, just as they are necessary for effective living, and life as well as literature has gone on because people have passionately believed—on quite insufficient evidence—

that art, God, justice, duty, righteousness, and the rest consisted in this or that.

Human society depends upon those various artificial structures which are known as law, religion, philosophy, morality, and the rest, but what it requires is merely *a* law, *a* religion, *a* philosophy, and so on. It can not only exist but flourish upon the basis of the most varied theoretical foundations so long as it has genuinely accepted one or another, and what is true of the social arts is equally true of those which are representative. The convictions of Flaubert and the convictions of Verlaine each promoted the development of one sort of literature, just as the convictions of Saint Francis and the convictions of Cellini each promoted the development of one sort of life. Whole societies as well as mere individual lives or individual poems may be executed in very different manners, but successful works of literature no less than successful lives or successful societies are always faithful to some style, and the esthetic theories which profess to define the aims and methods of literature as a whole actually do, very often, accurately define one of these possible styles—just as ethical systems which profess to define the whole duty of man actually do lay down the rules in accordance with which a style of living may successfully be achieved.

It is therefore neither surprising nor wholly unfortunate that theories of art should develop as inevitably and as variously as do theories of law, of justice, and of morality. It is not even surprising that a certain long unfashionable intransigence should now be making its reappearance among literary critics, and that a kind of authoritarianism should once more be defended—with grave dignity by the admirers of T. S. Eliot and with a bumptious truculence by the disciples of Irving Babbitt. The skeptic can reflect calmly that similar opinions have flourished before, and that they have even encouraged the production of various worthy works without having made impossible the development of other and quite interesting styles. Thus there were classicists before Mr. Babbitt who did not, nevertheless, prevent the appearance of Rousseau; and Pope no more prevented the development of Keats than the contempt of Keats annihilated the merits of Pope. But when this same skeptic is driven to defend his own unwillingness to leap upon any particular bandwagon, he may take comfort in the fact that skepticism still has the best of the argument at least, and that by logical methods it is still as difficult to establish absolutes in the field of literary criticism as it is to establish them in the field of politics or morality.

As Shakespeare has it, "The prosperity of a jest lies in the ear of the hearer," and esthetics is concerned with the effect which a work of art has upon us. But this effect is the result of an apperception; it is conditioned by the associations set up between the various elements of the vicarious experience afforded by the work in question and our own individual memories, opinions, and experiences. It differs, therefore, from person to person, and two critics who appear to be passing different judgments upon the same poem or tale are in reality passing judgment upon two different things which may bear very little resemblance to each other. Nor is there any way to avoid this, since art is in its nature suggestive, since it can function only by calling attention to something in ourselves, and any book which we read becomes, inevitably, as we read it, a collaboration between its author and ourselves.

Even the most dogmatic of critics commonly recognize the more obvious conclusions to be drawn from the fact that the value of a work of literature depends upon the intelligibility of its symbols and upon the existence of some one to whom those symbols are, at a given moment, intelligible. Thus no one would deny that it would be useless to discuss the value of an epic composed in a completely lost language, and few, if any, would fail to recognize another aspect of the same fact by admitting that a certain maturity of knowledge and experience, a certain age in years, must be reached before *Othello* becomes a greater work of literature than the story of Jack and the Beanstalk. Yet once this fact is admitted, the whole attempt to assign an absolute value to a work of art falls heavily to the ground unless it is buttressed by the assumption that it is possible to find and use some "normal" and normally cultured man whose temperament, experience, and knowledge have been standardized, and whose apperception of the work to be judged may therefore be identified with the work itself. But men do differ; and this standard man who may be taken to represent the whole of humanity at its best is, of course, always that particular man, the individual absolutist himself.

Thus at the very beginning of any attempt to find an absolute standard by which to judge a work of art we are met by something relative in its value—the relativity of a jest to the ear for which it is destined. And the further we go the more clearly we shall realize that at every step in our analysis we come upon some further relativity, so that, for example, the value of a work of art is relative, not only to the individual, but to the stage which he has reached in his individual development. No sensitive person who recalls the history of the evolution of his own taste can fail to remember how at one time he was dazzled by certain writers, Shelley, for example, from whom (so far as he is concerned) the glory now seems to have departed, though it is doubtless still visible to others. It was once there because he perceived it. It is still there because others still see it. But it is no longer there *for him*. And again there is no escape from this relativity of judgment unless some arbitrary norm is established. Certain writers we know are appropriate to youth and certain others to age, but how shall we judge them absolutely? Surely the very oldest man yet unburied is not the most completely infallible, and it is surely difficult to say which one of the seven ages of man sees things most truly.

Nor is it, moreover, possible to consider the value of a work of art wholly apart from the society which forms its audience, though we need not, to be sure, overestimate either the rapidity or the completeness with which societies change. Dante was a great *man*, and by virtue of that fact much more conspicuously like than unlike a citizen of the twentieth century. The best book is not necessarily the newest or superficially the most pertinent. But if there is any connection whatever between literature and those more or less variable sensibilities, aspirations, and convictions which give their peculiar character to social groups, then the value of any particular work *for* that group must be in part relative *to* that group, and it is difficult to imagine how any judge can wholly detach himself from the group to which he belongs. The conscious urgency of the need which certain contemporaries feel for absolute standards in criticism was not, apparently, felt by the generation of critics against whose relativism they are rebelling; and hence their desire to establish such absolutes must constitute one of the characteristics which make their writings particularly valuable to their group.

Works of art are constructions serving to arrange fragments of observation and experience into patterns which are pleasing because they are understandable in terms of human thought and consistent in terms of human feeling. To a greater or less degree these patterns are usually influenced by the criticism of human experience as a whole, and for this reason they tend to represent some sort of compromise between the author's vision of "reality" and those aspirations, desires, and hopes which determine his temperament. Hence such works embody something of what this group believes concerning the universe in which it lives, while, at the same time, they both reflect and influence those particular desires, perceptions, emotions, and emphases which give to the human consciousness at any time its peculiar character.

But if all these things are true, then the central error of those who insist upon setting up absolute standards of judgment for literature is the error vulgarly known as putting the cart before the horse, of assuming that we can know what literature *ought* to be without knowing just what man and Nature and God *are*. Of any particular work we may say that it represents Nature as thus or so. We may say also that it is a construction gratifying to certain desires, likely to develop certain sensibilities, or even tending to encourage a certain kind of conduct. But to judge it absolutely is to maintain that one knows not only what Nature is, but also which desires are legitimate, what conduct is permissible, and what sensibilities were, are, or ever could be capable of contributing valuable elements to the general experience of living. Perhaps the blind disciple of some minutely and dogmatically all-inclusive religion, perhaps the subscriber to the provisions of some inconceivably exhaustive Koran or Talmud, might venture to rank works of art in a hierarchy which he would pronounce eternally fixed. But no one else consistently could, and such a Koran or Talmud does not exist, because even the best-codified faiths permit differences of opinion and judgment concerning some of those subtle shades with which literature is frequently concerned. A dogmatically established criterion for the judgment of art presupposes dogmas which have previously settled every conceivable question concerning science, religion, philosophy, and morals.

Perhaps the poet may—perhaps the poet must—forget the logical necessity of skepticism. It is his business to devise constructions, and such constructions always involve premises which can become acceptable only if they are asserted with a confident faith. But if the critic is to be distinguished from the creator, if he is to maintain even the relative detachment and objectivity which make his art more like the art of the scientist or the philosopher than it is like the art of the poet, then this critic is bound to recognize both the element of arbitrariness in any work of art and the fact that the value of the construction made possible by this arbitrary element is relative to the audience that will contemplate it.

The proponents of "standards" are fond of arguing that without them the critic becomes no better than that "stringed lute" of Oscar Wilde's upon which—and with disastrous results—"all winds could play." In his hands criticism degenerates into the random impression, and what he produces is only a derivative work of art based upon the drama or poem or tale which he is pretending to criticize. By insisting upon the duty of the critic to judge, they propose to give him a function superior to that of mere pale recreation; and that purpose is laudable enough, but it is hardly worth while to achieve it at the cost of making him believe that he—of all people—should be the one to attempt that most stupendous of all creative acts, which consists in establishing by a fiat of the imagination some absolute standard of value.

The imagination which creates works of art is, after all, not the most powerful sort of imagination. To a greater or less extent such works always include an element of confessed make-believe, and to a greater or less extent they always recognize some distinction between the kind of "poetic faith" which they seek to inspire and that simple "faith" which is inspired by religions and philosophies. Hence the poet who calls himself "poet" and the romancer who calls himself "romancer" have neither the presumption nor the effectiveness of the poet who calls himself "prophet" or of the romancer who gets himself accepted as the revealer of some system of law or duty or morals. Hence to insist that the critic should come forth with some series of absolutes is a very strange way of preventing him from meddling with the business of "creating," since "standards" of any kind are, as a matter of fact, the supreme achievements of the creative imagination. Doubtless he should guard himself against the tendency to rest content with a merely lyrical account of his "impressions," but it is, on the other hand, when he sets up standards or proposes absolutes that he is most clearly and most actively forsaking the effort to criticize for the effort to create.

### III

Such is the dilemma of the critic who is obliged to pronounce judgments at the same time that he distrusts the only basis upon which such judgments can be made. Literary history reminds him that mutually destructive theories of the nature of art have been held by the most distinguished critics of the past, and introspection makes it clear that when he pretends to discuss a work of literature as though it were an objective fact he is, in reality, discussing an apperception of it which is, in no small measure, influenced by his own experience and temperament. Yet he must strive for some sort of objectivity, for some degree of detachment, unless he is willing to sink to the level of the most arbitrary of impressionists and to rest content with so-called critiques which are, in fact, no more than mere reveries suggested by the theme of the work he is pretending to criticize.

Granted, then, that literary criticism must stop short of the plainly dogmatic, there does, nevertheless, remain a considerable field over which it may speculate with relative detachment as well as with some profit, and certain portions of that field may be described very briefly. In the first place, criticism may very legitimately concern itself with general theories of the nature and function of Art—provided only that these theories are sufficiently general to make room for all the variety which the corpus of literature actually includes and do not, like some, churlishly rule out Shakespeare because he has no social doctrine or Mr. Shaw because he has. In the second place, it may, when it leaves inclusive generalization to deal with either particular works or groups of work, certainly concern itself with what may be called "discrimination," in contradistinction to "judgment." It may, that is to say, seek to distinguish between various styles of literature and to aid the reader in his effort to enter into a work—both by analyzing the particular kind of satisfaction which it proposes to give and by investigating the premises upon which its structure is erected. Thus Racine's excellence may usefully be discriminated from Zola's. Finally, the critic may, still without ceasing to maintain a relative detachment, judge a work, not absolutely, but in accordance with what we shall call its functional effectiveness. He may, that is to say, seek to discover how successfully it achieves what appears to be its purpose—how thrillingly a melodrama wreaks our hate upon its villain, or how vividly a work of another class makes us aware of those sights, or sounds, or emotions, the sensitivity to which it is trying to cultivate.

Even such processes as those which have just been described are, moreover, only relatively impersonal, for it is obvious that even they involve the personal experience of a critic whose knowledge and susceptibility are individual, and who can judge of the effect which may be produced upon another only by the effect produced upon him. Literature differs from geometry by the fact that it inevitably deals with materials which have a human significance, and hence the criticism of it cannot wholly detach itself from the influence of those materials and the critic's attitude toward them. The latter is most nearly impersonal when he is "discriminating" rather than evaluating, or when he is attempting to judge the effectiveness rather than the worth of any particular work, but he is not absolutely impersonal even then, and criticism rarely has—or rarely should have—confined itself exclusively to those processes which may be carried on in even this relatively impersonal way. It passes almost imperceptibly to matters which more and more intimately involve the personality of the critic.

Consider, for example, the fact that both language and literature are in their very nature allusive. To the extent that the former is so, even the dictionary undertakes a kind of interpretative criticism when it endeavors to define the meaning of a word, and in so doing is obliged to indicate those associations and connotations which have grown up in the minds of various individuals and gradually been generalized to such an extent that they may fairly be called a part of the word's meaning, even though they are not so clearly defined or so inevitably understood as its primary significance. In a similar fashion the author of these explanatory notes which accompany the school text of a classic is doing the same sort of thing when he takes something out of his own mind and puts it into the mind of the pupil by explaining that Horace's "ab ovo" refers to the strange birth of Helen, or that Shakespeare refers to a "wooden O" because some Elizabethan theatres were oval. No one could accuse the lexicographer or the editor of mingling too much of himself in his exegesis or of mistaking what T. S. Eliot calls "a weak creative impulse" for a critical one. Yet the lexicographer is attempting to prepare the mind of the consultant by furnishing it with associations which will render its apperception identical with his own, and since the associations of all words are not fixed and unvarying, he is beginning to impose upon another "interpretations" which have some elements of the personal. What is true of words is, moreover, true to a much greater extent of all allusions to historical characters or familiar situations. Phrases like "the glory that was Greece" or "I fling my cap for polish and for Pope" actually have a content which varies from ear to ear, and yet it is, notoriously, upon such imperfectly defined contents that the effect of the more imaginative kinds of literature depends. In poetry, as Santayana has so brilliantly remarked, "feeling is transferred by contagion," and under its influence "minds radiate from a somewhat similar core of sensation, from the same vital mood, into the most diverse and incommunicable images."

Surely the most determined of impersonal critics could not stop short of the effort to describe what the phrase "the glory that was Greece" meant to the poet who wrote it, but it is nevertheless difficult to see how he can always be sure that he is distinguishing what it meant to its author from what it means to him. He might compile a list of the books which Poe is known to have read, and he might, by considering all the latter's knowledge of Greece in connection with all the circumstances under which he acquired it, seek to form some conception of just what—for Poe—this "glory" was. But he would nevertheless be compelled to feel the influence of his own associations, to describe—in part at least—what the phrase meant to him as well as what it meant to Poe. And once he has done that, the road, entirely deprived of landmarks, would lie open to the most personal of interpretations. If any book that is read becomes inevitably a kind of collaboration between author and reader; if the thing which happens in the reader's mind is the result of the associations formed between the words of the book and the ideas in his mind; if—in a word—the esthetic experience is the result of an apperception rather than of a perception, then any attempt to describe it must involve something personal, and what we must have is, after all, that now so much-despised something which was once admiringly described as "the adventures of the soul among masterpieces." All that a repudiation of it can amount to is a determination not to cultivate too extravagantly the idiosyncratic, a determination to keep as close as one can to the mind of the author and to concern oneself as far as possible with those associations which appear to be common to a considerable number of persons. And that is, indeed, all that can possibly be the result of attempting to heed the rhetorically effective pronunciamentos of that new school of critics who declare that a work of literature must be considered purely for what it is rather than for what it is capable of suggesting in the mental context of the critic. Actually it can never be detached from that context, and the difference between impressionism and "objective criticism" is merely the difference between a criticism which struggles against and a criticism which yields itself to the influence of the purely personal element in our reaction to any work of art.

Nor does it seem possible, once we have gone thus far, to assert that a critic becomes worthless just as soon as his opinions are seen to be influenced in even the slightest degree by his moral, social, or even political opinions. They inevitably influence his judgment of a literary work because they inevitably influence the effect which it has upon him, and, accordingly, help to determine what—for him— it *is*. How, to return again to a simple example, can the effect which a melodrama has upon us fail to be influenced in some degree by the things for which the hero and the villain stand, how can we possibly raise ourselves above the fact that the downfall of the latter will be more satisfying, more "right," and more "beautiful" if the hero happens to be "on our side"? And what is true of melodrama with its crude appeal to gross convictions is true to a less extent of those other forms of literature which make their appeal to more refined and less easily analyzed passions and preferences.

A "pure" esthetic emotion—if it still remains esthetic at all—is doubtless possible in contemplating the purely formal perfection of a mathematical demonstration which, because it *is* mathematical, is wholly without content. Perhaps also, and for the sake of argument, we may admit that such a "pure" esthetic experience is also possible in the presence of certain kinds of music and certain very abstract forms of painting. But as long as literature uses words, and as long as words refer to things which awaken desire or disgust or hate or love or fear, then just so long must the experience which it produces fall to some degree short of the "purely" esthetic. Just so long also will the criticism of it fail to achieve that "purity" of which the more fastidious critics often speak; and there is only one thing which we can reasonably expect. We can ask only that the critic shall be aware of the personal nature of his reactions as well as of the arbitrary character of his standards, and that, just in proportion as he fails to maintain an absolute detachment, he will cultivate that underlying skepticism which softens the dogmatism from which we cannot escape so long as we undertake to say anything at all.

# JOHN DEWEY

## (1859–1952)

JOHN DEWEY was born in Burlington, Vermont, on October 20, 1859. After graduating from the state university, he spent some time studying at home and then took up graduate work at Johns Hopkins, receiving his Ph.D. in 1884. His long and fruitful teaching career began at the University of Michigan where, with the exception of one year, he remained for ten years. The next decade he spent at the University of Chicago, where he had an opportunity, as director of the School of Education, to put his pioneering educational theories into practice. In 1904 he went to Columbia University, where he was one of the prominent members in the department of philosophy.

His faith in a philosophy rooted in experience has left a deep impress on the literature and literary criticism of the twentieth century. Though unlike Santayana he has never practiced the art of literary criticism, his philosophy has had a marked influence on the minds of many American critics. Whether they accept him *in toto* or in part, or reject him completely, their thinking has been shaped by his ideas. Critics so diverse in method and point of view as Randolph Bourne, Lewis Mumford, James T. Farrell, Max Eastman, and Kenneth Burke, have acknowledged their indebtedness to his work. A radical empiricist Dewey exposed the weakness of absolutism and fixed standards in ethics, religion, science, and metaphysics, showing how inadequate they were when applied to a world undergoing constant change. Having faith in the method of instrumentalism and in the power of science and technology to cope with the challenge of the environment, he insisted that life could be improved, especially if we are willing to breast the tides of change and break down the Chinese walls of tradition. His belief in experience and the experimental method as the best way of determining the truth of ideas, his stress on education not as a preparation for life but as life itself, and his faith in democratic liberalism as opposed to authoritarianism in politics, all this has greatly helped to shape the mind of his age. His insistence that the naturalistic method could

349

be applied to all fields of inquiry led him to explore not only logic but also ethics and aesthetics.

Based on a series of lectures delivered at Harvard University on the philosophy of art, *Art as Experience* (1934) is perfectly in keeping with Dewey's instrumental philosophy. In it he seeks to restore the lost continuity between the refined forms of experience embodied in works of art and the events which we designate as everyday experience. Art, far from being an esoteric experience, springs fundamentally from the same sources and manifests the same qualities as all human life on earth. Dewey's object is thus to dispel the aura of spirituality that has been conventionally associated with art. For art, in its multifarious incarnations, celebrates the experiences that men have, and it cannot do otherwise.

If life has a biological basis, so has art, and biological considerations also help to explain the relation of the aesthetic to normal experience. Life is a constant resolution of conflict, an overcoming of resistance, a release of tension. Intellectual and emotional reactions—these are but complementary modes in the flow of energy as man continually adjusts himself to his environment. Action, feeling, and meaning are one in the process of rhythmic interaction between man and nature, but the achievement of harmony is only temporary, the result of a truce with the environment. There are no enduring consummations. Art is implicit in the process of living.

Dewey would rescue critics from being led astray by false psychologies that distort our aesthetic philosophy. It is arbitrary and untenable to separate the intellectual from the sensory function, the emotional from the ideational. They form a psychological unity. An aesthetic experience does not imply exclusion. It is too rich and complex for that. Mind and body are not separate and opposed. The faculty of imagination, Dewey believes, is not peculiar to art but pervades all processes of observation.

Dewey is aware that abstract discussions of aesthetic problems are sterile and futile. Thrusting aside all fixed standards and rules, he holds that the work of art is always concrete and individual. All the vital and significant movements in art explore new areas of human experience. The critic must safeguard himself against the inertia of habit and routine. Even more effective is Dewey's analysis of the weakness of impressionistic criticism. If, after responding freely and fully to a work of art, we proceed to define and coordinate our impressions we can hit upon a reliable aesthetic judgment. Even if the critic gives a statement of his impressions, the reasons for his likes and dislikes—reasons inherent in his temperament—his work approximates the objective.

Criticism is a process of valuation. Values exist only in relation to a particular work of art. But criticism when it functions does not look for values in general but for the objective properties of a work. Since standards do not exist for works of art, there are none in criticism. This does not mean that there are no sound criteria in the act of judgment, for the work of art furnishes the material on which judgment is based. Judgments will therefore vary as the material evoking them varies. Analysis and synthesis represent in criticism an inseparable unity. Analysis studies the parts and their relation to the whole, while the unifying phase of judgment elicits the creative response of the critic, which calls for insight and illumination, not the application of rules. Creative criticism thus becomes an art, for every sound analysis also involves synthesis.

The personal equation must always be taken into account in criticism, since it is always present, but there need be nothing lawless or erratic about it. The critic's instinctive preferences and prejudices can be controlled by trained sensitivity and discriminating insight. Though the function of criticism is to arouse and heighten the aesthetic experience in other minds, each one must perform the task of appraisal for himself. All the critic can do for him is to subject him directly to the influence of the work of art.

The scientific method is too new as yet to become a normal and established part of our collective experience, our mental habits, our frame of reference, and it is wrong to conclude from this that science has a restrictive effect on the imagination. Though science analyzes and disintegrates the objects of experience, the world of immediate experience remains unchanged. Nor can the neutrality of scientific "laws" be used to argue that the death of poetry is imminent. Science shows that man is a part of nature, and this has important consequences for art, for it enables man to establish a better relation between himself and nature. Science will quicken, liberate, and enrich the human spirit, not only arousing a deeper intellectual curiosity and more alert and trained powers of observation but also awakening a wholesome respect for experience itself. As for industrialism in art, Dewey maintains that there is nothing in the machine to prevent the production and enjoyment of works of art.

BIBLIOGRAPHY

TEXT

*Studies in Logical Theory*. Chicago, 1903.
*The Influence of Darwin upon Philosophy*. New York, 1910.
*How We Think*. Boston and New York, 1916.
*Essays in Experimental Logic*. Chicago, 1916.

*Human Nature and Conduct*. New York, 1922.
*Experience and Nature*. Chicago, 1926.
*The Quest for Certainty*. New York, 1929.
*Individualism, Old and New*. New York, 1930.
*Philosophy and Civilization*. New York, 1931.
*Art as Experience*. New York, 1934.
*A Common Faith*. New Haven, 1934.
*Liberalism and Social Action*. New York, 1935.
*Logic, the Theory of Inquiry*. New York, 1938.
*Freedom and Culture*. New York, 1939.
*Problems of Men*. New York, 1946.

#### CRITICISM

Adler, Mortimer J., *Art and Prudence*. New York, 1937.
Eastman, Max, *Heroes I Have Known*. New York, 1942.
*Essays in Honor of John Dewey on the Occasion of His Seventieth Birthday*, New York, 1929.
Frank, Waldo, *The Re-discovery of America*. New York, 1929.
Hook, Sidney, *John Dewey*. New York, 1939.
Leander, Folke, "John Dewey and the Classical Tradition," *American Review*, IX, 504–527 (October, 1937).
——, *The Philosophy of John Dewey*. Göteborg (Sweden), 1939.
Mencken, H. L., *Prejudices, Fifth Series*. New York, 1929.
McGill, V. J., "Pragmatic Reconsidered," *Science and Society*, III, 289–322 (1939).
More, Paul Elmer, *On Being Human*. Princeton, 1936.
Schilpp, Paul Arthur (ed.), *The Philosophy of John Dewey*. Evanston and Chicago, 1939.
Tate, Allen, "The Aesthetic Emotion as Useful," *This Quarter*, V, 292–303 (December, 1932).
Thomas, Milton Halsey, *A Bibliography of John Dewey*. New York, 1939.
White, Morton Gould, *The Origin of Dewey's Instrumentalism*. New York, 1943.

## CRITICISM AND PERCEPTION*

CRITICISM is judgment, ideally as well as etymologically. Understanding of judgment is therefore the first condition for theory about the nature of criticism. Perceptions supply judgment with its ma-

* From *Art as Experience*, by John Dewey. Copyright, 1934, by John Dewey. Courtesy of G. P. Putnam's Sons.

terial, whether the judgments pertain to physical nature, to politics or biography. The subject-matter of perception is the only thing that makes the difference in the judgments which ensue. Control of the subject-matter of perception for ensuring proper data for judgment is the key to the enormous distinction between the judgments the savage passes on natural events and that of a Newton or an Einstein. Since the matter of esthetic criticism is the perception of esthetic objects, natural and artistic criticism is always determined by the quality of first-hand perception; obtuseness in perception can never be made good by any amount of learning, however extensive, nor any command of abstract theory, however correct. Nor is it possible to exclude judgment from entering into esthetic perception, or at least from supervening upon a first total unanalyzed qualitative impression.

Theoretically, it should therefore be possible to proceed at once from direct esthetic experience to what is involved in judgment, the clews being given on one side from the formed matter of works of art as they exist in perception, and, on the other side, from what is involved in judgment by the nature of its own structure. But, in fact, it is first necessary to clear the ground. For unreconciled differences as to the nature of judgment are reflected in theories of criticism, while diverse tendencies among the arts have given rise to opposed theories that are developed and asserted for the sake of justifying one movement and condemning another. Indeed, there is ground for holding that the most vital questions in esthetic theory are generally to be found in controversies regarding special movements in some art, like "functionalism" in architecture, "pure" poetry or free verse in literature, "expressionism" in the drama, the "stream of consciousness" in the novel, "proletarian art" and the relation of the artist to economic conditions and revolutionary social activities. Such controversies may be attended with heat and prejudice. But they are more likely to be conducted with an eye directed upon concrete works of art than are lucubrations upon esthetic theory in the abstract. Yet they complicate the theory of criticism with ideas and aims derived from external partisan movements.

It cannot be safely assumed at the outset that judgment is an act of intelligence performed upon the matter of direct perception in the interest of a more adequate perception. For judgment has also a legalistic meaning and import, as in Shakespeare's phrase, "a critic, nay, a night watchman." Following the signification supplied by the practice of the law, a judge, a critic, is one who pronounces an authoritative sentence. We hear constantly of the verdict of critics, and of the verdict of history pronounced upon works of art. Criticism is thought of as if its business were not explication of the content of an object as to substance and form, but a process of acquittal or condemnation on the basis of merits and demerits.

The judge—in the judicial sense—occupies a seat of social authority. His sentence determines the fate of an individual, perhaps of a cause, and upon occasion it settles the legitimacy of future courses of action. Desire for authority (and desire to be looked up to) animates the human breast. Much of our existence is keyed to the note of praise and blame, exculpation and disapproval. Hence there has emerged in theory, reflecting a widespread tendency in practice, a disposition to erect criticism into something "judicial." One cannot read widely in the outgivings of this school of criticism without seeing that much of it is of the compensatory type—the fact which has given rise to the gibe that critics are those who have failed in creation. Much criticism of the legalistic sort proceeds from subconscious self-distrust and a consequent appeal to authority for protection. Perception is obstructed and cut short by memory of an influential rule, and by the substitution of precedent and prestige for direct experience. Desire for authoritative standing leads the critic to speak as if he were the attorney for established principles having unquestionable sovereignty.

Unfortunately such activities have infected the very conception of criticism. Judgment that is final, that settles a matter, is more congenial to unregenerate human nature than is the judgment that is a development in thought of a deeply realized perception. The original adequate experience is not easy to attain; its achievement is a test of native sensitiveness and of experience matured through wide contacts. A judgment as an act of controlled inquiry demands a rich background and a disciplined insight. It is much easier to "tell" people what they should believe than to discriminate and unify. And an audience that is itself habituated to being told, rather than schooled in thoughtful inquiry, likes to be told.

Judicial decision can be made only on the basis of general rules supposed to be applicable to all cases. The harm done by particular instances of judicial sentence, as particular, is much less serious than the net result in developing the notion and antecedent authoritative standards and precedents are at hand by which to judge. The so-called classicism of the eighteenth century alleged that the ancients provided models from which rules could be derived. The influence of this belief extended from literature to other branches of art. Reynolds recommended to students of art the observance of the art-form of Umbrian and Roman painters, and, warning them against others, said of Tintoretto that his inventions are "wild, capricious, extravagant and fantastic."

A temperate view of the importance of the models furnished by the past is given by Matthew Arnold. He says that the best way to discover "what poetry belongs to the class of the truly excellent, and *can therefore do us the most good,* is to have always in one's mind lines and expressions of the great masters, and to apply them as a touchstone to other poetry." He denies that he means that other poetry should be reduced to imitation, but says that such lines are an "infallible touchstone for detecting the presence or absence of high poetic quality." Aside from the moralistic element involved in the words I have taken the liberty of italicizing, the idea of an "infallible" test is bound, if acted upon, to limit direct response in perception, to introduce self-consciousness and reliance upon extraneous factors, all harmful to vital appreciation. Moreover, there is involved the question as to whether the masterpieces of the past are accepted as such because of personal response or on the authority of tradition and convention. Matthew Arnold is really assuming an ultimate dependence upon some one's personal power of just perception.

Representatives of the school of judicial criticism do not seem to be sure whether the masters are great because they observe certain rules or whether the rules now to be observed are derived from the practice of great men. In general, it is safe to assume, I think, that reliance upon rules is a weakened, a mitigated, version of a prior, more direct, admiration, finally become servile, of the work of outstanding personalities. But whether they are set up on their own account or are derived from masterpieces, standards, prescriptions, and rules are general while objects of art are individual. The former have no locus in time, a fact naïvely stated in calling them eternal. They belong neither here nor there. In applying to everything, they apply to nothing in particular. In order to get concreteness, they have to be referred for exemplification to the work of the "masters." Thus in fact they encourage imitation. The masters themselves usually serve an apprenticeship, but as they mature they absorb what they have learned into their own individual experience, vision, and style. They are masters precisely because they do not follow either models or rules but subdue both of these things to serve enlargement of personal experience. Tolstoi spoke as an artist when he said that "nothing so contributes to the perversion of art as these authorities set up by criticism." Once an artist is pronounced great "all his works are regarded as admirable and worthy of imitation. . . . Every false work extolled is a door through which hypocrites of art creep in."

If judicial critics do not learn modesty from the past they profess to esteem, it is not from lack of material. Their history is largely the record of egregious blunders. The commemorative exhibition of paintings by Renoir in Paris in the summer of 1933 was the occasion for exhuming some of the deliverances of official critics of fifty years before. The pronouncements vary from assertions that the paintings cause a nausea like that of sea-sickness, are products of diseased minds—a favorite statement—that they mix at random the most violent colors, to an assertion that they "are denials of all that is *permissible* [characteristic word] in painting, of everything called light, transparence and shade, clarity and design." As late as 1897, a group of academicians (always the favorites of judicial criticism) protested against the acceptance by the Luxembourg Museum of a collection of paintings by Renoir, Cezanne, and Monet, and one of them stated that it was impossible that the Institute should be silent in the presence of such a scandal as reception of a collection of insanities since it is the guardian of tradition—another idea characteristic of judicial criticism.[1]

There is, however, a certain lightness of touch usually associated with French criticism. For real majesty of pronunciamento we may turn to the outgivings of an American critic on the occasion of the Armory exhibition in New York in 1913. Under the caption of the ineffectualness of Cezanne, it is said that the latter is "a second-rate impressionist who had now and then fair luck in painting a moderately good picture." The "crudities" of Van Gogh are disposed of as follows: "A moderately competent impressionist who was heavy-handed (!), and who had little idea of beauty and spoiled a lot of canvas with crude and unimportant pictures." Matisse is disposed of as one who has "relinquished all respect for technique, all feeling for his medium; content to daub his canvas with linear and tonal coarseness. Their negation of all that true art implies is significant of smug complacency. . . . They are not works of art but feeble impertinences." The reference to "true art" is characteristic of judicial criticism, never more injudicious than in this case with its reversal

---

[1] The greater part of the collection is now in the Louvre—a sufficient comment on the competency of official criticism.

of what is significant in the artists mentioned: Van Gogh being explosive rather than heavy-handed; Matisse being a technician almost to a fault, and inherently decorative rather than coarse; while "second rate" applied to Cezanne speaks for itself. Yet this critic had by this time accepted the impressionist painting of Manet and Monet—it was 1913 instead of twenty years earlier; and his spiritual offspring will doubtless hold up Cezanne and Matisse as standards by which to condemn some future movement in the art of painting.

The "criticism" just quoted was preceded by other remarks that indicate the nature of the fallacy that is always involved in legalistic criticism: confusion of a particular technique with esthetic form. The critic in question quoted from a published comment of a visitor who was not a professional critic. The latter said, "I never heard a crowd of people talk so much about meaning and about life and so little about technique, values, tones, drawing, perspective, studies in blue and white, etc." Then the judicial critic adds: "We are grateful for this bit of concrete evidence of the fallacy which more than others threatens to mislead and completely obfuscate the too confiding observers. To go to this exhibition with a solicitude about 'meaning' and about 'life' at the expense of matters of technique is not simply to beg the question; it is to give it away with both hands. In art, elements of 'meaning' and 'life' do not exist until the artist has mastered those technical processes by which he may or may not have genius to call them [*sic*] into being."

The unfairness of the implication that the author of the comment intended to rule out matters of technique is so characteristic of alleged judicial criticism that it is significant only because it indicates how completely the critic can think of technique only as it is identified with some one model of procedure. And this fact is deeply significant. It indicates the source of the failure of even the best of judicial criticism: its inability to cope with the emergence of new modes of life—of experiences that demand new modes of expression. All of the post-impressionist painters (with the partial exception of Cezanne) had shown in their early works that they had command of the techniques of the masters that immediately preceded them. The influence of Courbet, Delacroix, even of Ingres, pervades them. But these techniques were suited to the rendering of old themes. As these painters matured, they had new visions; they saw the world in ways to which older painters were insensitive. Their new subject-matter demanded a new form. And because of the relativity of technique to form, they were compelled to experiment with the development of new technical procedures.[2] An environment that is changed physically and spiritually demands new forms of expression.

I repeat that here we have exposed the inherent defect of even the best of judicial criticism. The very meaning of an important new movement in any art is that it expresses something new in human experience, some new mode of interaction of the live creature with his surroundings, and hence the release of powers previously cramped or inert. The manifestations of the movement therefore cannot be judged but only misjudged when form is identified with a familiar technique. Unless the critic is sensitive first of all to "meaning and life" as the matter which requires its own form, he is helpless in the presence of the emergence of experience that has a distinctively new character. Every professional person is subject to the influence of custom and inertia, and has to protect himself from its influences by a deliberate openness to life itself. The judicial critic erects the very things that are the dangers of his calling into a principle and norm.

The blundering ineptness of much that calls itself judicial criticism has called out a reaction to the opposite extreme. The protest takes the form of "impressionist" criticism. It is in effect, if not in words, a denial that criticism in the sense of judgment is possible, and an assertion that judgment should be replaced by statement of the responses of feeling and imagery the art object evokes. In theory, though not always in practice, such criticism reacts from the standardized "objectivity" of ready-made rules and precedents to the chaos of a subjectivity that lacks objective control, and would, if logically followed out, result in a medley of irrelevancies—and sometimes does. Jules Lemaître has given an almost canonical statement of the impressionistic point of view. He said: "Criticism, whatever be its pretensions, can never go beyond defining the impression which, at a given moment, is made on us by a work of art wherein the artist has himself recorded the impression which he received from the world at a certain hour."

The statement includes an implication which, when it is made explicit, goes far beyond the intention of the impressionist theory. To *define* an impression signifies a good deal more than just to utter it. Impressions, total qualitative unanalyzed effects that things and events make upon us, are the antecedents and beginnings of all judgments.[3] The beginning of a new idea, terminating perhaps in an

2 See *Art as Experience* (New York, 1934), p. 142.
3. See *Ibid.*, p. 191.

elaborate judgment following upon extensive inquiry, is an impression, even in the case of a scientific man or philosopher. But to define an impression is to analyze it, and analysis can proceed only by going beyond the impression, by referring it to the grounds on which it rests and the consequences which it entails. And this procedure is judgment. Even if the one who communicates his impression confines his exposition of it, his demarcation and delimitation, to grounds that lie in his own temperament and personal history, taking the reader frankly into his confidence, he still goes beyond the bare impression to something objective to it. Thus he gives the reader ground for an "impression" on his own part that is more objectively grounded than any impression can be that is founded on a mere "it seems to me." For the experienced reader is then given the means of discriminating among different impressions of different persons on the basis of the bias and experience of the person who has them.

The reference to objective grounds having begun with statement of personal history cannot stop there. The biography of the one who defines his impression is not located inside his own body and mind. It is what it is because of interactions with the world outside, a world which in some of its aspects and phases is common with that of others. If the critic is wise, he judges the impression that occurs at a certain hour of his own history by considering the objective causes that have entered into that history. Unless he does so, at least implicitly, the discriminating reader has to perform the task for him—unless he surrenders himself blindly to the "authority" of the impression itself. In the latter case, there is no difference among impressions; the insight of a cultivated mind and the gush of the immature enthusiast stand on the same level.

The sentence quoted from Lemaître has another significant implication. It sets forth a proportion that is objective: as his subject-matter is to the artist, so is the work of art to the critic. If the artist is numb and if he does not impregnate some immediate impression with meanings derived from a prior rich funded experience, his product is meager and its form is mechanical. The case is not otherwise with a critic. There is an illicit suggestion contained in the reference to the impression of the artist as occurring at a "certain hour" and that of the critic as taking place "at a given moment." The suggestion is that because the impression exists at a particular moment, its import is limited to that brief space of time. The implication is the fundamental fallacy of impressionist criticism. Every experience, even that containing a conclusion due to long processes of inquiry and reflection, exists at a "given moment." To infer from this fact that its import and validity are affairs of that passing moment is to reduce all experience to a shifting kaleidoscope of meaningless incidents.

Moreover, the comparison of the attitude of a critic toward a work of art to that of the artist toward his subject-matter is so just as to be fatal to the impressionist theory. For the impression the artist has does not consist of impressions; it consists of objective material rendered by means of imaginative vision. The subject-matter is charged with meanings that issue from intercourse with a common world. The artist in the freest expression of his own responses is under weighty objective compulsions. The trouble with very much criticism, aside from the impressionist label, is that the critic does *not* take an attitude toward the "impressions he has received from the world." The critic can go off into irrelevancies and arbitrary dicta much more readily than the artist, while failure to be controlled by subject-matter is much more evident to eye and ear than is a corresponding failure on the part of the critic. The tendency of the critic to dwell in a world apart is great enough in any case without being sanctioned by a special theory.

Were it not for the blunders made by the judicial critic, blunders that proceed from the theory he holds, the reaction of the impressionist theory would hardly have been called forth. Because the former set up false notions of objective values and objective standards, it was made easy for the impressionist critic to deny there are objective values at all. Because the former has virtually adopted a conception of standards that is of an external nature, derived from use of standards developed for practical ends, and legally defined, the latter has assumed there are no criteria of any sort. In its precise signification, a "standard" is unambiguous. It is a quantitative measure. The yard as a standard of length, the gallon as a standard of liquid capacity, are as precise as legal definitions can make them. The standard of liquid measure for Great Britain was defined, for example, by an act of Parliament in 1825. It is a container holding ten pounds avoirdupois of distilled water, weighed in air with the barometer at thirty inches and the Fahrenheit thermometer at sixty-two degrees.

There are three characteristics of a standard. It is a particular physical thing existing under specified physical conditions; it is *not* a value. The yard is a yard-stick, and the meter is a bar deposited in Paris. In the second place, standards are measures of definite things, of lengths, weights, capacities. The things measured are not values, although it is of great social value to be able to measure them, since the properties of things in the way of size, volume, weight, are important for commercial exchange. Finally, as standards of measure, standards define things with respect to *quantity*. To be able to measure quantities is a great aid to further judgments, but it is not itself a mode of judgment. The standard, being an external and public thing, is applied *physically*. The yard-stick is physically laid down upon the things measured to determine their length.

When, therefore, the word "standard" is used with respect to judgment of works of art, nothing but confusion results, unless the radical difference in the meaning now given standard from that of standards of measurement is noted. The critic is really judging, not measuring physical fact. He is concerned with something individual, not comparative—as is all measurement. His subject-matter is qualitative, not quantitative. There is no external and public thing, defined by law to be the same for all transactions, that can be physically applied. The child who can use a yard-stick can measure as well as the most experienced and mature person, if he can handle the stick, since measuring is not judgment but is a physical operation performed for the sake of determining value in exchange or in behalf of some further physical operation—as a carpenter measures the boards with which he builds. The same cannot be said of judgment of the value of an idea or the value of a work of art.

Because of failure of critics to realize the difference between the meaning of standard as applied in measurement and as used in judgment or criticism, Mr. Grudin can say of a critic who is a believer in a fixed standard with respect to works of art: "His procedure has been that of an excursion for words and notions to support his claims, wherever he could find them; and he has had to trust to the meanings he could read into already available odds and ends belonging to various fields and gathered into a makeshift critical doctrine." And this, he adds with not too great severity, is the usual procedure followed by literary critics.

Yet it does not follow because of absence of an uniform and publicly determined external object, that objective criticism of art is impossible. What follows is that criticism is judgment; that like every judgment it involves a venture, a hypothetical element; that it is directed to qualities which are nevertheless qualities of an *object;* and that it is concerned with an individual object, not with making comparisons by means of an external preëstablished rule between different things. The critic, because of the element of venture, reveals himself in his criticisms. He wanders into another field and confuses values when he departs from the object he is judging. Nowhere are comparisons so odious as in fine art.

Appreciation is said to occur with respect to values, and criticism is currently supposed to be a process of valuation. There is, of course, truth in the conception. But it is fraught, in current interpretation, with a host of equivocations. After all, one is concerned with the values of a poem, a stage-play, a painting. One is aware of them as qualities-in-qualitative-relations. One does not at the time categorize them *as* values. One may pronounce a play fine or "rotten." If one term such direct characterization valuing, then criticism is *not* valuing. It is a very different sort of thing than a direct ejaculation. Criticism is a search for the properties of the object that may justify the direct reaction. And yet, if the search is sincere and informed, it is not, when it is undertaken, concerned with values but with the objective properties of the object under consideration—if a painting, with its colors, lights, placings, volumes, in their relations to one another. It is a survey. The critic may or may not at the end pronounce definitely upon the total "value" of the object. If he does, his pronouncement will be more intelligent than it would otherwise have been, because his perceptive appreciation is now more instructed. But when he does sum up his judgment of the object, he will, if he is wary, do so in a way that is a summary of the outcome of his objective examination. He will realize that his assertion of "good" or "bad" in this and that degree is something the goodness or badness of which is itself to be tested by other persons in their direct perceptual commerce with the object. His criticism issues as a social document and can be checked by others to whom the same objective material is available. Hence the critic, if he is wise, even in making pronouncements of good and bad, of great and small in value, will lay more emphasis upon the objective traits that sustain his judgment than upon values in the sense of excellent and poor. Then his surveys may be of assistance in the direct experience of others, as a survey of a country is of help to the one who travels through it, while dicta about worth operate to limit personal experience.

If there are no standards for works of art and hence none for criticism (in the sense in which there are standards of measurement), there are nevertheless criteria in judgment, so that criticism does not fall in the field of mere impressionism. The discussion of form in relation to matter, of the meaning of medium in art, of the nature of

the expressive object, has been an attempt on the part of the writer
to discover some of these criteria. But such criteria are not rules or
prescriptions. They are the result of an endeavor to find out what a
work of art is as an experience: the kind of experience which constitutes it. As far as the conclusions are valid, they are of use as instrumentalities of personal experience, not as dictations of what the
attitude of any one should be. Stating what a work of art is as an
experience, may render particular experiences of particular works of
art more pertinent to the object experienced, more aware of its own
content and intent. This is all any criterion can do; and if and as far
as the conclusions are invalid, better criteria are to be set forth by
an improved examination of the nature of works of art in general as
a mode of human experience.

Criticism is judgment. The material out of which judgment grows
is the work, the object, but it is this object as it enters into the experience of the critic by interaction with his own sensitivity and his
knowledge and funded store from past experiences. As to their content, therefore, judgments will vary with the concrete material that
evokes them and that must sustain them if criticism is pertinent and
valid. Nevertheless, judgments have a common form because they all
have certain functions to perform. These functions are discrimination
and unification. Judgment has to evoke a clearer consciousness of
constituent parts and to discover how consistently these parts are
related to form a whole. Theory gives the names of analysis and
synthesis to the execution of these functions.

They cannot be separated from each other, because analysis is dis-
closure of part as parts of a whole; of details and particulars as belonging to total situation, a universe of discourse. This operation is
the opposite of picking to pieces or dissection, even when something
of the latter sort is required in order to make judgment possible. No
rules can be laid for the performance of so delicate an act as determination of the significant parts of a whole, and of their respective
places and weights in the whole. This is the reason, perhaps, why
scholarly dissertations upon literature are so often merely scholastic
enumerations of minutiæ, and so-called criticisms of paintings are of
the order of analyses of handwriting by experts.

Analytic judgment is a test of the mind of the critic, since mind,
as organization into perceptions of meanings derived from past intercourse with objects, is the organ of discrimination. Hence the safeguard of the critic is a consuming informed interest. I say "consum-

ing" because without natural sensitivity connected with an intense liking for certain subject-matters, a critic, having even a wide range of learning, will be so cold that there is no chance of his penetrating the heart of a work of art. He will remain on the outside. Yet, unless affection is informed with the insight that is the product of a rich and full experience, judgment will be one-sided or not rise above the level of gushy sentimentalism. Learning must be the fuel of warmth of interest. For the critic in the field of art, this informed interest signifies acquaintance with the tradition of his particular art; an acquaintance that is more than knowledge about them since it is derived from personal intimacy with the objects that have formed the tradition. In this sense acquaintance with masterpieces, and with less than masterpieces, is a "touchstone," of sensitiveness, though not a dictator of appraisals. For masterpieces themselves can be critically appreciated only as they are placed in the tradition to which they belong.

There is no art in which there is only a single tradition. The critic who is not intimately aware of a variety of traditions is of necessity limited and his criticisms will be one-sided to the point of distortion. The criticisms of post-impressionistic painting that were cited came from persons who thought they were expert because of exclusive initiation into a single tradition. In the plastic arts, there is the tradition of Negro, of Persian, of Egyptian, of Chinese and Japanese art, as well as the Florentine and Venetian traditions—to mention a few outstanding ones. It is because of lack of sense for the variety of traditions that unstable swings of fashion mark the attitude of different periods toward works of art—the overestimation of Raphael and the Roman school, for example, at the expense of Tintoretto and El Greco once current. Much of the unending and sterile controversy of critics adhering exclusively to "classicism" and "romanticism" has a like source. In the field of art, there are many mansions; artists have built them.

Through knowledge of a variety of conditions, the critic becomes aware of the vast variety of materials that are usable (since they have been used) in art. He is saved from the snap judgment that this or that work is esthetically wrong because it has matter to which he is not accustomed, and when he comes across a work whose matter has no discoverable precedent he will be wary of uttering an offhand condemnation. Since form is always integral with matter, he will also, if his own experience is genuinely esthetic, appreciate the multitude of special forms that exist and be safeguarded against identifying form with some technique that he has come to prefer. In short, not only will his general background be broadened, but he will become familiar, to the point of saturation, with a more fundamental matter, the conditions under which the subject-matter of varied modes of experience move to fulfillment. And this movement constitutes the objective and publicly accessible content of all works of art.

This knowledge of many traditions is no foe to discrimination. While I have spoken for the most part of the condemnations passed by judicial criticisms, it would be easily possible to quote as great egregious blunders in misplaced laudations. Absence of sympathetic acquaintance with a number of traditions leads the critic to a ready appreciation of academic works of art provided they are done with excellent technical facility. Seventeenth century Italian painting was met with an acclaim that it was far from deserving simply because it pushed to an extreme, with technical skill, factors that earlier Italian art had held within bounds. Knowledge of a wide range of traditions is a condition of exact and severe discrimination. For only by means of such a knowledge can the critic detect the intent of an artist and the adequacy of his execution of intent. The history of criticism is filled with charges of carelessness and willfulness that would never have been brought if an adequate knowledge of traditions had been present, just as it is filled with praise for works that have no merit beyond a skillful use of materials.

In most cases, the discrimination of a critic has to be assisted by a knowledge of the development of an artist, as that is manifested in the succession of his works. Only rarely can an artist be criticized by a single specimen of his activity. The inability is not merely because Homer sometimes nods, but because understanding of the logic of the development of an artist is necessary to discrimination of his intent in any single work. Possession of this understanding broadens and refines the background without which judgment is blind and arbitrary. The words of Cezanne about the relation of exemplars of tradition to the artist are applicable to the critic. "Study of the Venetians, especially of Tintoretto, sets one upon a constant search for means of expression which will surely lead one to experience from nature one's own means of expression. . . . The Louvre is a good book to consult, but it is only an intermediary. The diversity of the scene of nature is the real prodigious study to be undertaken. . . . The Louvre is a book where we learn to read. But we should not be content to keep the formulæ of our illustrious predecessors. Let us leave them so as to study beautiful nature and search to express it

according to our personal temperament. Time and reflection gradually modify vision, and at last comprehension comes." Change the
terms that need to be changed, and the procedure of the critic stands
forth.

Critic and artist alike have their predilections. There are aspects
of nature and life that are hard and others that are soft; that are
austere, even bleak, and that have attractive charm; that are exciting and that are pacifying, and so on almost without end. Most
"schools" of art exhibit a tendency in one direction or another. Then
some original mode of vision seizes upon the tendency and carries it
to its limit. There is, for example, the contrast between the "abstract"
and the "concrete"—that is, the more familiar. Some artists work for
extreme simplification, feeling that internal complexity leads to a
superfluity that distracts attention; others take as their problem the
multiplication of internal specifications to the utmost point consistent
with organization.[4] There is again the difference between the frank
and open approach and the indirect and allusive approach to vague
matter that goes by the name of symbolism. There are artists who
tend toward what Thomas Mann calls the dark and death and others
who rejoice in light and air.

It goes without saying that every direction has difficulties and
dangers that increase as it approaches its limit. The symbolic may
lose itself in unintelligibility and the direct method in the banal. The
"concrete" method ends in mere illustration and the "abstract" in
scientific exercise, and so on. But yet each is justified when form and
matter achieve equilibrium. The danger is that the critic, guided by
personal predilection or more often by partisan conventionalism, will
take some one procedure as his criterion of judgment and condemn
all deviations from it as departures from art itself. He then misses the
point of all art, the unity of form and matter, and misses it because
he lacks adequate sympathy, in his natural and acquired one-sided-
ness, with the immense variety of interactions between the live
creature and his world.

There is a unifying as well as a discriminating phase of judgment
—technically known as synthesis in distinction from analysis. This
unifying phase, even more than the analytic, is a function of the
creative response of the individual who judges. It is insight. There
are no rules that can be laid down for its performance. It is at this
point that criticism becomes itself an art—or else a mechanism

4 While the two examples of animal art are given primarily to indicate the
nature of "essence" in art, they also exemplify these two methods.

worked by precept according to a ready-made blue print. Analysis, discrimination, must result in unification. For to be a manifestation of judgment it must distinguish particulars and parts with respect to their weight and function in formation of an integral experience. Without a unifying point of view, based on the objective form of a work of art, criticism ends in enumeration of details. The critic operates after the manner of Robinson Crusoe when he sat down and made a credit and debit list of his blessings and troubles. The critic points out so many blemishes and so many merits, and strikes a balance. Since the object is an integral whole, if it is a work of art at all, such a method is as boring as it is irrelevant.

That the critic must discover some unifying strand or pattern running through all details does not signify that he must himself produce an integral whole. Sometimes critics of the better type substitute a work of art of their own for that they are professedly dealing with. The result may be art but it is not criticism. The unity the critic traces must be in the work of art as its characteristic. This statement does not signify that there is just one unifying idea or form in a work of art. There are many, in proportion to the richness of the object in question. What is meant is that the critic shall seize upon some strain or strand that is actually there, and bring it forth with such clearness that the reader has a new clue and guide in his own experience.

A painting may be brought to unity through relations of light, of planes, of color structurally employed, and a poem through predominant lyric or dramatic quality. And one and the same work of art presents different designs and different facets to different observers—as a sculptor may see different figures implicit in a block of stone. One mode of unification on the part of the critic is as legitimate as another—provided two conditions are fulfilled. One of them is that the theme and design which interest selects be really present in the work, and the other is the concrete exhibition of this supreme condition: the leading thesis must be shown to be consistently maintained throughout the parts of the work.

Goethe, for example, gave a notable manifestation of "synthetic" criticism in his account of the character of Hamlet. His conception of the essential character of Hamlet has enabled many a reader to see things in the play that otherwise would have escaped attention. It has served as a thread, or better as a centralizing force. Yet his conception is not the only way in which the elements of the play may be brought to a focus. Those who saw Edwin Booth's portrayal of

the character may well have carried away the idea that the key to
Hamlet as a human being is found in the lines spoken to Guilden-
stern after the latter had failed to play on a reed. "Why, look you
now, how unworthy a thing you make of me! You would play upon
me; would seem to know my stops; you would pluck out the heart
of my mystery; you would sound me from my lowest note to the top
of my compass; and there is much music, excellent voice, in this
little organ; yet cannot you make it speak. 'S blood, do you think I
am easier to be played upon than a pipe?"

It is customary to treat judgment and fallacies in intimate connection with each other. The two great fallacies of esthetic criticism
are reduction, and confusion of categories. The reductive fallacy results from oversimplification. It exists when some constituent of the
work of art is isolated and then the whole is reduced to terms of this
single isolated element. Generalized examples of this fallacy have
been considered in previous chapters: for example, in the isolation
of a sense-quality, like color or tone, from relations; isolation of the
purely formal element; or again when a work of art is reduced to the
exclusive representative values. The same principle applies when
technique is taken apart from its connection with form. A more
specific example is found in criticism made from a historical, political
or economic point of view. There can be no doubt that the cultural
milieu is inside as well as outside works of art. It enters as a genuine
constituent, and acknowledgment of it is one element in a just discrimination. The sumptuousness of Venetian aristocracy and commercial wealth is a genuine constituent of the painting of Titian.
But the fallacy of reducing his pictures to economic documents, as
I once heard done by a "proletarian" guide in the Hermitage in
Leningrad, is too evident to need mention were it not that it is a
gross case of what often happens in modes so subtle as not to be
readily perceptible. On the other hand, the religious simplicity and
austerity of French twelfth century statues and paintings, which
come into them from their cultural milieu, is held up, apart from
the strictly plastic qualities of the objects in question, as their essential esthetic quality.

A more extreme form of the reductive fallacy exists when works
of art are "explained" or "interpreted" on the basis of factors that
are incidentally inside them. Much of so-called psycho-analytic "criticism" is of this nature. Factors that may—or may not—have played
a part in the causative generation of a work of art are treated as if

they "explained" the esthetic content of the work of art itself. Yet the latter is just what it is whether a father or mother fixation, or a special regard for the susceptibilities of a wife, entered into its production. If the factors spoken of are real and not speculative, they are relevant to biography, but they are wholly impertinent as to the character of the work itself. If the latter has defects, they are blemishes to be detected in the construction of the object itself. If an Œdipus complex is part of the work of art, it can be discovered on its own account. But psycho-analytic criticism is not the only kind that falls into this fallacy. It flourishes wherever some alleged occasion in the life of the artist, some biographical incident, is taken as if it were a kind of substitute for appreciation of the poem that resulted.[5]

The other chief mode in which this type of the reductive fallacy prevails is in so-called sociological criticism. Hawthorne's "Seven Gables," Thoreau's "Walden," Emerson's "Essays," Mark Twain's "Huckleberry Finn" have an undoubted relation to the respective milieus in which they were produced. Historical and cultural information may throw light on the causes of their production. But when all is said and done, each one is just what it is artistically, and its esthetic merits and demerits are within the work. Knowledge of social conditions of production is, when it is really knowledge, of genuine value. But it is no substitute for understanding of the object in its own qualities and relations. Migraine, eyestrain, indigestion may have played a part in the production of some works of literature; they may even account, from a casual point of view, for some of the qualities of the literature produced. But knowledge of them is an addition to medical lore of cause and effect, not to judgment of what was produced, even though the knowledge induce towards the author a moral charity we might not otherwise share.

We are thus brought to the other great fallacy of esthetic judgment which indeed is mixed with the reductive fallacy: the confusion of categories. The historian, the physiologist, the biographer, the psychologist, all have their own problems and their own leading conceptions that control the inquiries they undertake. Works of art provide them with relevant data in the pursuit of their special investigations. The historian of Greek life cannot construct his report of Greek life except by taking into account the monuments of Greek

---

[5] Martin Schuetze, in his "Academic Illusions," gives pertinent detailed examples of this kind of fallacy and shows them to be the stock-in-trade of entire schools of esthetic interpretation.

art; they are at least as relevant and as precious for his purpose as the political institutions of Athens and Sparta. The philosophic interpretations of the arts provided by Plato and Aristotle are indispensable documents for the historian of the intellectual life of Athens. But historic judgment is not esthetic judgment. There are categories —that is, controlling conceptions of inquiry—appropriate to history, and only confusion results when they are used to control inquiry into art which also has its own ideas.

What is true of historical approach is true of the other modes of treatment. There are mathematical aspects of sculpture and painting as well as of architecture. Jay Hambridge has produced a treatise on the mathematics of Greek vases. An ingenious work has been produced on the mathematically formal elements of poetry. The biographer of Goethe or Melville would be derelict if he did not use their literary products when he is constructing a picture of their lives. The personal processes involved in construction of works of art are as precious data for the study of certain mental processes as records of procedures used by scientific inquirers are significant in the study of intellectual operations.

The phrase "confusion of categories" has an intellectualistic sound. Its practical counterpart is confusion of values.[6] Critics as well as theorists are given to the attempt to translate the distinctively esthetic over into terms of some other kind of experience. The commonest form of this fallacy is to assume that the artist begins with material that has already a recognized status, moral, philosophic, historical or whatever, and then renders it more palatable by emotional seasoning and imaginative dressing. The work of art is treated as if it were a reëditing of values already current in other fields of experience.

There can be no doubt, for example, that religious values have exercised an almost incomparable influence upon art. For a long period in European history, Hebrew and Christian legends formed the staple material of all the arts. But this fact of itself tells us nothing about distinctively esthetic values. Byzantine, Russian, Gothic and early Italian paintings are all equally "religious." But esthetically each has its own qualities. Doubtless the different forms are connected with difference of religious thought and practice. But esthetically the influence of the mosaic form is a more pertinent consideration. The question involved is the difference between material

6 There is a significant chapter with this title in Buermeyer's "The Æsthetic Experience."

and matter so often referred to in previous discussions. The medium and effect are the important matters. For this reason, later works of art that have no religious content have a profoundly religious effect. I imagine the majestic art of "Paradise Lost" will be more, not less, admitted, and the poem be more widely read, when rejection of its themes of Protestant theology has passed into indifference and forgetfulness. And this opinion does not imply that form is independent of matter. It implies that *artistic* substance is not identical with theme—any more than the form of the "Ancient Mariner" is identical with the story that is its theme. The *mis-en-scène* of Milton's portrayal of the dramatic action of great forces need not be esthetically troublesome, any more than is that of the "Iliad," to the modern reader. There is a profound distinction between the vehicle of a work of art, the intellectual carrier through which an artist receives his subject-matter and transmits it to his immediate audience, and both the form and matter of this work.

The direct influence of scientific upon artistic values is much less than that of religion. It would be a brave critic who would assert that the artistic qualities of either Dante's or Milton's works are affected by acceptance of a cosmogony that no longer has scientific standing. As to the future, I think Wordsworth spoke truly when he said: ". . . if the labours of Men of science should ever create any material revolution, direct or indirect, in our condition and in the impressions which we habitually receive, the Poet will sleep then no more than at present . . . he will be at his side, carrying sensation into the midst of the objects of science itself. The remotest discoveries of the Chemist, the Botanist, or Mineralogist, will be as proper objects of the Poet's art as any upon which it can be employed if the time should ever come when these things shall be familiar to us, and the relations under which they are contemplated by the followers of these respective sciences shall be manifestly and palpably material to us as enjoying and suffering beings." But poetry will not on that account be a popularization of science, nor will its characteristic values be those of science.

There are critics who confuse esthetic values with philosophic values, especially with those laid down by philosophic moralists. T. S. Eliot, for example, says that "the truest philosophy is the best material for the greatest poet," and implies that what the poet does is to make philosophic content more viable by addition of sensuous and emotional qualities. Just what the "truest philosophy" is, is a matter of some dispute. But critics of this school do not lack definite, not to say dogmatic, convictions on this point. Without any particular special competency in philosophic thought, they are ready to pronounce *ex cathedra* judgments, because they are committed to some conception of the relation of man to the universe that flourishes in some past epoch. They regard its restoration as essential to the redemption of society from its present evil state. Fundamentally their criticisms are moral recipes. Since great poets have had different philosophies, acceptance of their point of view entails that if we approve the philosophy of Dante we must condemn the poetry of Milton, and if we accept that of Lucretius we must find the poetry of both the others woefully defective. And where, upon the basis of any of these philosophies, does Goethe come in? And yet these are our great "philosophic" poets.

Ultimately all confusion of values proceeds from the same source: —neglect of the intrinsic significance of the medium. The use of a particular medium, a special language having its own characteristics, is the source of every art, philosophic, scientific, technological and esthetic. The arts of science, of politics, of history, and of painting and poetry all have finally the same *material;* that which is constituted by the interaction of the live creature with his surroundings. They differ in the media by which they convey and express this material, not in the material itself. Each one transforms some phase of the raw material of experience into new objects according to the purpose, each purpose demands a particular medium for its execution. Science uses the medium that is adapted to the purpose of control and prediction, of increase of power; it is an art.[7] Under particular conditions, its matter may also be esthetic. The purpose of esthetic art being the enhancement of direct experience itself, it uses the medium fit for the accomplishment of that end. The necessary equipment of the critic is, first, to have the experience and then to elicit its constituent in terms of the medium used. Failure in either of these respects results inevitably in confusion of values. To treat poetry as having a philosophy, even a "true" philosophy, for its especial material is like supposing that literature has grammar for its material.

An artist may, of course, *have* a philosophy and that philosophy may influence his artistic work. Because of the medium of words, which are already the product of social art and are already pregnant with moral meanings, the artist in literature is more often influenced by a philosophy than are artists who work with a plastic medium.

7 This point I have emphasized in the "Quest for Certainty," Chapter IV.

Mr. Santayana is a poet who is also a philosopher and a critic. Moreover, he has stated the criterion which he employs in criticism, and the criterion is just the thing most critics do not state and apparently are not even aware of. Of Shakespeare he says, ". . . the cosmos eludes him; he does not seem to feel the need of framing that idea. He depicts human life in all its richness and variety, but leaves that life without a setting and consequently without a meaning." Since the various scenes and characters presented by Shakespeare have each its own setting, the passage evidently implies lack of a particular setting, namely of a total cosmic setting. That this absence is what is implied is not left a matter of conjecture; it is definitely stated. "There is no *fixed* conception of any forces, natural or moral, *dominating and transcending* our mortal energies." The complaint is of lack of "totality"; fullness is not wholeness. "What is required for *theoretic wholeness* is not *this or that* system but *some* system."

In contrast with Shakespeare, Homer and Dante had a faith that "had enveloped the world of experience in a world of imagination in which *the ideals of the reason,* of the fancy and the heart had a natural expression." (None of the italics are in the original text.) His philosophic point of view, perhaps, is best summed up in a sentence occurring in a criticism of Browning: "The value of experience is not in experience but in the ideals which it reveals." And of Browning it is said that his "method is to penetrate by sympathy rather than to portray by intelligence"—a sentence one might suppose to be an admirable description of a dramatic poet rather than the adverse criticism it is intended to be.

There are philosophies and philosophies as well as criticisms and criticisms. There are points of view from which Shakespeare had a philosophy, and had a philosophy that is more pertinent to the work of an artist than one which conceives the ideal of philosophy to be the enclosure of experience within and domination of its varied fullness by a transcendent ideal that only reason beyond experience can conceive. There is a philosophy which holds that nature and life offer in their plenitude many meanings and are capable through imagination of many renderings. In spite of the scope and dignity of the great historic philosophic systems, an artist may be instinctively repelled by the constraint imposed by acceptance of any system. If the important thing is "not this or that system but some system," why not accept, with Shakespeare, the free and varied system of nature itself as that works and moves in experience in many and diverse organizations of value? As compared with the movement and change of nature, the form that "reason" is said to prescribe may be that of a particular tradition which is a premature and one-sided synthesis in terms of a single and narrow aspect of experience. Art that is faithful to the many potentialities of organization, centering about a variety of interests and purposes, that nature offers—as was that of Shakespeare—may have not only a fullness but a wholeness and sanity absent from a philosophy of enclosure, transcendence, and fixity. The question for the critic is the adequacy of form to matter, and not that of the presence or absence of any particular form. The value of experience is not only in the ideals it reveals, but in its power to disclose many ideals, a power more germinal and more significant than any revealed ideal, since it includes them in its stride, shatters and remakes them. One may even reverse the statement and say the value of ideals lies in the experience to which they lead.

THERE is one problem that artist, philosopher, and critic alike must face: the relation between permanence and change. The bias of philosophy in its more orthodox phase throughout the ages has been toward the unchanging, and that bias has affected the more serious critics—perhaps it is this bias which generates the judicial critic. It is overlooked that in art—and in nature as far as we can judge it through the medium of art—permanence is a function, a consequence, of changes in the relations they sustain to one another, not an antecedent principle. There is to be found in Browning's essay on Shelley what seems to me to come as near as criticism can come, to a just statement of the relations between the unified and "total"; between the varied and moving, the "individual," and the "universal," so that I shall quote it at length. "If the subjective might seem to be the ultimate requirement of every age, the objective in its strictest sense must still retain its original value. For it is with this world, as starting point and basis alike, that we shall always have to concern ourselves; the world is not to be learned and thrown aside, but reverted to and relearned. The spiritual comprehension may be infinitely subtilized but its raw material must remain."

"There is a time when the general eye has, so to speak, absorbed its full of the phenomena around it, whether spiritual or material, and desires rather to learn the exacter significance of what it possesses than to receive any augmentation of what it possesses. Then is the opportunity for the poet of loftier vision to lift his fellows, with their half-apprehensions, up to his own sphere, by intensifying the import of details and rounding out the universal meaning. The influence of such an achievement will not soon die out. A tribe of successors (Homerides) working more or less in the same spirit dwell on his discoveries and reenforce his doctrine till, at unawares, the world is found to be subsisting wholly on the shadow of a reality, on sentiments diluted from passions, on the tradition of a fact, the convention of a moral, the straw of last year's harvest. Then is the imperative call for the appearance of another sort of poet, who shall at once replace this intellectual rumination of food swallowed long ago by a supply of fresh and living swathe; getting at new substance by breaking up the assumed wholes into parts of independent and unclassed value, careless of the unknown laws for recombining them (it will be the business of yet another poet to suggest these hereafter), prodigal of objects for men's outer and not inner sight, shaping for their use a new and different creation from the last, which it displaces by the right of life over death—to endure till, in the inevitable process, its very sufficiency to itself shall require, at length, an exposition of its affinity to something higher—when the positive yet conflicting facts shall again precipitate themselves under a harmonizing law." . . .

"All the bad poetry in the world (accounted poetry, that is by its affinities) will be found to result from some one of the infinite degrees of discrepancies between the attributes of the poet's soul, occasioning a want of correspondency between his work and the varieties of nature—issuing in poetry, false under whatever form, which shows a thing not as it is to mankind generally, nor as it is to the particular describer, but as it is supposed to be for some unreal neutral mood, midway between both and of value to neither, and living its brief minute simply through the indolence of whoever accepts it in his inability to denounce a cheat."

Nature and life manifest not flux but continuity, and continuity involves forces and structures that endure through change; at least when they change, they do so more slowly than do surface incidents, and thus are, relatively, constant. But change is inevitable even though it be not for the better. It must be reckoned with. Moreover, changes are not all gradual; they culminate in sudden mutations, in transformations that at the time seem revolutionary, although in a later perspective they take their place in a logical development. All of these things hold of art. The critic, who is not as sensitive to signs of change as to the recurrent and enduring, uses the criterion of tradition without understanding its nature and appeals to the past for patterns and models without being aware that every past was once the imminent future of its past and is now the past, not absolutely, but of the change which constitutes the present.

Every critic, like every artist, has a bias, a predilection, that is bound up with the very existence of individuality. It is his task to convert it into an organ of sensitive perception and of intelligent insight, and to do so without surrendering the instinctive preference from which are derived direction and sincerity. But when his especial and selective mode of response is allowed to harden in a fixed mold, he becomes incapacitated for judging even the things to which his bias draws him. For they must be seen in the perspective of a world so multiform and so full that it contains an infinite variety of other qualities that attract and of other ways of response. Even the bewildering aspects of the world in which we live are material for art when they find the form through which they are actually expressed. A philosophy of experience that is keenly sensitive to the unnumbered interactions that are the material of experience is the philosophy from which a critic may most safely and surely draw his inspiration. How otherwise can a critic be animated by that sensitiveness to the varied movements toward completion in different total experiences that will enable him to direct the perceptions of others to a fuller and more ordered appreciation of the objective content of works of art?

For critical judgment not only grows out of the critic's experience of objective matter, and not only depends upon that for validity, but has for its office the deepening of just such experience in others. Scientific judgments not only end in increased control but for those who understand they add enlarged meanings to the things perceived and dealt with in daily contact with the world. The function of criticism is the reëducation of perception of works of art; it is an auxiliary in the process, a difficult process, of learning to see and hear. The conception that its business is to appraise, to judge in the legal and moral sense, arrests the perception of those who are influenced by the criticism that assumes this task. The moral office of criticism is performed indirectly. The individual who has an enlarged and quickened experience is one who should make for himself his own appraisal. The way to help him is through the expansion of his own experience by the work of art to which criticism is subsidiary. The moral function of art itself is to remove prejudice, do away with the scales that keep the eye from seeing, tear away the veils due to wont and custom, perfect the power to perceive. The critic's office is to further this work, performed by the object of art.

Obtrusion of his own approvals and condemnations, appraisals and ratings, is sign of failure to apprehend and perform the function of becoming a factor in the development of sincere personal experience. We lay hold of the full import of a work of art only as we go through in our own vital processes the processes the artist went through in producing the work. It is the critic's privilege to share in the promotion of this active process. His condemnation is that he so often arrests it.

# R. P. BLACKMUR

## (1904–    )

R. P. BLACKMUR was born in Springfield, Massachusetts, in 1904. From 1927 to 1934 he served as one of the editors of *Hound & Horn*. In 1937 he was awarded a Guggenheim fellowship. In addition to his two books of criticism, *The Double Agent* (1935) and *The Expense of Greatness* (1940), and his contribution to the recent volume, *Lectures in Criticism* (1949), he has published two volumes of poetry. Many of his critical essays have appeared in the leading literary journals. After serving a term as a member of the Institute for Advanced Study at Princeton, he became a Resident Fellow in Creative Writing at that university.

*The Double Agent* is typical of his method of attack: to consider not ideas in the abstract but as they are embodied in the literary work. This necessarily implies a full examination and analysis of the relation between intelligence and expression, language and communication, language and convention. In his first essay, "Notes on E. E. Cummings' Language," he sets out to disprove the romantic theory that the unintelligible—the negation of rational control in composition—is the seat of creative originality. His intent is to show that by discarding intelligence and relying on instinct and immediacy, the neo-romantic poet simply substitutes one convention for another. Blackmur has no doubt as to which convention is less desirable and nourishing. The true convention makes possible tension, interanimation within an organically unified context, whereas the cult of immediacy produces a surface without depth. Blackmur is interested in studying the relations between words and feelings and the part that intelligence plays in establishing these relations. Like I. A. Richards he believes that in a poem words should contain in suspension all the meanings which cling to them as the result of their past history, but rendered concrete in an individual context. If words in a poetic context fail to appeal to the senses, then the poem must in that respect be considered defective. The words have been transformed—or deformed—into ideas. The concrete, the sensuous, the particular, these are the gateways

378

to the art of reading the spirit. That is the central problem facing the poet: to transmute a private experience into a conventional form.

This critical method is applied with equal skill to the work of Hart Crane. Blackmur's underlying critical philosophy is that the typically great poet "is profoundly rational, integrating, and, excepting minor accidents and incapacity, a master of ultimate verbal clarity. Light, radiance, and wholeness remain the attributes of serious art."[1] He employs the method of analysis and comparison to point out how serious was Crane's failure in the use and control of poetic language. Blackmur's criticism proceeds on a rational plane, the plane, as he puts it, of competent technical analysis and appreciation, testing every judgment by the examination of minute particulars. The poet cannot work successfully without invoking the aid of technique, and the reader, too, must have a thorough awareness of technique before he can hope to read poetry with full understanding. Technical competence presupposes content, just as there can be no communicable content without a corresponding technical medium.

Though Blackmur in the thirties was in sympathy with Malcolm Cowley's political ideas, he cannot accept his Marxist exhortations as a satisfactory critical method. Similarly, in reviewing Granville Hicks' *The Great Tradition,* he exposes the signal limitations and defects of Marxism as a critical method, its tendency, for example, to judge all American literature in the light of an antecedent political theory, namely, Communism. Thus economic doctrine becomes the measure of value, orthodoxy the final test of aesthetic achievement. It is beside the point to attack Blackmur for not making use of Marxist criteria, when he is concerned primarily—indeed, first and last—with the improvement of literature, not the reform of society, which is a different and separate endeavor. In criticism, the efficient, hard-working critic concentrates on minute particulars and seeks to elucidate their meaning, their relationship to the whole, and then to determine the value of the final product thus analyzed. The artwork is the court of last resort when issues are at stake, and good criticism tends to make the reader both more curious and more intelligently perceptive in his appreciation. Invariably it is the aesthetic interest to which Blackmur devotes his full attention, refusing to be sidetracked by extraneous or peripheral considerations.

*The Double Agent* is notable chiefly for its patient analysis of the textual quality of poetry, the implications of style and language, the meanings that emerge from the content, the demands of structure and coherence, the discipline imposed by unified form. All this is made clear not in terms of generalities but by the documented elucidation of repre-

[1] R. P. Blackmur, *The Double Agent* (New York, 1935), p. 121.

sentative or significant passages of poetry. D. H. Lawrence is severely condemned for his sins against the ideal of organic form that Blackmur considers supremely important in poetry. The victim of the romantic fallacy of expressive form, Lawrence fell into the vice of self-expression, and thus dispensed with the aid and support of rational structure, formal discipline.[2]

### BIBLIOGRAPHY

#### TEXT

*The Double Agent.* New York, 1935.
*The Expense of Greatness.* New York, 1940.
"The Enabling Act of Criticism," *American Issues,* ed. by Willard Thorp, Merle Curti, and Carlos Baker. Chicago and Philadelphia, 1944, II, 876–879.
"Notes on Four Categories in Criticism," *Sewanee Review,* LIV, 576–589 (Autumn, 1946).
"A Burden for Critics," *Hudson Review,* I, 170–185 (Summer, 1948).

#### CRITICISM

Baker, Carlos, "R. P. Blackmur: A Checklist," *Princeton University Library Chronicle,* III, 99–106 (April, 1942).
Gregory, Horace, "Two Critics in Search of an Absolute," *Nation,* CXXXVIII, 189–191 (February 14, 1934).
Hyman, Stanley Edgar, "R. P. Blackmur and the Expense of Greatness," *The Armed Vision,* New York, 1948, pp. 239–271.
Schwartz, Delmore, "The Critical Method of R. P. Blackmur," *Poetry,* LIII, 28–39 (October, 1938).
Tate, Allen, "R. P. Blackmur," *Southern Review,* III, 183–198 (Summer, 1937).
West, R. B., Jr., "An Examination of Modern Critics: R. P. Blackmur," *Rocky Mountain Review,* VIII, 139–145 (Summer, 1945).

## A CRITIC'S JOB OF WORK*

CRITICISM, I take it, is the formal discourse of an amateur. When there is enough love and enough knowledge represented in the discourse it is a self-sufficient but by no means an isolated art. It witnesses constantly in its own life its interdependence with the other

---

[2] As for the meaning of the ambiguous title, *The Double Agent,* see Stanley Edgar Hyman, *The Armed Vision* (New York, 1948), p. 249.

* Reprinted from *The Double Agent* by permission of the author.

arts. It lays out the terms and parallels of appreciation from the outside in order to convict itself of internal intimacy; it names and arranges what it knows and loves, and searches endlessly with every
fresh impulse or impression for better names and more orderly arrangements. It is only in this sense that poetry (or some other art)
is a criticism of life; poetry names and arranges, and thus arrests
and transfixes its subject in a form which has a life of its own forever separate but springing from the life which confronts it. Poetry
is life at the remove of form and meaning; not life lived but life
framed and identified. So the criticism of poetry is bound to be occupied at once with the terms and modes by which the remove was
made and with the relation between—in the ambiguous stock phrase
—content and form; which is to say with the establishment and appreciation of human or moral value. It will be the underlying effort of
this essay to indicate approaches to criticism wherein these two problems—of form and value—will appear inextricable but not confused
—like the stones in an arch or the timbers in a building.

These approaches—these we wish to eulogise—are not the only
ones, nor the only good ones, nor are they complete. No approach
opens on anything except from its own point of view and in terms
of its own prepossessions. Let us set against each other for a time the
facts of various approaches to see whether there is a residue, not of
fact but of principle.

The approaches to—or the escapes from—the central work of
criticism are as various as the heresies of the Christian church, and
like them testify to occasional needs, fanatic emphasis, special interest, or intellectual pride, all flowing from and even the worst of
them enlightening the same body of insight. Every critic like every
theologian and every philosopher is a casuist in spite of himself. To
escape or surmount the discontinuity of knowledge, each resorts to
a particular heresy and makes it predominant and even omnivorous.[1]

For most minds, once doctrine is sighted and is held to be the completion of insight, the doctrinal mode of thinking seems the only one
possible. When doctrine totters it seems it can fall only into the gulf
of bewilderment; few minds risk the fall; most seize the remnants
and swear the edifice remains, when doctrine becomes intolerable
dogma.[2] All fall notwithstanding; for as knowledge itself is a fall

[1] The rashest heresy of our day and climate is that exemplified by T. S. Eliot
when he postulates an orthodoxy which exists whether anyone knows it or not.

[2] Baudelaire's sonnet *Le Gouffre* dramatises this sentiment at once as he saw it
surmounted in Pascal and as it occurred insurmountably in himself.

from the paradise of undifferentiated sensation, so equally every formula of knowledge must fall the moment too much weight is laid upon it—the moment it becomes omnivorous and pretends to be omnipotent—the moment, in short, it is taken literally. Literal knowledge is dead knowledge; and the worst bewilderment—which is always only comparative—is better than death. Yet no form, no formula, of knowledge ought to be surrendered merely because it runs the risk in bad or desperate hands of being used literally; and similarly, in our own thinking, whether it is carried to the point of formal discourse or not, we cannot only afford, we ought scrupulously to risk the use of any concept that seems propitious or helpful in getting over gaps. Only the use should be consciously provisional, speculative, and dramatic. The end-virtue of humility comes only after a long train of humiliations; and the chief labour of humbling is the constant, resourceful restoration of ignorance.

The classic contemporary example of use and misuse is attached to the name of Freud. Freud himself has constantly emphasised the provisional, dramatic character of his speculations: they are employed as imaginative illumination, to be relied on no more and no less than the sailor relies upon his buoys and beacons.[3] But the impetus of Freud was so great that a school of literalists arose with all the mad consequence of schism and heresy and fundamentalism which have no more honorable place in the scientific than the artistic imagination. Elsewhere, from one point of view, Caesarism in Rome and Berlin is only the literalist conception of the need for a positive state. So, too, the economic insights of Marxism, merely by being taken literally in their own field, are held to affect the subject and value of the arts, where actually they offer only a limited field of interest and enliven an irrelevant purpose. It is an amusing exercise —as it refreshes the terms of bewilderment and provides a common clue to the secrets of all the modes of thinking—to restore the insights of Freud and Fascism and Marxism to the terms of the Church; when the sexual drama in Freud becomes the drama of original sin, and the politics of Hitler and Lenin becomes the politics of the City of God in the sense that theology provides both the sanctions of economics and the values of culture. Controversy is in terms abso-

---

[3] Santayana's essay "A Long Way Round to Nirvana" (in *Some Turns of Thought in Modern Philosophy*) illustrates the poetic-philosophic character of Freud's insight into death by setting up its analogue in Indian philosophy; and by his comparison only adds to the stimulus of Freud.

lutely held, when the problems argued are falsely conceived because necessarily abstracted from "real" experience. The vital or fatal nexus is in interest and emotion and is established when the terms can be represented dramatically, almost, as it were, for their own sakes alone with only a pious or ritualistic regard for the doctrines in which they are clothed. The simple, and fatal, example is in the glory men attach to war; the vital, but precarious example, is in the intermittent conception of free institutions and the persistent reformulation of the myth of reason. Then the doctrines do not matter, since they are taken only for what they are worth (whatever rhetorical pretensions to the contrary) as guides and props, as aids to navigation. What does matter is the experience, the life represented and the value discovered, and both dramatised or enacted under the banner of doctrine. All banners are wrong-headed, but they make rallying points, free the impulse to cry out, and give meaning to the cry itself simply by making it seem appropriate.

It is on some analogue or parallel to these remarks alone that we understand and use the thought and the art of those whose doctrines differ from our own. We either discount, absorb, or dominate the doctrine for the sake of the life that goes with it, for the sake of what is *formed* in the progressive act of thinking. When we do more— when we refine or elaborate the abstracted notion of form—we play a different game, which has merit of its own like chess, but which applied to the world we live in produces false dilemmas like solipsism and infant damnation. There is, taking solipsism for example, a fundamental distinction. Because of the logical doctrine prepared to support it, technical philosophers employ years[4] to get around the impasse in which it leaves them; whereas men of poetic imagination merely use it for the dramatic insight it contains—as Eliot uses it in the last section of the *Wasteland;* or as, say, everyone uses the residual mythology of the Greek religion—which its priests nevertheless used as literal sanctions for blood and power.

Fortunately, there exist archetypes of unindoctrinated thinking. Let us incline our minds like reflectors to catch the light of the early Plato and the whole Montaigne. Is not the inexhaustible stimulus and fertility of the Dialogues and the Essays due as much as anything to the absence of positive doctrine? Is it not that the early Plato always holds conflicting ideas in shifting balance, presenting them

---

[4] Santayana found it necessary to resort to his only sustained labour of dialectic, *Scepticism and Animal Faith,* which, though a beautiful monument of intellectual play, is ultimately valuable for its *incidental* moral wisdom.

in contest and evolution, with victory only the last shift? Is it not that Montaigne is always making room for another idea, and implying always a third for provisional, adjudicating irony? Are not the forms of both men themselves ironic, betraying in its most intimate recesses the duplicity of every thought, pointing it out, so to speak, in the act of self-incrimination, and showing it not paled on a pin but in the buff life?. . . Such an approach, such an attempt at vivid questing, borrowed and no doubt adulterated by our own needs, is the only rational approach to the multiplication of doctrine and arrogant technologies which fills out the body of critical thinking. Anything else is a succumbing, not an approach; and it is surely the commonest of ironies to observe a man altogether out of his depth do his cause fatal harm merely because, having once succumbed to an idea, he thinks it necessary to stick to it. Thought is a beacon not a life-raft, and to confuse the functions is tragic. The tragic character of thought—as any perspective will show—is that it takes a rigid mould too soon; chooses destiny like a Calvinist, in infancy, instead of waiting slowly for old age, and hence for the most part works against the world, good sense, and its own object: as anyone may see by taking a perspective of any given idea of democracy, of justice, or the nature of the creative act.

Imaginative scepticism and dramatic irony—the modes of Montaigne and Plato—keep the mind athletic and the spirit on the stretch. Hence the juvenescence of the *Tempest,* and hence, too, perhaps, the air almost of precocity in *Back to Methuselah.* Hence, at any rate, the sustaining power of such varied works as *The Brothers Karamazoff, Cousine Bette,* and *The Magic Mountain.* Dante, whom the faithful might take to the contrary, is yet "the chief imagination of Christendom"; he took his doctrine once and for all from the Church and from St. Thomas and used it as a foil (in the painter's sense) to give recessiveness, background, and contrast. Virgil and Aristotle, Beatrice and Bertrans de Born, have in their way as much importance as St. Thomas and the Church. It was this security of reference that made Dante so much more a free spirit than were, say, Swift and Laurence Sterne. Dante had a habit (not a theory) of imagination which enabled him to dramatise with equal ardour and effect what his doctrine blessed, what it assailed, and what, at heart, it was indifferent to. Doctrine was the seed and structure of vision, and for his poems (at least to us) never more. The Divine Comedy no less than the Dialogues and the Essays is a true Speculum Mentis.

With lesser thinkers and lesser artists—and in the defective works

of the greater—we have in reading, in criticising, to supply the
scepticism and the irony, or, as may be, the imagination and the
drama, to the degree, which cannot be complete since then we should
have had no prompts, that they are lacking. We have to rub the
looking-glass clear. With Hamlet, for example, we have to struggle
and guess to bring the motive out of obscurity: a struggle which, aiming at the wrong end, the psychoanalysts have darkened with counsel.
With Shelley we have to flesh out the Platonic Ideas, as with Blake
we have to cut away, since it cannot be dramatised, all the ex-
crescence of doctrine. With Baudelaire we have sometimes to
struggle with and sometimes to suppress the problem of belief, working out the irony implicit in either attitude. Similarly, with a writer
like Pascal, in order to get the most out of him, in order to compose
an artistic judgment, we must consider such an idea as that of the
necessity of the wager, not solemnly as Pascal took it, but as a
dramatised possibility, a savage, but provisional irony; and we need
to show that the scepticisms of Montaigne and Pascal are not at all
the same thing—that where one produced serenity the other produced
excruciation.

Again, speaking of Andre Gide, we should remind ourselves not
that he has been the apologist of homosexuality, not that he has become a communist, but that he is par excellence the French puritan
chastened by the wisdom of the body, and that he has thus an acutely
scrupulous ethical sensibility. It is by acknowledging the sensibility
that we feel the impact of the apologetics and the political conversion.
Another necessity in the apprehension of Gide might be put as the
recognition of similarity in difference of the precocious small boys
in Dostoieffsky and Gide, e.g. Kolya in *Karamazoff* and young
George in *The Counterfeiters:* they are small, cruel engines, all
naked sensibility and no scruple, demoniacally possessed, and used
to keep things going. And these in turn may remind us of another
writer who had a predilection for presenting the *terrible* quality of
the young intelligence: of Henry James, of the children in *The Turn
of the Screw,* of Maisie, and all the rest, all beautifully efficient
agents of dramatic judgment and action, in that they take all things
seriously for themselves, with the least prejudice of preparation,
candidly, with an intelligence life has not yet violated.

Such feats of agility and attention as these remarks illustrate
seem facile and even commonplace, and from facile points of view
there is no need to take them otherwise. Taken superficially they
provide escape from the whole labour of specific understanding; or,

worse, they provide an easy vault from casual interpretation to an omnivorous world-view. We might take solemnly and as of universal application the two notions of demonic possession and inviolate intelligence in the children of Gide, Dostoieffsky, and James, and on that frail nexus build an unassailable theory of the sources of art, wisdom, and value; unassailable because affording only a stereotyped vision, like that of conservative capitalism, without reference in the real world. The maturity of Shakespeare and of Gertrude Stein would then be found on the same childish level.

But we need not go so far in order to draw back. The modes of Montaigne and Plato contain their own safety. Any single insight is good only at and up to a certain point of development and not beyond, which is to say that it is a provisional and tentative and highly selective approach to its field. Furthermore, no observation, no collection of observations, ever tells the whole story; there is always room for more, and at the hypothetical limit of attention and interest there will always remain, quite untouched, the thing itself. Thus the complex character—I say nothing of the value—of the remarks above reveals itself. They flow from a dramatic combination of all the skills and conventions of the thinking mind. They are commonplace only as criticism—as an end-product or function. Like walking, criticism is a pretty nearly universal art; both require a constant intricate shifting and catching of balance; neither can be questioned much in process; and few perform either really well. For either a new terrain is fatiguing and awkward, and in our day most men prefer paved walks or some form of rapid transit—some easy theory or outmastering dogma. A good critic keeps his criticism from becoming either instinctive or vicarious, and the labour of his understanding is always specific, like the art which he examines; and he knows that the sum of his best work comes only to the pedagogy of elucidation and appreciation. He observes facts and he delights in discriminations. The object remains, and should remain, itself, only made more available and seen in a clearer light. The imagination of Dante is for us only equal to what we can know of it at a given time.

Which brings us to what, as T. S. Eliot would say,[5] I have been

---

[5] . . . that when "morals cease to be a matter of tradition and orthodoxy—that is, of the habits of the community formulated, corrected, and elevated by the continuous thought and direction of the Church—and when each man is to elaborate his own, then *personality* becomes a thing of alarming importance." (*After Strange Gods*.) Thus Mr. Eliot becomes one of those viewers-with-alarm whose next step forward is the very hysteria of disorder they wish to escape. The hysteria of institutions is more dreadful than that of individuals.

leading up to all the time, and what has indeed been said several times by the way. Any rational approach is valid to literature and may be properly called critical which fastens at any point upon the work itself. The utility of a given approach depends partly upon the strength of the mind making it and partly upon the recognition of the limits appropriate to it. Limits may be of scope, degree, or relevance, and may be either plainly laid out by the critic himself, or may be determined by his readers; and it is, by our argument, the latter case that commonly falls, since an active mind tends to overestimate the scope of its tools and to take as necessary those doctrinal considerations which habit has made seem instinctive. No critic is required to limit himself to a single approach, nor is he likely to be able to do so; facts cannot be exhibited without comment, and comment involves the generality of the mind. Furthermore, a consciously complex approach like that of Kenneth Burke or T. S. Eliot, by setting up parallels of reference, affords a more flexible, more available, more stimulating standard of judgment—though of course at a greater risk of prejudice—than a single approach. What produces the evil of stultification and the malice of controversy is the confused approach, when the limits are not seen because they tend to cancel each other out, and the driving power becomes emotional.

The worse evil of fanatic falsification—of arrogant irrationality and barbarism in all its forms—arises when a body of criticism is governed by an *idée fixe,* a really exaggerated heresy, when a notion of genuine but small scope is taken literally as of universal application. This is the body of tendentious criticism where, since something is assumed proved before the evidence is in, distortion, vitiation, and absolute assertion become supreme virtues. I cannot help feeling that such writers as Maritain and Massis—no less than Nordau before them—are tendentious in this sense. But even here, in this worst order of criticism, there is a taint of legitimacy. Once we reduce, in a man like Irving Babbitt, the magnitude of application of such notions as the inner check and the higher will, which were for Babbitt paramount,—that is, when we determine the limits within which he really worked—then the massive erudition and acute observation with which his work is packed become permanently available.

And there is no good to be got in objecting to and disallowing those orders of criticism which have an ulterior purpose. Ulterior is not in itself a pejorative, but only so when applied to an enemy. Since criticism is not autonomous—not a light but a process of elucidation—it cannot avoid discovering constantly within itself a purpose or purposes ulterior in the good sense. The danger is in not knowing what is ulterior and what is not, which is much the same as the cognate danger in the arts themselves. The arts serve purposes beyond themselves; the purposes of what they dramatise or represent at that remove from the flux which gives them order and meaning and value; and to deny those purposes is like asserting that the function of a handsaw is to hang above a bench and that to cut wood is to belittle it. But the purposes are varied and so bound in his subject that the artist cannot always design for them. The critic, if that is his bent, may concern himself with those purposes or with some one among them which obsess him; but he must be certain to distinguish between what is genuinely ulterior to the works he examines and what is merely irrelevant; and he must further not assume except within the realm of his special argument that other purposes either do not exist or are negligible or that the works may not be profitably discussed apart from ulterior purposes and as examples of dramatic possibility alone.

## II

Three examples of contemporary criticism primarily concerned with the ulterior purposes of literature should, set side by side, exhibit both the defects and the unchastened virtues of that approach; though they must do so only tentatively and somewhat invidiously —with an exaggeration for effect. Each work is assumed to be a representative ornament of its kind, carrying within it the seeds of its own death and multiplication. Let us take then, with an eye sharpened by the dangers involved, Santayana's essay on Lucretius (in *Three Philosophical Poets*), Van Wyck Brooks' *Pilgrimage of Henry James,* and Granville Hicks' *The Great Tradition.* Though that of the third is more obvious in our predicament, the urgency in the approach is equal in all three.

Santayana's essay represents a conversion or transvaluation of an actually poetic ordering of nature to the terms of a moral philosophy which, whatever its own responsibilities, is free of the special responsibility of poetry. So ably and so persuasively is it composed, his picture seems complete and to contain so much of what was important in Lucretius that *De Rerum Natura* itself can be left behind. The philosophical nature of the insight, its moral scope and defect, the influence upon it of the Democritan atom, once grasped intellectually as Santayana shows us how to grasp them, seem a good substitute for the poem and far more available. But, what Santayana remembers but does not here emphasise since it was beyond his immediate interest, there is no vicar for poetry on earth. Poetry is idiom, a special and fresh saying, and cannot for its life be said otherwise; and there is, finally, as much difference between words used about a poem and the poem as there is between words used about a painting and the painting. The gap is absolute. Yet I do not mean to suggest that Santayana's essay—that any philosophical criticism —is beside the point. It is true that the essay may be taken as a venture in philosophy for its own sake, but it is also true that it reveals a body of facts about an ulterior purpose in Lucretius' poem—doubtless the very purpose Lucretius himself would have chosen to see enhanced. If we return to the poem it will be warmer as the facts come alive in the verse. The re-conversion comes naturally in this instance in that, through idioms differently construed but equally imaginative, philosophy and poetry both buttress and express moral value. The one enacts or represents in the flesh what the other reduces to principle or raises to the ideal. The only precaution the critic of poetry need take is negative: that neither poetry nor philosophy can ever fully satisfy the other's purposes, though each may seem to do so if taken in an ulterior fashion. The relationship is mutual but not equivalent.

When we turn deliberately from Santayana on Lucretius to Van Wyck Brooks on Henry James, we turn from the consideration of the rational ulterior purpose of art to the consideration of the irrational underlying predicament of the artist himself, not only as it predicts his art and is reflected in it, but also, and in effect predominantly, as it represents the conditioning of nineteenth century American culture. The consideration is sociological, the method of approach that of literary psychology, and the burden obsessive. The conversion is from literary to biographical values. Art is taken not as the objectification or mirroring of social experience but as a personal expression and escape-fantasy of the artist's personal life in dramatic extension. The point for emphasis is that the cultural situation of Henry James' America stultified the expression and made every escape ineffectual—even that of Europe. This theme— the private tragedy of the unsuccessful artist—was one of Henry James' own; but James saw it as typical or universal—as a characteristic tragedy of the human spirit—illustrated, as it happened for him, against the Anglo-American background. Brooks, taking the same theme, raises it to an obsession, an omnivorous concept, under which all other themes can be subsumed. Applied to American cultural history, such obsessive thinking is suggestive in the very exaggeration of its terms, and applied to the private predicament of Henry James the man it dramatically emphasises—uses for all and more than it is worth—an obvious conflict that tormented him. As history or as biography the book is a persuasive imaginative picture, although clearly not the only one to be seen. Used as a nexus between James the man and the novels themselves, the book has only possible relevance and cannot be held as material. *Hamlet,* by a similar argument, could be shown to be an unsuccessful expression of Shakespeare's personality. To remain useful in the field of literary criticism, Brooks' notions ought to be kept parallel to James' novels but never allowed to merge with them. The corrective, the proof of the gap, is perhaps in the great air of freedom and sway of mastery that pervades the Prefaces James wrote to his collected edition. For James art was enough because it moulded and mirrored and valued all the life he knew. What Brooks' parallel strictures can do is to help us decide from another point of view whether to choose the values James dramatised. They cannot affect or elucidate but rather —if the gap is closed by will—obfuscate the values themselves.

In short, the order of criticism of which Brooks is a masterly exponent, and which we may call the psycho-sociological order, is primarily and in the end concerned less with the purposes, ulterior or not, of the arts than with some of the ulterior *uses* to which the arts can be appropriately put. Only what is said in the meantime, by the way—and does not depend upon the essence of argument but only accompanies it—can be applied to the arts themselves. There is nothing, it should be added, in Brooks' writings to show that he believes otherwise or would claim more; he is content with that scope and degree of value to which his method and the strength of his mind limit him; and his value is the greater and more urgent for that.

Such tacit humility, such implicit admission of contingency, are not immediate characteristics of Granville Hicks' *The Great Tradition,* though they may, so serious is his purpose, be merely virtues of which he deliberately, for the time being and in order to gain his point, deprives himself of the benefit. If that is so, however expedient his tactics may seem on the short view they will defeat him on the long. But let us examine the book on the ground of our present concern alone. Like Brooks, Hicks presents an interpretation of Ameri-

BLACKMUR                                    391

can literature since the Civil War, dealing with the whole body
rather than single figures. Like Brooks he has a touchstone in an
obsessive idea, but where we may say that Brooks *uses* his idea—as
we think for more than it is worth—we must say that Hicks is
victimised by his idea to the point where the travail of judgment is
suspended and becomes the mere reiteration of a formula. He judges
literature as it expressed or failed to express the economic conflict of
classes sharpened by the industrial revolution, and he judges individual writers as they used or did not use an ideology resembling the
Marxist analysis as prime clue to the clear representation of social
drama. Thus Howells comes off better than Henry James, and Frank
Norris better than Mark Twain, and, in our own day, Dos Passos is
stuck on a thin eminence that must alarm him.

Controversy is not here a profitable exercise, but it may be said for
the sake of the record that although every period of history presents
a class struggle, some far more acute than our own, the themes of
great art have seldom lent themselves to propaganda for an economic
insight, finding, as it happened, religious, moral, or psychological—
that is to say, interpretative—insights more appropriate impulses. If
*Piers Plowman* dealt with the class struggle, *The Canterbury Tales*
did not, and Hicks would be hard put, if he looked sharp, to make
out a better case of social implication in Dostoieffsky than in Henry
James.

What vitiates *The Great Tradition* is its tendentiousness. Nothing
could be more exciting, nothing more vital, than a book by Hicks
which discovered and examined the facts of a literature whose major
theme hung on an honest, dramatic view of the class struggle—and
there is indeed such a literature now emerging from the depression.
And on the other hand it would be worth while to have Hicks sharpen
his teeth on all the fraudulent or pseudo art which actually slanders
the terms of the class and every other struggle.

The book with which he presents us performs a very different
operation. There is an initial hortatory assumption that American
literature ought to represent the class struggle from a Marxist view
point, and that it ought thus to be the spur and guide to political action. Proceeding, the point is either proved or the literature dismissed
and its authors slandered. Hicks is not disengaging for emphasis and
contemporary need an ulterior purpose; he is not writing criticism
at all; he is writing a fanatic's history and a casuist's polemic, with
the probable result—which is what was meant by suggesting above

that he had misconceived his tactics—that he will convert no one who retains the least love of literature or the least knowledge of the themes which engage the most of life. It should be emphasised that there is no more quarrel with Hicks' economic insight as such than there was with the insights of Santayana and Van Wyck Brooks. The quarrel is deeper. While it is true and good that the arts may be used to illustrate social propaganda—though it is not a great use—you can no more use an economic insight as your chief critical tool than you can make much out of the Mass by submitting the doctrine of transubstantiation to chemical analysis.

These three writers have one great formal fact in common, which they illustrate as differently as may be. They are concerned with the separable content of literature, with what may be said without consideration of its specific setting and apparition in a form; which is why, perhaps, all three leave literature so soon behind. The quantity of what can be said directly about the content alone of a given work of art is seldom great, but the least saying may be the innervation of an infinite intellectual structure, which, however valuable in itself, has for the most part only an asserted relation with the works from which it springs. The sense of continuous relationship, of sustained contact, with the works nominally in hand is rare and when found uncommonly exhilarating; it is the fine object of criticism: as it seems to put us in direct possession of the principles whereby the works move without injuring or disintegrating the body of the works themselves. This sense of intimacy by inner contact cannot arise from methods of approach which hinge on seized separable content. We have constantly—if our interest is really in literature—to prod ourselves back, to remind ourselves that there was a poem, a play, or a novel of some initial and we hope terminal concern, or we have to falsify facts and set up fictions[6] to the effect that no matter what we are saying we are really talking about art after all. The question must often be whether the prodding and reminding is worth the labour, whether we might not better assign the works that require it to a different category than that of criticism.

---

[6] Such a fiction, if not consciously so contrived, is the fiction of the organic continuity of all literature as expounded by T. S. Eliot in his essay, "Tradition and the Individual Talent." The locus is famous and represents that each new work of art slightly alters the relationships among the whole order of existing works. The notion has truth, but it is a mathematical truth and has little relevance to the arts. Used as Eliot uses it, it is an experimental conceit and pushes the mind forward. Taken seriously it is bad constitutional law, in the sense that it would provoke numberless artificial and insoluble problems.

## III

Similar strictures and identical precautions are necessary in thinking of other, quite different approaches to criticism, where if there are no ulterior purposes to allow for there are other no less limiting features—there are certainly such, for example, for me in thinking of my own. The ulterior motive, or the limiting feature, which ever it is, is a variable constant. One does not always know what it is, nor what nor how much work it does; but one always knows it is there—for strength or weakness. It may be only the strength of emphasis —which is necessarily distortion; or it may be the worse strength of a simplifying formula, which skeletonises and transforms what we want to recognise in the flesh. It may be only the weakness of what is unfinished, undeveloped, or unseen—the weakness that follows on emphasis; or it may be the weakness that shows when pertinent things are deliberately dismissed or ignored, which is the corresponding weakness of the mind strong in formula. No mind can avoid distortion and formula altogether, nor would wish to; but most minds rush to the defence of qualities they think cannot be avoided, and that, in itself, is an ulterior motive, a limiting feature of the mind that rushes. I say nothing of one's personal prepossessions, of the damage of one's private experience, of the malice and false tolerance they inculcate into judgment. I know that my own essays suffer variously, but I cannot bring myself to specify the indulgences I would ask; mostly, I hope, that general indulgence which consists in the task of bringing my distortions and emphases and opinions into balance with other distortions, other emphases, and better opinions.

But rather than myself, let us examine briefly, because of their differences from each other and from the three critics already handled, the modes of approach to the act of criticism and habits of critical work of I. A. Richards, Kenneth Burke, and S. Foster Damon. It is to characterise them and to judge the *character* of their work—its typical scope and value—that we want to examine them. With the objective validity of their varying theories we are not much here concerned. Objective standards of criticism, as we hope them to exist at all, must have an existence anterior and superior to the practice of particular critics. The personal element in a given critic— what he happens to know and happens to be able to understand— is strong or obstinate enough to reach into his aesthetic theories; and as most critics do not have the coherence of philosophers it seems doubtful if any outsider could ever reach the same conclusions as the critic did by adopting his aesthetics. Aesthetics sometimes seems only as implicit in the practice of criticism as the atomic physics is present in sunlight when you feel it.

But some critics deliberately expand the theoretic phase of every practical problem. There is a tendency to urge the scientific principle and the statistical method, and in doing so to bring in the whole assorted world of thought. That Mr. Richards, who is an admirable critic and whose love and knowledge of poetry are incontestable, is a victim of the expansiveness of his mind in these directions, is what characterises, and reduces, the scope of his work as literary criticism. It is possible that he ought not to be called a literary critic at all. If we list the titles of his books we are in a quandary: *The Foundations of Aesthetics, The Meaning of Meaning* (these with C. K. Ogden), *The Principles of Literary Criticism, Science and Poetry, Practical Criticism, Mencius on the Mind,* and *Coleridge on Imagination.* The apparatus is so vast, so labyrinthine, so inclusive—and the amount of actual literary criticism is so small that it seems almost a by-product instead of the central target. The slightest volume, physically, *Science and Poetry,* contains proportionally the most literary criticism, and contains, curiously, his one obvious failure in appreciation—since amply redressed—, his misjudgment of the nature of Yeats' poetry. His work is for the most part *about* a department of the mind which includes the pedagogy of sensibility and the practice of literary criticism. The matters he investigates are the problems of belief, of meaning, of communication, of the nature of controversy, and of poetic language as the supreme mode of imagination. The discussion of these problems is made to focus for the most part on poetry because poetry provides the only great monuments of imagination available to verbal imagination. His bottom contention might I think be put as this: that words have a synergical power, in the realms of feeling, emotion, and value, to create a reality, or the sense of it, not contained in the words separately; and that the power and the reality as experienced in great poetry make the chief source of meaning and value for the life we live. This contention I share; except that I should wish to put on the same level, as sources of meaning and value, modes of imagination that have no medium in words—though words may call on them—and are not susceptible of verbal reformulation: the modes of great acting, architecture, music, and painting. Thus I can assent to Mr. Richards' positive statement of the task of criticism, because I can add to it positive tasks in analogous fields: "To recall that poetry is the supreme use of language, man's chief co-ordinating instrument, in the service of the most integral purposes of life; and to explore, with thoroughness, the intricacies of the modes of language as working modes of the mind." But I want this criticism, engaged in this task, constantly to be confronted with examples of poetry, and I want it so for the very practical purpose of assisting in pretty immediate appreciation of the use, meaning, and value of the language in that particular poetry. I want it to assist in doing for me what it actually assists Mr. Richards in doing, whatever that is, when he is reading poetry for its own sake.

Mr. Richards wants it to do that, too, but he wants it to do a great deal else first. Before it gets to actual poetry (from which it is said to spring) he wants literary criticism to become something else and much more: he wants it to become, indeed, the master department of the mind. As we become aware of the scope of poetry, we see, according to Mr. Richards that "the study of the modes of language becomes, as it attempts to be thorough, the most fundamental and extensive of all inquiries. It is no preliminary or preparation for other profounder studies. . . . The very formation of the objects which these studies propose to examine takes place through the processes (of which imagination and fancy are modes) by which the words they use acquire their meanings. Criticism is the science of these meanings. . . . Critics in the future must have a theoretical equipment which has not been felt to be necessary in the past. . . . But the critical equipment will not be *primarily* philosophical. It will be rather a command *of the methods of general linguistic analysis*."[7] I think we may take it that *Mencius on the Mind* is an example of the kind of excursion on which Mr. Richards would lead us. It is an excursion into multiple definition, and it is a good one if that is where you want to go and are in no hurry to come back: you learn the enormous variety and complexity of the operations possible in the process of verbally describing and defining brief passages of imaginative language and the equal variety and complexity of the result; you learn the practical impossibility of verbally ascertaining what an author means—and you hear nothing of the other ways of apprehending meaning at all. The instance is in the translation of Mencius, because Mr. Richards happens to be interested in Mencius, and because it is easy to see the difficulties of translating Chinese; but the principles and method of application would work as well on passages

7 All quoted material is from the last four pages of *Coleridge on Imagination*.

from Milton or Rudyard Kipling. The real point of Mr. Richards' book is the impossibility of understanding, short of a lifetime's analysis and compensation, the mechanism of meaning in even a small body of work. There is no question of the exemplary value and stimulus of Mr. Richards' work; but there is no question either that few would care to emulate him for any purpose of literary criticism. In the first place it would take too long, and in the second he does not answer the questions literary criticism would put. The literal adoption of Mr. Richards' approach to literary criticism would stultify the very power it was aimed to enhance—the power of imaginative apprehension, of imaginative coördination of varied and separate elements. Mr. Richards' work is something to be aware of, but deep awareness is the limit of use. It is notable that in his admirable incidental criticism of such poets as Eliot, Lawrence, Yeats, and Hopkins, Mr. Richards does not himself find it necessary to be more than aware of his own doctrines of linguistic analysis. As philosophy from Descartes to Bradley transformed itself into a study of the modes of knowing, Mr. Richards would transform literary criticism into the science of linguistics. Epistlemology is a great subject, and so is linguistics; but they come neither in first nor final places; the one is only a fragment of wisdom and the other only a fraction of the means of understanding. Literary criticism is not a science—though it may be the object of one; and to try to make it one is to turn it upside down. Right side up, Mr. Richards' contribution shrinks in weight and dominion but remains intact and preserves its importance. We may conclude that it was the newness of his view that led him to exaggerate it, and we ought to add the probability that had he not exaggerated it we should never have seen either that it was new or valuable at all.

From another point of view than that of literary criticism, and as a contribution to a psychological theory of knowledge, Mr. Richards' work is not heretical, but is integral and integrating, and especially when it incorporates poetry into its procedure; but from our point of view the heresy is profound—and is far more distorting than the heresies of Santayana, Brooks, and Hicks, which carry with them obviously the impetus for their correction. Because it is possible to apply scientific methods to the language of poetry, and because scientific methods engross their subject matter, Mr. Richards places the whole burden of criticism in the application of a scientific approach, and asserts it to be an implement for the judgement of poetry. Actually, it can handle only the language and its words and cannot touch—except by assertion—the imaginative product of the words which is poetry: which is the object revealed or elucidated by criticism. Criticism must be concerned, first and last—whatever comes between—with the poem as it is read and as what it represents is felt. As no amount of physics and physiology can explain the *feeling* of things seen as green or even certify their existence, so no amount of linguistic analysis can explain the *feeling* or existence of a poem. Yet the physics in the one case and the linguistics in the other may be useful both to the poet and the reader. It may be useful, for example, in extracting the facts of meaning from a poem, to show that, whether the poet was aware of it or not, the semantic history of a word was so and so; but only if the semantics can be resolved into the ambiguities and precisions created by the poem. Similarly with any branch of linguistics; and similarly with the applications of psychology—Mr. Richards' other emphasis. No statistical description can either explain or demean a poem unless the description is translated back to the imaginative apprehension or feeling which must have taken place without it. The light of science is parallel or in the background where feeling or meaning is concerned. The Oedipus complex does not explain *Oedipus Rex;* not that Mr. Richards would think it did. Otherwise he could not believe that "poetry is the supreme use of language" and more, could not convey in his comments on T. S. Eliot's *Ash Wednesday* the actuality of his belief that poetry is the supreme use.

It is the interest and fascination of Mr. Richards' work in reference to different levels of sensibility, including the poetic, that has given him both a wide and a penetrating influence. No literary critic can escape his influence; an influence that stimulates the mind as much as anything by showing the sheer excitement as well as the profundity of the problems of language—many of which he has himself made genuine problems, at least for readers of poetry: an influence, obviously, worth deliberately incorporating by reducing it to one's own size and needs. In T. S. Eliot the influence is conspicuous if slight. Mr. Kenneth Burke is considerably indebted, partly directly to Mr. Richards, partly to the influences which acted upon Mr. Richards (as Bentham's theory of Fictions) and partly to the frame of mind which helped mould them both. But Mr. Burke is clearly a different person—and different from anyone writing today; and the virtues, the defects, and the élan of his criticism are his own.

Some years ago, when Mr. Burke was an animating influence on the staff of *The Dial,* Miss Marianne Moore published a poem in that magazine called "Picking and Choosing" which contained the following lines.

<blockquote>
and Burke is a

psychologist—of acute and raccoon-

like curiosity. *Summa diligentia;*

to the humbug, whose name is so amusing—very young

and ve-

ry rushed, Caesar crossed the Alps on the 'top of a

*diligence.'* We are not daft about the meaning but this

familiarity

with wrong meanings puzzles one.
</blockquote>

In the index of Miss Moore's *Observations,* we find under Burke that the reference is to Edmund, but it is really to Kenneth just the same. There is no acuter curiosity than Mr. Burke's engaged in associating the meanings, right and wrong, of the business of literature with the business of life and vice versa. No one has a greater awareness —not even Mr. Richards—of the important part wrong meanings play in establishing the consistency of right ones. The writer of whom he reminds us, for the buoyancy and sheer remarkableness of his speculations, is Charles Santiago Saunders Peirce; one is enlivened by them without any *necessary* reference to their truth; hence they have truth for their own purposes, that is, for their own uses. Into what these purposes or uses are it is our present business to inquire.

As Mr. Richards in fact uses literature as a springboard or source for a scientific method of a philosophy of value, Mr. Burke uses literature, not only as a springboard but also as a resort or home, for a philosophy or psychology of moral possibility. Literature is the hold-all and the persuasive form for the patterns of possibility. In literature we see unique possibilities enacted, actualised, and in the moral and psychological philosophies we see the types of possibility generalised, see their abstracted, convertible forms. In some literature, and in some aspects of most literature of either great magnitude or great possibility, we see, so to speak, the enactment or dramatic representation of the type or patterns. Thus Mr. Burke can make a thrilling intellectual pursuit of the subintelligent writing of Erskine Caldwell: where he shows that Caldwell gains a great effect of humanity by putting in *none himself,* appealing to the reader's common stock: i.e., what is called for so desperately by the pattern of the story must needs be generously supplied. Exactly as thrilling is his demonstration of the great emotional role of the outsider as played in the supremely intelligent works of Thomas Mann and André Gide. His common illustrations of the pervasive spread of symbolic pattern are drawn from Shakespeare and from the type of the popular or pulp press. I think that on the whole his method could be applied with equal fruitfulness either to Shakespeare, Dashiell Hammet, or Marie Corelli; as indeed he does apply it with equal force both to the field of anarchic private morals and to the outline of a secular conversion to Communism—as in, respectively, *Toward a Better Life* and *Permanence and Change*.

The real harvest that we barn from Mr. Burke's writings is his presentation of the types of ways the mind works in the written word. He is more interested in the psychological means of the meaning, and how it might mean (and often really does) something else, than in the meaning itself. Like Mr. Richards, but for another purpose, he is engaged largely in the meaning of meaning, and is therefore much bound up with considerations of language, but on the plane of emotional and intellectual patterns rather than on the emotional plane; which is why his essays deal with literature (or other writings) as it dramatises or unfolds character (a character is a pattern of emotions and notions) rather than with lyric or meditative poetry which is Mr. Richards' field. So we find language containing felt character as well as felt coördination. The representation of character, and of aspiration and symbol, must always be rhetorical; and therefore we find that for Mr. Burke the rightly rhetorical is the profoundly hortatory. Thus literature may be seen as an inexhaustible reservoir of moral or character philosophies in action.

It is the technique of such philosophies that Mr. Burke explores, as he pursues it through curiosities of development and conversion and duplicity; it is the technique of the notions that may be put into or taken out of literature, but it is only a part of the technique of literature itself. The final reference is to the psychological and moral possibilities of the mind, and these certainly do not exhaust the technique or the reality of literature. The reality in literature is an object of contemplation and of feeling, like the reality of a picture or a cathedral, not a route of speculation. If we remember this and make the appropriate reductions here as elsewhere, Mr. Burke's essays become as pertinent to literary criticism as they are to the general ethical play of the mind. Otherwise they become too much a methodology for its own sake on the one hand, and too much a philosophy at one remove on the other. A man writes as he can; but those who use his writings have the further responsibility of redefining their scope, an operation (of which Mr. Burke is a master) which alone uses them to the full.

It is in relation to these examples which I have so unjustly held up of the philosophical, the sociological or historical, the tendentious, the semasiological, and the psychological approaches to criticism that I wish to examine an example of what composes, after all, the great bulk of serious writings about literature: a work of literary scholarship. Upon scholarship all other forms of literary criticism depend, so long as they are criticism, in much the same way that architecture depends on engineering. The great editors of the last century—men such as Dyce and Skeat and Gifford and Furness—performed work as valuable to the use of literature, and with far less complement of harm, as men like Hazlitt and Arnold and Pater. Scholarship, being bent on the collection, arrangement, and scrutiny of facts, has the positive advantage over other forms of criticism that it is a coöperative labour, and may be completed and corrected by subsequent scholars; and it has the negative advantage that it is not bound to investigate the mysteries of meaning or to connect literature with other departments of life—it has only to furnish the factual materials for such investigations and connexions. It is not surprising to find that the great scholars are sometimes good critics, though usually in restricted fields; and it is a fact, on the other hand, that the great critics are themselves either good scholars or know how to take great advantage of scholarship. Perhaps we may put it that for the most part dead critics remain alive in us to the extent that they form part of our scholarship. It is Dr. Johnson's statements of fact that we preserve of him as a critic; his opinions have long since become a part of that imaginative structure, his personality. A last fact about scholarship is this, that so far as its conclusions are sound they are subject to use and digestion not debate by those outside the fold. And of bad scholarship as of bad criticism we have only to find means to minimise what we cannot destroy.

It is difficult to find an example of scholarship pure and simple, of high character, which can be made to seem relevant to the discussion in hand. What I want is to bring into the discussion the omnipresence of scholarship as a background and its immediate and necessary availability to every other mode of approach. What I want is almost anonymous. Failing that, I choose S. Foster Damon's *William Blake* (as I might have taken J. L. Lowes' *Road to Xanadu*) which, because of its special subject matter, brings its scholarship a little nearer the terms of discussion than a Shakespeare commentary would have done. The scholar's major problem with Blake happened to be one which many scholars could not handle, some refused to see, and some fumbled. A great part of Blake's meaning is not open to ordinarily well-instructed readers, but must be brought out by the detailed solution of something very like an enormous and enormously complicated acrostic puzzle. Not only earnest scrutiny of the poems as printed, but also a study of Blake's reading, a reconstruction of habits of thought, and an industrious piecing together into a consistent key of thousands of clues throughout the work, were necessary before many even of the simplest appearing poems could be explained. It is one thing to explain a mystical poet, like Crashaw, who was attached to a recognised church, and difficult enough; but it is a far more difficult thing to explain a mystical poet like Blake, who was so much an eclectic in his sources that his mystery as well as his apprehension of it was practically his own. All Mr. Damon had to go on besides the texts, and the small body of previous scholarship that was pertinent, were the general outlines of insight to which all mystics apparently adhere. The only explanation would be in the facts of what Blake meant to mean when he habitually said one thing in order to hide and enhance another; and in order to be convincing—poetry being what it is—the facts adduced had to be self-evident. It is not a question here whether the mystery enlightened was worth it. The result for emphasis is that Mr. Damon made Blake exactly what he seemed least to be, perhaps the most intellectually consistent of the greater poets in English. Since the chief weapons used are the extended facts of scholarship, the picture Mr. Damon produced cannot be destroyed even though later and other scholarship modifies, re-arranges, or adds to it with different or other facts. The only suspicion that might attach is that the picture is too consistent and that the facts are made to tell too much, and direct, but instructed, apprehension not enough.

My point about Mr. Damon's work is typical and double. First, that the same sort of work, the adduction of ultimately self-evident facts, can be done and must be done in other kinds of poetry than Blake's. Blake is merely an extreme and obvious example of an unusually difficult poet who hid his facts on purpose. The work must be done to the appropriate degree of digging out the facts in all orders of poetry—and especially perhaps in contemporary poetry, where we tend to let the work go either because it seems too easy or because it seems supererogatory. Self-evident facts are paradoxically the hardest to come by; they are not evident till they are seen; yet the meaning of a poem—the part of it which is intellectually formulable —must invariably depend on this order of facts, the facts about the meanings of the elements aside from their final meaning in combination. The rest of the poem, what it is, what it shows, its final value as a created emotion, its meanings, if you like, *as* a poem, cannot in the more serious orders of poetry develop itself to the full without this factual or intellectual meaning to show the way. The other point is already made, and has been made before in this essay, but it may still be emphasised. Although the scholarly account is indispensable it does not tell the whole story. It is only the basis and perhaps ultimately the residue of all the other stories. But it must be seen to first.

My own approach, such as it is, and if it can be named, does not tell the whole story either; the reader is conscientiously left with the poem with the real work yet to do; and I wish to advance it—as indeed I have been advancing it *seriatim*—only in connection with the reduced and compensated approaches I have laid out; and I expect, too, that if my approach is used at all it will require its own reduction as well as its compensations. Which is why this essay has taken its present form, preferring for once, in the realm of theory and apologetics, the implicit to the explicit statement. It is, I suppose, an approach to literary criticism—to the discourse of an amateur—primarily through the technique, in the widest sense of that word, of the examples handled; technique on the plane of words and even of linguistics in Mr. Richards' sense, but also technique on the plane of intellectual and emotional patterns in Mr. Burke's sense, and technique, too, in that there is a technique of securing and arranging and representing a fundamental view of life. The advantage of the technical approach is I think double. It readily admits other approaches and is anxious to be complemented by them. Furthermore, in a sense, it is able to incorporate the technical aspect, which always exists, of what is secured by other approaches—as I have argued elsewhere that so unpromising a matter as T. S. Eliot's religious convictions may be profitably considered as a dominant element in his technique of revealing the actual. The second advantage of the technical approach is a consequence of the first; it treats of nothing in literature except in its capacity of reduction to literary fact, which is where it resembles scholarship, only passing beyond it in that its facts are usually further into the heart of the literature than the facts of most scholarship. Aristotle, curiously, is here the type and master; as the *Poetics* is nothing but a collection and explanation of the facts of Greek poetry, it is the factual aspect that is invariably produced. The rest of the labour is in the effort to find understandable terms to fit the composition of the facts. After all, it is only the facts about a poem, a play, a novel, that can be reduced to tractable form, talked about, and examined; the rest is the product of the facts, from the technical point of view, and not a product but the thing itself from its own point of view. The rest, whatever it is, can only be known, not talked about.

But facts are not simple or easy to come at; not all the facts will appear to one mind, and the same facts appear differently in the light of different minds. No attention is undivided, no single approach sufficient, no predilection guaranteed, when facts or what their arrangements create are in question. In short, for the arts, *mere* technical scrutiny of any order, is not enough without the direct apprehension—which may come first or last—to which all scrutinies that show facts contribute.

It may be that there are principles that cover both the direct apprehension and the labour of providing modes for the understanding of the expressive arts. If so, they are Socratic and found within, and subject to the fundamental scepticism as in Montaigne. There must be seeds, let us say—seeds, germs, beginning forms upon which I can rely and to which I resort. When I use a word, an image, a notion, there must be in its small nodular apparent form, as in the peas I am testing on my desk, at least prophetically, the whole future growth, the whole harvested life; and not rhetorically nor in a formula, but stubbornly, pervasively, heart-hidden, materially, in both the anterior and the eventual prospect as well as in the small handled form of the nub. What is it, what are they, these seeds of understanding? And if I know, are they logical? Do they take the processional form of the words I use? Or do they take a form like that of the silver backing a glass, a dark that enholds all brightness? Is every metaphor—and the assertion of understanding is our great metaphor—mixed by the necessity of its intention? What is the mixture of a word, an image, a notion?

The mixture, if I may start a hare so late, the mixture, even in the fresh use of an old word, is made in the pre-conscious, and is by hypothesis unascertainable. But let us not use hypotheses, let us not desire to ascertain. By intuition we adventure in the pre-conscious; and there, where the adventure is, there is no need or suspicion of certainty or meaning; there is the living, expanding, *prescient* sub-stance without the tags and handles of conscious form. Art is the looking-glass of the pre-conscious, and when it is deepest seems to participate in it sensibly. Or, better, for purposes of criticism, our sensibility resumes the division of the senses and faculties at the same time that it preens itself into conscious form. Criticism may have as an object the establishment and evaluation (comparison and analysis) of the modes of making the pre-conscious *consciously* available.

But this emphasis upon the pre-conscious need not be insisted on; once recognised it may be tacitly assumed, and the effort of the mind will be, as it were, restored to its own plane—only a little sensitive to the tap-roots below. On its own plane—that is the plane where almost everything is taken for granted in order to assume adequate implementation in handling what is taken for granted by others; where because you can list the items of your bewilderment and can move from one to another you assert that the achievement of motion is the experience of order;—where, therefore, you must adopt always an attitude of provisional scepticism; where, imperatively, you must scrutinise and scrutinise until you have revealed, if it is there, the in-scrutable divination, or, if it is not, the void of personal ambition; where, finally, you must stop short only when you have, with all the facts you can muster, indicated, surrounded, detached, somehow found the way demonstrably to get at, in pretty conscious terms which others may use, the substance of your chosen case.

1935

# GRANVILLE HICKS
## (1901–     )

GRANVILLE HICKS was born in Exeter, New Hampshire, on September 9, 1901. In 1923 he graduated from Harvard University. After graduating from the Harvard Divinity School in 1925, he took a position teaching biblical literature and English at Smith College. He taught for a number of years as assistant professor of English at Rensselaer Polytechnic Institute. He started writing for the *New Masses* and other radical periodicals in 1931. He served for a time as literary editor of the *New Masses*, becoming one of the most articulate and influential spokesmen for Marxist criticism in the United States. When the Munich Pact was signed, he decided to sever his connections with the Communist Party and resign his position on the *New Masses*.

Hick's first book, *Eight Ways of Looking at Christianity*, was published in 1926. In a few years he passed by various stages from religious faith, through intellectual doubt, to orthodox Communism. As soon as he embraced Communism, he assumed that the Marxist world-attitude is the only correct and desirable one for the writer to adopt. The writer must choose on which side he is going to fight, on the side of life triumphant, as represented by the militant proletariat, or on the side of death, as represented by the capitalist class. During his Marxist period, Hicks was austerely consistent in his method of critical evaluation. Convinced that the class struggle could not be solved peacefully, Hicks sounds the call to revolution as the only effectual means of social salvation. And the purpose of literature is nothing less than to arouse a sacred revolutionary ardor in the mind of the workers.

In *The Great Tradition* (1933) the Marxist yardstick is applied with rigorous consistency to a critical period of American literature. Every work is judged in the light of the ubiquitous class struggle. Aesthetic values are generally ignored or minimized in favor of socio-economic coordinates of judgment. If writers failed to deal with the implications of industrialism, the ruthless exploitation of labor, the violence of the class conflict, then no excellence in terms of artistic value can redeem them for

405

posterity. *The Great Tradition* stresses the single thesis that the major American writers in the nineteenth century failed to shoulder their social responsibility; that is to say, they had no grasp of Marxist theory and failed to join forces with the workers.

Writing on "Problems of American Fellow Travelers," in *International Literature* (No. 3, July, 1933), Granville Hicks discusses a number of American novelists, poets, and critics, and their attitude toward the class struggle. He was then convinced that many of the' problems the fellow travelers faced could be solved if they would but draw closer to the working class, participate in the struggle, and profit from the discipline of Marxism. In "The Writer Faces the Future," which he contributed to *The Writer in a Changing World,* he sings the same refrain, insisting that the cause of Communism must be defended against all attack, and that any writer who holds back is derelict in his duty. In a series of articles on "Revolution and the Novel," published in 1934 in the *New Masses,* Hicks argued that for the proletarian novelist, fictional authenticity resides in a faithful documented recording of the life of a period interpreted in the light of the Marxian conception of history. Hicks' judgment of literature in general and of the novel in particular is based on the assumption that what is most important about an individual is not his mind or character or philosophy but the social class to which he belongs. Until the classless society is established, the revolutionary writer can effect an artistic integration of his complex and refractory material only by being militantly class-conscious, by taking into consideration the needs, aspirations, and purposes of the proletariat.

In *Figures of Transition* (1939), Hicks is interested in certain changes, literary and social, that took place in England at the end of the last century. In writing about the eighties and nineties, he tells us, he tries "to use history as an aid to the understanding of literature and literature as an aid to the understanding of history."[1] He interprets Victorianism, not as an aberration, an historical "sport," but in terms of the rising middle class, the progress of industrial capitalism. *I Like America* (1938) reveals a great deal about the author, his ancestry, his family life, his occupations and interests, but all that is preliminary to the elaboration of his thesis that though he likes America, there are many things in it he wants to change, and the only effective method of changing America is by establishing a form of Communism.

Hicks' disillusionment with the practical politics of Communism led him not only to resign from the Party but also to revise his critical principles. Now he realizes the damage that left criticism has done. He acknowledges,

1 Granville Hicks, *Figures of Transition* (New York, 1939), pp. xii–xiii.

in an article on "The Failure of 'Left' Criticism," that duruing his period of service with the *New Masses,* he accepted the party position and was not guilty of major heresy. His most revealing observation is that left criticism did not produce a critic "capable of consistent analysis and mature, well-rounded evaluations."[2] The literary disputes were predominantly sectarian in character, and the turbulent political atmosphere was not conducive to the development of a useful critical method. Hicks concludes that Marxist critics were naive in their faith that literary criticism could be a formidable weapon in the resolutionary struggle to change the world.

In "Communism and the American Intellectuals," contributed to *Whose Revolution?,* edited by Irving DeWitt Talmadge (1941), Hicks attempts to discover why he and others like him blindly went astray as they took the road to Moscow. Now he perceives that the talk of Marxist-Leninist principles was but an ideological smokescreen. The government in Soviet Russia was a bureaucracy interested in consolidating and extending its power. Such a tendency, Hicks decided, was inherent in Leninism and in certain aspects of Marxism itself. The believer in democracy could not afford to take such shortcuts. Hicks now rejects *in toto* the theory of the dictatorship of the proletariat. Communism in Russia and Nazism in Germany are both examples of oppressive dictatorship.

Reviewing his past in *Small Town* (1946), he confesses that during his period of communist orthodoxy he disseminated more half-truths than the rest of his life can atone for. Though he has no illusions about the limitations of democracy in the United States, he believes "that what we have is too precious to be given up without a fight. I can approve of no reform, however attractive it may sound, if it is likely to break a path for totalitarianism."[3] Having abandoned the Marxist conception of the class struggle, he now declares that he has no faith in the automatic and inevitable operation of a dialectical materialism that will usher in the classless society. All this, of course, invalidates much of the critical writing Hicks had done during the thirties. It also marks an abatement, if not the end, of the Marxist debate in criticism.

## BIBLIOGRAPHY

### TEXT

*The Great Tradition.* New York, 1933.
*One of Us.* New York, 1935.

[2] Granville Hicks, "The Failure of 'Left' Criticism," *New Republic,* CIII (September 9, 1940), 345–347.

[3] Granville Hicks, *Small Town* (New York, 1946), pp. 227–228.

(ed.), *Proletarian Literature in the United States*. New York, 1935.
*John Reed*. New York, 1936.
*I Like America*. New York, 1938.
*Figures of Transition*. New York, 1939.
*Small Town*. New York, 1946.

CRITICISM

Farrell, James T., "Mr. Hicks: Critical Vulgarian," *American Spectator*,
    IV, 21–26 (April, 1936).
——, *A Note on Literary Criticism*. New York, 1936.
Glicksberg, Charles I., "Granville Hicks and Marxist Criticism," *Sewanee
    Review*, XLV, 129–140 (April, 1937).
Mathiessen, Francis O., "The Great Tradition," *New England Quarterly*,
    VII, 223–234 (June, 1934).

## LITERATURE AND REVOLUTION*

IT is not without hesitation that I speak on such a subject before such a gathering. I know that to do so invites misunderstanding, for the theories I shall try to expound are not isolated; they derive from and depend upon a body of thought that extnds into philosophy, history, economics, and political strategy. I do not mean that the Communist party has an official position on literature; nor, if it did, could I present myself as its spokesman. I mean merely that a full statement of my views would involve an exposition and defense of historical materialism, the Marxian conception of the class struggle, Marxian economics, and the Communist program for the overthrow of capitalism and the establishment of the dictatorship of the proletariat. Of course no aesthetic theory can be properly discussed without some consideration of its philosophical foundations and its social implications, but the foundations and implications of my theory are less familiar, and perhaps, to most of you, less acceptable than those that are ordinarily taken into account in aesthetic discourse. My exposition will, therefore, seem fragmentary, and you may well be

* Reprinted by permission of Granville Hicks, *College English*, and *The English Journal*. Copyright, 1935.

Address delivered before College Conference on English in the Central Atlantic States, December 1, 1934, conscious of assumptions that are not shared by you and cannot, within the limits of this paper, be defended by me.

To obviate this difficulty as far as is possible, I shall approach my subject by way of a rather elementary analysis of the nature and function of literature. I should describe a work of literature as the presentation of a particular fragment of experience in the light of the author's conception of the totality of experience. The definition is neither original nor uncommon. Something of the sort is implicit in most of the definitions, from Plato's and Aristotle's to those of contemporary aestheticians. Matthew Arnold said essentially the same thing when he called literature the criticism of life; to the experience that is his immediate theme the author brings the results of a larger experience, and it is the juxtaposition of the two that gives his work its value. Indeed, the simple proposition that selection is the basis of all art implies the existence of standards, beliefs, predispositions, and prejudices according to which the selection is made; and at their highest these ideas and moods are integrated into a world-view, or, if that is too abstract and intellectual a term to describe the mental processes of an artist, into a world-attitude.

The lyric poet is supposed to be, and indeed is, concerned with the immediate experience; and yet almost any lyric, certainly any body of lyrics, impresses the reader with a sense that the immediate experience draws its significance, for poet and reader alike, from the organized body of experience with which it is associated. Wordsworth, Shelley, and Tennyson occur to the mind at once as obvious examples; each saturated the least pretentious of his verses with all that he thought and felt about life. The sensation of the moment seems to occupy Keats, but careful reading reveals in his work the outlines of a clear and concrete world-attitude, and he comes to seem a more genuinely philosophical poet than Shelley or Tennyson. Baudelaire, to take another example at random, was once claimed by the theoreticians of pure poetry as their private possession, but now T. S. Eliot and his party describe him as an ethical and religious poet.

Nothing could be easier than to multiply examples from the lyricists, and lyric poetry is, by common consent, the least philosophical of literary forms. There is scarcely a novelist or dramatist of importance who has not provided material for a doctoral dissertation on his philosophy. A novel or play, by the mere fact that it binds into some sort of unity a variety of experiences, clearly reveals its author's assumptions. We come to know his personal tastes, his system of values, his conception of human nature, and his views on the destiny of the race. Any one of us could roughly define the world-attitude of hundreds of writers. Of course, our statements would be inadequate; they would be bare formulas, stripped of the substance that the artist's imagination gives; but they would symbolize a reality that we all could recognize.

Let us bear this definition in mind as we go on to discuss the effect of literature. Reading has, we all assume, some sort of effect. The crude conception of literature as either beneficial or detrimental to morals, and the value judgments based on that conception, have largely been discarded, but rather because of changing standards of morals than because of changing views of literature. The humanists, though scoffing at the black-and-white, good-bad verdicts of the moralists, postulate an ethical effect of literature and base their whole aesthetics on the assumption. Even the impressionists grant, and indeed emphasize, a personal effect, though refusing to generalize. The question is complex, and there is no easy solution. I. A. Richards, I believe, has come closer, in his *Principles of Literary Criticism,* to a comprehensive account than any other writer I know. "We pass as a rule," he says, "from a chaotic to a better organized state by ways we know nothing about. Typically through the influence of other minds. Literature and the arts are the chief means by which these influences are diffused."

This description, even without the evidence Richards adduces from psychology in support of it, commends itself because it recognizes both the many-sidedness and the subtlety of the effect that literature may have. We all realize that ordinarily a work of literature does not impel us to do some certain thing—neither to commit adultery, as the moralists fear, nor to lynch the nearest capitalist, as some propagandists seem to hope. Occasionally, under the right circumstances, a work of art may inspire in certain persons a sharp emotion that finds immediate outlet in action, but usually we sit calmly at home in our armchairs, read our masterpiece, put it down, turn out the lights, go to bed, and go to sleep. Yet we are all conscious that certain novels or plays or poems have influenced our lives, and we may suspect that every book has some influence, imperceptible though it may be.

To define this influence we have to consider the relation of reading to actual experience. Reading is not a substitute for experience. As Kenneth Burke says, the death by torture of some admired hero of fiction is less painful than one's own toothache, and the most beautiful description of a garden cannot give us the same sort of pleasure as a bunch of flowers. But it is equally true that the account of a toothache in a novel may linger in our minds when the memory of some painful accident we have endured has been dispelled, and the description of a single flower may rouse a sharper emotion than any experience in countryside or conservatory. The author cannot give us the experience with the intensity it would have, even for us insensitive beings, in real life, but he can reveal its relationship to other experiences in such a way that our own experiences, of similar and perhaps even of different sorts, take on new meaning. He can bring into truer perspective whole realms of emotion and thought, and the new perception we acquire conditions our subsequent responses to the events of our lives. This, I gather, is what Richards means when he speaks of passing from a chaotic to a better organized state.

Even this summary account should make clear why I have attached so much importance to the world-attitude of the author. I reiterate that this need not be an articulate philosophy; and in any case it must be more than that. It is a way of seeing, feeling, acting, and it may be completely non-intellectualized. The artist is important for civilization because he is not limited to intellectual formulas, because, if he is inferior to the scientist in precision, he is superior to him in scope, because he can include so much that is important in life but as yet baffles quantitative measurement or logical definition. And yet we must not be deceived into thinking that the responses of the artist are fragmentary or disorganized. Some critics speak of pure experience. There is no such thing, although great physical pain perhaps approximates it. Pure experience would be entirely physiological and absolutely ineffable. Experience has meaning when it is related to other experiences, and the wider the relationships the greater the meaning. Art is the representation—or perhaps I should say the discovery or even the creation—of these relationships, not in an abstract system, but in a dynamic, living integration.

You will perceive that I attach only secondary importance to the technical problems of communication. Form and content are so closely connected that one cannot be profitably discussed apart from the other. If I may appeal to our common experience, I should like to point out that English teachers must be particularly aware of the limitations of technical instruction. Nine out of ten faulty themes could be fundamentally improved only if we could change the mental operations of their authors, could make them see differently, feel differently, think differently. H. G. Wells's comments on the theories of

Henry James, in his *Experiment in Autobiography,* show that their quarrel was not really concerned with technique, though it seemed to be, but with their conception of the purpose of fiction, their understanding of the nature of life, and their active response to the world in which they lived. James's prefaces are extraordinary documents in the analysis of the novel, but they are also revelations of his world-attitude, and it may be doubted whether an author with an entirely different world-attitude could possibly avail himself of James's technical devices. Much criticism of poetry takes the form of painstaking dissection of figures of speech; such criticism obviously, if it is at all useful, is not merely technical; it concerns itself with the author's perceptive qualities. I do not want to seem to claim too much, but I think you will grant that Theodore Dreiser's sentence structure could be improved only if you eradicate his muddle-headedness, and that Walt Whitman's stylistic weaknesses are closely related to the confusion and the diffuseness of his mind. At the same time, I would maintain that Whitman and Dreiser are relatively great writers not only in spite of their technical defects, but in spite of the incoherence in their world-attitudes. The technical facility of minor writers seldom commands respect, for the reader realizes that they achieve it by restricting the scope of their imaginative efforts. The writer cannot communicate more than he has to say, and if he deliberately chooses to do less, so much the worse for him.

If what I have said is sound, it is on a writer's world-attitude that we must concentrate if we wish to understand him and to interpret and explain him to others. At this point there may be objection. Someone will say, "You can explain Shakespeare's attitude and you can explain Lyly's attitude, but will that explain Shakespeare's superiority to Lyly?" Not entirely, I grant. No writer, for that matter, can ever be completely explained, and it seems to be the elements that make the difference between genius and talent, as we ordinarily use the words, that are hardest to explain. No method has proved adequate. The psychoanalysts certainly have not succeeded. Joseph Wood Krutch explains, more or less convincingly, certain of the peculiarities of Poe's mind, but he would be the first to admit that he is a long way from showing the reasons for Poe's virtues as a poet. All that I can say is that the more fully we understand the author's world-attitude, not as it may be stated in some bare formula but in the rich and living complexity of his imaginative functioning, the closer we come to understanding his genius. And, moreover, if we can understand the way in which his world-attitude developed, we at least see him in relation to the men and movement of his own age, to the rest of humanity, in short. The explanation of literary phenomena, if it is more than an intellectual exercise, is intended to help the reader to understand and appreciate what he reads. Such understanding is accomplished, not by isolating the author from the world in which we live, but by finding his true place in it.

I have implied that the author's world-attitude is a social phenomenon. If the adjective is correctly understood, the fact is obvious. Certainly, the artist does not spin his world-attitude out of himself; it is something that is created by contact with his environment. The artist's mind grows as any mind grows, and that process, as Piaget, for example, has shown, is a social process. We need not go as far as the Behaviorists, and view the mind of the newborn infant as a *tabula rasa;* even if there are inherited instincts and aptitudes, their operation is environmentally determined.

No, the only question is what environmental influences are most important. The psychological critic carefully examines the artist's life from birth to maturity, seeking for clues in family relationships, physical conditions, and personal contacts. The social critic examines the currents of thought and emotion in the artist's era. Both are concerned with social phenomena; both examine the artist's environment. The two methods are complementary, and adequate explanation requires that both shall be used. It is, however, possible to argue that one is more important than the other. I think the social method is more useful, and fortunately so, since the facts essential to satisfactory psychological analysis are rarely available.

Illustration cannot prove my contention but may clarify it. Ludwig Lewisohn makes much of the point that Walt Whitman was homosexual, and thinks that this explains the peculiarly emotional form that Whitman's theory of human brotherhood assumed. He may be right, but how much less important this is than the democratic theory itself, which obviously cannot be explained in terms of sexual abnormality! Whitman's father was a workingman, and Whitman was definitely a part of the masses about whom he wrote. From the first he inclined to the theories of the Jacksonians, and these theories were the foundation of the conception of democratic comradeship that he made his theme. American conditions in the decades before the Civil War created the whole philosophy of democratic individualism, and Whitman's work was that of elaboration and imaginative application. His putative homosexuality can at best only partly explain his enthusiasm for the democratic ideal, and it cannot at all explain the development of democratic sentiment and theory.

It is by way of the discovery of sexual aberrations that the psychological critics usually attempt to explain literary work. Mr. Lewisohn finds Emerson and Thoreau sexually frigid. Mr. Krutch believes that Poe suffered from a mother-fixation, and I understand that Amabel Williams-Ellis has maintained that Ruskin was the victim of a similar misfortune. Other authors have been similarly treated: Keats, Baudelaire, Emily Dickinson, D. H. Lawrence, and even Shakespeare. It would be foolish to ridicule this method, for it may have useful results, but it can explain relatively little.

If what we are seeking is understanding, the important thing is to see the artist in relation to his age: Marlowe against a background of Elizabethan expansiveness, Congreve in the setting of aristocratic reaction, Richardson in the midst of all the phenomena of bourgeois emergence, Shelley as part of the democratic revolution, Tennyson in terms of Victorian progress, and Joyce as a symptom of capitalist decline. The phrases I have chosen are deliberate oversimplifications, but they suggest what I mean: that the artist can be understood only if one understands the movements that dominated his age.

It is the reality behind such phrases that the critic must discover. To understand all the complex relationships of men and movements in any age is beyond the power of the human mind, but a usable comprehension may be possible. The Marxist believes that he has a method that provides such comprehension. He holds that one cannot understand the intellectual movements of a given period without understanding the class alignments of that period. He recognizes, of course, that class alignment is never a simple matter of division into exploiters and exploited. He distinguishes at the present time between the petty bourgeoisie and the big bourgeoisie, between industrial workers and farmers, between richer farmers and poorer. In considering certain periods of the past, he recognizes the distinctive psychology of the merchants, the industrialists, and the financiers. Still farther back he sees the feudal aristocracy as the dominant class, and he realizes that in Europe survivals of feudalism have remained to complicate the struggles of the bourgeoisie.

The Marxist also rejects the notion that it is possible to explain the world-attitude of a given author merely by stating his class affiliation. The dominant class colors the entire culture of a period. Individual authors may be led by class influences to diverge from the prevailing pattern, but its effect is nonetheless felt. In a period in which the ruling class is almost unchallenged, as in Elizabethan England, for example, or in seventeenth-century France, or in contemporary Russia, culture will tend to be homogeneous, for authors will start from much the same premises, however idiosyncratic their courses may be. In the mid-seventeenth century, in England, however, we find strongly marked differences in literature, reflecting the interests of two conflicting and nearly balanced classes. The same phenomenon has often appeared at other times in other places: in France just before the Revolution, in the United States before the Civil War, and in most countries of the Western world today. Today we have a vigorous proletarian literature in the United States, but it is by no means completely independent from bourgeois literature, which even in its decline determines the dominant pattern. Between these extremes of relative unity and nearly balanced opposition, there are innumerable variations, each producing its own manifestations in literature and the arts.

The influence of class alignment upon a writer is complex and difficult to trace. Marlowe clearly expresses the expansive spirit of the merchant-adventurers who, only recently escaped from the bonds of the feudal system, were building the British Empire, and yet there is in Marlowe, as in most of the Elizabethan dramatists, a kind of pessimism that ill accords with the achievements of his class. Richardson, to take a simpler case, eagerly accepts the prudence-morality of the rising petty-bourgeoisie, and condemns the indiscretion of the landowners, but at the same time he snobbishly aspires to aristocratic distinction. Whitman speaks for the hopeful masses of Americans, westward bound on the trail of prosperity, individualistic and self-reliant, and yet he welcomes the socialist ideals of the collective state. Such complexities raise problems that may not be insoluble but are not to be ignored.

Social conditions change, and artists change too, and the interaction of these changes may produce surprising results. William Wordsworth was one of the poets who most heartily welcomed the democratic dawn of the late eighteenth century. Though in England successive strata of the bourgeoisie had pushed themselves up to positions of power as the productive forces of capitalism had expanded, the process was not moving fast enough to suit the young idealists. Insurgent sections of the bourgeoisie have always employed the slogans of freedom, democracy, and equal opportunity, and there have always been those who took the slogans seriously. In

France, moreover, the bourgeois revolution, more violent because longer suppressed, had exploded into a volcanic fury of libertarian sentiment. But suddenly the process seemed to be going too fast. The democratic slogans of the French bourgeoisie, spreading to the proletariat, became a menace to the stability of the middle class. In England, too, workers were restless. Wordsworth did not consciously recant; he merely recoiled. If this was what his principles involved, he could not but see that his principles were wrong. He became the lost leader.

Social conditions are always changing. Mark Twain was early exposed to the democratic spirit of the frontier. When, later, he came to live in the industrialized society of the post-war East, he was bewildered. On the one hand, his own self-reliant and acquisitive impulses drove him to participate in the excesses of the Gilded Age; on the other, he saw quite clearly the tendency toward a snobbish oligarchy, based on injustice, and he did not hesitate to attack exploitation, class distinction, and imperialism from the frontiersman's egalitarian point of view. It is not, I think, unfair to attribute much of his pessimism to his uncertainty and to the conflicts that divided his mind. His friend Howells went through a similar experience, suddenly losing confidence in the society in which he had been so delighted to win a place for himself. Both Howells and Mark Twain called themselves socialists, but both, as the former bitterly remarked, continued to wear their fur coats. The changing shape of American life had involved them in contradiction, and their work suffered as a result in clarity and firmness.

Carlyle and Dickens were both born on the lower fringes of the petty-bourgeoisie. Both were opposed to the callous cruelty of the rising business class and to the utilitarian philosophy and laissez-faire economics that rationalized that brutality. Both sympathized with the working class, but the working class at that time was too weak to sustain a culture, too dependent on bourgeois religion, morality, and education to offer a real alternative to the business class. The one genuine alternative was the landowning class, and it was thither that Carlyle and Dickens turned for support. Carlyle might talk to captains of industry, but it was the feudal virtues that he praised in his attempt to create a more just social order for the oppressed. Dickens, more acutely sympathetic with the workers and perhaps more cognizant of their potentialities, could not envisage a happier solution than a benevolent paternalism. Kingsley made *Alton Locke* a plea for obedience to the church and the crown, attacking the ruthless business men, it is true, but opposing as well Chartist aspirations to working class independence. Observe that none of the novelists of the earlier Victorian period, except Harriet Martineau, adopted a world-attitude that made any place for utilitarianism and its economic corollaries. They sympathized with the working class, opposed the business men, and looked to the landowners for political action. Their attitude reflected the economic situation: after the Reform Bill of 1832 had given the balance of power to the industrialists, the workers were glad of any allies; the landowners saw that, for the moment, there was only one enemy, and the petty-bourgeois, crushed by the advance of industrial capitalism, could find but one refuge.

The unwillingness of the early Victorians to adhere to the principles on which industrialism was rising to power reminds us that writers have seldom been willing to adopt the psychology of capitalism. This does not mean that writers are uninfluenced by the theories and practices of the ruling class; on the contrary, that influence permeates their work from beginning to end, even, perhaps especially, when they repudiate it. All I am trying to point out is that artists have traditionally rejected the acquisitive way of life—at least in theory. Perhaps that is because most artists come from the petty-bourgeoisie, from the least prosperous section of the non-proletarian world. Perhaps it is because art, for which capitalism makes no place, therefore attracts the dissatisfied. Whatever the explanation, we see writers running away from an industrial world to romantic refuges, far away or long ago. We hear them asserting proudly that art has no connection with the world of affairs, as if that was the only way in which they could maintain their independence. They even deny that the function of literature is communication, in order to avoid difficulties that, on other terms, seem to make literature impossible. But they very, very seldom attempt to maintain that the prevailing way of life, the way of life that is led by the rulers of our civilization, is a good way.

At times this hostility to capitalist values takes a more direct form. At the turn of the century a literature developed, both in England and America, in which specific proposals for social reform played a large part: the novels of Wells and the plays of Shaw in England, the novels of Norris, Sinclair, and Herrick in this country. This reform movement expressed, I believe, the last insurgence of the petty-bourgeoisie, forced by the rise of monopoly capitalism to the recognition that equal opportunity was a myth. The class was caught in a contradictory position: it could not go back to earlier conditions, and to go ahead meant to surrender even more of its opportunities. The contradiction is reflected in the confusion of the reformist writers, as I have tried to show, so far as American writers are concerned, in *The Great Tradition,* and as John Strachey has shown, with regard to the British writers, in *The Coming Struggle for Power.*

It would not be difficult, of course, to swell the list of examples; indeed, it is my contention that, if one knows enough, the whole history of literature yields itself to such treatment. But perhaps it is time to recapitulate. The purpose of explaining literary phenomena is to understand them, to respond more fully to them. I favor using all methods that conduce to that end. If the study of literary influences is helpful, by all means let us study literary influences. If Freud has anything to teach us, let us turn to Freud, or to any other psychologist, for that matter, who can guide us through the mysteries of human personality. But for myself I believe, and I have tried to show, that we can understand an author best if we examine his relation to the social movements of his time and to the class alignments out of which they grow. This may not tell us all we should like to discover, but it will tell us what is most important for us to know.

But this is only half the story. The critic's task does not stop with explanation; it must go on to evaluation. Evaluation, I need scarcely remind you, is not a matter of passing out grades. It, too, has as its primary function the extension of the reader's capacity for appreciation. To that extent I agree with H. L. Mencken's catalyst theory, but I do not think that catalysis is accomplished by the random recording of transient impressions. In evaluating a work of art, the critic brings to it all his experience with other works, all his knowledge of human nature, all his understanding of the character and purpose of life. Two world-attitudes are brought face to face, and the result is, or should be, illuminating.

I fall back once more upon Mr. Richards, whose views, if not wholly acceptable, are helpful and serve as a convenient point of departure. If what literature does is to help us pass from a chaotic to a more organized state, it may be possible, not only to dismiss certain works as definitely disorganizing, but also to define the relative value of works that are not contributory to chaos. Mr. Richards maintains that the object of life is to satisfy as many appetencies as possible. In a chaotic state the fulfilment of one desire—to use a more common, if less exact, term—blocks the satisfaction of others. Not only are those desires dangerous that may grow into vices; intrinsically admirable pursuits may result in the disastrous warping of character. In particular, as Mr. Richards recognizes, the satisfaction of legitimate appetencies at the expense of other persons results ultimately in frustration. The ruthless man gets what he wants but finds that he has forever deprived himself of confidence and respect on the part of his associates. Literature, then, does not perform its organizing function unless it creates in us attitudes that permit us to live in fruitful concord with our fellow-men.

Mr. Richards assumes that it is possible to develop all-inclusive harmonious relationships. It is difficult, he knows, but he will not admit the existence of irreconcilable oppositions. I, however, believe that there is one conflict that permits of no peaceful solution. I refer, of course, to the class struggle. The proletariat can, in the long run, be satisfied with nothing less than all that it produces. Since, moreover, the developing contradictions of capitalism result in greater and greater deprivation for the proletariat, it is driven by sheer necessity to demand the abolition of exploitation. This demand the capitalists and those most closely associated with them in the sharing of profits cannot concede, since to do so would be absolute abdication. No ruling class in history has ever voluntarily surrendered its power, and there is reason to believe that there is not the least possibility of peaceful surrender by the masters of capitalism. Even abdication, however, would not invalidate my argument that there is an irreconcilable opposition between the exploiters and the exploited, since it would signify, quite as definitely as would involuntary liquidation, the triumph of one point of view over the other.

If this is true, it follows that, in certain respects at least, what capitalists regarded as a satisfactory integration could not be acceptable to proletarians. Let me take one example, to which I have already alluded, Kingsley's *Alton Locke*. A capitalist reader would find himself moved to pity the lot of the working class, but he would at the same time be confirmed in his conviction that it is wrong for workers to use violence to obtain their demands. These two attitudes could be adequately reconciled if he came to feel a greater responsibility toward his employees. He would still be the judge, however, of what constituted humane treatment, and it it reasonable to suppose that his conscience would be appeased more easily than the appetites of the workers. A working-class reader would be led to feel pity for himself and at the same time would learn to rely on the benevolence of his master rather than on the organized strength of his class. This would be a satisfactory integration from the capitalist's point of view. It would not, in the long run, serve the best interests of the worker.

This clear-cut example may suffice for the moment, for I shall shortly discuss in some detail the kind of integration that is desirable for the proletarian, and this discussion will touch upon less obvious influences. All I want to maintain now is that, if the critic recognizes the existence of such irreconcilable oppositions, he must decide where he stands and in whose interests he desires integration to take place. It is impossible for me to state fully why I personally have chosen the side of the proletariat and why I urge other intellectuals to make the same choice. I believe that the capitalist system is inherently unstable, and that such depressions as that which has just entered its sixth year are not only unavoidable under capitalism but are certain to grow worse. Capitalism itself cannot solve the problems that, as it becomes fully developed, it creates. Only socialization of industry will eliminate these ills and permit the enjoyment of the full resources of our productive machinery. Moreover, the desperate effort of the capitalist class to maintain its privileged position results in Fascism, which sacrifices the political and cultural gains of the period of industrial expansion without achieving stability. Socialization is the only preventive of both Fascism and war, and socialization can be brought about only by the proletariat, not because of some peculiar virtue resident in factory workers, but because it is the one class that stands to gain so much by socialization and to lose so much by the perpetuation, especially in a fascist form, of capitalism that it will be willing to make the sacrifices that revolution entails.

This is, in brief, the argument that has led me to make the proletariat my point of reference. Any critic, unless he accepts the complete irresponsibility of impressionism tries to transcend his own idiosyncrasies and speak in the name of some larger entity. To do so, he must, as Richards says, foster a kind of dual response to literature. He knows what a work of art does to and for him, but he also realizes the ways in which he deviates from what he regards as the norm, and he makes due allowance for these deviations in reaching his conclusions. So with the revolutionary critic. It has been charged that the proletariat is an abstraction, and the charge has some measure of truth, but the critic's norm is always an abstraction. Mr. Richards, for example, implies the existence of Man, with a capital letter, and the Humanists have a very precise but completely abstract conception of humanity. The revolutionary critic's idea of the normal proletarian is, in comparison, concrete and realistic, based both on an understanding of the historic rôle of the class and on first-hand experience of its spirit as displayed in crucial struggles.

I can realize how many objections might be introduced at this point, but let us see what, in practice, our conclusions involve. If we were to go to some militant leader of the working class and ask him what literature ought to do, he would probably tell us that it ought, first of all, to create a revolutionary spirit in the proletariat. Only that literature, he might well say, that prepares the class for the great task before it has any value.

This may seem a narrow and, perhaps, to some, an unworthy conception of literature. So thoroughly schooled have we been in the doctrine of the sacredness of art that we shrink from any association of literature and practical affairs. This response of ours results from the fact that any association of literature with the practical affairs of monopoly capitalism is debasing. Art under capitalism is so constantly in danger of Mammon-worship that, in order to maintain any sort of artistic integrity, we have built up these elaborate defenses. But actually in the course of human history literature has again and again been openly allied with church and state, and it may be argued that the periods of such alliance have not been unfruitful. The artists of Greece and Rome and those of the Middle Ages found no degradation in the serving of practical ends, and the rise of democracy has been aided by many of the greatest writers of modern times.

Nothing has so beclouded contemporary aesthetic discourse as the use of the word "propaganda." Because of its use during the war the term has come to connote chicanery and distortion. Yet it also has been employed to describe any sort of direct exhortation, and the aesthetes apply it to any work of art with a serious purpose. So often has the word been abusively hurled by aesthetes against revolutionaries that the latter have accepted the challenge and adopted the word as their own. Diego Rivera, for example, says that all art is propaganda. There is a sense of the term in which this is true, but it is not the meaning that is ordinarily understood.

Personally, I believe that the word ought to be used only in its pejorative sense, but in any case it ought to be kept out of discussions of literature. I have tried to maintain that any work of literature presents some sort of world-attitude, and that it must be judged in terms of the author's world-attitude and his success in communicating it. The most outrageous dadaist poem implies a certain attitude toward life; and the author, whether he admits it or not, wants others to adopt that attitude. If literature with a purpose is propaganda, then Rivera is right, but in that case the word is too inclusive to be useful. The conviction of most persons—that literature with a purpose one doesn't like is propaganda and literature with a purpose one does like is art—is obviously unsound. We are left, it seems to me, to hold that propaganda involves misrepresentation, and, since misrepresentation is intrinsically bad, it is unnecessary to talk about propaganda.

In serving the revolutionary cause the revolutionary writer is merely expressing his own world-attitude and fulfilling his own desires. To that extent he is like writers of all classes and all ages. And the critic, when he judges literature by its effect in preparing the proletariat for its struggle, is applying a criterion that does not differ in kind from the criteria of other critics. There is a danger, however, that he may demand immediate, concrete results. Such a demand is wrong simply because it is not in the nature of literature, as I have already remarked, to produce such results.

What we have to ask, it seems to me, is whether a work of literature contributes to a world-attitude that is compatible with the aims and tasks of the proletariat and whether it tends to build up a system of responses that will permit the proletarian to play his individual part in the coming struggle. We cannot approve, for example, a novel or a play that fosters an attitude of subservience. It may have incidental values, which we must point out, but fundamentally it is wrong. We cannot tolerate a defeatist literature, not merely because of the attitude it encourages, but also because, from our point of view, it distorts life by ignoring elements in human character and history that, for the proletariat, the ascendant class, make pessimism impossible. Escapism, too, must be resisted. The romantic satisfactions of the daydream are recognized as perilous by most psychologists, for they inhibit the forming of adjustments that make possible the permanent and progressive fulfilment of appetencies; but they are peculiarly menacing to the proletarian reader, both because the hardships of his present existence make them so tempting and because his future rôle is so exacting.

On the other hand, we are not to suppose that the literature of the past is to be condemned *en bloc*. Revolutionary leaders from Marx to Stalin have insisted on the preciousness of the cultural heritage with which history endows the proletariat. There is a class element in any work produced in a class society, and this bias, as found in past writers, is distressing to proletarian readers. The classic example is Shakespeare's treatment of the lower class, a treatment so derogatory that Upton Sinclair, in *Mammonart*, warns workers against reading his plays. Mr. Sinclair, I feel, underestimates the natural immunity of the modern worker to such suggestion, and he equally underestimates the valuable elements of Shakespeare's plays. The mysticism of Dostoyevsky is wholly unacceptable to the Marxist, and yet his novels are widely read in the Soviet Union. Wherever the author's class bias is negated by his insight, his work is important. In spite of both snobbishness and a quasi-mystical detachment, Marcel Proust left a richer and more detailed account of the breakdown of the leisure class than can be found elsewhere.

We recognize an element of distortion in all the literature of the past, but we see, too, much that is valid, and to that we cling. At first it seems a paradox to say that we find most enduring value in those writers who most completely responded to and represented their own times. But once you perceive that class limits cannot be transcended, you realize that human nature can best be understood in terms of the forces that at any given time condition it. The writer who sets out to rise above material circumstance and deal with the pure human spirit is occupying himself with an unreal abstraction. The great writer has always been wholly and unmistakably part of his age, and, by mastering it, has left something of value for succeeding ages.

What we demand of a writer is that he honestly confront the central issues of his own age. His world-attitude must embrace the whole of his world as his age knew it, and must organize that world in such a way as to place central issues in the center. If he does this he deserves our praise. But I hasten to repeat that literature is not primarily a matter of the intellect. It embraces the entire mind, and it must not be judged in purely intellectual terms. An author may have formulated a world-attitude that, if he were a philosopher, would be admirable, and yet his poem or story may be worthless. He may, on the other hand, have no conscious philosophy, or only a very banal one, and yet be a great writer. This is particularly necessary for me to say, for it is characteristic of revolutionary sentiment that it seems to reach the intellect first. The young revolutionary author, filled with a sense of the comprehensiveness of Marxist analysis, and unwilling to subject his imagination to the long process of quiet and largely unconscious assimilation that literature requires, is tempted to substitute dogma for experience. This explains the weaknesses of some revolutionary literature, but it is a fault that time will remedy.

As the critic sees it, the problem defines itself in terms of complete-ness of communication, so that the experience of the writer becomes an experience for the reader. I doubt if intensity of experience is, by itself, an adequate criterion of literary greatness, but it is an in-dispensable element. That is why we rightly attach importance to the successful communication of even a minor experience. An author who communicates to us the joy he feels in contemplating a daffodil has done more than the author who, in attempting to communicate a vision of epic scope, only frustrates and bewilders us. The kind of integration Richards speaks of depends on the full communication of every element of the various experiences that enter into the author's plan. Each part must reach us if the whole is to have its effect. Since all degrees are possible, the critic often has to weigh a complete suc-cess in a limited field against the partial failure of an ambitious at-tempt. Specifically, the revolutionary critic may have to say that a limited poet like Robert Frost is better than a more central but more superficial poet, such as Carl Sandburg. What Sandburg is trying to do is more important than what Frost is trying to do, but Frost achieves his aims much more completely than Sandburg.

Though he must keep this question of efficacy of communication always in mind, the critic is principally concerned with the author's world-attitude. It is my opinion, which I have tried to defend in *The Great Tradition,* that in the last hundred years the central ques-tion for Western man has been that posed by the rise of industrial-ism. I am far from demanding that every writer should write about factories, but I do believe that every writer, whatever his theme, must understand the relation of the particular fragment of experi-ence he chooses to describe to the fundamental and inescapable forces that have been affecting every phase of American life. I do not ask whether this author or that has read Karl Marx; I merely as-sume that a really sensitive author, whatever his political views, is bound to be aware of what is going on.

Today the issues created by the rise of industrialism have become so sharp that only conscious evasion can keep a writer from consider-ing them. As in various periods of the past, the central issue has be-come the obvious issue. And of course there has been a great in-crease in the number of novels, plays, and poems that deal directly with economic issues. Even romantic novels these days, such as *Anthony Adverse, So Red the Rose,* and *The Foolscap Rose,* have a conscious social purpose.

In this situation revolutionary writers have, I believe, a great advantage. Here, I admit, my argument must be double-edged. Obviously, from my point of view, they have an advantage, since they agree in their basic assumptions with the class whose needs and interests I take as my standard of reference. But I mean more than that. If, as I believe, victory will ultimately come to the working class, writers who are on its side are more likely to see the forces leading to that victory than are those on the other side. The capitalist writer is something of an apologist, however sincere he may try to be defending special privilege. To put it crudely, the author who chooses capitalism is betting on the losing side, and either he conceals the real reasons for his choice or else his real reasons are bad ones.

Certainly the vitality of contemporary revolutionary literature can scarcely be ignored. I do not hold that every novel written by a Communist is perfect and beyond criticism. I believe, on the contrary, that I am unusually sensitive to the defects of revolutionary literature because I have so vivid a conception of what it ought to be and so poignant a desire to see it realize its potentialities. But when I compare the young radical writers with the young aesthetes or the young regionalists or the young pessimists or the young romantics, I confess that the former seem to be far more alive and promising. To compare Dos Passos' career with Hemingway's, or Jack Conroy's first novel with Gladys Hasty Carroll's, or Isidor Schneider's poetry with Yvor Winters' is to see the difference between a healthy, courageous, resourceful confrontation of reality and a querulous or timid or snobbish preoccupation with petty personal problems.

But perhaps you do not agree with me; and if you do not, I suspect it is because we have different sets of values—because, indeed, our lives are organized toward different ends. I do not want to overemphasize these differences. I hope and believe that I have allies among you, and I have no desire to antagonize anyone. But I am sure that you cannot understand what I am trying to say unless you realize that I expect and desire and work for a revolution that will not only alter political and economic forms but will profoundly change the whole basis of our culture. A new class is coming into power, and the results of its emergence can only dimly be foreseen. I believe that, whatever hardships this revolution may entail, it will eventually be a powerful stimulus to cultural growth, for, by destroying exploitation and class division, it will make possible a truly human civilization. The process may be long and painful, but the goal is clear, and this is the only path by which it can be reached.

You may ask, of course, why you, who have no desire to identify yourselves with the proletariat, should be expected to show any interest in its literary achievements. I can answer on several grounds. In the first place, just as the proletariat finds in bourgeois literature, with all its class bias, a portrayal of human life that is intelligible and enriching, so the bourgeoisie can adjust itself to class differences and discover in proletarian literature a valuable extension and partial integration of experience. This adjustment is relatively easy at present because proletarian literature is still under the influence of the dominant class literature. And it is worth making the necessary effort, for, even if my theories are entirely wrong, these writers from the working class and their sympathizers are very close to movements that are affecting us all. In the second place, you ought to be willing to grant that my conception of the future may be right, and if it is right, these novels and poems, however crude, are certain to have historical importance. Finally, I must invite you to contemplate what not only Marxian theory but the practical experience of Europe has demonstrated to be the only alternative to Communism, Fascism. From my point of view, of course, it is not an alternative but merely a postponement. Nevertheless, within the span of our lives, its constitutes a kind of alternative. And if the choice does lie between Communism and Fascism, it does not seem difficult to decide which deserves the allegiance of those of us who find inspiration in the literature of the past and nourish hopes for the growth of literature in the future.

# JAMES T. FARRELL

## (1904–      )

JAMES T. FARRELL was born on February 27, 1904, in Chicago. He attended classes at De Paul University and the University of Chicago. He has had varied experiences working for an express company and as clerk in a cigar store. He has sold advertising and served as a reporter on a Hearst newspaper. A militant naturalist in fiction, he has also contributed articles on a wide variety of subjects to numerous magazines and newspapers. After intensive study he plunged into the critical debate that raged during the thirties and forties, determined to rid the literary scene of noxious error and to make the truth as he saw it prevail.

In *A Note on Literary Criticism* (1936) Farrell takes up the cudgels in behalf of logical consistency and naturalistically grounded common sense in the sphere of criticism. He objects strenuously to the application of mechanical Marxist principles to literature, and to the opposite, equally deplorable tendency, revolutionary sentimentalism, with its diffuse emotionalism and its febrile exaltation of the cause and character of the proletariat. That is how the actual function of literature is obscured and the formulation of standards external to the literary process becomes an end in itself. Vigorously he denounces the calculus of optimism and pessimism as a basis for literary evaluation. He sees great danger in the development of revolutionary extremism, and his object is to check it by the use of empirical logic and discriminating aesthetic insight. In literature as well as in science and culture as a whole there is an inescapable continuity of influence. Culture does not precede social change; there are no shortcuts; no stage of development can be jumped. Casting aside as irrelevant all questions of party loyalty, he attacks the simplifications advocated by critics like V. F. Calverton, Isidor Schneider, Granville Hicks, Michael Gold, and others.

Farrell lustily combats the effort to politicalize literature, which is not concerned with the dissemination of propaganda. Its object is the assimilation and presentation of life, not the tracking down of social and cultural

427

movements to their economic source. There is a fundamental difference between a political document like the *Communist Manifesto* and a profound, stirring novel like *Man's Fate*. Literature and politics serve different functions and aim to achieve different ends. Revolutionary critics have placed a false emphasis on class-conscious ideology, without stopping to consider the ideology of a work in relation to its formal organization of material. Left-wing critics often completely ignore the refreshment-value of literature, its power of affording us pleasure by enabling us to feel more deeply and with heightened understanding. The ideal critic will analyze and judge a book primarily as a literary work.

*The League of Frightened Philistines* (1945) does not seriously modify the position Farrell formerly held; there is evident, however, a sharpening of perspective, a clearer and more confident utterance on certain issues, a more determined effort to find out the role of the writer in society and the influence of literature on society. The title essay accuses critics like John Chamberlain, Archibald MacLeish, and Van Wyck Brooks of wearing ideological uniforms, of selling benign platitudes and moral panaceas for a living, without recognizing that the social conditions which breed poverty and war must first be changed from the bottom up. There is no substance, he argues, to the charge that the naturalistic novelists fouled their own nests and destroyed faith in American civilization. Respectable worshipers of the past, these critics use their new-won piety and love of tradition to draw a veil over ugly realities that exist at present. These attacks were led by frightened Philistines, reactionaries and traditionalists, and Farrell is determined to oppose them every inch of the way.

There was no shadow of correspondence between the categories harped on so fanatically by the Marxist critics and the actualities of life in America during the thirties. In "Literature and Ideology," first published in 1942, Farrell endeavors to prove that the "moral" critics spawned by the war are ideologically on the same side as those "proletarian" critics who a decade ago were screeching that literature is an instrument in the class struggle. He fails, however, to indicate concretely what Marxist literary criticism consists of, how it can be recognized and evaluated, or to give clinical specimens of such criticism. Though Farrell considers himself a true Marxist, he has no patience with the aberrations of the Marxist aesthetic. If literature becomes politicalized, whether under "moral" or "proletarian" auspices, there can be only one result: the formation of a state-controlled literature. Greatness in literature is not determined by the ideological content of a work. Neither *An American Tragedy* nor *War and Peace* can be dismissed simply because the reader happens to disagree with certain of the doctrines they express.

A powerful polemicist, Farrell has consistently championed the freedom of the artist to tell the truth uncompromisingly about life. In *Literature and Morality* (1947), the initial essay, which discusses the dualism between individual and social morality, expresses the conviction that the major evils of our time spring from the structural character of society itself. Though the mechanical application of Marxist theory may be legitimately assailed as deficient in many respects, the fundamental element of Marxism, its condemnation of the exploitation of man by man, remains sound. All this leads him to the conclusion that moral judgments of literature are inescapable, since we cannot avoid passing moral judgments whenever we discuss literature or life. He zealously defends realism as not only telling the truth about life but also as opening up new areas of experience for creative expression. Though literature is not a mode of action or a means of ushering in social reforms, realistic literature can help people to learn the truth about themselves and the world they live in. There can be no question that Farrell's work, though largely controversial in nature, has made a genuinely valuable contribution to the critical debate of our time.

BIBLIOGRAPHY

TEXT

*A Note on Literary Criticism.* New York, 1936.
*The League of Frightened Philistines.* New York, 1945.
*The Fate of Writing in America.* Norfolk, 1946. (Pamphlet)
*Literature and Morality.* New York, 1947.

CRITICISM

Adams, J. Donald, *The Shape of Books to Come.* New York, 1944.
Glicksberg, Charles I., "The Criticism of James T. Farrell," *Southwest Review,* XXXV, 189–196 (Summer, 1950).
Smith, Bernard, *Forces in American Criticism.* New York, 1939.

## THE CATEGORIES OF "BOURGEOIS" AND "PROLETARIAN"*

IF my analysis and demonstration be acceptable, we are forced to the conclusion that some elements of the thought and the creative literature of the past survive, carrying with them some degree of

* Reprinted by permission from *A Note on Literary Criticism* by James T. Farrell, Copyright, 1936, by Vanguard Press, Inc.

æsthetic and objective validity. It is, then, safe to assume that some of the art and some of the thought of the present will retain elements of intellectual or æsthetic validity after the process of history and the passage of time have eliminated or solved the problems created by the conditions and the burning needs of our impermanent system of capitalist democracy.

Further, if this line of reasoning be correct, what becomes of the categories *bourgeois* and *proletarian* in their application to art, literature, and thought? These categories have often been applied confusingly. Thus they have been used in a descriptive sense on the one hand, and on the other they have been transferred from the status of descriptive standards to that of categories of value *per se*.

Michael Gold, with his usual Marxmanship, has given us one interesting application. Writing on Gilbert and Sullivan[1] he says that "when a Nazi with hands dripping with the blood of workers begins to sentimentalize over Wagner, or an ex-Czarist officer who has hung and flogged peasants, tells us that Dostoevsky shakes him to the very soul, one is perhaps justified in suspecting both Wagner and Dostoievsky," because "it is difficult to separate a work of art from the class out of which it has sprung and the audience it affects." Here the class status of the audience, even years after the artist is dead, is made a category; and from being a category it is tacitly shifted, by the very phrasing itself, into a qualitative judgment *per se*. Mr. Gold continues: "It [Gilbert and Sullivan's opera] is all the most glorious nonsense, and the music has a happy folk-dance quality. Nobody has ever written better popular music; it hasn't a single vulgar flaw. . . . I can testify to the hypnotic spell these two magicians cast upon me." Despite this effect, however, he remained worried, because "true class culture grows by . . . subconscious accretion." And Gilbert, it must be remembered, was a Tory. And so, according to Mr. Gold, "Such men are the 'cultural' pioneers of Fascism." He therefore demands proletarian Gilbert-and-Sullivan operas. Here the category *bourgeois* is applied from a superficial recognition of the class-consciousness of the audience, connected with the subconscious and turned into an implicit judgment.

Granville Hicks[2] finds the bourgeois novel incompletely satisfying. Contrary to Isidor Schneider his adoption of a "Marxian" viewpoint has changed his literary outlook. Thus, he presents considerable

---

1 "The Gilbert-Sullivan Cult," *New Masses,* April 24, 1934.

2 "The Future of the Proletarian Novel"—final article in the series "Revolution and the Novel," *New Masses,* May 22, 1934.

detail to prove that he could not now be so impressed by Proust as he once was. He confesses: "There is no bourgeois novel that, taken as a whole, satisfies me. I am not merely conscious of omission and irrelevancies; I feel within myself a definite resistance, a counter-emotion, so to speak, that makes a unified esthetic experience impossible." The present is, however, a period of transition, and we have as yet no great proletarian novels to substitute for great bourgeois novels. Thus "the reason why revolutionary writers so often seem clumsy is that they are trying to communicate the operation of what deserves to be called a new type of sensibility."[3] In the future, they will achieve this expression in a socialist society. Until that society shall develop, "the integration toward which the revolutionary writer aims is limited by the outlook and needs of the proletariat. This means, obviously, an emphasis on class-consciousness and militancy, but the author most effectively creates such attitudes not by ignoring large sectors of life, but by integrating them with the class struggle."

Hicks spends considerable time discussing the themes about which a proletarian novelist might write; and he suggests that some themes, such as those dealing with the life of the petty bourgeoisie, will not generally satisfy the proletarian novelist. "The trouble is, of course, that such a theme does not give the author an opportunity to display the forces [the class-conscious vanguard of the proletariat and its leaders] that are working against the defeatism and incipient Fascism of the petty bourgeoisie."[4] Withal, Mr. Hicks does not impose restrictions on the proletarian novelist in choice of themes and material. On the contrary, he is as broad as life, and even declares that the proletarian novelist may write about the past, the present, or the future. However, he thinks it most likely that the proletarian novelist, in writing about the past, will select a subject in which the feature of "relevance" is fairly obvious.[5] He mentions probable historical subjects that clearly would be classified here—Shays's Rebellion, the Paris Commune, and the French Revolution. He predicts a future in which the proletarian novel will surpass the bourgeois novel, and he pens a prophetic picture of the future proletarian novel:

[3] *Ibid.*

[4] "Character and Classes" in the series "Revolution and the Novel," *New Masses,* April 24, 1934. In my opinion, the *greatest* American novel of our century is *An American Tragedy.* It may be considered as a case history of the American petty bourgeoisie. I wonder if many of our proletarian novelists would have been dissatisfied with such a theme if they had written *An American Tragedy.*

[5] *Ibid.*

"If we can imagine an author with Michael Gold's power of evoking scenes, and William Rollins'[6] structural skill, with Jack Conroy's wide acquaintance with the proletariat, with Louis Colman's[7] first-hand knowledge of the labor movement, with all the passion of these and a dozen other revolutionary novelists, with something of Dreiser's massive patience, we can see what shape a proletarian masterpiece might take. It would do justice to all the many-sided richness of the characters, exploring with Proustian persistence the deepest recesses of individuality and at the same time exhibiting that individuality as essentially a social phenomenon. And it would carry its readers toward life, not, as *The Remembrance of Things Past* does, toward death."[8]

Mr. Hicks here, as in *The Great Tradition*, reveals a strong tendency to use the categories of bourgeois and proletarian literature as standards, and within them to judge works of literature in terms of themes and of formal ideology.

Often, when they have contrasted bourgeois and proletarian literature, revolutionary critics have been pressed into a dilemma. Bourgeois literature, so-called, has developed through a long tradition, and its heritage now includes a number of great works. Proletarian literature, so-called, has not had that same historical development. Revolutionary critics, proceeding in terms of these categories, have therefore been forced to counter what has been accomplished in bourgeois literature with faith in the prospects and potentialities of proletarian literature. Through many prognostications, much theorizing, countless prophecies, we have found these critics again and again cooking up recipes for tomorrow's "great" literature. Mr. Hicks' description of a future proletarian Proust, greater than Marcel Proust himself, is one of many such prophecies. These efforts suggest a remark of Louis Grudin's. Speaking of the critic who applies standards of measurement instead of criteria of judgment, Mr. Grudin[9] comments: "His procedure has been that of an excursion for words and notions to support his claims, wherever he could find them; and he has had to trust to the meanings he could read into already available odds and ends belonging to various fields and gathered into a makeshift critical doctrine."

We can gain a further sense of the confusion in this aspect of the critical problem by considering the views of D. S. Mirsky on James

6 Author of *The Shadow Before.*
7 Author of *Lumber.*
8 In *New Masses*, May 23, 1934.
9 Quoted by John Dewey in *Art as Experience.*

Joyce.[10] After describing the social and ideological backgrounds and the personal history of Joyce, and proving that Joyce was introduced as a figure into the world of the international bourgeoisie by two millionaires, Mirsky asks the question whether or not Joyce offers any model for revolutionary writers:

"The answer is that his method is too inseparably connected with the specifically decadent phase of the bourgeois culture he reflects, is too narrowly confined within its limits. The use of the inner monologue (stream of consciousness method) is too closely connected with the ultra subjectivism of the parasitic, rentier bourgeoisie, and entirely unadaptable to the art of one who is building socialist society. Not less foreign to the dynamics of our [Russian] culture is the fundamentally static method in which the picture of Bloom is composed. . . . There remains still the most fundamental element of Joyce's art, his realistic grasp, his amazing exactness of expression, all that side in which he is of the school of the French naturalists, raising to its ultimate height their cult of the *mot juste*. It is this exactness which gives Joyce the wonderful realistic power in depicting the outer world for which he is famous. But this has its roots on the one hand in a morbid, defeatist delight in the ugly and repulsive and, on the other, in an aesthetico-proprietary desire for the possession of 'things'. So that even this one realistic element of Joyce's style is fundamentally foreign to the realism towards which Soviet art aims, mainly a mastery of the world by means of active, dynamic materialism—with the purpose of not merely understanding but also changing the reality of history."[11]

These quotations reveal the widespread confusion that has accompanied the applications of such categories to literature. Mirsky assumes such a direct tie-up between economics and literature that he finds Joyce's exactitude in description to be an acquisitive and an æsthetico-proprietary desire for "things"; and that Joyce's utilization of the interior monologue is too closely connected with a parasitic element of the bourgeoisie to be usable by revolutionary writers. Such discoveries enable Mirsky to legislate for writers at wholesale on what will or will not influence them.

Michael Gold, seeking to apply these categories, extends them to the audience, applies them retroactively to dead authors, and calls upon the subconscious for abetment in his damnation of bourgeois art. And Granville Hicks, in order to establish the importance of

10 "Joyce and Irish Literature," in the *New Masses*, April 3, 1934.
11 Mirsky's remarks on Joyce might be contrasted with Edmund Wilson's analysis in *Axel's Castle*.

proletarian literature, even relies on such badly subjective evidence as the flat statement that no bourgeois novel will provide him with a unified æsthetic experience. The proper duties of criticism are ignored, and the carry-over value of literature is almost completely disregarded. Functional extremism rampantly leads to one-sided formulæ, the rationalization of prejudices, and the concoction of meaningless recipes for the novelist of the classless society of the future.

Here it becomes necessary to re-emphasize a fairly apparent fact. The "bourgeois" novel has had a long history. It is possible to examine that history, to note the various types of novel that are included within the category, to arrive at some fairly accurate definitions, and even to make some fairly accurate descriptions of its growth and its methods. But with "proletarian" literature this cannot be done, because that literature is now only at the beginning of its history. It will grow and develop as part of the development of literature in general. It will not grow from the definitions of critics. In its growth it will—for some time to come—be constantly influenced by "bourgeois" literature. The assimilation will not be even and regular; it will not proceed according to the dictates of critical legislation. And since literature is a qualitative matter, and since it is æsthetic and subjective as well as functional and objective, the growth of future proletarian literature will not *per se* prove the failure of Joyce or Proust, let alone the failure of Dreiser or Melville. A proletarian classic in the future will not necessarily give rise to dispraise of *Ulysses*, any more than *Macbeth* can logically be cited in dispraise of Dante's *Divine Comedy,* or than Milton's *Paradise Lost* can be used to prove the failure of the author of *Beowulf.*

§ 2

It seems to me that there are the following possible definitions of proletarian literature: it can be defined as creative literature written by a member of the industrial proletariat, regardless of the author's political orientation; as creative literature that reveals some phase of the experience of the industrial proletariat, regardless of the political orientation of the author; as creative literature written by a member of the industrial proletariat who is class-conscious in the Marxian sense, and a member of the proletarian vanguard; as creative literature written by a class-conscious member of the proletariat and treating solely (or principally) of some phase of the life of that group; as creative literature written about that group within the proletariat regardless of the author's class status or his group status within his class; as creative literature written in order to enforce, through its conclusions and implications, the views of the proletarian vanguard; as creative literature read by the proletariat; as creative literature read by the proletarian vanguard; or as creative literature combining these features in differing combinations.

Irrespective of which of these definitions or combination of definitions one applies, it remains that they do not *per se* constitute a category of value. They do not constitute an *a priori* fiat for the critical destruction of works that will not slide into such a category. Moreover, it does not follow that works of literature snugly fitting into whichever of these definitions (or combinations of definitions) one adopts will be uninfluenced by literature that is unqualifiedly non-proletarian, like Proust's works, or unqualifiedly non-revolutionary, in the political sense, like T. S. Eliot's. For there is a continuity in literature and literary influences, just as there is in thought and in science. The literary process continues whether or not we are critically conscious of it. The tightening of categories into absolutes does not destroy this continuity; it merely diverts the literary influences into a subterranean channel. In so doing, it does not subject them to the test of sensible and intelligent critical evaluation. And this is precisely the error that "leftism" has committed in its effort to harden categories and to ignore the carry-over value in literature.

Since literature is not made by definitions of categories, the definition of proletarian literature presented by our revolutionary critics is not, objectively, so important as they assume it to be. The establishment of functional categories sets up standards of measurement rather than criteria of judgment. But—as is pertinently suggested by John Dewey in *Art as Experience*—it is criteria of judgment, not standards of measurement, that are the business of criticism. And the overemphasis of definitions and categories is least relevant when it is referred to a trend in literature that is only at the beginning of its history, only now preparing to spread its wings and fly in many directions.

Any revolutionary critic who would defend himself against my analysis, and argue that the categories of bourgeois and proletarian are more than descriptive, must take one of two positions: he must admit and adopt a double standard, a dual set of criteria, or else he must favor the destruction of one at the expense of the other. If he recognizes two different sets of criteria—one for proletarian values and proletarian literature, and another for bourgeois values and bourgeois literature—he is contradicting his own position, and consistency will demand that he make adjustments of it elsewhere. He sets a wall between bourgeois values and proletarian values in literature. Not advocating the destruction of bourgeois values, he can then grant them a right to existence only as bourgeois values. For him, this position is utterly untenable; he has only one resource— and that is to recognize that these categories are descriptive.

If he adopts the other position, advocating the destruction of bourgeois values and bourgeois influences, and the creation, enlargement, and solidification of proletarian values and proletarian influences, he must answer certain questions. Where is he to find the source from which he will develop his strictly proletarian values? The answer is—in the life and the needs of the proletariat. But the proletariat does not exist in total isolation from the bourgeoisie, nor from bourgeois influences; it does not, for one thing, live free from tradition.[12] And so, despite the critics' sternest defense, bourgeois values will be smuggled in. If barbed-wire fences are to be placed around the minds of the proletariat and its allies, what then of the stream of cultural continuity? If the critic would like to dam off this stream of cultural continuity, does he actually believe that he can?

12 In *What Is to Be Done?* Lenin writes: "Since there can be no talk of an independent ideology being developed by the masses of the workers in the process of their movement, then *the only choice is:* Either bourgeois or Socialist ideology. There is no middle course (for humanity has not created a third ideology, and moreover, in a society torn by class antagonism there can never be a non-class or above class ideology)." And in a footnote he adds: "This does not mean, of course, that the workers have no part in creating such an ideology. But they take part not as workers, but as Socialist theoreticians . . . in other words, they take part only to the extent that they are able, more or less, to acquire the knowledge of their age and advance that knowledge. And in order that working men *may be able to do this more often,* efforts must be made to raise the level of the consciousness of the workers generally; care must be taken that the workers do not confine themselves to the artificially restricted limits of *literature for workers* but that they study *general literature* to an increasing degree. It would even be more true to say, 'were not confined,' instead of 'not confine themselves', because the workers themselves wish to read and do read all that is written for the intelligentsia and it is only a few (bad) intellectuals who believe that it is sufficient 'for the workers' to tell them a few things about factory conditions, and to repeat over and over again what has long been known."

If the knowledge of an age must be mastered, what is the source of most of that knowledge? Obviously, in our age, it is bourgeois. If there can only be either a bourgeois or a Socialist ideology, what is the inference? Obviously, that that knowledge, so far as it has value, must be assimilated into socialist ideology, and used as the basis for advancing the knowledge of the age. Is not the same thing, then, true of culture in general? I contend that it is.

Yet it seems to me that a relentless enforcement of the view that the categories "bourgeois" and "proletarian" are disconnectably separable, that they are standards, and that the proletariat has all of its values created within the range of its own class experience, leads inevitably to that conclusion. For to say that bourgeois values are useless to the proletariat in culture, to say that proletarian values will take their place uninfluenced by bourgeois values, is to contend that the cultural values and achievements that have grown out of the past are useless to the proletariat, and must therefore be destroyed. But a relentlessly enforced leftist theory leads logically to this conclusion, and to follow it out in action and in criticism constitutes an effort toward such an achievement—if achievement it can be called. The critic who is faced with this interpretation will deny it. Yet what other conclusion can be drawn from his reasoning?

Obviously, this view was not held by the great revolutionary Marxist leaders. Further, it is a position that is today rapidly losing ground in America; though, because at one time it did exert a stronger influence on the revolutionary movement, remnants of it are still to be encountered. Such a theory is not one that preserves culture, for culture permits a more, rather than a less, conscious assimilation of the cultural heritage—which was the aim of all the great Marxist leaders.

André Gide has written:[13]

"In every enduring work of art . . . one that is capable of appealing to the appetites of successive generations, there is to be found a good deal more than a mere response to the momentary needs of a class or a period. It goes without saying that it is a good thing to encourage the reading of such masterpieces; and the U.S.S.R., by its reprints of Pushkin and its performances of Shakespeare, better shows its real love of culture than it does by the publication of a swarm of productions which, while they may be remarkable enough in kind, and while they may exalt its triumphs, are possessed, possibly, of but a passing interest. The mistake, I feel, lies in trying to indicate too narrowly, too precisely, just what is to be looked for in the great works of the past, the lesson that is to be learned from them."

When one freezes the categories of bourgeois and proletarian and insists that they be standards of measurement in literature, one shuts out the enduring element that Gide speaks of. This is, baldly,

[13] In a paper read before the First International Congress of Writers for the Defense of Culture, held in Paris in the summer of 1935. Printed in the *Partisan Review*, No. 9, translated by Samuel Putnam.

the position of leftism when it uses its categories in such a way. And it does not sponsor a method that preserves culture. It should remain, then, that the categories bourgeois and proletarian, when applied to literary criticism, are not the basis of value judgment *per se;* rather, they are descriptive categories. Within the category bourgeois, there will be found both progressive and regressive elements. One of the fundamental duties of revolutionary criticism is, as I have already suggested in my comments on Aquinas and Spinoza, to assimilate and further the understanding of the progressive elements, and to negate the influence of the regressive ones.[14] By performing such a task, which is his legitimate one, the critic does not dam up the stream of cultural continuity. Furthermore, his task—evaluating the literature of the present—is not simply and solely that of putting it into categories; nor that of legislating themes on the basis of such categories; nor that of grandiloquently describing future proletarian Prousts greater than Proust. It is rather the task of understanding, assimilating, evaluating, interpreting the literature of the present in a manner analogous to that in which he treats the literature of the past. And if he meets these obligations with intelligence and imagination, he is contributing toward the assimilation of cultural influences and cultural values.

[14] Marx in *The Poverty of Philosophy* criticizes Proudhon for assuming that "every economic category has two sides, the one good, the other bad. . . . The *good* and the *bad* side, the *advantage* and the *inconvenience,* taken together, form for M. Proudhon the contradiction in each economic category. The problem to solve: To conserve the good side while eliminating the bad." Slavery is cited as an example. "What will M. Proudhon do to save slavery? He puts the problem: Conserve the good side of this economic category, eliminate the bad." Marx then shows that Proudhon is here arbitrary. "It is not the category which poses and opposes itself by its contradictory nature, it is M. Proudhon who disturbs himself, argues with himself, strives and struggles between the two sides of the category. . . . He takes the first category to hand and arbitrarily attributes to it the quality of becoming a remedy to the inconveniences of the category which he wishes to purify . . . In thus taking successively the economic categories one by one and making one the antidote of the other, M. Proudhon makes of this mixture of contradictions and of antidotes to contradictions, two volumes of contradictions which he calls by their proper title: 'The System of Economic Contradictions'." (Pp. 121, 123.)

I quote this in order to make the point that I am not speaking here of such categories; I am dealing with larger ones. Also, I am not speaking of "good" and "bad" categories within these categories. I am speaking of "the succession of ideas" (the phrase is Marx's) and of the succession of cultural values.

# WALDO FRANK

## (1889–1967)

WALDO FRANK was born in Long Branch, New Jersey, on August 25, 1889. An amazingly precocious youngster, he had a novel accepted by a publisher when he was sixteen. During his senior year at Yale, from which he graduated in 1911, he gained some valuable journalistic experience by conducting a column of drama criticism in the New Haven *Courier-Journal*. After leaving Yale he did some newspaper work for the New York *Evening Post* and the *New York Times*. In addition he wrote some plays. In 1913, after a year spent abroad in Paris and Germany, where he studied the German and French stage, he became a free-lance writer. In 1916, he helped to found *The Seven Arts*, which he edited until it ceased publication. In addition to the books that flowed from his productive pen, he was active as a translator of works from the French and contributed steadily to magazines not only in this country but also in Mexico, South America, and France. His temporary alliance with the radical movement during the thirties was motivated by his passion for social justice. His work has attracted serious attention in Spain, France, Russia, and South America.

Though Waldo Frank agrees that criticism requires a method, he has done little to supply one; his approach to literature is intuitive and metaphysical rather than primarily aesthetic. In an article on "The Critic as Artist," he maintains that criticism must be practiced as an art, not a science. What the American critic needs is a metaphysical conviction founded on the belief "that the critical work *can* reach reality, that it *can* become part of the Real and as such function in and work upon a world of real values."[1] Waldo Frank is convinced that this is an essential act of affirmation which will make for seriousness and supply a helpful method. In short, he is seeking a morality or a metaphysic at the service of a method. Or as he prefers to state the problem: the critic will be engaged

[1] Waldo Frank, "The Critic as Artist," *New Republic*, XLVIII (August 25, 1926), 19.

439

in the major task of creating Wholes out of the modern chaos. A critic who is not supported by a steady metaphysical vision and implicit faith in the universal, inevitably falls a victim to the fragmentariness of existence, becoming the puppet rather than the master of circumstances. The artist is essentially religious in his vocation, and his responsibility is to transform America, unformed and immature, by means of his creative vision, shape it into organic Oneness.

*Time Exposure* (1926) is a series of sketches of a number of figures from different parts of Bohemia—wealthy patrons of the arts, painters, poets, novelists, musicians, some of whom he knew personally. *Our America* (1919) is an attempt to create a conceptually satisfying image of America and its people. Since art is the expression of life, the leaders in the spiritual discovery of this land will be men of letters. Like Van Wyck Brooks he wrongly interprets the life of the pioneers and attacks pragmatism because it holds up utility as the measure of value, thus setting a premium upon success and reducing life to a mechanical principle. His insight as a critic is limited by his mystical metaphysic, though his judgments are often luminous and, in concrete cases, usually correct. What he looks for, however, is not technical competence but the measure of vitality a work emanates, its creative vision and depth of intensity. He is indebted to Whitman and to Van Wyck Brooks for many of his critical ideas. *Our America* made discontent conscious and articulate.

*Salvos* (1924), an informal book about books and plays, communicates the excitement and impress of the times that it portrayed. An important part of Frank's critical program is his search for a leader with the intellectual and imaginative power to revolutionize our world on a spiritual plane. Criticism is imperative if we are to hasten this consummation. Frank is thoroughly in sympathy with the modern revolt against the past. Culture, however, implies unity, a Whole, which he identifies with health and wholeness. Modern man suffers abysmal despair because he has lost the power to believe wholeheartedly in this spiritual monism. An ardent idealist, Frank has adopted those tenets which are conformable to his prophetic and crusading temperament. Hence his irrational hostility to science, hence the peculiar brand of mysticism that informs his criticism, hence his belief that art is the unique language that conveys the heart of the Mystery. Art is thus rendered sovereign, superior to science and reason. If there is a science of man, it will be found in aesthetics, and nowhere else.

*The Re-Discovery of America* (1929) repeats the thesis, already stated in *Salvos*, that the foundations of modern thought, undermined by the inroads of science and philosophy, have broken down. If the health of society is to be preserved, then religion and politics, Church and State, must form an organic whole. Frank holds science directly responsible for having fathered the machine. Rejecting economic determinism, he inveighs against the deadly materialism that the worship of the machine generates. His philosophy of Wholeness is metaphorical, abstract, and elusive. He believes that the mission of the artist is to save the world. *In the American Jungle,* a collection of essays written over a period of eleven years, marks the course of his intellectual progress and his quest for wholeness and truth. Growth, Frank believes, is not possible without contradiction, rejection, and renewal. He is willing to experiment with himself, with experiences, with ideas, testing the metal of his faith in these adventures of the mind and spirit. To be critical, to be in the ranks of the opposition, to be uncompromisingly sincere and iconoclastic—that, too, is a form of affirmation, an essential part of the critic's as well as artist's task in America.

Waldo Frank is one of the few American critics who have achieved a truly international reputation. The two thinkers who have influenced him most deeply are Marx and Freud. From the former he derived a scheme of social values, a conception of social justice, though he is forced to reject a number of Marxist dogmas. Spinoza supplies the philosophical corrective. The philosophical wisdom of Spinoza chastens and restrains the ideological excesses of Marxism. Frank cannot accept a critical method based on dialectical materialism, which ignores the organic values of a work of art and concentrates instead on its political significance. He is not impressed by the mechanical, formula-ridden quality of so-called Marxist criticism. The American revolutionary writer must see life whole and not through doctrinal spectacles. Whatever his political outlook he must not ignore the individual with his inner struggles and aspirations, nor must he neglect the timeless, universal values of art. At all times, the aim of the writer is to tell the whole truth.

BIBLIOGRAPHY

TEXT

*Our America.* New York, 1919.
*Salvos.* New York, 1924.
*Virgin Spain.* New York, 1926.
*Time Exposures.* New York, 1926.
*The Re-Discovery of America.* New York, 1929.
*America Hispana.* New York, 1931.
*In the American Jungle.* New York, 1937.

*Chart for Rough Waters.* New York, 1940.
*The Jew in Our Day.* New York, 1944.

CRITICISM

Erro, Carlos Alberto, "Un filosofo americano: Waldo Frank," *Sur; revista,*
    No. 7, 45–95 (1933). (Argentina)
*Waldo Frank in America Hispana.* New York, 1930.
Glicksberg, Charles I., "Waldo Frank: Critic of America," *South Atlantic
    Quarterly,* XXXV, 13–26 (January, 1936).
Jocelyn, John, "Getting at Waldo Frank," *Sewanee Review,* XL, 405–413
    (October-December, 1932).
Lann, Evgenyl, "Waldo Frank: American Writer," *International Litera-
    ture,* No. 1, 63–82 (1936).
Munson, Gorham B. *Waldo Frank.* New York, 1923.
Rosenfeld, Paul, *Men Seen.* New York, 1925, pp. 89–109.
Salaberry, R. C. "Waldo Frank et le nouvel idéal américain," *Mercure
    de France,* CCXIX, 353–362 (April 15, 1930).

## VALUES OF THE REVOLUTIONARY WRITER*

(This address was read at the first session of the American Writers Congress held
in New York in April, 1935.)

### I. DEFINITIONS

THE world stands at the crossways. It goes forward into the
socialist order, or human culture, not as we know it but as we aspire
to create it, will perish. I do not say the way forward is certain. The
life of man is at issue; and with man the alternatives are present, at
all times, of life or of death. They are present now. But this is certain. To agonize within the present system, to refuse to get clear by
the social revolution of the working classes, means the plunge of
Western man into a darkness to which his productive and his intellectual forces, if they continue uncontrolled, must doom him: a
darkness from which even the intimations of light that have made
our present, will have vanished. This makes clear that the cause of
the socialist society is not, finally, a political-economic problem: it is
a cultural problem: it is *the* human problem.

I propose to show the specific value, in this crisis, of the literary

* From: *In the American Jungle.* Copyright, 1937, by Waldo Frank. Reprinted by
permission of Rinehart & Company, Inc., Publishers.

work of art—not as a chorus of revolutionary politics, not as an echo to action: but as *an autonomous kind of action*. I propose to show that above all in America today, owing to our peculiar cultural conditions, the revolutionary writer must not be a "fellow traveler": that his art must be co-ordinate with, not subordinate to, the political-economic aspects of the re-creation of mankind.

This requires some definition of history and of literary art (for we are engaged in making history). Fortunately, I may point to the historic sense of mankind, implicit in Marx, as of a body which, like all organic life, evolves by reason of inward assimilations of an objective world from which it wins sustenance and on which it reacts—all according to a pattern which is the nature of the organism: a pattern which in man is capable of great variations chiefly through the process of what, vaguely, we call consciousness.

The part of consciousness, or if you prefer, of *experience*, in historic evolution is important for us because it leads straight to the social function of art. The work of art is a means (among other things) for extending, deepening, our experience of relationship with life as this organic whole. The feeling of intimate kinship with any part of the objective world is what we mean by beauty. As this relationship expands to an inclusive social form, it is what we mean by culture. The basic social function of art is *so to condition men that they will, as a social body, be the medium for the actions of growth and change required by their needs*. These social actions, to be healthy, must be performed within the true experience of *the whole of life involved*—and the conveying, the naturalizing, of this experience is the especial function of art.

I will make this plain. Suppose a man needs to hammer nails for his new house. He must hit the nails square on the head. But in order to do this, the man must be in good general condition. If his eyes are poor, if his brain is dizzy, all his technical skill of wrist-action won't save him from hammering nails badly. No man, it is obvious, is in shape for even an act so simple as hitting a nail on the head unless his body and mind are a fit *medium* for the job. No society of men is in shape for any needed action, save in so far as it has been conditioned to become the *effective medium* for that action.

In simple societies, the prime conditioning arts are lyrical: they are music, the song, the dance. By means of the experience absorbed and sustained through them, the folk becomes the effective medium for the kind of action its emotional and economic needs, and the needs of its rulers, call for. In our world where a chaos of forces is breaking down the life of man before our eyes, the chief conditioning art—although all arts have their place—must be one to synthesize our complex pasts and present, and to direct them. This is the art of words, by which man captures the world and selves that have borne him, and renders them alive with his own vision.

We know now, roughly, the kind of social action to demand of our literary art. It is in general to condition men for the multitude of direct actions of which their life consists: it is, with us, the crucial task of conditioning our readers—who we hope will be the workers, the farmers, and their allies, to become the effective medium of revolution.

This subtle process of *conditioning* is not to be confused with the work of direct *preparation* for daily struggle: work which falls primarily to the teachers, the theorists, the organizers of party and of union, who are largely conditioned by the accumulated work of writers. And it must be clear that this work of conditioning the social body, however invisible it seems, is the direct action of the writers. Words, of course, are also instruments for "preparation": reportage, pamphlets, slogans, manifestoes (this paper is a kind of manifesto), have their legitimate uses in political work. But only in so far as the need of the revolutionary *medium* is understood; and as the main function of literary art, *which is to create this medium,* prevails. The writer who forgets this, in order to bend his art to some seemingly more immediate task, weakens the organic health and progress of mankind by betraying his integral part in it. And in a world full of hunger, of hideous injustice, of threatening war, only a clarity rare, hard and heroic, will hold the literary artist to his own often thankless, often obscured, yet fundamental, action.

## II. The American Writer Under Capitalism

I apply at once these definitions to the special problems of the American revolutionary writer. To this end, we must first glance at the general state of readers and writers in our country.

We have never lacked literary talents. But the economic soil in which they rooted was washed away ere the roots could hold. We have had great writers. They have been influential abroad, where an organic cultural life possessing what we still lack—memory and consciousness—could employ them. Here, a Poe, a Whitman, a Thoreau, a Melville, could win only sentimental disciples because the discontinuity of ethnic and industrial conditions made their message obsolete more quickly than a generation could mature to hear them. We Americans are weak—infinitely weaker than the peasants of China, America Hispana, or old Russia—in that intuitive connection with soil and self and human past, which makes of a folk an effective medium for creative action. In this, our common state of cultural malnutrition, the need of sound literary art cries aloud. But our writers have been attainted by the disease they must help to cure. A sense of impotence, derived from their unconnectedness with the vital classes of the American world, has delivered them up to a succession of European fads and dogmas; and their reflections of foreign literary styles, like the shallow glints of a kaleidoscope, have added up to nothing. When they have turned to our world, our writers have been unable to resist the overpowering pulls of the capitalist system. They have been entertainers, purveyors of candy and cocktails. When at the end of the War, they began to rebel in numbers, their revolt was hollow: an exhibitionistic beating of drums or a snarl and a sneer.

Now the deepest cause of their subjection as writers, and of their impotence, is the hidden ideology of the American system, which—liberal and conservative alike—most of our writers have absorbed. *And this is painfully to the point,* because—whether they know it or not—the same ideology prevails among our revolutionary writers. Far too many of us have taken over the philosophy of the American capitalist culture that we are sworn to overthrow.

### III. THE AMERICAN REVOLUTIONARY WRITER

This American ideology, which has ruled from the beginning—from the time of those prophets of bourgeois business: Benjamin Franklin and Alexander Hamilton, the true masters of our way of life—is a shallow, static rationalism derived from the thinnest, not the deepest, eighteenth-century minds of France and Britain: an empirical rationalism based on fact-worship, on a fetishism (both unscientific and unpoetic) of the finished cut-and-dried report of the five senses, which is not remotely related to the organic rationalism explicit in Spinoza and implicit in the historical dialectic of Marx. Had this vulgar rationalism ruled in seventeenth-century England and France, there would be no modern science. It is, since it ignores the organic and evolving nature of man, by definition the foe of all creative work: the foe, therefore, however hidden, of art and revolution.

Briefly, I will disclose symptoms and attitudes in our revolutionary writers, which reveal (although the writers know it not) this sterile philosophy. . . .

(1) Disbelief in the autonomy of the writer's art; in its integral place *as art* in the organic growth of man and specifically in the revolutionary movement. This self-distrust makes the writer capitulate *as artist:* leads him to take orders, *as artist,* from political leaders—much to the dismay of the more intelligent of said political leaders. It moves the American writer to misapply in his art borrowed foreign definitions of values which have cogence in their place and time of origin; but are meaningless here. This is a carry-over of the faddism of middle-class American writing.

(2) From the same inorganic view of life and hence of art, comes the servile or passive concept of revolutionary literature as primarily "informational," "reflective," "propaganda." This is, of course, borrowed from the mid-Victorian, middle-class idea of utilitarian or moralistic art. There is no reason why good literature should not be of high documentary importance, and have a strong political appeal. Indeed, in a dynamic age like ours, a profound literary art, insofar as it must reveal the deepest evolving forces of man at the time, must be "propaganda" for these forces and for the goal of these forces. But this kind of propaganda derives from the work's effectiveness as literary art and is dependent on it.

(3) What murders the effectiveness of so much of our revolutionary writing? The clue is the word "murder." We all know that murder is a conspicuous American trait: there are more murders, we are told, in the United States in a day than in some European countries in a month. Now murder is a sort of short cut: it is an oversimplified solution of a problem—say, a nagging wife or husband—by simply getting rid of them. It eliminates the *life* of which the problem is a factor. What murder is to the art of life, this dead philosophy is to knowledge; and translated into literary terms it becomes "oversimplification." Call it, if you prefer, a kind of misplaced or *forced* direct action. Here are some of its results:

(a) Novels, aiming to reveal the revolutionary portent and substance of our world, which are stuffed with stereotypes . . . or imitate the spiced journalese of newspaper reports of surface events . . . or echo the bravado (hiding weakness) of the Hemingway-Dashiell Hammett school . . . or borrow the drab pedestrian effects of Victorian realism—as if these were adequate to convey the body—

tragic, farcical, explosive, corybantic, tender, deep as hell and high as heaven, of American life!

(b) Proletarian tales and poems which portray the workers as half-dead people devoid of the imagination, soaring wills and laughter, which are the springs of creation—and of revolution.

(c) Laborious essays in criticism and literary history in which the organic bodies of the works of poets and prosemen are mangled and flattened to become mere wallpapering for the structure of a political argument.[1]

(4) In these refusals, often by men of genuine literary gift, to recognize the material for a deep revolutionary art, lies the one ideological taint. Its final evil is to turn Marxism itself into a dogmatically, mechanically *shut* philosophy. And the effect of this, were it to prevail on our eager, unschooled and sensitive youth (workers as well as writers), would be to repel them: indeed, to drive many of them (and not the worst because the worst bewildered) to seek a home in reactionary schools of thought which do lip service to old forms of man's organic intuitions.

If the youth of America are drawn by the decayed loyalties of nationalism and church into the ranks of fascism, it will be *in part* because our revolutionary writers have been thwarted, by this dead rationalism implicit in the dying capitalist culture, from making clear that life today— in the depths that call for sacrifice, loyalty and love—is on the side of revolution.

The American revolutionary writer . . . to act his part, which is to create the cultural medium for revolution . . . must see life whole. He will have a political creed; if he is a generous man, it will be hard for him to forgo some share of the daily political-industrial struggle. But his political orientation must be within, must arise from, his orientation to life as an artist. Any course of action, any creed, lives within the dynamic substance of life itself: *and this substance, in all its attributes, is the business of the artist.* Therefore it is proper to state that the artist's vision of life IS the material of his art.

There is much confusion among us as to "material" and "subject." The subject of a book is a mere label or container; it may mislead or be empty. Our revolutionary poet or proseman, by his loyalty to

[1] I have read only three volumes of Marxist literary criticism in the English language: "The Liberation of American Literature," by V. F. Calverton; "The Great Tradition," by Granville Hicks; and a short book by John Strachey. All three are of this category.

the working class (whether born in it or not) and by his natural selection of strong, expressive subjects, will write more and more of the struggles of farmer and worker. But if his vision be sound, it will make—*whatever his subject*—the material for revolutionary art. The term "proletarian" applied to art should refer to the key and vision in which the work is conceived, rather than to subject. It should be a qualitative, not a quantitative, term. A story of middle-class or intellectual life, or even of mythological figures, if it is alight with revolutionary vision, is more effective proletarian art—and more effective art for the proletarians—than a shelf full of dull novels about stereotyped workers.

I wish to characterize two of our specific problems.

We writers have two highways for reaching mastery of our material. We must go into life . . . in persons and in self. These two ways are really one; and the writer must follow them together, else he will make headway in neither. If we look upon persons or classes, save with the eye of self-knowledge, we will not see them; and if we look inward upon self, save with an eye disciplined by objective understanding, we will see only the mists of egoism which are the true self's denial. Even more complex is this double way we must take, and never cease from taking. If we look upon persons of one class we will not know them unless we see the class opposing. If we look upon the present of any scene, we will not know it unless we see within it the past . . . and its dynamic direction: its future. *This is the dialectic of the artist.*

Because classes are in mortal conflict, *and because we have taken sides,* does not mean they have nothing in common: it means they have life in common. The class struggle, for us, is a focus of light, a modern form, by which timeless ingredients of human nature common to every person are revealed. It is not a substitute for understanding, but a kind of *spectrum* wherein hunger, passion, love, pity, envy, worship, dream, fear, despair and ecstasy receive a dynamic modern order.

The other branch of our simultaneous highway is the self. Self is the integer of value and of social action, the norm and form of life as man may know it. The revolutionary writer must understand the *person*, or his portraits of social struggle will be flat and ephemeral as the poster on a billboard. As early as Shakespeare, Cervantes and Racine, the artists were creating the image of the "lonely Soul," the "atomic will"—an image which served to make the *medium* in which the Protestant-bourgeois, individualist economy could flourish. We must have poets to sing the image of the new and truer person: the person who knows his integration with group and cosmos; the person through whom the Whole speaks.

Only by bringing home the timeless human values in the class struggle to every member of the exploited classes and to the sensitive of all classes (for under capitalism all decent men and women are oppressed) can the writer stimulate the will to revolutionary action. Only by deepening his comprehension of cultural historic forms, such as religion, in which, however faultily and impurely, man's profoundest intuitions of his organic nature were embodied, can the writer touch the *spirit* of the American worker and farmer and middle class, to release their spirit from obsolete forms into new creative channels. And only thus can we save them from the decayed devotions which are the treacherous bait of the fascists.

Thus, for the American revolutionary writer to give less than the whole picture is poor philosophy, poor art—and poor strategy.

We are aware there is war; we have declared this war to be ours; and we know that in war strategy is important. But this is a war whose battleground is the world—the world of extension and, no less, the world of inward depth. In this battle are countless separate struggles. Many, engaged on their particular fronts, are forced by the crisis of their position to ignore its relativity in the whole; or to misprize and forget values which do not appear to apply to their one urgent need. Therefore we writers must know the breadth and depth of the whole struggle: know its background and its foreground: know its ultimate values within its immediate aims: in order that, by the common experience of our work, the balance and unity be kept; that in the fever of struggle no human heritage of truth and freedom languish; and that the great war for Man move, without error or blindness, to its issue.

*Our* special work is the universal. In our field there can be no strategy but the whole truth.

If a writer doubts this, I doubt he is an artist.

If we believe that communism is the organic next step of the world to be released by freeing the world's forces of health, we must believe in the art revealing man's depths which bear this destiny. We will embody in our work the substance of life: the blood, the bone, the eye, the conscious embrace of necessity whose child is freedom —knowing that in so far as we create this truth, we are moving, and moving those who hear us, toward the Revolution.

# JOHN CROWE RANSOM
## (1888–          )

JOHN CROWE RANSOM was born on April 30, 1888, in Pulaski, Tennessee. In 1909 he graduated from Vanderbilt University. As Rhodes Scholar he spent three years at Oxford; in 1913 he received the bachelor's degree from Christ Church College. From 1914 to 1937 he taught in the English department at Vanderbilt. During the First World War he served as a first lieutenant in the field artillery. In 1931–1932 he was awarded a Guggenheim Fellowship. In 1937 he was appointed Professor of English at Kenyon College, where he founded *The Kenyon Review*. In 1951 he won the Bollingen Prize in poetry.

Ransom's profound interest in poetry is motivated by his own activities as a poet. In nearly all his critical writing his object is to formulate a coherent system of poetics, one that will combat the excesses of romantic sentimentality. What he will not countenance is poetry written by the romantics, which is the expression of the heart's desire, the effort of a sick mind to idealize the real world. True poetry, as he sees it, is not concerned with projects for reforming or idealizing the world, its only object being to realize the world in all its freshness and fullness. Such an aesthetic, as set forth in *The World's Body* (1938), disposes of the pretensions of science and raises poetry to a discipline, firm-bodied, realistic, self-justifying, which furnishes knowledge of a kind that the sciences do not give and are incapable of giving. The latter are cognitive constructions; the former is organic and intuitive. Poetry is our way of creative regeneration and spiritual renewal, but in order to "know" the world in all its beauty and variety, poetry must overcome the resistance of technique and become an art.

A believer in tradition, Ransom would develop the aesthetic forms into a technique of restraint and impersonality. Aesthetic experience is designed to cut off the stream of direct action, defeat the cult of self-expression. In analyzing the function of poetry, Ransom becomes involved in a defence of manners and religion and launches a spirited attack on sociology, politics,

450

economic determinism, and particularly the hegemony of science. T. S. Eliot had come out in behalf of royalism in politics, Anglo-Catholicism in religion, and classicism in literature. Ransom would revise this formula to read as follows: "In manners, aristocratic; in religion, ritualistic; in art, traditional."[1] The banner around which this generation must rally is that of formalism, and like Tate he would go so far as to stress the need for becoming "reactionary," in the sense of returning to the traditional amenities of the past. For the function of traditional society is to humanize the natural man and lift him to the plane of the aesthetic. The aesthetic solution is the most comprehensive one, embracing religion as ritual and life as art.

His aesthetic emerges clearly in his confident belief that an aesthetic effect may exist by itself, without the intrusion of morality or any other body of useful ideas. Ransom combines a staunch intellectualism, which is part of the heritage of the classicist, with an overweening sense of the importance of poetry. Poetry is not some wild cry from the depths of the unconscious. On the contrary, it must make as good sense as prose; that is its fundamental obligation. Poetry calls into being and puts to use the highest powers of the intellect. The poet who is intellectual has learned the value of discipline, the necessity for the restraint provided by technique; the learning of the past serves as a standard of reference, a source of creative strength, a test of what is noblest in the cultural heritage.

Though poetry profits immensely from the fruits of learning and the activity of the intellect, it is not to be confused with ideas. For whereas poetry is invested with the freshness and purity of light on the dawn of creation, an idea is essentially an abstraction, desiccated, cerebral, bloodless. Integral to the poetic act is the natural and spontaneous image. Ransom's *bête noir* is Platonic poetry: namely, the poetry of ideas, causes, allegories. Its efficacy as a rule is derived from the faith of the poet in the validity of his ideas. All this is founded on the premise that man is inherently a rational animal and that his world is based upon reason. Such poetry, Ransom argues, is in reality a misnomer, Being wedded to the image, poetry is rooted in the soil of pure perceptions and is therefore opposed to the abstractions of science. Poetry, like science, seeks truth but it seeks it through the avenue of the imagination. Thus poetry as a form of knowledge and cognition cannot be extruded from the aesthetic experience. The poet makes assertions; even his images are assertions, implicit or explicit. He animates nature; he even animates the collective abstractions of his culture, imbuing them with life. Hence Ransom concludes that poetry is much more "creative" than science.

1 John Crowe Ransom, *The World's Body* (New York, 1938), p. 42.

*The New Criticism* (1941) consists of three studies devoted to I. A. Richards, T. S. Eliot, and Yvor Winters, together with an essay, "Wanted: An Ontological Critic." T. S. Eliot is cited as an example of the historical critic, Richards of the psychological critic, and Winters of the logical critic. One of the fallacies Ransom combats is the tendency to use the vocabulary of psychology to pass judgment on the emotions and attitudes of poems instead of focusing attention on their objects. Another fallacy he attacks is the moralistic attitude exemplified by the writings of Yvor Winters. Ransom is also opposed to the conception that the function of poetry is to arouse and communicate passions, to organize attitudes. He would root out the heresy that art deals immediately, not mediately, with the passions. The emotions in the good poem are psychically distanced; there is the problem of structure and form to be solved. Art implies control, restraint, the mastery of its material. Ransom conceives of poetry as containing an argument or logical foundation that is combined organically with a texture, with details that are interesting and important in themselves, apart from what they contribute to the development of the central argument. That is the heart of his critical theory, the main prop and pivot of his method.

The "new criticism" Ransom admires and practices is technical, "difficult," specialized, concerned with structural organization and textural details, and the dialectical interaction between the two. Such criticism is marked by depth and precision. Its "newness" consists in its explicit and coherently unified method, but while the "new critics" have accomplished a great deal, Ransom feels that much more remains to be done. It must be purged of some impurities and some of its defects must be corrected. Ransom will not accept the psychological approach to poetry, the assumption that the knowledge poetry furnishes is without an objective referent, that it is a subjective "science." Art is worthy of being classified among the cognitive activities. By stripping the poetic experience of the cognitive element we convert poetry into a form of play or make-believe. The good poets do not echo the commonplaces of science nor labor under the illusion that the conceptual structure of science comprises all of reality. The good critic concerns himself with the aesthetic context, with the study of texture as well as structure. The poem, in its particularity of details, is a true cognition. What Ransom is interested in is not the paraphrasable content but the dynamic interplay of determinate with indeterminate meaning, the relation that obtains between structure and texture. That is the heart of the critical act, its measure of technical competence.

BIBLIOGRAPHY

TEXT

*God Without Thunder.* New York, 1930.
*The World's Body.* New York, 1938.
*The New Criticism.* Norfolk, 1941.
"Criticism as Pure Speculation," *Intent of the Critic,* ed. by Donald
    Stauffer. Princeton, 1941.
"The Bases of Criticism," *Sewanee Review,* LII, 556–571 (Autumn, 1944).
(ed.), *The Kenyon Critics.* Cleveland and New York, 1951.


CRITICISM

Baker, J. E., "Philosopher and New Critic," *Sewanee Review,* L, 167–170
    (April-June, 1942).
Burgum, Edwin Berry, "An Examination of Modern Critics: John Crowe
    Ransom," *Rocky Mountain Review,* VIII, 87–93 (Spring, 1944).
Knickerbocker, W. S., "Mr. Ransom and the Old South," *Sewanee Re-
    view,* XXXIX, 222–238 (April-June, 1931).
Lynskey, Winifred, "A Critic in Action: Mr. Ransom," *College English,*
    V, 239–249 (February, 1944).
Roellinger, F., "Two Theories of Poetry as Knowledge," *Southern Review,*
    VII, 690–705 (Spring, 1942).
Schwartz, Delmore, "Instructed of Much Morality," *Sewanee Review,*
    LIV, 438–448 (Summer, 1946).
*Sewanee Review,* LVI (Summer, 1948). Contains tributes to Ransom.
Stallman, R. W., "John Crowe Ransom: A Checklist," *Sewanee Review,*
    LVI (Summer, 1948).
Stauffer, Donald, "Critical Principles and a Sonnet," *American Scholar,*
    XII, 52–62 (Winter, 1942).
Trowbridge, H., "Aristotle and the 'New Criticism,'" *Sewanee Review,*
    LII, 537–555 (Autumn, 1944).
Winters, Yvor, *The Anatomy of Nonsense.* Norfolk, 1942.

# CRITICISM, INC.*

IT is strange, but nobody seems to have told us what exactly is
the proper business of criticism. There are many critics who might
tell us, but for the most part they are amateurs. So have the critics
nearly always been amateurs; including the best ones. They have

* Reprinted from *The World's Body* by John Crowe Ransom; copyright 1938 by
Charles Scribner's Sons; used by permission of the publishers.

not been trained to criticism so much as they have simply undertaken a job for which no specific qualifications were required. It is far too likely that what they call criticism when they produce it is not the real thing.

There are three sorts of trained performers who would appear to have some of the competence that the critic needs. The first is the artist himself. He should know good art when he sees it; but his understanding is intuitive rather than dialectical—he cannot very well explain his theory of the thing. It is true that literary artists, with their command of language, are better critics of their own art than are other artists; probably the best critics of poetry we can now have are the poets. But one can well imagine that any artist's commentary on the art-work is valuable in the degree that he sticks to its technical effects, which he knows minutely, and about which he can certainly talk if he will.

The second is the philosopher, who should know all about the function of the fine arts. But the philosopher is apt to see a lot of wood and no trees, for his theory is very general and his acquaintance with the particular works of art is not persistent and intimate, especially his acquaintance with their technical effects. Or at least I suppose so, for philosophers have not proved that they can write close criticism by writing it; and I have the feeling that even their handsome generalizations are open to suspicion as being grounded more on other generalizations, those which form their prior philosophical stock, than on acute study of particulars.

The third is the university teacher of literature, who is styled professor, and who should be the very professional we need to take charge of the critical activity. He is hardly inferior as critic to the philosopher, and perhaps not on the whole to the poet, but he is a greater disappointment because we have the right to expect more of him. Professors of literature are learned but not critical men. The professional morale of this part of the university staff is evidently low. It is as if, with conscious or unconscious cunning, they had appropriated every avenue of escape from their responsibility which was decent and official; so that it is easy for one of them without public reproach to spend a lifetime in compiling the data of literature and yet rarely or never commit himself to a literary judgment.

Nevertheless it is from the professors of literature, in this country the professors of English for the most part, that I should hope eventually for the erection of intelligent standards of criticism. It is their business.

Criticism must become more scientific, or precise and systematic, and this means that it must be developed by the collective and sustained effort of learned persons—which means that its proper seat is in the universities.

Scientific: but I do not think we need be afraid that criticism, trying to be a sort of science, will inevitably fail and give up in despair, or else fail without realizing it and enjoy some hollow and pretentious career. It will never be a very exact science, or even a nearly exact one. But neither will psychology, if that term continues to refer to psychic rather than physical phenomena; nor will sociology, as Pareto, quite contrary to his intention, appears to have furnished us with evidence for believing; nor even will economics. It does not matter whether we call them sciences or just systematic studies; the total effort of each to be effective must be consolidated and kept going. The studies which I have mentioned have immeasurably improved in understanding since they were taken over by the universities, and the same career looks possible for criticism.

Rather than occasional criticism by amateurs, I should think the whole enterprise might be seriously taken in hand by professionals. Perhaps I use a distasteful figure, but I have the idea that what we need is Criticism, Inc., or Criticism, Ltd.

The principal resistance to such an idea will come from the present incumbents of the professorial chairs. But its adoption must come from them too. The idea of course is not a private one of my own. If it should be adopted before long, the credit would probably belong to Professor Ronald S. Crane, of the University of Chicago, more than to any other man. He is the first of the great professors to have advocated it as a major policy for departments of English. It is possible that he will have made some important academic history.

2

Professor Crane published recently a paper of great note in academic circles, on the reform of the courses in English. It appeared in *The English Journal,* under the title: "History Versus Criticism in the University Study of Literature." He argues there that historical scholarship has been overplayed heavily in English studies, in disregard of the law of diminishing returns, and that the emphasis must now be shifted to the critical.

To me this means, simply: the students of the future must be permitted to study literature, and not merely about literature. But

I think this is what the good students have always wanted to do. The wonder is that they have allowed themselves so long to be denied. But they have not always been amiable about it, and the whole affair presents much comic history.

At the University of Chicago, I believe that Professor Crane, with some others, is putting the revolution into effect in his own teaching, though for the time being perhaps with a limited programme, mainly the application of Aristotle's critical views. (My information is not at all exact.) The university is an opulent one, not too old to experience waves of reformational zeal, uninhibited as yet by bad traditions. Its department of English has sponsored plenty of old-line scholarship, but this is not the first time it has gone in for criticism. If the department should now systematically and intelligently build up a general school of literary criticism, I believe it would score a triumph that would be, by academic standards, spectacular. I mean that the alive and brilliant young English scholars all over the country would be saying they wanted to go there to do their work. That would place a new distinction upon the university, and it would eventually and profoundly modify the practices of many other institutions. It would be worth even more than Professor Crane's careful presentation of the theory.

This is not the first time that English professors have tilted against the historians, or "scholars," in the dull sense which that word has acquired. They did not score heavily, at those other times. Probably they were themselves not too well versed in the historical studies, so that it could be said with honest concern that they scarcely had the credentials to judge of such matters. At the same time they may have been too unproductive critically to offer a glowing alternative.

The most important recent diversion from the orthodox course of literary studies was that undertaken by the New Humanists. I regret to think that it was not the kind of diversion which I am advocating; nor the kind approved by Professor Crane, who comments briefly against it. Unquestionably the Humanists did divert, and the refreshment was grateful to anybody who felt resentful for having his literary predilections ignored under the schedule of historical learning. But in the long run the diversion proved to be nearly as unliterary as the round of studies from which it took off at a tangent. No picnic ideas were behind it.

The New Humanists were, and are, moralists; more accurately, historians and advocates of a certain moral system. Criticism is the attempt to define and enjoy the æsthetic or characteristic values of literature, but I suppose the Humanists would shudder at "æsthetic" as hard as ordinary historical scholars do. Did an official Humanist ever make any official play with the term? I do not remember it. The term "art" is slightly more ambiguous, and they have availed themselves of that; with centuries of loose usage behind it, art connotes, for those who like, high seriousness, and high seriousness connotes moral self-consciousness, and an inner check, and finally either Plato or Aristotle.

Mr. Babbitt consistently played on the terms classical and romantic. They mean any of several things each, so that unquestionably Mr. Babbitt could make war on romanticism for purely moral reasons; and his preoccupation was ethical, not æsthetic. It is perfectly legitimate for the moralist to attack romantic literature if he can make out his case; for example, on the ground that it deals with emotions rather than principles, or the ground that its author discloses himself as flabby, intemperate, escapist, unphilosophical, or simply adolescent. The moral objection is probably valid; a romantic period testifies to a large-scale failure of adaptation, and defense of that failure to adapt, to the social and political environment; unless, if the Humanists will consent, it sometimes testifies to the failure of society and state to sympathize with the needs of the individual. But this is certainly not the charge that Mr. T. S. Eliot, a literary critic, brings against romanticism. His, if I am not mistaken, is æsthetic, though he may not ever care to define it very sharply. In other words, the literary critic also has something to say about romanticism, and it might come to something like this: that romantic literature is imperfect in objectivity, or "æsthetic distance," and that out of this imperfection comes its weakness of structure; that the romantic poet does not quite realize the æsthetic attitude, and is not the pure artist. Or it might come to something else. It would be quite premature to say that when a moralist is obliged to disapprove a work the literary critic must disapprove it too.

Following the excitement produced by the Humanist diversion, there is now one due to the Leftists, or Proletarians, who are also diversionists. Their diversion is likewise moral. It is just as proper for them to ferret out class-consciousness in literature, and to make literature serve the cause of loving-comradeship, as it is for the Humanists to censure romanticism and to use the topic, and the literary exhibit, as the occasion of reviving the Aristotelian moral canon. I mean that these are procedures of the same sort. Debate could never occur between a Humanist and a Leftist on æsthetic grounds, for they are equally intent on ethical values. But the debate on ethical grounds would be very spirited, and it might create such a stir in a department conducting English studies that the conventional scholars there would find themselves slipping, and their pupils deriving from literature new and seductive excitements which would entice them away from their scheduled English exercises.

On the whole, however, the moralists, distinguished as they may be, are like those who have quarrelled with the ordinary historical studies on purer or more æsthetic grounds: they have not occupied in English studies the positions of professional importance. In a department of English, as in any other going business, the proprietary interest becomes vested, and in old and reputable departments the vestees have uniformly been gentlemen who have gone through the historical mill. Their laborious Ph.D.'s and historical publications are their patents. Naturally, quite spontaneously, they would tend to perpetuate a system in which the power and the glory belonged to them. But English scholars in this country can rarely have better credentials than those which Professor Crane has earned in his extensive field, the eighteenth century. It is this which makes his disaffection significant.

It is really atrocious policy for a department to abdicate its own self-respecting identity. The department of English is charged with the understanding and the communication of literature, an art, yet it has usually forgotten to inquire into the peculiar constitution and structure of its product. English might almost as well announce that it does not regard itself as entirely autonomous, but as a branch of the department of history, with the option of declaring itself occasionally a branch of the department of ethics. It is true that the historical and the ethical studies will cluster round objects which for some reason are called artistic objects. But the thing itself the professors do not have to contemplate; and only last spring the head of English studies in a graduate school fabulously equipped made the following impromptu disclaimer to a victim who felt aggrieved at having his own studies forced in the usual direction: "This is a place for exact scholarship, and you want to do criticism. Well, we don't allow criticism here, because that is something which anybody can do."

But one should never speak impromptu in one's professional capacity. This speech may have betrayed a fluttery private apprehension which should not have been made public: that you can never be critical and be exact at the same time, that history is firmer ground than æsthetics, and that, to tell the truth, criticism is a painful job for the sort of mind that wants to be very sure about things. Not in that temper did Aristotle labor towards a critique in at least one branch of letters; nor in that temper are strong young minds everywhere trying to sharpen their critical apparatus into precision tools, in this decade as never before.

It is not anybody who can do criticism. And for an example, the more eminent (as historical scholar) the professor of English, the less apt he is to be able to write decent criticism, unless it is about another professor's work of historical scholarship, in which case it is not literary criticism. The professor may not be without æsthetic judgments respecting an old work, especially if it is "in his period," since it must often have been judged by authorities whom he respects. Confronted with a new work, I am afraid it is very rare that he finds anything particular to say. Contemporary criticism is not at all in the hands of those who direct the English studies. Contemporary literature, which is almost obliged to receive critical study if it receives any at all, since it is hardly capable of the usual historical commentary, is barely officialized as a proper field for serious study.

Here is contemporary literature, waiting for its criticism; where are the professors of literature? They are watering their own gardens; elucidating the literary histories of their respective periods. So are their favorite pupils. The persons who save the occasion, and rescue contemporary literature from the humiliation of having to go without a criticism, are the men who had to leave the university before their time because they felt themselves being warped into mere historians; or those who finished the courses and took their punishment but were tough, and did not let it engross them and spoil them. They are home-made critics. Naturally they are not too wise, these amateurs who furnish our reviews and critical studies, but when they distinguish themselves, the universities which they attended can hardly claim more than a trifling share of the honor.

It is not so in economics, chemistry, sociology, theology, and architecture. In these branches it is taken for granted that criticism of the performance is the prerogative of the men who have had formal training in its theory and technique. The historical method is useful, and may be applied readily to any human performance whatever. But the exercise does not become an obsession with the university men working in the other branches; only the literary scholars wish to convert themselves into pure historians. This has gone far to nullify the usefulness of a departmental personnel larger, possibly, than any other, and of the lavish endowment behind it.

### 3

Presumably the departments of English exist in order to communicate the understanding of the literary art. That will include both criticism and also whatever may be meant by "appreciation." This latter term seems to stand for the kind of understanding that is had intuitively, without benefit of instruction, by merely being constrained to spend time in the presence of the literary product. It is true that some of the best work now being done in departments is by the men who do little more than read well aloud, enforcing a private act of appreciation upon the students. One remembers how good a service that may be, thinking perhaps of Professor Copeland of Harvard, or Dean Cross at Greeley Teachers College. And there are men who try to get at the same thing in another way, which they would claim is surer: by requiring a great deal of memory work, in order to enforce familiarity with fine poetry. These might defend their strategy by saying that at any rate the work they required was not as vain as the historical rigmarole which the scholars made their pupils recite, if the objective was really literary understanding and not external information. But it would be a misuse of terms to employ the word instruction for the offices either of the professors who read aloud or of those who require the memory work. The professors so engaged are properly curators, and the museum of which they have the care is furnished with the cherished literary masterpieces, just as another museum might be filled with paintings. They conduct their squads from one work to another, making appropriate pauses or reverent gestures, but their own obvious regard for the masterpieces is somewhat contagious, and contemplation is induced. Naturally they are grateful to the efficient staff of colleagues in the background who have framed the masterpieces, hung them in the proper schools and in the chronological order, and prepared the booklet of information about the artists and the occasions. The colleagues in their turn probably feel quite happy over this division of labor, thinking that they have done the really productive work, and that it is appropriate now if less able men should undertake a little salesmanship.

Behind appreciation, which is private, and criticism, which is public and negotiable, and represents the last stage of English studies, is historical scholarship. It is indispensable. But it is instrumental and cannot be the end itself. In this respect historical studies have the same standing as linguistic studies: language and history are aids.

On behalf of the historical studies. Without them what could we make of Chaucer, for instance? I cite the familiar locus of the "hard" scholarship, the center of any program of advanced studies in English which intends to initiate the student heroically, and once for all, into the historical discipline. Chaucer writes allegories for historians to decipher, he looks out upon institutions and customs unfamiliar to us. Behind him are many writers in various tongues from whom he borrows both forms and materials. His thought bears constant reference to classical and mediæval philosophies and sciences which have passed from our effective knowledge. An immense labor of historical adaptation is necessary before our minds are ready to make the æsthetic approach to Chaucer.

Or to any author out of our own age. The mind with which we enter into an old work is not the mind with which we make our living, or enter into a contemporary work. It is under sharp restraints, and it is quite differently furnished. Out of our actual contemporary mind we have to cancel a great deal that has come there under modern conditions but was not in the earlier mind at all. This is a technique on the negative side, a technique of suspension; difficult for practical persons, literal scientists, and aggressive moderns who take pride in the "truth" or the "progress" which enlightened man, so well represented in their own instance, has won. Then, on the positive side, we must supply the mind with the precise beliefs and ways of thought it had in that former age, with the specific content in which history instructs us; this is a technique of make-believe. The whole act of historical adaptation, through such techniques, is a marvellous feat of flexibility. Certainly it is a thing hard enough to justify university instruction. But it is not sufficient for an English program.

The achievement of modern historical scholarship in the field of English literature has been, in the aggregate, prodigious; it should be very proud. A good impression of the volume of historical learning now available for the students of English may be quickly had from inspecting a few chapters of the Cambridge History, with the bibliographies. Or, better, from inspecting one of a large number of works which have come in since the Cambridge History: the handbooks, which tell all about the authors, such as Chaucer, Shakespeare, Milton, and carry voluminous bibliographies; or the period books, which tell a good deal about whole periods of literature.

There is one sense in which it may be justly said that we can never have too much scholarship. We cannot have too much of it if the critical intelligence functions, and has the authority to direct it. There is hardly a critical problem which does not require some arduous exercises in fact-finding, but each problem is quite specific about the kind of facts it wants. Mountains of facts may have been found already, but often they have been found for no purpose at all except the purpose of piling up into a big exhibit, to offer intoxicating delights to the academic population.

To those who are æsthetically minded among students, the rewards of many a historical labor will have to be disproportionately slight. The official Chaucer course is probably over ninety-five per cent historical and linguistic, and less than five per cent æsthetic or critical. A thing of beauty is a joy forever. But it is not improved because the student has had to tie his tongue before it. It is an artistic object, with a heroic human labor behind it, and on these terms it calls for public discussion. The dialectical possibilities are limitless, and when we begin to realize them we are engaged in criticism.

## 4

What is criticism? Easier to ask, What is criticism not? It is an act now notoriously arbitrary and undefined. We feel certain that the critical act is not one of those which the professors of literature habitually perform, and cause their students to perform. And it is our melancholy impression that it is not often cleanly performed in those loose compositions, by writers of perfectly indeterminate qualifications, that appear in print as reviews of books.

Professor Crane excludes from criticism works of historical scholarship and of Neo-Humanism, but more exclusions are possible than that. I should wish to exclude:

1. Personal registrations, which are declarations of the effect of the art-work upon the critic as reader. The first law to be prescribed to criticism, if we may assume such authority, is that it shall be objective, shall cite the nature of the object rather than its effects upon the subject. Therefore it is hardly criticism to assert that the proper literary work is one that we can read twice; or one that causes in us some remarkable physiological effect, such as oblivion of the outer world, the flowing of tears, visceral or laryngeal sensations, and such

like; or one that induces perfect illusion, or brings us into a spiritual ecstasy; or even one that produces a catharsis of our emotions. Aristotle concerned himself with this last in making up his definition of tragedy—though he did not fail to make some acute analyses of the objective features of the work also. I have read that some modern Broadway producers of comedy require a reliable person to seat himself in a trial audience and count the laughs; their method of testing is not so subtle as Aristotle's, but both are concerned with the effects. Such concern seems to reflect the view that art comes into being because the artist, or the employer behind him, has designs upon the public, whether high moral designs or box-office ones. It is an odious view in either case, because it denies the autonomy of the artist as one who interests himself in the artistic object in his own right, and likewise the autonomy of the work itself as existing for its own sake. (We may define a chemical as something which can effect a certain cure, but that is not its meaning to the chemist; and we may define toys, if we are weary parents, as things which keep our children quiet, but that is not what they are to engineers.) Furthermore, we must regard as uncritical the use of an extensive vocabulary which ascribes to the object properties really discovered in the subject, as: *moving, exciting, entertaining, pitiful; great,* if I am not mistaken, and *admirable,* on a slightly different ground; and, in strictness, *beautiful* itself.

2. Synopsis and paraphrase. The high-school classes and the women's clubs delight in these procedures, which are easiest of all the systematic exercises possible in the discussion of literary objects. I do not mean that the critic never uses them in his analysis of fiction and poetry, but he does not consider plot or story as identical with the real content. Plot is an abstract from content.

3. Historical studies. These have a very wide range, and include studies of the general literary background; author's biography, of course with special reference to autobiographical evidences in the work itself; bibliographical items; the citation of literary originals and analogues, and therefore what, in general, is called comparative literature. Nothing can be more stimulating to critical analysis than comparative literature. But it may be conducted only superficially, if the comparisons are perfunctory and mechanical, or if the scholar is content with merely making the parallel citations.

4. Linguistic studies. Under this head come those studies which define the meaning of unusual words and idioms, including the foreign and archaic ones, and identify the allusions. The total benefit

of linguistics for criticism would be the assurance that the latter was based on perfect logical understanding of the content, or "interpretation." Acquaintance with all the languages and literatures in the world would not necessarily produce a critic, though it might save one from damaging errors.

5. Moral studies. The moral standard applied is the one appropriate to the reviewer; it may be the Christian ethic, or the Aristotelian one, or the new proletarian gospel. But the moral content is not the whole content, which should never be relinquished.

6. Any other special studies which deal with some abstract or prose content taken out of the work. Nearly all departments of knowledge may conceivably find their own materials in literature, and take them out. Studies have been made of Chaucer's command of mediæval sciences, of Spenser's view of the Irish question, of Shakespeare's understanding of the law, of Milton's geography, of Hardy's place-names. The critic may well inform himself of these materials as possessed by the artist, but his business as critic is to discuss the literary assimilation of them.

## 5

With or without such useful exercises as these, probably assuming that the intelligent reader has made them for himself, comes the critical act itself.

Mr. Austin Warren, whose writings I admire, is evidently devoted to the academic development of the critical project. Yet he must be a fair representative of what a good deal of academic opinion would be when he sees no reason why criticism should set up its own house, and try to dissociate itself from historical and other scholarly studies; why not let all sorts of studies, including the critical ones, flourish together in the same act of sustained attention, or the same scheduled "course"? But so they are supposed to do at present; and I would only ask him whether he considers that criticism prospers under this arrangement. It has always had the chance to go ahead in the hands of the professors of literature, and it has not gone ahead. A change of policy suggests itself. Strategy requires now, I should think, that criticism receive its own charter of rights and function independently. If he fears for its foundations in scholarship, the scholars will always be on hand to reprove it when it tries to function on an unsound scholarship.

I do not suppose the reviewing of books can be reformed in the

sense of being turned into pure criticism. The motives of the reviewers are as much mixed as the performance, and indeed they condition the mixed performance. The reviewer has a job of presentation
and interpretation as well as criticism. The most we can ask of him
is that he know when the criticism begins, and that he make it as
clean and definitive as his business permits. To what authority may
he turn?

I know of no authority. For the present each critic must be his
own authority. But I know of one large class of studies which is certainly critical, and necessary, and I can suggest another sort of
study for the critic's consideration if he is really ambitious.

Studies in the technique of the art belong to criticism certainly.
They cannot belong anywhere else, because the technique is not
peculiar to any prose materials discoverable in the work of art, nor
to anything else but the unique form of that art. A very large volume
of studies is indicated by this classification. They would be technical
studies of poetry, for instance, the art I am specifically discussing,
if they treated its metric; its inversions, solecisms, lapses from the
prose norm of language, and from close prose logic; its tropes; its
fictions, or inventions, by which it secures "æsthetic distance" and
removes itself from history; or any other devices, on the general
understanding that any systematic usage which does not hold good
for prose is a poetic device.

A device with a purpose: the superior critic is not content with
the compilation of the separate devices; they suggest to him a much
more general question. The critic speculates on why poetry, through
its devices, is at such pains to dissociate itself from prose at all, and
what it is trying to represent that cannot be represented by prose.

I intrude here with an idea of my own, which may serve as a starting point of discussion. Poetry distinguishes itself from prose on the
technical side by the devices which are, precisely, its means of escap-
ing from prose. Something is continually being killed by prose which
the poet wants to preserve. But this must be put philosophically.
(Philosophy sounds hard, but it deals with natural and fundamental
forms of experience.)

The critic should regard the poem as nothing short of a desperate
ontological or metaphysical manœuvre. The poet himself, in the
agony of composition, has something like this sense of his labors.
The poet perpetuates in his poem an order of existence which in
actual life is constantly crumbling beneath his touch. His poem celebrates the object which is real, individual, and qualitatively infinite.

He knows that his practical interests will reduce this living object to a mere utility, and that his sciences will disintegrate it for their convenience into their respective abstracts. The poet wishes to defend his object's existence against its enemies, and the critic wishes to know what he is doing, and how. The critic should find in the poem a total poetic or individual object which tends to be universalized, but is not permitted to suffer this fate. His identification of the poetic object is in terms of the universal or commonplace object to which it tends, and of the tissue, or totality of connotation, which holds it secure. How does he make out the universal object? It is the prose object, which any forthright prosy reader can discover to him by an immediate paraphrase; it is a kind of story, character, thing, scene, or moral principle. And where is the tissue that keeps it from coming out of the poetic object? That is, for the laws of the prose logic, its superfluity; and I think I would even say, its irrelevance.

A poet is said to be distinguishable in terms of his style. It is a comprehensive word, and probably means: the general character of his irrelevances, or tissues. All his technical devices contribute to it, elaborating or individualizing the universal, the core-object; likewise all his material detail. For each poem even, ideally, there is distinguishable a logical object or universal, but at the same time a tissue of irrelevance from which it does not really emerge. The critic has to take the poem apart, or analyze it, for the sake of uncovering these features. With all the finesse possible, it is rude and patchy business by comparison with the living integrity of the poem. But without it there could hardly be much understanding of the value of poetry, or of the natural history behind any adult poem.

The language I have used may sound too formidable, but I seem to find that profound criticism generally works by some such considerations. However the critic may spell them, the two terms are in his mind: the prose core to which he can violently reduce the total object, and the differentia, residue, or tissue, which keeps the object poetical or entire. The character of the poem resides for the good critic in its way of exhibiting the residuary quality. The character of the poet is defined by the kind of prose object to which his interest evidently attaches, plus his way of involving it firmly in the residuary tissue. And doubtless, incidentally, the wise critic can often read behind the poet's public character his private history as a man with a weakness for lapsing into some special form of prosy or scientific bondage.

Similar considerations hold, I think, for the critique of fiction, or of the non-literary arts. I remark this for the benefit of philosophers who believe, with propriety, that the arts are fundamentally one. But I would prefer to leave the documentation to those who are better qualified.

# ALLEN TATE
## (1899–   )

BORN in Kentucky, Allen Tate attended Vanderbilt University, from which he graduated in 1922. He has taught English in various universities. In 1942 he was appointed to the chair of poetry in the Library of Congress. He edited, or helped to edit, a number of literary magazines. A Guggenheim Fellowship enabled him to live abroad from 1928 to 1930. As a member of "The Fugitives," and as founder and editor of *The Fugitive* from 1922 to 1925, he composed poetry that was notable for its hard intellectual content as opposed to the emotional and rhetorical vagueness of nineteenth-century writing. The Agrarians, as can be seen in the symposium, *I'll Take My Stand* (1930), were making a positive plea for regionalism, a return to the soil, rural civilization, protesting against the fallacy that industrialism could be equated with progress or that it was a panacea for the ills of the South.

As a consistent "reactionary," Allen Tate has striven to recapture and reaffirm the living values of the past, especially those to be found in the Southern cultural tradition and in religious orthodoxy. His critical essays have appeared in such magazines as *The Southern Review, The Kenyon Review,* and *The Sewanee Review.* The literary criticism contributed by men like Tate, Cleanth Brooks, and John Crowe Ransom was remarkable chiefly for its insistence that the critic must concern himself with the dynamic structure and internal properties of poetry. Thus they helped to focus attention on literature itself as the source of value instead of seeking literary values in a consideration of historical, political, and social forces. The major objection to formalist criticism as practised by these men is that it carries technical virtuosity to extreme lengths and, as Van Wyck Brooks and others have pointed out, cuts literature off from life.

Allen Tate fought against the Marxist view that socio-economic factors were of primary importance in the analysis and evaluation of literature. Steadily he waged war against the practical, utilitarian, political dogmas which, particularly during the "ideological thirties," had done so much to muddy the waters of criticism. If he denied the claims of revolutionary Marxist criticism, he also took exception, in *Reactionary Essays* (1936), to the Humanistic emphasis on moralistic criteria and to the psychological and psychoanalytic school of criticism which portrayed man in terms of a stimulus-response pattern. He tried to formulate a system of aesthetics that would not neglect the fundamental needs of the intellect. Hence he concluded that poetry, far from preempting the realm of the irrational, is an autonomous world, a special, unique, self-contained form of knowledge. The poet is capable of imposing order, an organic and meaningful unity, upon the chaotic flux of experience. Poetry is therefore superior to science, offering us the most complete and most responsible version of human experience. From this it follows that this autonomous realm must not be profaned by the importation of standards from such alien disciplines as sociology, politics, science, ethics, and psychology. In the consideration of poetry, which has its own laws of organization and its own techniques and traditions, these are only of secondary importance. Poetry must be studied and evaluated according to its own inherent standards.

Unlike impressionistic critics like Huneker and Mencken, Tate is a believer in absolutes, and his utterances are presumably grounded, as in *Reason in Madness* (1940), in universal and abiding truths. Tradition is his god, and what he means by tradition is quite plain. It is the tradition of the aristocratic South when the ownership of property carried with it a measure of social responsibility, when leisure was a virtue and manners were gracious and culture was a prized though exclusive possession of an elite. If our age is disrupted by violence and anarchy, then that, according to Tate, is due to the decay of manners, morals, and religion. How, he inquires, can men be human when they have lost the stay of a common religion, a common Church? The source of the mischief lies in the fact that they have capitulated to the philosophy of pragmatism; in other words, that they have adoped the scientific method.

Tate denounces science on moral as well as intellectual grounds. His belief is that "historicism, scientism, psychologism, biologism, in general the confident use of the scientific vocabularies in the spiritual realm, has created or at any rate is the expression of a spiritual disorder."[1] What he prescribes as a remedy is to have literature in its highest forms serve as the interpreter and organizer of human experience. He is opposed not only to the intrusion of the scientific outlook in poetry but also to the influence of the sociological. Why should a poet hope to deal more adequately with sociology than with physics?

In a sympathetic presentation of the viewpoint of the Southern critics,

[1] Allen Tate, *Reason in Madness* (New York, 1940), p. 4.

"The New Criticism and the Southern Critics," by Robert Wooster Stallman, Tate is called

"a disciple of Hulme in his campaign against the modern age of science, the age of romanticism, the post-Renaissance self-sufficient spirit of humanism, humanitarianism, protestantism, capitalism, progress, the economic and perfectible man."[2]

Tate insists upon a supernatural system of religion if man, realizing his own imperfections and limitations, is to strive for and achieve a higher synthesis. Whatever its serious defects as a critical philosophy and method, the work of the formalist critics has given a decided impetus to the practice of contemporary criticism. One must question, however, whether it deserves the encomium Robert Wooster Stallman lavishes upon it in his conclusion:

"The structure of critical ideas that Blackmur, Winters, Leavis, Empson, Brooks, Warren, Ransom, and Tate have contrived upon the foundations of Eliot and Richards constitutes an achievement in *criticism* the like of which has not been equaled by literary critics in our time or any previous period in our literary history."[3]

## BIBLIOGRAPHY

### TEXT

*Reactionary Essays on Poetry and Ideas.* New York, 1936.
*Reason in Madness.* New York, 1941.
(ed.), *The Language of Poetry.* Princeton, 1942.
(ed.), *A Southern Vanguard.* New York, 1947.
*On the Limits of Poetry.* New York, 1948.
*The Hovering Fly.* Cummington (Mass.), 1948.

### CRITICISM

Abraham, E., "The Reading of Poetry," *English Literary History,* IX, 235–244 (September, 1942).
Glicksberg, Charles I., "Allen Tate and Mother Earth," XLV, *Sewanee Review,* 284–295 (July-September, 1937).
Roelling, F., "Two Theories of Poetry as Knowledge," *Southern Review,* VII, 690–705 (Spring, 1942).
Stallman, R. W., "The Southern Critics," *A Southern Vanguard,* New York, 1947, pp. 28–51.

[2] Allen Tate (ed.), *A Southern Vanguard* (New York, 1947), p. 36.
[3] *Ibid.,* p. 51.

Thorp, Willard, "Allen Tate: A Checklist," *Princeton University Library Chronicle*, III, 85–98 (April, 1942).

Trowbridge, H., "Aristotle and the 'New Criticism,'" *Sewanee Review*, LII, 537–555 (Autumn, 1944).

## THE PRESENT FUNCTION
## OF CRITICISM*

### 1940

*Nous avons une impuissance de prouver,
invincible à tout le dogmatisme. Nous avons une idée
de la vérité, invincible à tout le pyrrhonisme.*

. . . PASCAL

WE are not very much concerned when we confess that communication among certain points of view is all but impossible. Let us put three persons together who soon discover that they do not agree. No matter; they quickly find a procedure, a program, an objective. So they do agree that there is something to be *done*, although they may not be certain why they are doing it, and they may not be interested in the results, the meaning of which is not very important: before they can consider the meaning they have started a new program. This state of mind is positivism. It assumes that the communication of ideas towards the formulation of truths is irrelevant to action; the program is an end in itself. But if we are interested in truth I believe that our intellectual confusion is such that we can merely write that interest upon the record of our time.

This essay represents a "point of view" which seems to have little in common with other points of view that are tolerated, and even applauded, today. It cannot be communicated at the level of the procedure and the program; it cannot, in short, be communicated to persons whose assumptions about life come out of positivism. (For positivism is not only a scientific movement; it is a moral attitude.) It has moved to contempt and rage persons whose intelligence I respect and admire.

* From "Reason in Madness" in *On the Limits of Poetry*, by Allen Tate, copyright 1941, 1948, by Allen Tate, by permission of The Swallow Press and William Morrow and Company, Inc.

The point of view here, then, is that historicism, scientism, psychologism, biologism, in general the confident use of the scientific vocabularies in the spiritual realm, has created or at any rate is the expression of a spiritual disorder. That disorder may be briefly described as a dilemma.

On the one hand, we assume that all experience can be ordered scientifically, an assumption that we are almost ready to confess has intensified if it has not actually created our distress; but on the other hand, this assumption has logically reduced the spiritual realm to irresponsible emotion, to what the positivists of our time see as irrelevant feeling; it is irrelevant because it cannot be reduced to the terms of positivist procedure. It is my contention here that the high forms of literature offer us the only complete, and thus the most responsible, versions of our experience. The point of view of this essay, then, is influenced by the late, neglected T. E. Hulme (and not this essay alone). It is the belief, philosophically tenable, in a radical discontinuity between the physical and the spiritual realms.

In our time the historical approach to criticism, in so far as it has attempted to be a scientific method, has undermined the significance of the material which it proposes to investigate. On principle the sociological and historical scholar must not permit himself to see in the arts meanings that his method does not assume. To illustrate some of the wide implications of this method I will try to see it as more than a method: it is the temper of our age. It has profoundly influenced our politics and our education.

What will happen to literature under the totalitarian society that is coming in the next few years—it may be, so far as critical opinion is concerned, in the next few months? The question has got to be faced by literary critics, who as men of explicit ideas must to a great extent define for imaginative literature the *milieu* in which it will flourish or decay. The first ominous signs of this change are before us. The tradition of free ideas is as dead in the United States as it is in Germany. For at least a generation it has suffered a slow extinction, and it may receive the *coup de grâce* from the present war. The suppression of the critical spirit in this country will have sinister features that the official Nazi censorship, with all its ruthlessness, has not yet achieved, for the Nazis are, towards opinion, crude, objective, and responsible. Although it has only a harsh military responsibility, this censorship is definite, and it leaves the profession of letters in no doubt of its standing. Under this regime it has no standing at all. Increasingly since 1933 the critical intelligence under

National Socialism has enjoyed the choice of extinction or frustration in exile.

Could the outlook be worse for the future of criticism? In the United States we face the censorship of the pressure group. We have a tradition of irresponsible interpretation of patriotic necessity. We are entering a period in which we shall pay dearly for having turned our public education over to the professional "educationists" and the sociologists. These men have taught the present generation that the least thing about man is his intelligence, if he have it at all; the greatest thing his adjustment to Society (not to a good society): a mechanical society in which we were to be conditioned for the realization of a *bourgeois* paradise of gadgets and of the consumption, not of the fruits of the earth, but of commodities. Happily this degraded version of the myth of reason has been discredited by the course of what the liberal mind calls "world events"; and man will at any rate be spared the indignity of achieving it. What else can he now achieve? If history had dramatic form we might be able to see ourselves going down to destruction, with a small standard flying in the all but mindless hollow of our heads; and we should have our dignity to the end.

But this vision is too bright, too optimistic; for the "democracy" of appetites, drives, and stimulus-and-response has already affected us. What we thought was to be a conditioning process in favor of a state planned by Teachers College of Columbia University will be a conditioning equally useful for Plato's tyrant state. The actuality of tyranny we shall enthusiastically greet as the development of democracy, for the ringing of the democratic bell will make our political glands flow as freely for dictatorship, as, hitherto, for monopoly capitalism.

This hypocrisy is going to have a great deal to do with literary criticism because it is going to have a very definite effect upon American thought and feeling, at every level. There is no space here to track down the intellectual pedigree of the attitude of the social scientist. As early as 1911 Hilaire Belloc published a neglected book called *The Servile State,* in which he contended that the world revolution would not come out of the Second International. Nobody paid any attention to this prophecy; the Marxists ignored it for the obvious reason, and the liberals took it to mean that the world revolution would not happen at all. Belloc meant that the revolution was inherent in our pseudo-democratic intellectual tradition, buttressed by monopoly capitalism, and that the revolution would not proceed towards social justice, but would achieve the slave state. The point of view that I am sketching here looks upon the rise of the social sciences and their influence in education, from Comtism to Dewey-ism, as a powerful aid to the coming of the slave society. Under the myth of reason all the vast accumulation of *data* on social behavior, social control, social dynamics, was to have been used in building a pseudo-mystical and pseudo-democratic utopia on the Wellsian plan. In this vision of mindless perfection an elementary bit of historical insight was permitted to lapse: Plato had this insight, with less knowledge of history than we have. It is simply that, if you get a society made up of persons who have surrendered their humanity to the predatory impulses, the quickest way to improve matters is to call in a dictator; for when you lose the moral and religious authority, the military authority stands ready to supervene. Professor Dewey's social integration does not supervene. Under the actuality of history our sociological knowledge is a ready-made weapon that is now being used in Europe for the control of the people, and it will doubtless soon be used here for the same purpose.

To put this point of view into another perspective it is only neces-sary to remember that the intellectual movement variously known as positivism, pragmatism, instrumentalism, is the expression of a middle-class culture—a culture that we have achieved in America with so little consciousness of any other culture that we often say that a class description of it is beside the point. Matthew Arnold—in spite of his vacillating hopes for the middle class—said that one of its leading traits was lack of intelligence, and that industrialism, the creation of the middle class, had "materialized the upper class, vulgarized the middle class, and brutalized the lower class."

This lack of intelligence in our middle class, this vulgarity of the utilitarian attitude, is translatable into other levels of our intellec-tual activity. It is, for example, but a step from the crude sociologism of the normal school to the cloistered historical scholarship of the graduate school. We are all aware, of course, of the contempt in which the scholars hold the "educationists": yet the historical scholars, once the carriers of the humane tradition, have now merely the genteel tradition; the independence of judgment, the belief in intelligence, the confidence in literature, that informed the humane tradition, have disappeared; under the genteel tradition the scholars exhibit timidity of judgment, disbelief in intelligence, and suspicion of the value of literature. These attitudes of scholarship are the atti-tudes of the *haute bourgeoisie* that support it in the great universities; it is now commonplace to observe that the uncreative money-culture of modern times tolerates the historical routine of the scholars. The routine is "safe," and it shares with the predatory social process at large a naturalistic basis. And this naturalism easily bridges the thin gap between the teachers' college and the graduate school, between the sociologist and the literary source-hunter, between the comptometrist of literary "reactions" and the enumerator of influences.

The naturalism of the literary scholar is too obvious to need demonstration here; his substitution of "method" for intelligence takes its definite place in the positivistic movement which, from my point of view, has been clearing the way for the slave state; and the scholar must bear his part of the responsibility for the hypocrisy that will blind us to the reality of its existence, when it arrives.

The function of criticism should have been, in our time, as in all times, to maintain and to demonstrate the special, unique, and complete knowledge which the great forms of literature afford us. And I mean quite simply *knowledge,* not historical documentation and information. But our literary critics have been obsessed by politics, and when they have been convinced of the social determinism of literature, they have been in principle indistinguishable from the academic scholars, who have demonstrated that literature does not exist, that it is merely history, which must be studied as history is studied, through certain scientific analogies. The scholars have not maintained the tradition of literature as a form of knowledge; by looking at it as merely one among many forms of social and political expression, they will have no defense against the censors of the power state, or against the hidden censors of the pressure group. Have the scholars not been saying all along that literature is only politics? Well, then, let's suppress it, since the politics of poets and novelists is notoriously unsound. And the scholars will say, yes, let's suppress it—our attempt to convert literature into science has done better than that: it has already extinguished it.

## II

What the scholars are saying, of course, is that the meaning of a work of literature is identical with their method of studying it—a method that dissolves the literature into its history. Are the scholars studying literature, or are they not? That is the question. If they are not, why then do they continue to pretend that they are? This is the scholars' contribution to the intellectual hypocrisy of the positivistic movement. But when we come to the individual critics, the word hypocrisy will not do. When we think of the powerful semi-scientific method of studying poetry associated with the name of I. A. Richards, we may say that there is a certain ambiguity of critical focus.

Mr. Richards has been many different kinds of critic, one kind being an extremely valuable kind; but the rôle I have in mind here is that of *The Principles of Literary Criticism,* a curious and ingenious *tour de force* of a variety very common today. The species is: literature is not really nonsense, it is in a special way a kind of science. This particular variety is: poetry is a kind of applied psychology. I am not disposing of Mr. Richards in two sentences; like everybody else of my generation I have learned a great deal from him, even from what I consider his errors and evasions; and if it is these that interest me now, it is because they get less attention than his occasional and profound insights into the art of reading poetry.

In *The Principles of Literary Criticism* there is the significant hocus-pocus of impulses, stimuli, and responses; there are even the elaborate charts of nerves and nerve-systems that purport to show how the "stimuli" of poems elicit "responses" in such a way as to "organize our impulses" towards action; there is, throughout, the pretense that the study of poetry is at last a laboratory science. How many innocent young men—myself among them—thought, in 1924, that laboratory jargon meant laboratory demonstration! But for a certain uneasiness evinced by Mr. Richards in the later chapters, one could fairly see this book as a typical instance of the elaborate cheat that the positivistic movement has perpetrated upon the human spirit. For the uneasy conscience of one Richards, a thousand critics and scholars have not hesitated to write literary history, literary biography, literary criticism, with facile confidence in whatever scientific analogies came to hand.

With the candor of a generous spirit Mr. Richards has repudiated his early scientism: the critical conscience that struggled in the early work against the limitations of a positivist education won out in the end. What did Mr. Richards give up? It is not necessary to be technical about it. He had found that the picture of the world passed on to us by the poetry of the pre-scientific ages was scientifically false. The *things* and *processes* pointed to by the poets, even the modern poets, since they too were backward in the sciences, could not be verified by any of the known scientific procedures. As a good positivist he saw the words of a poem as *referents,* and referents have got to refer to something—which the words of even the best poem failed to do. If Mr. Richards could have read Carnap and Morris in the early twenties, he would have said that poems may *designate* but they do not *denote,* because you can designate something that does not exist, like a purple cow. Poems designate things that do not exist, and are compacted of *pseudo-statements,* Mr. Richard's most famous invention in scientese; that is, false statements, or just plain lies.

Perhaps the best way to describe Mr. Richards's uneasiness is to say that, a year or two later, in his pamphlet-size book, *Science and Poetry,* he came up short against Matthew Arnold's belief that the future of poetry was immense, that, religion being gone, poetry would have to take its place. The curious interest of Arnold's argument cannot detain us. It is enough to remember that even in *The Principles of Literary Criticism* Mr. Richards was coming round to that view. Not that poetry would bring back religion, or become a new religion! It would perform the therapeutic offices of religion, the only part of it worth keeping. In short, poetry would "order" our minds; for although science was true, it had failed to bring intellectual order—it had even broken up the older order of pseudo-statement; and although poetry was false, it would order our minds, whatever this ordering might mean.

To order our minds with lies became, for a few years, Mr. Richards's program, until at last, in *Coleridge on Imagination* (1935), the Sisyphean effort to translate Coleridge into naturalistic terms broke down; and now, I believe, Mr. Richards takes the view that poetry, far from being a desperate remedy, is an independent form of knowledge, a kind of cognition, equal to the knowledge of the sciences at least, perhaps superior. The terms in which Mr. Richards frames this insight need not concern us here:[1] I have sketched his progress towards it in order to remind you that the repudiation of a literal positivism by its leading representative in modern criticism has not been imitated by his followers, or by other critics who, on a different road, have reached Mr. Richards's position of ten years ago. They are still there. Whether they are sociologists in criticism or practitioners of the routine of historical "correlation," they alike subscribe to a single critical doctrine. It is the Doctrine of Relevance.

[1] See pp. 41–48, 107–113, in *On the Limits of Poetry,* for more detailed discussions of this point.

## III

The Doctrine of Relevance is very simple. It means that the subject-matter of a literary work must not be isolated in terms of form; it must be tested (on an analogy to scientific techniques) by observation of the world that it "represents." Are the scene, the action, the relations of the characters in a novel, in some verifiable sense true? It is an old question. It has given rise in our time to various related sorts of criticism that frequently produce great insights. (I think here of Mr. Edmund Wilson's naturalistic interpretation of James's *The Turn of the Screw*. Mr. Wilson's view is not the whole view, but we can readily see that we had been missing the whole view until he added his partial view.)

The criterion of relevance, as we saw with Mr. Richards, has a hard time of it with an art like poetry. Of all the arts, poetry has a medium the most complex and the least reducible to any one set of correlations, be they historical, or economic, or theological, or moral. From the point of view of direct denotation of objects about all that we can say about one of Keats's odes is what I heard a child say— "It is something about a bird."

But with the novel the case is different, because the novel is very close to history—indeed, in all but the great novelists, it is not clearly set off from history. I do not intend here to get into Aristotle and to argue the difference between history and fiction. It is plain that action and character, to say nothing of place and time, point with less equivocation to observed or perhaps easily observable phenomena than even the simplest poetry ever does. The novel points with some directness towards history—or I might say with Mr. David Daiches, to the historical process.

I mention Mr. Daiches because his *The Novel and the Modern World* seems to me to be one of the few good books on contemporary fiction. Yet at bottom it is an example of what I call the Doctrine of Relevance, and I believe that he gains every advantage implicit in that doctrine, and suffers, in the range and acuteness of his perceptions, probably none of its limitations. I cannot do justice to Mr. Daiches's treatment of some of the best novelists of our time; my quotations from his final essay—which is a summary view of his critical position—will do him less than justice. His statement of his method seems to me to be narrower than his critical practice:

The critic who endeavors to see literature as a process rather than as a series of phenomena, and as a process which is bound up with an infinite series of ever wider processes, ought to realize that however wide his context, it is but a fraction of what it might be.

Admirable advice; but what concerns me in this passage is the assumption that Mr. Daiches shares with the historical scholar, that literature is to be understood chiefly as a part of the historical process. He goes on to say:

The main object is to indicate relevance and to show how understanding depends on awareness of relevance. That appreciation depends on understanding and that a theory of value can come only after appreciation, hardly need noting.

I must confess that after a brilliant performance of two hundred ten pages I feel that Mr. Daiches has let us down a little here. I am aware that he enters a shrewd list of warnings and exceptions, but I am a little disappointed to learn that he sees himself as applying to the novel a criterion of historical relevance not very different from the criterion of the graduate school. It is likely that I misunderstand Mr. Daiches. He continues:

The patterning of those events [in a novel], their relation to each other within the story, the attitude to them which emerges, the mood which surrounds them, the tone in which they are related, and the style of the writing are all equally relevant.

Yes: but relevant to what? And are they *equally* relevant? The equality of relevance points to historical documentation; or may we assume here that since the "main object is to indicate relevance," the critic must try to discover the relevance of history to the work? Or the work to history? What Mr. Daiches seems to me to be saying is that the function of criticism is to bring the work back to history, and to test its relevance to an ascertainable historical process. Does relevance, then, mean some kind of identity with an historical process? And since "understanding depends on awareness of relevance," is it understanding of history or of the novel; or is it of both at once? That I am not wholly wrong in my grasp of the terms relevance and process is borne out by this passage:

He [the critic] can neither start with a complete view of civilization and work down to the individual work of art, nor can he start with the particular work of art and work up to civilization as a whole; he must try both methods and give neither his complete trust.

Admirable advice again; but are there actually two methods here? Are they not both the historical method? When Mr. Daiches says that it is possible to start from the individual work of art and work *up* (interesting adverb, as interesting as the *down* to which you go in order to reach the work of art), he doubtless alludes to what he and many other critics today call the "formalist" method. Mr. Daiches nicely balances the claims of formalist and historian. The formalist is the critic who doesn't work up, but remains where he started, with the work of art—the "work in itself," as Mr. Daiches calls it, "an end which, though attainable, is yet unreal." Its unreality presumably consists in the critic's failure to be aware of the work's relevance to history. There may have been critics like Mr. Daiches's formalist monster, but I have never seen one, and I doubt that Mr. Daiches himself, on second thought, would believe he exists. (Or perhaps he was Aristotle, who said that the nature of tragedy is in its structure, not its reception by the audience.) I am not sure. As a critic of the novel Mr. Daiches is acutely aware of unhistorical meanings in literature, but as a critical theorist he seems to me to be beating his wings in the unilluminated tradition of positivism. That tradition has put the stigma of "formalism" upon the unhistorical meaning. Critics of our age nervously throw the balance in favor of the historical lump. Mr. Daiches's plea for it rests upon its superior inclusiveness; the historical scholar can make formal analyses against the background of history; he has it both ways, while the formalist has it only one, and that one "unreal." But here, again, Mr. Daiches's insight into the vast complexity of the critic's task prompts at least a rueful misgiving about the "wider context"; he admits the superiority of the historian, "though it may be replied that inclusiveness is no necessary proof of such superiority." At this point Mr. Daiches becomes a little confused.

I have the strong suspicion in reading Mr. Daiches (I have it in reading the late Marxists and the sociological and historical scholars) that critics of the positivist school would not study literature at all if it were not so handy in libraries; they don't really like it; or they are at any rate ashamed of it—because it is "unreal." The men of our time who have the boldness and the logical rigor to stand by the implications of their position are the new logical positivists at Chicago—Carnap and Morris, whom I have already mentioned; they are quite firm in their belief—with a little backsliding on the part of Morris[2]—that poetry, and perhaps all imaginative literature, is, in Mr. Arthur Mizener's phrase, only "amiable insanity": it designates but it does not denote anything "real."

I respect this doctrine because it is barbarism unabashed and unashamed. But of the positivists who still hanker after literature with yearnings that come out of the humane tradition, what can be said? The ambiguity or—since we are in our mental climate and no longer with persons—the hypocrisy of our liberal intellectual tradition appears again; or let us say the confusion. Is Mr. Daiches wrestling with a critical theory, or is he only oscillating between the extremes of a dilemma? From the strict, logical point of view he is entitled merely to the positivist horn, as the general critical outlook of our age is so entitled.

This ought to be the end of literature, if literature were logical; it is not logical but tough; and after the dark ages of our present enlightenment it will flourish again. This essay has been written from a point of view which does not admit the validity of the rival claims of formalism and history, of art-for-art's-sake and society. Literature is the complete knowledge of man's experience, and by knowledge I mean that unique and formed intelligence of the world of which man alone is capable.

[2] Charles W. Morris, "Science, Art, and Technology," in *The Kenyon Review,* Autumn 1939. Mr. Morris argues that, although poetry is nonsense semantically, it is the realm of "value."

# EDMUND WILSON
## (1895–     )

EDMUND WILSON was born in Red Bank, New Jersey, on May 8, 1895. After graduating from Princeton University in 1916 he became a reporter on the *New York Evening Sun*. During the First World War he served in a hospital base in France and in the Intelligence Corps. Upon his return to civilian life at the end of the war, he worked on the staff of *Vanity Fair*. From 1926 to 1931 he was associate editor of *The New Republic*. He received a Guggenheim Fellowship in 1935, and another one in 1939, to complete his book, *To the Finland Station*.

*Axel's Castle* (1931), undoubtedly his most important contribution, first won him substantial recognition as a literary critic. The impact of the depression led him to take a deep interest in economic and social problems, which is reflected in *The American Jitters* (1932). Though he was for a time in warm sympathy with the Marxist interpretation of literature, he soon came to recognize its limitations. It could determine the origin and social relations of a work within a given culture but it was impotent to assess matters of literary value. As an historical critic Edmund Wilson worked in the tradition of Taine and the historical school, endeavoring to trace the inception and growth of a man's ideas in the light of the conditions which helped to shape them.

*Axel's Castle* studies the influence of Symbolism on writers like Proust, Joyce, and Yeats, but it is also concerned with the character of modern literature. The conclusions at which he arrives in this book reveal a growing conviction that literature and life must be fused. Humanism, as he makes clear in the essay he contributed to *The Critique of Humanism* (1930), does not offer the solution he seeks. At the time he wonders uneasily whether Communism will provide a means of salvation both for society and the artist who lives in it.

He attempted to formulate his critical credo in two articles, "The Literary Class War," in the *New Republic*, May 4 and May 11, 1932. He sets out to discover what proletarian art is as distinguished from bourgeois art, but he has still not reached the point where he is willing to pigeonhole the artist within class categories. The minds of the greatest artists reach out beyond the limits of their time and place. The artist, whose genius partakes of the character of the universal and the timeless, transcends the limitations imposed by economic conditions and social background. He cannot accept the extreme Marxist doctrine that everything depends on the socio-economic roots and relations of the writer. It is proper to ask, as the Marxists do, whether a literary work makes a definite social contribution, but the nature of the contribution must be properly defined, and those who presume to determine it must be duly qualified to judge in the realm of aesthetics. Like the Humanists, too many Marxists ignore the aesthetic experience and proceed to legislate according to fixed abstractions.

Wilson's trip to Soviet Russia, which he has recorded in *Travels in Two Democracies* (1936), helped to disillusion him. He is impatient with doctrinaire attempts on the part of theoreticians to dictate the manufacture of masterpieces according to rigid Marxist principles. Socialist realism cannot be created by fiat. While abroad, he felt strongly that American republican institutions constituted a unique phenomenon, and that they have some permanent and absolute value. In *The Triple Thinkers* (1938), we see Wilson at his best, incisive in his analysis, resourceful in calling upon his knowledge of European and classical literature to make pointed comparisons and illuminating evaluations. If he is appreciative of the heritage of the past, he is alert in responding to greatness and intensity in modern literature. There has been no more hospitable and enthusiastic yet acutely discriminating critic of modern writers and experimental literary movements. The essay on "Marxism and Literature" shows the distance Wilson has traveled in clarifying his thoughts and breaking away completely from the leading-strings of Marxist doctrine. It offers one of the best refutations of the dogmatic doctrines fathered by Marxist aestheticians. A knowledge of Marxism, however extensive and profound, is no substitute for a genuine, first-hand appreciation of literature. The unpardonable sin of the Marxist critics is that they sought to evaluate literature by canons that had no bearing on that field. There is no point, Wilson concludes, in trying to convert literature into a class weapon, a revolutionary instrument.

In *The Wound and the Bow* (1941), Wilson devotes himself to the concrete analysis and appreciation of a number of writers like Dickens and Kipling, trying to determine the secret of their power and the cause for the decline of their reputation. In doing so, he applies, when needed, psychological and psychoanalytic insights that help to explain the development of a man's mind and personality. In "Philoctetes: The Wound and the Bow," Wilson works out his theory that superior strength is inseparable from disability or disease. Carried further, as Gide does, this implies the notion that art and disease go together. In short, those who suffer from psychological disorders or handicaps derive strength from their constructive abnormality, their weakness, their strangeness.[1]

In *Europe without Baedekker: Sketches among the Ruins of Italy, Greece, and England* (1947), the critic is very much in evidence, not only in his brief but striking portraits of the literary figures he encounters in his travels—Silone, Malraux, Santayana—and of books he reads or literary movements he analyzes, but also in his interpretation of political trends and economic conflicts. In the light of what is going on in Soviet Russia, Wilson declares his conviction that the United States is at the present time more advanced politically than any other country in the world.

## BIBLIOGRAPHY

### TEXT

*Axel's Castle.* New York and London, 1931.
*The American Jitters.* New York and London, 1932.
*Travels in Two Democracies.* New York, 1936.
*The Triple Thinkers.* New York, 1938.
*To the Finland Station.* New York, 1940.
*The Boys in the Back Room.* San Francisco, 1941.
*The Wound and the Bow.* Boston, 1941.
(ed.), *The Shock of Recognition.* Garden City, 1943.
*Europe without Baedeker.* Garden City, 1947.
*Classics and Commercials.* New York, 1950.

### CRITICISM

Adams, R., "Masks and Delays: Edmund Wilson as Critic," *Sewanee Review,* LVI, 272–286 (Spring, 1948).
Brown, E.K., "The Method of Edmund Wilson," *University of Toronto Quarterly,* XI, 105–111 (October, 1941).
Fiess, Edward, "Edmund Wilson," *Antioch Review,* I, 356–367 (Fall, 1941).
Freeman, Joseph, "Edmund Wilson's Globe of Glass," *New Masses,* XXVII, 73–79 (April 12, 1938).
Glicksberg, Charles I., "Edmund Wilson: Radicalism at the Cross Roads," *South Atlantic Quarterly,* XXXVI, 466–477 (October, 1937).

---

[1] For a critical discussion of this theory, see Lionel Trilling, "A Note on Art and Neurosis," *Partisan Review,* XII (Winter, 1945), 40–48.

Hyman, Stanley Edgar, "Edmund Wilson and Translation in Criticism," *The Armed Vision*, New York, 1948, pp. 19–48.

Mizener, Arthur, "Edmund Wilson: A Checklist," *Princeton University Library Chronicle*, V, 62–78 (February, 1944).

Schwartz, Delmore, "The Writing of Edmund Wilson," *Accent*, I, 177–186 (Spring, 1942).

Snell, George, "An Examination of Modern Critics: Edmund Wilson," *Rocky Mountain Review*, VIII, 36–44 (Winter, 1944).

# THE HISTORICAL INTERPRETATION
# OF LITERATURE*

I WANT to talk about the historical interpretation of literature—that is, about the interpretation of literature in its social, economic and political aspects.

To begin with, it will be worth while to say something about the kind of criticism which seems to be furthest removed from this. There is a kind of comparative criticism which tends to be non-historical. The essays of T. S. Eliot, which have had such an immense influence in our time, are, for example, fundamentally non-historical. Eliot sees, or tries to see, the whole of literature, so far as he is acquainted with it, spread out before him under the aspect of eternity. He then compares the work of different periods and countries, and tries to draw from it general conclusions about what literature ought to be. He understands, of course, that our point of view in connection with literature changes, and he has what seems to me a very sound conception of the whole body of writing of the past as something to which new works are continually being added, and which is not thereby merely increased in bulk but modified as a whole—so that Sophocles is no longer precisely what he was for Aristotle, or Shakespeare what he was for Ben Jonson or for Dryden or for Dr. Johnson, on account of all the later literature that has intervened between them and us. Yet at every point of this continual accretion, the whole field may be surveyed, as it were, spread out before the critic. The critic tries to see it as God might; he calls the books to a Day of Judgment. And, looking at things in this way, he may arrive at in-

---

A lecture delivered at Princeton University, October 23, 1940.

teresting and valuable conclusions which could hardly be reached by approaching them in any other way. Eliot was able to see, for example—what I believe had never been noticed before—that the French Symbolist poetry of the nineteenth century had certain fundamental resemblances to the English poetry of the age of Donne. Another kind of critic would draw certain historical conclusions from these purely esthetic findings, as the Russian D. S. Mirsky did; but Eliot does not draw them.

Another example of this kind of non-historical criticism, in a somewhat different way and on a somewhat different plane, is the work of the late George Saintsbury. Saintsbury was a connoisseur of wines; he wrote an entertaining book on the subject. And his attitude toward literature, too, was that of the connoisseur. He tastes the authors and tells you about the vintages; he distinguishes the qualities of the various wines. His palate was as fine as could be, and he possessed the great qualification that he knew how to take each book on its own terms without expecting it to be some other book and was thus in a position to appreciate a great variety of kinds of writing. He was a man of strong social prejudices and peculiarly intransigent political views, but, so far as it is humanly possible, he kept them out of his literary criticism. The result is one of the most agreeable and most comprehensive commentaries on literature that have ever been written in English. Most scholars who have read as much as Saintsbury do not have Saintsbury's discriminating taste. Here is a critic who has covered the whole ground like any academic historian, yet whose account of it is not merely a chronology but a record of fastidious enjoyment. Since enjoyment is the only thing he is looking for, he does not need to know the causes of things, and the historical background of literature does not interest him very much.

There is, however, another tradition of criticism which dates from the beginning of the eighteenth century. In the year 1725, the Neapolitan philosopher Vico published *La Scienza Nuova,* a revolutionary work on the philosophy of history, in which he asserted for the first time that the social world was certainly the work of man, and attempted what is, so far as I know, the first social interpretation of a work of literature. This is what Vico says about Homer: 'Homer composed the *Iliad* when Greece was young and consequently burning with sublime passions such as pride, anger and vengeance— passions which cannot allow dissimulation and which consort with generosity; so that she then admired Achilles, the hero of force. But, grown old, he composed the *Odyssey,* at a time when the passions of Greece were already somewhat cooled by reflection, which is the mother of prudence—so that she now admired Ulysses, the hero of wisdom. Thus also, in Homer's youth, the Greek people liked cruelty, vituperation, savagery, fierceness, ferocity; whereas, when Homer was old, they were already enjoying the luxuries of Alcinoüs, the delights of Calypso, the pleasures of Circe, the songs of the sirens and the pastimes of the suitors, who went no further in aggression and combat than laying siege to the chaste Penelope—all of which practices would appear incompatible with the spirit of the earlier time. The divine Plato is so struck by this difficulty that, in order to solve it, he tells us that Homer had foreseen in inspired vision these dissolute, sickly and disgusting customs. But in this way he makes Homer out to have been but a foolish instructor for Greek civilization, since, however much he may condemn them, he is displaying for imitation these corrupt and decadent habits which were not to be adopted till long after the foundation of the nations of Greece, and accelerating the natural course which human events would take by spurring the Greeks on to corruption. Thus it is plain that the Homer of the *Iliad* must have preceded by many years the Homer who wrote the *Odyssey;* and it is plain that the former must belong to the northeastern part of Greece, since he celebrates the Trojan War, which took place in his part of the country, whereas the latter belongs to the southeastern part, since he celebrates Ulysses, who reigned there.'

You see that Vico has here explained Homer in terms both of historical period and of geographical origin. The idea that human arts and institutions were to be studied and elucidated as the products of the geographical and climatic conditions in which the people who created them lived, and of the phase of their social development through which they were passing at the moment, made great progress during the eighteenth century. There are traces of it even in Dr. Johnson, that most orthodox and classical of critics—as, for example, when he accounts for certain characteristics of Shakespeare by the relative barbarity of the age in which he lived, pointing out, just as Vico had done, that 'nations, like individuals, have their infancy.' And by the eighties of the eighteenth century Herder, in his *Ideas on the Philosophy of History,* was writing of poetry that it was a kind of 'Proteus among the people, which is always changing its form in response to the languages, manners, and habits, to the

temperaments and climates, nay even to the accents of different nations.' He said—what could still seem startling even so late as that
—that 'language was not a divine communication, but something
men had produced themselves.' In the lectures on the philosophy of
history that Hegel delivered in Berlin in 1822–23, he discussed the
national literatures as expressions of the societies which had produced them—societies which he conceived as great organisms continually transforming themselves under the influence of a succession
of dominant ideas.

In the field of literary criticism, this historical point of view came
to its first complete flower in the work of the French critic Taine, in
the middle of the nineteenth century. The whole school of historian-
critics to which Taine belonged—Michelet, Renan, Sainte-Beuve—
had been occupied in interpreting books in terms of their historical
origins. But Taine was the first of these to attempt to apply such
principles systematically and on a large scale in a work devoted
exclusively to literature. In the Introduction to his *History of
English Literature,* published in 1863, he made his famous pronouncement that works of literature were to be understood as the
upshot of three interfusing factors: *the moment, the race and the
milieu.* Taine thought he was a scientist and a mechanist, who was
examining works of literature from the same point of view as the
chemist's in experimenting with chemical compounds. But the difference between the critic and the chemist is that the critic cannot
first combine his elements and then watch to see what they will do:
he can only examine phenomena which have already taken place.
The procedure that Taine actually follows is to pretend to set the
stage for the experiment by describing the moment, the race and
the milieu, and then to say: 'Such a situation demands such and such
a kind of writer.' He now goes on to describe the kind of writer that
the situation demands, and the reader finds himself at the end confronted with Shakespeare or Milton or Byron or whoever the great
figure is—who turns out to prove the accuracy of Taine's prognosis
by precisely living up to this description.

There was thus a certain element of imposture in Taine; but it
was the rabbits he pulled out that saved him. If he had really been
the mechanist that he thought he was, his work on literature would
have had little value. The truth was that Taine loved literature for
its own sake—he was at his best himself a brilliant artist—and he
had very strong moral convictions which give his writing emotional
power. His mind, to be sure, was an analytic one, and his analysis,

though terribly oversimplified, does have an explanatory value. Yet his work was what we call creative. Whatever he may say about chemical experiments, it is evident when he writes of a great writer that the moment, the race and the milieu have combined, like the three sounds of the chord in Browning's poem about Abt Vogler, to produce not a fourth sound but a star.

To Taine's set of elements was added, dating from the middle of the century, a new element, the economic, which was introduced into the discussion of historical phenomena mainly by Marx and Engels. The non-Marxist critics themselves were at the time already taking into account the influence of the social classes. In his chapters on the Norman conquest of England, Taine shows that the difference between the literatures produced respectively by the Normans and by the Saxons was partly the difference between a ruling class, on the one hand, and a vanquished and repressed class, on the other. And Michelet, in his volume on the Regency, which was finished the same year that the *History of English Literature* appeared, studies the *Manon Lescaut* of the Abbé Prévost as a document representing the point of view of the small gentry before the French Revolution. But Marx and Engels derived the social classes from the way that people made or got their livings—from what they called the *methods of production;* and they tended to regard these economic processes as fundamental to civilization.

The Dialectical Materialism of Marx and Engels was not really so materialistic as it sounds. There was in it a large element of the Hegelian idealism that Marx and Engels thought they had got rid of. At no time did these two famous materialists take so mechanistic a view of things as Taine began by professing; and their theory of the relation of works of literature to what they called the *economic base* was a good deal less simple than Taine's theory of the moment, the race and the milieu. They thought that art, politics, religion, philosophy and literature belonged to what they called the *superstructure* of human activity; but they saw that the practitioners of these various professions tended also to constitute social groups, and that they were always pulling away from the kind of solidarity based on economic classes in order to establish a professional solidarity of their own. Furthermore, the activities of the superstructure could influence one another, and they could influence the economic base. It may be said of Marx and Engels in general that, contrary to the popular impression, they were tentative, confused and modest when it came down to philosophical first principles, where a materialist like Taine was cocksure. Marx once made an attempt to explain why the poems of Homer were so good when the society that produced them was from his point of view—that is, from the point of view of its industrial development—so primitive; and this gave him a good deal of trouble. If we compare his discussion of this problem with Vico's discussion of Homer, we see that the explanation of literature in terms of a philosophy of social history is becoming, instead of simpler and easier, more difficult and more complex.

Marx and Engels were deeply imbued, moreover, with the German admiration for literature, which they had learned from the age of Goethe. It would never have occurred to either of them that *der Dichter* was not one of the noblest and most beneficent of humankind. When Engels writes about Goethe, he presents him as a man equipped for 'practical life,' whose career was frustrated by the 'misery' of the historical situation in Germany in his time, and reproaches him for allowing himself to lapse into the 'cautious, smug and narrow' philistinism of the class from which he came; but Engels regrets this, because it interfered with the development of the 'mocking, defiant, world-despising genius,' 'der geniale Dichter,' 'der gewaltige Poet,' of whom Engels would not even, he says, have asked that he should have been a political liberal if Goethe had not sacrificed to his bourgeois shrinkings his truer esthetic sense. And the great critics who were trained on Marx—Franz Mehring and Bernard Shaw—had all this reverence for the priesthood of literature. Shaw deplores the absence of political philosophy and what he regards as the middle-class snobbery in Shakespeare; but he celebrates Shakespeare's poetry and his dramatic imagination almost as enthusiastically as Swinburne does, describing even those potboiling comedies, *Twelfth Night* and *As You Like It*—the themes of which seem to him most trashy—as 'the Crown Jewels of English dramatic poetry.' Such a critic may do more for a writer by showing him as a real man dealing with a real world at a definite moment of time than the impressionist critic of Swinburne's type who flourished in the same period of the late nineteenth century. The purely impressionist critic approaches the whole of literature as an exhibit of belletristic jewels, and he can only write a rhapsodic catalogue. But when Shaw turned his spotlight on Shakespeare as a figure in the Shavian drama of history, he invested him with a new interest as no other English critic had done.

The insistence that the man of letters should play a political role, the disparagement of works of art in comparison with political action, were thus originally no part of Marxism. They only became associated with it later. This happened by way of Russia, and it was due to special tendencies in that country that date from long before the Revolution or the promulgation of Marxism itself. In Russia there have been very good reasons why the political implications of literature should particularly occupy the critics. The art of Pushkin itself, with its marvelous power of implication, had certainly been partly created by the censorship of Nicholas I, and Pushkin set the tradition for most of the great Russian writers that followed him. Every play, every poem, every story, must be a parable of which the moral is *implied*. If it were stated, the censor would suppress the book as he tried to do with Pushkin's *Bronze Horseman,* where it was merely a question of the packed implications protruding a little too plainly. Right down through the writings of Chekhov and up almost to the Revolution, the imaginative literature of Russia presents the peculiar paradox of an art that is technically objective and yet charged with social messages. In Russia under the Tsar, it was inevitable that social criticism should lead to political conclusions, because the most urgent need from the point of view of any kind of improvement was to get rid of the tsarist regime. Even the neo-Christian moralist Tolstoy, who pretended to be non-political, was to exert a subversive influence, because his independent preaching was bound to embroil him with the Church, and the Church was an integral part of the tsardom. Tolstoy's pamphlet called *What Is Art?,* in which he throws overboard Shakespeare and a large part of modern literature, including his own novels, in the interest of his intransigent morality, is the example which is most familiar to us of the moralizing Russian criticism; but it was only the most sensational expression of a kind of approach which had been prevalent since Belinsky and Chernyshevsky in the early part of the century. The critics, who were usually journalists writing in exile or in a contraband press, were always tending to demand of the imaginative writers that they should dramatize bolder morals.

Even after the Revolution had destroyed the tsarist government, this state of things did not change. The old habits of censorship persisted in the new socialist society of the Soviets, which was necessarily made up of people who had been stamped by the die of the despotism. We meet here the peculiar phenomenon of a series of literary groups that attempt, one after the other, to obtain official recognition or to make themselves sufficiently powerful to establish themselves as arbiters of literature. Lenin and Trotsky and Luna-charsky had the sense to oppose these attempts: the comrade-dictators of Proletcult or Lev or Rapp would certainly have been just as bad as the Count Benckendorff who made Pushkin miserable, and when the Stalin bureaucracy, after the death of Gorky, got control of this department as of everything else, they instituted a system of repression that made Benckendorff and Nicholas I look like Lorenzo de' Medici. In the meantime, Trotsky, who was Commissar of War but himself a great political writer with an interest in belles-lettres, attempted, in 1924, apropos of one of these movements, to clarify the situation. He wrote a brilliant and valuable book called *Literature and Revolution,* in which he explained the aims of the government, analyzed the work of the Russian writers, and praised or rebuked the latter as they seemed to him in harmony or at odds with the former. Trotsky is intelligent, sympathetic; it is evident that he is really fond of literature and that he knows that a work of art does not fulfill its function in terms of the formulas of party propaganda. But Mayakovsky, the Soviet poet, whom Trotsky had praised with reservations, expressed himself in a famous joke when he was asked what he thought of Trotsky's book—a pun which implied that a Commissar turned critic was inevitably a Commissar still;[2] and what a foreigner cannot accept in Trotsky is his assumption that it is the duty of the government to take a hand in the direction of literature.

This point of view, indigenous to Russia, has been imported to other countries through the permeation of Communist influence. The Communist press and its literary followers have reflected the control of the Kremlin in all the phases through which it has passed, down to the wholesale imprisonment of Soviet writers which has been taking place since 1935. But it has never been a part of the American system that our Republican or Democratic administration should lay down a political line for the guidance of the national literature. A recent gesture in this direction on the part of Archibald MacLeish, who seems a little carried away by his position as Librarian of Congress, was anything but cordially received by serious American writers. So long as the United States remains happily a

---

2 Первый блин лег наркомом, *The first pancake lies like a narkom* (people's commissar)—a parody of the Russian saying, Первый блин комом, *The first pancake lies like a lump.*

non-totalitarian country, we can very well do without this aspect of the historical criticism of literature.

Another element of a different order has, however, since Marx's time been added to the historical study of the origins of works of literature. I mean the psychoanalysis of Freud. This appears as an extension of something which had already got well started before, which had figured even in Johnson's *Lives of the Poets,* and of which the great exponent had been Sainte-Beuve: the interpretation of works of literature in the light of the personalities behind them. But the Freudians made this interpretation more exact and more systematic. The great example of the psychoanalysis of an artist is Freud's own essay on Leonardo da Vinci; but this has little critical interest: it is an attempt to construct a case history. One of the best examples I know of the application of Freudian analysis to literature is in Van Wyck Brooks's book, *The Ordeal of Mark Twain,* in which Mr. Brooks uses an incident of Mark Twain's boyhood as a key to his whole career. Mr. Brooks has since repudiated the method he resorted to here, on the ground that no one but an analyst can ever know enough about a writer to make a valid psychoanalytic diagnosis. This is true, and it is true of the method that it has led to bad results where the critic has built a Freudian mechanism out of very slender evidence, and then given us what is really merely a romance exploiting the supposed working of this mechanism, in place of an actual study that sticks close to the facts and the documents of the writer's life and work. But I believe that Van Wyck Brooks really had hold of something important when he fixed upon that childhood incident of which Mark Twain gave so vivid an account to his biographer—that scene at the deathbed of his father when his mother had made him promise that he would not break her heart. If it was not one of those crucial happenings that are supposed to determine the complexes of Freud, it has certainly a typical significance in relation to Mark Twain's whole psychology. The stories that people tell about their childhood are likely to be profoundly symbolic even when they have been partly or wholly made up in the light of later experience. And the attitudes, the compulsions, the emotional 'patterns' that recur in the work of a writer are of great interest to the historical critic.

These attitudes and patterns are embedded in the community and the historical moment, and they may indicate its ideals and its diseases as the cell shows the condition of the tissue. The recent scientific experimentation in the combining of Freudian with Marxist method, and of psychoanalysis with anthropology, has had its parallel development in criticism. And there is thus another element added to our equipment for analyzing literary works, and the problem grows still more complex.

The analyst, however, is of course not concerned with the comparative values of his patients any more than the surgeon is. He cannot tell you why the neurotic Dostoevsky produces work of immense value to his fellows while another man with the same neurotic pattern would become a public menace. Freud himself emphatically states in his study of Leonardo that his method can make no attempt to account for Leonardo's genius. The problems of comparative artistic value still remain after we have given attention to the Freudian psychological factor just as they do after we have given attention to the Marxist economic factor and to the racial and geographical factors. No matter how thoroughly and searchingly we may have scrutinized works of literature from the historical and biographical points of view, we must be ready to attempt to estimate, in some such way as Saintsbury and Eliot do, the relative degrees of success attained by the products of the various periods and the various personalities. We must be able to tell good from bad, the first-rate from the second-rate. We shall not otherwise write literary criticism at all, but merely social or political history as reflected in literary texts, or psychological case histories from past eras, or, to take the historical point of view in its simplest and most academic form, merely chronologies of books that have been published.

And now how, in these matters of literary art, do we tell the good art from the bad? Norman Kemp Smith, the Kantian philosopher, whose courses I was fortunate enough to take at Princeton twenty-five years ago, used to tell us that this recognition was based primarily on an emotional reaction. For purposes of practical criticism this is a safe assumption on which to proceed. It is possible to discriminate in a variety of ways the elements that in any given department go to make a successful work of literature. Different schools have at different times demanded different things of literature: *unity, symmetry, universality, originality, vision, inspiration, strangeness, suggestiveness, improving morality, socialist realism,* etc. But you could have any set of these qualities that any school of writing has called for and still not have a good play, a good novel, a good poem, a good history. If you identify the essence of good

literature with any one of these elements or with any combination of
them, you simply shift the emotional reaction to the recognition of
the element or elements. Or if you add to your other demands the
demand that the writer must have *talent,* you simply shift this recog-
notion to the talent. Once people find some grounds of agreement in
the coincidence of their emotional reactions to books, they may be
able to discuss these elements profitably; but if they do not have this
basic agreement, the discussion will make no sense.

But how, you may ask, can we identify this élite who know what
they are talking about? Well, it can only be said of them that they
are self-appointed and self-perpetuating, and that they will compel
you to accept their authority. Imposters may try to put themselves
over, but these quacks will not last. The implied position of the
people who know about literature (as is also the case in every other
art) is simply that they know what they know, and that they are determined to impose their opinions by main force of eloquence or
assertion on the people who do not know. This is not a question, of
course, of professional workers in literature—such as editors, professors and critics, who very often have no real understanding of
the products with which they deal—but of readers of all kinds in all
walks of life. There are moments when a first-rate writer, unrecognized or out of fashion with the official chalkers-up for the market,
may find his support in the demand for his work of an appreciative
cultivated public.

But what is the cause of this emotional reaction which is the
critic's divining rod? This question has long been a subject of study
by the branch of philosophy called esthetics, and it has recently
been made a subject of scientific experimentation. Both these lines
of inquiry are likely to be prejudiced in the eyes of the literary critic
by the fact that the inquiries are sometimes conducted by persons
who are obviously deficient in literary feeling or taste. Yet one should
not deny the possibility that something of value might result from
the speculations and explorations of men of acute minds who take as
their given data the esthetic emotions of other men.

Almost everybody interested in literature has tried to explain to
himself the nature of these emotions that register our approval of
artistic works; and I of course have my own explanation.

In my view, all our intellectual activity, in whatever field it takes
place, is an attempt to give a meaning to our experience—that is, to
make life more practicable; for by understanding things we make
it easier to survive and get around among them. The mathematician

Euclid, working in a convention of abstractions, shows us relations between the distances of our unwieldy and cluttered-up environment upon which we are able to count. A drama of Sophocles also indicates relations between the various human impulses, which appear so confused and dangerous, and it brings out a certain justice of Fate—that is to say, of the way in which the interaction of these impulses is seen in the long run to work out—upon which we can also depend. The kinship, from this point of view, of the purposes of science and art appears very clearly in the case of the Greeks, because not only do both Euclid and Sophocles satisfy us by making patterns, but they make much the same kind of patterns. Euclid's *Elements* takes simple theorems and by a series of logical operations builds them up to a climax in the square on the hypotenuse. A typical drama of Sophocles develops in a similar way.

Some writers (as well as some scientists) have a different kind of explicit message beyond the reassurance implicit in the mere feat of understanding life or of molding the harmony of artistic form. Not content with such an achievement as that of Sophocles—who has one of his choruses tell us that it is better not to be born, but who, by representing life as noble and based on law, makes its tragedy easier to bear—such writers attempt, like Plato, to think out and recommend a procedure for turning it into something better. But other departments of literature—lyric poetry such as Sappho's, for example—have *less* philosophical content than Sophocles. A lyric gives us nothing but a pattern imposed on the expression of a feeling; but this pattern of metrical quantities and of consonants and vowels that balance has the effect of reducing the feeling, however unruly or painful it may seem when we experience it in the course of our lives, to something orderly, symmetrical and pleasing; and it also relates this feeling to the more impressive scheme, works it into the larger texture, of the body of poetic art. The discord has been resolved, the anomaly subjected to discipline. And this control of his emotion by the poet has the effect at second-hand of making it easier for the reader to manage his own emotions. (Why certain sounds and rhythms gratify us more than others, and how they are connected with the themes and ideas that they are chosen as appropriate for conveying, are questions that may be passed on to the scientist.)

And this brings us back again to the historical point of view. The experience of mankind on the earth is always changing as man develops and has to deal with new combinations of elements; and the writer who is to be anything more than an echo of his predecessors must always find expression for something which has never yet been expressed, must master a new set of phenomena which has never yet been mastered. With each such victory of the human intellect, whether in history, in philosophy or in poetry, we experience a deep satisfaction: we have been cured of some ache of disorder, relieved of some oppressive burden of uncomprehended events.

This relief that brings the sense of power, and, with the sense of power, joy, is the positive emotion which tells us that we have encountered a first-rate piece of literature. But stay! you may at this point warn: are not people often solaced and exhilarated by literature of the trashiest kind? They are: crude and limited people do certainly feel some such emotion in connection with work that is limited and crude. The man who is more highly organized and has a wider intellectual range will feel it in connection with work that is finer and more complex. The difference between the emotion of the more highly organized man and the emotion of the less highly organized one is a matter of mere gradation. You sometimes discover books—the novels of John Steinbeck, for example—that seem to mark precisely the borderline between work that is definitely superior and work that is definitely bad. When I was speaking a little while back of the genuine connoisseurs who establish the standards of taste, I meant, of course, the people who can distinguish Grade A and who prefer it to the other grades.

# CONSTANCE M. ROURKE

## (1865–1941)

CONSTANCE M. ROURKE was born in Cleveland, on November 14, 1865. Upon graduating from Vassar she received a grant from the Borden Fund, that permitted her to travel abroad for purposes of study. She spent her time profitably in research at the Sorbonne and at the library of the British Museum. After her return to the United States in 1910, she became an instructor in English at Vassar, a position which she retained until 1915. From then on she devoted her time to research into folk history in the United States, preferring to study a region at first hand and there discover the survivals of a once rich and flourishing tradition. Thus she traveled across the length and breadth of America, listening to the characteristic rhythm of folk-speech, collecting folk-songs and folk-tales, jotting down folk-memories and folk-history, as these persisted, enriched and embellished by time, in the memory of all sorts of men. Here was the material she was looking for, the oral tradition, the living history of a people, all of which needed but to be transcribed. It needed, in addition, a new interpretation, a new fund of historical knowledge and imaginative insight, which she was fortunately able to supply. In this work she found her vocation.

Her interests reached beyond the bellestristic and included the arts of all kinds, however humble, so long as they were indigenous and representative of the ongoing life of the American people. She directed research and selected material for the *Index of American Design,* making as complete a record as was then possible of the arts and the role they played in American life. This indeed is the sustaining spirit and animating purpose behind her work; she sought to render explicit and give proper emphasis to the organic connection between folk traditions, many of which actively survive, and national art. She set herself the monumental task of assembling and interpreting all the material of this sort that still remained so that the native roots of our culture might be widely known and serve to call forth the best in the creative workers of our land. Unfortunately she died before carrying out her ambition plan to compose a three-volume *History of American Culture,* but she had succeeded in discovering and making available an American folk tradition that American writers and artists could put constructively to use. This is her most distinctive contribution to the field of American criticism.

*American Humor* (1931) examines hitherto neglected and unappreciated but vital aspects of our native culture, studying closely such American types as the Yankee and backwoodsmen, the minstrel shows, religious cultists, Lincoln, writers of "humor." In all of this Rourke attempts to show how the past prepared the soil out of which contemporary literature has grown, the folk culture which is present in our major nineteenth-century writers. Here are the rich ingredients of a national tradition which can nourish and sustain the American artists and give them a precious sense of continuity with the perennially active and fecundating past. With genuine affection and fine insight based on first-hand knowledge and experience, Constance Rourke traces the development of native American humor in all its multifarious ramifications. Throughout she follows the eddies and main currents of the mythologizing process at work, from the days of pioneering to our own time. But tradition takes a long time to develop; it is not easy to recover and fruitfully assimilate the past. The task of the contemporary writer is to situate himself in the American grain; he must work hard if he is to earn as well as inherit the fruits of the American tradition.

Issued posthumously and compiled from a mass of manuscripts she left behind, *The Roots of American Culture* was edited in 1942 by Van Wyck Brooks. Rourke had planned this as a history of American culture, for which her earlier work had been a kind of preparation. Van Wyck Brooks had argued that what this country needed, if it was to produce a full-bodied, mature literature, was a strong suffusing sense of its own past, a tradition that was vital and usable, but his signal mistake was to find fault with the American past. Rourke sought to remedy the deficiencies of this well-intentioned but poorly documented theory. Patiently she labored to furnish the groundwork of a tradition the richness and scope of which neither Brooks nor Mumford suspected. She worked devotedly at the task of recovering whatever traces yet remained of the early Americans' rich contribution to the arts, the kind of communal life they led and the collective artistic expression to which that life gave birth. She knew that a people voices its creative instinct not only in formal letters or painting or sculpture but also in its homespun, day-to-day concerns. Like Herder she is convinced that history, whether social or literary, should concern itself not with the epic achievements of a people but with its varied, teeming life at various layers. Unfortunately none of the American writers, with the exception of Whitman, saw the important implications of this theory in its bearing on the autochthonous quality of the folk-arts. The result of this has been the commonly accepted assumption that America lacked folk-expression and that whatever traces of it were to be found could be safely attributed to European importation. Then the twentieth century suddenly discovered the singular value and virtue of the folk element, but even so

"the idea of a coninuous life of the folk running through the history of the nation has not as yet become a salient idea, nor have possible relationships of the folk-arts to the fine arts seemed basic."[1]

Accumulating a massive pile of evidence, she tried to dispel the dominant but dubious theory that we could not rise out of our cultural nonage until we had steeped ourselves in the European tradition. It is this false conception of culture as achieved by means of carriers or fertilizers, that she labored to refute, since the best America could achieve, according to this doctrine, was an extension of European culture. This theory of cultural diffusion, she was convinced, did not apply to the American scene. For what is important is not the pervasiveness of foreign influences but the degree to which they acclimate themselves and take root and flourish. A culture is the sum of its native growths, and to appraise it adequately one must see it as a whole, in its total configuration, and not judge it by a few separate, specially favored arts. Our early arts, however inferior in many respects, cannot be considered the groping fruits of imitation. Springing from a life peculiar to this land, they had their own fresh idiom and characteristic pattern. Rourke called attention to the neglected but profoundly fruitful resources of our folk-arts, the fundamental material they provide for building an authentically native culture.

Her roots were in the Middle West. She denied that America was culturally disinherited. On the contrary, she convincingly demonstrated that a creative tradition existed in this country. Since this was so, then American arts and letters could take on a new lease on life. She had no wish to deny the deep influence of European culture and saw no reason for rejecting it. Fundamentally, however, it was not a question of imitating Europe but of bringing our own native seeds to fruition in accordance with our cultural climate and indigenous conditions. That was her object: to demonstrate the continuous impact and impregnating force of our native tradition. That was her primary purpose in collecting a wide diversity of material throughout the country, for in this way she hoped to nourish the

[1] Constance Rourke, *The Roots of American Culture* (New York, 1942), p. 26.

artists to come. Though her work has its limitations, she was tending definitely and steadily toward a criticism that would prove constructive and integrated.

### BIBLIOGRAPHY

#### TEXT

*Trumpets of Jubilee.* New York, 1927.
*Troupers of the Gold Coast.* New York, 1928.
*American Humor.* New York, 1931.
*Davy Crockett.* New York, 1934.
*Audubon.* New York, 1936.
*Charles Sheeler.* New York, 1938.
*The Roots of American Culture.* New York, 1942.

#### CRITICISM

Allen, Gay W., "Humor in America," *Sewanee Review,* XXXVIII, 111–113 (January-March, 1932).
Hyman, Stanley Edgar, "Constance Rourke and Folk Criticism," *The Armed Vision,* New York, 1948, pp. 127–141.
Marshall, Margaret, "Constance Rourke in the Critic's Den," *Nation,* CLV, 418–420 (October 24, 1942).

## AMERICAN ART: A POSSIBLE FUTURE*

IN none of the arts has our full native inheritance been clarified. It has been our fortune to create briefly, hastily, insecurely, and then to press on to some new and not always clearly understood objective, with the result that the arts in this country have shown many brave beginnings and few developments, and even these have often been casually buried and are to be found now only by excavation, like the artifacts of a forgotten city.

These careless approaches may prove to have been excellent for a people whose intentions are still experimental and who, presumably, have been trying to create arts distinctively their own. Much has been made of our "cultural lag," our lack of consistent esthetic purposes. But it is doubtful whether the beginnings of any

* Reprinted from *The Roots of American Culture* by Constance M. Rourke. Copyright, 1942, by Harcourt, Brace and Company, Inc.

art are ever orderly, and when patterns have become sharply grooved they are usually lifeless. Our so-called "lag" may be nothing of the kind. Instead we may be moving with hesitation in new directions.

Within the last dozen years one of our periodic rushes of rediscovery of our past has occurred; and if the evaluations are conflicting, gradually many hidden facts have been coming to the surface. In music a whole continuous underply begins to emerge, pre-Handelian, based primarily upon the dance, continued in part by the religious songs of the early New England singing schools, by both white and Negro spirituals, and by the British ballads, spreading into fiddle-tunes and songs of the southern mountains and of the range and lumber-camp, often mixed with other musical materials and showing original variations on new soil and under new conditions, and consistently maintained even to the present day in widely scattered areas. Here indeed is a whole musical heritage, affording something more than folk-tunes for musical decoration, rather to be used as European composers of the past have used a similar but not identical music, for a fundamental native schooling.

For years critics have lamented the absence of an American folklore and, building from this hypothesis, have formed dreary conclusions as to the future of the American arts. But our folklore is now seen to be abundant. Enough of this has come to the surface to indicate that, whatever its derivations, it is unlike that of other peoples in its essential patterns. Through it our early fantasies and mythologies are coming back to us, showing the secure beginnings of a native poetry and a native language; and the flow of these patterns into literary expression can be traced from Hawthorne and Melville to Mark Twain and Emily Dickinson and Edwin Arlington Robinson.

Our painting seems to have behind it less consistent traditions than our music and literature, but it would be well not to dogmatize about this in view of unpredictable discoveries in the other arts. And interpretations have often been wide of the mark. A favorite argument has been that the Puritan builder suppressed ornament as the result of a deliberate process of theological reasoning and that the blight has spread among us down the years. But, though the average Puritan had considerable power as a dialectician, it seems doubtful whether with hammer and saw in hand he often exercised this power and blocked an earthy impulse. For one thing, those using hammer and saw in the seventeenth and eighteenth centuries were not likely to be Puritans. The proportion of yeomen and journeymen was very large who remained outside the fold of the theocracy, even though it was to their clear advantage to enter.

Puritan and non-Puritan alike were influenced in this long period by the tendency toward the abstract in Calvinistic theology, and equally by the general turn toward abstraction which came in England with the Reformation and took many speculative forms. Puritan or non-Puritan, the journeyman builder belonged pretty much to his time. Instead of his being thwarted, it seems likely that abstract values gave him an undefined pleasure, that he even took a sensuous delight in the elimination of ornamental detail. Certainly form, strict but apparently casual, was rarely lacking in what he created. Its quality may be traced in everything to which he and his race have turned their minds, from meeting houses and clipper ships to metaphor and idiom. And this circumstance can be pressed toward the conclusion that the New Englander, with his self-contained creative powers and his passion for migration, left his distinctive print wherever he went in this country, creating a tendency among us toward the abstract which has been strong if unconscious and not as yet fully developed.

As for the pioneer of all ancestries or regional affiliations, a familiar theory has it that he was destructive of the amenities and the arts, but like many other generalizations about American life and the American character this does not bear the test of a close scrutiny of the record. Women often carried portraits or clocks with glass paintings or delicate china on their laps in oxcarts over hundreds of miles into the Western wilderness, and their children often kept these intact. In a Tennessee cabin I have seen a silver luster cup of exquisite shape, which had been broken into small fragments and coarsely mended, but which had been preserved with pride and pleasure for its esthetic values and its symbol of a tradition; and similar evidences will be found on almost every one of our successive frontiers.

Perhaps too much has been made of the folk-handicrafts, the carvings, whittlings, wrought iron, flower paintings, hooked rugs, woven bedspreads, and homespun, of the pioneer. These often have lasting creative values and join with other evidences to suggest the basis for a native approach; but what becomes more important in retrospect is the recurrent proof that they afford of visual and tactile skills and the steady, widespread use of these. Pioneer experience was extraordinarily full of subtle preoccupations for the eye and hand. To follow a hardly discernible path or trace in the forests, to notice slight essential changes in vegetation, in falling light, in contours of the ground, in the undercurrents of watercourses, was part of a necessary habit which extended through several American generations and is still to be found among many whose break with the land seems almost complete. And the typical pioneer or frontiersman was master of those daily and primitive arts that have often afforded an ancestry for the fine arts. His supple handling of weapons, his use of skins and furs, his construction of necessary tools, and not least his free sense of personal decoration, were all firmly restricted by economy of use and means and indicate in outline the esthetic approach.

As for an outcome in larger forms of expression, did this exist? We are impatient for an outcome; we always have been. From an early day, almost from the close of the Revolution and possibly before, our expectations as to esthetic fulfillment have been nothing short of stupendous. All at once we were to have all the arts, on the epical scale. Small Western newspapers foretold the certain event in the eighteen thirties and forties. We are still strangely afflicted by that obsession. Because the grandiose fulfillment has been lacking we have failed to perceive small but hardy evidences of those fresh forms and fresh approaches which would seem the natural result of an era of discovery, and may form beginnings for distinctive arts.

Woodcuts revealing new native types of the frontier and the backwoods with a sure linear attack and a pungent humor may be found scattered in old almanacs. As one turns old engravings on some single subject, say that of the Indian, here and there a striking bit of composition will appear, with primitive qualities boldly transcribed in terms of light and arrangement. Often these effects will be incomplete, shown only in a single passage of a drawing, set against a trite, blurred notion of what the wilderness was like. These evidences are likely to be highly discontinuous. The name attached to an interesting piece may not easily be found again. Many are unsigned. To draw together those of genuine worth over a period of years would mean a long search through humble sources, and because of our odd bias away from the popular arts (odd in a democracy) they are often difficult to find. The casual fate that has overtaken Audubon's drawings, so sure and so original in color and design, is an indication of our established tendency to overlook any but the formal evidences of an art. And it is only recently, through the discoveries and interpretations of such critics as Mr. Holger Cahill and the Nadelmans, that American folk-painting and sculpture—"the art of the common man"—has received any recognition whatever.

Even in their own day this expression was probably brief and fragmentary. Experiment was continually being blotted out, not by the scornful and destructive pioneer but by forces beyond his control. Whatever was created, whatever took shape out of a formative culture, was likely to be destroyed by the mere force of migration, acting like a vast physical upheaval, destroying small, tangible things and always tending to eliminate them, whatever the wish of women in oxcarts with their clocks and their delicate china. The related destructive force was that of fire. Native beginnings, particularly in the visual arts because of their destructible character, were reduced by repeated holocausts which extended from the burning of cabins and stockades in New England, as the result of Indian raids, down to the mid-century bonfires of cloth-and-paper-towns in California, and onward to the action of Mrs. O'Leary's cow, and indeed to a very recent day. Fire in this country has been a large and obvious yet unreckoned anti-cultural agency, and must be counted as part of the cost of making new, rash, primitive beginnings. For the rather hazy, popular theory as to the destructive nature of the pioneer, another, simpler reading of the record can be substituted.

2

Naturally European esthetics and the European arts have been an influence upon all our creative expression; but in literature and music the invasion seems to have been more gradual than in painting, and perhaps more easily assimilated. For the visual arts the first great influx apparently began with the Crystal Palace Exhibition in London in 1851, when under the sway of Albert, the lush Victorian abundance began to burgeon and bloom with a vengeance. Immediately we had in New York our own feebler Crystal Palace, and a gaudy, insipid acreage of oils so quickly became the rage that the auction rooms of the infant town of San Francisco were filled with them, advertised as specially imported from abroad. What Lewis Mumford has called a "pillage of the past" followed so quickly and feverishly that the possibility of assimilation was excluded, and the drive from the American center was continued by the pull of the foreign schools.

In the practical arts, on the other hand, it was readily taken for granted in this country that native skills could be developed on native ground, and they were, as in the unique and cunning designs of clipper ships and in the widening number of mechanical inventions. But as to the fine arts a false notion was dominant, a notion that by no means was peculiarly American. The artificial division between the practical and the fine arts had long since taken place in Europe, with the result that the one tended to be lost or obscured and the other separated from vigorous and natural sources.

Let us lay this burden for a moment at the already overcrowded door of the *bourgeoisie*. The natural interpenetration of the fine and the practical arts had been broken by the recession of the guilds and the rise of the small capitalist class. An instinctive functioning had been left behind. A whole outcome cannot of course be given any single ascription, and the tendency of the Reformation (or the turn of thought that was most highly concentrated in the Reformation) had likewise a disruptive and divisive effect as abstract and intellectual elements were introduced into the concrete cultures of Europe.

In other words, American painting began to take shape in the midst of a thorough and widespread confusion of aims, and for us confusion has been worse confounded because a difficult cultural destiny has been upon us from the beginning. On the whole, the European groups among us have meant to cast Europe behind them; yet a persistent awareness of Europe, of European values, of what Europe has thought of us and what we have thought of Europeans has been steadily with us. This awareness has become the sharper because Europeans have bent themselves to the task of judging our attainments with thoroughness in a great amount of letterpress.

We have both fought these judgments and yielded to them. Our mixed attitudes—our languishing wish to conform to European standards and our sensitive belligerence—appear strongly even in the folk-plays of our early stage. They recur in the explosive, highly posed, toplofty humor of *Innocents Abroad* and *A Connecticut Yankee at King Arthur's Court*. Our relation to Europe is a subject which we have never been able to let alone. We have been obsessed by it, and we haven't known what to do about it.

In the visual arts and in art criticism the dilemma has been particularly acute. The more or less explicit idea governing most of our art criticism has been that our art would naturally become a sequence within the art of western Europe. With enough European schooling and a sufficiently large number of civilized contacts, it has been hoped that esthetically we might at last begin to develop. We had only to catch up with Europe, so to speak, by diligent study.

This is to disregard the ways in which cultures have grown and been sustained in the past. Most cultures have at some time been subject to foreign influences, but surely the center of growth of any distinctive culture is to be found within the social organism and is created by peculiar and irreducible social forces. It is plain, as Franz Boas says in his introduction to Ruth Benedict's recent *Patterns of Culture,* that "hardly any trait of culture can be understood taken out of its general setting." And Dr. Benedict insists as her major thesis upon "the importance of the study of the whole configuration as over against the continued analysis of its parts."

Dr. Benedict cites Worringer as showing "how fundamental a difference this approach makes in the field of esthetics," and Worringer's argument has its suggestion for ourselves. "He contrasts the highly developed art of two periods, the Greek and the Byzantine. The older criticism, he insists, which defined art in absolute terms and identified it with classical standards, could not possibly understand the processes of art as they are represented in Byzantine painting or mosaic. Achievement in one cannot be judged in terms of the other, because each was attempting to achieve quite different ends. The Greeks in their art attempted to give expression to their own pleasure in activity; they sought to embody an identification of their vitality with the objective world. Byzantine art, on the other hand, objectified abstraction, a profound feeling of separation in the face of outside nature. Any understanding of the two must take account, not only of comparisons of artistic ability, but far more of differences of artistic intention. The two were contrasting, integrated configurations, each of which could make use of forms and standards that were incredible to the other."

Now whether or not so positive a contrast exists between our artistic intention and that of European groups, the fact remains that our "configuration" is not the European "configuration," either socially or geographically. And whether or not we derived our early motivating ideas from Europe, these have been shaped to our own distinctive ends. It would seem obvious that our art, if we are to have one, must spring from the center rather than from the periphery of our social pattern. Yet our criticism on the whole has considered European art in the absolute terms to which Worringer refers, and has related American art to this as if no basic differences existed between the groups of civilizations. Oriental influences have been discussed as though it were a mere matter of individual cleverness to assimilate them. To follow a single phase of Worringer's argument, a general attitude toward nature may prevail among us (and probably does) which is wholly different from that which prevails in England or in Spain, and this should lead to differences in expression; yet certain artistic achievements in England or in Spain are considered as absolutes which we should imitate. The results of such experiments will necessarily be faltering.

Our painting has never been fully considered in its native cultural relations and implications or basic intentions, nor is this strange, since the elements of our culture are only now being discovered and defined, and indeed the whole movement toward such explicit cultural definitions anywhere is comparatively a new one.

3

A fumbling effort to create an indigenous art appeared early in stress upon the American subject. The spectacular Indian was brought to the fore, and painting on this theme was largely bad because we never in any sense assimilated the Indian, and because Americans of an early period were governed by two extreme ideas, that Indians were savages who must be exterminated, and that they were figures in a primitive idyll.

This last, deriving from Rousseau, still obtains among many Americans who are creatively adrift, and may persist because certain tribal cultures, particularly that of the Pueblos of New Mexico, present definition and completion while ours is chaotic. Dr. Benedict might go further and suggest that what she calls the balanced Apollonian culture of the Pueblos offers a resting place for imperfect Dionysians like ourselves. Undoubtedly there is a good deal of wear and tear in being Dionysian, and our efforts in that direction have sometimes been particularly strenuous. But whether this small group of Apollonians—the Pueblos—can offer us a point of artistic departure is another matter. We should be obliged to go the whole way with Mary Austin as to the fundamental American rhythm, and then find a reason for selecting this one, highly distinctive tribe as a prototype for ourselves.

Consciousness of the American subject continued intermittently through the nineteenth century, in the abundant production of the Hudson River School, in those great mossy, green and brown dioramic landscapes that seem inspired by the American poems of

Felicia Hemans but that do somehow convey something characteristic of the American scene. The paintings of Inness reveal that "proprietary sense" of our landscape which Mr. Gutheim has noted. But though that geographic adaptation and expression which Mr. Gutheim has outlined appeared in all the arts, there were plenty of divergences. Church, Hunt, Washington Allston, LaFarge, both the Giffords, Martin, Whistler, used alien or remotely symbolical subjects, sometimes to the exclusion of others, and the emphasis soon began to shift to techniques.

At the turn of the century came the overwhelming discovery that subject was unimportant. The American subject was tacitly, sometimes openly derided; it was certainly left behind by American art students in the foreign schools as they began to thread the mazes of highly intellectualized modern theory and experiment. The powerful innovations of post-impressionism, *surréalisme*, and the rest became magnets. Now by another whirl we seem to have returned to the American subject as primary. This emphasis may have been dictated by recent necessity, but a school of renewed conviction has apparently arisen as part of the general move toward—or back to—a sometimes militant regionalism.

The apparently simple approach for the American artist by way of the American subject can offer plenty of pitfalls. The painting of Grant Wood, with its American types and regional backgrounds and themes, has all the orthodox elements of a native art, but this painter many times used superficial and transient elements of the American subject without touching its core. To make paintings look like crewel work, presumably because crewels were a familiar American medium (usually a bad one) is a regression quite as definite as would be another orgy of burnt wood, undertaken because the poker and the oak plank were easy to come by in the American home before the passing of the stove. To give a portrait in oils the style of a daguerreotype even to the shine of the copper base, presumably because the daguerreotype has played a large part among us, is an extreme sentimentalism that has nothing to do with the art of painting. Grant Wood seems at his best in some of his more casual decorations where a conscious purpose has less play, or in direct satire, for which a solid native tradition exists in the precise field which he has chosen, the portraiture of the type—a tradition which has established itself through many forms of our folk humor.

Yet a wide use of the environmental subject would seem peculiarly necessary for us because of our situation as a people whose culture is still undefined and incomplete. We do not know our land as peoples of older, smaller countries know theirs. Because of our continual mobility we lack a deeply rooted and instinctive knowledge of the underlying natural forms by which we are surrounded. We have rarely submitted for long to the discipline of place, though in the large we have been shaped by its earthy elements. Turner, Huntington, Ellen Semple and others have analyzed the power of the land in the formation of our societies, and its force appears outside social economics. Rhythms of hill and bottom land and prairie and mountain, native qualities of light or murk, have left their print upon the social mind and imagination. They have been—they still are—among our esthetic and cultural determinants.

It is not that we require mere faithful transcriptions of our sharply varied landscape or shore, or of the peculiar, stratified aggregations which make the American city, though these might offer more to a people still in process of self-recognition than the exponents of "pure" art would be willing to admit. Socially considered, there would seem to be a wide place for the honest journeyman painter—for the honest and simple pleasures of recognition. Beyond this, the land remains formative in a strict esthetic sense. Outer subject—the mere American scene—may fall away. Many artists may soon leave this behind, but the inalienable patterns will remain.

In the same way the American type and its many variations may become something more than visual material. Posture, gesture, movement, bone structure, ranges of individual expression—these inevitably suggest underlying social ideas and emotions and motives in terms of typical form. They provide clues to the governing complexes which belong to us and which make our culture distinctive from that of others.

Those who have derided subject are in a sense right. Our eager young art students who have been swept away by every new theory have their justification. They have sought a perception by means of which the final transcendence of art over its materials may be accomplished. It is obvious that in any final expression subject becomes secondary. Their mistake has been to suppose that such perceptions can be discovered in a vacuum anywhere. They have failed to notice that the young foreign artists with whom they have associated have all had an initial, unconscious schooling which the American lacks. The young foreign artist has of course long traditions in the arts which may be used in sequence or for departure: but even more significantly, he knows his environment and his native culture through association with others who look upon the outer world with eyes not unlike his own, and who suggest identities by a thousand communicative means—idiom, intonation, gesture, dress, social choices. Whatever his individual variation, he can draw unconsciously from a whole flux of basic social patterns. With us such patterns are not yet abundantly established, or are still unrecognized.

## 4

Let us lay down the principle that the American artist cannot take off from the same points of departure as the European artist. Let us accept the fact that it is futile for the American artist to try to "catch up" with Europeans because at best he is trying, often obscurely, to do something of his own.

In his complicated but really rather thrilling dilemma, the environmental subject will be one clue to native forms—an elementary discipline. His further and more difficult problem is to draw upon the many subtle evidences of an unfolding tradition. A process of discovery and rediscovery is going on, just now with acceleration, but until the materials of all our culture become known and are easily possessed the creative worker in any of the arts will necessarily be thwarted.

Here and there indications appear as to the stimulus and reinforcement which these materials may give to the painter. Our still half-buried folklore abounds in the purely legendary, and in this, essential American types, rather than characters, have been drawn and redrawn. Basic traceries are there which might be full of suggestion to the mural painter. This is not at all to propose that he should apotheosize Mike Fink and Davy Crockett, John Henry and Paul Bunyan, though these legendary heroes might lend themselves well to mural treatment. But the strong, prevailing legendary quality, with its native biases, naturally would have much to say to him, because the sense of legend lies broadly at the base of mural painting. From this special abundance he could gain a quite positive sense of direction.

As one reads consistent signs in our cultural history it would seem that very great sequences of mural painting should develop among us. This is a highly social art, and we have always gathered easily in crowds. A dozen reasons—timidity among them—might be mentioned as to why we have left empty the walls of our many gathering-places. An acute sense of the more conspicuous phases of social expression among us, as in revivals, camp-meetings, political demonstrations, lodges, parades, and even lynching, might give the American muralist a knowledge of basic social outlines as well as an extended range of materials. Thomas Benton has used some of these. A wide understanding of the dominating social forces might reveal subjects of quite a different order from those which he has chosen. And if our painters were fortunate enough to know well some of the folk-satire directed against our early flamboyant oratory, it may be that the lack of control, the tendency toward excess, which often afflicts our artists when they approach large subjects or utilize large spaces, would be objectified and reduced.

The American painter might gain assurance in a contemporary mode if he knew by heart the spare abstract as this appears in many phases of our folk-expression, particularly within the New England tradition. Woven into all our folklore is an acute observation of the external world which any artist could afford to know well, and this tends to be poetic rather than naturalistic. It is typically in key with the abstract. Indeed a full knowledge of our folklore and folk-song would reveal the subordinate place that naturalism constantly took in our early free expression. This absense in itself may constitute a tradition, and the underlying poetry and humor might give the artist something of the lift which he must have if subject and technique are not to leave him in chains.

This is by no means to lay down the thesis that the painter must be schooled in all the arts. The talent of many painters seems to be channeled in the single mode. But in the large, the problem for the American artist is a cultural problem, and it is only through a full appropriation of our cultural tendencies that the sound frame of native reference, which major painting requires, can be provided.

If such appropriations cannot easily become an individual matter, it is true that certain artists have accomplished them. In our own time Marin has overpassed the demands of subject and has used that turn toward purity of color and abstraction, which have a secure place in our traditions, with a humorous assertion of personal idio-syncrasy which anyone familiar with forms of our character will immediately recognize. I know that Burchfield has been regarded as an unsparing realist and even as a satirist, but it seems to me that what he accomplishes is not an exposure of facts but a synthesis of certain deep-lying qualities in American life. He is acutely aware of its melodrama, which has often appeared with a kind of driving poetry, infusing ugly materials. If, as has been said, his deserted mansions stand aloof from the earth on which they are planted, this separation from environment has been a large part of our experience.

The individual artist must always make his own special discoveries, but we shall gain if he is not pressed too hard to attain them, if he need not make them alone. The greater ones will survive the effort, but wastage and bewilderment will continue among lesser men who are too good to lose. A sensitive historical criticism would seem a major necessity, broadly grounded in native research as well as in esthetics. A prodigious amount of work is still to be done in the way of unearthing, defining, and synthesizing our traditions, and finally in making them known through simple and natural means. Beneath this purpose must probably lie fresh reconstructions of our notion as to what constitutes a culture, with a removal of ancient snobberies and with new inclusions.

This is not in any conceivable sense to advocate a policy of artistic isolation. With all the support that definitions of our own traditions may give him, the American artist will necessarily run full-on sooner or later into the uncertainties and over-pliant ambitions which now seem to cut across all expression everywhere. He cannot escape his fate all at once, as an American with a partially illegible and syncopated history behind him, or as a citizen of a world that now seems to face many economic, social, and cultural crossroads. Yet recognition of the peculiar elements which form American culture would seem fundamental for both the artist and the critic, whether or not they wholly like what they find.

The intellectualized self-consciousness which was a partial outcome of the Reformation and which has developed through the intervening centuries is apparently besetting all artists everywhere. With all his handicaps the American artist has at least the advantage of a fairly complete background for this mode. It began for us with the landing of the Pilgrims and was continued by fine-spun arguments in all the theologies. The intellectualized, self-conscious attack has become in a general way a national habit, even a rough technique. This technique can be turned toward the definition and solution of our difficult cultural problems. Perhaps the American artist cannot now assume those simple and intuitive attitudes which the artist always wants—which most of us want—but he may consciously work toward a discovery of our traditions, attempt to use them, and eventually take his inevitable place.

# CLEANTH BROOKS

## (1906–    )

CLEANTH BROOKS, born in 1906 in Kentucky, taught for a number of years at Louisiana State University. He is now a professor of English at Yale University. While at Louisiana State University he edited, in collaboration with Robert Penn Warren, *The Southern Review* (1935–1942). He also composed, again in collaboration with Warren, three brilliant anthologies: *Understanding Poetry* (1938), *An Approach to Literature* (1941), and *Understanding Fiction* (1943). In 1945 he published, this time in collaboration with Robert B. Heilman, *Understanding Drama*. In these works Brooks elucidates and applies the critical principles which are elaborated at greater length in *Modern Poetry and the Tradition* (1939) and *The Well Wrought Urn* (1947).

He carries on the work initiated in part by T. S. Eliot's revolt against the ideas and attitudes popularized by the romantic poets. In *Modern Poetry and the Tradition,* a study of the relation of modern poets to "the tradition," they are defended on curiously unmodernistic grounds. Cleanth Brooks breaks a lance with famous critics like Samuel Johnson, Wordsworth, Coleridge, and Matthew Arnold over the question whether the intrusion of the intellect interferes with the poetic communication of deep emotions. He endeavors to dispose of the fallacy that there is a range of material inherently poetic or that there are words and objects peculiarly unsuited to the high seriousness of poetry. In his efforts to trace a line of continuity between the seventeenth-century poets and the moderns, he takes up the metaphor for clinical dissection, for it is in the handling of the metaphor that the moderns are closely related to their predecessors. Persuaded that nothing is intrinsically unpoetic, the metaphysical poets, with their nimble imagination and daring wit, could transform material which, in isolation from the context, might seem barren of promise and poetic power. Modern poets accept the play of conscious volition and conscious control, without thereby sacrificing the vitality and integrity of their imagination. Cleanth Brooks makes a sober plea for the necessity and

514

rightness of wit, which makes for psychological subtlety and increases the range of the poet's mastery of the world of sensation, feeling, and thought.

The poet approaches his subject by indirection and accomplishes the feat of paradox and irony by the way in which he conjoins words in a given order, thus producing ever new and surprising combinations. Each word receives its particular evocative power from the words which surround it, its semantic environment. The creative imagination, in its kindling moments, achieves a true miracle of transubstantiation, the metaphor uniting the discrepant, the seemingly discordant. In *The Well Wrought Urn* Brooks indicates what can be done with *Macbeth,* for example, by carefully tracing one pattern of symbolism which runs through the play.

That in brief is his general method: to inspect each poem at close range for its felicities of meaning and structure. Poetry must be read as poetry, not as doctrine or edifying truth. In their headlong impatience for the direct paraphrasable meaning, the overt theme, the surface content, many modern readers miss the finest and most precious part of poetry. Yet in their eagerness to display the hidden intentions and cunning artistry of the poet, the formalist critics sometimes overreach themselves. Pope is rehabilitated as a consummate artist, a master of deft irony and *double entendre,* and "The Rape of the Lock" is alleged to give off Freudian overtones.

Brooks applies his method with aggressive consistency: the text's the thing whereby to catch the conscience of the paradox, whether intended or not. Even Gray's "Elegy" is shown to be full of paradox. The ironic overtones and ambiguities of a poem must be studied within the body of the text. The method comes into its own with Brooks' analysis of Wordsworth's "Ode on Intimations of Immortality," which is treated as an autonomous poem, an independent structure, without reference to other sources. Poems read in and for themselves communicate their own rich message. For Brooks an ambiguity is an invitation to the dance, the sound of hound and horn, an irritation that forces him to scratch. He will break the poem apart into a thousand pieces until he has discovered its inner structural secret, hunting through every line and the implications of every word in order to gather the telltale evidence. Ever beneath the surface flows the vital movement of imagery, doing things which escape the naked eye and which are not to be found in the literal meaning of the poem. It does not matter one bit whether Wordsworth was aware of what he was doing; the main thing is that he did it. In short, it is the aesthetic experience that counts supremely; the rest is but tangential commentary.

Brooks reads not only between the lines but under and over and through the lines, and discovers all sorts of hidden connections, intentional or unintentional plays on words, interanimating paradoxes beautifully sustained, the lightning of irony flashing through the text, the clash and conflict of words mutually reinforcing and enriching each other's meaning, the amazing appropriateness of metaphors, and what not. Before we know it the critic has composed a gloss which is practically a revised edition of the poem, far more ingenious and complex than the innocent original. There is no need, Brooks holds, for reference to time or place or circumstance. The well-wrought urn outlives its original use, achieves an immortality that mocks at the ashes it contains and which it was designed to hold. Socio-economic coordinates are thus beside the point, since they do not give us any determinant of aesthetic value.

Formalist criticism represents a revolt against the relativism of our age and its sociologizing mania. It no longer labors to situate a poem within an historical, socially determined context. Repudiating historical relativism, the formalist critic wants to know what makes a poem aesthetically valuable, regardless of when and where it was written. Otherwise, Brooks contends, what we get, in the case of the older poetry, is cultural anthropology, and, in the case of contemporary poetry, discussions of ideology or morals or politics. Again and again, Brooks declares that the concern of the critic is not with what Keats, for example, was asserting about truth and beauty and their interrelation in "Ode on a Grecian Urn," but the way in which it is expressed in the poem and how this is integrally connected with the total context. In poetry no question of truth or falsity enters in. What determines the value of a poetic statement is its position in the context; that is the only legitimate test. The fundamental question is one of poetic propriety, aesthetic fitness. The poet usually knows precisely what he is doing. The task of the critic is to make all this clear.

## BIBLIOGRAPHY

### TEXT

*The Relation of the Alabama-Georgia Dialect to the Provincial Dialects of Great Britain.* Baton Rouge, 1935.

*Modern Poetry and the Tradition.* Chapel Hill, 1939.

"The Poem as Organism," *English Institute Annual, 1940.* New York, 1941.

*Understanding Fiction,* ed. by Cleanth Brooks and Robert Penn Warren. New York, 1943.

*Understanding Drama,* ed. by Cleanth Brooks and Robert B. Heilman. New York, 1945.

"The New Criticism and Scholarship," *Twentieth Century English,* ed. by W. S. Knickerbocker. New York, 1946.

"Criticism and Literary History," *Sewanee Review*, LV, 199–222 (Spring, 1947).

*The Well Wrought Urn*. New York, 1947.

"The Place of Creative Writing in the Study of Literature," *Association of American Colleges Bulletin*, XXXIV, 225–233 (May, 1948).

### CRITICISM

Crane, R., "Cleanth Brooks." *Modern Philology*, XLV, 226–245 (May, 1948).

Pearce, Roy Harvey, " 'Pure' Criticism and the History of Ideas," *The Journal of Aesthetics and Art Criticism*, VII, 122–132 (December, 1948).

Stallman, R. W., "Cleanth Brooks: A Checklist," *University of Kansas City Review*, XIV, 317–324 (Summer, 1948).

## THE LANGUAGE OF PARADOX*

FEW of us are prepared to accept the statement that the language of poetry is the language of paradox. Paradox is the language of sophistry, hard, bright, witty; it is hardly the language of the soul. We are willing to allow that paradox is a permissible weapon which a Chesterton may on occasion exploit. We may permit it in epigram, a special subvariety of poetry; and in satire, which though useful, we are hardly willing to allow to be poetry at all. Our prejudices force us to regard paradox as intellectual rather than emotional, clever rather than profound, rational rather than divinely irrational.

Yet there is a sense in which paradox is the language appropriate and inevitable to poetry. It is the scientist whose truth requires a language purged of every trace of paradox; apparently the truth which the poet utters can be approached only in terms of paradox. I overstate the case, to be sure; it is possible that the title of this chapter is itself to be treated as merely a paradox. But there are reasons for thinking that the overstatement which I propose may light up some elements in the nature of poetry which tend to be overlooked.

The case of William Wordsworth, for instance, is instructive on this point. His poetry would not appear to promise many examples

* First appeared in *The Language of Poetry*, edited by Allen Tate and published in 1942. Reprinted from *The Well Wrought Urn* by Cleanth Brooks, copyright, **1947, by Harcourt, Brace and Company, Inc.**

of the language of paradox. He usually prefers the direct attack. He insists on simplicity; he distrusts whatever seems sophistical. And yet the typical Wordsworth poem is based upon a paradoxical situation. Consider his celebrated

> It is a beauteous evening, calm and free,
> The holy time is quiet as a Nun
> Breathless with adoration. . . .

The poet is filled with worship, but the girl who walks beside him is not worshiping. The implication is that she should respond to the holy time, and become like the evening itself, nunlike; but she seems less worshipful than inanimate nature itself. Yet

> If thou appear untouched by solmn thought,
> Thy nature is not therefore less divine:
> Thou liest in Abraham's bosom all the year;
> And worship'st at the Temple's inner shrine,
> God being with thee when we know it not.

The underlying paradox (of which the enthusiastic reader may well be unconscious) is nevertheless thoroughly necessary, even for that reader. Why does the innocent girl worship more deeply than the self-conscious poet who walks beside her? Because she is filled with an unconscious sympathy for *all* of nature, not merely the grandiose and solemn. One remembers the lines from Wordsworth's friend, Coleridge:

> He prayeth best, who loveth best
> All things both great and small.

Her unconscious sympathy is the unconscious worship. She is in communion with nature "all the year," and her devotion is continual whereas that of the poet is sporadic and momentary. But we have not done with the paradox yet. It not only underlies the poem, but something of the paradox informs the poem, though, since this is Wordsworth, rather timidly. The comparison of the evening to the nun actually has more than one dimension. The calm of the evening obviously means "worship," even to the dull-witted and insensitive. It corresponds to the trappings of the nun, visible to everyone. Thus, it suggests not merely holiness, but, in the total poem, even a hint of Pharisaical holiness, with which the girl's careless innocence, itself a symbol of her continual secret worship, stands in contrast.

Or consider Wordsworth's sonnet, "Composed upon Westminster

Bridge." I believe that most readers will agree that it is one of Wordsworth's most successful poems; yet most students have the greatest difficulty in accounting for its goodness. The attempt to account for it on the grounds of nobility of sentiment soon breaks down. On this level, the poem merely says: that the city in the morning light presents a picture which is majestic and touching to all but the most dull of soul; but the poem says very little more about the sight: the city is beautiful in the morning light and it is awfully still. The attempt to make a case for the poem in terms of the brilliance of its images also quickly breaks down: the student searches for graphic details in vain; there are next to no realistic touches. In fact, the poet simply huddles the retails together:

> silent, bare,
> Ships, towers, domes, theatres, and temples lie
> Open unto the fields. . . .

We get a blurred impression—points of roofs and pinnacles along the skyline, all twinkling in the morning light. More than that, the sonnet as a whole contains some very flat writing and some well-worn comparisons.

The reader may ask: Where, then, does the poem get its power? It gets it, it seems to me, from the paradoxical situation out of which the poem arises. The speaker is honestly surprised, and he manages to get some sense of awed surprise into the poem. It is odd to the poet that the city should be able to "wear the beauty of the morning" at all. Mount Snowden, Skiddaw, Mont Blanc—these wear it by natural right, but surely not grimy, feverish London. This is the point of the almost shocked exclamation:

> Never did sun more beautifully steep
> In his first splendour, valley, rock, or hill . . .

The "smokeless air" reveals a city which the poet did not know existed: man-made London is a part of nature too, is lighted by the sun of nature, and lighted to as beautiful effect.

> The river glideth at his own sweet will . . .

A river is the most "natural" thing that one can imagine; it has the elasticity, the curved line of nature itself. The poet had never been able to regard this one as a real river—now, uncluttered by barges, the river reveals itself as a natural thing, not at all disciplined into a rigid and mechanical pattern: it is like the daffodils, or the mountain brooks, artless, and whimsical, and "natural" as they. The poem closes, you will remember, as follows:

> Dear God! the very houses seem asleep;
> And all that mighty heart is lying still!

The city, in the poet's insight of the morning, has earned its right to be considered organic, not merely mechanical. That is why the stale metaphor of the sleeping houses is strangely renewed. The most exciting thing that the poet can say about the houses is that they are *asleep*. He has been in the habit of counting them dead—as just mechanical and inanimate; to say they are "asleep" is to say that they are alive, that they participate in the life of nature. In the same way, the tired old metaphor which sees a great city as a pulsating heart of empire becomes revivified. It is only when the poet sees the city under the semblance of death that he can see it as actually alive—quick with the only life which he can accept, the organic life of "nature."

It is not my intention to exaggerate Wordsworth's own consciousness of the paradox involved. In this poem, he prefers, as is usual with him, the frontal attack. But the situation is paradoxical here as in so many of his poems. In his preface to the second edition of the *Lyrical Ballads* Wordsworth stated that his general purpose was "to choose incidents and situations from common life" but so to treat them that "ordinary things should be presented to the mind in an unusual aspect." Coleridge was to state the purpose for him later, in terms which make even more evident Wordsworth's exploitation of the paradoxical: "Mr. Wordsworth . . . was to propose to himself as his object, to give the charm of novelty to things of every day, and to excite a feeling analogous to the supernatural, by awakening the mind's attention from the lethargy of custom, and directing it to the loveliness and the wonders of the world before us . . ." Wordsworth, in short, was consciously attempting to show his audience that the common was really uncommon, the prosaic was really poetic.

Coleridge's terms, "the charm of novelty to things of every day," "awakening the mind," suggest the Romantic preoccupation with wonder—the surprise, the revelation which puts the tarnished familiar world in a new light. This may well be the *raison d'être* of most Romantic paradoxes; and yet the neo-classic poets use paradox for much the same reason. Consider Pope's lines from "The Essay on Man":

In doubt his Mind or Body to prefer;
Born but to die, and reas'ning but to err;
Alike in ignorance, his Reason such,
Whether he thinks too little, or too much . . .

Created half to rise, and half to fall;
Great Lord of all things, yet a Prey to all;
Sole Judge of Truth, in endless Error hurl'd;
The Glory, Jest, and Riddle of the world!

Here, it is true, the paradoxes insist on the irony, rather than the
wonder. But Pope too might have claimed that he was treating the
things of everyday, man himself, and awakening his mind so that he
would view himself in a new and blinding light. Thus, there is a
certain awed wonder in Pope just as there is a certain trace of irony
implicit in the Wordsworth sonnets. There is, of course, no reason
why they should not occur together, and they do. Wonder and irony
merge in many of the lyrics of Blake; they merge in Coleridge's
*Ancient Mariner*. The variations in emphasis are numerous. Gray's
"Elegy" uses a typical Wordsworth "situation" with the rural scene
and with peasants contemplated in the light of their "betters." But
in the "Elegy" the balance is heavily tilted in the direction of irony,
the revelation an ironic rather than a startling one:

Can storied urn or animated bust
Back to its mansion call the fleeting breath?
Can Honour's voice provoke the silent dust?
Or Flatt'ry sooth the dull cold ear of Death?

But I am not here interested in enumerating the possible variations;
I am interested rather in our seeing that the paradoxes spring from
the very nature of the poet's language: it is a language in which the
connotations play as great a part as the denotations. And I do not
mean that the connotations are important as supplying some sort of
frill or trimming, something external to the real matter in hand. I
mean that the poet does not use a notation at all—as the scientist
may properly be said to do so. The poet, within limits, has to make up
his language as he goes.

T. S. Eliot has commented upon "that perpetual slight alteration
of language, words perpetually juxtaposed in new and sudden combinations," which occurs in poetry. It *is* perpetual; it cannot be kept
out of the poem; it can only be directed and controlled. The tendency
of science is necessarily to stabilize terms, to freeze them into strict

denotations; the poet's tendency is by contrast disruptive. The terms are continually modifying each other, and thus violating their dictionary meanings. To take a very simple example, consider the adjectives in the first lines of Wordsworth's evening sonnet: *beauteous, calm, free, holy, quiet, breathless*. The juxtapositions are hardly startling; and yet notice this: the evening is like a nun breathless with adoration. The adjective "breathless" suggests tremendous excitement; and yet the evening is not only quiet but *calm*. There is no final contradiction, to be sure: it is *that* kind of calm and *that* kind of excitement, and the two states may well occur together. But the poet has no one term. Even if he had a polysyllabic technical term, the term would not provide the solution for his problem. He must work by contradiction and qualification.

We may approach the problem in this way: the poet has to work by analogies. All of the subtler states of emotion, as I. A. Richards has pointed out, necessarily demand metaphor for their expression. The poet must work by analogies, but the metaphors do not lie in the same plane or fit neatly edge to edge. There is a continual tilting of the planes; necessary overlappings, discrepancies, contradictions. Even the most direct and simple poet is forced into paradoxes far more often than we think, if we are sufficiently alive to what he is doing.

But in dilating on the difficulties of the poet's task, I do not want to leave the impression that it is a task which necessarily defeats him, or even that with his method he may not win to a fine precision. To use Shakespeare's figure, he can

> with assays of bias
> By indirections find directions out.

Shakespeare had in mind the game of lawnbowls in which the bowl is distorted, a distortion which allows the skillful player to bowl a curve. To elaborate the figure, science makes use of the perfect sphere and its attack can be direct. The method of art can, I believe, never be direct—is always indirect. But that does not mean that the master of the game cannot place the bowl where he wants it. The serious difficulties will only occur when he confuses his game with that of science and mistakes the nature of his appropriate instrument. Mr. Stuart Chase a few years ago, with a touching naïveté, urged us to take the distortion out of the bowl—to treat language like notation.

I have said that even the apparently simple and straightforward poet is forced into paradoxes by the nature of his instrument. Seeing this, we should not be surprised to find poets who consciously employ it to gain a compression and precision otherwise unobtainable. Such a method, like any other, carries with it its own perils. But the dangers are not overpowering; the poem is not predetermined to a shallow and glittering sophistry. The method is an extension of the normal language of poetry, not a perversion of it.

I should like to refer the reader to a concrete case. Donne's "Canonization" ought to provide a sufficiently extreme instance.[1] The basic metaphor which underlies the poem (and which is reflected in the title) involves a sort of paradox. For the poet daringly treats profane love as if it were divine love. The canonization is not that of a pair of holy anchorites who have renounced the world and the flesh. The hermitage of each is the other's body; but they do renounce the world, and so their title to sainthood is cunningly argued. The poem then is a parody of Christian sainthood; but it is an intensely serious parody of a sort that modern man, habituated as he is to an easy yes or no, can hardly understand. He refuses to accept the paradox as a serious rhetorical device; and since he is able to accept it only as a cheap trick, he is forced into this dilemma. Either: Donne does not take love seriously; here he is merely sharpening his wit as a sort of mechanical exercise. Or: Donne does not take sainthood seriously; here he is merely indulging in a cynical and bawdy parody.

Neither account is true; a reading of the poem will show that Donne takes both love and religion seriously; it will show, further, that the paradox is here his inevitable instrument. But to see this plainly will require a closer reading than most of us give to poetry.

The poem opens dramatically on a note of exasperation. The "you" whom the speaker addresses is not identified. We can imagine that it is a person, perhaps a friend, who is objecting to the speaker's love affair. At any rate, the person represents the practical world which regards love as a silly affectation. To use the metaphor on which poem is built, the friend represents the secular world which the lovers have renounced.

Donne begins to suggest this metaphor in the first stanza by the contemptuous alternatives which he suggests to the friend:

> . . . chide my palsie, or my gout,
> My five gray haires, or ruin'd fortune flout. . . .

1 This poem is given in a supplement at the end of this essay.

The implications are: (1) All right, consider my love as an infirmity, as a disease, if you will, but confine yourself to my other infirmities, my palsy, my approaching old age, my ruined fortune. You stand a better chance of curing those; in chiding me for this one, you are simply wasting your time as well as mine. (2) Why don't you pay attention to your own welfare—go on and get wealth and honor for yourself. What should you care if I do give these up in pursuing my love.

The two main categories of secular success are neatly, and contemptuously epitomized in the line

> Or the Kings reall, or his stamped face . . .

Cultivate the court and gaze at the king's face there, or, if you prefer, get into business and look at his face stamped on coins. But let me alone.

This conflict between the "real" world and the lover absorbed in the world of love runs through the poem; it dominates the second stanza in which the torments of love, so vivid to the lover, affect the real world not at all—

> What merchants ships have my sighs drown'd?

It is touched on in the fourth stanza in the contrast between the word "Chronicle" which suggests secular history with its pomp and magnificence, the history of kings and princes, and the word "sonnets" with its suggestions of trivial and precious intricacy. The conflict appears again in the last stanza, only to be resolved when the unworldly lovers, love's saints who have given up the world, paradoxically achieve a more intense world. But here the paradox is still contained in, and supported by, the dominant metaphor: so does the holy anchorite win a better world by giving up this one.

But before going on to discuss this development of the theme, it is important to see what else the second stanza does. For it is in this second stanza and the third, that the poet shifts the tone of the poem, modulating from the note of irritation with which the poem opens into the quite different tone with which it closes.

Donne accomplishes the modulation of tone by what may be called an analysis of love-metaphor. Here, as in many of his poems, he shows that he is thoroughly self-conscious about what he is doing. This second stanza, he fills with the conventionalized figures of the Petrarchan tradition: the wind of lovers' sighs, the floods of lovers' tears, etc.—extravagant figures with which the contemptuous secular

friend might be expected to tease the lover. The implication is that
the poet himself recognizes the absurdity of the Petrarchan love
metaphors. But what of it? The very absurdity of the jargon which
lovers are expected to talk makes for his argument: their love, however absurd it may appear to the world, does no harm to the world.
The practical friend need have no fears: there will still be wars to
fight and lawsuits to argue.

The opening of the third stanza suggests that this vein of irony is
to be maintained. The poet points out to his friend the infinite fund
of such absurdities which can be applied to lovers:

> Call her one, mee another flye,
> We'are Tapers too, and at our owne cost die. . . .

For that matter, the lovers can conjure up for themselves plenty of
such fantastic comparisons; *they* know what the world thinks of
them. But these figures of the third stanza are no longer the threadbare Petrarchan conventionalities; they have sharpness and bite.
The last one, the likening of the lovers to the phoenix, is fully serious,
and with it, the tone has shifted from ironic banter into a defiant
but controlled tenderness.

The effect of the poet's implied awareness of the lovers' apparent
madness is to cleanse and revivify metaphor; to indicate the sense in
which the poet accepts it, and thus to prepare us for accepting seriously the fine and seriously intended metaphors which dominate the
last two stanzas of the poem.

The opening line of the fourth stanza,

> Wee can dye by it, if not live by love,

achieves an effect of tenderness and deliberate resolution. The lovers
are ready to die to the world; they are committed; they are not
callow but confident. (The basic metaphor of the saint, one notices,
is being carried on; the lovers in their renunciation of the world,
have something of the confident resolution of the saint. By the bye,
the word "legend"—

> . . . if unfit 'for tombes and hearse
> Our legend bee—

in Donne's time meant "the life of a saint.") The lovers are willing
to forego the ponderous and stately chronicle and to accept the
trifling and insubstantial "sonnet" instead; but then if the urn be
well wrought, it provides a finer memorial for one's ashes than does

the pompous and grotesque monument. With the finely contemptuous, yet quiet phrase, "halfe-acre tombes," the world which the
lovers reject expands into something gross and vulgar. But the
figure works further; the pretty sonnets will not merely hold their
ashes as a decent earthly memorial. Their legend, their story, will
gain them canonization; and approved as love's saints, other lovers
will invoke them.

In this last stanza, the theme receives a final complication. The
lovers in rejecting life actually win to the most intense life. This
paradox has been hinted at earlier in the phoenix metaphor. Here it
receives a powerful dramatization. The lovers in becoming hermits,
find that they have not lost the world, but have gained the world in
each other, now a more intense, more meaningful world. Donne is
not content to treat the lovers' discovery as something which comes
to them passively, but rather as something which they actively
achieve. They are like the saint, God's athlete:

> Who did the whole worlds soule contract, and drove
> Into the glasses of your eyes. . . .

The image is that of a violent squeezing as of a powerful hand. And
what do the lovers "drive" into each other's eyes? The "Countries,
Townes," and "Courtes," which they renounced in the first stanza of
the poem. The unworldly lovers thus become the most "worldly" of
all.

The tone with which the poem closes is one of triumphant achievement, but the tone is a development contributed to by various earlier
elements. One of the more important elements which works toward
our acceptance of the final paradox is the figure of the phoenix,
which will bear a little further analysis.

The comparison of the lovers to the phoenix is very skillfully related to the two earlier comparisons, that in which the lovers are
like burning tapers, and that in which they are like the eagle and
the dove. The phoenix comparison gathers up both: the phoenix is
a bird, and like the tapers, it burns. We have a selected series of
items: the phoenix figure seems to come in a natural stream of association. "Call us what you will," the lover says, and rattles off in
his desperation the first comparisons that occur to him. The comparison to the phoenix seems thus merely another outlandish one,
the morst outrageous of all. But it is this most fantastic one,
stumbled over apparently in his haste, that the poet goes on to develop. It really describes the lovers best and justifies their renuncia-

tion. For the phoenix is not two but one, "we two being one, are it"; and it burns, not like the taper at its own cost, but to live again. Its death is life: "Wee dye and rise the same . . ." The poet literally justifies the fantastic assertion. In the sixteenth and seventeenth centuries to "die" means to experience the consummation of the act of love. The lovers after the act are the same. Their love is not exhausted in mere lust. This is their title to canonization. Their love is like the phoenix.

I hope that I do not seem to juggle the meaning of *die*. The meaning that I have cited can be abundantly justified in the literature of the period; Shakespeare uses "die" in this sense; so does Dryden. Moreover, I do not think that I give it undue emphasis. The word is in a crucial position. On it is pivoted the transition to the next stanza,

> Wee can dye by it, if not live by love,
> And if unfit for tombes . . .

Most important of all, the sexual submeaning of "die" does not contradict the other meanings: the poet is saying: "Our death is really a more intense life"; "We can afford to trade life (the world) for death (love), for that death is the consummation of life"; "After all, one does not expect to live *by* love, one expects and wants, to die *by* it." But in the total passage he is also saying: "Because our love is not mundane, we can give up the world"; "Because our love is not merely lust, we can give up the other lusts, the lust for wealth and power"; "because," and this is said with an inflection of irony as by one who knows the world too well, "because our love can outlast its consummation, we are a minor miracle, we are love's saints." This passage with its ironical tenderness and its realism feeds and supports the brilliant paradox with which the poem closes.

There is one more factor in developing and sustaining the final effect. The poem is an instance of the doctrine which it asserts; it is both the assertion and the realization of the assertion. The poet has actually before our eyes built within the song the "pretty room" with which he says the lovers can be content. The poem itself is the well-wrought urn which can hold the lovers' ashes and which will not suffer in comparison with the prince's "halfe-acre tomb."

And how necessary are the paradoxes? Donne might have said directly, "Love in a cottage is enough." "The Canonization" contains this admirable thesis, but it contains a great deal more. He might have been as forthright as a later lyricist who wrote, "We'll build a sweet little nest, / Somewhere out in the West, / And let the rest of the world go by." He might even have imitated that more metaphysical lyric, which maintains, "You're the cream in my coffee." "The Canonization" touches on all these observations, but it goes beyond them, not merely in dignity, but in precision.

I submit that the only way by which the poet could say what "The Canonization" says is by paradox. More direct methods may be tempting, but all of them enfeeble and distort what is to be said. This statement may seem the less surprising when we reflect on how many of the important things which the poet has to say have to be said by means of paradox: most of the language of lovers is such —"The Canonization" is a good example; so is most of the language of religion—"He who would save his life, must lose it;" "The last shall be first." Indeed, almost any insight important enough to warrant a great poem apparently has to be stated in such terms. Deprived of the character of paradox with its twin concomitants of irony and wonder, the matter of Donne's poem unravels into "facts," biological, sociological, and economic. What happens to Donne's lovers if we consider them "scientifically," without benefit of the supernaturalism which the poet confers upon them? Well, what happens to Shakespeare's lovers, for Shakespeare uses the basic metaphor of "The Canonization" in his *Romeo and Juliet?* In their first conversation, the lovers play with the analogy between the lover and the pilgrim to the Holy Land. Juliet says:

> For saints have hands that pilgrims' hands do touch
> And palm to palm is holy palmers' kiss.

Considered scientifically, the lovers become Mr. Aldous Huxley's animals, "quietly sweating, palm to palm."

For us today, Donne's imagination seems obsessed with the problem of unity; the sense in which the lovers become one—the sense in which the soul is united with God. Frequently, as we have seen, one type of union becomes a metaphor for the other. It may not be too far-fetched to see both as instances of, and metaphors for, the union which the creative imagination itself effects. For that fusion is not logical; it apparently violates science and common sense; it welds together the discordant and the contradictory. Coleridge has of course given us the classic description of its nature and power. It "reveals itself in the balance or reconcilement of opposite or discordant qualities: of sameness, with difference; of the general, with the concrete; the idea, with the image; the individual, with the representative; the sense of novelty and freshness, with old and familiar objects; a more than usual state of emotion, with more than usual order. . . ." It is a great and illuminating statement, but is a series of paradoxes. Apparently Coleridge could describe the effect of the imagination in no other way.

Shakespeare, in one of his poems, has given a description that oddly parallels that of Coleridge.

> Reason in it selfe confounded,
> Saw Division grow together,
> To themselves yet either neither,
> Simple were so well compounded.

I do not know what his "The Phoenix and the Turtle" celebrates. Perhaps it *was* written to honor the marriage of Sir John Salisbury and Ursula Stanley; or perhaps the Phoenix is Lucy, Countess of Bedford; or perhaps the poem is merely an essay on Platonic love. But the scholars themselves are so uncertain, that I think we will do little violence to established habits of thinking, if we boldly pre-empt the poem for our own purposes. Certainly the poem is an instance of that magic power which Coleridge sought to describe. I propose that we take it for a moment as a poem about that power;

> So they loved as love in twaine,
> Had the essence but in one,
> Two distincts, Division none,
> Number there in love was slaine.
>
> Hearts remote, yet not asunder;
> Distance and no space was seene,
> Twixt this Turtle and his Queene;
> But in them it were a wonder. . . .
>
> Propertie was thus appalled,
> That the selfe was not the same;
> Single Natures double name,
> Neither two nor one was called.

Precisely! The nature is single, one, unified. But the name is double, and today with our multiplication of sciences, it is multiple. If the poet is to be true to his poetry, he must call it neither two nor one: the paradox is his only solution. The difficulty has intensified since Shakespeare's day: the timid poet, when confronted with the prob-

lem of "Single Natures double name," has too often funked it. A
history of poetry from Dryden's time to our own might bear as its
subtitle "The Half-Hearted Phoenix."

In Shakespeare's poem, Reason is "in it selfe confounded" at the
union of the Phoenix and the Turtle; but it recovers to admit its
own bankruptcy:

> Love hath Reason, Reason none,
> If what parts, can so remaine. . . .

and it is Reason which goes on to utter the beautiful threnos with
which the poem concludes:

> Beautie, Truth, and Raritie,
> Grace in all simplicitie,
> Here enclosde, in cinders lie.
>
> Death is now the Phoenix nest,
> And the Turtles loyall brest,
> To eternitie doth rest. . . .
>
> Truth may seeme, but cannot be,
> Beautie bragge, but tis not she,
> Truth and Beautie buried be.
>
> To this urne let those repaire,
> That are either true or faire,
> For these dead Birds, sigh a prayer.

Having pre-empted the poem for our own purposes, it may not be
too outrageous to go on to make one further observation. The urn
to which we are summoned, the urn which holds the ashes of the
phoenix, is like the well-wrought urn of Donne's "Canonization"
which holds the phoenix-lovers' ashes: it is the poem itself. One is
reminded of still another urn, Keats's Grecian urn, which contained
for Keats, Truth and Beauty, as Shakespeare's urn encloses "Beautie,
Truth, and Raritie." But there is a sense in which all such well-
wrought urns contain the ashes of a phoenix. The urns are not meant
for memorial purposes only, though that often seems to be their
chief significance to the professors of literature. The phoenix rises
from its ashes; or ought to rise; but it will not arise for all our mere
sifting and measuring the ashes, or testing them for their chemical
content. We must be prepared to accept the paradox of the imagina-

tion itself; else "Beautie, Truth, and Raritie" remain enclosed in their cinders and we shall end with essential cinders, for all our pains.


## SUPPLEMENT

### THE CANONIZATION

For Godsake hold your tongue, and let me love,
   Or chide my palsie, or my gout,
My five gray haires, or ruin'd fortune flout,
    With wealth your state, your minde with Arts improve,
      Take you a course, get you a place,
      Observe his honour, or his grace,
Or the Kings reall, or his stamped face
   Contemplate, what you will, approve,
   So you will let me love.

Alas, alas, who's injur'd by my love?
   What merchants ships have my sighs drown'd?
Who saies my teares have overflow'd his ground?
    When did my colds a forward spring remove?
      When did the heats which my veines fill
      Adde one more to the plaguie Bill?
Soldiers finde warres, and Lawyers finde out still
   Litigious men, which quarrels move,
   Though she and I do love.

Call us what you will, wee are made such by love;
   Call her one, mee another flye,
We'are Tapers too, and at our owne cost die,
    And wee in us finde the'Eagle and the Dove.
      The Phœnix ridle hath more wit
      By us, we two being one, are it.
So to one neutrall thing both sexes fit,
   Wee dye and rise the same, and prove
   Mysterious by this love.

Wee can dye by it, if not live by love,
   And if unfit for tombes and hearse
Our legend bee, it will be fit for verse;
   And if no peece of Chronicle wee prove,
      We'll build in sonnets pretty roomes;
      As well a well wrought urne becomes
The greatest ashes, as halfe-acre tombes,
   And by these hymnes, all shall approve
   Us *Canoniz'd* for Love:


And thus invoke us; You whom reverend love
   Made one anothers hermitage;
You, to whom love was peace, that now is rage;
   Who did the whole worlds soule contract, and drove
      Into the glasses of your eyes
      (So made such mirrors, and such spies,
That they did all to you epitomize,)
   Countries, Townes, Courts: Beg from above
   A patterne of your love!

# .YVOR WINTERS

## (1900–      )

YVOR WINTERS was born in Chicago on October 17, 1900. He attended four quarters at the University of Chicago. Upon contracting tuberculosis he spent three years in Santa Fé, New Mexico. For two years he was employed as a school teacher in the coal camps at Madrid and Cerillos, south of Santa Fé. In 1925 he received his M.A. in Romance languages at the University of Colorado. From 1925 to 1927 he taught French and Spanish at the University of Idaho. In 1927 he entered Stanford University as a graduate student in English and was appointed the following year to an instructorship in English. In 1934 he was granted his Ph.D. at Stanford, where he still teaches English. He contributed frequently to *Hound & Horn* and other literary magazines.

Intensely in earnest about his critical beliefs, Yvor Winters applies his standards with rigid conscientiousness. Forthright, uncompromisingly sincere in his utterances, he wages, like the Humanists, unremitting warfare against the romantic impulse in all its varied manifestations. Instead of being merely impressionistic, he attempts to formulate a single, thoroughly consistent, and logically coherent theory of literature. He has no use for the didactic, the hedonistic, and the romantic conception of literature, yet he believes that literature exerts a profound and permanent influence on the human mind and on human conduct. If he objects to the romantic interpretation of art and human nature, he is even more opposed to the philosophy of determinism, the notion that everything in the world is mechanically preordained and that the individual is but a bundle of conditioned reflexes, an automatic system of causes and effects. Carried to an extreme, determinism, like romanticism, ends up in psychic automatism. In opposition to the relativists and instrumentalists, Winters holds that there are absolute truths, absolute values.

Winters specializes in the techniques of evaluation, which he considers the culminating act of the critical process. Not only art but criticism as well, he maintains, is moral in nature. In both *Primitivism and Decadence*

(1937) and *Maule's Curse* (1938) he is concerned with the moral significance of literature. Even though he professes not to be a Humanist, there is no question of his indebtedness to the Humanism of Irving Babbitt. In his contribution to *The Critique of Humanism* (1930) he found much to assail in the New Humanist movement, yet at heart he has much in common with it. He is definitely aligned with classicism and traditionalism, and he frequently uses his critical evaluations to support the cause of "reaction." His use of the term "moral" is ambiguous, confusing, and often contradictory. At any rate, for Winters the essence of poetry lies in the fact that it offers a moral discipline, not an evasion of moral responsibility. Both the rational and the emotional content of language should be given expression in poetry, not one at the expense of the other. The form a poem assumes is a gauge of the extent to which the poet has evaluated and mastered his experience, the spiritual control he has succeeded in establishing. Poetry, in short, serves to enrich our awareness of human experience, increase our intelligence, and strengthen our moral fibre.

Winters works out an ambitious system of comparative literary values by means of which categories of major and minor, great and inferior, can be determined. Traditional verse, he argues, is superior because it permits variation. In *Primitivism and Decadence* (1937) he denounces the fallacy of imitative form, namely, the abortive effort to imitate the formless. By standards Winters means those feelings of rightness, of completeness, which we gain through a study of the masters. Just as *Primitivism and Decadence* studied the technical forms of American experimental poetry during the twentieth century and the obscurantism, conscious or unconscious, which informed it, *Maule's Curse* undertakes to trace the antecedents of this dangerous obscurantism in the earlier literary history of America and to show how and why it took root in the American mind. The generations after the Puritans, the generation of Hawthorne and Emerson, bore out the truth of Maule's prophecy that they would drink their heart's blood.

In *The Anatomy of Nonsense* (1943) Winters takes vigorous exception to Henry Adams' theory of human nature and his relativism in matters of criticism. Winters is convinced that a work of art has an absolute value, and it is the duty of the well-trained, conscientious critic to arrive at true judgments. Either that or one man's judgment is as good as another's, and everything is relative—but that, according to Winters, is unthinkable. Reputations do persist through time. For a critic who sets so much store by moral judgments and the right use of reason, the critical evaluations he draws up are nothing less than extraordinary. It is his failure to reckon with the relativity of taste that lands him in error. In his essay on "Jones

Very and R. W. Emerson," Emerson is ridiculed and deflated. He can find no better means of exalting Very than by dragging Emerson down, calling him a fraud and a sentimentalist. A man who can compose such vitriolic diatribes is scarcely entitled to pose as a defender of reason. Most happy when he is engaged in attacking a writer or a movement, he finds little in American literature that pleases his severe taste. One is bound to wonder how much value a critical method can possess that results in the practically wholesale rejection of such writers as Hawthorne, Eliot, Poe, Emerson, and Henry Adams.

Though Winters, in his theory of criticism, regards the element of feeling as fused organically with the conceptual content, in practice he seems to ignore the factor of technical excellence and concentrate his ammunition on the ideological content. If it fails to satisfy him he is prepared not only to condemn the poem but also to preach a lengthy sermon on the harmful consequences of following a wrong system of aesthetics. Thus he comes to the conclusion that a confused or illogical conceptual content—and he leaves us in no doubt as to what he considers confused and illogical—is bound to result in poetry that is confused or illogical, or to use his terms, decadent or primitivistic, whereas a rational content that is properly controlled makes for indubitable excellence in poetry.

Winters' chief quarrel is with romanticism, the cult of expressing the emotions, without attempting to understand them or to discipline them. Just as Rousseau was the villain in Babbitt's universe of discourse, so Emerson, invariably followed by Whitman, his disciple, is the chief villain in Winters' moral cosmos. The central mistake in Winters' conception of aesthetics lies in his loose use of the term "moral," which he applies to everything under the sun. He finds fault, for example, with Parrington's history of literature because it confines itself exclusively to ideas, without considering the value of works of art as art, yet he is guilty of a parallel and equally bad error: that of judging and rejecting—there is far more of rejection than of acceptance in his critical writing—literature, particularly poetry, by moral criteria.

The mistake of the moralistic critics who attempt to construct a foursquare philosophical justification for their position is that they assume they are right and all other points of view wrong. They confuse aesthetic values with those extracted from the work of philosophers in the past. To assume that the greater the poetry the sounder is the philosophy it voices is to fall into a crude fallacy, for obviously no one can say which philosophy is nearest to the truth. Though the poet may, of course, be supported by some philosophy, he can get along just as well if he is repelled by the limitations that the acceptance of some metaphysical system necessarily imposes.

BIBLIOGRAPHY

TEXT

*Notes on the Mechanics of the Poetic Image.* Vienna, 1925. (Pamphlet)
*Primitivism and Decadence.* New York, 1937.
*Maule's Curse.* Norfolk, 1938.
*The Anatomy of Nonsense.* Norfolk, 1943.
*Edwin Arlington Robinson.* Norfolk, 1946.
*In Defense of Reason.* New York, 1947.

CRITICISM

Barrett, William, "Temptations of St. Yvor," *Kenyon Review,* IX, 532–
551 (Autumn, 1947).
Blackmur, R. P., *The Expense of Greatness.* New York, 1940.
Hyman, Stanley Edgar, "Yvor Winters and Evaluation in Criticism," *The
Armed Vision,* New York, 1948, pp. 49–72.
Howells, Thomas, "Yvor Winters, Anatomist of Nonsense," *Poetry,* LVII,
144–152.
Ransom, John Crowe, *The New Criticism.* Norfolk, 1941.
Swallow, Alan, "Yvor Winters," *Rocky Mountain Review,* IX, 31–37
(Fall, 1944).
——, "The Sage of Palo Alto," *Rocky Mountain Review,* IV, 1–3 (Sum-
mer, 1940).
West, R. B., "The Language of Criticism," *Rocky Mountain Review,* VIII,
12–13 (Fall, 1943).

## PRELIMINARY PROBLEMS*

### FIRST PROBLEM

Is it possible to say that Poem A (one of Donne's *Holy Sonnets,*
or one of the poems of Jonson or of Shakespeare) is better than
Poem B (Collins' *Ode to Evening*) or vice versa?

If not, is it possible to say that either of these is better than Poem
C (*The Cremation of Sam Magee,* or something comparable)?

If the answer is no in both cases, then any poem is as good as any
other. If this is true, then all poetry is worthless; but this obviously
is not true, for it is contrary to all our experience.

If the answer is yes in both cases, then there follows the question of whether the answer implies merely that one poem is better than another for the speaker, or whether it means that one poem is intrinsically better than another. If the former, then we are impressionists, which is to say relativists; and are either mystics of the type of Emerson, or hedonists of the type of Stevens and Ransom. If the latter, then we assume that constant principles govern the poetic experience, and that the poem (as likewise the judge) must be judged in relationship to those principles. It is important, therefore, to discover the consequences of assuming each of these positions.

If our answer to the first question is no and to the second yes, then we are asserting that we can distinguish between those poems which are of the canon and those which are not, but that within the canon all judgment is impossible. This view, if adopted, will require serious elucidation, for on the face of it, it appears inexplicable. On the other hand, one cannot deny that within the canon judgment will become more difficult, for the nearer two poems may be to the highest degrees of excellence, the harder it will be to choose between them. Two poems, in fact, might be so excellent that there would be small profit in endeavoring to say that one was better, but one could arrive at this conclusion only after a careful examination of both.

## SECOND PROBLEM

If we accept the view that one poem can be regarded as better than another, the question then arises whether this judgment is a matter of inexplicable intuition, or whether it is a question of intuition that can be explained, and consequently guided and improved by rational elucidation.

If we accept the view that the judgment in question is inexplicable, then we are again forced to confess ourselves impressionists and relativists, unless we can show that the intuitions of all men agree at all times, or that the intuitions of one man are invariably right and those of all others wrong whenever they differ. We obviously can demonstrate neither of these propositions.

If we start, then, with the proposition that one poem may be intrinsically superior to another, we are forced to account for differences of opinion regarding it. If two critics differ, it is possible that one is right and the other wrong, more likely that both are partly right and partly wrong, but in different respects: neither the native gifts nor the education of any man have ever been wholly adequate to many of the critical problems he will encounter, and no two men are ever the same in these respects or in any others. On the other hand, although the critic should display reasonable humility and caution, it is only fair to add that few men possess either the talent or the education to justify their being taken very seriously, even of those who are nominally professional students of these matters.

But if it is possible by rational elucidation to give a more or less clear account of what one finds in a poem and why one approves or disapproves, then communication between two critics, though no doubt imperfect, becomes possible, and it becomes possible that they may in some measure correct each other's errors and so come more near to a true judgment of the poem.

### Third Problem

If rational communication about poetry is to take place, it is necessary first to determine what we mean by a poem.

A poem is first of all a statement in words.

But it differs from all such statements of a purely philosophical or theoretical nature, in that it has by intention a controlled content of feeling. In this respect, it does not differ from many works written in prose, however.

A poem differs from a work written in prose by virtue of its being composed in verse. The rhythm of verse permits the expression of more powerful feeling than is possible in prose when such feeling is needed, and it permits at all times the expression of finer shades of feeling.

A poem, then, is a statement in words in which special pains are taken with the expression of feeling. This description is merely intended to distinguish the poem from other kinds of writing; it is not offered as a complete description.

### Fourth Problem

What, however, are words?

They are audible sounds, or their visual symbols, invented by man to communicate his thoughts and feelings. Each word has a conceptual content, however slight; each word, exclusive, perhaps, of the particles, communicates vague associations of feeling.

The word *fire* communicates a concept; it also connotes very vaguely certain feelings, depending on the context in which we happen to place it—depending, for example, on whether we happen to think of a fire on a hearth, in a furnace, or in a forest. These feelings may be rendered more and more precise as we render the context more and more precise; as we come more and more near to completing and perfecting our poem.

### FIFTH PROBLEM

But if the poem, as compared to prose, pays especial attention to feeling, are we to assume that the rational content of the poem is unimportant to its success?

The rational content cannot be eliminated from words; consequently the rational content cannot be eliminated from poetry. It is there. If it is unsatisfactory in itself, a part of the poem is unsatisfactory; the poem is thus damaged beyond argument. If we deny this, we must surely explain ourselves very fully.

If we admit this, we are faced with another problem: is it conceivable that rational content and feeling-content may both be perfect, and yet that they may be unrelated to each other, or imperfectly related? To me this is inconceivable, because the emotional content of words is generated by our experience with the conceptual content, so that a relationship is necessary.

This fact of the necessity of such relationship may fairly return us for a moment to the original question: whether imperfection of rational content damages the entire poem. If there is a necessary relationship between concept and feeling, and concept is unsatisfactory, then feeling must be damaged by way of the relationship.

### SIXTH PROBLEM

If there is a relationship between concept and feeling, what is the nature of that relationship?

To answer this, let us return to the basic unit, the word. The concept represented by the word, motivates the feeling which the word communicates. It is the concept of fire which generates the feelings communicated by the word, though the sound of the word may modify these feelings very subtly, as may other accidental qualities, especially if the word be used skillfully in a given context. The accidental qualities of a word, however, such as its literary history, for example, can only modify, cannot essentially change, for these will be governed ultimately by the concept; that is, *fire* will seldom be used to signify *plum-blossom,* and so will have few opportunities to gather connotations from the concept, *plum-blossom.* The relationship, in the poem, between rational statement and feeling, is thus seen to be that of motive to emotion.

## SEVENTH PROBLEM

But has not this reasoning brought us back to the proposition that all poems are equally good? For if each word motivates its own feeling, because of its intrinsic nature, will not any rational statement, since it is composed of words, motivate the feeling exactly proper to it?

This is not true, for a good many reasons, of which I shall enumerate only a few of the more obvious. In making a rational statement, in purely theoretical prose, we find that our statement may be loose or exact, depending upon the relationships of the words to each other. The precision of a word depends to some extent upon its surroundings. This is true likewise with respect to the connotations of words. Two words, each of which has several usably close rational synonyms, may reinforce and clarify each other with respect to their connotations or they may not do so.

Let me illustrate with a simple example from Browning's *Serenade at the Villa:*

> So wore night; the East was gray,
> White the broad-faced hemlock flowers.

The lines are marred by a crowding of long syllables and difficult consonants, but they have great beauty in spite of the fault. What I wish to point out, for the sake of my argument, is the relationship between the words *wore* and *gray*. The verb *wore* means literally that the night passed, but it carries with it connotations of exhaustion and attrition which belong to the condition of the protagonist; and grayness is a color which we associate with such a condition. If we change the phrase to read: "Thus night passed," we shall have the same rational meaning, and a meter quite as respectable, but no trace of the power of the line: the connotation of *wore* will be lost, and the connotation of *gray* will remain merely in a state of ineffective potentiality. The protagonist in seeing his feeling mirrored in the landscape is not guilty of motivating his feeling falsely, for we know his general motive from the poem as a whole; he is expressing a portion of the feeling motivated by the total situation through a more or less common psychological phenomenon. If the poem were such, however, that we did not know why the night *wore* instead of *passed,* we should have just cause for complaint; in fact, most of the strength of the word would probably be lost. The second line contains other fine effects, immediately with reference to the first line, ultimately with reference to the theme; I leave the reader to analyze them for himself, but he will scarcely succeed without the whole poem before him.

Concepts, as represented by particular words, are affected by connotations due to various and curious accidents. A word may gather connotations from its use in folk-poetry, in formal poetry, in vulgar speech, or in technical prose: a single concept might easily be represented by four words with these distinct histories; and any one of the words might prove to be proper in a given poetic context. Words gain connotation from etymological accidents. Something of this may be seen in the English word *outrage,* in which is commonly felt, in all likelihood, something associated with *rage,* although there is no rage whatever in the original word. Similarly the word *urchin,* in modern English, seldom connotes anything related to hedgehogs, or to the familiars of the witches, by whose intervention the word arrived at its modern meaning and feeling. Yet the connotation proper to any stage in the history of such a word might be resuscitated, or a blend of connotations effected, by skillful use. Further, the connotation of a word may be modified very strongly by its function in the metrical structure, a matter which I shall discuss at length in connection with the theories of Ransom.

This is enough to show that exact motivation of feeling by concept is not inherent in any rational statement. Any rational statement will govern the general possibilities of feeling derivable from it, but the task of the poet is to adjust feeling to motive precisely. He has to select words containing not only the right relationships within themselves, but the right relationships to each other. The task is very difficult; and this is no doubt the reason why the great poetry of a great poet is likely to be very small in bulk.

## EIGHTH PROBLEM

Is it not possible, however, to escape from this relationship of motive to emotion by confining ourselves very largely to those words which denote emotion: love, envy, anger, and the like?

This is not possible, for these words, like others, represent concepts. If we should confine ourselves strictly to such a vocabulary, we should merely write didactic poetry: poetry about love in general, or about anger in general. The emotion communicated would result from our apprehension of the ideas in question. Such poetry is perfectly legitimate, but it is only one kind of poetry, and it is scarcely the kind which the Romantic theorist is endeavoring to define.

Such poetry has frequently been rendered particular by the use of allegory. The playful allegorizing of minor amoristic themes which one encounters in the Renaissance and which is possibly descended from certain neo-Platonic elements in medieval poetry may serve as illustration. Let us consider these and the subsequent lines by Thomas Lodge:

> Love in my bosom like a bee
> 　Doth suck his sweet;
> Now with his wings he plays with me,
> 　Now with his feet.

Love itself is a very general idea and might include many kinds of experience; the idea is limited by this allegory to the sentimental and sensual, but we still have an idea, the subdivision of the original idea, and the feeling must be appropriate to the concept. The concept is rendered concrete by the image of Cupid, whose actions, in turn, are rendered visible by comparison to the bee: it is these actions which make the poem a kind of anticipatory meditation on more or less sensual love, a meditation which by its mere tone of expression keeps the subject in its proper place as a very minor one. Sometimes the emphasis is on the mere description of the bee, sometimes on the description of Cupid, sometimes on the lover's feeling; but the feeling motivated in any passage is governed by this emphasis. The elements, once they are united in the poem, are never really separated, of course. In so far as the poet departs from his substantial theme in the direction of mere bees and flowers, he will achieve what Ransom calls irrelevance; but if there is much of this the poem will be weakened. Whether he so departs or not, the relation of motive to emotion must remain the same, within each passage. I have discussed this problem in my essay on Ransom.

A common romantic practice is to use words denoting emotions, but to use them loosely and violently, as if the very carelessness expressed emotion. Another is to make a general statement, but seem to refer it to a particular occasion, which, however, is never indicated: the poet thus seems to avoid the didactic, yet he is not forced to understand the particular motive. Both these faults may be seen in these lines from Shelley:

Out of the day and night
A joy has taken flight;
   Fresh spring, and summer, and winter hoar,
Move my faint heart with grief, but with delight
    No more—oh, never more.

The poet's intention is so vague, however, that he achieves nothing but stereotypes of a very crude kind.

The Romantics often tried other devices. For example, it would be possible to write a poem on fear in general, but to avoid in some measure the effect of the purely didactic by illustrating the emotion along the way with various experiences which might motivate fear. There is a danger here, though it is merely a danger, that the general idea may not dominate the poem, and that the poem may thus fall apart into a group of poems on particular experiences. There is the alternative danger, that the particular quality of the experiences may be so subordinated to the illustrative function of the experiences, that within each illustration there is merely a stereotyped and not a real relationship of motive to feeling: this occurs in Collins' *Ode to Fear,* though a few lines in the Epode come surprisingly to life. But the methods which I have just described really offer no semblance of an escape from the theory of motivation which I am defending.

Another Romantic device, if it is conscious enough to be called a device, is to offer instead of a defensible motive a false one, usually culled from landscape. This kind of writing represents a tacit admission of the principle of motivation which I am defending, but a bad application of the principle. It results in the kind of writing which I have called pseudo-reference in my volume, *Primitivism and Decadence.* One cannot believe, for example, that Wordsworth's passions were charmed away by a look at the daffodils, or that Shelley's were aroused by the sight of the leaves blown about in the autumn wind. A motive is offered, and the poet wants us to accept it, but we recognize it as inadequate. In such a poem there may be fragments of good description, which motivate a feeling more or less purely appropriate to the objects described, and these fragments may sustain our liking for the poem: this happens in Collins' *Ode to Evening;* but one will find also an account of some kind of emotion essentially irrelevant to the objects described, along with the attempt, more or less explicit, to deduce the emotion from the object.

There remains the method of the Post-Romantics, whether French

Symbolists or American Experimentalists: the method of trying to extinguish the rational content of language while retaining the content of association. This method I have discussed in *Primitivism and Decadence,* and I shall discuss it again in this book.

### NINTH PROBLEM

The relationship in the poem of rational meaning to feeling we have seen to be that of motive to emotion; and we have seen that this must be a satisfactory relationship. How do we determine whether such a relationship is satisfactory? We determine it by an act of moral judgment. The question then arises whether moral judgments can be made, whether the concept of morality is or is not an illusion.

If morality can be considered real, if a theory of morality can be said to derive from reality, it is because it guides us toward the greatest happiness which the accidents of life permit: that is, toward the fullest realization of our nature, in the Aristotelian or Thomistic sense. But is there such a thing, abstractly considered, as full realization of our nature?

To avoid discussion of too great length, let us consider the opposite question: is there such a thing as obviously unfulfilled human nature? Obviously there is. We need only turn to the feeble-minded, who cannot think and so cannot perceive or feel with any clarity; or to the insane, who sometimes perceive and feel with great intensity, but whose feelings and perceptions are so improperly motivated that they are classed as illusions. At slightly higher levels, the criminal, the dissolute, the unscrupulously selfish, and various types of neurotics are likely to arouse but little disagreement as examples.

Now if we are able to recognize the fact of insanity—if in fact we are forced to recognize it—that is, the fact of the obvious maladjustment of feeling to motive, we are forced to admit the possibility of more accurate adjustment, and, by necessary sequence, of absolutely accurate adjustment, even though we admit the likelihood that most people will attain to a final adjustment but very seldom indeed. We can guide ourselves toward such an adjustment in life, as in art, by means of theory and the critical examination of special instances; but the final act of judgment is in both life and art a unique act—it is a relationship between two elements, the rational understanding and the feeling, of which only one is classificatory and of which the other has infinite possibilities of variation.

## Tenth Problem

If the final act of adjustment is a unique act of judgment, can we say that it is more or less right, provided it is demonstrably within the general limits prescribed by the theory of morality which has led to it? The answer to this question is implicit in what has preceded; in fact the answer resembles exactly that reached at the end of the first problem examined. We can say that it is more or less nearly right. If extreme deviation from right judgment is obvious, then there is such a thing as right judgment. The mere fact that life may be conducted in a fairly satisfactory manner, by means of inaccurate judgment within certain limits, and that few people ever bother to refine their judgment beyond the stage which enables them to remain largely within those limits, does not mean that accurate judgment has no reality. Implicit in all that has preceded is the concept that in any moral situation, there is a right judgment as an ultimate possibility; that the human judge, or actor, will approximate it more or less nearly; that the closeness of his approximation will depend upon the accuracy of his rational understanding and of his intuition, and upon the accuracy of their interaction upon each other.

## Eleventh Problem

Nothing has thus far been said about human action, yet morality is supposed to guide human action. And if art is moral, there should be a relationship between art and human action.

The moral judgment, whether good, bad, or indifferent, is commonly the prelude and instigation to action. Hastily or carefully, intelligently or otherwise, one arrives at some kind of general idea of a situation calling for action, and one's idea motivates one's feeling: the act results. The part played by will, or the lack of it, between judgment and act, the possibility that action may be frustrated by some constitutional or habitual weakness or tendency, such as cowardice or a tendency to anger, in a person of a fine speculative or poetic judgment, are subjects for a treatise on ethics or psychology; a treatise on poetry stops with the consideration of the speculative judgment, which reaches its best form and expression in poetry. In the situations of daily life, one does not, as a rule, write a poem before acting: one makes a more rapid and simple judgment. But if the poem does not individually lead to a particular act, it does not prevent action. It gives us a better way of judging representative acts than we should otherwise have. It is thus a civilizing influence: it trains our power of judgment, and should, I imagine, affect the quality of daily judgments and actions.

## TWELFTH PROBLEM

What, then, is the nature of the critical process?

It will consist (1) of the statement of such historical or biographical knowledge as may be necessary in order to understand the mind and method of the writer; (2) of such analysis of his literary theories as we may need to understand and evaluate what he is doing; (3) of a rational critique of the paraphrasable content (roughly, the motive) of the poem; (4) of a rational critique of the feeling motivated—that is, of the details of style, as seen in language and technique; and (5) of the final act of judgment, a unique act, the general nature of which can be indicated, but which cannot be communicated precisely, since it consists in receiving from the poet his own final and unique judgment of his matter and in judging that judgment. It should be noted that the purpose of the first four processes is to limit as narrowly as possible the region in which the final unique act is to occur.

In the actual writing of criticism, a given task may not require all of these processes, or may not require that all be given equal emphasis; or it may be that in connection with a certain writer, whether because of the nature of the writer or because of the way in which other critics have treated him previously, one or two of these processes must be given so much emphasis that others must be neglected for lack of space. These are practical matters to be settled as the occasions arise.

# LIONEL TRILLING
## (1905–    )

LIONEL TRILLING, professor of English at Columbia University, has written literary criticism for *The Nation, Partisan Review, The Kenyon Review,* and other influential periodicals. In addition to his critical work, he has written short stories and is the author of a novel, *The Middle of the Journey.* He was elected in 1951 to the National Institute of Arts and Letters.

A gracious, constructive critic, Lionel Trilling loves literature too well to maltreat it or confine it within the Procrustean bed of some dogmatic theory. Eclectic without being Laodicean or uncommitted, he is alert to every new doctrine or technique, responsive to all vital currents of thought which can help to illuminate and invigorate the creative spirit. Lionel Trilling speaks with the accent of authority, the mellowed wisdom and mature insight which characterized the utterances of Matthew Arnold, from whom he has evidently learned a great deal. Author of two distinguished books of criticism, *Matthew Arnold* (1939) and *E. M. Forster* (1943), he has produced in *The Liberal Imagination* (1950), which consists of essays on literature written over the last ten years, a work which virtually puts him at the head of the critical brotherhood in this country.

This book is unified by his interest in the liberal imagination, by his effort to determine how the complex of ideas loosely known as liberalism is related to literature. He is convinced that liberalism, at this dark hour of history, is not only the dominant but the sole intellectual tradition. He believes, however, that liberalism will be rendered more constructive and valuable if it subjects its leading ideas to periodic re-examinations and appraisals, so that it does not fall into the trap of rationalistic righteousness or easy-going complacency. The only trouble with Trilling's liberalism is that it remains abstract, almost disembodied, without ever making close contact with the earth of experience and the specific necessities of our social existence.

Though he underscores the connection between literature and politics,

547

he uses "politics" in the wider sense, as the politics of culture, the organization of human life toward some end. Hence a literary critic is inescapably committed to a consideration of politics. Liberalism for Trilling is not merely a matter of ideation, an attachment purely of the intellect; it is intimately tied up with the emotions, the sentiments. That is how he hopes to combat the tendency of liberalism to reduce everything to abstract ideas. Poetry is needed too, the seminal contribution of the creative imagination, the poetry of earth, the redeeming sense of the variousness and untapped potentialities of life. If the emotions are the motive power of the intellect, then the conscious and unconscious life, the emotional and intellectual values, must be allowed to merge and fuse. Without the creative ferment of the imagination, the intellect atrophies. The job of liberalism, Trilling declares,

"would seem to be, then, to recall liberalism to its first essential imagination of variousness and possibility, which implies the awareness of complexity and difficulty. To the carrying out of this job of criticizing the liberal imagination, literature has a unique relevance, not merely because so much of modern literature has explicitly directed itself upon politics, but more importantly because literature is the human activity that takes the fullest and most precise account of variousness, possibility, complexity, and difficulty."[1]

The essay on "Freud and Literature," penetrating in its insights and wisely balanced in its evaluations, does not deny that Freudianism has exerted a pronounced, if not always happy, influence on literature, and literary criticism has undoubtedly learned much that is of distinct value from the Freudian system. But there is no basis for the assumption, favored by some literati, that Freud was the explorer who legitimized the myth and the irrational forces of the unconscious. Freud's intention was to drive back the legions of darkness, to subdue the primordial instincts, to conquer the irrational. But Trilling, chiefly interested in examining the relationship of Freudianism to literature and art, recognizes all too well the signal defects of the Freudian approach, its undisguised attitude of contempt, its conception of art as a sublimation of instinctual needs, an illusion in contrast to reality, and its interpretation of the artist as neurotic. Trilling, objecting to this dichotomy between reality and illusion, between what manifestly exists and can be empirically confirmed and what does not exist in the external world, drives home the thesis that there is a fundamental difference between the dream and the neurosis on the one hand and art on the other.

In the essay, "Art and Neurosis," he seeks to establish order in a realm

[1] Lionel Trilling, *The Liberal Imagination* (New York, 1950), p. xv.

characterized at present by a great deal of vagueness, confusion, and contradiction. Trilling deplores the way in which Freud's early belief in the essential neuroticism of the artist took root and gave rise to the myth of the sick artist. While the artist may be neurotic and his neurotic suffering play some part in his work, this influence is not to be mechanically dissected out nor is its presence to be held as a vitiating, discreditable judgment upon the art produced. The source of an artist's specific power and greatness cannot be sought in an elaborate analysis of his neurotic symptoms. There is no reason why power must be achieved at the expense of sickness and suffering. In short, knowledge of neurotic symptoms tells us nothing about a writer's characteristic talent, his degree of creative power, his technical skill, his devotion to his art, his patience, his interest in fields which have no relation to his neurotic involvement. To call the artist neurotic does not define his function.

Trilling's reaction to what is known as the New Criticism is to the point. The formalists labored to restore autonomy to the work of art, to emancipate it from the tendency that regarded it as an object of knowledge, but their fault was "that they make the elucidation of poetic ambiguity or irony a kind of intellectual calisthenic ritual."[2] Moreover, in reacting against the historical method, they forget that literature cannot repudiate or shuffle off its own past, of which it is, necessarily, continuously aware. In every work of the past is its historicity an important factor, for we are inescapably creatures of time, moulded by the historical sense. The secrets of a work of art are not to be discovered exclusively within the confines of the work itself. On the contrary, Trilling argues, with Matthew Arnold, that the elements of art reach into life, and that the critic can learn much, aesthetically, by research into the historical context of the work and into the personal life and development of the artist. In "The Sense of the Past," Trilling, though taking issues with the pseudo-scientific literary historians, still defends the genetic method as not being in the least inimical to the proper appreciation of works of art.

The concluding essay of *The Liberal Imagination*, "The Meaning of a Literary Idea," sets forth Trilling's ideas on the nature of literature and its inevitable involvement with ideas, since it concerns itself with human behavior in a social context. Though contemporary American literature is democratic in sentiment, he does not feel that it is of lasting interest. Literature stemming from the liberal democratic tradition does not move us deeply, fails to engage our imagination, lacks the sense of transcendence, the power of penetrating to the deepest corners of our mind, but this is no reflection on the adequacy or viability of these liberal ideas. The remedy

[2] Lionell Trilling, *The Liberal Imagination* (New York, 1950), p. 183.

lies in revising our conception of the nature and function of ideas in our culture. Ideas are "living things, inescapably connected with our wills and desires,"[3] and they can grow and develop just as they can decline and become corrupt and die. Only if we conceive of them in this way, declares Trilling, can literature as an active force again become possible.

BIBLIOGRAPHY

TEXT

*Matthew Arnold.* New York, 1939.
*E. H. Forster.* Norfolk, 1943.
(ed.), *The Portable Matthew Arnold.* New York, 1949.
*The Liberal Imagination.* New York, 1950.

## ART AND NEUROSIS*

THE question of the mental health of the artist has engaged the attention of our culture since the beginning of the Romantic Movement. Before that time it was commonly said that the poet was "mad," but this was only a manner of speaking, a way of saying that the mind of the poet worked in different fashion from the mind of the philosopher; it had no real reference to the mental hygiene of the man who was the poet. But in the early nineteenth century, with the development of a more elaborate psychology and a stricter and more literal view of mental and emotional normality, the statement was more strictly and literally intended. So much so, indeed, that Charles Lamb, who knew something about madness at close quarters and a great deal about art, undertook to refute in his brilliant essay, "On the Sanity of True Genius," the idea that the exercise of the imagination was a kind of insanity. And some eighty years later, the idea having yet further entrenched itself, Bernard Shaw felt called upon to argue the sanity of art, but his cogency was of no more avail than Lamb's. In recent years the connection between art and mental illness has been formulated not only by those who are openly or covertly hostile to art, but also and more significantly by those who are most intensely partisan to it. The latter willingly and even

3 *Ibid.,* p. 303.

* From *The Liberal Imagination* by Lionel Trilling. Copyright 1945, 1947 by Lionel Trilling. Reprinted by permission of The Viking Press, Inc., New York.

eagerly accept the idea that the artist is mentally ill and go on to make his illness a condition of his power to tell the truth.

This conception of artistic genius is indeed one of the characteristic notions of our culture. I should like to bring it into question. To do so is to bring also into question certain early ideas of Freud's and certain conclusions which literary laymen have drawn from the whole tendency of the Freudian psychology. From the very start it was recognized that psychoanalysis was likely to have important things to say about art and artists. Freud himself thought so, yet when he first addressed himself to the subject he said many clumsy and misleading things. I have elsewhere and at length tried to separate the useful from the useless and even dangerous statements about art that Freud has made.[1] To put it briefly here, Freud had some illuminating and even beautiful insights into certain particular works of art which made complex use of the element of myth. Then, without specifically undertaking to do so, his "Beyond the Pleasure Principle" offers a brilliant and comprehensive explanation of our interest in tragedy. And what is of course most important of all— it is a point to which I shall return—Freud, by the whole tendency of his psychology, establishes the *naturalness* of artistic thought. Indeed, it is possible to say of Freud that he ultimately did more for our understanding of art than any other writer since Aristotle; and this being so, it can only be surprising that in his early work he should have made the error of treating the artist as a neurotic who escapes from reality by means of "substitute gratifications."

As Freud went forward he insisted less on this simple formulation. Certainly it did not have its original force with him when, at his seventieth birthday celebration, he disclaimed the right to be called the discoverer of the unconscious, saying that whatever he may have done for the systematic understanding of the unconscious, the credit for its discovery properly belonged to the literary masters. And psychoanalysis has inherited from him a tenderness for art which is real although sometimes clumsy, and nowadays most psychoanalysts of any personal sensitivity are embarrassed by occasions which seem to lead them to reduce art to a formula of mental illness. Nevertheless Freud's early belief in the essential neuroticism of the artist found an all too fertile ground—found, we might say, the very ground from which it first sprang, for, when he spoke of the artist as a neurotic, Freud was adopting one of the popular beliefs of his age. Most readers will see this belief as the expression of the indus-

[1] See "Freud and Literature."

trial rationalization and the bourgeois philistinism of the nineteenth century. In this they are partly right. The nineteenth century established the basic virtue of "getting up at eight, shaving close at a quarter-past, breakfasting at nine, going to the City at ten, coming home at half-past five, and dining at seven." The Messrs. Podsnap who instituted this scheduled morality inevitably decreed that the arts must celebrate it and nothing else. "Nothing else to be permitted to these . . . vagrants the Arts, on pain of excommunication. Nothing else To Be—anywhere!" We observe that the virtuous day ends with dinner—bed and sleep are naturally not part of the Reality that Is, and nothing must be set forth which will, as Mr. Podsnap put it, bring a Blush to the Cheek of a Young Person.

The excommunication of the arts, when it was found necessary, took the form of pronouncing the artist mentally degenerate, a device which eventually found its theorist in Max Nordau. In the history of the arts this is new. The poet was always known to belong to a touchy tribe—*genus irritabile* was a tag anyone would know—and ever since Plato the process of the inspired imagination, as we have said, was thought to be a special one of some interest, which the similitude of madness made somewhat intelligible. But this is not quite to say that the poet was the victim of actual mental aberration. The eighteenth century did not find the poet to be less than other men, and certainly the Renaissance did not. If he was a professional, there might be condescension to his social status, but in a time which deplored all professionalism whatever, this was simply a way of asserting the high value of poetry, which ought not to be compromised by trade. And a certain good nature marked even the snubbing of the professional. At any rate, no one was likely to identify the poet with the weakling. Indeed, the Renaissance ideal held poetry to be, like arms or music, one of the signs of manly competence.

The change from this view of things cannot be blamed wholly on the bourgeois or philistine public. Some of the "blame" must rest with the poets themselves. The Romantic poets were as proud of their art as the vaunting poets of the sixteenth century, but one of them talked with an angel in a tree and insisted that Hell was better than Heaven and sexuality holier than chastity; another told the world that he wanted to lie down like a tired child and weep away this life of care; another asked so foolish a question as "Why did I laugh tonight?"; and yet another explained that he had written one of his best poems in a drugged sleep. The public took them all at their word—they were not as other men. Zola, in the interests of science, submitted himself to examination by fifteen psychiatrists and agreed with their conclusion that his genius had its source in the neurotic elements of his temperament. Baudelaire, Rimbaud, Verlaine found virtue and strength in their physical and mental illness and pain. W. H. Auden addresses his "wound" in the cherishing language of a lover, thanking it for the gift of insight it has bestowed. "Knowing you," he says, "has made me understand." And Edmund Wilson in his striking phrase, "the wound and the bow," has formulated for our time the idea of the characteristic sickness of the artist, which he represents by the figure of Philoctetes, the Greek warrior who was forced to live in isolation because of the disgusting odor of a suppurating wound and who yet had to be sought out by his countrymen because they had need of the magically unerring bow he possessed.

The myth of the sick artist, we may suppose, has established itself because it is of advantage to the various groups who have one or another relation with art. To the artist himself the myth gives some of the ancient powers and privileges of the idiot and the fool, half-prophetic creatures, or of the mutilated priest. That the artist's neurosis may be but a mask is suggested by Thomas Mann's pleasure in representing his untried youth as "sick" but his successful maturity as senatorially robust. By means of his belief in his own sickness, the artist may the more easily fulfill his chosen, and assigned, function of putting himself into connection with the forces of spirituality and morality; the artist sees as insane the "normal" and "healthy" ways of established society, while aberration and illness appear as spiritual and moral health if only because they controvert the ways of respectable society.

Then too, the myth has its advantage for the philistine—a double advantage. On the one hand, the belief in the artist's neuroticism allows the philistine to shut his ears to what the artist says. But on the other hand it allows him to listen. For we must not make the common mistake—the contemporary philistine does want to listen, at the same time that he wants to shut his ears. By supposing that the artist has an interesting but not always reliable relation to reality, he is able to contain (in the military sense) what the artist tells him. If he did not want to listen at all, he would say "insane"; with "neurotic," which hedges, he listens when he chooses.

And in addition to its advantage to the artist and to the philistine, we must take into account the usefulness of the myth to a third group, the group of "sensitive" people, who, although not artists, are not philistines either. These people form a group by virtue of their passive impatience with philistinism, and also by virtue of their awareness of their own emotional pain and uncertainty. To these people the myth of the sick artist is the institutional sanction of their situation; they seek to approximate or acquire the character of the artist, sometimes by planning to work or even attempting to work as the artists does, always by making a connection between their own powers of mind and their consciousness of "difference" and neurotic illness.

The early attempts of psychoanalysis to deal with art went on the assumption that, because the artist was neurotic, the content of his work was also neurotic, which is to say that it did not stand in a correct relation to reality. But nowadays, as I have said, psycho-analysis is not likely to be so simple in its transactions with art. A good example of the pschoanalytical development in this respect is Dr. Saul Rosenzweig's well-known essay, "The Ghost of Henry James."[2] This is an admirable piece of work, marked by accuracy in the reporting of the literary fact and by respect for the value of the literary object. Although Dr. Rosenzweig explores the element of neurosis in James's life and work, he nowhere suggests that this element in any way lessens James's value as an artist or moralist. In effect he says that neurosis is a way of dealing with reality which, in real life, is uncomfortable and uneconomical, but that this judgment of neurosis in life cannot mechanically be transferred to works of art upon which neurosis has had its influence. He nowhere implies that a work of art in whose genesis a neurotic element may be found is for that reason irrelevant or in any way diminished in value. In-deed, the manner of his treatment suggests, what is of course the case, that every neurosis deals with a real emotional situation of the most intensely meaningful kind.

Yet as Dr. Rosenzweig brings his essay to its close, he makes use of the current assumption about the causal connection between the psychic illness of the artist and his power. His investigation of James, he says, "reveals the aptness of the Philoctetes pattern." He accepts the idea of "the sacrificial roots of literary power" and speaks of "the unhappy sources of James's genius." "The broader application of the inherent pattern," he says, "is familiar to readers of Edmund Wilson's recent volume *The Wound and the Bow*. . . . Reviewing the experience and work of several well-known literary masters,

2 First published in *Character and Personality*, December 1943, and reprinted in *Partisan Review*, Fall, 1944.

Wilson discloses the sacrificial roots of their power on the model of
the Greek legend. In the case of Henry James, the present account
. . . provides a similar insight into the unhappy sources of his
genius. . . ."

This comes as a surprise. Nothing in Dr. Rosenzweig's thoery requires it. For his theory asserts no more than that Henry James,
predisposed by temperament and family situation to certain mental
and emotional qualities, was in his youth injured in a way which he
believed to be sexual; that he unconsciously invited the injury in the
wish to identify himself with his father, who himself had been similarly injured—"castrated": a leg had been amputated—and under
strikingly similar circumstances; this resulted for the younger Henry
James in a certain pattern of life and in a preoccupation in his work
with certain themes which more or less obsurely symbolize his sexual
situation. For this I think Dr. Rosenzweig makes a sound case. Yet
I submit that this is not the same thing as disclosing the roots of
James's power or discovering the sources of his genius. The essay
which gives Edmund Wilson's book its title and cohering principle
does not explicitly say that the roots of power are sacrificial and that
the source of genius is unhappy. Where it is explicit, it states only
that "genius and disease, like strength and mutilation, may be
inextricably bound up together," which of course, on its face, says
no more than that personality is integral and not made up of detach-
able parts; and from this there is no doubt to be drawn the important
practical and moral implication that we cannot judge or dismiss a
man's genius and strength because of our awareness of his disease or
mutilation. The Philoctetes legend in itself does not suggest anything
beyond this. It does not suggest that the wound is the price of the
bow, or that without the wound the bow may not be possessed or
drawn. Yet Dr. Rosenzweig has accurately summarized the force
and, I think, the intention of Mr. Wilson's whole book; its several
studies do seem to say that effectiveness in the arts does depend on
sickness.

An examination of this prevalent idea might well begin with the
observation of how pervasive and deeply rooted is the notion that
power may be gained by suffering. Even at relatively high stages of
culture the mind seems to take easily to the primitive belief that
pain and sacrifice are connected with strength. Primitive beliefs must
be treated with respectful alertness to their possible truth and also
with the suspicion of their being magical and irrational, and it is
worth noting on both sides of the question, and in the light of what

we have said about the ambiguous relation of the neurosis to reality, that the whole economy of the neurosis is based exactly on this idea of the *quid pro quo* of sacrificial pain: the neurotic person unconsciously subscribes to a system whereby he gives up some pleasure or power, or inflicts pain on himself in order to secure some other power or some other pleasure.

In the ingrained popular conception of the relation between suffering and power there are actually two distinct although related ideas. One is that there exists in the individual a fund of power which has outlets through various organs or faculties, and that if its outlet through one organ or faculty be prevented, it will flow to increase the force or sensitivity of another. Thus it is popularly believed that the sense of touch is intensified in the blind not so much by the will of the blind person to adapt himself to the necessities of his situation as, rather, by a sort of mechanical redistribution of power. And this idea would seem to explain, if not the orgin of the ancient mutilation of priests, then at least a common understanding of their sexual sacrifice.

The other idea is that a person may be taught by, or proved by, the endurance of pain. There will easily come to mind the ritual suffering that is inflicted at the tribal initiation of youths into full manhood or at the admission of the apprentice into the company of journeyman adepts. This idea in sophisticated form found its way into high religion at least as early as Aeschylus, who held that man achieves knowledge of God through suffering, and it was from the beginning an important element of Christian thought. In the nineteenth century the Christianized notion of the didactic suffering of the artist went along with the idea of his mental degeneration and even served as a sort of countermyth to it. Its doctrine was that the artist, a man of strength and health, experienced and suffered, and thus learned both the facts of life and his artistic craft. "I am the man, I suffered, I was there," ran his boast, and he derived his authority from the knowledge gained through suffering.

There can be no doubt that both these ideas represent a measure of truth about mental and emotional power. The idea of didactic suffering expresses a valuation of experience and of steadfastness. The idea of natural compensation for the sacrifice of some faculty also says something that can be rationally defended: one cannot be and do everything and the whole-hearted absorption in any enterprise, art for example, means that we must give up other possibilities, even parts of ourselves. And there is even a certain validity to the belief that the individual has a fund of undifferentiated energy which presses the harder upon what outlets are available to it when it has been deprived of the normal number.

Then, in further defense of the belief that artistic power is connected with neurosis, we can say that there is no doubt that what we call mental illness may be the source of psychic knowledge. Some neurotic people, because they are more apprehensive than normal people, are able to see more of certain parts of reality and to see them with more intensity. And many neurotic or psychotic patients are in certain respects in closer touch with the actualities of the unconscious than are normal people. Further, the expression of a neurotic or psychotic conception of reality is likely to be more intense than a normal one.

Yet when we have said all this, it is still wrong, I believe, to find the root of the artist's power and the source of his genius in neurosis. To the idea that literary power and genius spring from pain and neurotic sacrifice there are two major objections. The first has to do with the assumed uniqueness of the artist as a subject of psychoanalytical explanation. The second has to do with the true meaning of power and genius.

One reason why writers are considered to be more available than other people to psychoanalytical explanation is that they tell us what is going on inside them. Even when they do not make an actual diagnosis of their malaises or describe "symptoms," we must bear it in mind that it is their profession to deal with fantasy in some form or other. It is the nature of the writer's job that he exhibit his unconscious. He may disguise it in various ways, but disguise is not concealment. Indeed, it may be said that the more a writer takes pains with his work to remove it from the personal and subjective, the more —and not the less—he will express his true unconscious, although not what passes with most for the unconscious.

Further, the writer is likely to be a great hand at personal letters, diaries, and autobiographies: indeed, almost the only good autobiographies are those of writers. The writer is more aware of what happens to him or goes on in him and often finds it necessary or useful to be articulate about his inner states, and prides himself on telling the truth. Thus, only a man as devoted to the truth of the emotions as Henry James was would have informed the world, despite his characteristic reticence, of an accident so intimate as his. We must not of course suppose that a writer's statements about his intimate life are equivalent to true statements about his unconscious, which, by definition, he doesn't consciously know; but they may be useful clues to the nature of an entity about which we can make statements of more or less cogency, although never statements of certainty; or they at least give us what is surely related to a knowledge of his unconscious—that is, an insight into his personality.[3]

But while the validity of dealing with the writer's intellectual life in psychoanalytical terms is taken for granted, the psychoanalytical explanation of the intellectual life of scientists is generally speaking not countenanced. The old myth of the mad scientist, with the exception of an occasional mad psychiatrist, no longer exists. The social position of science requires that it should cease, which leads us to remark that those partisans of art who insist on explaining artistic genius by means of psychic imbalance are in effect capitulating to the dominant mores which hold that the members of the respectable professions are, however dull they may be, free from neurosis. Scientists, to continue with them as the best example of the respectable professions, do not usually give us the clues to their personalities which writers habitually give. But no one who has ever lived observantly among scientists will claim that they are without an unconscious or even that they are free from neurosis. How often, indeed, it is apparent that the devotion to science, if it cannot be called a neurotic manifestation, at least can be understood as going very cozily with neurotic elements in the temperament, such as, for example, a marked compulsiveness. Of scientists as a group we can say that they are less concerned with the manifestations of personality, their own or others', than are writers as a group. But this relative indifference is scarcely a sign of normality—indeed, if we choose to regard it with the same sort of eye with which the characteristics of writers are regarded, we might say the indifference to matters of personality is in itself a suspicious evasion.

It is the basic assumption of psychoanalysis that the acts of *every* person are influenced by the forces of the unconscious. Scientists,

---

[3] I am by no means in agreement with the statements of Dr. Edmund Bergler about "the" psychology of the writer, but I think that Dr. Bergler has done good service in warning us against taking at their face value a writer's statements about himself, the more especially when they are "frank." Thus, to take Dr. Bergler's notable example, it is usual for biographers to accept Stendhal's statements about his open sexual feelings for his mother when he was a little boy, feelings which went with an intense hatred of his father. But Dr. Bergler believes that Stendhal unconsciously used his consciousness of his love of his mother and of his hatred of his father to mask an unconscious love of his father, which frightened him. ("Psychoanalysis of Writers and of Literary Productivity" in *Psychoanalysis and the Social Sciences,* vol. 1.)

bankers, lawyers, or surgeons, by reason of the traditions of their professions, practice concealment and conformity; but it is difficult to believe that an investigation according to psychoanalytical principles would fail to show that the strains and imbalances of their psyches are not of the same frequency as those of writers, and of similar kind. I do not mean that everybody has the same troubles and identical psyches, but only that there is no special category for writers.[4]

If this is so, and if we still want to relate the writer's power to his neurosis, we must be willing to relate all intellectual power to neurosis. We must find the roots of Newton's power in his emotional extravagances, and the roots of Darwin's power in his sorely neurotic temperament, and the roots of Pascal's mathematical genius in the impulses which drove him to extreme religious masochism—I choose but the classic examples. If we make the neurosis-power equivalence at all, we must make it in every field of endeavor. Logician, economist, botanist, physicist, theologian—no profession may be so respectable or so remote or so rational as to be exempt from the psychological interpretation.[5]

[4] Dr. Bergler believes that there is a particular neurosis of writers, based on an oral masochism which makes them the enemy of the respectable world, courting poverty and persecution. But a later development of Dr. Bergler's theory of oral masochism makes it *the* basic neurosis, not only of writers but of everyone who is neurotic.

[5] In his interesting essay, "Writers and Madness" (*Partisan Review,* January–February 1947), William Barrett has taken issue with this point and has insisted that a clear distinction is to be made between the relation that exists between the scientist and his work and the relation that exists between the artist and his work. The difference, as I understand it, is in the claims of the ego. The artist's ego makes a claim upon the world which is personal in a way that the scientist's is not, for the scientist, although he does indeed want prestige and thus "responds to one of the deepest urges of his ego, it is only that his prestige may come to attend his person through the public world of other men; and it is not in the end his own being that is exhibited or his own voice that is heard in the learned report to the Academy." Actually, however, as is suggested by the sense which mathematicians have of the *style* of mathematical thought, the creation of the abstract thinker is as deeply involved as the artist's—see *An Essay on the Psychology of Invention in the Mathematical Field* by Jacques Hadamard, Princeton University Press, 1945—and he quite as much as the artist seeks to impose *himself,* to *express* himself. I am of course not maintaining that the processes of scientific thought are the same as those of artistic thought, or even that the scientist's creation is involved with his total personality *in the same way* that the artist's is—I am maintaining only that the scientist's creation is as *deeply* implicated with his total personality as is the artist's.

This point of view seems to be supported by Freud's monograph on Leonardo. One of the problems that Freud sets himself is to discover why an artist of the highest endowment should have devoted himself more and more to scientific investigation, with the result that he was unable to complete his artistic enterprises. The particular reasons for this that Freud assigns need not be gone into here; all

Further, not only power but also failure or limitation must be accounted for by the theory of neurosis, and not merely failure or limitation in life but even failure or limitation in art. Thus it is often said that the warp of Dostoevski's mind accounts for the brilliance of his psychological insights. But it is never said that the same warp of Dostoevski's mind also accounted for his deficiency in insight. Freud, who greatly admired Dostoevski, although he did not like him, observed that "his insight was entirely restricted to the workings of the abnormal psyche. Consider his astounding helplessness before the phenomenon of love; he really only understands either crude, instinctive desire or masochistic submission or love from pity."[6] This, we must note, is not merely Freud's comment on the extent of the province which Dostoevski chose for his own, but on his failure to understand what, given the province of his choice, he might be expected to understand.

And since neurosis can account not only for intellectual success and for failure or limitation but also for mediocrity, we have most of society involved in neurosis. To this I have no objection—I think most of society is indeed involved in neurosis. But with neurosis accounting for so much, it cannot be made exclusively to account for one man's literary power.

We have now to consider what is meant by genius when its source is identified as the sacrifice and pain of neurosis.

In the case of Henry James, the reference to the neurosis of his personal life does indeed tell us something about the latent intention of his work and thus about the reason for some large part of its interest for us. But if genius and its source are what we are dealing with, we must observe that the reference to neurosis tells us nothing about James's passion, energy, and devotion, nothing about his architectonic skill, nothing about the other themes that were important to him which are not connected with his unconscious concern with castration. We cannot, that is, make the writer's inner life exactly equivalent to his power of expressing it. Let us grant for the sake of argument that the literary genius, as distinguished from other men, is the

---

that I wish to suggest is that Freud understands these reasons to be the working out of an inner conflict, the attempt to deal with the difficulties that have their roots in the most primitive situations. Leonardo's scientific investigations were as necessary and "compelled" and they constituted as much of a claim on the whole personality as anything the artist undertakes; and so far from being carried out for the sake of public prestige, they were largely private and personal, and were thought by the public of his time to be something very like insanity.

6 From a letter quoted in Theodor Reik's *From Thirty Years With Freud,* p. 175.

victim of a "mutilation" and that his fantasies are neurotic.[7] It does not then follow as the inevitable next step that his ability to express these fantasies and to impress us with them is neurotic, for that ability is what we mean by his genius. Anyone might be injured as Henry James was, and even respond within himself to the injury as James is said to have done, and yet not have his literary power.

The reference to the artist's neurosis tells us something about the material on which the artist exercises his powers, and even something about his reasons for bringing his powers into play, but it does not tell us anything about the source of his power, it makes no causal connection between them and the neurosis. And if we look into the matter, we see that there is in fact no causal connection between them. For, still granting that the poet is uniquely neurotic, what is surely not neurotic, what indeed suggests nothing but health, is his power of using his neuroticism. He shapes his fantasies, he gives them social form and reference. Charles Lamb's way of putting this cannot be improved. Lamb is denying that genius is allied to insanity; for "insanity" the modern reader may substitute "neurosis." "The ground of the mistake," he says, "is, that men, finding in the raptures of the higher poetry a condition of exaltation, to which they have no parallel in their own experience, besides the spurious resemblance of it in dreams and fevers, impute a state of dreaminess and fever to the poet. But the true poet dreams being awake. He is not possessed by his subject but has dominion over it. . . . Where he seems most to recede from humanity, he will be found the truest to it. From beyond the scope of nature if he summon possible existences, he subjugates them to the law of her consistency. He is beautifully loyal to that sovereign directress, when he appears most to betray and desert her. . . . Herein the great and the little wits are differenced; that if the latter wander ever so little from nature or natural existence, they lose themselves and their readers. . . . They do not create, which implies shaping and consistency. Their imaginations are not active—for to be active is to call something into act and form—but passive as men in sick dreams."

The activity of the artist, we must remember, may be approximated by many who are themselves not artists. Thus, the expressions

---

[7] I am using the word *fantasy*, unless modified, in a neutral sense. A fantasy, in this sense, may be distinguished from the representation of something that actually exists, but it is not opposed to "reality" and not an "escape" from reality. Thus the idea of a rational society, or the image of a good house to be built, as well as the story of something that could never really happen, is a fantasy. There may be neurotic or non-neurotic fantasies.

of many schizophrenic people have the intense appearance of creativity and an inescapable interest and significance. But they are not works of art, and although Van Gogh may have been schizophrenic he was in addition an artist. Again, as I have already suggested, it is not uncommon in our society for certain kinds of neurotic people to imitate the artist in his life and even in his ideals and ambitions. They follow the artist in everything except successful performance. It was, I think, Otto Rank who called such people half-artists and confirmed the diagnosis of their neuroticism at the same time that he differentiated them from true artists.

Nothing is so characteristic of the artist as his power of shaping his work, of subjugating his raw material, however aberrant it be from what we call normality, to the consistency of nature. It would be impossible to deny that whatever disease or mutilation the artist may suffer is an element of his production which has its effect on every part of it, but disease and mutilation are available to us all—life provides them with prodigal generosity. What marks the artist is his power to shape the material of pain we all have.

At this point, with our recognition of life's abundant provision of pain, we are at the very heart of our matter, which is the meaning we may assign to neurosis and the relation we are to suppose it to have with normality. Here Freud himself can be of help, although it must be admitted that what he tells us may at first seem somewhat contradictory and confusing.

Freud's study of Leonardo da Vinci is an attempt to understand why Leonardo was unable to pursue his artistic enterprises, feeling compelled instead to advance his scientific investigations. The cause of this Freud traces back to certain childhood experiences not different in kind from the experiences which Dr. Rosenzweig adduces to account for certain elements in the work of Henry James. And when he has completed his study Freud makes this *caveat:* "Let us expressly emphasize that we have never considered Leonardo as a neurotic. . . . We no longer believe that health and disease, normal and nervous, are sharply distinguished from each other. We know today that neurotic symptoms are substitutive formations for certain repressive acts which must result in the course of our development from the child to the cultural man, that we all produce such substitutive formations, and that only the amount, intensity, and distribution of these substitutive formations justify the practical conception of illness. . . ." The statement becomes the more striking when we remember that in the course of his study Freud has had occasion to observe that Leonardo was both homosexual and sexually inactive. I am not sure that the statement that Leonardo was not a neurotic is one that Freud would have made at every point in the later development of psychoanalysis, yet it is in conformity with his continuing notion of the genesis of culture. And the *practical*, the quantitative or economic, conception of illness he insists on in a passage in the *Introductory Lectures*. "The neurotic symptoms," he says, ". . . are activities which are detrimental, or at least useless, to life as a whole; the person concerned frequently complains of them as obnoxious to him or they involve suffering and distress for him. The principal injury they inflict lies in the expense of energy they entail, and, besides this, in the energy needed to combat them. Where the symptoms are extensively developed, these two kinds of effort may exact such a price that the person suffers a very serious impoverishment in available mental energy which consequently disables him for all the important tasks of life. This result depends principally upon the amount of energy taken up in this way; therefore you will see that 'illness' is essentially a practical conception. But if you look at the matter from a theoretical point of view and ignore this question of degree, you can very well see that we are all ill, i.e., neurotic; for the conditions required for symptom-formation are demonstrable also in normal persons."

*We are all ill:* the statement is grandiose, and its implications—the implications, that is, of understanding the totality of human nature in the terms of disease—are vast. These implications have never been properly met (although I believe that a few theologians have responded to them), but this is not the place to attempt to meet them. I have brought forward Freud's statement of the essential sickness of the psyche only because it stands as the refutation of what is implied by the literary use of the theory of neurosis to account for genius. For if we are all ill, and if, as I have said, neurosis can account for everything, for failure and mediocrity—"a very serious impoverishment of available mental energy"—as well as for genius, it cannot uniquely account for genius.

This, however, is not to say that there is no connection between neurosis and genius, which would be tantamount, as we see, to saying that there is no connection between human nature and genius. But the connection lies wholly in a particular and special relation which the artist has to neurosis.

In order to understand what this particular and special connection is we must have clearly in mind what neurosis is. The current literary conception of neurosis as a *wound* is quite misleading. It inevitably suggests passivity, whereas, if we follow Freud, we must understand a neurosis to be an *activity*, an activity with a purpose, and a particular kind of activity, a *conflict*. This is not to say that there are no abnormal mental states which are not conflicts. There are; the struggle between elements of the unconscious may never be instituted in the first place, or it may be called off. As Freud says in a passage which follows close upon the one I last quoted, "If regressions do not call forth a prohibition on the part of the ego, no neurosis results; the libido succeeds in obtaining a real, although not a normal, satisfaction. But if the ego . . . is not in agreement with these regressions, conflict ensues." And in his essay on Dostoevski Freud says that "there are no neurotic complete masochists," by which he means that the ego which gives way completely to masochism (or to any other pathological excess) has passed beyond neurosis; the conflict has ceased, but at the cost of the defeat of the ego, and now some other name than that of neurosis must be given to the condition of the person who thus takes himself beyond the pain of the neurotic conflict. To understand this is to become aware of the curious complacency with which literary men regard mental disease. The psyche of the neurotic is not equally complacent; it regards with the greatest fear the chaotic and destructive forces it contains, and it struggles fiercely to keep them at bay.[8]

We come then to a remarkable paradox: we are all ill, but we are ill in the service of health, or ill in the service of life, or, at the very least, ill in the service of life-in-culture. The form of the mind's dynamics is that of the neurosis, which is to be understood as the ego's struggle against being overcome by the forces with which it coexists, and the strategy of this conflict requires that the ego shall incur pain

[8] In the article to which I refer in the note on page 559, William Barrett says that he prefers the old-fashioned term "madness" to "neurosis." But it is not quite for him to choose—the words do not differ in fashion but in meaning. Most literary people, when they speak of mental illness, refer to neurosis. Perhaps one reason for this is that the neurosis is the most benign of the mental ills. Another reason is surely that psychoanalytical literature deals chiefly with the neurosis, and its symptomatology and therapy have become familiar; psychoanalysis has far less to say about psychosis, for which it can offer far less therapeutic hope. Further, the neurosis is easily put into a causal connection with the social maladjustments of our time. Other forms of mental illness of a more severe and degenerative kind are not so widely recognized by the literary person and are often assimilated to neurosis with a resulting confusion. In the present essay I deal only with the conception of neurosis, but this should not be taken to imply that I believe that other pathological mental conditions, including actual madness, do not have relevance to the general matter of the discussion.

and make sacrifices of itself, at the same time seeing to it that its pain and sacrifice be as small as they may.

But this is characteristic of all minds: no mind is exempt except those which refuse the conflict or withdraw from it; and we ask wherein the mind of the artist is unique. If he is not unique in neurosis, is he then unique in the significance and intensity of his neurosis? I do not believe that we shall go more than a little way toward a definition of artistic genius by answering this question affirmatively. A neurotic conflict cannot ever be either meaningless or merely personal; it must be understood as exemplifying cultural forces of great moment, and this is true of any neurotic conflict at all. To be sure, some neuroses may be more interesting than others, perhaps because they are fiercer or more inclusive; and no doubt the writer who makes a claim upon our interest is a man who by reason of the energy and significance of the forces in struggle within him provides us with the largest representation of the culture in which we, with him, are involved; his neurosis may thus be thought of as having a connection of concomitance with his literary powers. As Freud says in the Dostoevski essay, "the neurosis . . . comes into being all the more readily the richer the complexity which has to be controlled by his ego." Yet even the rich complexity which his ego is doomed to control is not the definition of the artist's genius, for we can by no means say that the artist is pre-eminent in the rich complexity of elements in conflict within him. The slightest acquaintance with the clinical literature of psychoanalysis will suggest that a rich complexity of struggling elements is no uncommon possession. And that same literature will also make it abundantly clear that the devices of art—the most extreme devices of poetry, for example—are not particular to the mind of the artist but are characteristic of mind itself.

But the artist is indeed unique in one respect, in the respect of his relation to his neurosis. He is what he is by virtue of his successful objectification of his neurosis, by his shaping it and making it available to others in a way which has its effect upon their own egos in struggle. His genius, that is, may be defined in terms of his faculties of perception, representation, and realization, and in these terms alone. It can no more be defined in terms of neurosis than can his power of walking and talking, or his sexuality. The use to which he puts his power, or the manner and style of his power, may be discussed with reference to his particular neurosis, and so may such matters as the untimely diminution or cessation of its exercise. But its essence is irreducible. It is, as we say, a gift.

We are all ill: but even a universal sickness implies an idea of health. Of the artist we must say that whatever elements of neurosis he has in common with his fellow mortals, the one part of him that is healthy, by any conceivable definition of health, is that which gives him the power to conceive, to plan, to work, and to bring his work to a conclusion. And if we are all ill, we are ill by a universal accident, not by a universal necessity, by a fault in the economy of our powers, not by the nature of the powers themselves. The Philoctetes myth, when it is used to imply a causal connection between the fantasy of castration and artistic power, tells us no more about the source of artistic power than we learn about the source of sexuality when the fantasy of castration is adduced, for the fear of castration may explain why a man is moved to extravagant exploits of sexuality, but we do not say that his sexual power itself derives from his fear of castration; and further the same fantasy may also explain impotence or homosexuality. The Philoctetes story, which has so established itself among us as explaining the source of the artist's power, is not really an explanatory myth at all; it is a moral myth having reference to our proper behavior in the circumstances of the universal accident. In its juxtaposition of the wound and the bow, it tells us that we must be aware that weakness does not preclude strength nor strength weakness. It is therefore not irrelevant to the artist, but when we use it we will do well to keep in mind the other myths of the arts, recalling what Pan and Dionysius suggest of the relation of art to physiology and superabundance, remembering that to Apollo were attributed the bow and the lyre, two strengths together, and that he was given the lyre by its inventor, the baby Hermes—that miraculous infant who, the day he was born, left his cradle to do mischief: and the first thing he met with was a tortoise, which he greeted politely before scooping it from its shell, and, thought and deed being one with him, he contrived the instrument to which he sang "the glorious tale of his own begetting." These were gods, and very early ones, but their myths tell us something about the nature and source of art even in our grim, late human present.

# INDEX

# INDEX